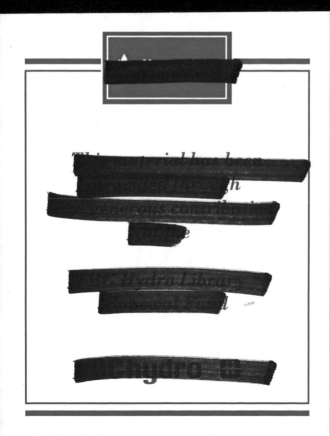

THE BLACKWELL ENCYCLOPEDIA OF MANAGEMENT

ORGANIZATIONAL BEHAVIOR

THE BLACKWELL ENCYCLOPEDIA OF MANAGEMENT

SECOND EDITION

Encyclopedia Editor: Cary L. Cooper
Advisory Editors: Chris Argyris and William H. Starbuck

Volume I: *Accounting*
Edited by Colin Clubb (and A. Rashad Abdel-Khalik)

Volume II: *Business Ethics*
Edited by Patricia H. Werhane and R. Edward Freeman

Volume III: *Entrepreneurship*
Edited by Michael A. Hitt and R. Duane Ireland

Volume IV: *Finance*
Edited by Ian Garrett (and Dean Paxson and Douglas Wood)

Volume V: *Human Resource Management*
Edited by Susan Cartwright (and Lawrence H. Peters, Charles R. Greer, and Stuart A. Youngblood)

Volume VI: *International Management*
Edited by Jeanne McNett, Henry W. Lane, Martha L. Maznevski, Mark E. Mendenhall, and John O'Connell

Volume VII: *Management Information Systems*
Edited by Gordon B. Davis

Volume VIII: *Managerial Economics*
Edited by Robert E. McAuliffe

Volume IX: *Marketing*
Edited by Dale Littler

Volume X: *Operations Management*
Edited by Nigel Slack and Michael Lewis

Volume XI: *Organizational Behavior*
Edited by Nigel Nicholson, Pino G. Audia, and Madan M. Pillutla

Volume XII: *Strategic Management*
Edited by John McGee (and Derek F. Channon)

Volume XIII: *Index*

THE BLACKWELL ENCYCLOPEDIA OF MANAGEMENT

SECOND EDITION

ORGANIZATIONAL BEHAVIOR

Edited by
Nigel Nicholson, Pino G. Audia,
and Madan M. Pillutla
London Business School, Haas School of Business,
University of California,
and London Business School

Blackwell
Publishing

BLACKWELL PUBLISHING
350 Main Street, Malden, MA 02148-5020, USA
9600 Garsington Road, Oxford OX4 2DQ, UK
550 Swanston Street, Carlton, Victoria 3053, Australia

First published 1997 by Blackwell Publishers Ltd
Published in paperback in 1999 by Blackwell Publishers Ltd
Second edition published 2005 by Blackwell Publishing Ltd

2   2006

Library of Congress Cataloging-in-Publication Data

The Blackwell encyclopedia of management. Organizational
behavior/edited by Nigel Nicholson, Pino G. Audia, and Madan M. Pillutla.
p. cm.—(The Blackwell encyclopedia of management ; v. 11)
Includes bibliographical references and index.
ISBN 0-631-23536-1 (hardcover : alk. paper)
1. Organizational behavior—Dictionaries. I. Nicholson, Nigel.
II. Audia, Pino G. III. Pillutla, M. M. (Madan M.) IV. Series.
HD30.15 .B455 2005 vol. 11
[HD58.7]
658′.003 s—dc22
[658′.003]
2004018333

ISBN-13: 978-0-631-23536-1 (hardcover : alk. paper)

ISBN for the 12-volume set 0-631-23317-2

A catalogue record for this title is available from the British Library.

Set in 9.5/11pt Ehrhardt
by Kolam Informations Services Pvt. Ltd, Pondicherry, India
Printed and bound in the United Kingdom
by TJ International Ltd, Padstow, Cornwall

The publisher's policy is to use permanent paper from mills that operate a sustainable forestry policy, and
which has been manufactured from pulp processed using acid-free and elementary chlorine-free practices.
Furthermore, the publisher ensures that the text paper and cover board used have met acceptable
environmental accreditation standards.

For further information on
Blackwell Publishing, visit our website:
www.blackwellpublishing.com

For Adèle, Archana, and Billie

Contents

Preface	viii
Acknowledgments	x
About the Editors	xi
Contributors	xii
Dictionary Entries A–Z	1
Index	425

Preface

The first edition of the *Blackwell Encyclopedia of Management: Organizational Behavior* (titled the *Blackwell Encyclopedic Dictionary of Management* or abbreviated to BEDOB), some 10 years ago, was written to a formula that proved to be uniquely powerful, flexible, and attractive for readers and writers alike – a large number of short entries, most 500 to 1,000 words in length, each designed to capture the essence of a topic and give guidance for further follow-up. Each entry follows a similar format: *definition – state of knowledge – current significance – future trends and applications*. This is designed to be especially useful to people new to the field, cutting through the jargon barrier with clear, concise, and informative explanations of key concepts and issues. It is a challenge to write to the level of succinctness required without loss of content, but it is one of the great achievements of the last edition that it did so to such evident reader satisfaction. I have lost count of the number of readers – from professors through to business readers – who have acclaimed the BEDOB as a treasure trove of enlightenment, entertainment, and utility.

In the decade since the last edition, a great deal has changed, and the entries in this edition reflect these developments. Yet much has not altered, in terms of the core of organizational behavior (OB) as a confluence of disciplines and the fundamental nature of its contribution. In the last edition we also claimed that OB had come of age, as an interdisciplinary subject area, and that its project – what could be summarized as analyzing the impact of people on organizations and the effects of organizations on people – has never been more important. The last 10 years have underlined this conclusion. The climate of acceptance of the OB mission is such that now most business people would endorse the statement that every business problem is at root a people problem.

Perhaps proof of the maturity of the field is the increasing blurring of the boundaries of disciplines and subject areas, as occurred among the natural sciences in the last decades of the twentieth century. Now we see in management such examples as behavioral finance becoming one of the fast growing sub-fields of applied economics, incorporating many of the ideas represented in this volume (*see* BEHAVIORAL DECISION RESEARCH). There is also increasing interest in the relevance of new ideas from contemporary biology (*see* EVOLUTIONARY PSYCHOLOGY and ORGANIZATIONAL ECOLOGY) and the physical sciences (*see* COMPLEXITY THEORY). This infusion and exchange reflects increasing sophistication in analytical techniques, theory development, modeling, and practical understanding. In OB there is another important bi-directional flow between theory and practice. It has long been common for theoretical ideas to assume importance to practitioners (EMOTIONAL INTELLIGENCE is perhaps a current example) but there are also reverse flows. The work of the best consultants has often highlighted phenomena that beg to be explained, for example EXECUTIVE DERAILMENT and the functioning of TOP MANAGEMENT TEAMS.

The current volume's contents differ from its predecessor's in several respects. First, there are the new emerging topics and fields, for example NETWORK THEORY AND ANALYSIS, ORGANIZATIONAL GEOGRAPHY, and KNOWLEDGE MANAGEMENT. Second, there are topics whose importance has grown or where work has developed at a high rate of intensity, such as NEGOTIATION, GAME THEORY, and TECHNOLOGY. There are also the major topics where the steady accretion of knowledge has continued; traditional areas where one can find new concepts and applications, such as MOTIVATION, ORGANIZATIONAL CULTURE, and LEADERSHIP. Additionally, there are a small number of entries that are unchanged from the previous edition – mainly because they are of historical importance, but not the subject of new thought and development (e.g., HAWTHORNE EFFECT). Among the unchanged entries, there are some timeless gems from the previous edition which require no addition or updating (e.g., Karl Weick's cogent entry on THEORY).

We have retained many outstanding leading thinkers from the last edition, and recruited this time many new young scholars at the leading edge of their subjects, to help ensure this work is as fresh and sharp as the previous edition. The author list thus represents a galaxy of current and future stars of OB, since this is an enterprise that has always attracted the very best minds in the field. This would not have been possible without fresh editorial inputs, and this new edition benefits from the partnership of three co-editors, rather than just relying on advisory editors. My colleagues Pino Audia and Madan Pillutla bring a broad range of expertise to help ensure that the headword list is fully representative of the field, that we have the newest and brightest stars as well as the most established authorities, and that our editing maintains the highest standards of disciplined feedback.

We have shed quite a large number of topics. A few have become obsolete, and the field has moved on away from them. Some of these were at the end of a historical trend: for example, "dual careers," an important phenomenon, is no longer treated as a topic meriting specific and separate theoretical or empirical interest, but has become largely incorporated within more generic areas (see WOMEN AT WORK; NON-WORK/WORK). In other areas subtopics have grown substantial enough to merit being spun off as separate entries, such as the FIVE FACTOR MODEL OF PERSONALITY. But the main reason for the elimination of entries from the first edition is overlap with the contents of other volumes, and we have omitted those that are outside core OB and that we judge are best and most fully represented in other volumes. The first edition of the BEDOB included work from strategic, international, and human resources management, as well as business ethics and operations management. We have streamlined the current volume to give more full representation to the increasing breadth and healthy vitality of OB from macro to micro perspectives from the most theoretical to the most applied, and to give as full representation to the rich past as much as to the promising future.

Our choice of entries and the space we have accorded them will not satisfy every reader's purview of the field. We apologize, though not much! We know we have represented the commanding heights and most of the foothills of the landscape. This is made possible by teamwork between the three of us as co-editors – building on the great work by the advisory editors to the last edition, Andy Van de Ven and Randy Schuler.

How to Use this Book

If you are new to the volume you will note that it differs from all other handbooks and dictionaries, apart from the others in this series, in the brevity of most of its entries. The great majority of entries are 500 to 1,000 words in length – the optimal for the scholar in a hurry who wants the essence of topic and to know where else to turn for deeper knowledge. Entries vary in length above and below this norm. We have taken care to classify entries according to our judgment about the significance, centrality, and enduring contribution of ideas, concepts, and topics. A few major sub-fields are accorded the maximum length of 4,000 words, and there are some minor or fringe topics allocated 200 words – enough to whet the appetite and point toward further resources.

A chief value of such a structure lies in its infinite possibilities as a "knowledge net" through cross-referencing. In every entry other topics represented in the volume are set in CAPITALS, and some further suggestions appear at the end of each entry. This makes the volume full of instructive and constructive possibilities for students, teachers, researchers, and other pathfinders.

Nigel Nicholson

Acknowledgments

In the Preface to the last edition we acknowledged the great team of people at Blackwell, colleagues at London Business School, and the administrative staff who helped manage the tremendous effort needed to keep track, control, and deliver a project of this breadth and complexity. We honor and appreciate their contribution, for the present edition builds on the great foundation that was laid then. Only three names will be repeated: Angie Quest at London Business School, who oversaw editorial administration, and Professors Andrew Van de Ven and Randall Schuler who helped to recruit contributors and advise on content.

This time the editorial burden has been fully shared between three of us, but the project is still one of daunting magnitude, and would not have been possible without the administrative support at London Business School of Florence Chan, whose precision, intelligence, and organizational capability kept all the forgetful academics on track. Finally, thanks again to all our professional colleagues whose efforts made this volume possible.

Nigel Nicholson, Pino G. Audia, and Madan M. Pillutla

About the Editors

Editor in Chief
Cary Cooper is based at Lancaster University as Professor of Organizational Psychology. He is the author of over 80 books, past editor of the *Journal of Organizational Behavior*, and Founding President of the British Academy of Management.

Advisory Editors
Chris Argyris is James Bryant Conant Professor of Education and Organizational Behavior at Harvard Business School.
William Haynes Starbuck is Professor of Management and Organizational Behavior at the Stern School of Business, New York University.

Volume Editors
Nigel Nicholson is Professor of Organizational Behavior at London Business School and an internationally renowned scholar and practitioner. In recent years he has been pioneering the application of evolutionary psychology to business, and his latest research is on leadership and the effectiveness of family firms. He has published 14 monographs and over 180 articles in the world's top scholarly and practitioner journals, in diverse areas such as managerial career transitions, behavioral risk in finance, leadership and personality, and leadership skills. He is a much sought-after executive speaker and directs two major leadership programs at London Business School: High Performance People Skills, and one of the world's most innovative programs, Proteus.

    Pino G. Audia is an Assistant Professor in the Organizational Behavior and Industrial Relations Group at the Haas School of Business, University of California, Berkeley. Prior to joining the Haas School, he was a faculty member in the Organizational Behavior department at the London Business School. His research focuses on micro explanations of macro phenomena such as organizational inertia and the emergence of industrial clusters. Pino is the recipient of the Outstanding Publication in Organizational Behavior award from the Academy of Management for the best research article published in the year 2000 for his article "The Paradox of Success" (with Edwin Locke and Kenneth Smith).

    Madan M. Pillutla is an Associate Professor of Organizational Behavior at the London Business School. His research focuses on negotiations and behavioral decision-making. In his recent work, he has looked at how trust develops between two interacting parties and at the debilitating effects of rewards and punishments on intrinsic desires to cooperate in work teams. His research has been featured in most of the top academic publications such as *Academy of Management Journal*, *Organizational Behavior and Human Decision Processes*, *Games and Economic Behavior*, and *Journal of Marketing Research*; in addition, he serves on the editorial board of *Administrative Science Quarterly*.

Contributors

Stuart Albert
University of Minnesota

Teresa M. Amabile
Harvard Business School

N. Anand
London Business School

Deborah Ancona
MIT

Philip Anderson
INSEAD

Chris Argyris
Harvard Business School

Richard D. Arvey
University of Minnesota

Blake Ashforth
Arizona State University

Pino G. Audia
University of California, Berkeley

Marcus Baer
University of Illinois,
Urbana-Champaign

Jessica Bagger
University of Arizona

James R. Bailey
London Business School

Stephen R. Barley
Stanford University

Bernard M. Bass
State University of New York
Binghamton

Max H. Bazerman
Harvard Business School

John D. Bigelow
Boise State University

Sally Blount-Lyon
New York University

Richard E. Boyatzis
Case Western Reserve University

Jill C. Bradley
Tulane University

Arthur P. Brief
Tulane University

Philip Bromiley
University of Minnesota

John G. Burgoyne
Lancaster University

W. Warner Burke
Columbia University

Kim Cameron
University of Michigan

John L. Campbell
Dartmouth College

Tiziana Casciaro
Harvard University

Robert B. Cialdini
Arizona State University

Chris W. Clegg
University of Sheffield

Stewart Clegg
University of Technology, Sydney

Jay Conger
London Business School

Thomas D. Cook
Northwestern University

Arnold C. Cooper
Purdue University

John Cordery
University of Western Australia

Thomas G. Cummings
University of Southern California

Carsten K. W. De Dreu
University of Amsterdam

David L. Deephouse
University of Alberta

Angelo DeNisi
Texas A&M University

Lex Donaldson
University of New South Wales

Linda M. Dunn-Jensen
New York University

W. Gibb Dyer, Jr.
Brigham Young University

Christopher P. Earley
London Business School

Jack E. Edwards
US General Accounting Office

Karen Holcombe Ehrhart
San Diego State University

Mark G. Ehrhart
San Diego State University

Aimee Ellis
Arizona State University

Miriam Erez
Technion, Israel Institute of Technology

Doris Fay
Aston University

Daniel C. Feldman
University of Georgia

Mark Fenton-O'Creevy
Open University

Stephen Fineman
University of Bath

Charles Fombrun
New York University

John Freeman
University of California, Berkeley

Michael Frese
University of Geissen

David Fryer
University of Stirling

Dana A. Gavrieli
Stanford University

Brenda Ghitulescu
University of Pittsburgh

Robert A. Giacalone
University of North Carolina at Charlotte

Jerald Greenberg
Ohio State University

Henrich R. Greve
BI Norwegian School of Management

Ricky W. Griffin
Texas A&M University

Amanda Griffiths
University of Nottingham

Rosanna E. Guadagno
University of California, Santa Barbara

David Guest
King's College

Barbara A. Gutek
University of Arizona

Colin Hales
University of Surrey

Donald C. Hambrick
Pennsylvania State University

Mary-Jo Hatch
University of Virginia

Erika Henik
University of California, Berkeley

Beth A. Hennessey
Wellesley College

E. Tory Higgins
Columbia University

Joyce Hogan
Hogan Assessment Systems

Daniel R. Ilgen
Michigan State University

Paul Ingram
Columbia University

Susan E. Jackson
Rutgers, The State University of New Jersey

Mariann Jelinek
College of William & Mary

Diana Jimeno-Ingrum
University of Illinois, Urbana-Champaign

Gary Johns
Concordia University

Timothy A. Judge
University of Florida

Ruth Kanfer
Georgia Institute of Technology

Christopher Kayes
George Washington University

John Kelly
London School of Economics

Manfred Kets de Vries
INSEAD

Richard Klimoski
George Mason University

Paul L. Koopman
Vrije Universiteit Amsterdam

Kenneth W. Koput
University of Arizona

Kathy E. Kram
Boston University School of Management

Roderick M. Kramer
Stanford University

Amy Kristof-Brown
University of Iowa

Gary P. Latham
University of Toronto

Barbara S. Lawrence
University of California, Los Angeles

Carrie Leana
University of Pittsburgh

Gerald E. Ledford, Jr.
Ledford Consulting Network

Karen Legge
University of Warwick

James R. Lincoln
University of California, Berkeley

Alessandro Lomi
University of Bologna

Brett Luthans
Missouri Western State College

Fred Luthans
University of Nebraska-Lincoln

Joanne Martin
Stanford University

Mark J. Martinko
Florida State University

Marshall W. Meyer
University of Pennsylvania

Stephen J. Mezias
New York University

Kevin Miliffe
Warrington College of Business, University of
Florida

George T. Milkovich
Cornell University

Susan Miller
University of Hull

Don Moore
Carnegie Mellon University

Robert H. Moorman
Creighton University

Timothy Morris
Templeton College, Oxford

Lisa M. Moynihan
London Business School

J. Peter Murmann
Northwestern University

J. Keith Murnighan
Northwestern University

Jayanth Narayanan
London Business School

Nigel Nicholson
London Business School

Stella M. Nkomo
University of South Africa

William Ocasio
Kellogg School of Business, Northwestern
University

Greg R. Oldham
University of Illinois,
Urbana-Champaign

Richard N. Osborn
Wayne State University

Layne Paddock
University of Arizona

Maury Peiperl
IMD, Lausanne

Lisa Penney
Personnel Decisions Research Institute,
Tampa, FL

Randall S. Peterson
London Business School

Madan M. Pillutla
London Business School

Mikolaj Jan Piskorski
Stanford University

Jeffrey T. Polzer
Harvard Business School

Marshall Scott Poole
Texas A&M University

Joseph Porac
New York University

Walter W. Powell
Stanford University

Phanish Puranam
London Business School

Elizabeth C. Ravlin
University of South Carolina

Peter Ring
Loyola Marymount University

Catherine A. Riordan
Central Michigan University

Karlene H. Roberts
University of California,
Berkeley

Ivan Robertson
Manchester Business School, University
of Manchester

Steven G. Rogelberg
University of North Carolina at Charlotte

Sarah Ronson
London Business School

Paul Rosenfeld
Navy Personnel Research, Studies and
Technology

Denise M. Rousseau
Carnegie Mellon University

Martin Ruef
Stanford University

Benjamin Schneider
University of Maryland

Randall S. Schuler
Rutgers,
The State University of New Jersey

Brent A. Scott
University of Florida

Craig Shepherd
The Institute of Work Psychology,
University of Sheffield

Sabine Sonnentag
University of Konstanz

Olav Sorenson
UCLA Anderson School of Management

Paul E. Spector
University of South Florida

Kannan Srikanth
London Business School

David Strang
Cornell University

Linda K. Stroh
Loyola University of Chicago

Kim Sutherland
University of Cambridge

Robert I. Sutton
Stanford University

Philip Tetlock
University of California, Berkeley

Marie D. Thomas
California State University,
San Marcos

Ginka Toegel
London School of Economics

Anne S. Tsui
Arizona State University

Michael Useem
University of Pennsylvania

Andrew H. Van de Ven
University of Minnesota

John Van Maanen
Massachusetts Institute of Technology

Toby D. Wall
University of Sheffield

John P. Wanous
Ohio State University

Karl E. Weick
University of Michigan

Keith Weigelt
University of Pennsylvania

Michael A. West
Aston University

Glen Whyte
University of Toronto

Charles R. Williams
Texas Christian University

Donna J. Wood
University of Northern Iowa

Robert Wood
Queensland University of Technology

Stephen J. Wood
University of Sheffield

Richard W. Woodman
Texas A&M University

Yoshio Yanadori
Sauder School of Business, University of British Columbia

Stuart A. Youngblood
Texas Christian University

Carolyn Youssef
University of Nebraska-Lincoln

Edward Zajac
Kellogg School of Management,
Northwestern University

Dale Zand
New York University

A

ability

Joyce Hogan

This important class of INDIVIDUAL DIFFER-
ENCES denotes competence in an activity (*see*
COMPETENCY). It is the capacity to act – it is
realized talent. Ability is a synonym for mental
power, although there are other human abilities
beyond the cognitive domain. Ability, a construct inferred from human performance, is a
product of inherited genetic predispositions and
acquired characteristics. Basic abilities interact
with PERSONALITY and MOTIVATION to predict performance across a range of tasks.

Historically, intelligence was seen as the basic
human ability, and perhaps the most classic
controversy in psychology is whether intelligence is a general ability (g) or a collection of
specific abilities. Spearman, at the turn of the
century, studied relations between mental measures and concluded that intelligence has one
general component and several secondary components. Lubinski (2003) provides an update on
the state of the field 100 years post-Spearman.
Thorndike and Thurstone argued that there are
multiple components of intelligence; the most
comprehensive conceptualization of intelligence
is Gilford's structure of intellect model, which
proposes 120 cognitive abilities. More recently,
Cattell and Horn suggest two dimensions:
fluid intelligence, based on biological inherit-
ance, and crystallized intelligence, based on
fluid ability combined with experience. Measures of intellectual abilities almost always include verbal comprehension and quantitative
reasoning. Item response theory advanced measurement of abilities by providing a model for
linking item responses and latent traits, as well
as providing efficient computerized adaptive
test procedures. In addition to the cognitive
domain, other abilities underlying task performance appear in the O*NET taxonomy of occupational information (US Department of Labor,
2001).

See also *aptitude; self-efficacy; skill*

Bibliography

Lubinski, D. (2003). Introduction to the special section on
cognitive abilities: 100 years after Spearman's (1904)
"General intelligence" objectively determined and
measured. *Journal of Personality and Social Psychology*,
86, 96–111.
US Department of Labor, Employment, and Training
Administration (2001). *O*NET Online* (online.
onetcenter.org). Washington, DC.

absenteeism

Gary Johns

Absenteeism is the failure to report for scheduled work. It can be distinguished from lateness,
which indicates a failure to show up for work on
time, and from turnover, which indicates a permanent break in the employment relationship.
Traditionally, managers have been interested in
absenteeism because of its cost to organizations,
while academics have been interested in absenteeism on the assumption that it indicates something about employees' social or psychological
attachment to the organization.

THE MEASUREMENT OF ABSENTEEISM

Organizations often codify absence instances
with attributions as to cause, which are of suspect
accuracy. Consequently, researchers most often
simply divide absenteeism into *time lost*, the
number of days missed over some period, and

frequency, the number of inceptions of absence over some period irrespective of the duration of each incident. To permit comparisons of employees with a different number of scheduled days or to characterize absenteeism at the group level, these figures can also be expressed as rates. Since absence is missing *scheduled* work, jury duty, vacation time, and maternity leave are not generally counted as absence.

Absence is a low base rate behavior, in that most employees exhibit relatively low absence levels while a few exhibit higher levels. Thus, a frequency distribution for absenteeism is truncated on the low end and positively skewed. Because it is a low base rate behavior, absence measures for individuals must be aggregated over a reasonably long period (3–12 months) to achieve adequate reliability of measurement. Even then, the reliability of absence measures (indexed by inter-period stability or internal consistency) is variable. Some validity evidence suggests that frequency of absence is more likely than time lost to reflect a voluntary component (Chadwick-Jones, Nicholson, and Brown, 1982; Hackett and Guion, 1985). Because of its non-normal distribution, managers should be aware that a few extreme absentees can have a disproportionate effect on means calculated from absence distributions.

CORRELATES AND CAUSES OF ABSENTEEISM

A longstanding tradition concerns the correlation between demographic variables and absenteeism. This research reveals reliable associations between age and absence among men (younger workers exhibit more absence), and gender and absence (women are absent more than men). However, little theory has emerged to explain these associations.

There is no dominant theory of absenteeism. Johns (1997) presents several "models" of absenteeism reflecting the fact that absence is the product of diverse causes and has been studied with a diversity of methodologies uncommon in the organizational sciences (Johns, 2003). Concerning the *medical model*, health-related behaviors such as smoking and problem drinking are associated with absence, as are migraine pain, back pain, and depression. Self-reported health status is correlated with absence, and people attribute the majority of their own absence to minor medical problems. The ultimate accuracy of such attributions is questionable, since "sickness" has motivational correlates, medical diagnoses often reflect prevailing community standards, and people sometimes adopt sick roles that manifest themselves in absence.

The *withdrawal model* suggests that absenteeism is an attempt to remove oneself temporarily from aversive working conditions. The literature on the relationship between job satisfaction and absenteeism reveals a modest association, with dissatisfaction with the work itself being the facet most associated with absenteeism (Hackett and Guion, 1985). Feelings of inequity and weak organizational support are especially likely to prompt absence. The progression-of-withdrawal hypothesis, for which there is fairly convincing evidence, posits a movement from lateness to absence to turnover.

The *deviance model* derives from the negative consequences of absence for organizations. In one form, it suggests that absentees harbor negative dispositional traits that render them unreliable. People tend to make negative attributions about the causes of others' absenteeism, and absenteeism is a frequent cause of employee–management CONFLICT. People also have a tendency to underreport their own absenteeism and to see their own behavior as exemplary compared to that of their co-workers and occupational peers. Evidence for a likely connection between negative traits and absenteeism includes the temporal and cross-situational stability of absence, its negative association with conscientiousness and PERSONALITY-based measures of integrity, and its positive correlation with other negative work behaviors such as poor performance (Bycio, 1992).

The *economic model* of absence suggests that attendance behavior is influenced by economic and quasi-economic constraints and opportunities. Those who value highly their non-work time are more likely to be absent, and looser contractual provisions regarding attendance result in more absence. Absenteeism is negatively associated with wages and the unemployment rate and positively associated with unionized status. Some industrial relations scholars have argued that absence is a form of unorganized conflict that substitutes for some of the functions of collective action.

The *cultural model* of absence begins with the observation that there is often more variance between aggregates of individuals (such as work groups, departments, organizations, occupations, industries, and nations) than within these aggregates. Mechanisms of social influence and control subsumed under the label *absence culture* have been advanced to account for these differences between groups (Chadwick-Jones, Nicholson, and Brown, 1982; Johns and Nicholson, 1982; Nicholson and Johns, 1985) (*see* ORGANIZATIONAL CLIMATE). Work unit absence has been shown to account for individual absence over and above individual-level predictors, and some rich case studies of absence cultures exist. The content of such cultures implicates absence norms, cohesiveness, management expectations, and shared views about the consequences of the behavior.

MANAGING ABSENTEEISM

The deviance model has dominated management approaches to absence. As a result, PUNISHMENT and discipline systems are the most common methods of controlling absence. Used alone, they are not especially effective because of negative side effects and because few employees are actually punished. More effective are mixed consequence systems that punish extreme offenders but reward good attenders with money or time off (Rhodes and Steers, 1990). JOB ENRICHMENT and flextime have both been associated with reduced absence, as have self-management programs that teach employees to regulate their own attendance behavior. Badly needed are theories that translate the likely causes of absenteeism into credible interventions and organizations with the foresight to experiment with these interventions. Obsession with extreme offenders has distracted managers from giving attention to the attendance behavior of all employees.

See also *hardiness; job satisfaction; motivation; performance appraisal/performance management; stress*

Bibliography

Bycio, P. (1992). Job performance and absenteeism: A review and meta-analysis. *Human Relations*, **45**, 193–220.

Chadwick-Jones, J. K., Nicholson, N., and Brown, C. (1982). *Social Psychology of Absenteeism*. New York: Praeger.

Goodman, P. S. and Atkin, R. S. (eds.) (1984). *Absenteeism*. San Francisco: Jossey-Bass.

Hackett, R. D. and Guion, R. M. (1985). A reevaluation of the absenteeism–job satisfaction relationship. *Organizational Behavior and Human Decision Processes*, **35**, 340–81.

Harrison, D. A., Johns, G., and Martocchio, J. J. (2000). Changes in technology, teamwork, and diversity: New directions for a new century of absenteeism research. *Research in Personnel and Human Resources Management*, **18**, 43–91.

Harrison, D. A. and Martocchio, J. J. (1998). Time for absenteeism: A 20-year review of origins, offshoots, and outcomes. *Journal of Management*, **24**, 305–30.

Johns, G. (1997). Contemporary research on absence from work: Correlates, causes, and consequences. *International Review of Industrial and Organizational Psychology*, **12**, 115–73.

Johns, G. (2003). How methodological diversity has improved our understanding of absenteeism from work. *Human Resource Management Review*, **13**, 157–84.

Johns, G. and Nicholson, N. (1982). The meanings of absence: New strategies for theory and research. *Research in Organizational Behavior*, **4**, 127–73.

Nicholson, N. and Johns, G. (1985). The absence culture and the psychological contract: Who's in control of absence? *Academy of Management Review*, **10**, 397–407.

Rhodes, S. R. and Steers, R. M. (1990). *Managing Employee Absenteeism*. Reading, MA: Addison-Wesley.

accountability

Philip Tetlock and Erika Henik

Accountability refers to the implicit or explicit expectation that one may be called on to justify one's beliefs, feelings, or actions to others (Scott and Lyman, 1968; Tetlock, 1985, 1992). Accountability links individuals to institutions by reminding them of the need to: (a) act in accordance with prevailing norms; and (b) advance compelling justifications or excuses for conduct that deviates from those norms (Edgerton, 1985). Thus defined, it plays a key role in everyday DECISION-MAKING.

Accountability represents a nexus of micro- and macro-organizational processes. Psychologists and micro-organizational behaviorists who study judgment and choice have focused on the cognitive and emotional strategies that decision-makers deploy to cope with constituencies' or audiences' specific requests for justification. AGENCY THEORISTS have focused on the perverse organizational and societal consequences that ensue when principals inadvertently give agents incentives to act in ways contrary to the principals' interests. Sociologists and cultural theorists have focused on accountability relationships as manifestations of broader organization norms, values, and operating routines.

Tetlock's (1992) social contingency model highlights individuals' relationships to social structures in decision-making contexts. This "meso" approach identifies the strategies people use to cope with accountability demands from external constituencies, as well as the personality and situational moderators of these coping strategies. The model expands the explanatory power of the micro- and macro-accounts of decision-making by adding considerations of the social and political contexts in which decisions are made and more psychologically nuanced options than strict norm adherence (*homo sociologicus*) and amoral rationality (*homo economicus*).

IDENTITY-DEFINING CHOICES AND COPING STRATEGIES

Accountability demands can represent challenges to one's social IDENTITY, according to self-presentation theorists. The ways in which people set priorities among potentially clashing social-identity goals and the strategies they use to achieve them are therefore key research foci. Recent studies have identified five identity-defining choices that arise in accountability predicaments and the antecedents likely to activate particular coping strategies.

(1) Attitude-shifting versus authenticity   Attitude-shifting is likely when the audience is powerful, firmly committed to its position and intolerant of others, and when the decision-maker lacks firm convictions and is socially insecure. However, it is feasible only when the decision-maker knows the views of the anticipated audience. Attitude-shifting becomes psychologically costly when it requires compromises of basic private beliefs (triggering cognitive dissonance) and socially costly when it requires backtracking on past commitments (making one look duplicitous).

But when these preconditions have been satisfied, attitude-shifting represents a cognitively efficient and politically expedient strategy that undermines neither one's self-concept as a principled being nor one's social reputation for integrity.

(2) Preemptive self-criticism versus defensive bolstering   One can respond to accountability pressures by trying to anticipate critics' reasonable objections and factoring them into one's own position (Tetlock, 1992) or by directing mental effort toward generating plausible reasons that bolster one's position (Staw, 1980). Accountability motivates thought in each case, but the thoughts take dialectically complex forms in the former coping strategy and evaluatively simpler forms in the latter.

Preemptive self-criticism is more likely when decision-makers are accountable to an audience with unknown views or to audiences with conflicting views that recognize the legitimacy of the other point of view, when decision-makers perceive the audience or audiences to be powerful or cognitively sophisticated (and equally so), and when decision-makers are not constrained by strong private views or past public commitments.

Defensive bolstering is most likely to be activated when decision-makers are accountable to powerful audiences that are not believed to be that knowledgeable about a topic, are accountable for past statements or acts that cast doubt on their competence or morality and that cannot be retracted or reversed, and recognize that it is impossible to deny responsibility for the conduct in question.

(3) Ducking, mediating, or plunging into controversy   Accountability theory posits that people will cope with contradictory constituency demands in one of three ways. First, they may engage in decision avoidance by buck-passing, procrastinating, or obfuscating, especially when they are accountable to conflicting constituencies that are powerful and equally so, when the constituencies deny the legitimacy of the other point of view, when there are no institutional precedents for evading taking a stand, and when decision-makers' own views are relatively weak. Second, aligning with one of the constituencies becomes tempting when the conflicting

entities deny each other's legitimacy, there are no institutional precedents for decision avoidance, one audience is more powerful than the other and favors a position similar to one's own preference, and the decision-makers hold strong views to which they are publicly committed. Third, trying to mediate the CONFLICT is likely when the clashing audiences are both powerful and equally so, when the audiences acknowledge the legitimacy of the other point of view, and when there are no precedents for decision evasion.

(4) Implementing versus resisting the collective mission This choice arises when people feel accountable for performance, rather than opinions or preferences. Thus, it pits good ORGANIZATIONAL CITIZENSHIP against resisting performance standards. The following preconditions have been found to promote the internalization of new performance standards: the perception that the standards are reasonable, were set through fair procedures, and are necessary for the survival of the organization, that burdens are shared fairly, and that strong cultural commitments to good citizenship exist within the organization, especially at the top. Research also sheds light on the forms resistance is likely to take when these conditions are systematically violated. Drawing on the work of Hirschman (1970) and Tyler (1990), accountability theory predicts that people will take advantage of opportunities to exercise the voice option, such as protesting burdensome standards, offering accounts for performance shortfalls, and appealing to higher authorities.

(5) Concentrating versus diffusing sacrifice Sacrifices (e.g., budget cuts) can be spread across many constituencies, avoiding severe impact on any one group, or targeted at subsets of constituencies based on efficiency or political grounds. Tetlock (1999) has argued that decision-makers who have internalized egalitarian values should be likely to spread a sacrifice widely when it is relatively small, when it is difficult to identify distinct pockets of inefficiency, and when the groups that have been singled out for deep cuts have demonstrated the ability to mobilize protest in the past. Decision-makers who have internalized the neoclassical economic value of efficiency should concentrate cuts on specific constituencies when they confront large budget cuts, can easily distinguish more from less efficient work units, and know that the groups singled out for deep cuts have little capacity to resist.

A BRIDGE BETWEEN COGNITIVISTS AND INSTITUTIONALISTS

Although cognitive social psychologists, sociologists, and economists all have explored accountability (see Lerner and Tetlock, 1999, for a review), not much cross-fertilization has occurred between the micro and macro camps, leaving many opportunities for future research.

For cognitivists, accountability theory clarifies empirical boundary conditions and suggests normative boundary conditions on the cognitive-miser portrait of human nature. It does so by explaining how people think, not just what they think. The theory specifies when people can be motivated to be thoughtful and resistant to various cognitive biases. For example, preexposure accountability (informing people that they will be held accountable for their judgments before they are exposed to the evidence on which they will base these judgments) is substantially more potent than post-exposure accountability in mitigating overattribution, primacy effects, and overconfidence, partly because it motivates effort-demanding self-critical thought.

The theory also suggests that response tendencies labeled errors or biases may in fact be appropriate or rational given particular accountability considerations. Escalating commitment to projects with large sunk costs (Staw, 1980) may be a rational course of action if one is judged on decisiveness or accountable to constituencies who benefit from continuing such projects (*see* COMMITMENT, ESCALATING). Sutton (1995) observes that unchecked public scrutiny can lead to perseverance at ongoing activities. Thus, the theory identifies combinations of micro-processes and accountability structures that can undermine macro-organizational goals like economic efficiency.

For institutionalists, accountability theory accounts for how individuals cope with cross-pressures and predicts which competing influence is likely to prevail, under what conditions, and for which subgroups of individuals. The theory predicts that most people will approximate *homo sociologicus*, responding to routine problems on normative autopilot, as long as they believe their social contract with the organization is being honored, but that they will shift into cognitive high gear when this bond is challenged.

Cognitive vigilance induced by cross-pressures need not lead to counter-normative conduct, though deviance may emerge when people assess that they have been treated contemptuously. Thus, accountability theory may be of use in generating hypotheses about the circumstances under which whistleblowing will occur to internal or external authorities (if at all) in the face of conflicting constituencies, performance standards that are perceived as legitimate or illegitimate, and the presence or absence of sanctioned channels for exercising voice. The theory has also implications for corporate governance because it predicts the effects that concentrated (e.g., boards) or diffuse (e.g., shareholders) constituencies may have on accountability structures, principal–agent dynamics, and opportunities for cooptation (*see* TOP MANAGEMENT TEAMS).

CONCLUSION

Early experimental work on accountability derived from the error-and-bias tradition of cognitive social psychology and focused on a narrow range of easily manipulated independent variables. Future research programs would do well to incorporate a broader array of reporting structures, organizational cultures, and coping strategies more reflective of real-world choice points and both institutional and individual constraints.

See also *bureaucracy; institutional theory*

Bibliography

Edgerton, R. B. (1985). *Rules, Exceptions, and Social Order.* Berkeley: University of California Press.
Hirschman, A. O. (1970). *Exit, Voice, and Loyalty: Responses to Declines in Firms, Organizations, and States.* Cambridge, MA: Harvard University Press.
Lerner, J. S. and Tetlock, P. E. (1999). Accounting for the effects of accountability. *Psychological Bulletin*, **125**, 255–75.
Scott, M. B. and Lyman, S. (1968). Accounts. *American Sociological Review*, 33, 46–62.
Staw, B. M. (1980). Rationality and justification in organizational life. In B. M. Staw and L. L. Cummings (eds.), *Research in Organizational Behavior*, Vol. 2. Greenwich, CT: JAI Press, 45–80.
Sutton, R. (1995). Public scrutiny. In N. Nicholson (ed.), *The Blackwell Encyclopedic Dictionary of Organizational Behavior.* Oxford: Blackwell, 458–9.
Tetlock, P. E. (1985). Accountability: A social check on the fundamental attribution error. *Social Psychological Quarterly*, **48**, 227–36.
Tetlock, P. E. (1992). The impact of accountability on judgment and choice: Toward a social contingency model. *Advances in Experimental Social Psychology*, **25**, 331–76.
Tetlock, P. E. (1999). Accountability theory: Mixing properties of human agents with properties of social systems. In L. L. Thompson, J. M. Levine et al. (eds.), *Shared Cognition in Organizations: The Management of Knowledge.* Mahwah, NJ: Lawrence Erlbaum Associates, 117–37.
Tyler, T. R. (1990). *Why People Obey the Law.* New Haven, CT: Yale University Press.

achievement, need for

Nigel Nicholson

Need theory flourished as a school of MOTIVATION theory from the 1930s to the 1970s, especially through the work of scholars such as Murray, Maslow, and Herzberg. These theories have mostly not survived critical review and empirical test, though arguably an exception to this is the work of David McClelland, who focused specifically on three sets of needs: achievement, affiliation, and power. It is the first of these needs (nAch) that has continued to remain central within the discourse of managerial psychology. McClelland used a clinical technique, the Thematic Apperception Test (TAT), to assess these needs. In this projective test, subjects supply a narrative to explain a series of line drawing depictions of individuals and groups in ambiguously interpretable situations. Although the technique is no longer in use within OB, mainly due to problems of RELIABILITY, the concept of achievement motivation remains popular. This is due to the programmatic work by followers of the theory (Heckhausen, 1977) and the evident applicability of its propositions to a range of issues and areas. These include the important idea that people with high nAch are the most likely to set themselves stretching, rather than easy or difficult goals (*see* GOAL-SETTING), to seek situations where they can control outcomes, and to be motivated by intrinsic rather than extrinsic rewards such as money, status or praise. High achievement motivated individuals are portrayed as seeking and welcoming FEEDBACK, especially if it is concrete and task focused. They are described as constantly contemplating goals and challenges, and seeking out situations where they have opportunities to find new problems to solve and areas in which they can implement improvements. McClelland maintained that nAch was formed through childhood socialization, especially by parents, but could be elevated by cognitive-behavioral training. Achievement motivation and power motivation have been used to distinguish CAREER orientations; for example, nAch is associated with sales orientation and performance, and nPow is linked with interest in line management positions. Researchers have decomposed achievement motivation into components, capable of discriminating between small business and economics students (Sagie and Elizur, 1999). Need for achievement has often been associated with ENTREPRENEURSHIP, and a recent meta-analysis has confirmed its predictive relevance to entrepreneurial orientation and behavior (Collins, Hanges, and Locke, 2004).

See also *affiliation; leadership; need for; power; self-efficacy;*

Bibliography

Collins, C. J., Hanges, P. J., and Locke, E. A. (2004). The relationship of achievement motivation to entrepreneurial behavior: A meta-analysis. *Human Performance*, 17, 95–117.

Heckhausen, H. (1977). Achievement motivation and its constructs: A cognitive model. *Motivation and Emotion*, 1, 283–329.

Langan-Fox, J. and Roth, S. (1995). Achievement motivation and female entrepreneurs. *Journal of Occupational and Organizational Psychology*, 68, 209–18.

McClelland, D. C. (1985). *Human Motivation*. Glenview, IL: Scott Foresman.

Sagie, A. and Elizur, D. (1999). Achievement motive and entrepreneurial orientation: A structural analysis. *Journal of Organizational Behavior*, 20, 375–87.

action research

David Fryer

Action research is "scientific social research which is participatory and practice-oriented, which aims to find solutions to social problems and to emancipate individuals and groups confronted with such problems" (Boog, Keune, and Tromp, 2003: 419). However, as Boog, Keune, and Tromp point out, there is disagreement among action researchers as to the degree of participation, emancipation, wider relevance, and practical impact required for something to count as "true" action research.

The theoretical origins of action research can be traced to Aristotle, Dewy, and Mead, but Kurt Lewin is generally thought to be the first to use the term "action research." Lewin certainly brought together all the key elements: the facilitation of change, the researcher as active participant, open systems assumptions, and iterative cycles of inquiry, action, and evaluation (Boog, 2003: 429). As early as 1946, Lewin wrote: "The research needed for social practice can best be characterized as research for social management or social engineering. It is a type of action-research, a comparative research on the conditions and effects of various forms of social action, and research leading to social action. Research that produces nothing but books will not suffice" (Lewin, 1946).

However, Marie Jahoda's classic action research in an unemployed Austrian community occurred 13 years earlier. In *Marienthal: The Sociography of an Unemployed Community*, first published in German in 1933, Jahoda describes how, among many other interventions, her interdisciplinary team distributed shoes and clothing, ran courses, provided free medical consultations and medication, and facilitated political party activity, to build close and insight-yielding research–community member relationships and in return for access to information. It was "a consistent point of policy that [none] of our researchers should be…a mere reporter or outside observer. Everyone was to fit naturally into the communal life by participating in some activity generally useful to the community" (Jahoda, Lazarsfeld, and Zeisel, 1972: 5).

Sociotechnical systems theorists (STSTs) used an action research base to redesign the work of coalminers and weavers in the 1950s and more recent organizational psychology job redesign studies have followed the tradition in also including action research components (e.g., Kemp et al., 1983). Participatory action research is also frequently favored by liberation psychology, critical psychology, and community psychology (e.g., Fryer and Fagan, 2003). *See* CRITICAL THEORY.

Pragmatically, when the action involved is meaningful to the potential participants, action research is a good way to investigate issues that are exceedingly complex or sensitive, or when working with people who would otherwise be unlikely to become constructively involved in research because of alienation, suspicion, "research fatigue," or disillusionment with "normal science" researchers. Because action researchers generally use a variety of methods in triangulation, because their field engagement is protracted over time, and because participants tend to cooperate enthusiastically, action research is also often methodologically sophisticated. The main attraction of action research is, however, that it facilitates the development of ethically and ideologically more progressive ways to engage simultaneously in collaborative, problem-driven, change oriented inquiry and intervention.

See also *research design; research methods*

Bibliography

Boog, B. W. M. (2003). The emancipatory character of action research, its history and the present state of the art. Pages 426–38 in B. W. M. Boog, L. Keune, and C. Tromp (guest eds.) (2003), Action research and emancipation. Special Issue, *Journal of Community and Applied Social Psychology*, 13 (6), 419–503.

Boog, B. W. M., Keune, L., and Tromp, C. (guest eds.) (2003). Action research and emancipation. Special Issue, *Journal of Community and Applied Social Psychology*, 13 (6), 419–503.

Fryer, D. and Fagan, R. (2003). Towards a critical community psychological perspective on unemployment and mental health research. *American Journal of Community Psychology*, 32 (1/2), 89–96.

Jahoda, M., Lazarsfeld, P. F., and Zeisel, H. (1972) [1933]. *Marienthal: The Sociography of an Unemployed Community*. London: Tavistock.

Kemp, N. J., Wall, T. D., Clegg, C. W., and Cordery, J. L. (1983). Autonomous work groups in a greenfield site: A comparative study. *Journal of Occupational Psychology*, 56, 271–88.

Lewin, K. (1946). Action research and minority problems. In Gertrud Weiss Lewin (ed.), *Resolving Social Conflicts: Selected Papers on Group Dynamics by Kurt Lewin*. New York: Harper and Row; Tokyo: John Weatherhill, ch. 13.

affect

see EMOTION IN ORGANIZATIONS

affiliation, need for

Nigel Nicholson

This is one of a trio of needs, along with power and achievement, extensively studied by David McClelland and followers. People identified as high nAff have been found to be motivated to seek colleagues for qualities of friendship before skill, to avoid CONFLICT, to seek approval, and to demonstrate high levels of CONFORMITY if it is instrumental to their social goals. McClelland also claimed it to be a component of a STRESS immunity syndrome.

See also *achievement, need for; hardiness; power, need for*

Bibliography

McClelland, D. C. (1989). Motivational factors in health and disease. *American Psychologist*, 44, 675–83.

age

Amanda Griffiths

Probabilistic forecasting methods suggest that by the end of the twenty-first century, the world's population will have stopped growing. This trend is already evident in many industrialized nations, with declining birth rates and increasing dependency ratios (an increasing number of pensioners per 100 working people). A stabilized or declining population is an aging population. This presents major economic and social challenges, not least for the world of work. Encouraging people to work for longer than has been traditional has been proposed as a solution to these challenges and as a result statutory retirement ages are rising. Thus, strategies need to be developed for enabling older people to stay on at work without risk to JOB SATISFACTION, performance, or health (Griffiths, 1997).

Research suggests that the widely held view that older employees perform less well may be inaccurate. Most of the relevant research has focused on age-related changes in cognitive and physical abilities (Warr, 2003). There are age related declines in skeletal, neuro-muscular, and energy-delivery systems, information processing speed, and certain aspects of memory. However, research has suggested that in many jobs, older workers compensate for these declines by means of experience, verbal and social skills, domain-specific knowledge and wisdom, such that overall performance does not decrease (Salthouse and Maurer, 1996).

Much so-called "age-related" deterioration can be countered once employers cease to regard chronological age as a predictor itself. Managers and supervisors play a key role in perpetuating myths about age related decline in competence; stereotypical ATTITUDES and discriminatory actions are not uncommon (Redman and Snape, 2002). These can affect selection, learning and development activities, CAREER DEVELOPMENT and promotion, as well as redundancy. However, longitudinal studies have shown that where supervisors are knowledgeable and have a positive attitude towards aging and where jobs are carefully designed, often involving team work, older employees (usually defined in research studies as 45+) continue to work successfully.

An extensive examination of this psychosocial work environment (employees' perceptions of the way their work is organized and managed) with regard to aging has not been conducted. Crucial questions that require answers include: (1) How do people's needs and behavior at work change as they age? (2) Do management practices and JOB DESIGN fairly reflect such changes? The fact that many countries are implementing anti-age DISCRIMINATION legislation suggests that the answer to these questions is "no."

Research also suggests that older workers, who traditionally receive little training, underachieve rapidly in changing jobs. They may require different training methodologies, and are more anxious about and less confident in their ability to learn (Maurer, 2001); these are all matters that can be resolved by non-discriminatory practices.

Contributions by older employees are influenced by organizational policies, age awareness programs, training, carefully designed work equipment and physical work environments, health promotion policies (particularly the promotion of physical exercise), flexible and part-time working options, horizontal job mobility, and gradual retirement. Many organizations, perhaps reflecting Western culture, have not yet evolved to the point where the potential contribution of older people is recognized and allowed to flourish. Once the current barriers are removed, and existing and developing knowledge is implemented, an optimistic picture for older workers may emerge.

See also *individual differences; job characteristics*

Bibliography

Griffiths, A. (1997). Aging, health, and productivity: A challenge for the new millennium. *Work and Stress*, 11, 197–214.

Maurer, T. (2001). Career-relevant learning and development, worker age, and beliefs about self-efficacy for development. *Journal of Management*, 27, 123–40.

Redman, T. and Snape, E. (2002). Ageism in teaching: Stereotypical beliefs and discriminatory attitudes towards the over fifties. *Work, Employment, and Society*, 16, 355–71.

Salthouse, T. and Maurer, T. (1996). Aging, job performance, and career development. In J. E. Birren and K. W. Schaie (eds.), *Handbook of the Psychology of Aging*. San Diego: Academic Press.

Warr, P. (2003). Age and work behavior: Physical attributes, cognitive abilities, knowledge, personality traits, and motives. In C. Cooper and I. Robertson (eds.), *International Review of Industrial and Organizational Psychology*. London: Wiley, 1–36.

agency theory

Edward Zajac

This theory examines the problems – and partial contractual solutions (*see* CONTRACTS) – that exist when a principal delegates DECISION-MAKING responsibility to an agent who is paid a fee, but whose own objectives may conflict with those of the principal. This economics-based theoretical perspective, like TRANSACTION COST ECONOMICS, has grown enormously in scope and influence (and with some controversy) since the 1970s, and has been used in analyses of executive compensation contracts and other corporate GOVERNANCE issues. In applying or adapting agency theory to these organizational issues, it is useful, however, to distinguish between what Jensen (1983: 334–5) refers to as two "almost entirely separate" agency literatures: a normative principal–agent literature emphasizing the design of compensation contracts with optimal risk sharing properties (Levinthal, 1988), and a positive, empirically based agency literature focusing primarily on questions relating to the separation of corporate ownership and control, and the role of boards of directors (Jensen and Murphy, 1990). This distinction still holds true today (cf. Bolton and Scharfstein, 1998; Gibbons, 1998).

Organizational research (as well as most of the research in financial economics) using agency theory has tended to draw from the positive, rather than the normative agency literature. For example, while the positive agency literature highlights the value of placing greater amounts of managerial compensation and managerial wealth at risk by tying it closer to firm performance, the normative agency literature stresses the need to consider the potential disadvantages of forcing managers to bear "excessive" compensation risk (Beatty and Zajac, 1994) (*see* RISK TAKING). Organizational research has generally placed greater emphasis on the importance – from an incentive and control standpoint – of imposing strong pay-for-performance linkages, rather than the possible disadvantages of imposing risk bearing on managers through their compensation contracts (*see* INCENTIVES). However, organizational researchers have recently begun to examine such questions more closely (Bloom and Milkovich, 1998; Miller, Wiseman, and Gomez-Mejia,

2002), studied through the familiar contingency lens in the organizational literature on compensation, which holds that different forms of compensation, such as pay-for-performance, vary in their attractiveness to individuals, and therefore, vary in their appropriateness as incentive–motivational tools .

Agency problems typically emerge because of two fundamental conditions that underlie principal–agent relationships: goal incongruence and information asymmetry (Zajac, 1990). Goal incongruence is an assumed condition, without which an agency problem reduces to a more easily solvable contracting problem. The second dimension, information asymmetry, is a critical variable in the principal–agent relationship, and has generated a substantial body of research within the information economics literature. Information asymmetry refers to the fact that in the typical principal–agent relationship, the principal has less information than the agent about (1) the characteristics of the agent and (2) the decisions made and the actions taken by the agent. These two aspects of information asymmetry have been labeled formally in the information economics literature as *adverse selection* and *moral hazard*, respectively.

The moral hazard problem is typically discussed in the positive agency literature that examines problems between owners and top managers (Fama and Jensen, 1983) or between boards and CEOs (Westphal and Zajac, 1994, 2001). For that literature, the issue is whether owners are able to adequately monitor and control the actions and decisions of self-interested CEOs. Most organizational research has tended to focus on the effectiveness (or ineffectiveness) of boards of directors as monitors of top management, without considering explicitly the possible cost-benefit trade-offs between the relative use of incentives versus monitoring as alternative sources of controlling managerial behavior (Zajac and Westphal, 1994). The search for a simple and direct relationship between indicators of board monitoring and firm performance has been elusive. One explanation is that three fundamental elements underlie agency relationships in organizations (incentives, monitoring, and risk bearing), and that all three should be included in theoretical and empirical analyses of contractual relations (Beatty and Zajac, 1994). Future research that considers these three elements jointly, and explicitly considers the conflicts, trade-offs, and substitution possibilities among them (as well as possible complementarities), may have the greatest potential to further advance our understanding of top executive compensation, ownership, and corporate governance.

See also *accountability; organizational effectiveness*

Bibliography

Beatty, R. P. and Zajac, E. J. (1994). Top management incentives, monitoring, and risk sharing: A study of executive compensation, ownership, and board structure in initial public offerings. *Administrative Science Quarterly*, **39**, 313–36.

Bloom, M. and Milkovich, G. T. (1998). Relationships among risk, incentive pay, and organizational performance. *Academy of Management Journal*, **41**, 283–97.

Bolton, P. and Scharfstein, D. S. (1998). Corporate finance, the theory of the firm, and organizations. *Journal of Economic Perspectives*, **12**, 95–114.

Fama, E. F. and Jensen, M. C. (1983). Separation of ownership and control. *Journal of Law and Economics*, **26**, 301–25.

Gibbons, R. (1998). Incentives in organizations. *Journal of Economic Perspectives*, **12**, 115–32.

Jensen, M. C. (1983). Organization theory and methodology. *Accounting Review*, **58** (3), 19–339.

Jensen, M. C. and Murphy, K. J. (1990). Performance pay and top-management incentives. *Journal of Political Economy*, **98**, 225–64.

Levinthal, D. (1988). A survey of agency models of organizations. *Journal of Economic Behavior and Organization*, **9**, 153–85.

Miller, J. S., Wiseman, R. M., and Gomez-Mejia, L. R. (2002). The fit between CEO compensation and firm risk. *Academy of Management Journal*, **45**, 745–56.

Westphal, J. D. and Zajac, E. J. (1994). Substance and symbolism in CEOs' long-term incentive plans. *Administrative Science Quarterly*, **39**, 367–90.

Westphal, J. D. and Zajac, E. J. (2001). Explaining institutional decoupling: The case of stock repurchase programs. *Administrative Science Quarterly*, **46**, 202–28.

Zajac, E. J. (1990). CEO selection, succession, compensation, and firm performance: A theoretical integration and empirical analysis. *Strategic Management Journal*, **11**, 217–30.

Zajac E. J. and Westphal, J. D. (1994). The costs and benefits of managerial incentives and monitoring in large US corporations: When is more not better? *Strategic Management Journal*, **15** (12), 1–192.

Zajac E. J. and Westphal, J. D. (1998). Toward a behavioral theory of the CEO/Board relationship. In D. C. Hambric, D. A. Nadler, and M. L. Tushman (eds.), *Navigating Change: How CEOs, Top Teams, and Boards Steer Transformation*. 256–77.

altruism

Nigel Nicholson

Altruistic acts are any behaviors enacted by an agent with the intention of conferring a benefit on another individual or group, that impose a cost on the actor without the expectation of any commensurate return or gain. It is truly unselfish behavior, and as such its existence has been challenged philosophically and empirically. The altruism motive – the assertion that human beings sometimes care about the welfare of others as an end in itself – is contrasted with the idea that self-interest is a human universal (*see* THEORY X AND Y). Contemporary EVOLUTIONARY PSYCHOLOGY claims to reconcile these two positions theoretically and empirically, along the lines that altruistic dispositions are motivated by a hardwired instinct to support the interest of those to whom we presume ourselves to be genetically related ("kin selection") and through the indirect reputational benefits that flow from costly signals about one's trustworthiness. In business, altruism is seen as an AGENCY hazard by economists, for whom it undermines rational DECISION-MAKING and the economic interests of the firm. It is seen as especially problematic in FAMILY FIRMS, though there is a contrary view that it is associated with advantageous aspects of organizational culture. Studies frequently identify "irrational" altruism as a commonly occurring phenomenon in bargaining and DECISION-MAKING, where sometimes it is associated with unexpected reciprocal gains.

See also *organizational citizenship behavior; reciprocal altruism; trust*

Bibliography

Schulze, W. S., Lubatkin, M. H., Dino, R. N., and Buchholtz, A. K. (2001). Agency relationships in family firms: Theory and evidence. *Organization Science*, **12**, 99–116.

Sober, E. and Wilson, D. S. (1998). *Unto Others: The Evolution and Psychology of Unselfish Behaviors.* Cambridge, MA: Harvard University Press.

ambiguity

see ROLE AMBIGUITY

anticipatory socialization

see CAREER DEVELOPMENT

anxiety

see STRESS

appraisal

see PERFORMANCE APPRAISAL/PERFORMANCE MANAGEMENT

aptitude

Joyce Hogan

Aptitude is the capacity to acquire SKILL – potential for talent. Traditionally, aptitudes reflect the cumulative experience of daily living under unknown conditions (Anastasi, 1988). Rooted in Thurstone's early interpretations of factor analytic findings on mental ability tests, aptitudes are the group factors or primary abilities that refer to relatively homogeneous and narrowly defined segments of ABILITY. Widely administered ability measures have incorporated this term; for example, the General Aptitude Test Battery (GATB) and the Armed Services Vocational Aptitude Battery (ASVAB), with factor analyses supporting a hierarchical solution with general mental ability underlying specific aptitudes (Carroll, 1993). Interest in measuring aptitude comes from the need to make special-

ized distinctions from the more general intelligence test. Aptitudes predict subsequent performance and can be used to forecast achievement in a new situation. From this practical need plus the availability of factor analysis and high-speed computing, distinctive aptitude measures were developed for educational advising, CAREER counseling, and occupational classification. Current multiple aptitude test batteries include assessments of mechanical reasoning, clerical speed and accuracy, spelling, language use, manual dexterity, and CREATIVITY; these are used widely by the armed services and civilian agencies for vocational counseling. It should be noted that tests of ability, aptitude, and achievement – where achievement is defined as learning information under controlled conditions – correlate very highly, making statistical distinctions between these test types difficult.

See also *individual differences; motivation*

Bibliography

Anastasi, A. (1988). *Psychological Testing.* New York: Macmillan.

Carroll, J. B. (1993). *Human Cognitive Abilities: A Survey of Factor Analytic Studies.* Cambridge: Cambridge University Press.

attitude theory

Ricky W. Griffin

This connotes the body of extant knowledge concerned with the structure of attitudes and the determination and consequences of attitudes. Attitude theory has generally tended to focus on the components of attitudes, the formation of attitudes, and the formation of quasi-consistent construct systems comprised of different attitudes, values, and beliefs.

Central to this body of knowledge is work concerned with attitudes that manifest themselves in and/or that are relevant to the workplace. An attitude is a relatively enduring feeling, belief, and behavioral tendency directed toward specific individuals, groups of individuals, ideas, philosophies, issues, or objects (Ajzen and Fishbein, 1980). Thus, in an organization, a person may (and likely will) have attitudes about various co-workers and colleagues, supervisors, subordinates, various organizational policies and practices, physical working conditions, rewards and other compensation, opportunities for advancement, the organization's culture and climate, and a wide variety of other organizational characteristics (*see* ORGANIZATIONAL CULTURE).

The dominant approach to characterizing the structure of an attitude is in terms of three components. The *affective component* of an attitude is the emotion, feeling, or sentiment the person has toward something. For example, the statement "I do not like that particular work group" reflects affect. The second component of an attitude, the *cognitive component*, is the actual belief or knowledge the individual presumes to have about something. The statement "The people in that work group are lazy and are too political" represents cognition (note that cognitions may or may not be accurate, or true, but are only believed to be by the individual). Third, the *behavioral intention component* of an attitude reflects how the individual intends to behave toward something. For example, the statement "I would resist a transfer to that work group" reflects a behavioral intention. These components are not discrete phenomena that are formed sequentially, but instead interact among themselves and are manifested in a variety of forms and mechanisms.

An alternative view of attitudes that has received moderate attention is the so-called situational model of attitudes (Salancik and Pfeffer, 1977). This approach suggests that attitudes represent socially constructed realities based on social information available in the workplace. Any given person's attitudes are seen as being a function of social cues about the object of the attitude that are provided by "significant others" in the workplace.

Attitudes are of interest in part because of their presumed connection with workplace behavior. Common sense suggests that attitudes will affect behaviors. In reality, this relationship is not straightforward. Only specific attitudes actually predict specific behaviors. For example, a strong attitude about one's pay being too low may cause that person to resign for a position with higher pay. General attitudes such as overall JOB SATISFACTION are not precise predictors of specific job behaviors. Likewise, specific attitudes such as satisfaction with one's vacation schedule are not precise predictors of overall job performance. While people develop a wide array of attitudes in the workplace, much organizational research on attitudes has tended to focus on the key attitude of job satisfaction (Fisher, 1980).

See also *cognitive dissonance; individual differences*

Bibliography

Ajzen, I. and Fishbein, M. (1980). *Understanding Attitudes and Predicting Social Behavior.* Englewood Cliffs, NJ: Prentice-Hall.

Fisher, C. D. (1980). On the dubious wisdom of expecting job satisfaction to correlate with performance. *Academy of Management Review*, 5, 607–12.

Salancik, G. and Pfeffer, J. (1977). An examination of need-satisfaction models of job attitudes. *Administrative Science Quarterly*, **22**, 427–56.

attribution

Mark J. Martinko

An attribution is a causal explanation. Fritz Heider (1958) is credited as the founder of attribution theory. His basic thesis was that people are "naive psychologists" who attempt to attain mastery of their environments by their abilities to explain and understand cause and effect relationships.

Although there are many variations of attribution theory (Martinko, 1995), research on attributions has focused on two primary areas: (1) the achievement motivation model, which emphasizes the intrapersonal process by which individuals explain their own successes and failures (see the work of Weiner (1986) and his colleagues) and (2) the social attribution process by which observers explain the behavior and outcomes of others (see Kelley, 1967; Green and Mitchell, 1979; Martinko, 2002a, b). Attribution theories have been applied to a wide range of organizational phenomena, including stereotyping, LEADERSHIP, performance appraisal processes, interpersonal conflict and aggression, IMPRESSION MANAGEMENT, and perceptions of justice and organizational responsibility.

Regardless of the model used, the basic premise of attribution theory is that people's beliefs about the causation affect their expectancies, emotions, and behaviors. More specifically, a causal explanation is the reason a person uses to explain success or failure. Effort, ABILITY, the difficulty of a task, and luck/chance are typical explanations. These explanations (i.e., attributions) can be classified according to a variety of underlying cognitive dimensions. The internal–external dimension affects emotion and is concerned with whether the cause of success or failure is inside the person or in the environment. Thus, when people attribute failure to their own internal inadequacies they tend to experience negative affect and helplessness. The stability dimension is concerned with whether the cause remains constant or changes over time and affects expectancies. Stable outcomes result in expectations of the same outcomes, whereas unstable outcomes allow for changes in expectations. Other dimensions such as intentionality, controllability, and globality have also been proposed and have had varying levels of empirical support.

Attribution theory has been found to be particularly efficacious in explaining dysfunctional behavior in organizations, including self-destructive behaviors such as learned helplessness, stress, and burnout, and other directed retaliatory behaviors, including violence, aggression, gossip, stealing, and sabotage (Martinko, Gundlach, and Douglas, 2002). This body of research essentially supports the hypothesis that inner-directed self-destructive behaviors are associated with stable and internal attributions such as a lack of ability. On the other hand, outward directed retaliatory behaviors are associated with external and stable attributions such as the belief that management is abusive and inflexible.

Another promising area of research is concerned with attribution styles and their relationships to both traits and behaviors. Attribution style is the tendency of individuals to be biased toward particular types of attributions regardless of situations. People with optimistic styles tend to explain success in terms of internal and stable attributions such as ability and explain failure with external and unstable attributions such as luck. On the other hand, pessimistic individuals tend to make external and unstable attributions for success and internal and stable attributions for failure. A variety of scales have been developed to measure attribution style and are reviewed by Kent and Martinko (1995). Research in this area has generally confirmed that attribution styles are related to the dysfunctional behaviors described above. In addition, there is both empirical and conceptual support for the notion that attributions and attribution styles are related to a variety of INDIVIDUAL DIFFERENCES such as SELF-ESTEEM, SELF-EFFICACY, GENDER, cultural background, and perceptions of organizational JUSTICE (Martinko, Gundlach, and Douglas, 2002). Thus, for example, females tend to make more external attributions than males for success and high self-efficacy is usually associated with internal and stable attributions for success. Finally, the positive psychology movement, which is now gaining attention within organizational behavior, asserts that moderate optimistic biases are associated with TRANSFORMATIONAL LEADERSHIP and healthy productive behavior by individuals.

Another major focus of attribution theory in the organizational sciences is social attributions, which are concerned with how individuals, and leaders in particular, make attributions for the behavior of others. These models generally use Kelley's Cube to explain the leader attribution process (Green and Mitchell, 1979), which posits that observers evaluate behavior along the dimensions of (1) the distinctiveness of the response – performance on this versus other tasks; (2) consistency – over time and occasions; and (3) consensus – comparison to others. The final assignment of responsibility is made according to the principle of covariation, which attempts to determine whether or not changes in causes are related to different outcomes. As Kelley (1967) indicated: "The effect is attributed to that condition which is present when the effect is present and which is absent when the effect is absent." In general, the research has documented that information regarding the dimensions described by Kelley's Cube is related to the nature and severity of leaders' reactions to poor subordinate performance.

Up to this point, researchers have most often used Kelley's model to explain social attributions and Weiner's model to explain intrapersonal achievement related attributions. Recently, Martinko and Thompson (1998) synthesized the Kelley and Weiner models, demonstrating that the same fundamental processes and dimensions of attributions apply to both intrapersonal and social attribution processes. This synthesis facilitates comparing the attributions of actors and observers and is particularly useful in explaining leader–member conflicts (Martinko, 2002a, b) and the process of interpersonal conflict and negotiations.

Promising areas for future research include more exploration of the effects of attribution styles on organizational behaviors and their relations to individual differences, exploration of the interactions of leader and members' attributions and their effects, the role of attributions in interpersonal conflicts and negotiations, the role of attributions in impression management, the contribution of attributional processes to the positive psychology movement, and the relationships between attribution styles and culture.

See also *attitude theory*

Bibliography

Green, S. and Mitchell, T. (1979). Attributional processes of leaders in leader–member interactions. *Organizational Behavior and Human Performance*, **23**, 429–58.

Heider, F. (1958). *The Psychology of Interpersonal Relations*. New York: Wiley.

Kelley, H. H. (1967). Attribution theory in social psychology. In D. Levine (ed.), *Nebraska Symposium on Motivation, 1967*. Lincoln: University of Nebraska Press.

Kent, R. and Martinko, M. J. (1995). The measurement of attributions in organizational research. In M. J. Martinko (ed.), *Attribution Theory: An Organizational Perspective*. Delray Beach, FL: St. Lucie Press, 17–34.

Martinko, M. J. (ed.) (1995). *Attribution Theory: An Organizational Perspective*. Delray Beach, FL: St. Lucie Press.

Martinko, M. J. (ed.) (2002a). *Advances in Attribution Theory*. Greenwich, CT: Information Age Publishing.

Martinko, M. J. (2002b). *Thinking Like a Winner: A Guide to High Performance Leadership*. Tallahassee, FL: Gulf Coast Publishing.

Martinko, M. J., Gundlach, M., and Douglas, S. C. (2002). An attributional explication of counterproductive behavior. *International Journal of Selection and Analysis*, **10** (1/2), 36–50.

Martinko, M. J. and Thompson, N. (1998). A synthesis of the Weiner and Kelley attribution models. *Journal of Basic and Applied Psychology*, **20** (4), 271–84.

Weiner, B. (1986). *An Attribution Theory of Motivation and Emotion*. New York: Springer-Verlag.

authoritarian personality

Nigel Nicholson

This personality syndrome was identified in the 1940s by émigré psychologist refugees from Nazism, in response to a felt need to understand the dynamics of anti-Semitism. Indeed, the F-scale measure of authoritarianism that was developed was a reworking of an earlier Fascism scale. The elements of the syndrome are excessive conformity, submissiveness to authority, intolerance, insecurity, superstition, and rigid stereotyped thought patterns. Although the measure has fallen into disuse the concept remains firmly in the lexicon. It has much overlap with dogmatism, which is associated with people who are intolerant of ambiguity and uncertainty, prone to absolutist ideologies, conservative values, and resistant to change. The originators of the syndrome saw it as the product of parenting styles and upbringing, though research also indicates it probably also has a significant degree of heritability (Olson et al., 2001). In OB there has been no notable recent applications of these ideas, though their key features would seem to be subsumed under Big Five characterizations of PERSONALITY (*see* FIVE FACTOR MODEL OF PERSONALITY).

See also *prejudice*

Bibliography

Adorno, T. W., Frenkel-Brunswick, E., Levinson, D. J., and Sanford, R. N. (1950). *The Authoritarian Personality*. New York: Harper and Row.

Olson, J. M., Vernon, P. A., and Harris, J. A. (2001). The heritability of attitudes: A study of twins. *Journal of Personality and Social Psychology*, **80**, 845–60.

authority

David L. Deephouse

This concept denotes the legitimate POWER in a social system associated with a particular person or position. Legitimate power is consented to or accepted by members of the social system. The power exercised by an authority includes not only the expectation of compliance or obedience with orders but also the ability to reward or punish (*see* PUNISHMENT).

Weber outlined four types of authority. Katz and Kahn (1978) condensed two of them into the rational–legal type; ideally, it is rule bound, formal, and based on positions, not personalities. Prevalent in modern organizations, rational–legal authority is manifested by hierarchy or BUREAUCRACY. Charismatic authority, Weber's second type, also is prevalent in organizations and is derived from the visionary characteristics of a particular leader (*see* LEADERSHIP, CHARISMATIC); this authority is personal and not characterized by rules. Weber's third form of authority is traditional, based on the sanctity of customs, VALUES, and experience; interest in traditional authority in organizations is evidenced by organizational culture.

See also *accountability; management, classical theory; organizational status*

Bibliography

Katz, D. and Kahn, R. L. (1978). *The Social Psychology of Organizations*, 2nd edn. New York: Wiley.

automation

see TECHNOLOGY

autonomous work groups

see SELF-MANAGING TEAMS

B

bargaining

see NEGOTIATION

bases of power

see POLITICS; POWER

batch production

see TECHNOLOGY

behavior modification

see BEHAVIORISM

behavioral decision research

Max H. Bazerman

The rational model of DECISION-MAKING is based on a set of assumptions prescribing how a decision *should* be made rather than describing how a decision *is* made. In contrast, behavioral decision research focuses on the systematic inconsistencies in the decision-making process which prevent humans from making fully rational decisions.

The field of behavior decision research has its roots in the Nobel Prize-winning work of Herbert Simon (1957; March and Simon, 1958). Simon suggested that decision-making is bounded in its rationality and that we can better understand decision-making by explaining actual, rather than normative ("what should be done"), decision processes. The model of bounded rationality sees individuals as attempting to make rational decisions, but acknowledges that decision-makers often lack important information to be fully rational. Time and cost constraints limit the quantity and quality of available information. Finally, limitations on intelligence and perceptions constrain the ability of decision-makers to accurately "calculate" the optimal choice from the information that is available. Together, these limitations prevent decision-makers from making the optimal decisions assumed by the rational model.

Kahneman and Tversky (1979; Tversky and Kahneman, 1974), also in Nobel Prize-winning work, have provided critical information about specific systematic biases that influence judgment. Their work, and work by subsequent researchers, has elucidated our modern understanding of judgment. People rely on a number of simplifying strategies, or rules of thumb, in making decisions. These simplifying strategies are called heuristics. Heuristics provide people with a simple way of dealing with a complex world, producing correct or partially correct judgments more often than not. In addition, it may be inevitable that humans will adopt some way of simplifying decisions. The only drawback of these heuristics is that individuals frequently are unaware that they rely on them. Unfortunately, the misapplication of heuristics to inappropriate situations leads people astray. When managers become aware of the potential adverse impact of using heuristics, they will be able to decide when and where to use them and, if it is to their advantage, eliminate certain heuristics from their cognitive repertoire.

People use a variety of types of heuristics. The poker player follows the heuristic "never play for an inside straight." The mortgage banker follows the heuristic "only spend 35 percent of your income on housing." Although an understanding of these specific heuristics is important to the poker player and mortgage banker, behavioral decision research is with more general cognitive heuristics that affect virtually all individuals. Thus, the heuristics explored in behavioral decision research are not specific to particular individuals; rather, research has shown that they can be applied across the population. The three general heuristics that have received the most attention are (1) the availability heuristic, (2) the representativeness heuristic, and (3) anchoring and adjustment.

The availability heuristic suggests that people assess the frequency, probability, or likely causes of an event by the degree to which instances or occurrences of that event are readily "available" in memory (Tversky and Kahneman, 1973). The representativeness heuristic argues that when making a judgment about an individual (or object or event), people tend to look for traits an individual may have that correspond with previously formed stereotypes. Finally, anchoring and adjustment argues that people make assessments by starting from an initial value and adjusting to yield a final decision.

Unfortunately, these heuristics lead to a number of biases. A number of the predominant biases described in this literature are reviewed below (this summary is based on Bazerman, 2001):

Ease of recall. Individuals judge events which are more easily recalled from memory, based upon vividness or recency, to be more numerous than events of equal frequency whose instances are less easily recalled.

Retrievability. Individuals are biased in their assessments of the frequency of events based upon how their memory structures affect search process.

Presumed associations. Individuals tend to overestimate the probability of two events co-occurring based upon the number of similar associations which are easily recalled, whether from experience or social INFLUENCE.

Insensitivity to base rates. Individuals tend to ignore base rates in assessing the likelihood of events when any other descriptive infor-mation is provided – even if the information is irrelevant.

Insensitivity to sample size. Individuals frequently fail to appreciate the role of sample size in assessing the RELIABILITY of sample information.

Misconceptions of chance. Individuals expect a sequence of data generated by a random process to look "random," even when the sequence is too short for those expectations to be statistically valid.

Regression to the mean. Individuals often ignore the fact that extreme events tend to regress to the mean on subsequent trials.

The conjunction fallacy. Individuals falsely judge that conjunctions (i.e., two events co-occurring) are more probable than a more global set of occurrences of which the conjunction is a subset.

Anchoring. Individuals make estimates for values based upon an initial value (derived from past events, random assignment, or whatever information is available) and typically make insufficient adjustments from that anchor when establishing a final value.

Conjunctive and disjunctive events bias. Individuals exhibit a bias toward overestimating the probability of conjunctive events and underestimating the probability of disjunctive events.

Overconfidence. Individuals tend to be overconfident in the infallibility of their judgments when answering moderately to extremely difficult questions.

The confirmation trap. Individuals tend to seek confirmatory information for what they think is true and neglect the search for disconfirmatory evidence.

Hindsight. After finding out whether or not an event occurred, individuals tend to overestimate the degree to which they would have predicted the correct outcome.

Framing. Individuals are influenced by irrelevant information concerning how questions are framed.

Thaler (2000) argues that there are three categories of ways in which humans deviate from pure rationality. One category is Simon's concept of bounded rationality. Second, we have bounded willpower: we tend to give greater weight to present concerns than to future concerns, leading to a variety of ways in which our temporary motivations are inconsistent with long-term interests (e.g., undersaving for retirement). Third, our self-interest is bounded: unlike the stereotypic economic actor, we care about the outcomes of others.

During the past twenty-five years, these biases have had a profound influence on the field of organizational behavior. Decision-making and a decision perspective to NEGOTI-ATION have emerged as central themes in OB research and the development of new OB courses. Negotiation research has been dominated by a behavioral decision research perspective. This work helps negotiators avoid errors in their own decision-making, and to anticipate errors in the decisions of others. Behavioral decision research has also been adopted in medical and legal education and research, and has been the foundation of contemporary consumer research and work on behavioral finance and economics. Our knowledge of biases has also been used to help organizational members better understand their limitations, and has been extended to the organizational level of analysis to help account for the systematic ERRORS of organizations.

Only recently, researchers have made progress on what professionals can do based on an understanding of this literature. It is clear that many of us are doing fine in making decisions that are good enough to get us by in everyday life. However, we all have plenty of room to improve our judgment. Behavioral decision researchers argue not that humans are "bad" decision-makers, but that they fall short of objectively rational behavior, and we do so in specific and systematic ways. What we can do to correct these deficiencies? Decision researchers have responded to this question with a variety of prescriptive advice that builds on their descriptive work. Research shows that simple experience is not sufficient to create lasting improvement – most biases continue despite massive experience (Bazerman, 2001). But some debiasing efforts are possible. For example, Thompson, Loewenstein, and Gentner (2000) show success in debiasing by having people draw analogies between related tasks where the same cognitive errors are made. Kahneman and

Lovallo (1993) show that people are far less biased when they step out of the emotion of the decision, and take an outsider's view. However, perhaps the most important role of behavioral decision research is in getting people to identify situations where they should not trust their intuition and to use systematic decision aids, independent judgment, and a host of tools made available by prescriptive decision researchers (Bazerman, 2001).

See also *attribution; bounded rationality; commitment, escalating; negotiation; prospect theory*

Bibliography

Bazerman, M. H. (2001). *Judgment in Managerial Decision Making*, 5th edn. New York: Wiley.

Kahneman, D. and Lovallo, D. (1993). Timid choices and bold forecasts: A cognitive perspective on risk taking. *Management Science*, **39**, 17–31.

Kahneman, D. and Tversky, A. (1979). Prospect theory: An analysis of decision under risk. *Econometrica*, **47**, 263–91.

March, J. G. and Simon, H. A. (1958). *Organizations*. New York: Wiley.

Simon, H. A. (1957). *Models of Man*. New York: Wiley.

Thaler, R. (2000). From homo economicus to homo sapiens. University of Chicago Working Paper.

Thompson, L., Loewenstein, J., and Gentner, D. (2000). Avoiding missed opportunities in managerial life: Analogical training more powerful than individual case training. *Organization Behavior and Human Decision Processes*, **82** (1), 60–75.

Tversky, A. and Kahneman, D. (1973). Availability: A heuristic for judging frequency and probability. *Cognitive Psychology*, **5**, 207–32.

Tversky, A. and Kahneman, D. (1974). Judgment under uncertainty: Heuristics and biases. *Science*, **185**, 1124–31.

behaviorism

Fred Luthans, Carolyn Youssef, and Brett Luthans

WHAT IS BEHAVIORISM?

Behaviorism is a theoretical foundation in psychology that emphasizes observable, measurable behavior as the primary unit of analysis and scientifically investigates the relationships between behavior and its environmental contingencies.

Unlike cognitive psychology theories, behaviorism is not concerned with internal mental processes, indirect measures of attitudes and feelings, and attempts to understand and explain the complex causes of human behavior. Instead, behaviorism focuses on the prediction and control/management of behavior and thus is especially relevant to organizational behavior. The primary historical building blocks of behaviorism as we know it today are Pavlov's (1849–1936) classical conditioning, Thorndike's (1874–1949) law of effect, Watson's (1878–1958) experiments with human conditioning, and Skinner's (1904–90) operant conditioning. The mainstream application of behaviorism to the field of organizational behavior is usually considered to be Luthans and Kreitner's (1975) book *Organizational Behavior Modification*.

WHAT DO WE KNOW ABOUT BEHAVIORISM?

Have you ever wondered how children, adults, and even animals learn? Early in the twentieth century, working mainly with cats in a puzzle box, Thorndike's studies resulted in the famous law of effect that states behaviors followed by positive consequences tend to be strengthened and increase in subsequent frequency, while those followed by negative consequences tend to weaken and decrease in frequency. Pavlov was able to condition dogs to salivate to the sounding of a bell associated with the presentation of food (stimulus–response). Watson a little later conditioned "little Albert" to fear white rats by associating them with a loud noise. Most significantly for modern behaviorism, in the 1930s Skinner, mostly using rats and pigeons in his studies, found that the consequences and not the antecedent stimuli were the key to understanding and predicting behavior. He made the important distinction between respondent conditioning (Pavlovian S-R connection) and operant conditioning (the organism operated on the environment to obtain the desired consequence, or the R-S connection). This work of Skinner led to the core basis of modern behaviorism: behavior is a function of its contingent consequences. Based on this premise, behaviorism suggests that we can shape and change people's behavior by managing the consequences associated with that behavior,

which has become known as "behavior modification."

Applying behaviorism and behavior modification to workplace applications has been termed by Luthans and Kreitner (1975) as "organizational behavior modification," or simply OB Mod. The OB Mod. approach involves five steps: (1) *identify* critical performance-related behaviors; (2) *measure* the frequency; (3) *analyze* the existing antecedents and consequences; (4) *intervene* with positive reinforcers; and (5) *evaluate* the results. Throughout three decades of extensive research studies, Luthans and colleagues (Stajkovic and Luthans, 1997, 2003), as well as many other behavioral management researchers, have been able to reach consistent, conclusive findings. First, three types of reinforcers result in significant improvements in workplace performance, if administered contingently. These are: money, performance FEEDBACK, and social recognition (Luthans and Stajkovic, 1999). Surprisingly, in many cases feedback and/or recognition, which usually involve no direct cost, can result in similar (and sometimes higher) performance outcomes than monetary reinforcers. However, for performance feedback to be effective, it should be positive, immediate, graphic, and specific. For social recognition to be effective, it should constitute personal one-on-one attention and appreciation, informing the employee that his or her behavior has been noticed and admired by management, rather than just a regular program of randomly selecting candidates for public spotlights (which is what many of the formal recognition programs become over time).

Second, positive reinforcement is substantially more effective than punishment in improving performance in the long run. Although PUNISHMENT may be effective when immediate ceasing of potentially destructive behavior is necessary (e.g., in cases of workplace safety violations), the potential long-term harm of punishment may be more than its potential benefits (e.g., stress, burnout, revenge, turnover, decrease in commitment). Third, behavioral management works across various organizational types and across cultures (Luthans and Stajkovic, 1999; Welsh, Luthans, and Sommer, 1993).

The Significance, Strengths, and Limitations of Behaviorism in the Workplace

The contributions of behaviorism in general, as well as behavioral management in particular, are enormous. The major leaps that behaviorism caused in our understanding of learning in education, child and adolescent development, clinical applications, performance management, and many other related areas of study cannot be denied. In the organizational behavior context, to take behavior out of organizational behavior is analogous to taking life out of an organism. Most organizations achieve their missions, visions, goals and objectives through the performance of people. Meta-analytical research findings show that the application of the OB Mod. model in the workplace increases performance on average 17 percent (Stajkovic and Luthans, 1997), and that behavioral management in organizational settings in general results in a 16 percent average increase in performance, with a 63 percent probability of success (Stajkovic and Luthans, 2003).

However, there are several limitations that should be noted. First, people are unique and so are the reinforcers they desire. Although not as big a problem in the workplace because of the generalizability of money, feedback, and recognition, people still vary in the weights they assign to these rewards. Behaviorism helps us predict, modify, and change behavior, but not to understand how or why it works, because it does not recognize the uniqueness of individual cognition. Second, in most cases, multiple contingencies are at play in the context within which behavioral management attempts take place, resulting in complex interactions. Behaviorism does not give direct attention to the social context within which contingent reinforcement (or punishment) takes place. In fact, modern behaviorism reduces the role of antecedent factors to only cues for the desired behavior. Third, in behaviorism, if the contingent reinforcement ceases to exist, the reinforced behavior is likely to decrease in frequency, and eventually fade away, which is referred to as "extinction." This implies that managers who would like to adopt a behaviorist approach to motivation need to at least maintain an intermittent reinforcement schedule, in order to avoid this "back to normal" limitation.

Recent Developments and Future Trends

In an attempt to combine the best of both worlds, and to present a more comprehensive and realistic view of human behavior in organizations, many previously radical behaviorists have "mellowed out" (Kreitner and Luthans, 1984; Luthans and Kreitner, 1985) to adopt a social cognitive approach to understanding behavior (Bandura, 1986). This approach asserts that behavior is the result of a continuous reciprocal interaction between the person (cognition), the environment (physical context, including organizational structure and design), social context (i.e., other people), and past behavior. Behavior is not only a function of its contingent consequences as under behaviorism, but is also influenced by the processes of symbolizing, forethought, observation, SELF-REGULATION, and self-reflection (Bandura, 1986; Stajkovic and Luthans, 1998). From a social cognitive perspective, the role of contingent reinforcement in enhancing performance can be understood in terms of outcome utility, informative content, and regulatory mechanisms (Stajkovic and Luthans, 2001).

The future of behaviorism is likely to continue along the lines of social cognition. Management practitioners and scholars now generally realize that we cannot afford to ignore the objectivity and predictive, performance impact of measurable, observable behavior as offered by behaviorism. However, in today's complex, ever-changing work environment, radical behaviorism cannot stand alone. With the increasing emphasis on human resources as the primary source of long-term competitive advantage, the confluence of behaviorism theory and cognitive theory through social cognitive theory may best accomplish the goals of understanding, prediction, and performance management.

See also *performance appraisal/performance management*

References

Bandura, A. (1986). *Social Foundations of Thought and Action*. Englewood Cliffs, NJ: Prentice-Hall.

Kreitner, R. and Luthans, F. (1984). A social learning approach to behavioral management: Radical behaviorists mellowing out. *Organizational Dynamics*, **13** (2), 47–65.

Luthans, F. and Kreitner, R. (1975). *Organizational Behavior Modification*. Glenview, IL: Scott, Foresman.

Luthans, F. and Kreitner, R. (1985). *Organizational Behavior Modification and Beyond*. Glenview, IL: Scott, Foresman.

Luthans, F. and Stajkovic, A. (1999). Reinforce (not necessarily pay) for performance. *Academy of Management Executive*, **13**, 49–57.

Stajkovic, A. and Luthans, F. (1997). A meta-analysis of the effects of organizational behavior modification on task performance, 1975–1995. *Academy of Management Journal*, **40**, 1122–49.

Stajkovic, A. and Luthans, F. (1998). Social cognitive theory and self-efficacy: Going beyond traditional motivational and behavioral approaches. *Organizational Dynamics*, 26, 62–74.

Stajkovic, A. and Luthans, F. (2001). Differential engagement effects of incentive motivators on work performance. *Academy of Management Journal*, **44**, 580–90.

Stajkovic, A. and Luthans, F. (2003). Behavioral management and task performance in organizations: Conceptual background, meta-analysis, and test of alternative models. *Personnel Psychology*, **56**, 155–94.

Welsh, D. H. B., Luthans, F., and Sommer, S. M. (1993). Managing Russian factory workers: The impact of US-based behavioral and participative techniques. *Academy of Management Journal*, **36**, 58–79.

bias

Kenneth W. Koput

Any systematic deviation of an estimate given by a statistical method from the true value the estimate is meant to represent is called bias (Oakes, 1986). As such, bias is a property of a procedure for estimating a value, rather than of any particular value of an estimate obtained from such a procedure. Bias can take many forms. The most common in organizational research are sample selection, aggregation, model selection, and omitted variable biases.

Sample selection bias occurs when an investigator selects a sample for observation without proper randomization. Examples of non-random selection abound, as when individual units are included in the sample because they are successful on the outcome variable of interest, because they are convenient, or because they are willing.

Researchers using the case method need to guard against bias in the process of selecting evidence. Studies done via SURVEYS, on the other hand, are especially prone to concerns about a particular sample selection problem known as response bias.

Aggregation biases can occur when observations on individual units or variables are combined. These biases are closely tied to questions concerning the choice among LEVELS OF ANALYSIS. Time aggregation bias is a particular form that arises in population ecology or similar work where continuous durations are rounded, either solely up or down, to discrete intervals.

Model selection bias occurs when an investigator presumes the relationship between the predictor and outcome variables follows a certain form without verifying that form for a particular set of data. Often, a convention emerges to use a particular model for reasons of expediency, and it becomes taken for granted. Omitted variable biases are extremely difficult to eliminate. These occur when an important predictor variable is unobserved, but at least partially correlated with other variables in a model.

COMPUTER SIMULATION is often used to demonstrate the bias of a statistical procedure or to explore ways of reducing biases in statistical methods. Other biases are of a non-statistical nature. Foremost among these are personal biases. Personal biases can only be mitigated through careful scrutiny of an investigator's entire methodology.

See also *error; errors; reliability; research design; research methods; statistical methods; validity*

Bibliography

Oakes, M. W. (1986). *Statistical Inference: A Commentary for the Social and Behavioral Sciences*. New York: Wiley.

big five

see FIVE FACTOR MODEL OF PERSONALITY

boards

see CORPORATE BOARDS

bonus payments

see INCENTIVES

boundary spanning

W. Warner Burke

To define this term we must first understand the idea of boundary. Boundary implies limit or separateness; a boundary therefore limits or establishes something to be separate from something else. This something can be physical (e.g., a wall), psychological or sociological (e.g., one's role, title, or ethnic identity), or even imaginary (e.g., "People who work in that part of the organization should be avoided"). Boundary spanning then becomes any process or activity that bridges, links, or perhaps even blurs the separateness of two or more boundaries.

Organizationally, boundaries exist interpersonally between and among individuals, particularly in the form of roles (*see* ROLE). Job descriptions also establish boundaries. Regardless of how desirable it might be to link if not blur roles, spanning a role can create stress and conflict. Kahn et al. (1964) defined a boundary role person as one located in two or more groups within the organization or within more than a single organization. Such a person can experience conflicting demands (*see* ROLE CONFLICT).

Organizational subsystems (*see* ORGANIZATIONAL DESIGN) establish boundaries within the organization. Marketing is one subsystem, finance another, etc. The classic organizational studies of Burns and Stalker (1961) and Lawrence and Lorsch (1964) distinguished between dividing labor (differentiation) and coordinating work (integration) (*see* MECHANISTIC/ ORGANIC). In one organization that Lawrence and Lorsch (1964) studied, product INNOVATION was desperately needed, requiring strong interdependence between research and sales groups and between research and production groups. They pointed out that management hierarchy alone could not bridge the gap across such wide differences. Consequently, Lawrence and Lorsch advocated the development of *integrating* roles and *cross-functional teams*, recommendations for spanning boundaries within the organization.

More recently, scholars of executive leadership have addressed the role of the CEO and fellow top executives as one of boundary spanning (e.g., Zaccaro and Klimoski, 2001). It is contended that organizational executives have two primary responsibilities: (1) boundary spanning, that is, linking the organization with its external environment, especially the organization's major constituents such as customers, professional and trade associations, capital market groups, vendors, etc., and (2) internal coordination (i.e., leading and managing within the organization). Top executives, then, spend considerable time and energy in boundary spanning activities, particularly (a) analyzing the external environment for needed actions regarding positioning their organizations more effectively to deal with forces impinging on them (e.g., changing governmental regulations, new technology, new products/services from competitors, etc.), and (b) relating with individuals and groups within the organization who are not part of the executive group, such as members of the board of directors, middle management, and members of the sales force, to name only a few.

Regarding boundary spanning across organizations, Kanter (1989) has identified at least three examples:

1 *Service alliances*, where a group of organizations bands together to create a new organization to serve some need for all of them (e.g., an industry research consortium).
2 *Opportunistic alliances*, where usually two organizations seize an opportunity to gain a competitive advantage by joining forces, typically referred to as a joint business venture.
3 STAKEHOLDER *alliances*, where preexisting interdependencies are strengthened, such as with suppliers, customers, and employees (i.e., between labor organizations and management).

Finally, since large organizations by their very nature are often overly hierarchical, protective of domains, and unnecessarily competitive and conflictual, spanning processes (e.g., cross-functional teams) are needed to alleviate the negative consequences noted above of boundaries not being sufficiently permeable for optimal organizational effectiveness.

See also *management, classical theory; managerial roles*

Bibliography

Burns, T. and Stalker, G. M. (1961). *The Management of Innovation.* London: Tavistock.
Kahn, R. L., Wolfe, D. M., Quinn, R. P., Snoek, J. D., and Rosenthal, R. A. (1964). *Organizational Stress: Studies in Role Conflict and Ambiguity.* New York: Wiley.
Kanter, R. M. (1989). *When Giants Learn to Dance: Mastering the Challenge of Strategy, Management, and Careers in the 1990s.* New York: Simon and Schuster.
Lawrence, R. R. and Lorsch, J. W. (1964). *Organization and Environment.* Homewood, IL: Irwin.
Zaccaro, S. J. and Klimoski, R. J. (eds.) (2001). *The Nature of Organizational Leadership: Understanding the Performance Imperatives Confronting Today's Leaders.* San Francisco: Jossey-Bass.

bounded rationality

Susan Miller

Classical economic theories assume that decision-makers make choices in completely rational ways, selecting the best alternative to achieve optimal outcomes. They assume a complete set of alternative solutions is readily available to the decision-maker, who has full knowledge of the consequences of each. The choice is arrived at after a thorough evaluation of each alternative against explicit criteria.

These assumptions are unrealistic in many cases and, although individuals are "intendedly" rational, their RATIONALITY is bounded – constrained by the environment in which they operate and by their own human limitations.

The complexity of the environment means that decision-makers have to simplify to make sense of it. It also means they are faced with uncertainty. Individuals cannot absorb all the information needed to formulate a complete set of alternatives from which to choose. Information may not be available and evaluation may be subject to personal biases.

A boundedly rational process involves limiting information to what can be easily managed. Alternative solutions are evaluated sequentially, not all together; if the first is acceptable, further search ceases. Decisions are made using "rules of thumb," heuristics, and, where possible, tried and tested routines for problem solving. A sub-optimal, or SATISFICING, decision is the result.

See also *behavioral decision research; perception; self-regulation*

Bibliography

March, J. G. and Simon, H. A. (1993). *Organizations.* Oxford: Blackwell

brainstorming

Randall S. Schuler

The brainstorming technique is an informal technique or tool for GROUP DECISION-MAKING. Group participants informally generate as many ideas, regardless of their apparent practicality or even relevance, as possible, without evaluation by others. In this way, brainstorming generates a large number of alternatives to issues, problems, and concerns. Using the same format, the brainstorming group is then used to generate creative solutions based upon those alternatives. Again, during the process of solutions generation (either face-to-face or electronically), evaluation is suspended until everyone has had the opportunity to contribute. By these means brainstorming generates, at relatively low cost and in an informal atmosphere, many potentially creative and useful alternatives and solutions (Paulus and Yang, 2000).

The method is used to help groups overcome barriers to DECISION-MAKING, such as hierarchy, which tends to suppress the contributions from lower status members. By generating contributions from all group members, the method creates member understanding, ownership of alternatives and solutions, and less resistance to solutions that require change (Delbecq, Van de Ven, and Gustafson, 1977) (*see* RESISTANCE TO CHANGE).

Used in conjunction with more formal and more structured techniques of group decision-making, brainstorming offers organizations an effective means to foster and facilitate CRE-ATIVITY in organizational and group decision-making.

See also *creativity; Delphi; innovation; nominal group technique*

Bibliography

Delbecq, A., Van de Ven, A. H., and Gustafson, D. (1977). *Group Techniques for Program Planning.* Glenview, IL: Scott, Foresman.

Paulus, P. B. and Yang, H.-C. (2000). Idea generation in groups. A basis for creativity in organizations. *Organizational Behavior and Human Decision Processes*, **82** (1), 76–87.

bureaucracy

Marshall W. Meyer

This widely used concept has a variety of meanings, some positive, some less so. The sociologist Max Weber (1946) thought bureaucracy was synonymous with rational organization (*see* RATIONALITY): bureaucracies embodied the ideals of rational–legal authority such that all but policy decisions are based on rules, which themselves are internally consistent and stable over time (*see* DECISION-MAKING). Political scientists tend to think of bureaucracy as governance by bureaus having the following characteristics: they are large, they are staffed by full-time employees who have careers within the organization, and they rely on budget allocations rather than revenues from sales, since their outputs cannot be priced in voluntary *quid pro quo* transactions in the market (Downs, 1967; Wilson, 1989). There is a third definition of bureaucracy, which is far less flattering: bureaucracy is inefficient organization, is inherently anti-democratic, cannot adapt to change, and, worse, exacerbates its own errors (Crozier, 1964). Discussion of bureaucracy tends to be ideologically tinged (*see* IDEOLOGY). The political left emphasizes the rationality and neutrality of government while downplaying the power of bureaucracy itself, while the right uses bureaucracy as an epithet or shibboleth and focuses on bureaucracy's anti-democratic tendencies and inefficiencies.

PROPERTIES OF BUREAUCRACY

The properties of bureaucracy are best understood in comparison with other forms of organization. Weber, for example, focuses on comparisons between bureaucracy and traditional forms of administration. Compared to traditional organizations, the structure of bureaucracy exhibits much greater differentiation and integration. With respect to differentiation, there is intensive division of labor, a hierarchy of authority, and, perhaps most importantly, a clear separation of official duties from personal interests and obligations – what Weber calls separation of home from office. With respect to integration, bureaucracies have written rules and regulations, codified procedures for selection and advancement of officials, and a specialized administrative staff charged with maintaining these rules and procedures. And compared to traditional organizations, bureaucracies constrain the conduct of officials while offering powerful incentives for compliance. The constraints lie in strict super- and subordination requiring all actions to be justified in terms of the larger purposes of the organization, the norm of impersonality that requires detachment and objectivity, and advancement contingent on both seniority and performance. The incentives consist of the prospect of a lifetime career, salaries paid in cash rather than in kind, and (in Europe if not the United States) a modicum of social esteem attached to the status of official or *fonctionnaire*. The elements of differentiation, integration, constraints, and INCENTIVES render bureaucratic organizations both more powerful and more responsive to central authority than traditional administration. The power of bureaucracies results from their capacity for coordinated action. Their responsiveness to centralized authority arises from the dependence of individual bureaucrats on their salaries and other emoluments of office. These four elements, according to Weber, also render bureaucracy more efficient than traditional forms of organization. "Precision, speed, unambiguity, knowledge of the files, continuity, discretion, unity, strict subordination, reduction of friction and of material and personal costs – these are raised to the optimum point in the strictly bureaucratic administration" (Weber, 1946: 214).

Compared to modern business organizations, bureaucracies have somewhat different and in some respects less attractive properties. One must ask, to begin, whether comparison of business and bureaucracy is warranted given Weber's insistence that the bureaucratic model describes both private and public administration. Public and private administration were remarkably similar at the time Weber was writing. Indeed, much of the United States' public sector was modeled explicitly after the private sector at the beginning of the twentieth century. It is not accidental that the reform movement in the United States, which called for administration devoid of politics, coincided with the emergence of scientific management, which called for active management of firms. Nor is it accidental that in the 1940s the same theory of organization was believed to apply to public and private sector enterprises. Public and private organizations have diverged in the last fifty years, however. Divergences have occurred in several domains, most notably ORGANIZATIONAL DESIGN, accounting practices, and performance measurement. With respect to organizational design, virtually all large firms have moved from functional to divisionalized organizational structures; that is, from designs in which the principal units are responsible for different activities (such as purchasing, manufacturing, and sales) to designs in which the principal units are self-contained businesses responsible for profit as well as for other objectives. To be certain, patterns of divisionalization have changed over time – firms typically have fewer and somewhat larger business units as a result of several waves of DOWNSIZING – but until very recent times there have been no comparable innovations in the public sector. For the most part, public agencies have retained the same organizing principles – organization by function – they used ninety years ago. With respect to accounting, public sector agencies have departed substantially from private sector practices. At the beginning of this century, public entities issues consolidated financial reports and maintained capital accounts just like private businesses. Consolidated accounting gave way to much more complicated fund accounting during the 1920s, when it was believed necessary to segregate revenues and expend-itures intended for different purposes into separate funds. Capital accounting has all but disappeared from the public sector, though accounting for long-term indebtedness remains out of necessity. With respect to performance measurement, the public sector lags substantially behind private businesses (see ORGANIZATIONAL EFFECTIVENESS). In business operations, not only is financial analysis necessary and universal, but also firms' internal operations are often typically gauged against industry benchmarks assembled by consultants and trade associations. By contrast, very little comparative performance assessment exists for government. In the United States, at least, performance comparisons across governmental units are strongly resisted. Just as at the beginning of the twentieth century, some efforts to make government more businesslike are now underway (see GOVERNMENT AND BUSINESS). Some services have been privatized altogether. Others have been placed in public corporations, which are held responsible for breaking even, if not making a profit. And some government agencies now measure customer satisfaction, just as businesses do.

LIABILITIES OF BUREAUCRACY

If public sector bureaucracies suffer in comparison with private sector management, one must ask whether these liabilities arise from systematic causes (that is, the structure of bureaucracies themselves) or from other causes. Both sociologists and economists have argued that at least some of the liabilities of bureaucracy are systematic, although for different reasons. Sociologists have focused on bureaucratic dysfunctions of various kinds, including displacement of goals, so-called vicious cycles in which different dysfunctions feed on one another, and spiraling bureaucratic growth. Economists, by contrast, have emphasized the efficiency disadvantages of bureaucracies compared to firms, asking whether, in general, non-market transactions are inefficient compared to market transactions and, specifically, the funding of bureaucracies through budgets rather than market transactions is conducive to overproduction of bureaucratic services. These potential liabilities of bureaucracy should be reviewed seriatim.

Displacement of goals Bureaucracies are known for rigid adherence to rules and procedures, even when rules and procedures appear to impede the objectives of the organization. The notion of goal displacement provides both a description and an explanation for this seemingly non-rational conduct. Goal displacement, following Merton (1958), describes the process whereby means become ends in themselves, or "an instrumental value becomes a terminal value." The displacement of goals is especially acute in settings, such as bureaucracies, where the following conditions obtain: the technical competence of officials consists of knowledge of the rules, advancement is contingent on adherence to the rules, and peer pressure reinforces the norm of impersonality, which requires rules and procedures to be applied with equal force in all cases. What is important is that goal displacement, at least as originally conceived, argues bureaucracies are efficient in general – under conditions anticipated by their rules and procedures – but inefficient in circumstances that cannot be anticipated. The implications of goal displacement for INNOVATION and new product development have been realized only gradually: bureaucracy can be antithetical to innovation.

Vicious cycles A more thoroughgoing critique of bureaucracy argues that dysfunctions are normal rather than exceptional and, moreover, that dysfunctions accumulate over time such that organizational stasis is the expected outcome. The elements of the vicious cycle of bureaucratic dysfunctions are impersonal rules that seek to limit the discretion of individual workers, centralization of remaining decisions, isolation of workers from their immediate supervisors as a consequence of limited decision-making authority, and the exercise of unofficial power in arenas where uncertainty remains. Thus, as Crozier (1964) observes, maintenance people exercise undue influence in state-owned factories because their work is inherently unpredictable and cannot be governed by rules. The logic of vicious cycles, it should be pointed out, yields several consequences. First, new rules will arise to eliminate whatever islands of POWER remain in the organization, but these rules will trigger further centralization, isolation, and power plays as new sources of uncertainty arise. Second, to

the extent that the organization is opened to uncertainties arising externally, line managers have the opportunity to reassert power that would otherwise erode through the dynamics of vicious cycles. External crisis (*see* CRISES/DISASTERS), in other words, may be an antidote to bureaucracies' tendency toward rigidity over time.

Spiraling growth Bureaucratic systems also tend toward growth, other things being equal (Meyer, 1985). Until recently, growth of government and of administrative staff in private firms was endemic. The causes of growth lie in several factors, but chief among them are people's motives for constructing organizations in the first place. People construct formal organizations in order to rationalize or make sense of otherwise uncertain environments; organizations, in fact, succeed at making the world more sensible; as a consequence, there is continuous construction of bureaucracy and hence bureaucratic growth as people attempt to perfect their rationalization of an inherently uncertain world. Two comments are in order. First, the logic of bureaucratic growth is built into administrative theory as developed by Simon (1976) and others (*see* ORGANIZATION THEORY). Irreducible uncertainty in the environment in conjunction with the belief that administrative organization can rationalize uncertainty will result in continuous growth in administration. Second, the growth imperative is so strong that deliberate campaigns to "downsize" or "restructure" organizations must be launched in order to achieve meaningful reductions in staff. Downsizing continues to occur at record rates in US firms, but may have reached a limit now that modest industrial expansion is underway.

Inefficiency Economists have asked persistently without resolution whether public sector bureaucracies are inherently less efficient than private sector enterprises. Several answers have been proffered, none fully satisfactory. From the 1940s to the present time, the Austrian school of economics, von Mises (1944) and others, have argued that any departure from market principles yields both inefficient transactions and anti-democratic tendencies. This position has proved difficult to reconcile with contemporary transaction cost theories (*see* TRANSACTION COST ECONOMICS), which argue that hierarchies may be more efficient than markets under some circumstances. In the 1970s the efficiency question was cast somewhat differently: might bureaus, which depend on budgets for their sustenance, overproduce compared to firms subject to the discipline of the market (Niskanen, 1971)? Here too the answer was equivocal, as analysis showed that rent maximizing monopolists would have similar incentives to overproduce whether they were located in public bureaucracies or private firms. Despite the absence of strong analytic underpinnings for the belief that bureaucracies are more apt to harbor inefficiencies than private sector organizations, privatization of governmental functions is occurring rapidly and with positive results in many countries. It is unclear whether the liabilities of public bureaucracies are simply the liabilities of established organizations that have been shielded from extinction for too long, or whether bureaucracies suffer disadvantages in comparison with private organizations regardless of their age.

RESEARCH ON BUREAUCRACY

Organizational research and research on bureaucracy were once synonymous or nearly so, as the bureaucratic model was believed to be descriptive of all organizations, for-profit and non-profit, and governmental not-for-profit organizations. Case studies of bureaucracy written during the 1950s and 1960s encompassed government agencies and industrial firms alike, as evidenced by titles like Gouldner's (1954) *Patterns of Industrial Bureaucracy*. Early quantitative research on organizations, such as the work of the Aston group and the studies emanating from the Comparative Organization Research Program in the United States, focused mainly on relations among elements of organizational structure (size, hierarchy, administrative ratio, formalization, centralization, etc.) that flowed from the bureaucratic model implicitly if not explicitly (Blau and Schoenherr, 1971). As attention shifted to external causes of organizational outcomes, the bureaucratic model lost some of its relevance to research. Thus, for example, the key causal variable in RESOURCE DEPENDENCE models of organizations is con-

trol of strategic resources, which is more germane to businesses than to government bureaus. The key dependent variables in organizational population ecology are births and deaths of organizations, which are infrequent in the public sector. And institutional organizational theory has very much downplayed Weber's notion of bureaucracy as rational administration and has substituted for it the notion that all organizations, bureaucratic and non-bureaucratic alike (but especially the former), seek social approval or legitimacy rather than efficiency outcomes.

Some research on bureaucracy remains. Development economists continue to study the role of national bureaucracies in promoting or retarding economic growth. Others, again mainly economists, pursue the comparative efficiency of private versus public sector service delivery and possible advantages of creating competition among public agencies. And the study of public administration remains a viable although by no means a growing field. But research on bureaucracy is no longer at the core of organizational theory even though most of the public sector and much of the administrative component of the private sector continue to be organized along bureaucratic lines.

See also *open systems*

Bibliography

Blau, P. M. and Schoenherr, R. (1971). The *Structure of Organizations*. New York: Basic Books.

Crozier, M. (1964). *The Bureaucratic Phenomenon*. Chicago: University of Chicago Press.

Downs, A. (1967). Inside Bureaucracy. Boston, MA: Little, Brown.

Gouldner, A. W. (1954). Patterns of Industrial Bureaucracy. Glencoe, IL: Free Press.

Merton, R. K. (1958). Bureaucratic structure and personality. In *Social Theory and Social Structure*, 2nd edn. Glencoe, IL: Free Press, 195–206.

Meyer, M. W. (1985). *Limits to Bureaucratic Growth*. New York: de Gruyter.

Niskanen, W. (1971). *Bureaucracy and Representative Government*. Chicago: Aldine.

Simon, H. A. (1976). *Administrative Behavior*, 3rd edn. New York: Free Press.

Weber, M. (1946). Bureaucracy. In H. Gerth and C. Wright Mills (eds.), *From Max Weber: Essays in Sociology*. Glencoe, IL: Free Press, 196–244.

von Mises, L. (1944). *Bureaucracy*. New Haven, CT: Yale University Press.

Wilson, J. Q. (1989). *Bureaucracy*. New York: Basic Books.

burnout

Nigel Nicholson

The concept of burnout denotes the negative psychological and physical consequences of chronic or prolonged exposure to stressors. It has wide currency. Occupational literatures (e.g., for the teaching and nursing professions) continue to make liberal use of the idea, though it remains unclear whether burnout can or should be distinguished from constructs such as exhaustion, depression, and negative affectivity. Operationally, burnout may be most productively viewed within a "conservation of resources" framework, of which stable individual differences may be one set of predictors.

See also *emotion in organizations; hardiness; personality; stress*

Bibliography

Grandey, A. and Cropanzano, R. (1999). The conservation of resources model and work–family conflict and strain. *Journal of Vocational Behavior*, **54**, 350–70.

Schaufeli, W. B., Maslach, C., and Marek, T. (eds.) (1993). *Professional Burnout: Recent Developments in Theory and Research*. London: Taylor and Francis.

C

career

Nigel Nicholson

The concept of career is central to the field of organizational behavior and raises a number of empirical, practical and theoretical challenges. The etymological root of the concept is that of a carriageway, and careers can be defined as pathways through working lives. The importance, interest, and complexity of the concept is that it represents the intersection between social structure and personal identity. The pathway is the product of both individuals' access to the opportunity structures in a given social system, and the capabilities, intentions, and characteristics of individuals. Traditionally, the main determinants of CAREER DEVELOPMENT have been external – once a career track is chosen then it follows a predictable socially constructed route – such as provided by an occupation or profession. The last century saw a weakening of these structures and moves towards what has been termed boundaryless careers (Arthur and Rousseau, 1996). In these circumstances, careers become much more variegated portfolio constructions, subject to less predictable patterning (*see* CAREER PLATEAU) and more the outcome of personal ENACTMENT.

However, it can be argued that boundaries for careers have become more mobile and permeable rather than removed altogether, and that traditional careers continue to populate a large part of the occupational landscape. The challenge for CAREER THEORY is therefore to find new ways of capturing the dynamism of person–environment interaction, explaining the growing complexity of observed career patterns, and predicting the outcomes of career development and change (Nicholson, 2000).

See also *career anchor; career theory; identity, personal; role transitions;*

Bibliography

Arthur, M. B. and Rousseau, D. M. (1996). *The Boundaryless Career: A New Employment Principle for a New Organizational Era*. New York: Oxford University Press.

Nicholson, N. (2000). Motivation–selection–connection: An evolutionary model of career development. In M. Peiperl, M. Arthur, R. Goffee, and T. Morris (eds.), *Career Frontiers: New Concepts of Working Life*. Oxford: Oxford University Press

career anchor

Barbara S. Lawrence

A career anchor is an individual's occupational self-concept composed of his or her self-perceived talents and abilities, motives and needs, and attitudes and VALUES (*see* MOTIVATION). Individuals discover their career anchors over time through personal work experiences in real-life settings.

> By definition, there cannot be an anchor until there has been work experience, even though motives and values may already be present from earlier experiences. It is the process of integrating into the total self-concept what one sees oneself to be more or less competent at, wanting out of life, one's value systems, and the kind of person one is that begins to determine the major life and occupational choices throughout adulthood. (Schein, 1993: 171)

Once identified, a career anchor provides a growing source of stability for individuals. Although individuals typically hold and explore many abilities and interests, when presented with occupational choices, they will make decisions congruent with the career anchor.

The career anchor concept emerged from a longitudinal panel study in 1961 and 1973 by Edgar H. Schein. Schein identified five career anchors: technical/functional competence, managerial competence, security, creativity, and autonomy/independence. Subsequent research in the 1980s added three career anchors: service or dedication to a cause, pure challenge, and lifestyle (Schein, 1996).

See also *career; career development; career theory*

Bibliography

Schein, E. H. (1993). *Career Anchors: Discovering Your Real Values*. San Francisco: Jossey-Bass/Pfeiffer.
Schein, E. H. (1996). Career anchors revisited: Implications for career development in the twenty-first century. *Academy of Management Executive*, 10, 80–8.

career development

Barbara S. Lawrence

Career development is the sequence of changes that occur throughout an individual's careers (*see* CAREER), usually with reference to either an individual's inner psychological evolution or their status within a social entity (for instance, functional area, hierarchical level, or degree of inclusion). Career development represents a subset of CAREER THEORY that focuses on individuals. The outcome of interest is the individual's career, and the time period involved is usually the individual's working life, although shorter segments are also studied.

The term career development generally assumes either an explanatory or prescriptive meaning. First, the term refers to theories or research that explain what happens to individuals over their careers. Thus, such work might include studies of career choice, CAREER STAGES, career typologies, socialization (*see* SOCIALIZATION), or MENTORING. Second, the term refers to programs designed to facilitate individuals' career growth. These programs are usually developed by career development specialists outside organizations or by human resource personnel within organizations. The emergence of boundaryless careers has refocused career development (Arthur and Rousseau, 1996). Instead of framing career development as an individual's evolution through jobs within a single occupation, career development now examines the individual's evolution through a portfolio of work activities requiring related skills, experience, and abilities.

See also *person–environment interaction; tournament theory*

Bibliography

Arthur, M. B. and Rousseau, D. M. (1996). *The Boundaryless Career: A New Employment Principle for a New Organizational Era*. New York: Oxford University Press.
Hall, D. T. (1990). Career development theory in organizations. In D. Brown, L. Brooks, and Associates (eds.), *Career Choice and Development*, 2nd edn. San Francisco: Jossey-Bass, 422–54.

career mobility

see CAREER DEVELOPMENT

career plateau

Nigel Nicholson

Plateauing has been defined in various ways: (1) amount of time spent in current position; (2) personal beliefs of an individual that they can expect little or no further hierarchical progression; and (3) the degree to which an individual's progress is on or off schedule in advancement relative to a reference group timetable norm. Each of these definitions has advantages and disadvantages in terms of objectivity, scope, and psychological content. Plateauing is an inevitable consequence of the logic of career advancement in pyramidal organizational structures, which also implies that it is more associated with traditional than new occupational and organizational forms (*see* ORGANIZATIONAL DESIGN). In traditional structures people who fall behind age-grade norms of advancement are the most likely to plateau early. However, plateauing is not always associated with negative psychological and behavioral consequences, such as reduced MOTIVATION, satisfaction, and effectiveness (Nicholson, 1993). These are more likely to arise in response to unchanging job content than to hierarchical immobility alone (Allen et al., 1999). Moreover, people's aspirations and interests change over the CAREER cycle. Early career ambition may decline, expectations realign to the realities of limited horizons, and primary goals become centered on other life spheres. Appropriate human resource management interventions to maintain the motivation and effectiveness of plateaued employees include MENTORING, project and team working, and expanded job responsibilities (Rotondo and Perrewe, 2000).

See also *age; career development; job satisfaction*

Bibliography

Allen, T. D., Russell, J. E. A., Poteet, M. L., and Dobbins, G. H. (1999). Learning and development factors related to perceptions of job content and hierarchical plateauing. *Journal of Organizational Behavior*, 20, 1113–37.

Nicholson, N. (1993). Purgatory or place of safety? The managerial career plateau and organizational age grading. *Human Relations*, 46, 1369–89.

Rotondo, D. M., and Perrewe, P. L. (2000). Coping with a career plateau: An empirical examination of what works and what doesn't. *Journal of Applied Social Psychology*, 30, 2622–46.

career stage

Maury Peiperl

The concept of CAREER stage denotes any period in the sequence of a person's life course that can be normatively characterized implicitly or explicitly along some dimension of contrast with other periods (e.g., "investing stage" or "reinvesting stage" for periods of education or other negative-income phases, "exploration stage" for periods of consideration of various career options at any time of life). There is no fixed sequence to career stages, though the term has been used to describe an individual's progress along a predetermined set of (usually vertical) job steps (e.g., trainee, junior professional, professional, manager, vice president/partner, president/chief executive) or life experiences (youth, young adulthood, parenthood, maturity, old age, retirement). Career stage is no longer limited to such linear characterizations.

See also *career development; career plateau*

Bibliography

Peiperl, M. and Arthur, M. (2000). Topics for conversation: Career themes old and new. In M. Peiperl, M. Arthur, R. Goffee, and T. Morris (eds.), *Career Frontiers: New Conceptions of Working Lives*. Oxford: Oxford University Press, 1–19.

career theory

Barbara S. Lawrence

Career theory is a generalizable explanation of a CAREER or career related phenomenon. The qualifier "generalizable" is used to distinguish career theory from situation-specific career descriptions derived from personal experience or local practices (Arthur, Hall, and Lawrence, 1989). An ethnographic study of an individual career may produce thick description that is critical in generating career theory, but the description itself is not a THEORY.

Career theory examines a fundamental component of management studies: the relationship between individuals, their work, and the social systems within which they work over time. Careers are a temporal product of what the individual contributes to the social system and what the social system returns to the individual (*see* PSYCHOLOGICAL CONTRACT). As a result, career theory involves a multidisciplinary perspective, which is evident in the many disciplines that study careers, including, but not limited to, psychology, sociology, economics, anthropology, and social psychology. Topics covered by career theory include phenomena as diverse as self-identity, work role transitions, occupational mobility, social networks, human capital, job selection, vacancy chains, labor markets, socialization, mentoring, and occupational demography.

Career theories are distinguished by six dimensions: work, time, level of analysis, perspective, social setting, and outcome. *Work* is any set of activities directed toward specific goals. Thus, one could study the work of a dishwasher, an architect, a volunteer fire fighter, or a delinquent. Each constitutes a set of activities that is recognized by the individual, or by others observing the individual, as connected and purposeful. One could also study the morning routine of a paper mill or the interactions on a movie set, which are not recognizable as occupations, but are recognizable as work. The goals towards which work is directed may be defined by individuals, those with whom they work, those for whom they work, or salient others outside the work environment.

Time is a measurable period during which actions, processes, or conditions occur. Time provides an important dimension for two reasons. First, time distinguishes careers from the standard conception of jobs. Careers unfold and are shaped over time. They involve the long-term consequences of work activities, such as the acquisition of social capital and learning, and the meaning of these consequences for the individual (*see* CAREER ANCHOR).

Second, work represents a process: a sequence of activities that begins at one time and ends at another. Work may involve a short time, such as the work of managing breaks in a blue collar job, or a long time, such as intergenerational changes in occupational status. Further, work may be defined by chronological time, that is, time as measured by a clock, or sociotemporal time, that is, time as measured by people's perceptions (Ancona et al., 2001). Time also captures work processes, such as the ENACTMENT, selection, and retention routines that shape and are shaped by individual action and interaction (Weick, 1996).

Level of analysis is a unit around which people have observed behavioral patterns and to which inferences will be made (Rousseau, 1985) (*see* LEVELS OF ANALYSIS). A small unit might be individuals and a large one might be a society. For example, careers can be studied at the individual level by examining individuals' self-concepts within work settings, at the organizational level by examining how vacancy chains influence mobility, at the social network level by examining how social contacts lead to jobs (*see* NETWORKING), or at the societal or national level by examining the impact of economic conditions on labor markets. Careers can also be studied as processes, such as job sequences, where the level of analysis is the process rather than the individual or social setting. Because careers are embedded within social systems, the study of careers encourages multi-level theory (e.g., Lawrence, 1990; Rosenbaum, 1984).

Independent of level of analysis is the *perspective* from which the career is studied. For instance, an individual's career can be viewed from the individual's perspective, that is, by how the individual sees him or herself, from the organization's perspective, that is, by how organizational managers perceive, define, or evaluate the individual's career, or from a regional perspective, that is, by how the inhabitants of a specific geographic area define or evaluate the individual's career. Other terms for distinctions in perspective include internal vs. external and objective vs. subjective.

A *social setting* is the context within which careers occur. Because careers include all points where the lives of individuals touch the social order, careers do not exist without social settings. Many scholars study career related phenomena without concurrent study of the social setting in which they occur: a typical example is studying individuals' promotions and career success without examining their organization or occupation. However, research suggests that social settings, such as occupations, organizations, social identity groups, social networks, national culture, and work–life arrangements, play an important role in careers.

A final dimension of career theory is *outcome*, the result or consequence of the work that individuals perform. Outcomes are specified either by the researcher, the individual, salient others, or social setting. For an individual, the defining outcome of an organizational career might be self-perceived career success or simply making a living. For an organization, the defining outcome might be organizational performance. For a network, the defining outcome might be a typology of boundaryless careers. For a significant other, a defining outcome might be work–family balance (Bailyn, 1993).

The history of career theory begins in psychology and sociology. In psychology, career theories grew rapidly in the 1940s and 1950s through studies of vocational choice (Super, 1963; Osipow, 1983). The aim was to understand how individual differences and self-knowledge translated into career choices characterized by job satisfaction and motivation. Two types of theories emerged: matching theories and process theories. Matching theories examine vocational choice as the match between the individual's traits and those of people currently in the occupation. These theories led to psychological instruments used for vocational counseling. In contrast, process theories focus on how people make vocational choices, examining the sequence of development and motivations involved in the decision process. Both matching and process theories focused on early adulthood, making the assumption that people choose careers and then remain in the same career for the remainder of their lives (*see* CAREER DEVELOPMENT; CAREER STAGE).

Sociologists started with a different notion of career. In the 1920s and 1930s, sociologists at the University of Chicago began using life histories to study the sequence of events underlying various social problems such as delinquency (Barley, 1989). These unfolding sequences were defined as "careers," and subsequent research by Everett Hughes and his students produced the beginnings of the sociology of work and occupations. Their studies included an array of ethnographies, embracing medical careers, funeral directors, marijuana users, and taxi dancers. The focus was on connecting the individual's interpretation and experience of career with institutional definitions. Later sociologists moved away from the breadth of this career vision and began narrowing their scope, concerned with providing depth about more focused topics, such as internal labor markets, the role of achieved and ascribed attributes in career success, and the function of occupations in distributing social status within the United States (Blau and Duncan, 1967).

In the early 1970s a group of management professors, energized by the connections they saw between these disciplinary approaches and armed with a view of careers as a fundamental component of social systems, began broadening the theoretical and research agenda once again. The development of this agenda can be seen in a series of books about career theory and research published during the subsequent two decades (Hall, 2002; Schein, 1978). The topics this group examined (for instance, career anchors, scientific and engineering careers, SOCIALIZATION, sense-making, MENTORING, and career "styles") emphasized professional careers within organizations (e.g., Dalton and Thompson, 1986; Howard and Bray, 1988).

More recently, scholars have turned their attention to boundaryless careers (Arthur and Rousseau, 1996). Reminiscent of Gouldner's (1957) cosmopolitan roles, boundaryless careers separate the individual from organizational constraints. Here, the social system within which work is embedded involves networks, economic systems, and value chains as well as organizations (e.g., Jones, 2001). Careers become sequences of work experiences whose common boundaries may involve multiple organizations, communities, contract work, economic marketability, and personal or family concerns. The potential chaos produced by such careers has refocused attention on the subjective career and quality of work life. Decisions about dual-career families, expatriate experiences, and gender, race, and national differences, take on increasing centrality in career theory when organizations no longer control career mobility and success.

This much abbreviated history presents a central dilemma of career theory. The dizzying breadth of topics and interactions encompassing career theory make it easy for big picture theories to be "a mile wide and an inch deep." From one perspective, career theory includes fundamental human phenomena: the work lives of individuals, their relationship to social systems, and the outcomes these relationships contribute to individuals, organizations, and societies. From another perspective, career theory is a specialized topic within management studies, focusing on individual careers within organizational promotion systems. As a result, interest in the topic waxes and wanes as scholars search for middle ground. Interest is highest when the concept remains broad, but narrowly defined studies produce more concrete results. However, when studies are narrowly defined, scholars seem to retreat toward disciplinary boundaries and the concept seems to lose its broad, general appeal.

Notwithstanding this dilemma, the importance of maintaining a broad definition of career theory has never been more significant than it is today. The global economy, corporate downsizing, massive shifts in job types, and technological changes have dramatically changed the nature of careers. These systemic changes in the fabric of work challenge all career theories and provide a potent reminder of the importance of historical period and cohort effects in theory and research. Those career theories that are truly generalizable will hold to the test of such change. Others may not, becoming more conditional, middle range theories. Certainly, these striking changes in modern work life are putting career theory to the test.

See also *career plateau; career stage; mentoring; motivation; non-work/work; role transitions*

Bibliography

Ancona, D. G., Goodman, P. S., Lawrence, B. S., and Tushman, M. L. (2001). Time: A new research lens. *Academy of Management Review*, **26**, 645–63.

Arthur, M. B., Hall, D. T., and Lawrence, B. S. (eds.) (1989). *Handbook of Career Theory*. Cambridge: Cambridge University Press.

Arthur, M. B. and Rousseau, D. M. (eds.) (1996). *The Boundaryless Career: A New Employment Principle for a New Organizational Era*. New York: Oxford University Press.

Bailyn, L. (1993). *Breaking the Mold: Women, Men, and Time in the New Corporate World*. New York: Free Press/Macmillan.

Barley, S. R. (1989). Careers, identities, and institutions: The legacy of the Chicago school of sociology. In M. B. Arthur, D. T. Hall, and B. S. Lawrence (eds.), *Handbook of Career Theory*. Cambridge: Cambridge University Press, 41–65.

Blau, P. and Duncan, O. D. (1967). *The American Occupational Structure*. New York: Wiley.

Dalton, G. W. and Thompson, P. H. (1986). *Novations: Strategies for Career Management*. Glenview, IL: Scott, Foresman.

Gouldner, A. (1957). Cosmopolitans and locals: Toward an analysis of latent social roles, Part I. *Administrative Science Quarterly*, **2**, 281–305.

Hall, D. T. (2002). *Careers In and Out of Organizations*. Thousand Oaks, CA: Sage.

Howard, A. and Bray, D. W. (1988). *Managerial Lives in Transition: Advancing Age and Changing Times*. New York: Guilford Press.

Jones, C. (2001). Co-evolution of entrepreneurial careers, institutional rules, and competitive dynamics in American film, 1895–1920. *Organization Studies*, **22**, 911–44.

Kanter, R. (1989). Careers and the wealth of nations: A macro-perspective on the structure and implications of career forms. In M. B. Arthur, D. T. Hall, and B. S. Lawrence (eds.), *Handbook of Career Theory*. Cambridge: Cambridge University Press, 506–21.

Lawrence, B. S. (1990). At the crossroads: A multiple-level explanation of individual attainment. *Organization Science*, **1**, 65–86.

Osipow, S. H. (1983). *Theories of Career Development*, 3rd edn. Englewood Cliffs, NJ: Prentice-Hall.

Peiperl, M., Arthur, M., Goffee, R., and Morris, T. (eds.) 2000. *Career Frontiers: New Conceptions of Working Lives*. New York: Oxford University Press.

Rosenbaum, J. E. (1984). *Career Mobility in a Corporate Hierarchy*. New York: Academic Press.

Rousseau, D. M. (1985). Issues of level in organizational research: Multi-level and cross-level perspectives. In L. L. Cummings and B. M. Staw (eds.), *Research in Organizational Behavior*, **7**, 1–37.

Schein, E. H. (1978). *Career Dynamics: Matching Individual and Organizational Needs*. Reading, MA: Addison-Wesley.

Super, D. E. (1963). *Career Development: Self-Concept Theory*. New York: CEEB.

Thomas, D. and Gabarro, J. (1999). *Breaking Through: The Making of Minority Executives in Corporate America*. Boston, MA: Harvard Business School.

Weick, K. (1996). Enactment and the boundaryless career: Organizing as we work. In M. B. Arthur and D. M. Rousseau (eds.), *The Boundaryless Career: A New Employment Principle for a New Organizational Era*. New York: Oxford University Press, 40–57.

case study research

see RESEARCH METHODS

CEOs

Donald C. Hambrick

The chief executive officer (CEO) is the executive who has overall responsibility for the conduct and performance of an entire organization, not just a subunit. The CEO designation has gained widespread use since about 1970, as a result of the need to draw distinctions among various senior executive positions in today's elaborate corporate structures. For example, sometimes a chief operating officer (COO), who is responsible for internal operational affairs, is among the executives who reports to a CEO; in such a case, the CEO primarily focuses on integrating internal and external, longer-term issues such as acquisitions, government relations, and investor relations.

In publicly traded corporations, sometimes the chairman of the board of directors is also the CEO, while the president (if such a title even exists) is the COO. In other cases (particularly European companies), the chairman is not an executive officer at all, but rather is an external overseer, while the president is the senior ranking employed manager or CEO. Other variations exist as well. Further complicating the scholar's task of identifying the CEO of a company is that the label may not be explicitly bestowed on anyone. Still, theorists and other observers of organizations are drawn to the idea that some one person has overall responsibility for the management of an enterprise and that, in turn, that person's characteristics and actions are of consequence to the organization and its stakeholders (Barnard, 1948).

CEO ROLES

The roles of a CEO are many and varied, including DECISION-MAKING (on major and sometimes minor issues), monitoring and transmitting information (both inside and outside the company), and interacting with internal and external parties (many constituencies believe they warrant the CEO's personal attention) (Mintzberg, 1973). CEO roles can also be thought of as spanning from the substantive (tangible actions) to the symbolic (the intangible, added meaning that is attached to a senior leader's behaviors, by virtue of the position he or she holds) (Pfeffer, 1981). Far more research has been done on CEO substantive actions than on symbolism, but recent theory and investigations have pointed to the great significance of the latter.

CEO EFFECTS ON ORGANIZATIONS

Most writings on senior executives, and CEOs in particular, have focused on the effects these individuals have on the form and fate of their companies. Some of these works attempt to describe the traits and behaviors of CEOs who have achieved remarkable successes – often referred to as the "Great Man" view. These inquiries are usually qualitative and, while rich in detail, are difficult to use as a reliable basis for a generalizable theory of LEADERSHIP.

Some research has taken a more limited approach, seeking to understand the associations between specific measurable CEO characteristics and actions taken or subsequent organizational profiles. For example, research has documented the tendencies of new CEOs hired from outside the company to make major immediate strategy and staffing changes; for CEOs with certain types of personalities to adopt certain structural characteristics for the organization; and for CEOs who are large shareholders of the company to take larger strategic risks than CEOs who are only paid employees. Significant findings from this stream of research are mounting (summarized in Finkelstein and Hambrick, 1996). But as the few illustrations here suggest, the patterns are diffuse and generally lacking a coherent theoretical framework – that is, unless the broadest possible perspective is taken, in which case it can be said that CEOs matter.

Actually, the issue of whether (or how much) CEOs matter to organizational outcomes is of longstanding debate among scholars. The earliest perspective, often called the strategic choice perspective, posits that executives engage in major adaptive decisions in the face of shifting environmental requirements and internal resources. Namely, CEOs make big choices and those choices matter. A contrary perspective, which gained currency in the 1970s and early 1980s, is that organizations are so confined by external constraints, institutional pressures, and internal inertia, that CEOs are not allowed (or choose not to undertake) many major strategic actions – that managers do not matter much.

A recent theoretical bridge between these two polar perspectives is the concept of "executive discretion," defined as latitude of action (Hambrick and Finkelstein, 1987). Executive discretion emanates from factors in the environment, in the organization, and within the executive; thus, sometimes CEOs have considerable discretion, sometimes none at all, and usually somewhere in between. This concept of executive discretion is proving very important for untangling the debate about whether CEOs matter and is further shedding light on other phenomena such as executive pay, executive TURNOVER, and executive demographic and personality characteristics.

CEO SELECTION AND SUCCESSION

The prevailing literature on CEOs has focused on the effects they have on their organizations, but a secondary and still notable stream has focused on the opposite causal direction, or the factors that affect CEO characteristics. Namely, why do certain people get appointed to CEO positions (Vancil, 1987)? When and why do they get dismissed? Theoretical perspectives for addressing these questions range widely. At the broadest level is the theory of social elites, arguing that individuals of the highest socioeconomic and educational backgrounds, as well as those who have the strongest connections with other elites, are chosen for CEO positions and are only reluctantly dismissed. A related theory, but narrower in its level of analysis, argues that successive CEOs are clones of each other – that there is a strong institutional tendency toward continuity of leadership profiles; moreover, CEOs who depart on good terms are allowed to influence, if not completely control, the selection of their replacements, who often strikingly resemble them. Finally, resource dependence theory argues that specific identifiable pressures from outside or from within the organization give rise to the appointment of CEOs who have characteristics that will lead them to deal successfully with these pressures. For example, trends in an industry may favor a certain type of perspective among top executives; strategic plans for a company may necessitate a certain CEO profile; and so on. Unfortunately, the actual processes of CEO selection, which are understandably very sensitive phenomena, are not well documented or understood.

See also *managerial roles; top management teams*

Bibliography

Barnard, C. (1948). *The Functions of the Executive*. Cambridge, MA: Harvard University Press.

Finkelstein, S. and Hambrick, D. C. (1996). *Strategic Leadership: Top Executives and Their Effects on Organizations*. Minneapolis/St. Paul: West Publishing.

Fredrickson, J. W., Hambrick, D. C., and Baumrin, S. (1988). A model of CEO dismissal. *Academy of Management Review*, 13, 255–70.

Hambrick, D. C. and Finkelstein, S. (1987). Managerial discretion: A bridge between polar views of organizational outcomes. In L. L. Cummings and B. M. Staw (eds.), *Research in Organizational Behavior*. Greenwich, CT: JAI Press, 369–406.

Hambrick, D. C. and Fukutomi, G. D. S. (1991). The seasons of a CEO's tenure. *Academy of Management Review*, 16 (4), 719–42.

Mintzberg, H. (1973). *The Nature of Managerial Work*. New York: Harper and Row.

Pfeffer, J. (1981). Management as symbolic action: The creation and maintenance of organizational paradigms. In L. L. Cummings and B. M. Staw (eds.), *Research in Organizational Behavior*. Greenwich, CT: JAI Press, 1–52.

Romanelli, E. and Tuchman, M. L. (1988). Executive leadership and organizational outcomes: An evolutionary perspective. In D. C. Hambrick (ed.), *The Executive Effect: Concepts and Methods for Studying Top Managers*. Greenwich, CT: JAI Press, 129–40.

Vancil, R. F. (1987). *Passing the Baton: Managing the Process of CEO Succession*. Boston, MA: Harvard Business School Press.

Westphal, J. D. (1999). Collaboration in the boardroom: The consequences of social ties in the CEO/board relationship. *Academy of Management Journal*, 43, 7–14.

change agents

see CHANGE, METHODS; CONSULTANCY; ORGANIZATION DEVELOPMENT

change, evaluation

Richard W. Woodman

To evaluate ORGANIZATIONAL CHANGE essentially refers to developing a systematic method of collecting information that will allow an assessment of the outcomes of an organizational change program. The field of organizational behavior needs effective methods for assessing organizational change for both practical and theory development reasons. From the perspective of change management, there is the obvious need to have a valid assessment of the effectiveness of organizational change programs: what changes are effective and under what conditions are they effective? At the same time, understanding change phenomena and processes in complex human systems can contribute to theory development in the organizational sciences (Woodman, 1989). In OB, we continue to draw heavily from the field of evaluation research for the design and execution of evaluation efforts (e.g., Lipsey and Cordray, 2000).

Evaluation of organizational change is likely to be most useful, for both practice and THEORY, when the following criteria are met.

1   The evaluation is planned in advance rather than being an *ad hoc* effort designed after the change intervention has occurred.
2   The evaluation is based upon theory.
3   The information is collected using measures with sound properties of RELIABILITY and VALIDITY.
4   The RESEARCH DESIGN utilized controls as much extraneous variation as possible, thus eliminating alternative explanations for the results.

See also *action research; change methods; innovation; organization development*

Bibliography

Lipsey, M. W. and Cordray, D. S. (2000). Evaluation methods for social intervention. In S. T. Fiske, D. L. Schacter, and C. Zahn-Waxler (eds.), *Annual Review of Psychology*, Vol. 51. Palo Alto, CA: Annual Reviews, 345–75.

Woodman, R. W. (1989). Evaluation research on organizational change: Arguments for a "combined paradigm" approach. In R. W. Woodman and W. A. Pasmore (eds.), *Research in Organizational Change and Development*, Vol. 3. Greenwich, CT: JAI Press, 161–80.

change, methods

Richard W. Woodman

Specific methods used to change organizations are often referred to as interventions – the planned change activities designed to increase an organization's effectiveness (Cummings and Worley, 2001). In the ORGANIZATION DEVELOPMENT paradigm, effectiveness includes both organizational performance and quality of work life.

FOCUS OF CHANGE EFFORTS

Effective change depends in large measure on a valid diagnosis of organizational functioning and problems. Valid identification of what the organization does well, less well, and poorly is a logical precursor for change. However, managers and change agents necessarily must have some means to link the findings from the diagnosis with effective action. Attempts to understand or identify such linkages have often taken the form of a model or typology that would categorize interventions by their focus or change targets. The seminal forerunner of many categorization schemes is the dichotomy of human processual and technostructural interventions developed by Friedlander and Brown (1974). Human processual interventions focus on processes through which individuals and groups accomplish the organization's work, such as DECISION-MAKING processes, COMMUNICATION processes, and so on. Technostructural interventions target task methods, TECHNOLOGY, and group and organizational structure. An elaborated example of such a categorization scheme was used by McMahan and Woodman (1992) in a survey of Fortune 500 industrial firms. They were able to identify the change methods used by these large organizations as fitting into one of the following four categories:

Human processual. Emphasis on human relationships, TEAM BUILDING, work team interaction (*see* WORK GROUPS/TEAMS), PROCESS CONSULTATION, or conflict resolution (*see* CONFLICT AND CONFLICT MANAGEMENT).
Technostructural. Emphasis on sociotechnical systems, task and technology work designs, or organization and group structure (*see* SOCIOTECHNICAL THEORY, JOB DESIGN, ORGANIZATIONAL DESIGN).
Strategic planning. Emphasis on strategic business planning processes, strategic change or

visioning; primarily top management involvement (*see* TOP MANAGEMENT TEAMS).

Systemwide. Emphasis on organization-wide improvement activities; LEADERSHIP, culture, quality improvement, and organizational transformation.

CONDITIONS FOR EFFECTIVE CHANGE

Regardless of the specific focus of the intervention activities, effective change methods seem to be characterized by certain conditions. In the "classic" statement of this observation, Argyris (1970) argued that effective ORGANIZATIONAL CHANGE depends upon three factors:

1   Valid and useful information about the organization and its problems.
2   Free and informed choice on the part of organizational members with regard to courses of action that they might take.
3   Internal commitment by participants in the change effort to the actions being pursued.

Absent these antecedents, effective change is seen as quite problematic.

Similarly, Porras and Robertson (1992) have reviewed the literature dealing with change methodology in order to identify conditions related to effective interventions. In brief, these conditions include:

1   The organization's members must be the key source of energy for the change, not some external consultant or change agent.
2   Key members of the organization must recognize the need for change and be attracted by the potential positive outcomes from the change program.
3   A willingness to change norms and procedures, in order to become more effective, must exist. Key members of the organization must exhibit both attitudes and behaviors that support new norms and procedures (*see* GROUP NORMS).

In addition to the above conditions, there is the notion that effective change needs to be system-wide (Woodman and Dewett, in press), a notion that is so widely accepted as to become almost reified. It is important to note, however, that careful systematic empirical work has supported its VALIDITY. For example, the Innovative Forms of Organizing (INNFORM) research program conducted in several countries concluded that there was a strong association between whole system change and firm performance (Pettigrew and Fenton, 2000). (Whole system change was defined as changing structures, work processes, and boundaries among units of the organization.) Firms that made partial changes (for example, changing structure, but not processes or boundaries) showed a negative association between change efforts and performance. This finding is bolstered by meta-analytic work in North America that found significant improvement from change programs required congruent changes in a wide array of organizational variables (Robertson, Roberts, and Porras, 1993) and utilized multiple change levers (Macy and Izumi, 1993). There are two related implications from these research studies: (1) effective organizational change requires the use of system-wide change methods, not piecemeal approaches, and (2) changes in various aspects or subsystems of the organization must be congruent (Woodman and Dewett, in press).

IMPLEMENTATION THEORY

The applied theories that can serve to guide change methods are called implementation theories (Porras and Robertson, 1992). Implementation theories can be further broken down into three categories, each corresponding to a different level of specificity in terms of prescribing change actions. At the most general level are *strategy theories*, which describe broad strategies that can be used to change complex human systems. *Procedure theories*, at a greater level of specificity, include descriptions of major steps taken in order to complete a change process. The most specific category of implementation theories, *technique theories*, focuses tightly on a single "step" or type of activity identified in a procedure theory.

Woodman (in press) has suggested that change methodology might be further enhanced if the field developed a more sophisticated typology concerning the types of changes needed. Woodman argued that the general capacity of the organization to change, the capacity to change in specific ways, the general capacity to innovate and create, and the capacity to create in specific ways exist, to a certain extent, in different "domains." While these domains are clearly related, nevertheless, change methods that are effective for improving the general capacity to change might be quite different, in important ways, from approaches to be used when change is more tightly focused on specific objectives. When does planned change need to focus on true creativity or innovation in addition to addressing change in general? Might there be crucial differences in intervention strategies, effective change methods, ways to evaluate the outcomes, and so on across these domains? Such a perspective suggests some additional refinements to implementation theories that could prove useful.

Many years ago, Kurt Lewin stated there was nothing as practical as a good THEORY. Implementation theories provide the field with a means for identifying the conditions and actions necessary for effective change. Further, implementation theories provide guidance for effective change management – linking organizational diagnosis with organizational actions needed for improved performance. In sum, implementation theory summarizes what the field knows about change methods, why they work, and how they might be successfully used.

Bibliography

Argyris, C. (1970). *Intervention Theory and Method: A Behavioral Science View*. Reading, MA: Addison-Wesley.

Cummings, T. R. and Worley, C. G. (2001). *Organization Development and Change*, 7th edn. Cincinnati, OH: South-Western College Publishing.

Friedlander, F. and Brown, L. D. (1974). Organization development. *Annual Review of Psychology*, 25, 313–41.

McMahan, G. C. and Woodman, R. W. (1992). The current practice of organization development within the firm. *Group and Organization Management*, 17, 117–34.

Macy, B. A. and Izumi, H. (1993). Organizational change, design, and work innovation: A meta-analysis of 131 North American field studies, 1961–1991. In R. W. Woodman and W. A. Pasmore (eds.), *Research in Organizational Change and Development*, Vol. 7. Greenwich, CT: JAI Press, 235–313.

Pettigrew, A. M. and Fenton, E. M. (eds.) (2000). *The Innovating Organization*. London: Sage.

Porras, J. I. and Robertson, P. J. (1992). Organizational development: Theory, practice, and research. In M. D. Dunnette and L. M. Hough (eds.), *Handbook of Industrial and Organizational Psychology*, Vol. 3, 2nd edn. Palo Alto, CA: Consulting Psychologists Press, 719–822.

Robertson, P. J., Roberts, D. R., and Porras, J. I. (1993). An evaluation of a model of planned organizational change: Evidence from a meta-analysis. In R. W. Woodman and W. A. Pasmore (eds.), *Research in Organizational Change and Development*, Vol. 7. Greenwich, CT: JAI Press, 1–39.

Woodman, R. W. (in press). Creativity and organizational change: Linking ideas and extending theory. In C. Ford (ed.), *Handbook of Organizational Creativity*. Mahwah, NJ: Lawrence Erlbaum Associates.

Woodman, R. W. and Dewett, T. (in press). Organizationally relevant journeys in individual change. In M. S. Poole and A. H. Van de Ven (eds.), *Handbook of Organizational Change and Innovation*. Oxford: Oxford University Press.

charismatic leadership

Jay Conger

To understand the qualities that shape perceptions of charisma in a leader, it is most appropriate to start with the early twentieth-century theories of German sociologist Max Weber, who first applied the term "charismatic" to leaders. His typology of three forms of AUTHORITY in society (the traditional, the rational–legal, and the charismatic) established charismatic LEADERSHIP as an important term to describe forms of authority based on perceptions of an extraordinary individual. In contrast to authority where traditions or rules or elections conferred legitimacy on individuals, the holder of charisma is "set apart from ordinary men and is treated as endowed with...exceptional powers and qualities...[which] are not accessible to the ordinary person but are regarded as of divine origin or as exemplary, and on the basis of them the individual concerned is treated as a leader" (Weber, 1947: 358–9).

Charismatic leadership is an ATTRIBUTION made by followers. The leadership ROLE behaviors displayed by a person make that individual (in the eyes of followers) not only a task leader or a social leader and a participative or directive leader but also a charismatic or non-charismatic leader. The leader's observed behavior can be interpreted by his or her own followers as expressions of charismatic qualities.

The behavioral components that lead to the attribution of charismatic leadership are interrelated, and the presence and intensity of these characteristics are expressed in varying degrees among different charismatic leaders. These components are associated with three stages of leadership. The first stage concerns the leader's sensitivity to the environment. Charismatic leaders can be distinguished from non-charismatic leaders in this stage by their heightened sensitivity to deficiencies and poorly exploited opportunities in the status quo. For this reason, we find that a number of reformers and entrepreneurs are charismatic leaders (*see* ENTREPRENEURSHIP). Charismatic leaders also tend to be highly sensitive to both the abilities and the emotional needs of followers – the most important resources for attaining organizational goals. This is especially true of social movement leaders like Gandhi, Martin Luther King, or Caesar Chavez. In addition, internal organizational deficiencies may be perceived by the charismatic leader as platforms for advocating radical change. Thus any context that triggers a need for a major change and/or presents unexploited market opportunities is relevant for the emergence of a charismatic leader.

Stage two of the leadership process concerns the act of formulating future goals or directions. Charismatic leaders are distinguished by a sense of strategic vision versus rational or purely tactical goals. Here the word *vision* refers to an idealized, highly aspirational goal that the leader wants the organization to achieve in the future. In articulating the vision, the charismatic leader's verbal messages construct reality such that only the positive features of the future vision and the negative features of the status quo are emphasized. The status quo is usually presented as intolerable, and the vision is presented in clear specific terms as the most attractive and attainable alternative. Charismatic leaders' use of rhetoric, high energy, persistence, unconventional and risky behavior, heroic deeds, and personal sacrifices all serve to articulate their own high motivation and enthusiasm, which then become contagious among their followers.

In the third and final stage of the leadership process – aligning followers' actions to realize goals – leaders in general build in followers a sense of trust in their abilities and clearly demonstrate the tactics and behaviors required to achieve the organization's goals. Charismatic leaders accomplish this by building TRUST through personal example and RISK TAKING and through unconventional expertise. They also engage in exemplary acts that are perceived by followers as involving great personal risk, cost, and energy.

See also *bureaucracy; CEOs; influence; leadership contingencies*

Bibliography

Bass, B. M. (1990). *Bass & Stogdill's Handbook of Leadership*, 3rd edn. New York: Free Press.

Conger, J. A. and Kanungo, R. N. (1987). Toward a behavioral theory of charismatic leadership in organizational settings. *Academy of Management Review*, **12**, 637–47.

Conger, J. A. and Kanungo, R. N. (1998). *Charismatic Leadership in Organizations*. Thousand Oaks, CA: Sage.

Shamir, B., House, R., and Arthur, M. B. (1993). The motivational effects of charismatic leadership: A self-concept based theory. *Organization Science*, **4** (4), 577–94.

Weber, M. (1947). *The Theory of Social and Economic Organizations*, trans. A. M. Henderson and T. Parsons. New York: Free Press.

citizenship

see ORGANIZATIONAL CITIZENSHIP BEHAVIOR (OCB)

classical design theory

see MANAGEMENT, CLASSICAL THEORY

coalition formation

J. Keith Murnighan

Coalition formation is typically a political act in which some but not all members of a group organize themselves to take a united position on an issue that affects the entire group (*see* GROUP DYNAMICS; POLITICS). Coalition formation is usually driven by the need to exert POWER in collective interactions.

In his classic book *Organizations in Action*, Thompson (1967: 126) wrote: "Coalition behavior is undoubtedly of major importance to our understanding of complex organizations." Although organizational theorists appropriately consider POWER as an essential force in organizational interactions and have often described organizations and organizational action as coalitional, organizational behavior has not incorporated the literature on coalitions in social psychology, GAME THEORY, or political science (Murnighan, 1978, 1994) into its normal discourse.

Early investigations of coalition formation suggested that the least endowed tended to coalesce and exclude the most endowed. These "strength is weakness" findings, which suggested the supremacy of the underdog, were eventually debunked. Instead, research showed that when power bases vary, strength is weakness only when parties with different resources are effectively interchangeable. Thus, parties whose resource bases are just sufficient become optimal coalition partners: fewer resources typically lead to smaller outcome demands, increasing a party's attractiveness as a coalition partner. When parties are not interchangeable, however, strength is extremely valuable.

Coalition founders tend to have a broad network of weak ties, rather than a few strong connections (*see* NETWORKING). Thus, a coalition's strength may rest on infrequent, nonrepetitive interactions with many others rather than on frequent interactions with a few close contacts. Political models suggest that coalitions form incrementally, via interconnected sets of interacting dyads. Put simply, coalitions form one person at a time (Murnighan and Brass, 1991). After achieving a critical mass, continued growth becomes much easier.

Surreptitious action may be critical to the success of organizational coalitions because silent action delays the formation of organized opposition. Von Neumann and Morgenstern's (1974) classic, original model of game theory assumed that such counter-coalitions would be a natural reaction to a coalition forming. Successful coalitions, then, may need to both form and disappear quickly (Murnighan and Brass, 1991).

Political models suggest that founders add similar members to protect their centrality in the final coalition. New parties are chosen to balance IDEOLOGY on either side of the founder's position. Coalitions grow to be just large enough, with narrow ideological ranges that increase the chances that the coalition's final position will closely reflect the founder's own preferences. This political strategy, which may be well understood by astute organizational tacticians, has not been documented in the research literature.

Within an organization, executives who are involved in many organizational coalitions are viewed as politically powerful (*see* POWER). Individuals who participate in several strong, organizationally dominant coalitions represent Thompson's (1967) concept of the *inner circle*, a select few whose interconnectedness gives them considerable influence (*see* INFLUENCE; LEADERSHIP).

See also *collaboration; intergroup relations; interorganizational relations*

Bibliography

Murnighan, J. K. (1978). Models of coalition formation: Game theoretic, social psychological, and political perspectives. *Psychological Bulletin*, 85, 1130–53.

Murnighan, J. K. (1994). Game theory and organizational behavior. In B. M. Straw and L. L. Cummings (eds.), *Research in Organizational Behavior*. Greenwich, CT: JAI Press.

Murnighan, J. K. and Brass, D. J. (1991). Intraorganizational coalitions. In M. H. Bazerman, R. J. Lewicki, and B. H. Sheppard (eds.), *Research on Negotiation in Organizations*. Greenwich, CT: JAI Press.

Thompson, J. D. (1967). *Organizations in Action*. New York: McGraw-Hill.

Von Neumann, J. and Morgenstern, O. (1974). *The Theory of Games and Economic Behavior*. Princeton, NJ: Princeton University Press.

cognition

see MANAGERIAL AND ORGANIZATIONAL COGNITION

cognitive dissonance

Ricky W. Griffin

This is an element of ATTITUDE THEORY, which arises when there is an inconsistency among an individual's attitudes, behaviors, and/or VALUES (Festinger, 1957). For example, an individual who strongly dislikes his or her job (i.e., who has a negative attitude toward his or her job) but who must work long hours in order to perform that job (i.e., a job-related behavior) will likely experience dissonance between intended behavior (as predicted by the negative attitude) and actual behavior (working long hours).

A person who experiences cognitive dissonance will be motivated to resolve it in some fashion. For example, the worker noted above may alter her or his attitude by focusing more on positive aspects of the work. Alternatively, the worker may alter her or his behavior by working fewer hours. Prolonged periods of dissonance tend to have dysfunctional consequences for the individual. For example, the worker is likely to experience higher levels of STRESS, frustration, and anxiety. Job performance may suffer. Extreme dissonance may also cause the individual to withdraw from the situation by being absent more frequently or resigning altogether.

See also *absenteeism; job satisfaction; self-regulation; turnover*

Bibliography

Festinger, L. (1957). *A Theory of Cognitive Dissonance*. Palo Alto, CA: Stanford University Press.

cognitive style

see PERSONALITY

cohesiveness

see GROUP COHESIVENESS

collaboration

Peter Ring

The richness and variety of collaborations between and among economic actors continue to grow. That growth is accompanied by intense interest among scholars with respect to the antecedents of their emergence, the dynamics and processes associated with their evolution, the structures of their governance, the implications of their performance, and causes of, and approaches to, their termination. The research into these diverse aspects of collaboration is grounded in a number of disciplines and a variety of theoretical frameworks within them. The overall academic literature on collaboration (or so-called strategic alliances) is extensive (well in excess of 2,000 articles since 1995 in peer reviewed journals) and it is grounded in rich and increasingly multi-disciplinary research streams: transaction cost theory, agglomeration economics, agency theory, game theory, real options theory, the resource-based view of the firm, the roles of trust, reliance on psychological contracts, negotiation techniques, relational contracting theory and neoclassical contract law, resource dependence theory, learning theory, justice theory, a number of process approaches and a wide variety of approaches based in social ecology, population ecology, sociology or on network techniques (for instance, relational and structural embeddedness perspectives, the role of social capital, the ability to bridge structural holes, etc.) (Ariño et al., 2001; Blaum, 2001; Das and Bing-Sheng, 2002).

Not surprisingly, it is still not possible to offer a single, widely accepted definition of a cooperative inter-organizational collaboration. In fact, given the increasing number of project-based collaborations (e.g., film production, IPOs, basic RandD, class-action lawsuits) involving individual economic actors, exploring collaboration from an inter-organizational basis is somewhat limiting. This is particularly so in light of the ability to explore the roles of interpersonal networks via network techniques as a way of shedding light on issues related to the emergence and evolution of collaborative efforts (*see* NET-WORKING).

Nonetheless it is possible to identify a number of recurring circumstances in which collaboration is likely to be found. One cause of collaboration is government action requiring it (as in cross-border joint ventures). Another is the need to access scarce or rare tangible resources (which also may be controlled by governments). Increasingly, however, collaboration is motivated by a need to gain access to know-how and other forms of tacit or knowledge-based resources. The disintegration of firms leading to increasing specialization is another motivation producing increased reliance on collaboration. This phenomenon is not limited to firms, as the fragmentation of states, the increase in non-profits intended to support single issue "causes" (e.g., specific types of cancer), the need to tackle "public interest" issues on a global basis (e.g., pollution issues, HIV/AIDs, water scarcity), and the rise in influence of supranational agencies (WTO, UN, OEDC, IMF, World Bank) has led to increased reliance on collaboration among and between these kinds of organizations. In some circumstances, large scale, multi-sectoral collaborations have given birth to entirely new "industries" (Murtha, Lenway, and Hart, 2001) or to new approaches to organizing knowledge-based economic activities (Doz, Santos, and Williamson, 2001). These approaches to collaboration, which are slightly outside the mainstream of management research, are likely to provide the more interesting new insights into the dynamics of collaboration in the foreseeable future.

See also *governance; inter-organizational relation*

Bibliography

Ariño, A., de la Torre, J., Doz, Y., Ring, P. S., and Lorenzoni, G. (2001). Process issues in international alliance management: A debate on the evolution of collaboration. In J. Cheng and M. A. Hitt (eds.), *Advances in International Management*, Vol. 14. London: Elsevier, 173–219.

Blaum, J. (2001). Part 3: Inter-organizational level. In J. Blaum (ed.), *The Blackwell Companion to Organizations*. Oxford: Blackwell.

Das, T. K. and Bing-Sheng, T. (2002). Alliance constellations: A social exchange perspective. *Academy of Management Review*, 27, 445–56.

Doz, Y., Santos, J., and Williamson, P. (2001). *From Global to Metanational: How Companies Win in the Knowledge Economy*. Boston, MA: Harvard Business School Press.

Murtha, T. P., Lenway, S. A., and Hart, J. A. (2001). *Managing New Industry Creation: Global Knowledge Formation and Entrepreneurship in High Technology*. Palo Alto, CA: Stanford University Press.

commitment

David Guest

Commitment is concerned with the level of identification with, and attachment and loyalty to, an organization, an occupation, or some other feature of work. Organizations increasingly need to motivate and retain talented staff, and those committed to the organization might be expected to work harder and have longer tenure. Indeed, Walton (1985) has contrasted a traditional employer–employee relationship based on control with one based on commitment, arguing that all organizations need to pursue a high commitment approach to survive. This has been a factor behind advocacy of human resource management.

Despite its intuitive appeal, commitment is a complex phenomenon. Interest has focused on four main issues: (1) the focus or target of commitment; (2) the definition and measurement of commitment; (3) the causes of variations in levels of commitment; (4) the consequences of commitment. The picture is made more complex by a distinction sometimes made between commitment as an attitude and commitment as behavior. However, Meyer and Herscovitch (2001) have argued these can be integrated into a general model of commitment in the workplace.

THE FOCUS OF COMMITMENT

Commitment may develop to a range of targets, including an organization, occupation, work team, or one's family. Indeed, the possibility of multiple and potentially competing commitments has led to a strand of research on dual commitment; and the interest in work–life conflict highlights the problem when a range of foci are present. However, most research has been directed to commitment to an organization.

The definition and measurement of commitment
Mowday, Porter, and Steers (1982) define organizational commitment as "the relative strength of an individual's identification with and involvement in an organization." They elaborate this to incorporate belief in the values and goals of the organization, willingness to exert effort on behalf of the organization, and desire to be a member of the organization. They developed the widely used Organizational Commitment Questionnaire (OCQ) to measure these elements. Both the definition and the measure have been criticized for conflating commitment with outcomes such as effort and propensity to stay.

Meyer and Allen (1997) proposed alternative definitions and measures, distinguishing affective, continuance, and normative commitment. Affective commitment emphasizes identification with the organization and is predicted to impact in particular on job performance. Continuance commitment focuses on the costs and benefits of staying with the organization and is expected to predict tenure. There appear to be two aspects of continuance commitment. First, it is suggested that individuals will stay with an organization as long as they gain a positive exchange. This exchange may be financial, but over time "side bets" such as pensions, CAREER prospects, and friendship develop. For both financial and non-financial reasons, staff cannot then "afford" to leave. The second aspect concerns the nature of the alternatives and it is anticipated that workers will be more likely to stay with an organization when they perceive a lack of attractive or feasible alternative jobs. The third dimension, normative commitment, is concerned with a sense of obligation to an organization, based perhaps on moral VALUES. The relationship between normative commitment and outcomes is less easy to predict. Meyer and Allen have developed and over time adapted measures of these dimensions of commitment. Despite a strong inter-correlation between affective and normative commitment, Meyer argues that they are conceptually and empirically distinct (Meyer et al. 2001).

The strand of research concerned with behavioral commitment explores the process whereby individuals become bound or committed to their actions. Drawing on COGNITIVE DISSONANCE theory, Salancik (1977) proposed that the propensity to act will be greater when an individual volunteers to act, when the action to be taken is explicit, when other people are present, and when the decision is hard to revoke. This approach underpins organizations such as Weight-watchers and Alcoholics Anonymous but can equally well be applied to decisions to join an organization or to decisions taken in work groups (*see* WORK GROUPS/TEAMS) and committees. A commitment to act is expected to increase the probability of subsequent action and of attitudes moving in line with behavior. This approach has successfully predicted tenure, based on analysis of the circumstances surrounding the process of career choice (Kline and Peters, 1991). Behavioral commitment, rather like goal setting, and in contrast to attitudinal commitment, is specific with respect to the conditions that must be met for behavior to ensue.

The antecedents of commitment
Research exploring the antecedents of organizational commitment indicates that individual variables such as age, gender, tenure, and education have only a modest influence on commitment. In contrast, work experiences, including organizational support, justice/fairness of treatment, TRANSFORMATIONAL LEADERSHIP, and role autonomy and clarity, are consistently strongly associated with affective commitment.

The consequences of commitment
Small but statistically significant associations are often reported between affective commitment and higher performance, greater organizational citizenship behavior, lower absence (particularly voluntary absence), and lower labor turnover. Contrary to the predictions of Meyer and Allen's three-dimensional model, affective commitment is consistently more strongly associated with all types of outcome than either continuance or normative commitment. A more limited amount of research indicates that affective commitment

is associated with lower STRESS and less work–non-work conflict, while the opposite is the case with respect to continuance commitment. Affective commitment to the organization is invariably highly correlated with occupational commitment, job satisfaction, and work involvement (Meyer et al., 2001). This suggests that high affective commitment to the organization may bring benefits for both the organization and individual workers.

After two decades of research on organizational commitment, there is a solid body of evidence indicating a significant, positive, but usually small association between organizational commitment and a range of outcomes. Furthermore, since commitment is largely influenced by organizational experiences that lie within the control of management, it can be "managed." Despite the efforts of Meyer and colleagues to justify several dimensions of commitment, attitudinal or affective commitment is consistently more strongly associated with outcomes than the other dimensions. One reason for the initial interest of some researchers was disillusion at the failure of job satisfaction to predict behavior. Yet in many studies where the two have been compared, commitment has fared no better than job satisfaction as a predictor of performance and tenure. More attention needs to be paid to the conditions under which organizational commitment and indeed commitment to other foci might be expected to affect behavior and in particular to change behavior. Finally, current trends in employment, including the decline in job security and continuing restructuring of organizations, challenge the viability of organizational commitment, increasing the possibility of a shift in the focus of individual commitment to profession, work group, or life outside work.

See also *motivation; non-work/work*

Bibliography

Kline, C. J. and Peters, L. H. (1991). Behavioral commitment and tenure of new employees: A replication and extension. *Academy of Management Journal*, **34** (1), 194–204.

Meyer, J. and Allen, N. (1997). *Commitment in the Workplace: Theory, Research, and Application.* Thousand Oaks, CA: Sage.

Meyer, J. and Herscovitch, L. (2001). Commitment in the workplace: Toward a general model. *Human Resource Management Review*, **11**, 299–326.

Meyer, J., Stanley, D., Herscovitch, L., and Topolnytsky, L. (2001). Affective, continuance, and normative commitment to the organization: A meta-analysis of antecedents, correlates, and consequences. *Journal of Vocational Behavior*, **61**, 20–52.

Mowday, R., Porter, L., and Steers, R. (1982). *Employee–Organizational Linkages.* New York: Academic Press.

Salancik, G. (1977). Commitment and the control of organizational behavior and belief. In B. M. Staw and G. R. Salancik (eds.), *New Directions in Organizational Behavior.* Chicago: St. Clair Press.

Walton, R. (1985). From control to commitment in the workplace. *Harvard Business Review*, **63**, 76–84.

commitment, escalating

Max H. Bazerman

Escalation is the degree to which an individual commits to a previously selected course of action beyond a level that a rational model of DECISION-MAKING would prescribe. We often face decisions of continuation. Should we add more resources into our old car? How long should we stay on hold waiting for someone to answer the phone? When an investment starts to fail, should we stick with it? Research suggests that decision-makers committed to a particular course of action have a tendency to make subsequent decisions which continue that COMMITMENT beyond the level that RATIONALITY would suggest is reasonable (Staw, 1976).

There are multiple reasons why escalation occurs (Bazerman, 2001). First, an individual's PERCEPTION may be biased by their previous decision (*see* BIAS). That is, the decision-maker may notice information that supports the decision, while ignoring information that contradicts the initial decision. Second, the decision-maker's biased judgments may cause them to perceive information in a way that justifies the existing position. Third, negotiators often make subsequent decisions which justify earlier decisions to themselves and others. Fourth, competitiveness adds to the likelihood of escalation; unilaterally giving up or even reducing demands may be viewed as a defeat, while escalating commitment leaves the future uncertain.

See also *behavioral decision research; game theory; negotiation; risk taking*

Bibliography

Bazerman, M. H. (2001). *Judgment in Managerial Decision-Making*, 5th edn. New York: Wiley.
Staw, B. M. (1976). Knee-deep in the big muddy: A study of escalating commitment to a chosen course of action. *Organizational Behavior and Human Performance*, 16, 27–44.

communication

Marshall Scott Poole

Through communication organizations and their members exchange information, form understandings, coordinate activities, exercise influence, socialize, and generate and maintain systems of beliefs, symbols, and values. Communication has been called the "nervous system of any organized group" and the "glue" which holds organizations together.

Claude Shannon's classic mathematical theory of communication defined seven basic elements of communication (Ritchie, 1991). Communication involves a *source* which *encodes* a *message* and *transmits* it through some *channel* to a *receiver*, which *decodes* the message and may give the sender some FEEDBACK. The sender and receiver may be individuals, machines, or collectives such as organizations or teams. The channel is subject to a degree of *noise* which may interfere with or distort the transmission of the message. Other distortions may come during encoding or decoding, if errors are introduced or if the source and receiver have different codes. The process of communication occurs through a series of transmissions among parties, so Shannon's single message is only the basic building block of larger interchanges among a system of two to *N* entities. This system may be represented as a *communication network* in which communicators are nodes and the various types of communication relationships are links (*see* NETWORK THEORY AND ANALYSIS). Message distortion may also be introduced as the message passes through multiple links, with small changes at each node. Communication is dependent on its *context*; many scholars argue that the interpretation of messages is only possible because the receiver has contextual cues to supplement message cues.

Due to the complexity of the organizational communication process and the many levels at which communication occurs, there is no generally agreed on theory of organizational communication. Different positions have been advanced on several issues.

A major controversy concerns what is communicated (i.e., the substance of communication). One position assumes that messages transmit *information*, defined as anything which reduces the receiver's uncertainty (Ritchie, 1991). This stance, first advanced in Shannon's theory, portrays communication as something amenable to precise analysis. The amount of information in a given message can, in theory, be measured, and messages can be compared on metrics of uncertainty reduction. This view has been adopted metaphorically by a wide range of analysts who view organizations as information processing systems or focus on uncertainty reduction. The information perspective has been criticized for reducing ideas, feelings, and symbols to a set of discrete bits pumped through a conduit from sender to receiver (Axley, 1984). An alternative position is that the essence of communication is *meaning*, encompassing ideas, emotions, values, and skills which are conveyed via symbolization and demonstration. Meaning cannot be reduced to information, because it depends on associations among symbols grounded in the surrounding culture and the communicators' experience. The meaning of a message or interaction is grasped through a process of interpretation which requires communicators to read individual signs in light of the whole message and its context, but simultaneously understand the whole by what its constituent signs signify. This *hermeneutic circle* implies that meaning can never be established finally or unequivocally. Interpretation is a continuing process, always subject to revision or qualification. The information-centered and meaning-centered conceptions of communication represent two quite different approaches, the former being favored by empirical social scientists and the latter by organizational culture and critical researchers.

There are also at least two positions on the role of communication in organizations. One regards communication as a *subprocess* which plays an important role in other organizational processes. For example, communication serves as a channel for the exercise of leadership or for the maintenance of inter-organizational linkages. The other position argues that communication is the process which *constitutes* the organization and its activities. Rather than being subsidiary to key phenomena such as LEADERSHIP, communication is regarded as the medium through which these phenomena and, more generally, organizations are created and maintained. This viewpoint in reflected in a wide range of organizational research, including Herbert Simon's *Administrative Behavior*, analyses of leadership as a language game, and most studies of organizational culture. The two positions have quite different implications for practice. For example, in the case of leadership communication the subprocess view implies that a leader should make sure that leadership functions are conveyed effectively, while the constitutive view implies that the leader should try to use communication to create and maintain leader–follower relationships and to generate a shared vision.

Another way of describing the role of communication is to delineate the functions it performs for organizations and their members. While the list is potentially endless, at least seven critical functions can be distinguished. Communication serves a *command and control* function in that it is the medium by which directives are given, problems identified, MOTIVATION encouraged, and performance monitored. The Weberian BUREAUCRACY emphasizes this function of communication, and the first wave of formal information systems for accounting attempted to automate it, with mixed results. The *linking* function of communication promotes a flow of information between different parts of the organization, enabling the organization to achieve a degree of coherency among disparate units and personnel. The linking function plays a key role in INNOVATION and in the diffusion of innovations within organizations. Important to linking are upward and lateral communication flows. A third function of communication is *enculturation*, which refers to the creation and maintenance of organizational cultures and to the

assimilation of members into the organization. RITUALS, myths, METAPHORS, mission statements, and other symbolic genres contribute to this function.

In addition to the three intra-organizational functions, communication also serves two additional inter-organizational functions. The fourth function is *inter-organizational linking*, which serves to create and maintain inter-organizational fields. This linking function is accomplished via BOUNDARY SPANNING personnel and units and through shared information systems used to monitor inter-organizational ventures. The fifth is *organizational presentation*, which defines the organization to key audiences, such as potential customers, other organizations, the state, and the public at large. This function contributes to the maintenance of an organization's institutional legitimacy. It is carried out through such diverse activities as public information campaigns, corporate advocacy advertisement, and maintenance of proper records and certifications.

Two functions of communication apply to both intra- and inter-organizational situations. The *ideational* function of communication refers to its role in the generation and use of ideas and knowledge in the organization. Simon's description of decision premises and their circulation through the organization is one example of the ideational function. This function is critical to the processes of social reasoning and organizational learning which contribute to organizational effectiveness. There is also an *ideological* function of communication: it is the vehicle for the development and promulgation of ideologies – systems of thought which normalize and justify relations of POWER and control. Postmodern analysis of organizations asserts that the reigning discourse in organizations defines what is correct and incorrect and who is able to decide matters of truth and falsehood. This arbitrary allocation of power leaves some groups with unquestioned control and omits others from consideration. Such processes are hard to uncover and change, because they occur in the course of normal, everyday communication and thus seem natural and nonproblematic.

Organizations have two distinct communication systems: formal and informal. The *formal* communication system is a part of the organizational structure and includes supervisory relationships, WORK GROUPS/TEAMS, permanent and *ad hoc* committees, and management information systems. In traditional organizations the major design concern was vertical communication, focusing on command and control; more contemporary forms such as matrix or networked organizations also focus on formal lateral communication. Formal channels, especially vertical ones, are subject to a number of communication problems. These include unintentional distortion and omission of information as it is passed up the hierarchy, delays in message routing, and intentional distortions by subordinates attempting to manipulate superiors or protect themselves.

The *informal* communication system emerges from day-to-day interaction among organizational members. Ties in the informal network are based on proximity, friendship, common interests, and political benefits more than on formal job duties. The informal system includes the "grapevine" and the "rumor mill." The informal communication network is usually more complex and less organized than the formal network. Messages pass through the informal network more rapidly, and members often regard them as more accurate and trustworthy than those from the formal system. An organization's informal communication system is important for several reasons. First, it often compensates for problems in formal communication. Members can use informal channels to respond to crises and exceptional cases rapidly. They can use informal contacts to make sense of uncertain, ambiguous, or threatening situations. Second, use of informal networks may improve organizational decision-making, because it allows members to talk "off the record" and "think aloud," hence avoiding the negative consequences of taking a public position. This is especially valuable when problems are ill-defined or solutions unclear. Third, informal networks foster innovation, because they are more open and rapid, and because they often connect people from different departments or professions.

The nature of *communication channels* exerts an important influence on its functions and effectiveness. The archetypal communication situations occur in face-to-face interactions or in public speeches to large audiences. However, communication occurs through many other media, including written formats, telephone, fax, electronic mail, teleconferencing, computer conferencing, and broadcast technologies. Information technologies such as electronic mail and computer networks vastly increase the connections among members and may stimulate a greater flow of ideas and innovations and change POWER relations. Studies have shown that the nature of the medium used affects the communication process; for example, NEGOTIATION generally is more effective through face-to-face and (to a lesser extent) audio media than through video or written media. In order to guide communicators' media choices, researchers have attempted to rank order these media in terms of their *social presence*, the degree to which they convey a sense of direct personal contact with another, and in terms of *media richness*, the degree to which a medium allows immediate feedback, multiple channels, variety of language, and personal cues (Sitkin, Sutcliffe, and Barrios-Chopin, 1992). Generally, face-to-face communication is classified as the richest and highest social presence medium, followed by meetings, video conferencing, telephone and teleconferencing, email, written memos, and, finally, numerical information. Achieving the correct match between media richness and the communication situation is an important determinant of effectiveness. Variables governing media choice include degree of equivocality and uncertainty in the situation (the more uncertain, the richer the medium needed), sender and receiver characteristics, and organizational norms. Also important in media choice is what the medium symbolizes; a personal meeting might signal the importance the convener attaches to an issue, whereas an electronic mail message might suggest the same issue is less critical. While social presence, richness, and symbolism are important to consider, studies have shown variations in the ranking of media on these dimensions; so, media choice is also dependent on the nature of the organization.

Numerous prescriptions and recommendations have been offered to improve organizational communication. Perhaps the most common is that the organization's communication system should be as open as possible. However, more communication is not necessarily better communication. At the personal level open communication can be threatening and exhausting to those who have to deal with difficult issues and personal problems they might otherwise avoid. At the organizational level open communication can result in communication overload and CONFLICT. Another common prescription emphasizes the importance of clarity and uncertainty reduction, but this too may be somewhat overrated. Eisenberg (1984) discusses the value of purposefully ambiguous communication. Its uses include the downplaying of differences in order to build consensus and masking negative consequences of organizational change in order to promote acceptance of innovations. A final common admonition is to promote rational argumentation and discussion. While this certainly is good currency, overemphasis can blind us to the creative potential of inconsistency and logical jumps and to the importance of the emotions. Like many things that seem simple and straightforward, communication conceals considerable complexity.

See also *communications technology; decision-making; learning organization*

Bibliography

Axley, S. (1984). Managerial and organizational communication in terms of the conduit metaphor. *Academy of Management Review*, 9, 428–37.

Conrad, C. and Poole, M. S. (2004). *Strategic Organizational Communication*, 6th edn. Belmont, CA: Wadsworth.

Eisenberg, E. M. (1984). Ambiguity as strategy in organizational communication. *Communication Monographs*, 51, 227–42.

Jablin, F. M. and Putnam, L. L. (2001). *The New Handbook of Organizational Communication*. Newbury Park, CA: Sage.

Monge, P. and Contractor, N. (2003). *Communication Networks*. New York: Oxford University Press.

Ritchie, L. D. (1991). *Information*. Newbury Park, CA: Sage.

Sitkin, S. B., Sutcliffe, J. M., and Barrios-Choplin, J. R. (1992). A dual-capacity model of communication media choice in organizations. *Human Communication Research*, 18, 563–98.

Weick, K. (1979). *The Social Psychology of Organizing*. Reading, MA: Addison-Wesley.

communications technology

Marshall Scott Poole

COMMUNICATION is the glue that binds organizations. As a result, there has been great incentive to develop and apply technologies that might enhance and speed communication. Communication technology refers to the hardware, software, organizational structures, and social procedures by which individuals collect, process, and exchange information with other individuals.

While it is natural to think of it in terms of modern electronic communication systems, communication technology has a long and complex history. The oldest communication technology, writing, fostered ancient empires and commerce. Later, the printing press laid the groundwork for literacy and education, which made Weber's BUREAUCRACY possible. In the late nineteenth and early twentieth centuries, techniques for systematic storage and retrieval of documents, such as vertical filing systems, greatly enhanced the ability of businesses to marshal information, while the evolution of communication genres such as the memo and the business letter changed the way in which internal and external communication was handled.

The first electronic technologies, the telegraph and the telephone, had profound effects on organizations, allowing them to spread over much greater distances and work more rapidly. Originally intended primarily as a business tool, the telephone also transformed interpersonal communication in general, changing both work and social relationships in organizations. Video conferencing came next, but it remained largely unsuccessful until the early 1990s, when the TECHNOLOGY finally matured. The most recent wave of communication technologies involves computer-supported communication. The earliest entries – electronic mail and computer conferencing – have already changed the nature of organizational communication. More recent developments – work group support, interpersonal messaging, blogging (internet conferencing) – promise even more profound changes. Communication technologies are becoming so important to modern organizations that some theorists have suggested that they are the limiting factor on ORGANIZATIONAL DESIGN and growth.

This brief overview hints at the complex nature of communication technologies. Their most obvious aspect is the ever-expanding array of hardware. However, reflection indicates that the hardware operates within a broader context of social norms which define adequate communication, organizational structures which influence the application of the hardware and motivate members to use it, and the larger societal and international systems within which technologies develop and standards for their design are set. This context is as essential to the communication technology as the hardware.

Media choice theories have attempted to define dimensions that help organizational members select among the wide variety of communication modes available to them. Communication technologies can be characterized in terms of their *social presence*, the degree to which they convey a sense of direct personal contact with another, and in terms of *media richness*, the degree to which a medium allows immediate FEEDBACK, multiple channels, variety of language, and personal cues (*see* COMMUNICATION for a more complete discussion). A related dimension is *interactivity*, which describes the degree to which a communication technology supports active participation in interchanges and interaction among users. While communication technologies may seem to have objective locations on these dimensions (e.g., video conferencing is classified as richer than email), users' social constructions influence their perceptions of these technologies. For instance, email may be perceived to allow the same degree of social presence as a phone call, depending on how the technology is used in the organization (Rice and Gattiker, 2000).

The expanding array of new communication technologies has had major impacts on organizations. These technologies have greatly influenced organizational design. The capacity of electronic mail, teleconferencing, video conferencing, and fax to enable coordination and collaboration at a distance permits organizations to adopt more dispersed forms. For example, Hewlett Packard product development teams are often spread around the world at several facilities and do much of their work via electronic media.

Various new organizational forms, such as the dynamic network and virtual organization, rely on new communication technologies to hold them together and to give them the ability to rapidly restructure. Combined with accounting and other information technologies, communication technologies greatly enhance the ability to coordinate and control a wide variety of contracting and joint venture relationships among individual firms. This has promoted the increasing use of "modular" organizations composed of temporary aggregations of firms and contractors who pursue a limited term project. Communication and information technologies also permit telecommuting and outsourcing of work to the home, both of which promise to alter the nature of work fundamentally.

New communication technologies also affect organizational behavior. If members are permitted to use technologies such as electronic mail with few restrictions, the result is often an "opening up" of the organization. Ideas flow more freely and innovation increases. Boundaries between different levels or parts of the organization become more permeable, and lower level members feel freer to engage in upward communication. The downside of this is that those at the top of the organization are often overloaded.

Communication technologies such as group support systems and computer conferencing alter decision-making, meeting, and negotiation processes. Their effects include (1) the possibility of enhanced member participation in meetings; (2) more thorough consideration of options, alternatives, and ideas; (3) greater surfacing of differences and conflict; (4) greater difficulty in achieving consensus if the systems do not have features which support conflict resolution, but greater ability to resolve conflict if the systems do have conflict management features; and (5) more organized meetings and negotiation processes. Accompanying these group level impacts are several on the individual level. Intially, users tend to report lower satisfaction with these technologies than with more traditional group methods, though this difference fades with continued use. Computer mediated communication technologies also seem to alter the individual's attentional focus, centering it more on the self and less on others. However, the widely discussed phenomenon of "flaming" –

the use of extreme, abusive, and negative language in computer mediated communication – is not as widespread as was originally presumed; generally, organizations and user communities develop norms that control or prohibit it.

With the exception of the telephone, new communication technologies are only just being integrated into society. From the onset, unmediated, face-to-face communication has been taken as the standard that should be emulated and achieved by communication technologies. However, as was true for the telephone, over time new norms develop and the ideal standard of effective communication changes. Novel communication technologies promise to change the nature of communication and of organizations in coming years.

See also *organizational effectiveness; systems theory*

Bibliography

Grant, A. E. and Meadows, J. H. (eds.) (2002). *Communication Technology Update*, 8th edn. Oxford: Focal Press.

Lievrouw, L. and Livingstone, S. (eds.) (2002). *Handbook of New Media*. London: Sage.

Rice, R. E. and Gattiker, U. E. (2000). New media and organizational structuring. In F. E. Jablin and L. L. Putnam (eds.), *The New Handbook of Organizational Communication: Advances in Theory, Research, and Methods*. Newbury Park, CA: Sage.

Sproull, L. and Keisler, S. (1991). *Connections: New Ways of Working in the Networked Organization*. Cambridge, MA: MIT Press.

Yates, J. (1989). *Control Through Communication: The Rise of System in American Management*. Baltimore, MD: Johns Hopkins University Press.

community ecology

John Freeman

Community ecology refers to the study of the ways in which communities of organizations manage relationships with their resource environments. It constitutes one branch of the human ecology tree. Another branch is population ecology of organizations. The two differ most concretely in unit of analysis.

Population ecologists study organizations by examining the vital rates of founding and failure that characterize the populations manifesting one or more organizational forms. The unit of analysis is the organizational population. Community ecology focuses on the interactions of organizational populations in distinct localized communities. Discussing how bio-ecologists use the term "community," Ricklefs (1973: 590) writes: "the community is spatially defined and is all-inclusive within its boundaries." For human ecologists, the pattern of competition and mutual support exhibited by these various organizational populations both enables and constrains the people who live in those communities. This is because organizations are the primary means by which sustenance is brought into the community. So to understand why a town or city works the way it does, one needs to understand the interplay of the various kinds of organizations that operate there. Further, to understand the operation of individual organizations one needs to consider the patterned scarcity or abundance of resources that come bundled in macro-structures. Strategic problems faced by managers, policy issues analyzed by government officials, and personal career or lifestyle decisions of individuals are all driven in part by community structure, and the ways in which resources flow into that community.

COMMUNITIES AND ORGANIZATIONS

Community ecology is by far the older branch of human ecology. It dates from the early 1920s, when sociologists such as Burgess (1925), McKenzie (1924), and Park (1925) began to study the structure of cities and towns. They wanted to know why such communities had neighborhoods characterized by clearly distinct patterns of economic and social life. They wanted to know why such communities were located where they were and especially how distance affected interaction. This line of research reached its zenith with the publication of Amos Hawley's *Human Ecology: A Theory of Social Structure* (1950). These early community ecologists were aware that organizations were important and readily labeled neighborhoods and regions by their dominant economic functions, referring to them as "retail centers" or "manufacturing areas." Their organizational focus was on competition for resources, especially for space.

However, community ecology was really about how human populations are concentrated in communities, and how those people go about their daily lives. So the connection of community ecology to the field of demography has always been strong. Organizations figure into the story mainly as mechanisms for attracting resources and for distributing them through the community.

Organizations were treated as more fundamental parts of the community's social organization by Hawley, who placed greater emphasis on the role of interdependencies in the generation of community organization than had his predecessors. So while people and organizations compete, they also depend on each other. They combine (organize) to increase their power of action. So people form organizations, and organizations build alliances and other BOUNDARY SPANNING structures to manage interdependencies. They do so on the basis of "complementary differences" (symbiosis), in which case the division of labor requires cooperation. Or they combine on the basis of "supplementary similarities" (commensalism) – what they have in common (Hawley, 1986).

Organizations are arrayed along a food chain in which those standing early in the flow of transactions create conditions under which succeeding organizations must operate. So power and "dominance" are enjoyed by those organizations that most directly mediate with the community's environment.

THE IMPORTANCE OF LOCATION AND SPACE

For all community ecologists, geography and distance are the crucial underlying organizing issues. Given some means of transport, distance can be understood as time, and time defines limitations on access. So a population ecologist might view the decision to start a particular kind of organization as primordial in the sense that many other decisions are implicit once organizational form is chosen; the community ecologist would view the location as a primordial decision.

For biological ecologists, "habitat" is the geographical unit of greatest relevance. It is assumed that creatures of all kinds live in a localized environment, in which resource scarcity or abundance is packaged. Organizations researchers are less likely to make such

assumptions. In fact, population ecologists often treat geographical boundaries in a cavalier fashion, taking them for granted as their data points come to them. While biologists derive much theoretical value from models of population density, these models are usually based on some fixed geographical referent. When geographical space is less clear, they often refer to "abundance" rather than density.

Organizations scholars who borrow concepts from community ecology without considering the spatial boundaries of ecological systems miss the point (Astley and Fombrun, 1983). In this sense, research on strategic groups (Carroll and Swaminathan, 1992) is closer to the population ecology tradition than it is to community ecology.

Fundamentally, the issue is the degree to which one believes that the resources, whose scarcity limits organizational populations, are localized, and whether the social support networks through which cooperation is effected are most intense at close quarters. This is no small matter, as increasingly efficient transportation and communications technologies bring remotely located organizations into contact.

SOCIAL SUPPORT

Population ecologists have spent considerable effort showing that patterns of density dependent selection conform to a simple model in which legitimation is juxtaposed with competition for resources. Social support in this treatment is legitimation in the phenomenological sense of social acceptance. More recently, this point of view has been generalized to focus on the creation of social identities for organizational forms (Ruef, 2000). People and other organizations use these identities to inform decisions about whether to cooperate with an organization or to withhold cooperation. Given that building and maintaining social ties takes time and effort, and involves investing the other with one's own reputational credit, this is a complex and risky decision.

The community level of analysis sheds light on the study of organizations to the degree that social contact, relationships, and material resources flow in ways that provide advantages to propinquity. At the same time, propinquity generates challenges as competition for resources may concentrate in space as well.

See also *evolutionary perspectives; organizational ecology*

Bibliography

Astley, W. G. and Fombrun, C. J. (1983). Collective strategy: Social ecology of organizational environments. *Academy of Management Review*, 8, 576–87.

Burgess, E. W. (1925). The growth of the city: An introduction to a research project. In R. E. Park, E. W. Burgess, and R. D. McKenzie (eds.), *The City*. Chicago: University of Chicago Press.

Carroll, G. R. and Swaminathan, A. (1992). The organizational ecology of strategic groups in the American brewing industry from 1975 to 1990. *Industrial and Corporate Change*, 1, 65–97.

Hawley, A. H. (1950). *Human Ecology: A Theory of Social Structure*. New York: Ronald.

Hawley, A. H. (1986). *Human Ecology: A Theoretical Essay*. Chicago: University of Chicago Press.

McKenzie, R. D. (1924). The ecological approach to the study of the human community. *American Journal of Sociology*, 30, 287–301.

Park, R. E. (1925). The urban community as a spatial pattern and a moral order. *Publications of the American Sociological Society*, 20, 1–14.

Ricklefs, R. E. (1973). *Ecology*. Newton, MA: Chiron.

Ruef, M. (2000). The emergence of organizational forms: A community ecology approach. *American Journal of Sociology*, 106, 658–714.

competency

Richard E. Boyatzis

A competency is an underlying characteristic of a person that leads to or causes effective or outstanding performance. In the last thirty years the study of competencies has moved from psychological research into a quest for a common basis for human resource management in most organizations to identify talent early. In some cultures these characteristics are also called abilities or capabilities. Each competency is a constellation of functionally related actions, linked by common, often unconscious, intent. For example, the competency called empathy can be observed by watching someone listen to others or asking questions about their feelings and thoughts. If demonstrating empathy, the

person would be undertaking these acts with the intent of trying to understand another person. On the other hand, someone could show these acts while cross-examining a witness in a criminal trial where the intent is to catch them in a lie – which is likely also to be the demonstration of another competency, INFLU-ENCE.

Competencies are more complex than skills and share many features with personality traits or abilities. Within a comprehensive PERSON-ALITY theory, competencies can be said to emanate from physiological dispositions and processes (e.g., neural circuitry and hormones), unconscious motives and traits, and VALUES and philosophy (Boyatzis, Goleman, and Rhee, 2000). Clusters of competencies appear to hold more promise in understanding and predicting performance than single competencies. Most competencies are functionally related to other competencies. As a result, the distinctions among them are often more conceptual than empirical. When separate competencies can be identified, it appears that using one or two competencies from each of the clusters is far more effective than using all of the competencies in one or two clusters (McClelland, 1998).

When hundreds of such performance validation studies are collected and integrated, whether empirically, or conceptually as in Spencer and Spencer (1993), about five clusters of competencies appear as consistently predictive of effective performance in management, LEAD-ERSHIP, and professional ROLES. They are (1) the Self-Awareness cluster with competencies such as emotional self-awareness and self-confidence; (2) the Self-Management cluster with competencies such as achievement orientation, emotional self-control, and adaptability; (3) the Social Awareness cluster with competencies such as empathy and cultural awareness; (4) the Relationship Management cluster with competencies such as influence, teamwork, and developing others; and (5) the Cognitive cluster with competencies such as systems thinking and pattern recognition. The first four clusters have been collectively called Emotional Intelligence (Goleman, Boyatzis, and McKee, 2002).

The specific competencies that are empirically validated as distinguishing outstanding performance in an organization will be context sensitive. That is, the particular organizational culture, industry, structure, and larger culture surrounding it will affect which of these abilities are important. The job or role will also affect which competencies are relevant and which are critical to performance.

First the military, and then executives in industry, government, and the not-for-profit sector, wanted to know how to identify people early to give them special development or opportunities. David McClelland attached the competency label to this emerging area of study and created an intellectual focus with his key article in 1973 called "Testing for competence rather than intelligence."

Competency-based human resource practices have gone from new techniques to common practice over the past twenty-five years. Major consulting companies have become worldwide practitioners in competency assessment and development, and conducted major international conferences, with competency validation studies conducted in over 160 countries. This work has focused on all types of occupations. Since most of this research is done by psychologists based in consulting companies, most of the studies remain unpublished, giving rise to an exaggerated perception in academic circles that there is a lack of empirical evidence on the topic.

Some competencies are growing in their importance, while others may be waning. Competency studies in the last ten years reveal a growing importance of empathy, cultural awareness, teamwork, and adaptability. The diversity of the workforce has increased dramatically over the last twenty years. With globalization, the diversity of customers and vendors has increased. To work with heterogeneous people, we need an ability to be sensitive to others (e.g., empathy and cultural awareness).

A major advance in understanding the effect of competencies on performance came from catastrophe theory, which is now considered a subset of complexity theory. Instead of asking the typical question, "Which competencies are needed or necessary for outstanding performance?" David McClelland, in a paper published posthumously in 1998, posed the question, "How often do you need to show a competency to 'tip' you into outstanding performance?" In other words, how frequently should a competency be demonstrated to be sufficient for maximum performance? He reported that presidents of divisions of a large food company enacting competencies above certain thresholds received significantly higher bonuses, which were proportional to the profitability of their divisions, as compared to their less profitable peers (McClelland, 1998). Other studies are emerging that are replicating these findings, potentially giving guidance to managers, leaders, and professionals about which competencies to coach in order to add value to performance. The thresholds or "tipping points" for each competency would be a function of the organization environment.

Studies in industry, government, and higher education have shown that competencies can be developed (Boyatzis, Cowen, and Kolb, 1995; Cherniss and Adler, 2000). These longitudinal studies are showing that the belief that many of these characteristics cannot be developed (i.e., they are innate) is founded on the results of inappropriate or ineffective development methods, and that the development of these competencies has been sustained over seven years (Goleman, Boyatzis, and McKee, 2002).

See also *emotional intelligence; impression management; interpersonal skills*

Bibliography

Boyatzis, R. E., Cowen, S. C., and Kolb, D. A. (1995). *Innovation in Professional Education: Steps on a Journey from Teaching to Learning*. San Francisco: Jossey-Bass.

Boyatzis, R. E., Goleman, D., and Rhee, K. (2000). Clustering competence in emotional intelligence: Insights from the Emotional Competence Inventory (ECI). In R. Bar-On and J. D. A. Parker (eds.), *Handbook of Emotional Intelligence*. San Francisco: Jossey-Bass, 343–62.

Cherniss, C. and Adler, M. (2000). *Promoting Emotional Intelligence in Organizations: Make Training in Emotional Intelligence Effective*. Washington, DC: American Society of Training and Development.

Goleman, D., Boyatzis, R. E., and McKee, A. (2002). *Primal Leadership: Realizing the Power of Emotional Intelligence*. Boston, MA: Harvard Business School Press.

Howard, A. and Bray, D. (1988). *Managerial Lives in Transition: Advancing Age and Changing Times*. New York: Guilford Press.

McClelland, D. C. (1973). Testing for competence rather than intelligence. *American Psychologist*, 78 (1), 1–14.

McClelland, D. C. (1998). Identifying competencies with behavioral event interviews. *Psychological Science*, 9 (5), 331–9.

Spencer, L. M., Jr. and Spencer, S. M. (1993). *Competence at Work: Models for Superior Performance*. New York: Wiley.

complexity theory

Olav Sorenson

Complexity theory refers to a loosely linked body of research examining the importance of interactions – in other words, interdependence among the elements – in dynamic systems, whether those systems represent small groups, organizations, industries, or entire economies. In the physical and biological sciences, where the term and most of the methods originated, the Santa Fe Institute has played a crucial role in promoting the perspective and in linking disparate groups of researchers working on fundamentally similar (from a mathematical point of view) problems; its working paper series (available at www.santafe.edu) provides an excellent resource for those interested in the technical details.

Though in many respects the subject matter and assumptions of this line of research harken back to earlier work (e.g., Simon, 1962, or general systems theory), the advent of cheap computing power has transformed the enterprise. Researchers working in the domain of complexity theory typically build an explicit formal model (i.e., equations specifying rules of action). Since the interactions in these models make them too difficult to solve analytically, researchers rely on simulations to understand the behavior of their models (an approach often referred to as computational modeling).

Though a wide variety of models exists (see Lomi and Larsen, 2001, for several applications to the social sciences), two models account for most of the research applicable to the field of organizations: the NK model and cellular automata.

The NK model, originally developed by physicists to analyze the properties of spin-glasses, uses only two parameters to describe systems: N, the number of elements in the system, and K, the average degree of interaction between these elements (for a thorough description, see Kauffman, 1993). Heuristically, we can think of these parameters as generating a "fitness landscape" on which actors search for the best positions. In systems with a low degree of interdependence, these landscapes look like a multidimensional hill, gradually ascending to a single peak. As the degree of interdependence rises, however, the number of hills and their steepness rises, making it increasingly difficult for actors (firms) to find the optima.

Although early work relied on relatively straightforward translation of the model to organizational issues – for example, Rivkin (2000) used it to demonstrate that complex strategies should be more difficult for rivals to imitate – more recent research has been focused on modifying the search algorithms or the pattern of interactions so that the model assumptions fit better with what we know about organizations. For example, Gavetti and Levinthal (2000) examine a case in which managers use frameworks (rather than a precise understanding of every organizational routine) to guide them. Interestingly, they find that these frameworks can improve firm performance. The intuition behind this result resides in the fact that these frameworks prevent managers from becoming trapped in sticking points (i.e., local optima; for a complete discussion see Rivkin and Siggelkow, 2002). In fact, much of the recent research could be characterized as identifying factors that allow organizations to escape these sticking points; for example, organizational restructuring, parallel experimentation, and the division of decision-making across members of the organization have all been shown to allow firms to find superior end states. Though as yet unverified, this work offers new ideas on how and why ORGANIZATIONAL DESIGN might influence firm performance.

The other main approach involves the use of cellular automata. Cellular automata generate more highly structured worlds – interacting only in local neighborhoods usually with a fixed degree of interdependence. To understand the dynamics of cellular automata, imagine a chessboard. In these models, the behavior of one position (square) would only depend on the eight adjacent squares (or maybe just the four squares sharing borders). This differs from the NK models in three respects: (1) researchers rarely vary the neighborhood size, hence the level of K remains fixed across their simulations; (2) the interactions only occur locally, so one can meaningfully represent them in a low-dimensional space (the chessboard has two dimensions; by comparison, representing an NK model with the same level of interdependence would require a 7-dimensional space); and (3) researchers specify the functional form of the interactions in cellular automata, while interactions have random effects in the NK model.

The primary application of cellular automata has thus been to situations in which researchers want to investigate the nature of the interactions themselves (rather than the search algorithms of firms facing uncertain interdependencies). Lomi and Larsen (1996), for example, have used cellular automata to add a spatial dimension to the models studied by organizational ecologists. One of the more interesting findings to date is that age dependence might be an ecological phenomenon; in other words, rising (or falling) mortality rates as a function of age might result from local interactions among firms rather than from any change in internal organizational processes (Lomi and Larsen, 2001: ch. 9).

Though theory has been developing at a rapid pace, relatively little work has been done in trying to corroborate these ideas empirically. One can, however, find a couple of notable exceptions in the technology management literature. For example, Fleming and Sorenson (2001) demonstrate through the analysis of patent data that the process of invention appears to fit well the predictions of the NK model, though subsequent research reveals that the model fails in situations in which the actors likely have a theory about the nature of the interactions between components (Fleming and Sorenson, 2004). Similarly, Frenken (2001), analyzing the usage of physical components in aircraft product, also finds support for the applicability of the NK model in the evolution of technology.

Though these results support some of the basic findings, the future development of this field depends crucially on empirical work corroborating theoretical findings and identifying conditions under which these models fail to explain the world. Researchers interested in this domain, however, should consider it an exciting opportunity for future research.

See also *computer simulation; organization theory; organizational ecology*

Bibliography

Fleming, L. and Sorenson, O. (2001). Technology as a complex adaptive system: Evidence from patent data. *Research Policy*, 30, 1019–39.

Fleming, L. and Sorenson, O. (2004). Science as a map in technological search. *Strategic Management Journal*, 25: forthcoming.

Frenken, K. (2001). *Understanding Product Innovation Using Complex Systems Theory*. Unpublished PhD dissertation, University of Amsterdam and University of Grenoble.

Gavetti, G. and Levinthal, D. (2000). Looking forward and looking backward: Cognitive and experimental search. *Administrative Science Quarterly*, 45, 113–37.

Kauffman, S. (1993). *The Origins of Order: Self-Organization and Selection in Evolution*. New York: Oxford University Press.

Lomi, A. and Larsen, E. (1996). Interacting locally and evolving globally: A computational approach to the dynamics of organizational populations. *Academy of Management Journal*, 39, 1287–321.

Lomi, A. and Larsen, E. (2001). *Dynamics of Organizations: Computational Modeling and Organization Theory*. Menlo Park, CA: AAAI/MIT Press.

Rivkin, J. (2000). Imitation of complex strategies. *Management Science*, 46, 824–44.

Rivkin, J. and Siggelkow, N. (2002). Organizational sticking points on NK landscapes. *Complexity*, 7, 31–43.

Simon, H. (1962). The architecture of complexity. *Proceedings of the American Philosophical Society*, 106, 467–82.

compliance

see INFLUENCE

computer simulation

Alessandro Lomi

Computer simulation is a distinctive approach to the representation of organizational theories.

Early theories of organizations were expressed in natural language. Examples of such verbal theories are still dominant in contemporary organization studies. The adoption of explicit algebraic representations has proceeded almost in parallel with the development of verbal theories. Somewhat more recently, mathematical formalization has become popular among economists interested in a broad range of organizational issues.

As a consequence of developments in the field of artificial intelligence, the last decade has witnessed the introduction of formal logic in an attempt to translate theoretical statements expressed in natural language into symbolic systems that can then be interpreted and manipulated through automatic theorem-provers. While not widely adopted, this particular style of symbolic representation is gaining legitimacy within organization studies.

In the context of this general discussion on theory and knowledge representation, computer simulation can be viewed as an approach to THEORY building and testing based on a symbolic representation expressible in executable computer code. As Michael Masuch wrote in the first edition of this volume (1995: 92): "As an approach to theory building computer simulation and the computer code that embodies the model differ from other representations only in the choice of formal constraints on the description language."

Computer simulation has played a central role in the intellectual development of the field of organization theory and behavior. Between the 1960s and early 1970s, some of the most influential and imaginative theoretical statements have been based on computer simulation. As a consequence, the intellectual legacies of works such as *Industrial Dynamics* (Forrester, 1961), *Behavioral Theory of the Firm*, and the "garbage can" model of organizational choice (*see* GARBAGE CAN MODEL) continue to shape the contemporary debate.

Simulation modeling was not much influenced by – and did not significantly influence – the developments of organizational theories during the 1970s and the 1980s. More recently, however, progress in computer technology and the emergence of a new generation of simulation models called agent-based models are beginning

to bridge the gap between theoretical problems and methodological possibilities (Bonabeau, 2002). The work of Epstein and Axtell (1996), the new computational and mathematical organization theory (CMOT) movement (Carley and Gasser, 1999), and the chapters collected in the volumes edited by Carley and colleagues collectively demonstrate the resurgence of interest in computer simulation across the social and organizational sciences.

As Herbert Simon (1969) recognized more than thirty years ago, the central question about computer simulation still remains: Can a computer model tell us anything that we do not already know? Recent advances in the related fields of pattern discovery, evolutionary computation, computational mechanics, and artificial life provide good reason for a cautious, but optimistic, positive answer to this fundamental question.

See also *decision-making; organization theory; research methods; technology*

Bibliography

Bonabeau, E. (2002). Agent based modeling: Methods and techniques for simulating human systems. *Proceedings of the National Academy of Science*, **99** (3), 7280–7.

Carley, K. M. and Gasser, L. (1999). Computational organization theory. In G. Weiss (ed.), *Multiagent Systems: A Modern Approach to Distributed Artificial Intelligence*. Cambridge, MA: MIT Press, 299–330.

Cohen, K. and Cyert, R. (1965). Simulation of organizational behavior. In J. G. March (ed.), *Handbook of Organizations*. Chicago: Rand McNally, 305–34.

Cyert, R. and March, J. G. (1963). *A Behavioral Theory of the Firm*. Englewood Cliffs, NJ: Prentice-Hall.

Epstein, J. and Axtell, R. (1996). *Growing Artificial Societies*. Washington, DC/Cambridge, MA: Brooking Institution Press/MIT Press.

Forrester, J. W. (1961). *Industrial Dynamics*. Cambridge, MA: MIT Press.

Lomi, A. and Larsen, E. (eds.) (2001). *Dynamics of organization: Computational Modeling and Organization Theories*. Boston, MA/Palo Alto, CA: MIT Press/AAAI Press.

Masuch, M. (1991). Formalization of Thompson's organization in action: Intermediate report. CCSOM Report 91-32.

Prietula, M., Carley, K., and Gasser, L. (1998). *Simulating Organizations: Computational Models of Institutions and Groups*. Boston, MA/Palo Alto, CA: MIT Press/AAAI Press.

conditioning

see BEHAVIORISM

conflict and conflict management

Carsten K. W. De Dreu

The current view of conflict is that it is a process that begins when Party (e.g., an individual, or group) feels Other did or will do something that negatively affects Party's interests, opinions, and beliefs, or norms and values. This conflict process entails conflict issues, conflict experiences, conflict management, and conflict outcomes (Thomas, 1992). Conflict issues refer to the content of the conflict: Is it about resources (power, money, time) or information (ideas, opinions, values), or according to another taxonomy, about task content, task process, or relationships (De Dreu, Harinck, and Van Vianen, 1999; Jehn and Mannix, 2001)? Conflict experiences involve the emotions and feelings, the motivational goals, and the cognitive structures that are elicited by and associated with the conflict issues, the context within which the conflict takes place, and the other party. Conflict management refers to the way parties manage their conflict experiences, and is usually aimed at mitigating or fueling the conflict. Conflict outcomes involve both performance related variables such as learning and innovation, individual or team effectiveness, and return on investment and market share, as well as health related variables such as psychosomatic complaints and BURNOUT (*see* STRESS).

Conflict in organizations occurs at four levels of analysis. Conflict is intrapersonal when an individual or group faces role conflict or ambiguity, or when choices between two negatives or two positives have to be made. In addition to these decisional conflicts, there is group conflict between individuals within a work unit or team, intergroup conflict between groups within the same organization (e.g., between departments, or between unionized workers and management), and inter-organizational conflict between different organizations.

Although conflict is inherent to organizations, it is embedded in some organizations more than in others, and may take different forms depending on organizational structure (Jaffee, 2000). For instance, matrix organizations have decisional conflict explicitly built in, and interpersonal conflict over the distribution and allocation of resources is repeatedly observed. Traditional bureaucracies face political, intergroup conflict between high and low power members. Team-based organizations face group conflict about task content, task process, and relationships.

CONFLICT AND OUTCOMES

Conflict is often associated with negative outcomes only, but a more balanced view has emerged in the past two decades. Two models of conflict and performance have been proposed. The inverted U-shape model assumes that extremely low and extremely high levels of conflict are bad for performance and health, whereas moderate levels of conflict stimulate individual and group performance (Walton, 1969). The idea is that at low levels individuals are not stimulated to process information, whereas at high levels there is too much arousal and cognitive load to accurately and creatively process information. As a result, at moderate levels of conflict individuals and groups are most creative and innovative, and perform most effectively. Empirical support is mostly indirect and circumstantial.

The task-relationship conflict model proposed by Jehn (e.g., Jehn and Mannix, 2001) considers team level processes. It assumes that whereas relationship conflict is bad for performance, task conflict is beneficial especially in non-routine, complex tasks (*see* GROUP DYNAMICS). The idea is that when performing complex and non-routine tasks, conflict related to task content and process stimulates team members to reconsider their assumptions, their routines, and their solutions, and this leads them to develop more innovative and better work processes. Relationship conflict may derive from dissimilarity among team members in terms of demographic differences (e.g., age, gender, cultural background), whereas task conflict may derive from diversity in terms of insights, educational background, and expertise. Although intriguing and stimulating, a meta-analysis of the research base to date uncovered no support for the model – both task and relationship conflict were negatively associated with team effectiveness (De Dreu and Weingart, 2003).

CONFLICT MANAGEMENT

Although it is obvious that conflict at work affects individual and group performance, and individual well-being, it also has become clear that these effects cannot be simply understood in terms of conflict intensity, or the task or relationship focus of the conflict. Instead, one needs to incorporate the way conflict is managed (Lovelace, Shapiro, and Weingart, 2001; Tjosvold, 1998). Conflict management is what people in conflict intend to do as well as what they actually do. Whereas an infinite number of conflict management strategies may be conceived of, conflict research and theory tend to converge on the idea that individuals in conflict can (1) ask for third party intervention (asking a judge, an arbitrator, their manager, or fate to make a decision), (2) engage in unilateral decision-making by trying to impose one's will on the other side (forcing), by accepting and incorporating other's will (yielding), or by remaining inactive, or (3) engage in joint decision-making (seeking a compromise, problem solving, negotiation, asking a mediator for help). Sometimes, different conflict management strategies are used sequentially (e.g., when mediation is followed by arbitration, or in a good-cop/bad-cop strategy), or simultaneously when forcing on one item is combined with yielding on another ("logrolling": see Pruitt and Rubin, 1986).

Realizing the importance of conflict management, many large companies have adopted Alternative Dispute Resolution to control and reduce the cost and resentment associated with prolonged conflict and associated lawsuits. These programs basically seek to stimulate employees and managers to handle their conflicts through joint decision-making, rather than through litigation and arbitration (Ury, Brett, and Goldberg, 1993). Obviously, to make these programs work employees and their managers should have strong conflict management competencies, and acquiring this requires investment by employees and their organization.

Two theories explicitly deal with the ways conflict management relates to individual and group performance. The theory of cooperation and competition (Deutsch, 1973; Tjosvold, 1998) assumes that individuals view their goals to be positively linked to those of others (cooperative interdependence: both sink or swim together), to be negatively linked to those of others (competitive interdependence: when one swims, the other sinks), or to be independent. Under cooperative goal interdependence, parties engage in "constructive controversy" and respect others' views and attitudes, approach the issues open-mindedly and try to work together to learn from the conflict. Under competitive goal interdependence, or when goals are independent, parties develop negative, hostile attitudes, they engage in lying and deception, and competitive exchanges characterize interaction. In general, constructive controversy is believed to be beneficial to individual participants and their teams: it fosters innovation, effectiveness, and interpersonal relations. The theory has received good support from both experimental and field research (Tjosvold, 1998).

Dual concern theory (Pruitt and Rubin, 1986), and the related conflict management grid (Blake and Mouton, 1964) predict when and why individuals engage in unilateral decision-making (forcing, yielding, inaction) or joint decision-making (problem solving, negotiation). The basic idea is that parties have a high or low concern for their own interests and, independently, a high or low concern for their counterpart's interests. Concern for self is high when realizing own interests is positively valued, instrumental, and feasible. Thus, while most individuals positively value their own interests, they can be judged more or less instrumental, and more or less feasible in a particular situation. This explains why concern for self can vary between high and low. Concern for other is high when realizing other's interests is positively valued (e.g., one likes the other), instrumental (e.g., one needs the opponent in future interaction), and feasible. Thus, concern for other may be rooted in genuinely pro-social motives, or in enlightened self-interest (i.e., by helping the other one serves one's own interests best).

When concern for self is high and the concern for other is low, parties engage in *forcing*, and they try to impose their goals upon the other party. Forcing can be rights-based when parties refer to standards, norms, and basic principles, or power-based when parties use their threat capacity to get their way (Ury, Brett, and Goldberg, 1993). When concern for self is low and concern for other is high, parties engage in *yielding* and give in to their opponent's demands and desires. When both concern for self and concern for other is low, parties engage in *inaction* and are predicted to remain passive. When both concern for self and concern for other is high, parties collaborate and engage in *problem solving*.

A meta-analysis of research on NEGOTIATION has provided strong support for Dual Concern Theory, and also revealed its predictive value to be superior to the Theory of Cooperation and Competition (De Dreu, Weingart, and Kwon, 2000). This and other work has also revealed that problem solving is associated with more integrative agreements, reduced probability of future conflict, greater SELF-EFFICACY, and enhanced interpersonal liking (e.g., Lovelace, Shapiro, and Weingart, 2001; for reviews, see Pruitt and Rubin, 1986; Thomas, 1992).

FUTURE RESEARCH

Although including conflict management into the equation leads to a much more powerful prediction of the relationship between conflict and performance, four issues require attention in future research. First, most of this work seems to rest on the implicit assumption that there exists a "one-best-way" to manage conflict. Although constructive controversy and problem solving are probably the most suited strategies in many cases, some conflicts require inaction, and others require forcing to insure high levels of performance. Work is needed to develop more sophisticated models of the interplay between types of conflict at work, conflict management strategies, and conflict outcomes in terms of performance. In addition, most work on conflict has a rather short-term focus, and more research is needed to understand the long-term effects of conflict on team performance, employee turnover, and individual health and well-being.

Second, cumulating research reveals that individuals from individualistic countries (e.g., Western Europe, US) are more confrontational and assertive in managing conflict, whereas individuals from collectivist culture (e.g., Southeast Asia, Africa) tend to value harmony and fairness (e.g., Gelfand and Realo, 1999). This work will gain applied value for multinational companies when it moves into the study of cross-cultural encounters – when individuals from different cultures have to manage conflict between them.

Third, research is needed also to better understand the possible negative effects of conflict on employee well-being. Although initial research suggests relatively weak effects only, individual differences and organizational characteristics may turn out to be important moderators. For example, prolonged, systematic bullying at work may lead victims to develop irreversible psychosomatic complaints prohibiting them from participating in the labor market, and conflict between manager and subordinate may have much stronger influence on the subordinate's health than conflict between two subordinates.

Fourth, and finally, we need to integrate research on conflict with two obviously related but currently dispersed literatures. Conflict research and theory can and should be integrated with research on leadership, power, and influence. Related to this is that conflict theory needs to be integrated with research on organizational change, resistance to change, and innovation. With regard to change, it is interesting and important to note that conflict theory implicitly assumes that both parties want change. Most organizational change programs involve some parties desiring change and some parties desiring to maintain the status quo. We have limited understanding of how these asymmetrical conflicts (Pruitt and Rubin, 1986) can and should be managed, and how ways of managing resistance to change affect future performance of individuals, groups, and entire organizations.

Taken together, we have a fairly solid idea about how conflicts are and should be managed, and when and why conflict hurts or stimulates performance. Most conflicts are detrimental to performance and health. Those concerned with task content can be productive, provided they are managed collaboratively and constructively. Cross-cultural comparisons, an enhanced focus on the psychosocial aspects of organizational life, and greater effort to understand asymmetrical conflicts will produce a more balanced and sophisticated conflict theory with strong implications for individual health, group performance, and organizational design.

See also *collaboration; exchange relations; group decision-making; politics; power*

Bibliography

Blake, R. and Mouton, J. S. (1964). *The Managerial Grid*. Houston, TX: Gulf.

De Dreu, C. K. W., Harinck, F., and Van Vianen, A. E. M. (1999). Conflict and performance in groups and organizations. In C. L. Cooper and I. T. Robertson (eds.), *International Review of Industrial and Organizational Psychology*, vol. 14. Chichester: Wiley, 369–414.

De Dreu, C. K. W. and Weingart, L. R. (2003). Task versus relationship conflict, team performance, and team member satisfaction: A meta-analysis. *Journal of Applied Psychology*, 88, 741–9.

De Dreu, C. K. W., Weingart, L. R., and Kwon, S. (2000). Influence of social motives in integrative negotiation: A meta-analytic review and test of two theories. *Journal of Personality and Social Psychology*, 78, 889–905.

Deutsch, M. (1973). *Conflict Resolution: Constructive and Destructive Processes*. New Haven, CT: Yale University Press.

Gelfand, M. J. and Realo, A. (1999). Individualism–collectivism and accountability in intergroup negotiations. *Journal of Applied Psychology*, 84, 721–36.

Jaffee, D. (2000). *Organization Theory: Tension and Change*. New York: McGraw Hill.

Jehn, K. and Mannix, E. (2001). The dynamic nature of conflict: A longitudinal study of intragroup conflict and group performance. *Academy of Management Journal*, 44, 238–51.

Lovelace, K., Shapiro, D. L., and Weingart, L. R. (2001). Maximizing cross-functional new product teams' innovativeness and constraint adherence: A conflict communications perspective. *Academy of Management Journal*, 44, 779–83.

Pruitt, D. G. and Rubin, J. Z. (1986). *Social Conflict: Escalation, Stalemate, and Settlement*. New York: Random House.

Thomas, K. W. (1992). Conflict and negotiation processes in organizations. In M. D. Dunnette and L. M. Hough (eds.), *Handbook of Industrial and Organizational Psychology*, 2nd edn. Palo Alto, CA: Consulting Psychologists Press, 651–717.

Tjosvold, D. (1998). Cooperative and competitive goal approaches to conflict: Accomplishments and challenges. *Applied Psychology: An International Review*, 47, 285–342.

Ury, W. L., Brett, J. M., and Goldberg, S. B. (1993). *Getting Disputes Resolved: Designing Systems to Cut the Costs of Conflict*. Cambridge, MA: PON.

Walton, R. E. (1969). *Interpersonal Peacemaking: Confrontations and Third Party Consultation*. Reading, MA: Addison-Wesley.

conflict resolution

see CONFLICT AND CONFLICT MANAGEMENT

conformity

Daniel C. Feldman

This is the shift of an individual's behaviors and attitudes toward the perceived standards of the group as a result of group pressure (Kelman, 1961; Asch, 1951; Sherif, 1936).

Substantial work has been conducted on distinguishing conformity from other responses to group pressure and social INFLUENCE (*see* IDENTIFICATION). For conformity to exist, the following conditions should be present:

1   The individual has a crystallized attitude or a regular behavior pattern before exposure to group influence.

2   The individual's attitude or behavior changes as a result of group influence.

3   The individual's attitude or behavior changes in the perceived desired direction of the group.

4   The individual's attitude or behavior changes soon after exposure to group pressure.

5   The individual's private beliefs change as well as his or her publicly stated attitudes and publicly observable behaviors (Nail, 1986) (*see* MINORITY GROUP INFLUENCE).

There has been considerable research on the factors which predispose individuals to conform to group pressure. The classic Yale Obedience Study (Milgram, 1974) and Stanford Prison Study (Haney and Zimbardo, 1973) suggest that individuals are more likely to conform when the work environment is uncertain and individuals need the group for information, when individuals have low self-esteem and need the group for affirmation, when the group is prestigious and individuals value group membership highly, when individuals have made a public COMMITMENT to the group, when individuals are new in the group or at lower levels of the organization, and when individuals are alone in their opposition to the group's position (Kiesler and Kiesler, 1969).

In general, the research suggests that situational factors have a greater impact on an individual's willingness to conform than individual PERSONALITY traits. For example, the Stanford Prison Study suggests that an individual's role demands can completely overwhelm other aspects of his or her self-identity under extreme social pressure (Haney and Zimbardo, 1973) (see ROLE-TAKING). Indeed, in studies of the conformity of individuals to immoral or unethical demands, it has been found that conformers are "ordinary people" who follow orders out of a sense of obligation to their leaders and not from any peculiarly aggressive tendencies (Milgram, 1974).

While individuals' conformity to group expectations may make daily functioning of the group more predictable and routine, there is substantial evidence that too much conformity can be detrimental to the quality of GROUP DECISION-MAKING (Janis, 1972) (see GROUPTHINK). In organizational settings, too much conformity can result in the group's inattention to flaws in its planning and DECISION-MAKING activities as well as intolerance of, and lack of acceptance of, fresh perspectives of new group members (Feldman, 1984; Dentler and Erikson, 1959). For this reason, researchers and practitioners have been investigating group process interventions (see ORGANIZATIONAL DEVELOPMENT) and group decision-making heuristics to help groups build in safeguards against overconformity.

See also *affiliation, need for; group dynamics*

Bibliography

Asch, S. (1951). Effects of group pressure upon the modification and distortion of judgment. In M. H. Guetzkow (ed.), *Groups, Leadership, and Men*. Pittsburgh, PA: Carnegie Institute of Technology Press, 117–90.

Dentler, R. A. and Erikson, K. T. (1959). The functions of deviance in groups. *Social Problems*, 7, 98–107.

Feldman, D. C. (1984). The development and enforcement of group norms. *Academy of Management Review*, 9, 47–53.

Haney, C. and Zimbardo, P. G. (1973). Social roles and role-playing: Observations from the Stanford Prison Study. *Behavioral and Social Science Teacher*, 1, 25–45.

Janis, I. L. (1972). *Victims of Groupthink: A Psychological Study of Foreign-Policy Decisions and Fiascos*. New York: Houghton Mifflin.

Kelman, H. C. (1961). Processes of opinion change. *Public Opinion Quarterly*, 25, 57–78.

Kiesler, C. A. and Kiesler, S. B. (1969). *Conformity*. Reading, MA: Addison-Wesley.

Milgram, S. (1974). *Obedience to Authority*. New York: Harper and Row.

Nail, P. R. (1986). Toward an integration of some models and theories of social response. *Psychological Bulletin*, 100, 190–206.

Sherif, M. (1936). *The Psychology of Social Norms*. New York: Harper.

congruence

Kim Cameron

This term refers to a condition where two elements match, fit with, or are in harmony with one another. In organizational behavior, congruence has been applied to at least two different phenomena: interpersonal COMMUNICATION and ORGANIZATIONAL DESIGN. Congruence in interpersonal communication means that a person's message (i.e., the words spoken) matches exactly the person's thoughts and feelings. Rogers (1961) claimed that the "fundamental law of interpersonal relationships" is centered on congruence: the more congruence in an interpersonal relationship, the stronger and more satisfying it is.

Congruence in organization design refers to consistency among various elements in an organization. Authors have focused on different organizational attributes, but the basic assumption is that when these elements are congruent, the organization is more effective (see Nadler and Tushman, 1997). The well-known 7-S framework, for example, proposes that ORGANIZATIONAL EFFECTIVENESS is enhanced when congruence exists among seven elements: strategy, structure, systems, staffing, SKILLS, style, and shared VALUES. This means that each element fits with, reinforces, or is consistent with all other elements. To attain high performance, organizations and teams must strive to develop congruence among these various elements.

See also *inter-organizational relations; organizational design*

Bibliography

Nadler, D. A. and Tushman, M. L. (1997). *Competing by Design*. New York: Oxford University Press.
Rogers, C. R. (1961). *On Becoming a Person*. Boston, MA: Houghton Mifflin.

consensus

J. Keith Murnighan

Consensus refers to an often used, informal group decision-making process (*see* GROUP DECISION-MAKING). Ideally, consensus means a clear, open discussion of many alternatives until the group chairperson suggests that one alternative is clearly favored. If no group member disagrees, this consensually supported alternative is taken as the group's decision. Typically, however, the consensus process is informal and unstructured, allowing for many attempts at INFLUENCE or political action within the group (*see* GROUP DYNAMICS; POLITICS).

True consensus can generate commitment to the decision and strong GROUP COHESIVENESS (*see* COMMITMENT). Unfortunately, the unstructured nature of the process leads to a variety of problems, including:

1 a small number of low quality alternatives or ideas;
2 potentially strong social pressure within the group, especially when someone with POWER states a consensus prematurely;
3 low task orientation, when group members spend more time interacting socially than attending to their task;
4 a high potential for CONFLICT if people disagree (Murnighan, 1981).

Nevertheless, consensus has such positive connotations, implying agreement, democracy, and informal unanimity, that many organizational groups, even very large groups, use it for many if not all of their decisions.

See also *decision-making; group norms; groupthink*

Bibliography

Murnighan, J. K. (1981). Group decision-making: What strategies should you use? *Management Review*, **70** (2), 55–62.

consultancy

Ginka Toegel

Management consulting can be defined as the provision of independent advice and help about the process of management to clients with management responsibilities (ICMCI, 2004). Consultants are not supposed to run organizations or to make decisions on behalf of their executives. The deeper connotation of the concept "consultation" is "helping" (Schein, 1999). While managers (principals) have direct power and responsibility over the action, consultants (agents) try to get things done by providing advisory service and assistance, without taking charge.

THE CONSULTING PROCESS

There are five generic *purposes* for using consultants: achieving organizational objectives (e.g., competitive advantage, growth, etc.), solving management and business problems (e.g., loss of important markets, high labor turnover, etc.), identifying and utilizing new opportunities (e.g., improving quality), enhancing learning, and implementing change.

The consulting process can be conceived as going through five phases. First is *entry*. This includes the first contact with the client, discussions on what the purpose of the assignment should be, clarification of the roles of both parties, preliminary problem diagnosis and negotiation of the consulting contract. In the second phase, *diagnosis*, the problem is studied in depth. This means that data are collected, analyzed, and fed back to the client. The third phase, *action planning*, focuses on the finding of a solution to the problem. It encompasses development and evaluation of alternatives, elaboration of strategies and tactics for implementing changes, and discussion of the proposals with the client. The fourth phase is *implementation*. When change starts happening, consultants may adjust the proposal, train staff, and assist management in the process of delivering change. The fifth and final phase is *termination*. Now performance has to be evaluated by both the client and the consultant, a final report is presented, and possible follow-ups are discussed. At the end of this phase, the consultant withdraws.

A Historical Overview

The development of consulting reflects the evolution of management. Researchers distinguish three different generations of management consultancies (Kipping, 2002). The first wave goes back to scientific management, when consultants such as Emerson, Maynard, and Bedaux focused on improving productivity and efficiency. The late 1950s was characterized by the dominance of a new generation of management consultancies (e.g., Booz Allen, McKinsey, BCG, A. T. Kearney) that focused on corporate strategy and organization. In the late 1970s, information technology opened new opportunities for value chain management. Accounting and auditing firms were quick to start implementing large-scale information and coordination systems. This gave rise to the third generation of network building consultancies such as the so-called "Big Five" accounting firms, plus EDS, CSC, and Gemini. Historical review suggests that consultancies from one wave have found it difficult to retain their dominant position in a subsequent wave and to compete with the newcomers. In the last decade, for example, second-generation consulting firms lost substantial market share. One reason is that reputation and brand equity are difficult to build or change. While consultants generally send the right signals to relevant constituencies during the expansion phase, they can be seen as outdated when the new generation of consultancies emerges. The second reason is the difficulty in changing the skills of consultants quickly or to adjust the internal organization of the consulting firm to fit the requirements of the new wave.

In recent decades, the consulting sector has experienced steady growth. Compared with 1992, the world consulting market in 1999 was up 260 percent and its total revenue amounted to $102 billion (Kubr, 2002). It is estimated that currently about 700,000 management, business, and IT consultants are operating worldwide. Nowadays, there are more than 50 large multinational consulting firms with more than 1,000 staff members. In 2000, twenty of those giants labeled as "full-service consulting firms" providing "total service packages" earned over $1 billion each.

Perspectives on Management Consulting

There are two main perspectives on the content of management consulting practice (Fincham and Clark, 2002). The first one is the ORGANIZATION DEVELOPMENT (OD) approach, which began in the 1950s and dominated until the mid-1980s. The second one is the critical perspective (see CRITICAL THEORY). The major goal of the OD approach was to increase an organization's effectiveness through a planned and participative intervention process. While OD focuses on the management consulting activity itself, the critical perspective suggests that the real problem faced by consultants is to demonstrate their value to clients in the first place. It argues that management consulting is not a profession and that references to effectiveness and success are a form of rhetoric used by consultants to legitimize their claimed core product, namely knowledge (see Alvesson, 1993).

Organizational researchers have turned their attention to the role of consultants as knowledge brokers, to their expertness, or to their contribution to management fads. An interesting stream of studies tries to explain why management consulting exists and the roles management consultants play. With the proliferation of management consulting, a substantial body of literature concerned with the litany of complaints about its inefficiency has accumulated.

Typologies of Management Consulting Interventions

In the last decade, sociologists realized that the modern profession of consulting has been largely ignored compared with the traditional ones, like law and medicine. The short institutional his-

Table 1 Overview of the typologies of management consulting

Typology	Authors	Description
Dichotomy	Greiner and Metzger, 1983	Content vs. process consultants
	Kubr, 2002	Resource vs. process roles
	Hargadon, 1998	Generalists vs. functionalists
	Ganesh, 1978	Human vs. system orientations
Continuum	Margulies and Raia, 1972	Task (technical expert) – process (facilitator)
	Lippitt and Lippitt, 1978	Directive – non-directive approach
	Turner, 1982	Hierarchy of 8 task categories, which reflect consultant's involvement
	Tilles, 1961	3 roles: sellers of services, suppliers of information, and business doctors
	Steele, 1975	9 roles: teacher, student, detective, barbarian, clock, monitor, talisman, advocate, and ritual pig
Roles and metaphors	Nees and Greiner, 1985	5 roles: the mental adventurer, the strategic navigator, the management physician, the system architect, and the friendly co-pilot
	Schein, 1999	3 models: purchase of information, doctor-patient, and process consultation

tory of this profession is reflected in its poorly defined boundaries, hence typologies are necessarily broad. They are of two main types: dichotomies/continua and metaphors. An overview of these current typologies (see table 1) shows that they focus, variously, on the nature of the consulting problem, on the consulting process itself, and on the style of consultants. Not all are conceived as normative or prescriptive in intent. The goal of many of them is to help us apprehend the different inputs, processes, and outcomes in consulting interventions.

FUTURE TRENDS

During the last decade, clients have become more competent in using consulting services. There is a trend to involve consultants more actively in the phase of implementation and to make their remuneration contingent on results. E-consulting and outsourcing have become the fastest growing areas of service. Current trends reflect the growing complexity of national and international business environments and the rapid advancement of information technologies. Five main trends can be discerned:

1 *Redefinition and restructuring.* Services have become more integrated and multidisciplinary. This has triggered a redefinition of management consulting in terms of widening the service portfolio and establishing working alliances with other consultants and service firms. Some consultants even prefer to define their field as business consulting, consulting to whole sectors or stratas of firms. This has led to increased concentration of service provision from among the top consulting firms, which have grown fastest. One emerging trend is to couple consulting with another business such as airline operation, banking, insurance, or manufacturing. In 2000, for example, IBM employed 50,000 consultants and provided management consulting alongside IT services.

2 *Joint teams of internal and external consultants.* There is a rapid growth of internal consultants, mainly in large business operators. While critics contend that in-house consulting cannot provide independence, objectivity, and knowledge from other companies in the industry, supporters point out advantages such as intimate knowledge of the com-

pany, confidentiality, and substantially lower costs. In future, we will see more joint teams of internal and external consultants, because the arrangement satisfies all parties: it lowers costs, knowledge gets transferred to internal consultants, while the external ones diagnose problems more quickly talking to colleagues (*see* KNOWLEDGE MANAGEMENT).

3 *Avoiding conflict of interest.* Following the financial scandal of Enron, the analysis of Anderson's audit failures revealed conflict of interest. Since 2001 there is a growing pressure from regulatory authorities in different countries to separate management and other business services from audit services in order to guarantee impartiality and objectivity.

4 *Commoditization.* The essence of consulting is the creation, transfer, sharing, and application of management and business knowledge (Kubr, 2002). Especially in the field of IT and e-business, commoditization of business knowledge in terms of developing standard procedures and delivering standard products has led to spectacular growth. The use of standard instruments permits the employment of more junior consultants, often criticized by clients as "the school bus approach."

5 *Flexible arrangements.* Some practices reflect some new modes of purchasing consulting services for a longer period of time. A retainer contract, for example, implies that the client purchases a certain amount of consultant's time. It can be used to review periodically results and trends of the client's business or to provide a constant flow of information in a certain area. Under these more flexible arrangements, consultants may become permanent board members, personal advisors to top management, and providers of new ideas.

See also *change methods; organizational change; outsourcing;*

Bibliography

Alvesson, M. (1993). Organizations as rhetoric: Knowledge-intensive firms and the struggle with ambiguity. *Journal of Management Studies*, **30** (6), 997.

Fincham, R. and Clark, T. (2002). Introduction: The emergence of critical perspectives on consulting. In T. Clark and R. Fincham (eds.), *Critical Consulting: New Perspectives on the Management Advice Industry*. Oxford: Blackwell, 1–18.

Ganesh, S. (1978). Organizational consultants: A comparison of styles. *Human Relations*.

Greiner, L. and Metzger, R. (1983). *Consulting to Management*. Englewood Cliffs, NJ: Prentice-Hall.

Hargadon, A. (1998). Firms as knowledge brokers: Lessons in pursuing continuous innovation. *California Management Review*, **40** (3), 209–27.

ICMCI (2004). The International Council of Management Consulting Institutes. http://www.icmci.org/AboutUs/defs.htm, visited on Jan 13.

Kipping, M. (2002). Trapped in their wave: The evolution of management consultancies. In T. Clark and R. Fincham (eds.), *Critical Consulting: New Perspectives on the Management Advice Industry*. Oxford: Blackwell, 28–49.

Kubr, M. (2002). *Management Consulting: A Guide to the Profession*, 3rd revd. edn. Geneva: International Labor Office.

Lippitt, G. and Lippitt, R. (1978). *The Consulting Process in Action*. California: University Associates.

Margulies, N. and Raia, A. (eds.) (1972). *Organizational Development: Its Theory and Practice*. New York: McGraw-Hill.

Nees, D. and Greiner, L. (1985). Seeing behind the look-alike management consultants. *Organizational Dynamics*, **13**, 68–79.

Schein, E. (1999). *Process Consultation Revisited*. Reading, MA: Addison Wesley.

Steele, F. (1975). *Consulting for Organizational Change*. Amherst, MA: University of Massachusetts Press.

Tilles, S. (1961). Understanding the consultant's role. *Harvard Business Review*, **39**, 87–99.

Turner, A. (1982). Consulting is more than giving advice. *Harvard Business Review*, **60**, 120–9.

consultancy intervention models

see CONSULTANCY

contingency theory

John Freeman

This denotes a body of literature that seeks to explain the structure of organizations by analyzing their adjustment to external factors, particularly changing circumstances that introduce uncertainty in DECISION-MAKING.

Prior to the development of contingency theory, organizations were usually understood as closed systems (*see* SYSTEMS THEORY), with ORGANIZATIONAL DESIGN based primarily on maxims for organizing that emerged from literature on public BUREAUCRACY and military organization. Contingency theory drew attention to the organization's environment and to its TECHNOLOGY, both of which were understood as outside the organization and as subjects of independent or exogenous causation; hence, the term OPEN SYSTEMS. Contingency theory viewed organizations as reacting to the environments and technologies around and within them, rather than to the effects of organizations on their environments. Conceptualization of these sources of contingency tended to be broad, with frequent reference to "the environment" without specifying the sources of such effects. So while open systems perspectives continue to figure prominently in organizational research, most succeeding theory has focused on the reciprocal relationship between internal organization and its context. In addition, contingency theory often viewed organizations in a static way, assuming that adjustment to contingencies would happen in a straightforward, often rationally designed and managed way.

The primary argument of contingency theory is that when activity in the organization is routinized, bureaucratic organization prevails. The fixed structure of bureaucracy is undermined when contingencies generate high levels of uncertainty. This happens either when technological factors or the environment are unstable, producing numerous unanticipated events requiring a response, or when the pattern of inputs to the organization is complex. In either case, structure becomes more complex with a finer division of labor, more highly trained and skilled personnel, fewer written rules, and less direct vertical supervision. Organizations in unstable environments, or those using rapidly changing technologies, display patterns of interdependency that are characterized by large numbers of non-routine problems whose solutions have implications for many parts of the organization. Because the parts affected by each problem differ, and the problems do not repeat themselves in precisely the same way, a customized response is required. This leads to a fluid mode of organization or an organic system as opposed to a mechanistic system (Burns and Stalker, 1961) (*see* MECHANISTIC/ORGANIC).

Contingency theory was undermined when its empirical base was called into question. Technology loomed less large to subsequent researchers when it was shown that research designs mixed partial organizations, such as factories owned by larger corporations, with free-standing organizations with a full complement of support functions (e.g., finance, marketing). Size seemed to matter as much as technology and many effects that appeared to emanate from the technology were as much a function of size. In addition, the reactive nature of contingency theory drew criticism from those who saw many issues of technology and environment as subject to managerial choice. Finally, the relatively undifferentiated conceptualization of the environment drew criticism as subsequent researchers focused attention on the flow of resources and the tendency for POWER in organizations to emanate from resource flows.

See also *leadership; organizational change; organization theory; resource dependence*

Bibliography

Burns, T. and Stalker, G. M. (1961). *The Management of Innovation*. London: Tavistock.

Lawrence, P. R. and Lorsch, J. W. (1967). *Organization and Environment*. Cambridge, MA: Harvard University Press.

Pugh, D. S., Hickson, D. J., Hinings, C. R., and Turner, C. (1969). The context of organization structures. *Administrative Science Quarterly*, **14**, 91–114.

Thompson, J. D. (1967). *Organizations in Action*. New York: McGraw-Hill.

continuous improvement

Gerald E. Ledford, Jr.

The view that organizations should strive ceaselessly to improve is a basic principle of TOTAL QUALITY MANAGEMENT. Continuous improvement has long been advocated by the two leading gurus of the quality movement, J. M. Juran and the late W. Edwards Deming. One of

Deming's famous Fourteen Points was "improve constantly and forever the system of production and service."

Japanese students of Deming and Juran readily embraced the concept, translated as kaizen, decades ago. Continuous improvement today is fundamental to the Japanese management style. Continuous improvement "is a pervasive concept linked to all Japanese manufacturing practices" (Young, 1992).

The notion of continuous improvement is not obvious from the perspective of organization theory. For example, the concept of continuous improvement contrasts with the concept of dynamic homeostasis in open systems theories (*see* SYSTEMS THEORY). Open systems theories treat changes to the system as disruptions or threats to survival. The system is seen as constantly striving to return to an equilibrium state that preserves its basic character. By contrast, the idea of continuous improvement suggests that there may be no state of dynamic equilibrium. Rather, organizational members consciously choose to keep the organization in a chronically unfrozen state.

A number of texts provide specific tools and techniques for the practice of continuous improvement (e.g., Imai, 1987; Robson, 1991; Schonberger, 1982). These tend to emphasize work analysis, production techniques, and group problem solving techniques.

Employees do not always embrace the concept of continuous improvement. Some in the labor movement characterize it as part of a pattern of "management by stress" (e.g., Parker and Slaughter, 1988), in which managers cajole employees into surrendering ideas that may eliminate their jobs. Without employment guarantees, the productivity increases that result from continuous improvement may indeed threaten jobs. Thus, Young (1992) hypothesized that continuous improvement will be adopted faster and will be more successful where there is a lower likelihood that workers will be laid off from their jobs. It is also possible to reward employees directly for offering suggestions leading to improvement. This is a common practice in Japan (Imai, 1987). Young (1992) hypothesized that the availability of monetary and non-monetary rewards would enhance the adoption and effectiveness of continuous improvement efforts.

Many theories of organizational change contrast gradual, incremental, or routine change with a more dramatic form of change, variously called strategic, punctuated, discontinuous, or radical. The experience of continuous improvement challenges theories that equate incremental changes with minor ones. Such perspectives often underestimate the cumulative power of incremental changes to transform organizations and even industries over time. For example, firms in the automobile industry have been radically transformed over the last 25 years even though it is difficult to point to radical changes, such as new technology, that have created this change. Rather, decades of continuous improvement have increased productivity and quality dramatically and have led to changes in virtually every aspect of the management of these firms as companies have responded to and fostered more continuous improvement.

See also *empowerment; innovation; job design; organizational effectiveness*

Bibliography

Imai, M. (1987). *Kaizen: The Key to Japan's Competitive Success*. New York: Random House.

Parker, M. and Slaughter, J. (1988). *Choosing Sides: Unions and the Team Concept*. Boston, MA: South End Press.

Robson, G. D. (1991). *Continuous Process Improvement: Simplifying Work Flow Systems*. New York: Free Press.

Schonberger, R. J. (1982). *Japanese Manufacturing Techniques: Nine Hidden Lessons in Simplicity*. New York: Free Press.

Young, S. M. (1992). A framework for successful adoption and performance of Japanese manufacturing practices in the United States. *Academy of Management Review*, 17 (4), 677–700.

contracts

Madan M. Pillutla

Contracts are collections of commitments, duties, and rights, which establish specific obligations and entitlements for each party (Farnsworth, 1980). According to Parks and Smith (1998), these commitments are created through one of two contractual mechanisms:

promissory or social contracting. Promissory contracts refer to the explicit exchange of commitments about tangible factors such as future behaviors, goods, and services, and non-tangible ones such as loyalty and fidelity. Social contracts refer to the common understanding of the appropriateness of particular behaviors, and provide the normative background against which promissory contracts are created, maintained, and executed.

Within the organizational literature, those interested in PSYCHOLOGICAL CONTRACTS, which refer to the reciprocal expectations and obligations that characterize the relationship between employees and their organizations, examine social contracts. Promissory contracts are central to economic theories of organization such as AGENCY THEORY and transaction cost economics (see TRANSACTION COST ECONOMICS). The basic assumptions in organizational economics models are that complex contracts are necessarily incomplete (because of BOUNDED RATIONALITY) and that individuals are opportunistic. Thus organizations (or individuals) should design contractual relationships by taking *ex ante* safeguards to deter *ex post* opportunism. Transaction cost economics proposes that organizations choose to locate a transaction either in a market or within a hierarchy depending on the relative costs of bureaucratic inefficiency or of contract remediability in the market (e.g., through the courts).

Recent research suggests that in addition to bringing transactions within a hierarchy, organizations attempt to resolve the incomplete contracts problems with relational contracts through which the parties reach accommodations when unforeseen or uncontracted events occur. Relational contracts are common in the networks of firms in the fashion industry or the diamond trade, and in strategic alliances, joint ventures, and business groups. Formal contracts must be specified *ex ante* in terms that can be verified *ex post* by the third party, whereas a relational contract can be based on outcomes that are observed by only the contracting parties *ex post*, and also on outcomes that are prohibitively costly to specify *ex ante* (Baker, Gibbons, and Murphy, 2002).

The economic approach towards contracting would consider relational contracts to be a prom-

issory one, as it emphasizes that these contracts are worth undertaking only if the value of the future relationship is sufficiently large that the parties to the contract do not renege. Relational contracts, within this tradition, are therefore more a matter of self-interested, profit seeking behavior rather than willful commitment or altruistic attachment (Macneil, 1978). The embeddedness approach (e.g., Uzzi, 1997), on the other hand, emphasizes the non-calculative, psychological processes, primarily TRUST, in the maintenance of relational contracts (see NETWORK THEORY AND ANALYSIS). Within this tradition, relational contracts appear to be social rather than promissory.

Despite these differences, both approaches agree that relational contracts tend to be particularistic, involve long-term investments, and are mutually understood and enforced. They are likely to be characterized by a willingness to honor the spirit of the contract rather than the letter, and when disputes arise they are expected to be resolved through internal mechanisms that are designed to preserve the long-term relationship rather than the legalistic remedies that characterize formal contracts. A relational contract thus allows the parties to utilize their detailed knowledge of their specific situation and to adapt to new information as it becomes available (Baker, Gibbons, and Murphy, 2002).

See also *bureaucracy; inter-organizational relations*

Bibliography

Baker, G., Gibbons, R., and Murphy, K. (2002). Relational contracts and the theory of the firm. *Quarterly Journal of Economics*, 117, 39–83.

Farnsworth, E. A. (1980). *Contracts*. Boston, MA: Little, Brown.

Macneil, I. (1978). Contracts: Adjustment of long-term economic relations under classical, neoclassical, and relational contract law. *Northwestern University Law Review*, 72, 854–905.

Parks, J. M. and Smith, F. (1998). Organizational contracting: A "rational" exchange? In J. Halpern and R. Stern (eds.), *Debating Rationality: Non-Rational Aspects of Organizational Decision-Making*. Ithaca, NY: Cornell University Press, 125–54.

Uzzi, B. (1997). Social structure and competition in interfirm networks: The paradox of embeddedness. *Administrative Science Quarterly*, 42, 35–67.

corporate boards

William Ocasio

Corporate boards are the top-level decision-making bodies in corporate forms of organization. Typically composed of a chairperson and directors from inside and outside the corporation, as well as several committees, the study of corporate boards has been an active area of research in macro-organizational behavior for over 30 years.

Despite their formal authority over corporate decisions, the role and importance of boards of directors remains a subject of theoretical and empirical controversy. Building on Berle and Mean's classic study of the separation of ownership and control in large US corporations, the study of corporate boards is closely associated with research on the relative power and control of managers, shareholders, and financial capitalists. With the rise of agency theory perspectives in macro theory (Walsh and Seward, 1990), research on boards has focused on the ability of boards of directors to monitor and control the activities of corporate managers.

Early research on boards undertaken from a resource dependence perspective (Pfeffer and Salancik, 1978) viewed boards as mechanisms for mitigating external control of organizations, allowing for the firm to adapt to its environment. This view of the board was challenged by power elite theorists (Useem, 1984; Mizruchi, 1992) who focused on the role of boards in maintaining the intercorporate power structure. Useem viewed board members in large corporations in Great Britain and the United States as an "inner circle," a group of selected business elites who typically have ties to multiple numbers of big corporations, who transcend the boundaries of one particular firm or company, and who act to make fairly concerted actions to push for the interests of the big businesses as a whole. They give coherence and direction to the politics of business. Useem also notes that their activities have become particularly influential politically in the 1970s and 1980s in Great Britain and the United States. Adopting a structural model of social action, Mizruchi (1992) examined the effects of factors such as geographic proximity, common industry membership, stock ownership, interlocking directorates, and interfirm market relations on the extent to which firms behave similarly and found that both organizational and social network factors contribute to similar behavior among board members.

Network and intercorporate approaches to boards continue to influence research on boards and interlocking directorates. The most important finding is that boards serve as a mechanism of intercorporate diffusion and imitation. However, while some innovations diffuse through the network of interlocking directors, others do not. For example, Davis and Greve (1997) find that while poison pills diffused quickly through board interlocks, golden parachutes diffused slowly through mechanisms other than board membership. Davis and Greve argue that boards provide a mechanism for cognitive legitimacy at the intercorporate level, providing evidence that other board members in similar roles make similar decisions.

Following both agency theory and political perspectives on board behavior, much research on boards has focused on the effects of board structure and composition, particularly the role of insiders versus outsiders in the board and CEO-chairperson duality. While various measures of board structure, particularly CEO-chairperson duality, affect important board decisions such as CEO succession (Ocasio, 1994), the impact of insiders versus outsiders or board independence on board decision-making and board performance seems overstated. Board independence has been a subject of both public policy and research concern since at least the late 1970s, but the research fails to support conventional views that "independent" boards perform better, are better aligned with shareholder interests, or are more likely to monitor CEO performance. For example, Ocasio (1994) found that under conditions of poor economic performance, CEOs are more likely to be replaced with a *greater* number of insiders in the board, the opposite of what would be expected from views that "independence" leads to greater monitoring of CEOs. Other research also questions the importance of board independence on board performance or behavior. For example, a meta-analysis by Dalton et al. (1998) found that board independence did not lead to higher financial performance.

While the importance of board structure and composition has been increasingly questioned, recent research has highlighted the importance of board processes. For example, Westphal (1998) examined the use of social influence processes, including CEO persuasion and ingratiation, as CEOs adapted to structural measures of board independence. Westphal (1998) found the effects of board processes to be more significant than that of board structure, further suggesting that research and policy concerns with board structure and composition may be misplaced. Theoretical perspectives on corporate boards have highlighted the importance of cognitive processes in board DECISION-MAKING, viewing corporate boards as strategy-making groups (Forbes and Milliken, 1999).

During the last decade, research has also focused on the institutional and symbolic functions of boards of directors. In a series of studies, Westphal and Zajac looked at the interplay between the substantive and symbolic role of board decisions, and the decoupling between public announcements of decisions made by the board and their actual implementation. For example, Westphal and Zajac (1994) found decoupling between announcements of CEO's long-term incentive plans and actual adoption of those plans. Follow-up studies found similar findings for stock buybacks. They find that decoupling of announcements and implementation is moderated by the power of the CEO over the board of directors. Ocasio (1999) emphasizes the institutional function of corporate boards, as boards serve to affirm and reproduce the norms of appropriate corporate behavior. In a study of the insider versus outsider succession, Ocasio found that boards serve to reproduce precedents of insider succession and affirm the continuation of the internal labor market for CEOs.

Given the recent interest in institutional perspectives on boards, an important area for research is how board structures and board processes are endogenous and subject to institutional and historical contingencies. For example, despite the lack of an adequate empirical base for the importance of board independence for corporate boards, normative pressures from institutional investors and more recently regulatory pressures have led to a decline in inside directors in large corporations.

See also *governance; interlocking boards; organizational design; stakeholders*

Bibliography

Dalton, D. R., Daily, C. M, Ellstrand, A. E., and Johnson, J. L. (1998). Meta-analytic reviews of board composition, leadership structure, and financial performance. *Strategic Management Journal*, 19 (3), 269–90.

Davis, G. F. and Greve, H. R. (1997). Corporate elite networks and governance changes in the 1980s. *American Journal of Sociology*, 103, 1–37.

Forbes D. P. and Milliken, F. J. (1999). Cognition and corporate governance: Understanding boards of directors as strategic decision-making groups. *Academy of Management Review*, 24 (3), 489–505.

Mizruchi, M. S. (1992). *The Structure of Corporate Political Action: Interfirm Relations and their Consequences*. Cambridge, MA: Harvard University Press.

Ocasio, W. (1994). Political dynamics and the circulation of power: CEO succession in United States industrial corporations, 1960–1990. *Administrative Science Quarterly*, 39, 285–312.

Ocasio, W. (1999). Institutionalized action and corporate governance: The reliance on rules of CEO succession. *Administrative Science Quarterly*, 44 (2), 384–416.

Pfeffer, J. and Salancik, G. (1978). *The External Control of Organizations: A Resource Dependence Perspective*. New York: Harper and Row.

Useem, M. (1984). *The Inner Circle: Large Corporations and the Rise of Business Political Activity in the US and UK*. New York: Oxford University Press.

Walsh, J. P. and Seward, J. K. (1990). On the efficiency of internal and external corporate control mechanisms. *Academy of Management Review*, 15 (3), 421–58.

Westphal, J. D. (1998). Board games: How CEOs adapt to increases in structural board independence from management. *Administrative Science Quarterly*, 43 (3), 511–37.

Westphal J. D and Zajac, E. J. (1994). Substance and symbolism in CEOs long-term incentive plans. *Administrative Science Quarterly*, 39 (3), 367–90.

corporate reputation

see REPUTATION

corporate social performance

Donna J. Wood

Corporate social performance (CSP) is defined as a business organization's configuration of principles of social responsibility, processes of social responsiveness, and observable outcomes as they relate to the firm's societal relationships (Wood, 1991). CSP scholars envision societies as complex webs of interconnected cause and effect, and conceive of business as a social institution with both power and responsibility. CSP, then, has to do with the full range of antecedents and outcomes of business organization operations, and does not focus narrowly on maximizing shareholder wealth.

In the CSP model, three principles of corporate social responsibility – institutional legitimacy, public responsibility, and managerial discretion – define structural relationships among society, the business institution, business organizations, and people.

The principle of institutional legitimacy states that society grants legitimacy and power to business, and that business must use its power in a way that society considers responsible. General *institutional* expectations are made of any business organization, and organizational legitimacy is achieved and maintained by complying with these institutional expectations.

The principle of public responsibility states that business organizations are responsible for outcomes related to their primary (mission or operations derived) and secondary (related to, but not derived from, mission or operations) areas of societal involvement (Preston and Post, 1975). Each business *organization* has unique responsibilities because of its size, industry, markets, product/service mix, etc.

The principle of managerial discretion states that managers are moral actors and are obligated to exercise all available discretion toward socially responsible outcomes. This principle of *individual* responsibility emphasizes that within various domains of business activity (economic, legal, ethical, charitable) (Carroll, 1979), managers are responsible for balancing their moral decision-making autonomy and their AGENCY relationship to the firm and its stakeholders.

Processes of corporate social responsiveness, the second dimension of CSP, represent characteristic boundary spanning behaviors of businesses. These processes, linking social responsibility principles and behavioral outcomes, include (a) environmental assessment: gathering and assessing information about the external environment; (b) stakeholder management: managing the organization's relationships with relevant persons, groups, and organizations; and (c) issues management: tracking and developing responses to social issues that may affect the company.

In neoclassical economics, business outcomes are thought of as narrow financial measures such as profit, share value, and market share. In the stakeholder view of organizations, outcomes are defined as consequences to stakeholders, including product safety, human rights, pollution, and effects on local communities as well as profitability, and to the firm itself as policies and practices are adapted to achieve better CSP.

Current research focuses on linking CSP to theories of stakeholders, ethics, and organizations; systematizing the assumptions and theoretical implications of the CSP model; empirically testing ideas about how people perceive, interpret, and enact CSP; using a CSP framework to broaden causal investigations of financial performance (Margolis and Walsh, 2001); examining the validity of the CSP model in cross-cultural and multinational settings; and critiques of existing CSP theory. Current issues relevant to CSP include corporate GOVERNANCE, ethics in practice, accountability, and transparency via social reporting.

See also *institutional theory; organizational citizenship behavior; stakeholders; values*

Bibliography

Carroll, A. B. (1979). A three-dimensional model of corporate performance. *Academy of Management Review*, **4**, 497–505.

Margolis, J. D. and Walsh, J. P. (2001). *People and Profits? The Search for a Link Between a Company's Social and Financial Performance*. New York: Lawrence Erlbaum Associates.

Preston, L. E. and Post, J. E. (1975). *Private Management and Public Policy: The Principle of Public Responsibility*. Englewood Cliffs, NJ: Prentice-Hall.

Wartick, S. L. and Cochran, P. R. (1985). The evolution of the corporate social performance model. *Academy of Management Review*, **10**, 758–69.

Wood, D. J. (1991). Corporate social performance revisited. *Academy of Management Review*, **16**, 691–718.

creativity

Teresa M. Amabile

Organizational researchers and high level managers in organizations have displayed growing interest in creativity in recent years, perhaps because creativity is seen as the primary means by which organizations can maintain competitive advantage. Creativity is generally defined as the generation of ideas or products that are both novel and appropriate (correct, useful, valuable, or meaningful) (Amabile, 1996). Within an organization, creativity can arise in the work of an individual or a small team working closely together. INNOVATION occurs when an organization successfully implements the creative ideas emerging from individuals or teams. Clearly, successful implementation often requires creative (novel and useful) ideas. Thus, although a strict distinction between creativity and innovation is inappropriate, it is useful to think of creativity as the early part and innovation as the later part of a continuous process in organizations.

THE NATURE AND ASSESSMENT OF CREATIVITY

The assessment of creativity is important for both researchers and management practitioners. For these purposes, creativity can be viewed as the *outcome* of a *process* by which *persons* produce novel, useful ideas that are viewed as valuable by credible observers (Cskiszentmihalyi, 1999). Ultimately, most researchers and practitioners are reluctant to identify something as creative purely on the basis of characteristics of the persons who produced it, or the process by which it was produced. The hallmark of creativity is the outcome – the resulting idea, new product, new service, or process improvement. Moreover, creativity is not dichotomous, in the sense of being either present or absent in an individual. Rather, there is a continuum of creativity in any realm, from ideas that shatter previous conceptions and ways of doing something, to ideas that are more modestly novel and useful. Thus, creativity is not limited to only a few geniuses deemed "creative" by dint of their eccentric personalities or outstanding cognitive capacities; rather, all humans with normal capacities have the potential to produce creative work in some degree in

some domain. Creativity is not limited to certain domains, such as marketing, advertising, or research and development; new and appropriate ideas can be generated and applied to any human activity, including organizational behavior.

Researchers have developed a straightforward process for assessing creativity: asking people who should know (Amabile and Mueller, in press). This "consensual assessment technique" involves having knowledgeable people in a particular domain (such as branding techniques) examine and rate the creativity of ideas in that domain (such as particular advertising campaigns) relative to one another. In most contemporary organizational research, the creativity of individuals or teams is assessed by supervisors, peers, or some other group of experts within the organization. Although such judges often find it difficult to articulate exactly what defines a creative idea or outcome, it is something they can confidently recognize and rate when asked to compare different individuals or projects. Thus, generally, the use of multiple, knowledgeable, independent raters yields reliable and replicable assessments of creativity in organizations.

THE COMPONENTS OF CREATIVITY

Contemporary theorists of organizational creativity assume that it is best conceptualized not as a personality trait or a general ability but as a behavior resulting from particular constellations of personal characteristics, cognitive abilities, and social-environmental factors within the organization (Amabile, 1988; Ford, 1996; Woodman, Sawyer, and Griffin, 1993). According to the componential theory of organizational creativity (Amabile, 1988), there are three components within the individual, and one component outside the individual, that determine a person's creativity. The three intra-individual components are expertise in the domain, creative thinking skills, and intrinsic motivation. The external component is the organizational work environment.

The first intra-individual component, expertise, depends on a person's innate talent for learning and thinking in a given domain, as well as the person's formal education, informal training, and experience in the domain. The second component, creative thinking skill, depends to some extent on the individual's PERSONALITY. A cluster of personal characteristics has been repeatedly identified as important to high level creative behavior: (a) self-discipline in matters concerning work; (b) an ability to delay gratification; (c) perseverance in the face of frustration; (d) independence of judgment; (e) a tolerance for ambiguity; (f) a high degree of autonomy; (g) an absence of sex-role stereotyping; (h) an internal LOCUS OF CONTROL; (i) an orientation toward RISK TAKING; and (j) a high level of self-initiated, task-oriented striving for excellence. Creative thinking skill also depends on a person's cognitive style. Generally, creativity will be higher when the person's cognitive style is marked by (a) perceptual flexibility; (b) cognitive flexibility; (c) understanding complexities; (d) keeping response options open as long as possible; (e) suspending judgment; (f) using "wide" categories; (g) remembering accurately; (h) breaking out of performance scripts; and (i) perceiving creatively. Although personality and cognitive style are shaped by an individual's innate characteristics, creative thinking skills and work styles can be improved through training and practice.

The third intra-individual component – MOTIVATION – is, in some respects, the most important, because it determines what people will do with their expertise and creative thinking skill, and because it can be affected most immediately by the social environment. Research with both children and adults, in a variety of settings and across a range of creative activities, suggests that intrinsic motivation (engaging in an activity because of interest, involvement, or personal challenge) is more conducive to creativity than extrinsic motivation (engaging in an activity to achieve some external goal) (Amabile, 1996) (*see* EXTRINSIC AND INTRINSIC MOTIVATION). Social-psychological experiments on the effect of particular environmental factors on the creativity of adults and children has demonstrated that evaluative pressures, surveillance, contracted-for-reward, competition, and restricted choice can undermine intrinsic motivation and creativity by focusing the individual on external reasons for doing the task (Amabile, 1996). These findings are summarized in the Intrinsic Motivation Principle of Creativity: People will be most creative when they feel motivated primarily by the interest, enjoyment, satisfaction, and challenge of the work itself – and not by external pressures. There are some notable exceptions. Recent research has revealed that, under certain conditions, external motivators may support intrinsic motivation and creativity rather than undermining them. Specifically, external rewards that provide competence information or enable individuals to more deeply engage in their creative work can have positive effects. This phenomenon is termed "motivational synergy" (Amabile, 1993).

WORK ENVIRONMENT INFLUENCES

The final component of creativity is the work environment surrounding the individual or team. Research suggests that, generally, it is the social environment, not the physical environment, that exerts the stronger influence on creativity. Researchers have identified a number of aspects of the work environment that distinguish highly creative from less creative work in organizations (Amabile et al., 1996; Scott and Bruce, 1994). Expanding beyond experimental methods, this research has utilized the observational methods of interviews and questionnaires to examine the complex effects of the work environment on individual and team creativity. Work environments most conducive to the fulfillment of creative potential appear to be characterized by a high level of worker autonomy in carrying out the work; encouragement to take risks from higher level managers; reward and recognition for creative efforts; mechanisms for developing new ideas in the organization; WORK GROUPS/TEAMS that are both diversely skilled and cooperative; supervisors who serve as good work models, clearly set overall strategic goals for a project, and protect the team within the organization; COMMUNICATION and collaboration within and across work groups in the organization; sufficient resources for getting the work done; and a substantial degree of challenge in the work.

Work environments least conducive to the fulfillment of creative potential appear to be characterized by political problems and turf battles within the organization; a conservative, status quo orientation from top management; a history of harsh criticism of new ideas; and most forms of extreme time pressure. Recent research suggests that high levels of creativity are possible under extreme time pressure, if the stimulants to creativity are in place and if people are protected from distractions as they work to solve the problem at hand.

Taking all of the work environment stimulants and obstacles into account, there appear to be four "balance factors" handled effectively by managers who promote creativity: *goals* that are set clearly at the overall strategic level, but left loose at the operational level; rewards that are neither ignored nor overly emphasized; PERFORMANCE APPRAISAL systems that provide constructive, frequent FEEDBACK on work without generating threatening negative criticism; and *pressure* arising from the challenging, urgent nature of the work rather than from arbitrary time pressure or intra-organizational competitive pressure.

Creativity enhancement in organizations
Since the 1950s, a growing number of creativity enhancement training programs have been offered to organizations. The oldest and most widely used program, and the source from which most such programs have been developed, is the Creative Problem Solving process. This process, developed during the 1950s and 1960s from the brainstorming technique, involves the use of checklists and forced relationships in addition to the brainstorming principles of deferred judgment and quantity of idea generation (see Parnes, 1992.)

Synectics, a somewhat similar process, relies more heavily on the use of metaphor and analogy in the generation of novel ideas. The guiding principle of synectics is to "make the familiar strange and strange familiar" – to use cognitive techniques for distancing oneself from habitual thought patterns, and to also attempt to see connections between something new and something that is already understood. The prescribed cognitive techniques include personal analogy, direct analogy, symbolic analogy, and fantasy analogy.

Although research on the long-term effectiveness of creativity training programs is limited, many managers and human resource management professionals utilize such programs for employee development.

CURRENT APPROACHES

In order to gain a more comprehensive understanding of creativity in organizational contexts, contemporary theorists are attempting to integrate personality, cognitive, and work environment factors. Researchers have recently begun to take comprehensive views of organizational creativity, simultaneously examining multiple influences. As predicted by the componential theory, creativity appears to flourish when individuals having expertise, creative thinking skill, and intrinsic motivation operate in stimulating, supportive work environments (e.g., Oldham and Cummings, 1996). It is likely that research methods will continue to broaden beyond experiments, interviews, and surveys, to include naturalistic, ethnographic studies of creativity in organizational contexts (e.g., Sutton and Hargadon, 1996). Moreover, with the increasing pace and scope of international business competition, it is likely that both the scope of organizational creativity research, and the depth of management interest in such research, will continue to expand.

See also *brainstorming; Delphi; group decision-making; nominal group technique*

Bibliography

Amabile, T. M. (1988). A model of creativity and innovation in organizations. In B. M. Staw and L. L. Cummings (eds.), *Research in Organizational Behavior*, Vol. 10. Greenwich, CT: JAI Press.

Amabile, T. M. (1993). Motivational synergy: Toward new conceptualizations of intrinsic and extrinsic motivation in the workplace. *Human Resource Management Review*, 3, 185–201.

Amabile, T. M. (1996). *Creativity in Context*. Boulder, CO: Westview Press.

Amabile, T. M., Conti, R., Coon, H., Lazenby, J., and Herron, M. (1996). Assessing the work environment for creativity. *Academy of Management Journal*, 39, 1154–84.

Amabile, T. M. and Mueller, J. M. (in press). Assessing creativity and its antecedents: An exploration of the componential theory of creativity. In C. Ford (ed.), *Handbook of Organizational Creativity*. Mahwah, NJ: Lawrence Erlbaum Associates.

Cskiszentmihalyi, M. (1999). Implications of a systems perspective for the study of creativity. In R. J. Sternberg (ed.), *Handbook of Creativity*. Cambridge: Cambridge University Press, 313–35.

Ford, C. M. (1996). A theory of individual creative action in multiple social domains. *Academy of Management Review*, **21**, 1112–42.

Oldham, G. R. and Cummings, A. (1996). Employee creativity: Personal and contextual factors at work. *Academy of Management Journal*, **39**, 607–34.

Parnes, S. J. (ed.) (1992). *Source Book for Creative Problem Solving*. Buffalo, NY: Creative Education Foundation Press.

Scott, S. G. and Bruce, R. A. (1994). Determinants of innovative behavior: A path model of individual innovation in the workplace. *Academy of Management Journal*, **37**, 580–607.

Sternberg, R. J. (ed.) (1999). *Handbook of Creativity*. Cambridge: Cambridge University Press.

Sutton, R. I. and Hargadon, A. (1996). Brainstorming groups in context: Effectiveness in a product design firm. *Administrative Science Quarterly*, **41**, 685–718.

Woodman, R. W., Sawyer, J. E., and Griffin, R. W. (1993). Toward a theory of organizational creativity. *Academy of Management Review*, **18**, 293–321.

crises/disasters

Richard N. Osborn

The terms *crisis* and *disaster* are frequently used but often not precisely defined. Here, a crisis refers to a radical change in status that threatens survival with little time for response, while a disaster characterizes a sudden, often unforeseen, misfortune with dire consequences. The terms evoke mixed interpretations concerning causality and intentions since crises and disasters stem from known and unknown uncontrollable causes as well as from carelessness, ignorance, and/or lack of due diligence.

Historically, analyses of crises and disasters have often attempted to isolate specific causal factors with deterministic models (e.g., from engineering, as in the WASH-1400, a.k.a. the Rasmussen Report, 1975). Here, researchers are asked to isolate a proximate, primary cause as well as contributing factors from a list of categories. The lists often include such categories as human error (*see* ERRORS) and mechanical/electrical failure, among others.

OB research recognizes that increasing numbers of crises and disasters are embedded in organizations. Thus, Pauchant and Mitroff (1992) define a crisis in terms of disturbance to a whole system coupled with challenges to the basic assumptions of that system (*see* SYSTEMS THEORY). One can envision four severity levels of crises/disasters:

Level 1   Dramatic reduction in financial and/or reputational well-being (*see* REPUTATION); substantial destruction of property; serious injury to persons and/or the physical environment (e.g., the 2001 Enron scandal and the 1979 Three Mile Island nuclear accident).

Level 2   Death of involved individuals; injury to the general public or destruction of a habitat with disruption of an ecosystem (e.g., the 1989 Exxon Valdez oil spill).

Level 3   Death in the general public, extinction of a species or destruction of an ecosystem (e.g., the 9/11 events in the US; the 1986 Bophal chemical accident).

Level 4   Alteration of future generations such as by changes in the gene pool of a species (e.g., the 1986 Chernobyl nuclear disaster).

Collectively, the literature presents a rich series of concepts to isolate dynamics within organizations associated with dysfunctional outcomes. These concepts include both unintended and intended dynamic patterns of interaction among elements of a complex system. Perrow (1984) was among the first to emphasize a systems view in his analysis of "normal accidents." The concept of a normal accident stresses that "given systems characteristics, multiple and unexpected interactions of failure are inevitable." Perrow emphasized the inherent inconsistencies among technical requirements in high risk systems with their "tight coupling" and administrative capability (*see* LOOSE COUPLING). Using Perrow's terminology, for example, plants that transform raw materials into marketable products may have numerous interactive "tight couplings" among technical systems, equipment, and components so that a small change in one part of the production process quickly alters another. To manage usual conditions, administrative systems are often rigid, procedural-driven mechanistic systems with sufficient detail to tell operators and supervisors what to do (*see* MECHANISTIC/OR-GANIC). When an anomaly occurs, however, individual initiative, a keen sense of problem identification, and other individualistic attributes fostered by more decentralized organic systems may be necessary. Since executives cannot now develop administrative systems that are simultaneously mechanistic and organic, Perrow recommends that high risk transformation systems should be altered or abandoned if catastrophes are to be avoided.

Many scholars also stress the importance of multiple minor events and how they can quickly escalate into a catastrophe with high risk technologies. This theme was a central feature of Starbuck and Milliken's (1988) analysis of the Challenger disaster (the 1986 explosion of a US space shuttle). They introduced the concept of "fine-tuning to disaster." As with "normal accidents," "fine-tuning to disaster" attempts to explain a system's dynamic that underlies accidents. Starbuck and Milliken argued that engineers and managers are expected to improve technical and administrative systems. Unfortunately, these improvements may have unintended consequences because:

1 specific improvements may be implemented in isolation but tightly coupled in operation;
2 the causal models linking prior success (failure) and future success (failure) are faulty.

Thus, partially contradictory attempts to improve different system features are continued even though the effects of the changes cannot be completely understood. "Improvements" are continued until the system mysteriously breaks. Both "normal accidents" and "fine-tuning to disaster" emphasize unintended consequences arising from the complexities and limitations of modern organizations. Both are in the qualitative tradition of this literature where one or a few exemplary disasters are examined in detail.

In contrast, Osborn and Jackson (1988) suggest that high risk systems may be prone to "purposeful unintended consequences." Here, it is assumed that executives have an influence on administrative systems. The concept of "purposeful unintended consequences" is based on a combination of PROSPECT THEORY, institutional inertia, and AGENCY THEORY. Although executives claim they make choices or at least modify recommendations by subordinates, they were found to purposively deny (a) potential trade-offs among economic, executive, and social outcomes; (b) organizational inadequacies; and (c) their own risk biases (*see* RISK TAKING). Executives promulgated a series of myths suggesting that (a) efficiency and safety are positively linked (e.g., a reliable plant is a safe plant); (b) their organizations are highly competent; and (c) they are risk neutral. Extensive data analyses concerning the safeness of all operating commercial nuclear power plants in the US showed that not only were the myths inaccurate (e.g., safeness and efficiency measures were not related), but also that executives' risk biases and organizational inadequacies combined to yield a potentially serious pattern of safety deficiencies. While the risk bias and organizational inadequacies (e.g., Perrow, 1984; Starbuck and Milliken, 1988) are knowable, the threats to the public may continue because executives continue to perpetuate criteria myths.

Pauchant and Mitroff (1992) also show that mythology, in the form of rationalizations, can combine with vicious cycles (*see* LEARNING, ORGANIZATIONAL) to yield a crisis prone organization. A crisis prone organization is subject to vicious cycles because it has:

1 too narrow a strategic focus;
2 an inappropriately rigid structure with few provisions to deal with a crisis;
3 a culture replete with rationalizations and myths;
4 a collective psyche filled with defense mechanisms, among other factors.

Recently, these views have been extended by using complexity theory (e.g., Anderson, 1999) to delve more intricately into the dynamic interplay among externally uncontrollable factors and human agency in an attempt to both prevent and deal with Level 1 crises and disasters (e.g. Osborn, Hunt, and Jauch, 2002). While the concepts discussed here were developed to help understand and prevent some of the most deleterious consequences of organizational activity, this line of research also appears relevant to examining ORGANIZATIONAL CHANGE, ORGANIZATIONAL DESIGN, high reliability and, of course, accidents.

See also *behavioral decision research; communication; stress; technology*

Bibliography

Anderson, P. (1999). Complexity theory and organizational science. *Organization Science*, **10** (3), 233–6.
Osborn, R. N. and Jackson, D. H. (1988). Leaders, riverboat gamblers, or purposeful unintended consequences in the management of complex dangerous technologies. *Academy of Management Journal*, **20** (4), 924–47.
Osborn, R. N., Hunt, J. G., and Jauch, L. R. (2002). Toward a contextual theory of leadership. *Leadership Quarterly*, **13**, 797–817.
Pauchant, T. C. and Mitroff, I. I. (1992). *Transforming the Crisis-Prone Organization*. San Francisco: Jossey-Bass.
Perrow, C. (1984). *Normal Accidents: Living with High-Risk Technologies*. New York: Basic Books.
Starbuck, W. H. and Milliken, F. J. (1988). Challenger: Fine-tuning the odds until something breaks. *Journal of Management Studies*, **25** (4), 319–40.
WASH-1400, a.k.a. the Rasmussen Report (1975). *Reactor Safety Study: An Assessment of Accident Risks in US Commercial Nuclear Power Plants*. Washington, DC: US Nuclear Regulatory Commission.

critical theory

Stewart Clegg

Critical theory challenges traditional approaches to the study of organizations and management. The term is associated with the Frankfurt School and its most significant proponent has been Habermas (1984). The critical theory view is that organization and management, and their theory, are not simply neutral instruments but instruments of domination. Marcuse (1964) argued that critical theory should articulate the interests of marginalized or repressed voices, such as those of women, the ecology, workers, blacks, etc. Following this logic, critical theory seeks to serve the interests of the repressed or the exploited rather than the rich and powerful and to unmask the rhetoric and facade of pseudo-science that conventional theory uses to cloak its interests. Critical theory demands that management not be isolated from other discursive currents in social science, and thus runs counter to programs that see management as a clearly delineated area of research forming a separate and self-contained paradigm with little connection to the wider framework of social science.

Critical theory has a strong empirical component, especially as Habermas's ideas have been translated into the work of Forrester and developed into a coherent methodology by Alvesson and Skoldberg (1999). They propose a democratic method of inquiry in which as many potential stakeholders as possible become involved in the research process: it does not just talk to top managers. Not all critical theory follows the democratic imperative that Forrester demands. There is another more elitist vein, which is in many respects closer to Marcuse. We find this where critical theory assumes that it knows what the interests of others "really" are in a way that is better than conventional or orthodox theory. Critical theory seeks to reveal to people what their real interests are, buried behind the facades of both everyday understanding and the normal procedures of orthodox science. Hardly anyone would credit Marxian theory with such powers of revelation any more. It is hard to accept that only certain theoretical positions, such as a favored brand of Marxism, feminism, or whatever, can unlock truth. If research protocols can demonstrate a broader sampling, deeper investigation, and wider theorization, then that will be their source of competitive advantage (Clegg and Hardy, 1996). Increasingly, it is on these empirical grounds that critical theory in organizations and management stands, rather than the claim to a specific theoretical competence (Alvesson and Skoldberg, 1999).

See also *postmodernism; research methods; theory*

Bibliography

Alvesson, M. and Skoldberg, K. (1999). *Reflexive Methodology: New Vistas for Qualitative Research*. London: Sage.
Clegg, S. R. and Hardy, C. (1996). Representations. In S. R. Clegg, C. Hardy, and W. Nord (eds.), *Handbook of Organization Studies*. London: Sage.
Habermas, J. (1984). *The Theory of Communicative Action: Reason and the Rationalization of Society*. Boston, MA: Beacon Press.

Marcuse, H. (1964). *One-Dimensional Man*. London: Routledge and Kegan Paul.

cross-cultural research

P. Christopher Earley

When a researcher examines how organizational forms manifest themselves in different economies or how merit systems operate in individualistic versus collectivistic cultures, what they are really assessing is the generalizability and universality of a given organizational model across multiple, shared systems of meaning, belief, and action (Earley and Singh, 1995). The purpose of such an examination is a more fundamental understanding of organizational phenomena. Uncovering universal and idiosyncratic aspects of management practices is the focus of cross-cultural research.

Earley and Singh (1995) proposed a framework for understanding cross-cultural management based on two dimensions: relevance to international management and relevance to cross-cultural management. The differences between these two dimensions are often attributed to level of analysis, but they argued that the differences can be thought of as examining a whole system versus component elements of a system. They proposed four basic types of research approaches that might classify existing research and guide future work.

First, in a Unitary Form, a researcher is neither concerned with cultural or national systems, nor reductionist from a comparative perspective, and an emphasis is on a phenomenon unique to a single culture, or what Berry (1990) and Earley and Mosakowski (2002) call "emic." By emic, we mean that the emphasis is on understanding a single cultural group or nation on its own terms using its own constructs. Second, in a Gestalt Form, a researcher emphasizes a whole interdependent system rather than breaking it apart. Interpretations of findings from a given cultural or national system must be developed with reference to specifics of the system. Third, in a Reduced Form, a researcher emphasizes breaking down a system into component parts to understand the functioning of processes within the system. Relationships are not interpreted in terms of the overall system; rather, they are interpreted using specific aspects of the system. Fourth, in a Hybrid Form, a researcher uses aspects of both a gestalt and a reduced perspective. Constructs and relationships are assumed to be separable from the system in which they are embedded, but the mapping back onto an existing system may not be simply linear or additive and specific relationships are interpreted using reduced parts of the system.

These approaches to cross-cultural research represent a wide array of styles that researchers may use in their work. Although it is not clear that one style is better than the others, Earley and Singh suggest that the hybrid form is advantageous because it combines positive features of the other forms. This suggestion is echoed in the multiple methods approach described by Brett et al. (1997) and Earley and Mosakowski (2002), as well as Leung and Bond (1989).

See also *culture, national; organizational culture; research methods*

Bibliography

Berry, J. W. (1990). Imposed-etics, emics, and derived-etics: Their conceptual and operational status in cross-cultural psychology. In T. N. Headland, K. L. Pike, and M. Harris (eds.), *Emics and Etics: The Insider/ Outsider Debate*. Newbury Park, CA: Sage Publications.

Brett, J. M., Tinsley, C. H., Janssens, M., Barsness, Z. I., and Lytle, A. L. (1997). New approaches to the study of culture in industrial/organizational psychology. In P. C. Earley and M. Erez (eds.), *New Perspectives in International Industrial/ Organizational Psychology*. San Francisco: New Lexington, 75–129.

Earley, P. C. and Mosakowski, E. (2002). Linking culture and behavior in organizations: Suggestions for theory development and research methodology. In F. Dansereau and F. Yammarino (eds.), *Advances in Cross-Level Organizational Research*. Greenwich, CT: JAI Press.

Earley, P. C. and Singh, H. (1995). International and intercultural research: What's next? *Academy of Management Journal*, 38, 1–14.

Leung, K. and Bond, M. (1989). On the empirical identification of dimensions for cross-cultural comparison. *Journal of Cross-Cultural Psychology*, **20**, 133–51.

culture, national

P. Christopher Earley

A core concept in much of the current work on international aspects of organizational behavior is that of culture (Erez and Earley, 1993). There are a number of ways that researchers have defined culture. A widely accepted definition was proposed by Clyde Kluckhohn, who summarized the anthropologist's definition of culture as "Culture consists in patterned ways of thinking, feeling and reacting, acquired and transmitted mainly by symbols, constituting the distinctive achievements of human groups, including their embodiments in artifacts; the essential core of culture consists of traditional (i.e., historically derived and selected) ideas and especially their attached values."

There are many other commonly applied definitions of culture as well, including Herskovits (1955: 305), who defined culture as the human-made part of the environment, whereas Triandis (1994) and Osgood (1974) define it as a perception of the human-made part of the environment. Definitions vary from a very limited and focused view that culture is a set of shared meaning systems, to a broad and encompassing view that it consists of the untested assumptions of how and why to behave. Hofstede (1991) defines culture as a set of mental programs that control an individual's responses in a given context.

The most general view of culture is that it is some shared set of characteristics in common to a particular group of people. We can view culture as a function of interrelated systems (Erez and Earley, 1993) including the ecology, subsistence, sociocultural, individual, and inter-individual systems. The ecological system refers to the physical environment, resources, and geography of a people. The subsistence system refers to how individuals in a society use ecological resources to survive; namely, how people hunt and fish, gather food, or create industry. The sociocultural system refers to the institutions, norms, roles, and values as they exist around the individual. The individual and inter-individual systems refer to the individual (e.g., motivation, perception, and learning) and social aspects of behavior (e.g., child-rearing, social networks).

There are a variety of influences of culture on the institutional and organizational levels of human endeavor. Culture shapes the type of organizations that evolve and the nature of social structures as they grow and adapt (Hofstede, 1991). Societies shape their collectivities and social aggregates according to the rules implied by culture. Just as a highly individualistic society has a low emphasis on broad, social networks of extended families and friends, their organizations reflect an emphasis on individual reward and action (Triandis, 1994).

See also *cross-cultural research; organisational culture; values*

Bibliography

Erez, M. and Earley, P. C. (1993). *Culture, Self-Identity, and Work*. New York: Oxford University Press.

Herskovits, M. J. (1955). *Cultural Anthropology*. New York: Knopf.

Hofstede, G. (1991). *Culture and Organizations: Software of the Mind*. London: McGraw-Hill.

Osgood, C. E. (1974). Probing subjective cultures: Parts 1 and 2. *Journal of Communication*, **24**, 21–34, 82–100.

Triandis, H. C. (1994). *Culture and Social Behavior*. New York: McGraw-Hill.

D

decentralization

see ORGANIZATIONAL DESIGN

decision-making

Henrich R. Greve

Organizational decision-making occurs when individuals or groups make decisions on behalf of an organization. Decision-making is integral to organized behavior in general, and to managerial work in particular. In organizational theory, decision-making is represented by a bounded rationality branch rooted in the Carnegie School (Cyert and March, 1963), a full rationality branch rooted in economics (*see* RATIONALITY), and a behavioral branch rooted in psychology (Mellers, Schwartz, and Cooke, 1999) (*see* BEHAVIORAL DECISION RESEARCH). In addition, cultural and interpretive perspectives are sometimes applied to decision-making (*see* ORGANIZATIONAL CULTURE).

Decision-making is a problem-solving activity, and the problem to be solved differs depending on the context. Accordingly, theory of decision-making comes in different flavors depending on the number of decision-makers involved and whether multiple decision-makers have shared preferences or conflicts. It also differs depending on whether the procedure for evaluating alternatives is maximization, satisficing, or identity confirmation (March, 1994). Maximization means that each decision-maker seeks to get as much as possible of one or multiple goal variables. It requires clear preferences and knowledge about the consequences of alternatives (at least a probability distribution). Satisficing means that each decision-maker seeks to fulfill target levels of one or multiple goal variables. Like maximizing it is a consequence-driven form of decision-making, but it has weaker requirements of preferences and knowledge. Identity confirmation means that the decision-maker is seeking to fulfill expectations associated with an individual or group role (like a judge, accountant, or doctor). It refers back to rule-like precedence and norms more than forward to consequences of alternatives, though rules may be made in ways that incorporate estimates of consequences.

CONTEXTS

The decision-making procedure may be crossed with the number of decision-makers and extent of conflict to give a matrix of nine decision-making contexts (table 1). Each of these is associated with a body of theoretical and empirical work.

Table 1 Decision-making contexts

	Maximization	*Satisficing*	*Identity*
Individual	rational	boundedly rational	rule
Multiple, shared	team	routine	clan
Multiple, conflict	game	negotiation	enactment

Rational An individual maximizing a goal is the classic rational-behavior context described in the economic theory of choice. Multiple goals are handled by assuming that they can be translated into a single metric of utility, and uncertainty is handled by taking the expectation (which means that the individual is neutral to risk) or by explicitly formulating a risk preference (usually an aversion). Rationality is a procedure for making decisions given a set of preferences and beliefs, and needs to be coupled with assumptions on the preferences and beliefs in order to make predictions. Rational decision-making in management may thus lead to different predictions depending on whether managers are assumed to pursue their own interests or those of the firm. A rational theory of firm decision-making is difficult to construct because the rational decision-maker in economic theory is an individual rather than a collective actor, and Arrow's impossibility theorem shows that the preferences of multiple individuals cannot be combined into a well-behaved collective utility function. Thus the classical theory can only be directly applied to an organization led by an owner-entrepreneur.

Boundedly rational An individual satisficing goals stated as constraints is the boundedly rational context (*see* BOUNDED RATIONAL-ITY). Bounded rationality was launched as an alternative to full rationality, which demands knowledge of all alternatives, all consequences of alternatives, and preferences over the consequences (March, 1994). Individuals lacking this knowledge or ability to integrate it are likely to use goal fulfillment as a shortcut in the decision-making. Satisficing handles multiple goals by setting constraints on each one, and handles risk by positing choices that minimize the risk of falling short of each goal (*see* RISK TAKING). Because the goals can be set by others than the focal decision-maker, such as a board of directors setting goals for a chief executive officer or a manager setting goals for subordinates, bounded rationality is well suited for explaining decision-making within organizational hierarchies. As in rationality, predictions in bounded rationality come from combining the decision-making procedure with knowledge of goals, but researchers from a bounded rationality perspective can often start from knowledge of formal organizational goals when making predictions about managerial behavior.

Rule Whereas rationality is completely selfish and bounded rationality is consequential based on internal or assigned goals, rule-based decision-making is based on norms and roles (*see* ROLE). Rule-based decision-making occurs in contexts where procedural requirements are more important than outcomes. Fairness and due process are important to a judge, accounting standards are important to an accountant, and treatment of illness is important to a doctor. Making convictions, approving financial statements, and curing patients are results of these procedures rather than goals to be maximized. The question of what consequences the decisions have is lifted up to the system in which the rules are decided or allowed to evolve. Rules are used in many jobs, but professionals working in organizations are particularly frequent rule users whose behaviors tend to standardize decisions across organizations. Because organizations contain both explicitly stated formal rules and informal rules, researchers from a rule-based perspective investigate the extent to which formal rule systems are elaborated and control behavior, and also whether deviations from the rule-specified behavior are sufficiently systematic to indicate that informal rules are in use.

Team Rational individuals with a shared goal differ from a single individual with the same goal when they hold different information and communication is costly. Team theory is about how individuals can predetermine work procedures such that they generate the best possible outcome based on all possible future information they may receive. The original team theory specified procedures for making rational decisions on how to coordinate joint production, and has been overshadowed in economics by game theory, which assumes conflicting interests. Its principles are still in use when designing systems for optimal multi-person decision-making, as in many applications of operations research.

Routine Boundedly rational individuals with shared preferences cannot specify the optimal reaction to all contingencies in advance, and instead develop routines through learning from experience. The quality of the routines becomes a function of the extent of experimentation, the form of feedback, and the reaction to feedback (Levitt and March, 1988). This learning process underlies important phenomena such as the learning curve in production (Argote, 1999), which is a result of teams of boundedly rational workers making decisions to modify routines in the production process. Managerial routines for decision-making include budgeting cycles and periodic strategy reviews, which specify the timing and participation of certain decisions. Routines related to production and support functions potentially encompass every repeated behavior in organizations, especially when considering that a routine can have a complex structure including selection of subroutines depending on information obtained during execution.

Clan   Organizations where strong and shared identities guide the decision-making may be called clans (Ouchi, 1980). Such organizations rely on norms just as role-based decision-making does, and are capable of group decision-making because of interpersonal consistency of norms. The main forms of clans are ideological organizations, in which individual identities are submerged in the organizational identity, and organizations dominated by a single profession, in which individuals have few organizational constraints on acting according to the professional identity (*see* PROFESSIONAL SERVICE FIRMS).

Game   Rational actors making decisions in a situation with conflicting preferences can be analyzed using GAME THEORY, which predicts the joint decisions a set of rational and selfish actors will make in a given reward structure. AGENCY THEORY applies game theory to problems of delegated decision-making in organizations to discover which reward and monitoring mechanisms a manager can use to make subordinates implement instructions in spite of private incentives to choose other actions (Milgrom and Roberts, 1992) (*see* INCENTIVES). It has led to significant research on how the composition of boards of directors affects organizational governance, including CEO replacement and strategic changes, and organizational performance.

Negotiation   Group decision-making by boundedly rational actors with conflicting preferences is a major topic in social psychology. The focus is less on different preferences, as in game theory, and more on disagreements about the correct course of action for the organization. Much work has examined whether the decisions reach the center of the preference distribution or are drawn away from it by vocal minorities, on the one hand, or dominance by the majority, on the other hand (*see* GROUP DECISION-MAKING; GROUPTHINK). This theory has been applied to decision-making in management teams and boards of directors through work on how diversity affects the quality of decisions. There is also work on coalition building that examines how managers may use political techniques such as logrolling (trading of concessions across decisions) to form majorities in contentious decision-making situations (March, 1994) (*see* POLITICS).

Enactment   Identity-based   decision-making with conflicting interests is found in multi-profession organizations such as hospitals. The conflict stems from how professions make competing claims of autonomy and decision-making rights, often coupled with status competition. These claims are resolved through enactment processes where different-profession individuals interact with each other and with task characteristics, and the conflict makes the resolution process complex and lengthy (Barley, 1986) (*see* ENACTMENT).

FINDINGS

Research on organizational decision-making has been particularly active and successful in investigating how routines are modified over time and affect organizational decisions. Significant progress has been made in the areas of (1) risk taking, (2) performance feedback, (3) rules, (4), momentum, and (5) social influence.

Risk taking by boundedly rational individuals has been an active research tradition for some time, and has tested hypotheses from PROSPECT THEORY. Extensions of this work to organizational decision-making have shown that managers take more risks following low performance and reduce it following high performance (Shapira, 1994). The increased risk taking after low performance often leads to losses, leading to the risk-return paradox of firms that take high risk having low financial returns on average. This is a paradox according to rational investment theory, which predicts that managers will demand high expected returns in order to take high risks (Nickel and Rodriguez, 2002).

Following a similar argument, performance feedback theory predicts that managers are likely to make major organizational changes if the performance falls below expectations (Cyert and March, 1963). Firms make more market niche changes, innovations, and investments following low performance (Greve, 2003), as predicted, showing that managers make changes in order to solve problems rather than to pursue opportunities. This pattern of change offers opportunities for firms to catch up with the competition, but also involves the risk of further losses. Conversely, the conservativeness of successful firms is often helpful in stable environments, but prevents adaptation when major environmental changes suggest a need for strategic changes (Audia, Locke, and Smith, 2000). Change and inertia are both risky, and the managerial dilemma is to determine which offers better risk/return relations in a given situation.

Organizational rules can be viewed as formalized decision-making routines that predetermine how the organization will respond to given situations. Rules evolve in competition with other rules, as a given problem area has limited capacity for rules, and rules are also results of external pressures on the organization (March, Schulz, and Zhou, 2000). Rule research suggests that organizational decision-making is strongly conditioned by history, and especially by periods of environmental pressure. Rule systems summarize and store organizational knowledge, and evolve when organizational participants encounter problems whose solutions result in new knowledge that can be formalized through rule addition, rule change, or rule deletion.

Even in the absence of formal rules, organizational learning through precedence, interpretation of past actions, and an incremental approach to making changes causes organizations to repeat and extend major decisions. This tendency is a form of decision-making momentum (Amburgey and Miner, 1992).

Momentum is especially influential when managers select from a wide range of possible responses, as it causes repetition of responses that are still prominent in the organizational memory.

While momentum occurs because of influence from the organization's own past, social influence from other organizations also affects organizational decision-making. The impact is particularly strong in visible actions such as adoption of new structures, technologies, and strategies. Organizational behaviors that catch the attention of decision-makers spread easily through social influence, leading to diffusion of novel organizational structures or routines (such as total quality management, personnel departments, and golden parachutes), entry into new market niches, acquisitions, and adoption of new technologies (Strang and Soule, 1998). Social influence in decision-making is selective because managers appear to favor imitation of prominent organizations or organizations similar to their own, and managers appear to avoid imitation that would intensify competitive relations.

QUESTIONS

Some unanswered questions on decision-making appear ripe for further exploration. First, organizational decision-making is done by individuals, often working in groups, in an organizational structure that includes authority relations, informal social networks, rules, and routines for information collection and decision-making. Clearly, it is important to understand how individuals make decisions in given situations, but it is also important to understand how the organizational structure influences which situations individuals are faced with. This problem is not addressed by research on group decision-making, because groups operate under a layer of organizational rules and routines that affects whether a group will meet to make decisions and what the agenda and information of the group will be. The interaction of individual behaviors and organizational context is staggeringly complex and has led to a split between theory focusing on individuals or groups, and theory focusing on the organization. This is done for analytical convenience and usually without claiming that one level of analysis trumps the other. This analytical separation leaves much room for developing theory integrating causal mechanisms at multiple levels. Investigation of organizational routines for creating decision-making occasions and providing information to decision-makers is an important research topic with potential for integrating individual and organization level research on decision-making.

Second, much work on bounded rationality in individual or multi-person contexts is motivated by an immediate concern for examining when boundedly rational decision-making gives adaptive results and an ultimate concern for improving decision-making rules. An important tool is simulation of the rewards to empirically observed decision-making rules under given environmental conditions. Problems in making and interpreting simulations include specification of realistic decision-making rules and calibration of the parameters that guide them, and specification of realistic reward rules from the environment. As empirical work progresses on the types of decision rules used in organizations and the usual environmental responses to decisions, model construction can get a stronger empirical foundation. Currently, it is difficult to simulate the effect of organizational change on performance because the empirical literature has not reached a firm answer on whether there is a penalty for changing organizations.

Third, disproportionate attention appears to have been given to evaluation and selection of alternatives, with less work on the generation of alternatives. How decision-makers search for alternatives from existing organizational or societal repertoires or construct new alternatives is a question that currently has seen so little empirical attention that it calls for more work. Research on the generation of alternatives might explore the question of when managers focus on internally generated alternatives versus externally generated alternatives such as innovations that spread through the population of organizations. Such work might integrate the research on organizational learning from own experience and organizational learning through social influence among organizations.

In addition to these three major unexplored questions, much work also remains in the five active areas of research noted above. The findings so far indicate strong effects of satisficing procedures in organizational decision-making, and further work will no doubt uncover the mechanisms in greater detail. The three identity-based decision-making contexts have also yielded interesting findings, and deserve further investigation. Organizational decision-making has fundamental theoretical interest and high practical importance, and researchers have taken notice of this.

See also *group decision-making; nominal group technique*

Bibliography

Amburgey, T. L. and Miner, A. S. (1992). Strategic momentum: The effects of repetitive, positional, and contextual momentum on merger activity. *Strategic Management Journal*, 13, 335–48.

Argote, L. (1999). *Organizational Learning: Creating, Retaining, and Transferring Knowledge*. Boston, MA: Kluwer Academic Publishers.

Audia, P. G., Locke, E. A., and Smith, K. G. (2000). The paradox of success: An archival and a laboratory study of strategic persistence following a radical environmental change. *Academy of Management Journal*, 43, 837–53.

Barley, S. R. (1986). Technology as an occasion for restructuring: Evidence from observations of CT scanners and social order of radiology departments. *Administrative Science Quarterly*, 31, 24–60.

Cyert, R. M. and March, J. G. (1963). *The Behavioral Theory of the Firm*. Englewood Cliffs, NJ: Prentice-Hall.

Davis, J. H. (1992). Some compelling intuitions about group consensus decisions, theoretical and empirical research, and interpersonal aggregation phenomena: Selected examples, 1950–1990. *Organizational Behavior and Human Decision Processes*, 52, 3–38.

Greve, H. R. (2003). *Organizational Learning from Performance Feedback: A Behavioral Perspective on Innovation and Change*. Cambridge: Cambridge University Press.

Levitt, B. and March, J. G. (1988). Organizational learning. *Annual Review of Sociology*, 14, 319–40.

March, J. G. (1994). *A Primer on Decision-Making: How Decisions Happen*. New York: Free Press.

March, J. G., Schulz, M., and Zhou, X. (2000). *The Dynamics of Rules: Change in Written Organizational Codes*. Stanford, CA: Stanford University Press.

Mellers, B. A., Schwartz, A., and Cooke, A. D. J. (1999). Judgment and decision-making. *Annual Review of Psychology*, 49, 447–77.

Milgrom, P. and Roberts, J. (1992). *Economics, Organization, and Management*. Englewood Cliffs, NJ: Prentice-Hall.

Nickel, M. N. and Rodriguez, M. C. (2002). A review of research on the negative accounting relationship between risk and return: Bowman's paradox. *Omega*, **30**, 1–18.

Ouchi, W. (1980). Markets, bureaucracies, and clans. *Administrative Science Quarterly*, **25**, 129–41.

Shapira, Z. (1994). *Risk Taking*. New York: Russel Sage.

Strang, D. and Soule, S. A. (1998). Diffusion in organizations and social movements: From hybrid corn to poison pills. *Annual Review of Sociology*, **24**, 265–90.

delayering

see ORGANIZATIONAL CHANGE

Delphi

Randall S. Schuler

The Delphi group format continues to be an important technique by which a wide array of expert opinion can be generated to maximize the range of alternative solutions to issues and problems (Sahakian, 1997). In the Delphi group format for DECISION-MAKING, invited experts typically respond to questionnaires about issues and problems, which are then used to generate multiple expert opinions, without the need for face-to-face contact. Of course, the lack of face-to-face contact reduces the possibility of interactive discussion and challenge, but Delphi groups can be adapted to enable the experts to react to a second round of opinion, in response to the expert input from the first round (Rowe and Wright, 1999).

The Delphi group technique for GROUP DECISION-MAKING was originally developed by the Rand Corporation for the US Air Force in the 1950s. It has since been adapted in business organizations as an effective alternative to traditional methods of decision-making, especially in relation to complex and long-term issues, problems, and concerns.

The Delphi group technique for decision-making continues to serve business and governmental organizations alike in a way that other

similar techniques, such as the nominal group, are unable to. These other techniques, however, should not be thought of as competing alternatives, but rather as complementary alternatives.

See also *brainstorming; creativity; innovation; nominal group technique*

Bibliography

Rowe, G. and Wright, G. (1999). The Delphi technique as a forecasting tool: Issues and analysis. *International Journal of Forecasting*, **15** (4), 353–75.

Sahakian, C. E. (1997). *The Delphi Method*. Skokie, IL: Corporate Partnering Institute.

density

see COMMUNITY ECOLOGY; ORGANIZATIONAL ECOLOGY

departmentalization

see ORGANIZATIONAL DESIGN; ORGANIZATIONAL STRUCTURE

derailment

see EXECUTIVE DERAILMENT

deskilling

see JOB DESKILLING

deviance

Jerald Greenberg

In the workplace, deviance refers to a type of behavior by members of organizations that is enacted with the intent of harming either other individuals in the organization or the legitimate interests of the organization itself. Over a dozen concepts that are either highly similar or identical in meaning have been identified since the late 1990s (for reviews, see Bennett and Robinson, 2003; Robinson and Greenberg, 1998; Vardi and Weitz, 2003), the most popular of which are antisocial behavior, counterproductive work behavior, and organizational misbehavior. However labeled, workplace deviance costs businesses around the world untold billions of dollars due both to direct causes (e.g., theft of cash) and indirect causes (e.g., lost productivity due to absenteeism) (see statistics in Bennett and Robinson, 2003).

Gruys and Sackett (2003) have identified 11 major forms of deviant behavior: theft of cash or property, destruction of property, misuse of information, wasting time and other resources, unsafe behavior, intentionally poor attendance, intentionally substandard work, alcohol use on the job, drug use on the job, inappropriate verbal actions, and inappropriate physical actions. These researchers also examined the extent to which these forms of deviance co-occur within work samples. Using multidimensional scaling, they found that co-occurrence was strong to the extent that the behaviors were similar along each of two dimensions: individuals versus organizations as targets of harm, and the extent to which the behavior is performed on or off the job. So, for example, misuse of time and poor attendance tended to co-occur because they are both organizationally focused, and inappropriate physical actions and inappropriate verbal actions tended to co-occur because both took place on the job (as opposed to abusing drug and alcohol, which occurred predominantly off the job).

Another orientation to identifying the underlying dimensions of deviance is the perceptual approach taken by Robinson and Bennett (1995). These researchers used multidimensional scaling to assess people's perceptions of the similarity between various forms of deviance. Like Gruys and Sackett (2003), they found a distinction between organizational and individual targets of deviance. However, unlike Gruys and Sackett (2003), Robinson and Bennett's second dimension was the degree of seriousness of the action. Further evidence for the construct validity of the Robinson and Bennett (1995) taxonomy was provided by Bennett and Robinson (2003).

Researchers have paid considerable attention to the antecedents of deviant behavior in the hope of curtailing the behavior by eliminating the antecedents, or at least minimizing their impact. One class of antecedents is experiential in nature, focusing on events that trigger deviant behavior. Among the most popularly studied have been aggressive behaviors brought on by events that thwart people's efforts to attain goals and acts of theft undertaken in an effort to restore justice among workers who believe themselves to be underpaid (Greenberg, 1990). Researchers also have found that one of the most prominent experiences that trigger deviant behavior comes from the social comparisons workers make with others in the workplace – that is, workers tend to model the deviant behavior of their workmates (Robinson and O'Leary-Kelly, 1998).

A second class of antecedents focuses on PERSONALITY variables that are predictive of deviant behavior. Research exploring this possibility has met with mixed results (Robinson and Greenberg, 1998), as no clear personality profile has emerged of the person likely to commit deviant behavior in the workplace. However, because efforts to predict deviant behavior from standard psychological measures of personality are becoming more widespread (e.g., Hakstain, Farrell, and Tweed, 2002), there is reason to believe that reliable constellations of personality based predictors will be discovered.

A formidable problem in predicting deviant behavior involves measuring such acts in the first place. After all, because many deviant acts are conducted in private, they are difficult to observe (a state of affairs which Gruys and Sackett (2003) refer to as this field's "Achilles heel"). And because they are socially undesirable in nature, the validity of self-reports using standard self-report measures is open to question. To get around these limitations researchers studying workplace deviance have resorted to using special techniques. First, when available, company records have proven to be invaluable measures of deviant behavior (such as used by Greenberg (1990) in his field experiment on employee theft, which relied on records of inventory shrinkage). Second, to enhance the validity of self-report, paper-and-pencil measures of deviance by reducing fears of disclosure, some researchers (e.g., Bennett and Robinson, 2003) have relied on anonymous mail-in surveys from the general population. Still other researchers have relied on various masked-response questionnaires, such as the unmatched block technique and the unmatched count technique (for a review, see Robinson and Greenberg, 1998). Bennett and Robinson (2003) have identified several research methods that hold promise for future research on workplace deviance. These include event sampling, computer and video monitoring (despite potential ethical questions), reports of critical incidents, and policy capturing.

Recently, several large-scale survey studies have linked deviant behavior to other forms of voluntary behavior that occurs in the workplace, such as ORGANIZATIONAL CITIZENSHIP BEHAVIOR (OCB; for a review, see Sackett, 2002). In all studies, very strong negative correlations were found between deviant behavior and positive forms of organizational citizenship (e.g., helping a co-worker in need). In a newly proposed theory, Spector and Fox (2002) introduced a model integrating both of these forms of behavior by describing the environmental and personal factors that lead to positive behavior (OCB) or negative behavior (deviant acts) through the mediating processes of perception and emotion. This work is typical of emerging efforts in this field to examine the processes underlying the occurrence of deviant behavior.

Because it has begun to mature, research on workplace deviance is rapidly approaching the point at which scientific knowledge can be used as the basis for making informed decisions about how to control deviant behavior. Lacking, however, have been systematic, long-term studies assessing the impact of interventions aimed at minimizing deviance. Such efforts would not only make it possible to offer more accurate practical advice about controlling deviance, but also promise to shed light on the theoretical bases underlying such behavior.

See also *absenteeism*

Bibliography

Bennett, R. J. and Robinson, S. L. (2003). The past, present, and future of workplace deviance research. In J. Greenberg (ed.), *Organizational Behavior: The State of the Science*. Mahwah, NJ: Lawrence Erlbaum Associates, 247–81.

Greenberg, J. (1990). Employee theft as a reaction to underpayment inequity: The hidden cost of pay cuts. *Journal of Applied Psychology*, 75, 561–8.

Gruys, M. J. and Sackett, P. R. (2003). Investigating the dimensionality of counterproductive work behavior. *International Journal of Selection and Assessment*, 11, 30–42.

Hakstain, A. R., Farrell, S., and Tweed, R. G. (2002). The assessment of counterproductive tendencies by means of the California Psychological Inventory. *International Journal of Selection and Assessment*, 10, 58–86.

Robinson, S. L. and Bennett, R. J. (1995). A typology of deviant workplace behaviors: A multidimensional scaling study. *Academy of Management Journal*, 38, 555–72.

Robinson, S. L. and Greenberg, J. (1998). Employees behaving badly: Dimensions, determinants, and dilemmas in the study of workplace deviance. In C. L. Cooper and D. M. Rousseau (eds.), *Trends in Organizational Behavior*, Vol. 5. New York: Wiley, 1–30.

Robinson, S. L. and O'Leary-Kelly, A. (1998). Monkey see, monkey do: The influence of work groups on the antisocial behavior of employees. *Academy of Management Journal*, 41, 658–72.

Sackett, P. R. (2002). The structure of counterproductive work behaviors: Dimensionality and relationships with facets of job performance. *International Journal of Selection and Assessment*, 10, 5–11.

Spector, P. E. and Fox, S. (2002). An emotion-centered model of voluntary work behaviors: Some parallels between counterproductive work behavior (CWB) and organizational citizenship behavior. *Human Resources Management Review*, 12, 269–92.

Vardi, Y. and Weitz, E. (2003). *Misbehavior in Organizations: Theory, Research, and Management*. Mahwah, NJ: Lawrence Erlbaum Associates.

discretion

see JOB DESIGN

discrimination

Stella M. Nkomo

This concept can be generally defined as any behavior that denies persons certain rights because they belong to specific groups. It includes verbal and non-verbal acts, whether intended or unintended. Most theorists distinguish between discrimination at the individual level and at the institutional level (Dovidio et al., 1996). The former refers to actions carried out by individuals based on negative attitudes (for example, a manager who will not hire women for middle management positions because of a belief that women are less competent than men). Institutional discrimination pertains to institutional norms, practices, and policies that help to create or perpetuate sets of advantages or privileges for dominant group members and to the exclusion or unequal access of subordinate groups.

Institutions can produce discriminatory consequences intentionally or unintentionally. For example, job seniority practices implemented during a recession can yield negative consequences for minority employees who have lower seniority because of their historical exclusion from certain jobs. Institutional procedures such as hiring and promotion and evaluation are central features of institutional discrimination. The distinction between institutional discrimination and individual discrimination is problematic. First, it is important to point out that some scholars in the field argue that the term discrimination should not be used in lieu of terms like racism or sexism (*see* GENDER) because it underrates the significance of IDEOLOGY in the way systems of domination are structured in society (Essed, 1991; Back and Solomos, 2000). Second, the concept of individual discrimination detaches the individual from the institutions in which rules, procedures, and policies flourish.

Theories of discrimination are centered upon explaining its continued persistence. Most of these theories can be classified as order theories, person-centered theories, or power-conflict and structural theories (Farley, 1995). Order theories tend to accent assimilation and concentrate on the progressive assimilation of subordinate groups into the dominant culture. As groups are assimilated, they should experience less discrimination. Person-centered theories focus on the argument that there are real differences between majority group members and subordinate group members and these differences explain the differential treatment of each group. A corollary strand of person-centered theories is that discrimination is largely a function of prejudiced behavior of individuals (*see* PREJUDICE). In contrast, power-conflict theories place emphasis

upon economic stratification, structural and power issues, and patriarchy in maintaining systems of domination (*see* CRITICAL THEORY). Prominent among these latter groups of theories are class-based theories, feminist theories, and Marxist and neo-Marxist theories. These theories suggest the need to examine the policies and practices in social systems or in organizations, which create and perpetuate systemic barriers for certain groups.

Since the passage of extensive civil rights and equal employment legislation in many countries, the concept of institutional discrimination has developed largely as a technical notion, particularly in the United States. Two theories of discrimination growing out of this legislation, disparate impact and disparate treatment, have heavily informed the way discrimination has been studied in organizational behavior and personnel psychology. Disparate treatment theory holds that discrimination occurs when those belonging to a protected category (women, racial minorities, the disabled, etc.) are in some way intentionally treated differently regarding employment practices (for example, rejecting women applicants of childbearing age for certain jobs). Under disparate impact theory, facially neutral employment practices (e.g., standardized tests, height and weight requirements) which have an adverse impact on members of a protected group may constitute discrimination if they cannot be shown to be job related and essential to the organization's operations.

Much organizational research on discrimination has involved a search for objective and quantifiable evidence of discrimination in staffing, selection predictors, performance evaluation ratings, compensation, and promotion (*see* PERFORMANCE APPRAISAL/MANAGEMENT). Race and sex discrimination have garnered the most attention, although more research is appearing on age and disability discrimination (Duncan and Loretto, 2004). The results across studies on race and sex discrimination are often inconsistent, with some studies reporting discriminatory effects and others finding none. The failure to find consistent results may be a function of methodological inadequacies, ranging from an over-reliance on laboratory studies to underdeveloped theoretical frames and weak measures (*see* RESEARCH METHODS;

RESEARCH DESIGN). Additionally, the subtle nature of modern discrimination may also contribute to the mixed results.

The literature on discrimination in organizations suggests that considerable progress has been made to address discriminatory barriers to job entry for women and minorities. Yet current research reports that subtle discrimination influences their chances for upward mobility, where they encounter "glass ceiling" effects on their careers (Bell and Nkomo, 2001; Burke and Nelson, 2002) (see WOMEN AT WORK; WOMEN MANAGERS; CAREER DEVELOPMENT). For instance, women and minorities have less access to many informal networks in organizations and still suffer from the effects of solo and token status (Ibarra, 1993).

The persistence of discrimination in organizational settings suggests that it is no longer adequate to study discrimination as though it were purely a technical question or solely the product of attitudes, stereotypes, or interpersonal relations. Some scholars have called for more attention to research that explores the phenomenology of discrimination in organizations. Understanding the process of discrimination and structural properties of exclusion is important for changing organizational policies and practices operating to the detriment of some groups (Cockburn, 1991; Maier, 1999). An approach that combines micro and macro influences is needed. In the case of discrimination based on race, Essed (1991) introduced the concept of everyday racism to capture the structural-cultural properties of racial discrimination as well as the micro-inequities that perpetuate the system.

See also gender; intergroup relations; women at work; women managers

Bibliography

Back, L. and Solomos, J. (eds.) (2000). *Theories of Race and Racism*. New York: Routledge.

Bell, E. and Nkomo, S. M. (2001). *Our Separate Ways: Black and White Women and the Struggle for Professional Identity*. Boston, MA: Harvard Business School Press.

Burke, R. and Nelson, D. L. (2002). *Advancing Women's Careers*. Oxford: Blackwell.

Cockburn, C. (1991). *In the Way of Women*. London: Macmillan.

Dovidio, J. F., Brigham, J. C., Johnson, T. T., and Gaertner, S. L. (1996). Stereotyping, prejudice, and discrimination: Another look. In N. Macrae, C. Stangor, and M. Hewstone (eds.), *Stereotypes and Stereotyping*. New York: Guilford Press, 276–319.

Duncan, C. and Loretto, W. (2004). Never the right age? Gender and age-based discrimination in employment. *Gender, Work and Organization*, 11, 95–116.

Essed, P. (1991). *Everyday Racism: An Interdisciplinary Theory*. Newbury Park, CA: Sage.

Farley, J. (1995). *Majority–Minority Relations*. Englewood Cliffs, NJ: Prentice-Hall.

Ibarra, H. (1993). Personal networks of women and minorities in management. *Academy of Management Review*, 18, 56–87.

Maier, M. (1999). On the gendered substructure of organizations: Dimensions and dilemmas of corporate masculinity. In G. N. Powell (ed.), *Handbook of Gender and Work*. Thousand Oaks, CA: Sage, 69–94.

distributive justice

see JUSTICE, DISTRIBUTIVE

diversity management

Susan E. Jackson

The phrase "management of diversity" refers to practices aimed at improving the effectiveness with which organizations utilize diverse human resources (Ashkanasy, Hartel, and Dass, 2002). In the era when mass production methods dominated business activity, many organizations managed diversity simply by avoiding it. Product specialization helped keep costs low, a function-based organizational form was almost universal, and the employees in most organizations all looked much alike; often those employees who were in the minority (for example, in terms of ethnicity or gender) worked together in occupational groups that were segregated from majority employees in the company. Nowadays many mass product markets have been replaced by smaller more precisely defined specialty consumer markets, while large businesses operate in multiple niches. The latter case often means that distinctly different business units – each with its own unique structure, strategy, management processes, and organizational subculture – must synergistically coexist under one corporate roof. At the same time, the diversity of human resources within organizations is increasing. Due to changing workforce demographics, globalization, and a desire to employ people who reflect their customer base, organizations in many countries are becoming more diverse in terms of gender, race, ethnicity, religion, national origin, AGE, and many other personal characteristics. In modern organizations around the world, managers need to embrace diversity to insure business success.

THE NATURE OF DIVERSITY IN ORGANIZATIONS

Demographic and cultural diversity are two important types of diversity in modern organizations. Throughout the world, women are entering the workforce in growing numbers, with men and women increasingly found working side-by-side (see GENDER; WOMEN MANAGERS; WOMEN AT WORK). In some countries, age diversity is also increasing, as declining rates of population growth push employers to hire older employees to work alongside the younger intakes. As organizations allow the higher education of younger employees to substitute for the job experience that previous cohorts of employees had to accrue in order to be promoted, relatively young employees are found more often in higher level jobs. Ethnic and cultural diversity also are increasingly important. For example, in the US, approximately 10 percent of the total workforce immigrated from other countries, and approximately 15 percent of all new workforce entrants are immigrants. In many European countries, ethnic and cultural diversity are increasing due to the consolidation of economic markets and related changes in immigration and employment policies. Throughout the world, managing cultural diversity has become essential as corporations have expanded their operations into foreign countries and/or developed strategic alliances with foreign-owned firms.

Managing diversity is important even in organizations where the workforce has not become more demographically and/or culturally diverse because many organizations are utilizing WORK GROUPS/TEAMS to pursue new business strategies. These often bring together employees from previously segregated areas of the company, creating occupational and knowledge-based diversity. Teams may also bring together employees from two or more organizations. For example, manufacturers may include their suppliers and end users as part of a product design team. Such teams must develop a mode of operating that fits with the differing organizational cultures in which the subunits are embedded.

THE CONTENT AND STRUCTURE OF DIVERSITY

Individual attributes such as gender, age, religion, and occupational background reflect the *content* of diversity; in contrast, the configuration of attributes within a social unit reflects the *structure* of diversity. Concepts to capture the structure of diversity differ across levels of analysis: for dyads it is interpersonal (dis)similarity, for small groups it is relational demography and team diversity, and for larger entities it is ORGANIZATIONAL DEMOGRAPHY. At the team and organizational levels, attention has focused on such issues as the inclusion of demographic "token" or "solo" members, the presence of small minority factions, and bipolar team composition (where there are two equal-size coalitions). Such configurations can be particularly influential in affecting GROUP DYNAMICS (see also COALITION FORMATION; MINORITY GROUP INFLUENCE; GROUP DECISION-MAKING).

CONSEQUENCES OF DIVERSITY

Workplace diversity has many short-term and longer-term consequences for employees and employers, some positive and others negative. Detailed reviews of relevant research (e.g., Jackson, May, and Whitney, 1995; Jackson, Joshi and Erhardt, 2003; Milliken and Martins, 1996) indicate that the consequences of diversity depend on its content, its structure, and the organizational context. For example, the amount and type of stereotyping and bias that people engage in depends on the composition of a group. When two clear factions are present, stereotyping, bias, and CONFLICT will be greater than when the group is homogeneous or when there are so many differences present that there are no clear subgroups. Furthermore, demographic (e.g., age, sex, ethnicity) diversity is often associated with interpersonal conflict and may interfere with COMMUNICATIONS and stimulate employee TURNOVER. On the other hand, diversity with respect to task-related cognitions is likely to improve the quality and CREATIVITY of a group's decision-making processes, reduce GROUPTHINK, and improve an organization's ability to adapt quickly to a changing environment.

MANAGEMENT IMPLICATIONS

No single theory explains the full set of beneficial and detrimental effects of diversity in work organizations and this makes it difficult to develop effective means for managing diversity. Nevertheless, in recognition of the growing importance of the topic, many large and prominent firms began to implement "managing diversity" initiatives during the late 1980s. Such initiatives have proliferated since then and are now a major human resource management activity.

Table 1 describes several of the approaches used by employers as they strive to manage diversity more effectively. These programs often are implemented in organizations that have already been proactive in their attempts to reduce DISCRIMINATION and provide equal opportunities to a broad array of employees. They are also found in some organizations with large numbers of expatriates working abroad. Ultimately, the best approach to managing diversity will depend on the types of diversity present in an organization and the outcomes of most concern to the organization. Therefore, those who wish to improve the ability of an organization to manage diversity effectively need to develop a comprehensive approach tailored to their specific situation. It is impossible to prescribe interventions that will be universally acceptable, but organizations that have been successful in their efforts to effectively manage diversity appear to use the following principles to guide the process of ORGANIZATIONAL CHANGE (for several case descriptions, see Jackson and Associates, 1992; for more general discussions of how organizations are approaching the management of diversity, see Cox, 1993; Carr-Ruffina, 1999).

Diagnosis Before launching diversity initiatives such as these, managers should study their organizations to understand the nature of diversity present, and they should evaluate current practices to understand whether any of them have unintended negative consequences for employees from diverse backgrounds. Questions to be answered include: What are the backgrounds of people in the organization and how

Table 1 Initiatives used for the management of diversity

Diversity awareness training: Provides accurate information about subcultures present in the organization and educates employees about the negative consequences of stereotypes.

Harassment training: Educates employees about the meaning of harassment and the actions the company will take when someone complains of being harassed.

Teamwork training: Builds relationships among diverse employees and improves the team's ability to leverage their diversity.

Caucus groups (also called network or affinity groups): Employees with common backgrounds and interests (e.g., based on gender, ethnicity, sexual orientation, disability, area of expertise) sponsor activities such as training workshops, conferences, and mentoring programs for their members.

Succession planning: Insures that employees from all backgrounds are identified, developed, and given equal opportunity to assume leadership roles in the company. May involve setting numerical targets that specify the percentages of men and women, ethnic groups, people with disabilities, and so on, to be hired and promoted into each major job category.

Work–family balance programs: Designed to support the diverse family responsibilities of employees. Common initiatives include alternative work schedules such as job sharing, flextime, and compressed workweeks, childcare and elder care resources and referral services, adoption assistance, and employee counseling.

Community outreach and development: Includes a variety of community activities intended to benefit people other than the company's current employees. Examples include science education days for young school children to combat early occupational stereotyping, and partnerships with schools to provide academic counseling, part-time employment, mentoring, and tutoring for at-risk students (who often are ethnic minorities).

is diversity distributed throughout the organization? Do people from diverse backgrounds work closely together, or are they segregated into homogeneous subgroups based on occupations, hierarchical levels, or geographic locations? How do the backgrounds of people relate to their attitudes and behaviors? Do subgroups of employees report different degrees of satisfaction with their co-workers or the supervision they receive? Are turnover patterns different among different groups of employees? Does career mobility appear to differ across subgroups? Do diverse work teams perform the same as (or better or worse than) homogeneous teams? In order to design initiatives that fit their organizational circumstances, and subsequently evaluate the effectiveness of those initiatives, managers must first develop a sophisticated understanding of how diversity influences employees and work groups within the organization.

Objectives   The next task is to set objectives and prioritize the dimensions of diversity that are important for the organization to address. These objectives might include meeting social and legal responsibilities, attracting and retaining a qualified workforce, facilitating teamwork, creating synergy between dispersed and diverse work units, and spanning the boundary between the organization and its markets (*see* BOUNDARY SPANNING). Which objectives are top priorities for an organization will influence the types of diversity that must be managed and the types of initiatives likely to be most useful.

Design interventions that fit the situation   To be effective, new initiatives require buy-in from all relevant constituents, who include those who are targeted as the direct users (e.g., those attending a workshop) as well as those in a position to encourage the direct customers' use of a service (e.g., managers and supervisors of the users). Involving constituents in the design of diversity interventions is one way to increase their support during the change process.

Hold managers accountable   When an organization offers a new product (good or service) in the marketplace, it almost always uses one or more numerical indicators to measure its success. This plays a part in determining managers' raises, bonuses, and promotions. When the development and sale of a product is successful, the people who contributed to that success often are recognized and rewarded. It is possible to apply these same principles to the introduction of diversity-related changes. Organizations that have done so say it seems to pay off. Research shows that the success of diversity training initiatives is greater in organizations that evaluate the effectiveness of the training and in those that offer rewards to managers who make diversity-related improvements in their business units.

Anticipate challenges   Any organizational change effort can run into unanticipated problems, and diversity programs are no exception. Cultural awareness training programs may backfire if they seem to reinforce stereotypes or highlight cultural differences that employees have tried to erase in order to fit into the company's culture. Special skill-building programs offered only to some subgroups also can feed negative stereotyping, or they may be viewed as showing the target group an unfair advantage. Employees assigned to work in markets that match their cultural backgrounds may view that as limiting the contributions that they can make. Staffing plans that include targets for promoting employees from various backgrounds may create a stigma for those targeted to benefit, with the result that qualified people are presumed to have acquired their positions because of their demographic attributes rather than on the basis of merit. Caucus or networking groups may lead to increased segregation and fragmentation. Ultimately, managing diversity successfully involves developing a strong organizational culture that values cultural differences and insures that the talents of all employees are used to their fullest extent. Implementing the variety of changes that may be needed to manage diversity more effectively will take many years in most organizations.

CONCLUSION

Diversity is a complex and potentially "hot" issue. Although there are few generalizations about what are the most effective ways to manage diversity within organizations, it is clear that almost all organizations must learn to do so. As is true for most strategic issues, the most effective method is a learn-as-you-go approach that fits their unique situation. Inevitably, the learning process will be challenging at times, as change agents, supervisors, subordinates, and co-workers realize the need for changes within themselves, in their organization's culture, and in the basic human resource management systems of the organization.

See also *cross-cultural research; culture, national; individual differences*

Bibliography

Ashkanasy, N. M., Hartel, C. E. J., and Dass, C. S. (2002). Diversity and emotion: The new frontiers in organizational behavior research. *Journal of Management*, 28, 307–38.
Carr-Ruffina, N. (1999). *Diversity Success Strategies*. Concord, MA: Butterworth-Heinemann.
Cox, T. H. (1993). *Cultural Diversity in Organizations*. San Francisco: Berrett-Koehler.
Hofstede, G. (1991). *Cultures and Organizations: Software of the Mind*. London: McGraw-Hill.
Jackson, S. E. and Associates (1992). *Diversity in the Workplace: Human Resources Initiatives*. New York: Guilford Press.
Jackson, S. E., Joshi, A., and Erhardt, N. L. (2003). Recent research on team and organizational diversity: SWOT analysis and implications. *Journal of Management*, 29 (6), 801–30.
Jackson, S. E., May, K. E., and Whitney, K. (1995). Understanding the dynamics of diversity in decision-making teams. In R. A. Guzzo and E. Salas (eds.), *Team Effectiveness and Decision-Making in Organizations*. San Francisco: Jossey-Bass.
Milliken, F. J. and Martins, L. L. (1996). Searching for common threads: Understanding the multiple effects of diversity in organizational groups. *Academy of Management Review*, 21, 402–33.
Williams, K. Y. and O'Reilly, C. A., III (1998). Demography and diversity in organizations: A review of 40 years of research. In B. M. Staw and L. L. Cummings (eds.), *Research in Organizational Behavior*, Vol. 20. Greenwich, CT: JAI Press, 77–140.

double-loop learning

Chris Argyris

Learning occurs whenever errors are detected and corrected. An error is any mismatch between intentions and actual consequences. Discovery of a mismatch is only a first step in learning. Additional steps occur when the error is corrected in such a way that the correction is maintained. Furthermore, there are at least two ways to correct errors. One is to change the behavior. This kind of correction requires single-loop learning. The second way to correct errors is to change the underlying program, or master program, that leads individuals to *believe as they do* about their error correction strategies.

Theories of action inform actors of the strategies they should use to achieve their intended consequences. Theories of action are governed by sets of values which provide the framework for the action strategies chosen. Thus, human beings are designing beings. They create, store, and retrieve designs that advise them how to act if they are to achieve their intentions and act consistently with their governing values.

There are two types of theories of action. One is the theory that individuals espouse and that comprise their beliefs, attitudes, and values. The second is their *theory-in-use* – the theory that they actually employ.

Model I theory-in-use is the design we find throughout the world. It has four governing values: achieve your intended purpose; maximize winning and minimize losing; suppress negative feelings; and behave according to what you consider rational (*see* RATIONALITY). Model I tells individuals to craft their positions, evaluations, and attributions in ways that inhibit inquiries into them or tests of them with others' logic. The consequences of these Model I strategies are likely to be defensiveness, misunderstanding, and self-fulfilling and self-sealing processes.

Organizations come alive through the thoughts and actions of individuals acting as organizational agents and creating the organizational behavioral world in which work gets done. If it is true that most individuals use Model I, then a consequence of this use will be the creation of organizational defensive routines (*see* ORGANIZATIONAL NEUROSIS).

An organizational defensive routine is any action, policy, or practice preventing organizational participants from experiencing embarrassment or threat and, at the same time, preventing them from discovering the causes of the embarrassment or threat. Organizational defensive routines, like Model I theories-in-use, inhibit double-loop learning and overprotect the individuals and the organizations.

Model II theories-in-use are hypothesized to produce double-loop learning. The governing values of Model II are valid information, informed choice, and vigilant monitoring of the implementation of the choice in order to detect and correct error. As in the case of Model I, the three most prominent behaviors are advocate, evaluate, and attribute. However, unlike Model I behaviors, Model II behaviors are crafted into action strategies which openly illustrate how the actors reach their evaluations or attributions and how they craft them to encourage inquiry and testing by others. As a consequence, defensive routines that are anti-learning are minimized and double-loop learning is facilitated. Embarrassment and threat are not bypassed and covered up; they are engaged. Model II action will interrupt organizational defensive routines and begin to create organizational learning processes and systems that encourage double-loop learning in ways that persist.

For example, the director–owners of a professional firm wanted to reduce the destructive politics at, and eventually below, their present levels. Through observations and interviews a map was developed of the organizational defensive routines. Next, through the use of specially designed cases, the directors became aware of their Model I theories-in-use. Then they learned to make Model II an additional theory-in-use. Five years of observations and tape recordings indicate that the dysfunctional politics have been reduced significantly, that issues that were considered undiscussable (e.g., financial ownership) have become discussable and alterable, and that the process is spreading at all levels of the organization (Argyris, 1993).

See also *feedback; learning organization*

Bibliography

Argyris, C. (1993). *Knowledge for Action.* San Francisco: Jossey-Bass.
Argyris, C. (2000). *Flawed Advice.* New York: Oxford University Press.
Argyris, C. (2004). *Reasons and Rationalizations: The Limits to Organizational Knowledge.* Oxford: Oxford University Press.

downsizing

Kim Cameron

This term refers to a set of activities, undertaken on the part of the management of an organization, designed to reduce expenses or enhance competitiveness. This is usually, but not exclusively, accomplished by shrinking the size of the workforce. However, downsizing is a term used to encompass a wide range of activities from personnel layoffs and hiring freezes to consolidations and mergers of organizational units.

Beginning in the 1980s, downsizing came into prominence as a topic of both practical and scholarly interest. This is because, on a practical basis, more than three fourths of all medium and large sized companies in North America and Europe downsized in that decade. Two thirds of companies that engaged in downsizing did so more than once. The popularity of downsizing brought into question the common assumptions that increased size, complexity, and resources are inherently associated with organizational effectiveness. Smaller and leaner became associated with success, not largesse and over-abundance.

The concept of downsizing has arisen out of popular usage, not precise theoretical construction. In fact, identifying the definition and conceptual boundaries of downsizing is more relevant for theoretical purposes than for practical ones. The terminology used to describe downsizing activities is relatively unimportant to practicing managers, and many terms are used as synonyms – for example, rationalizing, restructuring, rightsizing, re-engineering.

For scholarly purposes, precise conceptual meaning is required in order for cumulative and comparative research to occur. For example, on the surface, downsizing can be interpreted as merely a reduction in organizational size. When this is the case, downsizing is often confused with the concept of organizational decline, which also is interpreted as a reduction in organizational size. Important differences exist, of course, and decline is a separate phenomenon conceptually and empirically. Attributes of downsizing also make it distinct from other related concepts such as lay-offs, maladaptation, or reverse growth. These distinguishing attributes of downsizing are (1) intent, (2) personnel, (3) efficiency, and (4) work processes.

Intent. Downsizing is not something that happens to an organization, but it is something that managers and organization members undertake purposively as an intentional set of activities. This differentiates downsizing from loss of market share, loss of revenues, or the unwitting loss of human resources through turnover, acquisition, or organizational demise. Downsizing is distinct from the encroachment of the environment on performance or resources because it implies organizational action.

Personnel. Second, downsizing usually involved reductions in personnel, although it is not limited solely to headcount reductions. A variety of personnel reduction strategies are associated with downsizing, such as transfers, outplacements, retirement incentives, buyout packages, layoffs, attrition, and job banks. These reductions may occur in one part of an organization but not in others, yet are still labeled organizational downsizing. Downsizing does not always involve reductions in employees, however, because some instances occur in which new products are added, new sources of revenue opened up, or additional work acquired without a commensurate number of employees being added. Fewer numbers of workers are then employed per unit of output compared to some previous level of employment.

Efficiency. A third characteristic of downsizing is its focus on improving the efficiency of the organization. Downsizing occurs either proactively or reactively in order to contain costs, to enhance revenue, or to bolster competitiveness. That is, downsizing may be implemented as a defensive reaction to financial pressures, or it may be a proactive strategy to enhance performance. During its first decade as an organizational strategy, most downsizing was defensive in orientation. More recently, a majority of downsizing has occurred in firms that are not losing money and are, instead, attempting to enhance competitiveness and profitability by reducing costs.

Work processes. Fourth, downsizing affects work processes, wittingly or unwittingly. When the workforce contracts, for example, fewer employees are left to do the same amount of work, and this has an impact on which work gets done and how it gets done. A common mistake of the architects of downsizing is to expect that work processes will remain the same even though employment is reduced. Overload, burnout, inefficiency, and conflict are frequent consequences. On the other hand, positive outcomes may result – including improved productivity or speed – as a consequence of restructuring, eliminating work (such as discontinuing functions, abolishing hierarchical levels, merging units), or redesigning tasks (*see* JOB DESIGN). Downsizing almost always requires process redesign to be successful.

The level of analysis being discussed when using the term downsizing is the organization itself, not the individual or the industry. A substantial literature exists on the psychological impacts of layoffs and cutbacks on individuals, including financial well-being, health, personal attitudes, family relationships, worker interactions, and other personal factors (see Kozlowski et al., 1993). At the industry level of analysis, a substantial literature also exists on MERGERS AND ACQUISITIONS and industry consolidation, including market segmentation, divesting unrelated businesses, and consolidating industry structure.

In general, therefore, organizational downsizing refers to an intentionally instituted set of activities within the organization designed to improve efficiency and performance. These activities affect the size of the organization's workforce, costs, and work processes. Downsizing's goal is usually enhanced financial performance, and it may be reactive and defensive, or it may be proactive and anticipatory. The presence of ineffectiveness or impending financial exigency are common defensive motivations for downsizing, whereas lowering costs or enhancing market competitiveness are common offensive motivations.

Surprisingly, most research to date indicates that the overall effects of downsizing on organizational performance are negative. For example, fewer than half the companies that downsized between 1990 and 2000 had short or long-term profit increases. Three years after downsizing, the market share prices of downsized companies were an average of 26 percent below the share prices of their competitors, and a decade later share prices of firms that downsized continued to lag the industry average. Among companies with similar growth rates, those that did not downsize consistently outperformed those that did during the recessionary years beginning in 2001. Moreover, fewer than 10 percent of downsizing firms reported improvements in product and service quality, innovation, and organizational climate, and more than 70 percent of senior managers in downsized companies reported that morale, trust, and productivity suffered after downsizing. Half of the firms in a survey of 1,500 firms indicated that productivity deteriorated after downsizing, and a third of executives reported that their downsizing efforts failed to achieve desired results (Cameron, 1994, 1998; Cascio, Young, and Morris, 1997).

These negative outcomes are not universal, of course, since the way downsizing occurs is more important than the fact that downsizing is implemented (Cameron, 1998). Organizations whose performance improves as a result of downsizing tend to manage the process as a renewal, revitalization, and culture change effort, not merely as a strategy to reduce expenses or organizational size.

See also *organizational change; organizational effectiveness*

Bibliography

Cameron, K. S. (1994) Strategies for successful organizational downsizing. *Human Resource Management Journal*, 33, 89–112.

Cameron, K. S. (1998). Strategic organizational downsizing: An extreme case. *Research in Organizational Behavior*, 20, 185–229.

Cascio, W. F., Young, C. E., and Morris, J. R. (1997). Financial consequences of employment change decisions in major US corporations. *Academy of Management Journal*, 40, 1175–89.

Kozlowski, S. W. J., Chao, G. T., Smith, E. M., and Hedlund, J. (1993). Organizational downsizing: Strategies, interventions, and research implications. In C. L. Cooper and I. T. Robertson (eds.), *International Review of Industrial and Organizational Psychology*, Vol. 8. New York: Wiley.

E

ecology

see COMMUNITY ECOLOGY; ORGANIZA-TIONAL ECOLOGY

emergent properties

see INSTITUTIONAL THEORY

emotion management

Stephen Fineman

Emotion management refers to the way that emotion is expressed and "used" in the workplace. It is an area that has developed significantly in recent years, drawing insights from a range of disciplines, especially organizational psychology, sociology, and anthropology. More broadly, it has moved the study of emotion away from a preoccupation with job satisfaction, to the ways emotions penetrate, and define, much of organizational life (Fineman, 2003).

The concept of emotional labor has been at the forefront of emotion management ideas. Originally outlined by Arlie Hochschild, emotional labor refers to the explicit or implicit work undertaken to present the appropriate emotion "face" or appearance to a customer or client – such as smiling, being "nice," and appearing "professional." Hochschild (1983) described the "deep acting" or "surface acting" that has to be accomplished to make this possible. The former involves internalizing the corporate or professional codes about what is required – taking them to heart. The latter requires a convincing act that can be dropped when off-stage, where different emotional display rules apply.

Varied "emotional zones," physical or symbolic areas of the workplace, allow for different kinds of off-stage, emotional presentation (such as in the galley of an aircraft, a school staff room, around the water cooler, or in washrooms) (Fineman, 1993).

The bulk of early research on emotional labor focused on front-line service workers, but interest has now expanded into different occupations, exposing unacknowledged, and unremunerated, emotional labor. These include paralegals, managers, lecturers, politicians, and medical professionals. Emotional labor was originally thought to be especially costly in terms of personal distress, especially to the deep actors. It is now acknowledged that there are different ways of coping, or insulating oneself, from the corporate script and its stresses (Adelman, 1995; Korczynski, 2003).

Emotional labor has generated a number of controversies and developments. For example, when are we "really authentic" at work if management and customers/clients are pulling our emotional strings? One view is that the authentic, core self has to fight for space. Another view is that all our self-presentations are equally authentic, or real. All are discourses of self and feelings drawn from a cultural bundle of possibilities. That we take some as more real than others is no more (or less) than a socially constructed illusion which draws upon structural and ideological emotion scripts: what a man, woman, novice, or competent professional "ought" to feel or express. It becomes oppressive when one voice, such as that of management, insists on a way of being that we find unacceptable but inescapable (Sturdy and Fineman, 2001).

A related development concerns aesthetic labor (Witz, Warhurst, and Nickson, 2003).

Aesthetic laborers physically represent the product or service they are dealing with. They are obliged to "live" the corporate uniform, to wear the clothes they are selling, to appear in the company's colors. Uniforms and accessories are designed to blend work identities and feelings with corporate ideologies. Having to look "right" may or may not be self-enhancing, but it completes the way emotion can be shaped by a third party and, literally, be connected with body.

The role of emotion and its management can be seen in a variety of other work practices (Barry, 1999; Fineman, 2000; Frost, 2003; Matthews, Zeider, and Roberts, 2002). They include the strategic use of emotion in DECI-SION-MAKING and LEADERSHIP, the way EMOTIONAL INTELLIGENCE has been promoted, how anxiety in CHANGE settings is stirred and contained, and the emotional cultures that ferment harassment and bullying. Overall, our study of emotion management has stimulated an important and exciting new area, bringing emotion firmly out of the organizational closet.

See also *critical theory; emotion in organizations; role*

Bibliography

Adelman, P. K. (1995). Emotional labor as a potential source of job stress. In S. L. Sauter and L. R. Murphy (eds.), *Organizational Risk Factors for Job Stress*. Washington, DC: American Psychological Association.

Barry, B. (1999). The tactical use of emotion in negotiation. *Research on Negotiation in Organizations*, 7, 93–121. Stamford, Connecticut: JAI Press.

Fineman, S. (1993). Organizations as emotional arenas. In S. Fineman (ed.), *Emotion in Organizations*. London: Sage.

Fineman, S. (2000). Commodifying the emotionally intelligent. In S. Fineman (ed.), *Emotion in Organizations*, 2nd edn. London: Sage, 101–15.

Fineman, S. (2003). *Understanding Emotion at Work*. London: Sage.

Frost, P. J. (2003). *Toxic Emotions at Work*. Harvard, MA: Harvard Business School Press.

Hochschild, A. (1983). *The Managed Heart*. Berkeley: University of California Press.

Korczynski, M. (2003). Communities of coping: Collective emotional labor in service work. *Organization*, 10 (1), 55–79.

Matthews, G., Zeider, M., and Roberts, R. D. (2002). *Emotional Intelligence: Science and Myth*. Cambridge, MA: MIT Press.

Sturdy, A. and Fineman, S. (2001). Struggles for the control of affect – resistance as politics and emotion. In A. Sturdy, I. Grugulis, and H. Willmott (eds.), *Customer Service: Empowerment and Entrapment*. Basingstoke: Palgrave.

Witz, A., Warhurst, C., and Nickson, D. (2003). The labor of aesthetics and the aesthetics of labor. *Organization*, 10 (1), 33–54.

emotion in organizations

Jill C. Bradley and Arthur P. Brief

Work experiences both impact and are impacted by people's emotions (or affect). Beginning in the 1930s, researchers have sought to answer questions regarding the role of emotions in the workplace. Early research yielded a number of ideas, methods, and findings that remain relevant but largely not attended to by contemporary researchers (Weiss and Brief, 2001). Hersey (1932), for example, tracked the relationships between daily affect and job performance as well as those between emotions at home and work. Yet Hersey's work is cited rarely.

During the succeeding 50 years or so, the focus of workplace affect research narrowed almost exclusively to JOB SATISFACTION. Researchers in this era explored various job satisfaction precursors and outcomes, such as task characteristics, workplace justice, attitudes of co-workers, turnover, and job performance. The theoretical approach guiding much research during this period was one of "fit" between the person and his or her work environment, with fit leading to satisfaction and lack of fit leading to dissatisfaction (*see* PERSON–ENVIRONMENT INTERACTION). In recent years, the "fit" approach and the focus on job satisfaction have been shown to be overly narrow (Brief and Weiss, 2002).

Currently, promising developments in the study of workplace affect include such innovative theoretical statements as Weiss and Cropanzano's (1996) Affective Events Theory, emerging methodologies concerned with the affective component of job satisfaction, and perhaps, most of all, a concern with discrete emotions such as anger, surprise, and fear. Arguably, the current state of the field can be described as an "affective revolution" (Barsade, Brief, and Spartaro, 2003). Part of this revolution entails alternative construals of affect. Trait affect, for example, is viewed as an enduring disposition that predisposes an individual to experience a particular mood state. A seminal work by Staw, Bell, and Clausen (1986) demonstrated that trait affect measured during adolescence could predict job satisfaction nearly 50 years later! Less stable than trait affect, moods are seen as generalized feeling states not typically associated with a particular stimulus. More intense and short-lived than moods are emotions, which generally are linked to an event.

Despite unimpressive past results concerning affect–performance relationships, researchers continue to be engrossed in this line of investigation. One new strategy, however, has been to examine affect–performance relationships at the level of the work group or organization rather than the individual worker. Additionally, some researchers have broadened the definition of performance in these studies to include so-called "organizational citizenship" behaviors. Another trend is the exploration of the social aspects of emotion, including ways in which people influence each other's emotions. Researchers also have taken an interest in the interaction between work and home life, long ago investigated by Hersey (1932). Other "hot" topics include emotional labor, or the attempt of individuals to manage their own displayed affect at work, and "emotional intelligence," or the monitoring of self and others' emotions to guide behavior. Clearly, recent years have signaled a time of development and revolution in affective research. Continued theoretical and methodological advancements are sure to follow from the momentum built during the past decade.

See also *emotion management; motivation; stress*

Bibliography

Barsade, S. G., Brief, A. P., and Spartaro, S. E. (2003). The affective revolution in organizational behavior: The emergence of a paradigm. In J. Greenberg (ed.), *Organizational Behavior: The State of the Science*, 2nd edn. Mahwah, NJ: Lawrence Erlbaum Associates, 3–51.

Brief, A. P. and Weiss, H. M. (2002). Organizational behavior: Affect in the workplace. *Annual Review of Psychology*, 53, 279–307.

Hersey, R. B. (1932). *Workers' Emotions in Shop and Home: A Study of Individual Workers from the Psychological and Physiological Standpoint*. Philadelphia, PA: University of Philadelphia Press.

Staw, B. M., Bell, N. E., and Clausen, J. A. (1986). The dispositional approach to job attitudes: A lifetime longitudinal test. *Administrative Science Quarterly*, 31, 56–77.

Weiss, H. M. and Brief, A. P. (2001). Affect at work: A historical perspective. In R. L. Payne and C. L. Cooper (eds.), *Emotions at Work: Theory, Research, and Applications for Management*. Chichester: John Wiley and Sons, 133–71.

Weiss, H. M. and Cropanzano, R. (1996). Affective events theory: A theoretical discussion of the structure, causes, and consequences of affective experiences at work. *Research in Organizational Behavior*, 18, 1–74.

emotional intelligence

Richard E. Boyatzis

Salovey and Mayer (1990) first introduced EI into the academic literature, defining it as a set of abilities in awareness of and handling of one's emotions. Here it will be defined as the intelligent use of one's emotions (*see* EMOTION IN ORGANIZATIONS). Given that emotions are a constant element in cognitive processes, a more technical definition of EI is that it is a set of thoughts, feelings, and behaviors driven by a neural circuitry located in the limbic system, mediated by the control functions of the prefrontal cortex (Goleman, Boyatzis, and McKee, 2002). The concept of EI achieved prominence through Goleman's bestselling book in 1995. In this, he made the concept more behavioral than originally conceived, defining EI as a set of COMPETENCIES that enable a person to be effective in a job, successful in life, happy as a person, and a contributing member of society. Specifically, EI is composed of four clusters of competencies (Goleman, Boyatzis, and McKee, 2002). They are (1) the Self-Awareness cluster of competencies such as emotional self-awareness and self-confidence; (2) the Self-Management cluster of competencies such as achievement orientation, initiative, emotional self-control, and adaptability; (3) the Social Awareness cluster of competencies such as empathy and cultural awareness; and (4) the Relationship Management or Social Skills cluster of competencies such as influence, teamwork, communications, and developing others.

Although there are differences among the theories and models offered by various authors, these distinctions have more to do with the measurement of EI with the three most popular instruments, such as the MSCEIT, EQ-I, and ECI, than the underlying theory. Controversy in the field has emerged as to whether there is one concept called EI, whether it should be called an "intelligence," and how best to measure it. Regardless, the concept of EI has allowed scholars to create a holistic personality theory with roots in neuroscience. It has also provided a label that makes it easy for many to classify non-cognitive characteristics. Because the Goleman (1995) model of EI is based on competencies, applications of EI are relevant to a wide range of human resource and education contexts.

See also *individual differences; personality*

Bibliography

Bar-On, R. and Parker, J. (eds.). *Handbook of Emotional Intelligence*. San Francisco: Jossey-Bass.

Cherniss, C. and Adler, M. (2000). *Promoting Emotional Intelligence in Organizations: Make Training in Emotional Intelligence Effective*. Washington, DC: American Society of Training and Development.

Goleman, D. (1995). *Emotional Intelligence*. New York: Bantam Books.

Goleman, D., Boyatzis, R. E., and McKee, A. (2002). *Primal Leadership: Realizing the Power of Emotional Intelligence*. Boston, MA: Harvard Business School Press.

Salovey, P. and Mayer, J. D. (1990). Emotional intelligence. *Imagination, Cognition and Personality*, **9**, 185–211.

employee involvement

Mark Fenton-O'Creevy

The term *employee involvement* (EI) has been used to denote a wide range of practices in organizations which increase employees' influence over how their work is carried out, or increase employees' influence over other areas of organizational policy and practice. A key distinction can be made between employee involvement as a form of work organization and employee involvement as a form of PARTICIPATION in organization governance (usually via representative structures such as labor organizations or works councils). The economic benefits claimed for involvement in work organization are most often benefits to the organization from greater individual effort and effectiveness via increased commitment, job satisfaction, and clarity about goals. The economic benefits most often claimed for participation in governance are at the level of the economy: industrial conflict is reduced and the conditions are created for greater investment in human capital. There is also some evidence that representative employee involvement in organization governance may enhance perceived legitimacy of management decisions among employees and lead to enhanced perceptions of procedural justice. Debates about the role of employee involvement as participation in organization governance are central to discussions about the relative merits of the liberal market approach to economic organization practiced in countries such as the USA and the coordinated market approach practiced in countries such as Germany.

The most common practices that aim to increase (work organization) employee involvement are COMMUNICATION programs (e.g., employee attitude surveys), QUALITY CIRCLES, quality of working life programs, consultative committees, gainsharing, JOB ENRICHMENT/work redesign, and SELF-MANAGED TEAMS. Key dimensions on which EI efforts differ are:

- Individually based (e.g., job redesign) versus team based (e.g., quality circles, self-managing work teams), or organization based (e.g., gainsharing).
- Changes to core organization (e.g., self-managing work teams, job redesign) or collateral organization (e.g., quality circles, attitude surveys). The distinction here is whether the EI effort requires changes in the way the core work of the organization is carried

out or whether the EI activities are "added on."

- Direct involvement versus indirect (i.e., through representatives).

Research evidence concerning the outcomes of EI is mixed. The most consistent finding is of successfully implemented EI leading to increased JOB SATISFACTION. Evidence for productivity improvements is weak, although it is stronger for self-managed work teams and some forms of work redesign (*see* JOB DESIGN).

The most successful forms of EI are those that imply changes to the core work of the organization. Collateral or parallel organization forms of EI, such as quality circles, often have a limited lifespan. Their impact is often quickly absorbed by the more enduring organization structures and systems. While many organizations have benefited considerably from the introduction of EI practices, in others EI efforts founder or deliver only minor benefits.

Several barriers to the successful application of EI are frequently cited. These include lack of clearly communicated COMMITMENT from top management, resistance from middle managers who see their interests threatened, opposition from unions, and failure to adapt organizational systems to new ways of working.

See also *continuous improvement; empowerment; participation; survey feedback*

Bibliography

Cotton, J. L. (1993). *Employee Involvement*. London: Sage.

Fenton-O'Creevy, M. P. (2002). Seeking success by involving workers. In J. Pickford (ed.), *Mastering People Management*. London: Prentice-Hall, 165–70.

Freeman, R. B. and Kleiner, M. M. (2000). Who benefits most from employee involvement: Firms or workers? *American Economic Review*, **90** (2), 219–23.

Lawler, E. E. (1986). *High-Involvement Management* San Francisco: Jossey-Bass.

employee participation

see EMPLOYEE INVOLVEMENT; PARTICIPATION

empowerment

Mark Fenton-O'Creevy

Prior to its adoption as a management term, the word *empowerment* was most often used in fields such as politics, social work, feminist theory, and Third World aid. Writers in these fields have taken it to mean providing (usually disadvantaged) individuals with the tools and resources to further their own interests, as they see them. Within the field of management, empowerment is commonly used with a different meaning: providing employees with tools, resources, and discretion to further the interests of the organization (as seen by senior management). Conger and Kanugo (1988) define empowerment as a psychological construct. They suggest that empowerment is the process of fostering SELF-EFFICACY beliefs among employees. This implies both removing sources of powerlessness and providing employees with positive FEEDBACK and support. Empowerment, in this sense of a psychological construct, is a principal goal of most forms of EMPLOYEE INVOLVEMENT. Much writing on empowerment has been criticized as obscuring the divergence of interests between organizations and their employees (e.g., Wilkinson, 1998). A critical practical implication is that an important precondition for organizations to benefit from empowerment initiatives is the generation of common purpose across the organization.

See also *decision-making; employee involvement; influence; participation; power*

Bibliography

Conger, J. A. and Kanugo, R. N. (1988). The empowerment process: Integrating theory and practice. *Academy of Management Review*, **13**, 471–82.

Wilkinson, A. (1998) Empowerment: Theory and practice. *Personnel Review*, **27** (1–2), 40–58.

enactment

Nigel Nicholson

This concept was first developed by Weick in his influential and innovative monograph, *The*

Social Psychology of Organizing (1969), to connote an organism's adjustment to its environment by directly acting upon the environment to change it. Enactment thus has the capacity to create ecological change to which the organism may have subsequently to adjust, possibly by further enactment. Weick discusses this process in the context of active sensemaking by the individual manager or employee, but also notes how one may enact "limitations," for example, by avoidance of disconfirming experience, or "charades," by acting-out in order to test understanding. Enactment is thus often a species of self-fulfilling prophecy. It may also be deviation amplifying, where consequences are successively multiplied by actions on the environment. Weick also identifies enactment as a form of social constructionism: the reification of experience and environment through action.

Since Weick's origination of the concept, it has found most use in strategic management, to capture the dynamics of relations between organization and environment (e.g., Abolafia and Kilduff, 1988). The notion of strategic choice was developed in the 1970s with this intent (i.e., to show how organizational adaptation should not be seen as entirely exogenously directed, but as the agentic response of "purposeful systems" seeking to modify and if possible master the environmental contingencies bearing down upon them). This idea reinforces a model of organizations as akin to willful actors, a construction that challenges the behaviorist paradigm of OPEN SYSTEMS' actions being determined by environmental conditioning.

One can expect enactment processes to be most visible in large and powerful organizations that have the capacity to shape their markets, but they are no less relevant to the way smaller enterprises conceive their contexts and make choices about how they will act in relation to them. This draws attention to such strategies of accommodating environmental forces as creating buffers to diffuse impact, negotiation with STAKEHOLDERS, co-opting influential agencies, and avoidance. Enactment is equally relevant to individual or group behavior, where it is analogous to the dynamic equilibria of SELF-REGULATION where action reconfigures the relationship between goals, states, context, perceptions, and affect.

As an operational concept, enactment could be said to lack precision, though for Weick (2003) this is a helpful "roominess" that encourages the reconciliation, analytically, of cognition, constraint, reciprocal action, and purpose. It is "the glue that joins organizing with sensemaking" and allows people "to replace uncertainty with meaning." As such it embodies an important recognition of how agency and constructive cognitive processes are essential elements in our understanding of the behavior of individuals and organizations.

See also *organizational ecology; structuration*

Bibliography

Abolafia, M. Y. and Kilduff, M. (1988). Enacting market crisis: The social construction of a speculative bubble. *Administrative Science Quarterly*, 33, 177–93.

Weick, K. E. (1969). *The Social Psychology of Organizing*. Reading, MA: Addison-Wesley.

Weick, K. E. (2003). Enacting an environment: The infrastructure of organizing. In R. Westwood and S. Clegg (eds.), *Debating Organization*. Oxford: Blackwell.

enterprise resource planning

Craig Shepherd

Enterprise resource planning, or ERP systems, are computer-based systems comprising a centralized database and integrated software modules designed to manage all of an enterprise's work processes. The past decade has witnessed an exponential growth in their popularity. Yen, Chou, and Chang (2002) highlight that 70 percent of Fortune 1000 companies have implemented ERP applications in some form, with the expected growth for the next 5 years at 37 percent. They are presented as a panacea by many enterprises, since implementations are often combined with business process reengineering, in attempts to harmonize working practices and replace aging legacy systems. Benefits cited by vendors include enhanced profitability, efficiency, and business agility. In common with many information technologies, implementations are typified by over-expenditure, time delays, unrealized business benefits and, in extreme cases, failure (Davenport, 1998).

While these represent concerns for practitioners, the research agenda has been dominated by studies of the implementation process, with few studies critically examining the ability of these technologies to transform organizations and deliver the promised benefits. Also, research thus far has offered few insights into their impacts on end users, or how these technologies are being used in practice. Given their likely longevity, this represents an opportunity for future research.

See also *performance appraisal/management; technology*

Bibliography

Davenport, T. H. (1998). Putting the enterprise into the enterprise system. *Harvard Business Review*, **76** (4), 121–31.

Yen, D. C., Chou, D. C., and Chang, J. (2002). A synergic analysis for web-based enterprise resource planning systems. *Computer Standards and Interfaces*, **24** (4), 337–46.

entrainment

Deborah Ancona

This term means the adjustment of the pace, cycle, and rhythm of one activity to match that of another (Ancona and Chong, 1993). A cycle is a pattern of events over time and a rhythm is a recurrent cyclical pattern. Managers who shorten product development time or speed up their DECISION-MAKING processes to match accelerated innovation cycles within an industry are exhibiting entrainment. Similarly, managers who consistently align ORGANIZATIONAL CHANGE with major technological discontinuities are entraining to their environment.

Entrainment can be deliberate, as managers try to adjust pace, cycle, and rhythm to key environmental patterns, or unintentional, as dominant cycles and rhythms "capture" other cycles. An example of the latter is the coupling of performance appraisal, budgeting, sales activity, and hiring practices to the fiscal year.

Entrainment to cycles in the workplace is very common. Shift workers' families often change meal times, leisure activities, and play patterns to accommodate sleep during the day (McGrath and Rotchford, 1983). Parents often sacrifice time with children to accommodate to intense work periods in their careers.

Entrainment appears to be inertial and initial entrainment appears to be the strongest. Once set, pace, cycles, and rhythm are hard to change. In a series of studies Kelly and McGrath (1985) showed that individuals and groups that were given 5, 10, and 20 minutes, respectively, to complete a task learned to work at decreasing rates of speed. The shorter the time limit, the higher the rate at which anagrams were solved. McGrath, Kelly, and Machatka (1984) argue "that groups and individuals attune their rates of work to fit the conditions of their work situations." Once established, this pace becomes inertial. The groups maintained their initial pace even when the time limits were subsequently changed to 20, 10, and 5 minutes, respectively.

Huygens was the first to write about entrainment in the seventeenth century (Minorsky, 1962). He observed that when two pendulum clocks that separately ran at different speeds were both hung on the same thin wooden board, they came to swing in perfect synchrony. The term entrainment is most commonly used in biology, whereby endogenous biological rhythms are modified in their phase and periodicity by powerful exogenous influences called external pacers. An example is the circadian (meaning about 1 day) rhythm where most bodily cycles are entrained to the external light–dark, 24-hour cycle of the earth. Individuals who are isolated from these cycles revert back to their "natural" periodicities, which are usually an hour or so longer than 24 hours.

As the pace of organization change quickens, the cycles of time to market and product development shrink, and technological innovation accelerates, issues of speed and meshing of cycles become increasingly important. Similarly, organizations are subject to variant cycles, such as the quarterly and annual accounting cycles, the seasonal cycles of demand, and the roughly 4-year business cycle, and contain processes with intrinsic response times that vary substantially (order fulfillment may take seconds while capacity expansion may take years) (Sterman and Mosekilde, 1993). Organizations are filled with individuals going through various career and life cycles, and teams that pace themselves to temporal milestones (*see* CAREER STAGE). They exist in environments with technological, market, and business cycles in which pace seems to be ever quickening. These characteristics call for analysis through the entrainment lens.

Entrainment helps us to focus on how fast activities occur and the impact of how cycles and rhythms interact. It focuses on non-linear patterns whereby you may have to act quickly, for if you wait too long the world will have changed and you have to do something different. It focuses on multilevel phenomena, examining how CEO, team, organizational, and environmental cycles interact over time. It also focuses on coordination by time rather than by activity; that is, rather than looking at whose activities are interdependent and finding appropriate coordination mechanisms, it specifies when activity must be completed, letting activities be reconfigured as necessary to meet deadlines.

Research on entrainment is just beginning. Many issues remain unresolved, including the mechanisms that cause entrainment to occur, the methods that are best able to measure entrainment, and how entrainment differs from related concepts of coordination, scheduling, and time allocation. Nonetheless, society's increased obsession with speed and timing suggests an increasing role for entrainment in a theory of organizations.

See also *organization theory; technology*

Bibliography

Ancona, D. and Chong, C. (1993). Time and timing in top management teams. MIT Sloan School of Management Working Paper No. 3591–93–BPS.

Kelly, J. and McGrath, J. (1985). Effects of time limits and task types on task performance and interaction of four-person groups. *Journal of Personality and Social Psychology*, 49, 395–407.

McGrath, J. E., Kelly, J. R., and Machatka, D. E. (1984). The social psychology of time: Entrainment of behavior in social and organizational settings. *Applied Social Psychology Annual*, 5, 21–44.

McGrath, J. E. and Rotchford N. L. (1983). Time and behavior in organizations. In L. L. Cummings and B. M. Staw (eds.), *Research in Organizational Behavior*, Vol. 5. Greenwich, CT: JAI Press.

Minorsky, N. (1962). *Nonlinear Oscillations*. Princeton, NJ: Van Nostrand.

Sterman, J. D. and Mosekilde, E. (1993). Business cycles and long waves: A behavioral disequilibrium perspective. MIT Sloan School of Management Working Paper No. 3528–93–MSA.

entrepreneurship

Arnold C. Cooper

Entrepreneurship is a term that has been used in different ways. One usage views entrepreneurship as concerned with the processes leading to new venture creation, without regard to the type or potential of the organizations created. Another view sees entrepreneurship as primarily concerned with developing innovative ventures, whether these are independent or occur within already established organizations. Entrepreneurship inside organizations has sometimes been termed "corporate entrepreneurship" or "intrapreneurship." Both usages emphasize the role of the entrepreneur as one who organizes a venture and bears some degree of risk in return for rewards.

Interest in entrepreneurship has increased for several reasons. As large organizations have "downsized," much of the net new job creation has occurred in new and small firms (*see* DOWNSIZING). (One study (Birch, 1987) found that about 88 percent of the net new jobs created in the United States economy from 1981–5 were in firms with less than 20 employees.) New firms have served as centers of innovation, developing products or services attuned to a changing environment. For many individuals, entrepreneurship has been the vehicle by which they pursue personal goals and achieve independence. In countries which have been moving from state-owned to private enterprise, entrepreneurship has been supported as a means to transform these economies. In regard to corporate entrepreneurship, managements of large organizations have recognized that one of their greatest challenges is to become more innovative and more responsive to changes in markets and TECHNOLOGY (*see* ORGANIZATIONAL DESIGN).

The entrepreneur seeking to develop an independent venture must recognize an opportunity;

in fact, some would regard the identification of opportunities as the essence of entrepreneurship. The entrepreneur must then develop a strategy or way of competing, investigate the venture's requirements and potential, assemble resources, and move forward to start and manage that organization. There is some evidence that, at any point in time, about 4 percent of the adult population are nascent entrepreneurs, but that only about 10 percent of these actually proceed to the point of creating new firms (Reynolds and White, 1993). New organizations may differ widely in scale or potential as well as in the resources and technical or management sophistication required. Small scale ventures may be started with the financial resources, contacts, and "sweat equity" of the founder. Large scale and high potential ventures often involve founding teams and the attraction of outside resources, sometimes provided by sophisticated investors. Although some founders might be viewed as "habitual entrepreneurs," many engage in this process only once, and therefore must learn how to put a venture together and how to manage a particular line of business as they proceed.

New ventures start with ideas; the sources of these ideas are often previous jobs or personal interests – 43 percent and 18 percent, respectively, in one study (Cooper et al., 1990). Strategies must be developed which take into account the limited resources available to the start-up and the nature of existing competitors. The entrepreneur must then try to assemble resources, at a time when risks appear high to potential investors, customers, employees, and suppliers. Entrepreneurs often proceed sequentially – gathering information, revising plans, and making commitments in stages, with attempts to minimize exposure at each stage.

Industries and geographical areas vary in the extent to which they offer entrepreneurial opportunities. In general, growth, change, and market segmentation lead to opportunities. The scale of operations needed to compete is also a factor, with industries which require limited investment to get started being more likely to have high rates of new firm formation. Within a geographical area, establishment of clusters of related firms sometimes leads to locational advantages and higher startup rates.

Corporate entrepreneurship can involve efforts to encourage INNOVATION and RISK TAKING throughout the organization (see ORGANIZATIONAL CHANGE). It can also focus upon developing entirely new businesses, in which case it involves many of the same challenges that arise in starting independent ventures. Opportunities must be identified; strategies must be developed; and resources must be committed, all within the context of an existing organization. Important issues include whether ventures "fit" with corporate strategy and how resources not directly controlled by the corporate entrepreneurs can be accessed for the new venture. Other issues relate to how internal corporate entrepreneurs should be rewarded. Should they have the same prospects for wealth (and failure) that independent entrepreneurs experience, or should their rewards (and job security) be similar to those of other employees? The corporate strategy, including the extent to which the organization is expanding and diversifying, and the degree of personal sponsorship by influential senior executives are among the major influences which bear upon whether venture activities are supported (Fast, 1978) (see CEOs). It should be recognized that corporate entrepreneurship may take place in widely different contexts. Some venture activities occur within relatively separate subsidiaries or venture departments, which have control of their own assets and the freedom to depart from corporate policies. Others are embedded in the existing organization, and involve shared resources and sponsorship by existing departments.

One stream of research on independent venturing has emphasized traits of entrepreneurs, seeking to determine whether they are "different" in certain ways. Such PERSONALITY attributes as risk-taking propensity, internal LOCUS OF CONTROL, and ACHIEVEMENT, NEED FOR have been examined. There have been problems with this research stream, including lack of comparability of samples, inappropriate test instruments, and lack of consideration of contextual factors. Demographic characteristics have also been considered, including AGE, whether there were entrepreneurial parents, and membership in particular subgroups. In general, some of the strongest findings reflect relationships between entrepreneurial activity and achievement motivation, as well as having had entrepreneurial parents. Some have urged that research should focus less upon traits and more upon MAN-AGERIAL AND ORGANIZATIONAL COGNI-TION or the behaviors of entrepreneurs. Research on cognitive processes of entrepreneurs suggests that entrepreneurs appear to differ from general managers in large organizations in being more likely to use cognitive heuristics in analyzing problems. In particular, they were more likely to demonstrate overconfidence and to generalize from limited observations (Busenitz and Barney, 1997). Furthermore, when presented with scenarios describing business situations, they appear more inclined to frame them as opportunities, rather than problems. Interestingly, entrepreneurs did not demonstrate greater propensity to take risks (Palich and Bagby, 1995).

Study of the processes followed by entrepreneurs has included how they minimized initial resource needs through borrowing, trading, or sharing resources, as well as using creative ways to minimize initial assets needed (Starr and MacMillan, 1990).

A growing body of research has considered how entrepreneurs develop and utilize their networks of contacts to gather information, to increase trust, and to access resources. Networks can be described as involving strong or weak ties and as being densely connected or having "holes," with some members of the network not being connected to others. Strong ties are usually long-term, two-way relationships and involve emotional closeness. They are more likely to lead to joint problem solving and exchange of detailed information. Weak ties and structural holes generate opportunities for entrepreneurs by bridging contacts between different groups. Both kinds of ties are utilized as ventures are formed. Diversity in network ties provides greater access to information and resources (Aldrich, 1999). Entrepreneurs within corporations also utilize their contacts inside and outside the corporation to gain access to resources and information and to persuade others to support the developing venture.

Venture finance has been a focal point for research since the earliest days of the academic study of entrepreneurship. A literature has developed examining the costs and benefits as-sociated with different sources of financing, including the roles of angel investors and corporate investors (Dennis, 2004). Venture capitalists contribute capital, but also add value through monitoring, shaping management teams, and certifying quality through their willingness to be associated with a venture. Typically they invest in stages, giving them the right to abandon an investment if it no longer seems promising. Angel investors are high net worth individuals who invest privately. They often invest in early stage ventures. Corporations sometimes invest directly in new ventures, in part to allow them to monitor developments in new technologies and markets.

Other research frameworks have considered how environmental influences and resource availability bear upon birth and survival (see ORGANIZATIONAL ECOLOGY). A considerable body of research has sought to determine how founding processes, initial firm characteristics, business strategies, and management methods influence later patterns of development. It appears that early venture characteristics may "imprint" the firm and shape its later strategy. Findings relating to performance have been mixed to date, but research suggests that higher performance is associated with ventures started by entrepreneurs who have a high need for achievement, who take explicit steps to manage risk, and who engage in relatively systematic planning. Furthermore, ventures may do better if they are closely related to the organizations which the entrepreneurs had left, if they are started by teams, entail larger amounts of capital, and involve industries in the growth stage (Cooper and Gimeno-Gascon, 1992).

See also *family firms; innovation; organizational effectiveness*

Bibliography

Aldrich, H. (1999). *Organizations Evolving*. London: Sage.

Birch, D. L. (1987). *Job Creation in America*. New York: Free Press.

Busenitz, L. W. and Barney, J. B. (1997). Difference between entrepreneurs and managers in large organizations: Biases and heuristics in strategic decision-making. *Journal of Business Venturing*, 12 (1), 9–30.

Cooper, A. C., Dunkelberg, W. C., Woo, C. Y., and Dennis, W. (1990). *New Business in America: The Firms and Their Owners*. Washington, DC: NFIB Foundation.

Cooper, A. C. and Gimeno-Gascon, J. (1992). Entrepreneurs, processes of founding, and new firm performance. In D. Sexton and J. Kasarda (eds.), *State of the Art in Entrepreneurship Research*. Boston, MA: PWS-Kent, 301–40.

Dennis, D. J. (2004). Entrepreneurial finance: An overview of the issues and evidence. *Journal of Corporate Finance*.

Fast, N. D. (1978). *The Rise and Fall of Corporate New Venture Divisions*. Ann Arbor, MI: UMI Research Press.

Palich, L. E. and Bagby, D. R. (1995). Using cognitive theory to explain entrepreneurial risk taking: Challenging conventional wisdom. *Journal of Business Venturing*, **10** (6), 425–38.

Reynolds, P. D. and White, S. B. (1993). *Wisconsin's Entrepreneurial Climate Study*. Final report. Madison, WI: Wisconsin Housing and Economic Development Authority.

Starr, J. A. and MacMillan, I. C. (1990). Resource cooptation via social contracting: Resource acquisition strategies for new ventures. *Journal of Business Venturing*, **11** (Supp. issue), 79–92.

environment

see CONTINGENCY THEORY

equity theory

Jerald Greenberg

Introduced by Adams (1965) as an extension of distributive justice and COGNITIVE DISSONANCE, equity theory proposes that people's attitudes and behavior are affected by their assessment of their work contributions (referred to as *inputs*) and the rewards they receive (referred to as *outcomes*). Inputs may include such contributions as effort, SKILL, and seniority. Outcomes may include such rewards as pay, status, and recognition.

People are said to compare the ratios of their own perceived outcomes/inputs to the corresponding ratios of other people or groups. Reference comparisons may be made to such others as co-workers on the job, industry standards, or oneself at an earlier point in time (*see* SOCIAL COMPARISON). The theory focuses on individuals' perceptions of their own and others' outcomes and inputs rather than actual states. When one's own outcome/input ratio is believed to be greater than another's, the individual is theorized to experience a state of *overpayment inequity*, leading to feelings of guilt. In contrast, when one's own outcome/input ratio is believed to be less than another's, the individual is theorized to experience a state of *underpayment inequity*, resulting in feelings of anger. When one's own outcome/input ratio is believed to match the comparison standard, a state of equitable payment is said to exist, resulting in feelings of satisfaction (*see* JOB SATISFACTION).

Because the negative emotions associated with inequitable states are undesirable, people are motivated to alter their own or the other's outcomes or inputs (if possible), either behaviorally or cognitively, so as to achieve an equitable state. For example, workers who feel underpaid may be motivated to lower their own outcomes (a behavioral reaction) or to convince themselves that their work contributions are not as great as another who is believed to receive higher outcomes (a cognitive reaction). Likewise, people may respond to overpayment by raising their own inputs or by convincing themselves that relative to the comparison other, their own contributions are sufficiently great to merit the higher reward received. Research has generally supported these claims (for a review, see Mowday and Colwell, 2003). Although early tests of equity theory were conducted in the laboratory, more recent research has been successful in finding support for equity theory in a wide variety of work settings. For example, researchers have used equity theory to explain such work related behaviors as reactions to job titles, office assignments, pay cuts, and layoffs (Greenberg, 1996).

Attempting to refine equity theory and extend it to a wide variety of social situations (beyond the work context on which Adams originally focused), Walster, Walster, and Berscheid (1978) proposed equity theory as a general theory of social behavior. Notably, they used equity theory to explain behavior in marriage and romantic relationships as well as parent–child relationships.

Equity theory has been criticized on several grounds, including the necessity of distress as a motivator of attempts to redress inequities, uncertainties regarding the choice of a comparison other, vagueness regarding the choice of a mode of inequity redress, and difficulties in quantifying inequities (see Adams and Freedman, 1976). However, equity theory has inspired a more general interest in justice in the workplace that is popular today.

See also *justice, distributive; motivation*

Bibliography

Adams, J. S. (1965). Inequity in social exchange. In L. Berkowitz (ed.), *Advances in Experimental Social Psychology*, Vol. 2. New York: Academic Press, 267–99.

Adams, J. S. and Freedman, S. (1976). Equity theory revisited: Comments and annotated bibliography. In L. Berkowitz and E. Walster (eds.), *Advances in Experimental Social Psychology*, Vol. 8. New York: Academic Press, 43–90.

Greenberg, J. (1996). *The Quest for Justice on the Job: Essays and Experiments.* Thousand Oaks, CA: Sage.

Mowday, R. T. and Colwell, K. A. (2003). Employee reactions to unfair outcomes in the workplace: The contributions of Adams's equity theory to understanding work motivation. In L. W. Porter, G. A. Bigley, and R. M. Steers (eds.), *Motivation and Work Behavior*, 7th edn. Burr Ridge, IL: McGraw-Hill/Irwin, 65–81.

Walster, E., Walster, G. W., and Berscheid, E. (1978). *Equity: Theory and Research.* Boston, MA: Allyn and Bacon.

ERP

see ENTERPRISE RESOURCE PLANNING

error

Kenneth W. Koput

This term has two uses in statistics. In the first use, error is defined as any variation not assigned a cause. In other words, error is any deviation of an actual value from that predicted by the deterministic part of a statistical model. In experimental studies of GOAL SETTING, for example, any variation in individual perform-

ance from the average for all those in a common condition, such as level of FEEDBACK, is referred to as error. Similarly, in field studies of job design, the deviation of an individual's value on an outcome, such as INTRINSIC MOTIVATION, from that predicted for all those who share the same inputs (e.g., job characteristics) is also called error (*see* ERRORS).

The second use of the term occurs in hypothesis testing. In this sense, error is a logical condition in which an inference drawn from a statistical procedure is incongruent with what is actually true – though the latter may be unknown. There are two well-known kinds of error in hypothesis testing. An error of the first kind, often denoted as a Type I error, occurs when a researcher rejects a hypothesis that is true. The second kind, often denoted as Type II, happens if a researcher fails to reject a hypothesis when it is false. For example, a researcher who, on the basis of a particular sample, rejects the hypothesis that LOOSE COUPLING increases INNOVATION, when it in fact does, would be making a Type I error.

These kinds of errors in hypothesis testing can occur due to the probabilistic nature of statistical inference. The probability of making an error of the first kind is referred to as the size of a hypothesis test. The size can be chosen by the researcher. The probability of making an error of the second kind is called the power of a hypothesis test. POWER is a property of a second hypothesis that is an alternative to the focal hypothesis. Due to the nature of hypothesis testing in organizational research, in which an alternative is often not well explicated, power is usually indeterminate and subject to neither control nor scrutiny. Exceptions occur when concerns about sample sizes lead to considerations of power.

Many statisticians also admit to a third variety of error. Any statistical method requires a model. A model is a set of assumptions sufficient to specify a probability distribution for the statistic on which an inference is to be based. An incorrect model invalidates any inference or conclusions drawn from the associated method. This error propagates mistakes in subsequent interpretation and use of the results. Errors of this kind may be the most problematic in organizational research, since issues of model selection and VALIDITY are often set aside in favor of convention and expediency. One criterion for evaluating statistical models is the minimization of errors – in the first use of the term, above.

See also *bias; reliability; research design; research methods; statistical methods*

Bibliography

Gigerenzer, G., Swijtink, Z., Porter, T., Daston, L., Beattz, J., and Kruger, L. (1989). *The Empire of Chance: How Probability Changed Science and Everyday Life*. New York: Cambridge University Press.

errors

Michael Frese

Errors are unintentional deviations from a goal, caused by some act or omission that is in principle avoidable (Zapf et al., 1992). They are self-evidently important to management, since they can cause considerable losses, such as cases of environmental catastrophe (Reason, 1997) and planning disasters (Hartley, 1997).

Violations (intentional deviations from some norm and value), faults (manifestations of errors in some machine or software), and inefficiencies (reaching the goal with higher effort than called for) can be differentiated from errors. Some error researchers distinguish between mistakes (errors of a conscious intention) and slips and lapses (errors in routine behaviors) (Reason, 1997). Errors appear as a result of the interaction of the individual and the environment such that no root cause can be deduced (because there is a potentially unending causal chain). For every cause of a particular error, it is possible to find further causes; for example, in the agent's psychological makeup, in the usability of the system that is employed as a tool, and in the organizational support functions. A final important distinction is between manifest errors (which happened obviously) and latent errors ("resident pathogens") related to errors against which the organization has no defenses.

An analysis of errors, violations, and near misses (negative consequences could have happened but did not or were trivial) can be used to develop better technical and organiza-tional systems (Reason, 1997; Zapf et al., 1992).

Errors are the other side of the coin of cognitive efficiency. Since our cognitive capacity is limited, humans cannot calculate all opportunities and threats, think of all routes to a goal, or hold all information in memory. Therefore, we have to take cognitive shortcuts. This makes cognitive processing very fast and efficient, but at the cost of occasional errors (Dörner, 1996; Kahneman, Slovic, and Tversky, 1982). Errors appear more frequently under environmental or personal/human conditions. Environmental conditions that lead to more errors are complexity, dynamism (changes take place without intervention by the target person), non-transparency, and exponential rather than linear changes (Dörner, 1996). The human conditions that lead to an increased frequency of errors are fatigue, high or very low SELF-EFFI-CACY, prior success, distraction from the primary task, fear of being punished for errors, and low self-reflections. Errors of omission seem to be more likely than errors of commission or, at least, lead to more negative consequences (Reason, 1997). Perrow (1984) has argued that two factors increase the chance of catastrophes following from errors: complexity of technical systems or organizations, and tightly coupled subsystems where errors in one subsystem lead to unpredictable consequences in other subsystems.

As shown in figure 1, there are in principle two strategies that can be used to deal with errors: (a) error prevention, which is to reduce the occurrence of errors and (b) error management. The strategy most frequently used is error prevention because people wish to avoid the negative personal reputational consequences. People do not like to be caught making an error, a phenomenon extensively studied in social psychology under the rubrics of the fundamental attribution error and hindsight bias: the "knew-it-all-along-effect." The fundamental attribution error implies that whenever a person is seen to make an error, others will assume that internal causes led to the error (lack of competence or MOTIV-ATION, and PERSONALITY deficits). In contrast, the agents themselves will tend to attribute the causes of errors to the situation. Similarly, hindsight BIAS implies that when a

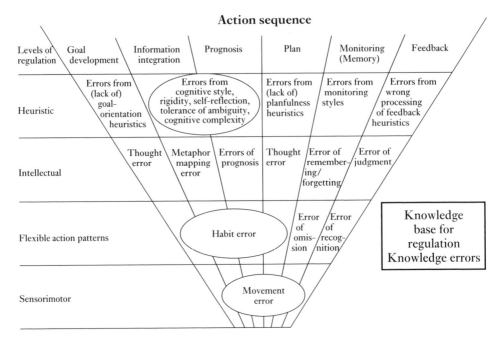

Figure 1   A taxonomy of action errors.

Note: This taxonomy consists of two dimensions – the action sequence and the levels of regulation – plus the knowledge base for regulation (important for knowledge errors). The reverse pyramid shape signifies that one cannot differentiate the action sequence on the lower levels of regulation.

negative event (such as an error) has occurred, observers will tend to see it as a sign of inherent weakness in the person that they had failed to predict a negative event that they, the observers, had seen coming. For these reasons, people tend to prevent errors and/or they attempt to disguise their errors (reattribute them to others or to the situation, or seek to conceal them). Additional potential consequences of error prevention in organizations are low expectations of the likelihood of errors and, therefore, reduced reaction time to correct an error, little use of systematic error detection, and concealment of errors to avoid sanctions. These factors contribute to increases in latent errors in an organization and low learning from errors.

Thus, a strategy focusing narrowly on error prevention may not help organizational learning. This has led some scholars to argue for an error management approach (Sitkin, 1992) that has the aim of "reducing future errors, of avoiding negative error consequences, and of dealing quickly with error consequences, once they

occur" (Frese, 1995: 113). An error management strategy aims to alleviate or avert negative error consequences, by such means as training to enhance people's ability to recognize and deal with errors efficiently, and by changes to system and organizational design. This approach seeks to avoid the negative error consequences of errors, but not necessarily the errors themselves. Figure 1 explains the differences between error prevention and error avoidance, as one of relative emphasis on causes vs. consequences. Effective error management should support error detection and increase the speed of the reaction of systems and individuals so as to minimize negative consequences. System design can play a part in reducing the negative consequences (such as the UNDO function in computing). Learning from errors is enhanced by means of better understanding, less inappropriate personal attribution, and better use of error correction strategies. Many quality improvement concepts (such as kaizen, or continuous improvement) are implicitly based on such error management principles.

The most important benefit of error management is its effect on organizational learning. Evidence shows that people have to be instructed to view errors as learning opportunities to counter negative emotional and self-regulatory effects (Heimbeck et al., 2003). At a different level of analysis, error management as a cultural condition in organizations has been shown to be positively related to profitability (Van Dyck et al., 2003).

See also *crises/ disasters; double-loop learning; feedback; learning, individual; learning organization;*

Bibliography

Dörner, D. (1996). *The Logic of Failure.* Reading, MA: Addison Wesley.

Frese, M. (1995). Error management in training: Conceptual and empirical results. In C. Zuccchermaglio, S. Bagnara, and S. U. Stucky (eds.), *Organizational Learning and Technological Change.* Berlin: Springer, 112–24.

Hartley, R. F. (1997). *Management Mistakes and Successes.* New York: Wiley.

Heimbeck, D., Frese, M., Sonnentag, S., and Keith, N. (2003). Integrating errors into the training process: The function of error management instructions and the role of goal orientation. *Personnel Psychology,* 56, 333–62.

Kahneman, D., Slovic, P., and Tversky, A. (eds.) (1982). *Judgment Under Uncertainty: Heuristics and Biases.* Cambridge, MA: Cambridge University Press.

Perrow, C. (1984). *Normal Accidents: Living with High Risk Technologies.* New York: Cambridge University Press.

Reason, J. (1997). *Managing the Risks of Organizational Accidents.* Aldershot: Ashgate.

Sitkin, S. B. (1992). Learning through failure: The strategy of small losses. *Research in Organizational Behavior,* 14, 231–66.

Van Dyck, C., Frese, M., Baer, M., and Sonnentag, S. (2003). Organizational error management culture and its impact on profitability: A two study replication. Submitted for publication. Giessen: Dept. of Psychology, University of Giessen.

Zapf, D., Brodbeck, F. C., Frese, M., Peters, H., and Prümper, J. (1992). Errors in working with computers: A first validation of a taxonomy for observed errors in a field setting. *International Journal of Human–Computer Interaction,* 4, 311–39.

ethics

see CORPORATE SOCIAL PERFORMANCE

ethnicity

see DISCRIMINATION

ethnography

Stephen R. Barley

This has traditionally been the methodology of choice in cultural anthropology, although numerous sociologists and an increasing number of organizational theorists have pursued ethnographic research (*see* RESEARCH DESIGN; RESEARCH METHODS). The aim of ethnography is to comprehend and portray the culture of a collective, or the activities that occur in a circumscribed setting from the point of view of an insider. Accordingly, ethnographers rely heavily on participation and observation as means of data collection. Doing ethnography requires a researcher to spend long periods of time observing, interviewing, and interacting with the people he or she studies. Ethnographers therefore measure periods of fieldwork in months and even years. Most ethnographers collect data in the form of fieldnotes – written records of the activities they have observed and the conversations in which they have engaged. Ethnographers may supplement their observations with data from surveys, archives, video tapes, audio tapes, and formal interviews. Although ethnography is frequently equated with "qualitative" research, the equation is misguided. Many forms of qualitative research, such as textual analysis, conversational analysis, and interpretive deconstruction (*see* POSTMODERNISM), do not qualify as ethnography because they have little to say about the way of life in a social collective. Moreover, numerous ethnographers make use of quantitative data. For instance, ethnographers were among the first social scientists to make extensive use of graph theory and NETWORK ANALYSIS (Hage and Harary 1983). The distinguishing marks of ethnography are therefore long periods of fieldwork and the intent to portray the culture of a group or setting from the inside.

As documents, ethnographies can be divided into two broad types: emic or etic. These terms derive from "phonetic" and "phonemic" and were coined by Pike (see Pike,1990, for a review of the history of and debate on the distinction). An emic ethnography attempts to communicate the "native's point of view," to portray a culture or setting entirely from the perspective of an insider. Emic ethnographies frequently organize information using the terminology and conceptual systems of a participant. In contrast, etic ethnographies organize information according to an analytic scheme developed by the researcher and tend to make more liberal use of concepts drawn from sociological or anthropological theory. In both cases, however, the analysis is presented in a discursive or narrative form. Van Maanen (1988) explicated several genres of ethnographic narrative that reflect ontological stances ranging from realism to interpretive relativism. The particular power of ethnography for organization studies is its ability to reveal processes and phenomena largely ignored by the field. Exemplary ethnographies in this regard are Kunda's (1991) study of the contradictions of life in a high-technology company and Jackall's (1988) investigation of how managers conceptualize and handle moral dilemmas.

See also *organizational culture; symbolism*

Bibliography

Agar, M. H. (1980). *The Professional Stranger: An Informal Introduction to Ethnography*. New York: Academic Press.
Hage, P. and Harary, F. (1983). *Structural Models in Anthropology*. Cambridge: Cambridge University Press.
Jackall, R. (1988). *Moral Mazes: The World of Corporate Managers*. New York: Oxford University Press.
Kunda, G. (1991). *Engineering Culture: Control and Commitment in a High-Tech Corporation*. Philadelphia, PA: Temple University Press.
Pike, K. (1990). *Emics and Etics: The Insider–Outsider Debate*. Newbury Park, CA: Sage.
Van Maanen, J. (1988). *Tales of the Field: On Writing Ethnography*. Chicago: University of Chicago Press.

ethnomethodology

see ETHNOGRAPHY; RESEARCH METHODS

evolutionary perspectives

J. Peter Murmann

Evolutionary perspectives contend that complex structures in the social and the biological world have developed over time through causal processes that require little or no foresight but considerable trial and error. Evolutionary thought in organizational analysis comprises two distinct intellectual lines. The first, concerned with organizational change, relies to a considerable extent on a selection logic in which change comes about through the birth and death of individual entities that make up a population of similar things. This account of change contrasts sharply with theories in which omniscient actors perfectly transform individual entities to meet new environmental conditions. The second line of evolutionary thought draws on EVOLUTIONARY PSYCHOLOGY to explain the behavior of human beings in organizational settings in terms of the evolved nature of the human mind and body. The key idea in this more recent second line of thought is that the functions and processes of the human mind stopped evolving long ago when they were adapted to the life of Stone Age hunter-gatherer societies living in the African savannas. According to this theory, because today's physical and social world is so different from that of our Stone Age ancestors, our brains are ill adapted for many life patterns in present-day industrial societies. Management scholars in this tradition are developing detailed knowledge about the properties of the human brain (e.g., the role of emotions and cognitive heuristics in decision making) and how they shape our behavior at work. At the same time, these scholars aim to develop principles for designing work places that are more consistent with and compensate for some of the evolved shortcomings of human nature.

As Donald Campbell pointed out in the 1960s, one can formulate a model of stability and change at a high level of abstraction that applies across a large variety of domains, ranging from culture to biology. On the level of pure logic, the three processes of variation, selection, and retention (VSR) collectively constitute a complete model for explaining both persistence and change in structures. The two lines of evolutionary thought in organizational analysis differ most fundamentally in terms of the time scales they examine. For evolutionary psychologists, the time scale is hundreds of thousands of years; for theorists of organizational change, the time scale ranges from minutes to hundreds of years. Because of the different time scales used, scholars drawing on evolutionary psychology focus on stable features of the brain (retention), whereas organizational theorists focus more on processes that generate novelty and competition (variation and selection), which bring about change. Over the past three decades, the latter theorists have developed detailed and complementary VSR-based models of change ranging from the micro to macro levels of organization: Weick at the level of the group, Burgelman at the level of the individual organization, and Aldrich and Nelson and Winter at the level of the industry and the economy. Because an evolutionary perspective – in contrast to essentialist ontologies – always involves a population of entities, the appeal and the future promise of this perspective lie in the possibility that change is already built into the basic structure of the theory. Unlike a Newtonian-type of science, the evolutionary perspective belongs firmly to the historical sciences. The ever-growing number of evolutionary-minded scholars will increasingly draw on historical methods to identify more detailed causal mechanisms that are transforming diverse arenas in the social and economic landscape.

See also *community ecology; organizational ecology*

Bibliography

Aldrich, H. (1999). *Organizations Evolving*. London: Sage.

Murmann, J. P. (2003). *Knowledge and Competitive Advantage: The Coevolution of Firms, Technology, and National Institutions* New York: Cambridge University Press.

Nelson, R. R. and Winter, S. G. (1982). *An Evolutionary Theory of Economic Change*. Cambridge, MA: Belknap Press of Harvard University Press.

Nicholson, N. (2000). *Executive Instinct: Managing the Human Animal in the Information Age*. New York: Crown Business.

Weick, K. E. (1979). *The Social Psychology of Organizing*. Reading, MA: Addison-Wesley.

evolutionary psychology

Nigel Nicholson

Evolutionary psychology (EP) is the body of thought that has emerged from major and rapid development in Darwinian theorizing over the last 30 years. It concerns how our evolved biology affects the way we think and act, and what this implies for our social life and institutions. The core proposition is that the human species evolved by retaining key features of psychological and physical design, including a range of heritable biases, goals, dispositions, impulses, and capabilities that were shaped for survival and reproduction in our ancestral hunter-gatherer environment. The new paradigm challenges the long taken-for-granted *tabula rasa* assumptions of traditional social science, about the extreme malleability of human thought and action. By implication this also challenges much optimism in management about the range of outcomes for which people can be developed and the demands of organizational roles and designs to which people can readily adapt. Rather, it suggests that we need to design and implement processes, systems, and institutions that are compatible with an unchanging human nature.

Psychology, neuroscience, and anthropology are at the core of EP theorizing, but despite its name it is an interdisciplinary field, bringing together scholars from biological sciences, all the social sciences including law and economics, humanities such as law and archeology, as well as philosophers and ethicists. Its ideas have radical implications for all of these areas. It builds upon, but departs in significant respects from, what was called "sociobiology." Contemporary EP has moved on with much more sophisticated theoretical precepts and empirical supporting evidence, especially through the work of Robert Trivers, John Tooby, and Leda Cosmides, and popular writings by Robert Wright and Stephen Pinker. Through their work the ideas have gained much wider acceptance, though they remain deeply controversial for many.

Only in the 1990s were the ideas first applied to business (Nicholson, 1997). Since then they have been slowly gaining attention, but less in management science than other disciplines. The implications for OB are as wide as the field (Nicholson, 2000). In considering ORGANIZA-

TIONAL DESIGN the neo-Darwinian perspective suggests that small size and flexible hierarchies are optimal for human satisfaction and coordination, and that these properties relate directly to channels of resource availability (Pierce and White, 1999). It also indicates the importance of perceived CONTRACT violations in organizational life, and highlights the great importance attached by people to issues of procedural and distributive injustice in the workplace (see JUSTICE, PROCEDURAL).

An EP framework can also be claimed to integrate research and theory in the areas of cognition, affect, and SELF-REGULATION. For example, many of the biases recorded by BEHAVIORAL DECISION RESEARCH, the persistence of economically irrational behaviors in NEGOTIATION such as ALTRUISM, and varieties of risk behavior can be conceived as heritable and favorable to fitness. The same reasoning applies to various social judgments, such as stereotyping, in-group out-group biases, and various ATTRIBUTION processes, which are extensions of the human capacity and imperative for what psychologists call "everyday mindreading" applied to complex social environments.

Status variations are also predicted to be major determinants of both physical and psychological well-being in all primates, and large scale occupational studies have shown consistent parallels among human populations of subordinate rank. It is said that human sensitivities to rank are adaptively oriented to fluid hierarchies with an egalitarian ethos. The consequence is that major inequalities such as are prevalent in modern societies – indexed by the *Gini coefficient* in economics – are predictive of loss of social cohesion and deleterious consequences for social well-being and life expectancy.

Perhaps the most controversial area of application is in the area of sex differences. EP asserts that the different optimal reproductive strategies of men and women also equip them with distinctive dispositions and orientations, often reflected in work-related preferences and styles (Browne, 1998). This is perhaps most manifest in male propensities for competitive striving and women's predilection for networking and co-operative endeavor. The small number of women in top business positions has been attrib-

uted to this difference, a by-product of the male bias inherent in organizational design and career systems (Nicholson, 2000). More idiosyncratic individual differences are also of interest. The Big Five PERSONALITY dimensions have been claimed to be a highly general species adaptation, and heritable individual variations are thought to be the result of frequency dependent selection – the comparative advantage for social roles and mating opportunities of having a distinctive profile. (see FIVE FACTOR MODEL OF PERSONALITY).

EP offers a radical and rich alternative to traditional theories of organizational behavior, but suffers from a lack of specificity in its ability to generate novel testable hypotheses in OB. These are hard to articulate, for various reasons, though scholars have done so successfully in a range of topics, especially in the realms of cognitive and social behavior. Perhaps for the moment the greatest value that can be claimed for the perspective in relation to OB is as a novel, powerful, consistent, and simplifying explanatory framework for reviewing topics and themes in the field. The future prospects are for steady growth in application of the paradigm, though continued opposition to its assumptions is also likely to persist.

See also *decision-making; evolutionary perspectives; stress; women at work*

Bibliography

Barkow, J. H, Cosmides, L., and Tooby, J. (eds.) (1992). *The Adapted Mind: Evolutionary Psychology and the Generation of Culture*. Oxford: Oxford University Press.

Barrett, L., Dunbar, R., and Lycett, J. (2002). *Human Evolutionary Psychology*. New York: Palgrave.

Browne, K. (1998). *Divided Labors: An Evolutionary View of Women at Work*. London: Wiedenfeld and Nicolson.

Markóczy, L. (ed.) (1998). Management, organization, and human nature. Special issue of *Managerial and Decision Economics*, 19 (7–8).

Nicholson, N. (1997). Evolutionary psychology: Toward a new view of human nature and organizational society. *Human Relations*, 50, 1053–78.

Nicholson, N. (2000). *Managing the Human Animal*. London: Texere.

Nicholson, N. and White, R. (2005). Darwinian perspectives on behavior in organizations. *Journal of Organizational Behavior*. Special issue: in press.

Pierce, B. and White, R. (1999). The evolution of social structure: Why biology matters. *Academy of Management Review*, **24**, 843–53.

Pinker, S. (2002). *The Blank Slate*. New York: Viking.

Wright, R. (1994). *The Moral Animal: Evolutionary Psychology and Everyday Life*. New York: Little, Brown.

excellence

see REPUTATION

exchange relations

J. Keith Murnighan

Exchange relations is a theoretical perspective that analyzes interpersonal interactions and relationships on the basis of their costs and benefits. Our constant interactions with one another are conceptualized as a series of exchanges (*see* GROUP DYNAMICS). Analyzing exchange relations can determine who has POWER over whom, and how much power they have.

Early exchange theorists (Homans, 1961; Thibaut and Kelley, 1961; Blau, 1964) assumed that people maximize their own utilities by weighing the costs and benefits of their actions. Analysis includes the costs and benefits of both parties. The power in a relationship could then be determined by the mutual interdependence of the parties. If person X depended upon person Y for positive outcomes and person Y did not depend on X, then exchange theory says that Y has power over X (e.g., Cook and Emerson. 1978). As X's outcomes from Y become more unique, Y's power over X grows. Not surprisingly, changes in the balance of power between two parties also tend to change the dynamics and processes within their relationship. Thus, dependent parties, for instance, tend to initiate interactions more than powerful actors do.

Organizationally, supervisors not only control the financial outcomes of their employees (termed "fate control" by Thibaut and Kelley, 1961) but they also influence employees' behavior ("behavior control") by rewarding particular sets of behaviors. At the same time, employees can organize (*see* COALITION FORMATION) and generate additional alternatives for themselves, thereby controlling their employers' outcomes ("mutual fate control"; see Mechanic, 1962).

Interpersonally, Thibaut and Kelley (1961) suggested that people use comparison levels (alternative states) to determine their happiness and satisfaction: they compare their current situation with alternative states, including their own past or their anticipated future (*see* SOCIAL COMPARISON). People use "a comparison level for alternatives" to determine how satisfied they might be if they made a change (in their job, their home, etc.). When a person's comparison level for alternatives is better than his or her current state, a change will provide benefits that more than compensate for the costs of change. Thus, people should change jobs when an alternative provides so many benefits that it also covers the costs of changing (*see* COMMITMENT; TURNOVER). When employees do not have such alternatives (e.g., during poor economies or job scarcity), employers' fate and behavior control increases. When jobs are plentiful and the economy is booming, however, employees' power increases and their employers' fate and behavior control over them decreases.

Research on the value of others' costs and benefits – the relatively new area of social utility – indicates that individuals are attuned to others' outcomes as well as their own and that others' outcomes provide individuals with additional utility. This line of analysis expands the fundamental notion that the parties to an interaction will make many of their decisions on the basis of their own individual costs and benefits. More generally, exchange theory and its extensions provide a particularly rational basis for understanding the complex interplay within and between organizations and individuals.

See also *game theory; negotiation; resource dependence*

Bibliography

Blau, P. M. (1964). *Exchange and Power in Social Life*. New York: Wiley.

Cook, K. S. and Emerson, R. M. (1978). Power, equity, and commitment in exchange networks. *American Sociological Review*, **43**, 721–39.

Homans, G. C. (1961). *Social Behavior: Its Elementary Forms.* New York: Harcourt, Brace, and World.

Mechanic, D. (1962). Sources of power of lower participants in complex organizations. *Administrative Science Quarterly*, 7, 349–64.

Thibaut, J. and Kelley, H. H. (1961). *The Social Psychology of Groups.* New York: Wiley.

executive derailment

Sarah Ronson and Randall S. Peterson

Derailed executives are those who show high promise up to a general management level, but then find limited opportunity for further advancement because their skill set has not grown in line with the demands of increasing responsibility (Van Velsor and Leslie, 1995). Ironically, many of these executives will have advanced quickly and performed well above average early in their careers because of their technical skills (Ference, Stoner, and Warren, 1977). Executive derailment occurs due to a misalignment between an executive's skill set and the changing job requirements of moving from managing in a technical environment into general management (Van Velsor and Leslie, 1995). Five interrelated skill deficiencies have been identified consistently across time and national culture as likely to derail executives careers: (1) problems with developing strong interpersonal relationships; (2) failure to build and lead a team; (3) too narrow or technical an approach in the face of changing circumstances; (4) failure to meet business objectives at the new organization level coupled with a blaming reaction to the failure; and (5) unwillingness to learn (McCall, 1997; Van Velsor and Leslie, 1995). Many derailed executives demonstrated at least one of these failures early in their career, but were promoted despite the failing in the belief that they would address the failure as they learned their new position (McCall, 1997).

The concept of derailment originated largely with McCall when he conducted a series of studies in the 1980s and 1990s at the Center for Creative Leadership (McCall, 1997; Van Velsor and Leslie, 1995). Since then, the notion of derailment and the factors affecting derailment have been found to be relevant across many cultures and over a quarter of a century of research (Van Velsor and Leslie, 1995). However, derailment should be viewed as a dynamic interaction between personality and context, not simply as resulting from an individual characteristic. Skills, particularly technical or functional expertise, that are valued early in a career can become weakness as a manager progresses, blinding the manager to the bigger picture. Certain flaws, such as arrogance, are tolerated in some contexts, but not in others; success can lead to overconfidence and result in poor decisions (McCall, 1997).

The issue of executive derailment seems likely to become increasingly important for managers. The gap between skill sets required at lower and higher organization levels is likely to increase, particularly in knowledge industries, in which deep and specialized knowledge is required for high levels of performance at lower organization levels. This focus may provide little opportunity to develop the general management and interpersonal skills required at higher levels of the organization. As the pace of technological and economic change increases, managers will need to be more flexible and willing to learn than ever before. Finally, globalization also demands higher levels of flexibility for international executives, both as they enter new cultural contexts and when they return to their home country (McCall, 1997).

Research to date on executive derailment has focused primarily on empirical studies of practitioners, resulting in a reasonable understanding of the phenomenon, but a relative lack of theoretical development. Now that robust effects have been found and replicated, future scholarly attention needs to focus on theoretical development to better integrate the literature on executive derailment with theoretical perspectives in careers, leadership, and human resources management.

See also *CEOs; deviance; leadership; personality*

Bibliography

Ference, T. P., Stoner, J. A. F., and Warren, E. K. (1977). Managing the career plateau. *Academy of Management Review*, 2, 602–13.

McCall, M. W. (1997). *High Flyers: Developing the Next Generation of Leaders.* Cambridge, MA: Harvard Business School.

Van Velsor, E. and Leslie, J. B. (1995). Why executives derail: Perspectives across time and cultures. *Academy of Management Executive*, 9, 62–73.

executive succession

William Ocasio

The process of selection and removal, and the transfer of power of senior organizational managers is a topic of long and continuing interest in macro-organizational behavior. As macro theories have focused since the late 1970s on the effects of the environment on organizations, research on the topic has examined whether and how executive succession serves to align the organization's environment with the internal POWER structures and strategic orientations of senior executives.

Various theoretical perspectives in macro-organizational behavior have viewed executive succession as critical for organizational adaptation and strategic choice, including RESOURCE DEPENDENCE theory (Pfeffer and Salancik, 1978), AGENCY THEORY (Zajac, 1990), organizational learning (Viranyi, Tushman, and Romanelli, 1992), TOP MANAGEMENT TEAM theory (Boeker, 1992), political coalition theory (Ocasio, 1994), and ORGANIZATIONAL DEMOGRAPHY (Zajac and Westphal, 1996). More recently, INSTITUTIONAL THEORY has also focused on executive succession, viewing succession as a mechanism of both stability and change (Ocasio 1999; Thornton and Ocasio 1999) in organizations and organizational fields.

The adaptive effects of executive succession were first highlighted by Pfeffer and Salancik (1978), who view the selection and removal of executives as the outcome of a political process and the distribution of power in organizations. Building on both resource dependence and strategic contingencies' view of power, they posited the tenure and removal of executives as a function of the ability of executives to cope with environmental contingencies, and executive succession as a political process, resolved by sub-unit power. According to Pfeffer and Salancik (1978), however, organizational adaptation through executive succession is moderated by political entrenchment and the institutionalization of power of senior executives.

Empirical research supports the general contours of a resource dependence view on executive succession. Executive succession is determined in part by organizational performance, but the effects are moderated by the power of CEOs relative to members of corporate boards and other senior executives (Boeker 1992; Ocasio 1994). Changes in sub-unit power serve to align the organization with changing strategic contingencies. During the 1960s and 1970s, US industrial organizations experienced the rise of financial CEOs to power in large corporations, as finance executives were more oriented towards strategies of diversification and mergers and acquisitions under a "finance conception of control" and the rise of portfolio management strategies and large conglomerates (Fligstein, 1987). In the 1980s and 1990s, financial CEOs declined in power, as foreign competitive threats took hold, conglomerates became illegitimate, and portfolio management strategies were abandoned (Ocasio and Kim, 1999).

The effects of executive succession on organizational adaptation have also received empirical support. For example, Viranyi, Tushman, and Romanelli (1992), show that executive succession is a mechanism for organizational learning as turnover of senior executives is associated with strategic reorientations and organizational change. They show that it is important to distinguish between CEO succession and executive-team change, which independently improve subsequent organization performance. They further find that positive impact of succession is accentuated when it coincides with strategic reorientation. Boeker (1992) also distinguishes between CEO succession and the succession of other members of the top management team. He finds that changes in other top managers are subject to scapegoating, as powerful CEOs displace blame for poor performance onto their subordinates, the top managers of the organization, who subsequently are replaced, while the chief executive remains.

Resource dependence perspectives on executive succession have been complemented with approaches that focus on internal political processes and demographic characteristics of senior executives and board members. Viewing firms as political coalitions, Ocasio (1994) high-lights internal power struggles as determinants of succession and posits a model of circulation of power, where the power of the CEO is subject to obsolescence and contestation. The circulation of power emphasizes the internal contests for control and opposition to the CEO that emerge with increased executive tenure and under conditions of economic adversity. Ocasio (1994) finds support for an increasing rate of CEO succession during the first decade of tenure, consistent with the model of circulation, followed by a slow decline afterward, consistent with the institutionalization of the CEO's power. The model was extended by Ocasio and Kim (1999). They find evidence of an ideological and political obsolescence of financial CEOs and a change in the strategic contingencies that previously favored finance and the financial conception of control. In their model, circulation of power is contingent on both changes in environmental contingencies and on ideological challenges to existing conceptions of control.

An important issue in studies of executive succession has been the selection of insiders versus outsiders, particularly with respect to CEO succession. Most CEO successions are by insiders, with the rate of outsider succession increasing under poor economic performance (Ocasio, 1999). The selection of insiders versus outsiders as CEO has incorporated lessons drawn from agency theory (Zajac, 1990), organizational demography (Zajac and Westphal, 1996) and institutional theories (Ocasio, 1999). Zajac (1990) focuses on the information asymmetries that result in superior performance for insider CEOs. Zajac and Westphal (1996) examine the effects of CEO–board power and that outside CEOs are demographically similar to board members. Ocasio (1999) found that boards rely on both past precedents and formal internal labor markets for executive succession and the selection of insiders versus outsiders as CEOs.

While most research on executive succession has focused on the interplay between micropolitics and environmental contingencies, institutional perspectives focus on how executive succession is shaped by rules and logics at the level of the organization (Ocasio, 1999) and organizational field. Thornton and Ocasio (1999) found that the determinants of executive succession were historically contingent on the institutional logics that prevailed in the field. Under a professional logic, power POLITICS are shaped by hierarchical relationships and internal growth, and executive succession is determined by organization size and structure. Under a market logic, power politics are directed toward issues of resource competition and acquisition growth, and executive succession is determined by the product market and the market for corporate control.

Research on executive succession continues in the twenty-first century, with renewed focus on both power dynamics and the role of succession on strategic orientations.

See also *career development; organizational change; role transitions*

Bibliography

Boeker, W. (1992). Power and managerial dismissal: Scapegoating at the top. *Administrative Science Quarterly*, 37, 400–21.
Fligstein, N. (1987). The intraorganizational power struggle: Rise of finance personnel to top leadership in large corporations, 1919–1979. *American Sociological Review*, 52, 44–58.
Ocasio, W. (1994). Political dynamics and the circulation of power: CEO succession in United States industrial corporations, 1960–1990. *Administrative Science Quarterly*, 39, 285–312.
Ocasio, W. (1999). Institutionalized action and corporate governance: The reliance on rules of CEO succession. *Administrative Science Quarterly*, 44 (2), 384–416.
Ocasio W. and Kim, H. (1999). The circulation of corporate control: Selection of functional backgrounds of new CEOs in large US manufacturing firms, 1981–1992. *Administrative Science Quarterly*, 44, 532–62.
Pfeffer, J. and Salancik, G. (1978) *The External Control of Organizations: A Resource Dependence Perspective*. New York: Harper and Row.
Thornton, P. H. and Ocasio, W. (1999). Institutional logics and the historical contingency of power in organizations: Executive succession in the higher education publishing industry, 1958–1990. *American Journal of Sociology*, 105, 801–43.
Viranyi, B., Tushman, M. L., and Romanelli, E. (1992). Executive succession and organization outcomes in turbulent environments: An organization learning approach. *Organization Science*, 3, 72–91.
Zajac, E. J. (1990). CEO selection, succession, compensation and firm performance: A theoretical integration

and empirical analysis. *Strategic Management Journal*, 11, 217–30.

Zajac, E. J. and Westphal, J. D. (1996). Who shall succeed? How CEO board preferences and power affect the choice of new CEOs. *Academy of Management Journal*, 39, 64–90.

expectancy

see MOTIVATION

expected utility theory

see EXCHANGE RELATIONS; GAME THEORY; PROSPECT THEORY

extinction

see BEHAVIORISM

extraversion

see FIVE FACTOR MODEL OF PERSONALITY; PERSONALITY

extrinsic and intrinsic motivation

Beth A. Hennessey and Teresa M. Amabile

Intrinsic MOTIVATION is the motivation to do something for its own sake, for the sheer enjoyment of the task itself. Extrinsic motivation is the motivation to do something in order to attain some external goal or meet some externally imposed constraint. Theorists have emphasized the role of certain psychological states in the experience of intrinsic motivation, including a sense of self-determination or perceived control over task engagement (Deci and Ryan, 1985) and a sense of optimal challenge (Csikszentmihalyi, 1997) that enhances self-perceptions of competence (Deci and Ryan, 1985). The highest level of intrinsic motivation state has been labeled "optimal experience" or "flow" (Csikszentmihalyi, 1997). Extrinsic motivation can be engendered by a number of social-environmental factors, including expected reward, expected evaluation, competition, surveillance, time limits, and external control over task engagement (Amabile, 1996; Deci and Ryan, 1985). Research reveals that, although general intrinsic and extrinsic motivational orientations toward one's work are relatively stable traits, both intrinsic and extrinsic motivational states can vary considerably above or below an individual's baseline level as a function of the immediate social environment (Amabile et al., 1994).

There is considerable experimental evidence that extrinsic motivators in the social environment can undermine intrinsic motivation. Because people are often not fully aware of their own motivations, they are sometimes in the same position as outside observers of their own actions. Thus, in situations where their behavior is *overjustified* (where both a plausible internal cause and a plausible external cause are present), people tend to *discount* the internal cause (intrinsic motivation) in favor of the external cause (extrinsic motivation). For example, under expected reward or evaluation or external control over the way in which they do an activity, people may perceive themselves as engaging in the activity not because it interests them but because they have been coerced.

However, there is recent evidence that, under some circumstances, certain forms of reward may enhance intrinsic motivation through a process of motivational synergy (Amabile, 1996; Hennessey and Zbikowski, 1993). This process is more likely to the extent that initial intrinsic motivation is strong and salient, as well as the extent to which extrinsic rewards confirm a person's competence and the value of the person's work, or enable the person to become more deeply engaged in work that was already intrinsically interesting.

Research has demonstrated that intrinsic and extrinsic motivation have a number of performance consequences for a wide variety of subject populations. Children who are more intrinsically motivated toward an activity are more likely to undertake that activity voluntarily, more likely to learn complex material effectively, and more likely to be creative in the activity (see Deci and Ryan, 1985). Adults who are more intrinsically motivated are also more likely to be creative in their work, in domains as diverse as writing poetry, doing artwork, and inventing new products in corporations (Amabile, 1996). This phenomenon is summarized by the Intrinsic Motivation Principle of Creativity: people will be most creative when they feel motivated primarily by the interest, enjoyment, satisfaction, and challenge of the work itself – and not by external pressures or inducements.

See also *incentives; job satisfaction; personal initiative*

Bibliography

Amabile, T. M. (1996). *Creativity in Context*. Boulder, CO: Westview Press.

Amabile, T. M., Hill, K. G., Hennessey, B. A., and Tighe, E. M. (1994). The Work Preference Inventory: Assessing intrinsic and extrinsic motivational orientations. *Journal of Personality and Social Psychology*, **66**, 950–67.

Csikszentmihalyi, M. (1997). *Creativity: Flow and the Psychology of Discovery and Invention*. New York: Harper Collins.

Deci, E. L. and Ryan, R. M. (1985). *Intrinsic Motivational and Self-Determination in Human Behavior*. New York: Plenum.

Hennessey, B. A. and Zbikowski, S. (1993). Immunizing children against the negative effects of reward: A further examination of intrinsic motivation training techniques. *Creativity Research Journal*, **6**, 297–307.

extrinsic satisfaction

see EXTRINSIC AND INTRINSIC MOTIVATION; JOB SATISFACTION

F

family firms

Nigel Nicholson

Defining the family firm is not straightforward, though the general consensus is that they are businesses where families have a controlling interest, which may be quite a modest ownership share in a large publicly quoted business. Family firms, according to how one defines them, account for a substantial proportion of all businesses and the GDP of most economies (Shanker and Astrachan, 1999). In many parts of the world they are among the largest, most long-lived and most successful firms. They differ greatly in form, with distinctive issues absorbing them at their various stages of development (Gersick et al. 1997): the controlling owner phase, the sibling partnership, the cousin consortium, and the open family firm, where ownership is highly diffused.

Research into family firms has tended to be specialized rather than integrated into the mainstream of organizational and management science. Even in the field of ENTREPRENEUR-SHIP there is little mention of them. A recent exception to this neglect has been the attention of economists interested in AGENCY problems in business, who assert that while family firms have the advantage of unifying ownership and control, they are vulnerable to a range of unique fresh hazards essentially to do with a malign influence on DECISION-MAKING of sentiment, family favor, and other biases (Schulze et al., 2001). It is certainly the case that family firms are vulnerable to unique threats to their viability, the most common being failure to prepare for or effectively implement leadership succession, inability to integrate family and non-family interests, intra-family conflict, and diffusion or loss of ownership.

However, scholars and commentators in the area frequently assert that family firms, when they survive these hazards, have unique advantages over non-family firms, such as powerful and integrated cultures, long-term strategic perspectives and "patient capital," value driven LEADERSHIP with high social responsibility concerns, high trust and loyalty in stakeholder relationships, and speed and pragmatism in operational decision-making. Much of the evidence to support this is anecdotal or case based, though a recent systematic comparison of family and non-family publicly quoted US firms found the family firms significantly outperformed their counterparts (Anderson and Reeb, 2003), and also fared better when the CEO was family rather than non-family.

It can be argued that the agency hazards can be overstated and that there is a performance premium to be extracted from the unique qualities of a culture that rests upon a "genetic" identity between a business and its owners and executives (Nicholson, 2000). However, to secure this requires GOVERNANCE mechanisms that enable leadership and decision-making to resolve the special challenges family firms face (Neubauer and Lank, 1998). It has become common for special devices such as family councils and constitutions to be implemented that enable the family to speak with a single voice, for family and non-family interests to be aligned, for values and principles to be made explicit, and for transitions (leadership, ownership, and strategic) to be planned and delivered smoothly.

One can predict increased interest in family firms, because of the growing diversity of types of business beyond traditional corporate forms, and because of the theoretical and empirical richness of the challenge to understand what underlies their success and failure. A major future issue in the area will be how they adapt and preserve their strengths through radical demographic changes that are transforming the structure, size, and cultural values of families worldwide.

See also *corporate boards; organizational culture*

Bibliography

Anderson, R. C. and Reeb, D. M. (2003). Founding family ownership and firm performance: Evidence from the SandP 500. *Journal of Finance*.

Gersick, K. E., Davis, J. A., Hampton, M. M., and Lansberg, I. (1997). *Generation to Generation*. Cambridge, MA: Harvard Business School Press.

Neubauer, F. and Lank, A. G. (1998). *The Family Business: Its Governance and Sustainability*. London: Macmillan.

Nicholson, N. (2000). *Managing the Human Animal*. London: Texere.

Shanker, M. C. and Astrachan, J. H. (1999). Myths and realities: Family businesses' contribution to the US economy: A framework for assessing family business statistics. *Family Business Review*, 9, 107–24.

Schulze, W. S., Lubatkin, M. H., Dino, R. N., and Buchholtz, A. K. (2001). Agency relationships in family firms: Theory and evidence. *Organization Science*, 12, 99–116.

feedback

Angelo DeNisi

Feedback refers to information a person receives about his or her performance or behavior. This may include some evaluation, or it may simply indicate the level of performance or the nature of the behavior. Feedback may be intrinsic to the task at hand, or it may require some external source. Feedback may or may not include information on how to improve performance, but it is most effective when such information is included.

For many years, it was assumed that performance feedback generally facilitated performance improvements, especially when that feedback was positive. Much of what we knew or believed to be true was based on the conclusions from a major review of the feedback literature conducted by Ammons (1956). But, by the 1970s, a number of scholars were arguing that reactions

to feedback were more complex than had been suspected. For example, Herold and Greller (1977) noted that reactions to feedback were dependent, to a large extent, upon the credibility of the source of the feedback, and the psychological closeness of that source. Soon afterwards, a very influential theoretical paper (Ilgen, Fisher and Taylor, 1979) outlined a series of issues that were proposed to influence feedback effectiveness, emphasizing both the source of the feedback and the sign of the feedback. Specifically, these authors noted that there were mechanisms through which recipients could discount negative feedback, and so argued that it would be less effective.

For the most part, however, feedback was widely accepted as being either effective or, perhaps, neutral, but there were only a few arguments that feedback could ever be destructive or harmful for subsequent performance. One exception to this view (DeNisi, Randolph, and Blencoe, 1983) dealt with feedback from peers. Those authors reported that negative feedback from peers was extremely harmful to subsequent group processes and cohesiveness and resulted in significant performance decrements. In fact, the effects of feedback from multiple sources have become much more important with the increased reliance upon multi-rater or 360 Degree appraisal systems, and the effectiveness of feedback in these settings appears to be mixed (see, for example, Brett and Atwater, 2001; Seifert, Yukl, and McDonald, 2003).

Based on a meta-analysis of hundreds of studies on feedback effectiveness, published over the previous hundred years, Kluger and DeNisi (1996) concluded that, in roughly one-third of the cases, feedback (regardless of its sign) actually *harmed* subsequent performance. That is, in most cases, feedback worked as most expected (both positive and negative feedback exhibited an ability to improve performance), but, in a significant number of cases, providing feedback results in performance getting worse – not remaining the same and certainly not improving. Those authors also noted, however, that most published studies dealing with feedback actually lacked the data needed to draw any firm conclusions about effectiveness. Specifically, they found that surprisingly few studies made a direct comparison between a group of individuals receiving feedback and a comparable group receiving no feedback (i.e., a control group). Instead, most studies simply examined the effectiveness of different types of feedback, while assuming that, in general, feedback worked as intended. The results of the Kluger and DeNisi (1996) meta-analysis and theoretical review were important because they indicated that feedback was not always effective and because they revealed the absence of rigorous evaluations of feedback effectiveness.

Kluger and DeNisi also developed a contingent model of feedback effectiveness (Feedback Intervention Theory; Kluger and DeNisi, 1989; 1996; DeNisi and Kluger 2000), based on their data and relevant theory, which proposed some parameters for when feedback should work as intended, and when it probably won't. For example, feedback (regardless of sign) is most likely to be problematic when a person is working on a new or extremely complex task. That is because the person needs all his or her cognitive resources to master performance on the task, and any attention paid to the feedback is a distraction. In addition, feedback that is threatening to one's self-image is especially problematic, as the recipient tends to focus on aspects of that identity rather than on improving performance. Feedback is more likely to be helpful and effective when it is directed at behavior rather than at a person; when it is provided in a timely and regularly scheduled fashion; when it allows the recipient to see improvement; when the recipient is also told about ways to improve performance; and when the recipient is encouraged to set goals for improvement.

This work has led to scholars (and managers) thinking more about what makes feedback more or less effective. It is important to realize that feedback does not always work as intended (even if it usually does). This means that it is critical that organizations actually evaluate the effectiveness of any feedback intervention, rather than simply assume that it works. The increased reliance upon teams at work makes it especially critical that we come to understand how feedback works. As noted earlier, there is evidence that negative feedback from peers may be especially harmful, and yet such feedback is critical for team performance and in the case of multi-source feedback. Therefore, it is important that we learn more about the exact nature of the effects of negative feedback from peers and come to understand how to make such feedback more effective.

Also, given the fact that there is evidence that feedback can be harmful when a person is working on a novel task, and given the fact that the nature of work is rapidly changing, we also need to develop a better understanding of how and when to provide performance feedback as work changes. In general, it should now be clear that organizations and individual managers must be concerned with questions about the nature of the feedback they give, and even whether they should provide feedback in every case. Sweeping recommendations that feedback is universally helpful and useful are clearly not appropriate.

See also *goal setting; incentives; performance appraisal/performance management*

Bibliography

Ammons, R. B. (1956). Effects of knowledge of performance: A survey and tentative theoretical formulation. *Journal of General Psychology*, **54**, 279–99.

Brett, J. F. and Atwater, L. E. (2001). 360 Degree feedback: Accuracy, reactions, and perceptions of usefulness. *Journal of Applied Psychology*, **86**, 930–42.

DeNisi, A. S. and Kluger, A. N. (2000). Feedback effectiveness: Can 360 Degree appraisals be improved? *Academy of Management Executive*, **14**, 129–39.

DeNisi, A. S., Randolph, W. A., and Blencoe, A. G. (1983). Potential problems with peer ratings. *Academy of Management Journal*, **26**, 457–67.

Herold, D. M. and Greller, M. M. (1977). Feedback: The definition of a construct. *Academy of Management Journal*, **20**, 142–7.

Ilgen, D. R., Fisher, C. D., and Taylor, M. S. (1979). Consequences of individual feedback on behavior in organizations. *Journal of Applied Psychology*, **64**, 340–71.

Kluger, A. N. and DeNisi, A. S. (1989). Feedback interventions: Toward the understanding of a double-edged sword. *Current Directions in Psychological Science*, 7, 67–72.

Kluger, A. N. and DeNisi, A. S. (1996). The effects of feedback interventions on performance: Historical review, meta-analysis, a preliminary feedback intervention theory. *Psychological Bulletin*, 119, 254–84.

Seifert, C. F., Yukl, G., and McDonald, R. A. (2003). Effects of multi-source feedback and a feedback facilitator on the influence behavior of managers towards subordinates. *Journal of Applied Psychology*, **88**, 561–9.

feminism

see GENDER

five factor model of personality

Timothy A. Judge and Brent A. Scott

Consensus is emerging that a five factor model of PERSONALITY (often termed the "Big Five") can be used to describe the most salient aspects of personality (Goldberg, 1992). The first researchers to replicate the five factor structure were Norman (1963) and Tupes and Christal, who are generally credited with founding the five factor model. The five factor structure has been recaptured through analyses of trait adjectives in various languages, factor analytic studies of existing personality inventories, and decisions regarding the dimensionality of existing measures made by expert judges. The cross-cultural generalizability of the five factor structure has been established through research in many countries. Evidence indicates that the Big Five are heritable and stable over time.

The traits comprising the five factor model are:

Extraversion. Extraversion represents the tendency to be outgoing, assertive, active, and excitement seeking, and is comprised of three major components: sociability, dominance, and positive emotionality. Whereas neuroticism is related to the experience of negative life events, extraverts are predisposed to experience positive emotions (Costa and McCrae, 1992). Evidence also indicates that extraverts have more friends and spend more time in social situations than do introverts (*see* EMOTION IN ORGANIZATIONS).

Agreeableness. Agreeableness consists of tendencies to be kind, gentle, trusting and trustworthy, and warm. It has been argued that agreeableness should be related to happiness because agreeable individuals have greater motivation to achieve interpersonal intimacy, which should lead to greater levels of well-being. Organ and Lingl note that agreeableness "involves getting along with others in pleasant, satisfying relationships."

Conscientiousness. Conscientiousness is comprised of two major facets: achievement and dependability. The subjective well-being literature suggests a positive relationship between conscientiousness and life satisfaction. Evidence even indicates that conscientious individuals live longer.

Neuroticism. Neuroticism, often labeled by the positive pole of the trait, emotional stability, is the tendency to show poor emotional adjustment in the form of STRESS, anxiety, depression, and fear. Due to their essentially negative nature, neurotic individuals experience more negative life events than other individuals, in part because they select themselves into situations that foster negative affect.

Openness to experience. Openness to experience is defined by being intellectual (as opposed to unreflective or narrow), artistic, imaginative, and polished or cultured. Openness to experience is related to scientific and artistic creativity, divergent thinking, low religiosity, and political liberalism. Openness to experience is a "double-edged sword" that predisposes individuals to feel both the good and the bad more deeply.

RELEVANCE OF FACETS

One of the most prominent criticisms of the five factor model is that it provides too coarse a description of personality. Although some researchers have argued for fewer than five traits, most personality psychologists who criticize the number of factors do so on the basis of too few factors. As Block has noted: "for an adequate understanding of personality, it is necessary to think and measure more specifically than at this global level if behaviors and their mediating variables are to be sufficiently, incisively represented." In industrial-organizational (I-O) psychology, the relative merits of broad versus specific traits (framed in terms of the bandwidth-fidelity issue) also have been debated with respect to the Big Five traits. Some researchers have argued in favor of traits more numerous or specific than the Big Five. Hough argued that the Big Five obscures important relations between traits and criteria. She concludes: "If prediction of life outcomes or criteria is important in evaluating personality taxonomies, the Big Five is an inadequate taxonomy of personality constructs." Conversely, Ones and Viswesvaran argued that broader and richer personality traits will have higher predictive validity than narrower traits.

MEASUREMENT

There are a variety of measures of the Big Five that researchers have at their disposal. The Revised NEO Personality Inventory (NEO-PI-R; Costa and McCrae, 1992) is a standardized measure of the Big Five, meaning that it has published norms and an established track record of reliability and VALIDITY. The NEO-PI-R was revised from the NEO-PI (Costa and McCrae, 1985) to include facets of agreeableness and conscientiousness. Overall, the full NEO-PI-R contains 30 facets of the Big Five and consists of 240 items. A shorter version of the NEO consists of 40 items measuring conscientiousness, agreeableness, neuroticism, openness to experience, and extraversion; however, this scale cannot be used to compute the facets contained in the full measure. The NEO-PI-R is a proprietary measure, so researchers must obtain permission from the authors in order to utilize it in their research.

In contrast, Goldberg (1992) developed a non-proprietary personality inventory based on adjectives of the Big Five identified previously by Norman (1963). Goldberg identified 100 unipolar descriptors of the Big Five, with 20 items per factor. Although this scale cannot be used to compute facets of the Big Five, its robust yet simplistic design makes this scale attractive to researchers. To facilitate greater ease of use, Saucier (1994) subsequently developed "mini-markers" of the full unipolar scale. The "mini-markers" scale consists of 40 unipolar adjectives taken from the full set of Big Five markers. Saucier (1994) demonstrated the comparative validity of the mini-markers to the full set of unipolar markers.

The Big Five Inventory (BFI; John, Donahue, and Kentle, 1991) is a 44-item, non-proprietary measure developed with the goal of creating a brief inventory that would allow assessment of the five factors when specific facets were not needed. In contrast to the unipolar markers scale developed by Goldberg (1992), the BFI uses short phrases based on prototypical adjectives of the Big Five. The BFI has demonstrated convergent validity with other Big Five measures.

While self-report has been the traditional means by which to assess personality, a number of researchers have found utility in using reports from individuals other than the person of interest. These observer ratings can come from a variety of sources, but supervisors and significant others are typically used. Although one may question the VALIDITY of observer ratings on such an internal characteristic as personality, research has demonstrated that these ratings can match or even exceed the predictive validity of self-report measures. For example, Mount, Barrick, and Strauss (1994) found that supervisor, co-worker, and customer ratings of conscientiousness and extraversion predicted performance ratings over and above self-report ratings. In addition, Judge et al. (1999) utilized observations by trained psychologists to measure personality in a longitudinal analysis of the relationship between personality and CAREER success. These observer ratings possessed good reliability and demonstrated predictive validity. Taken together, the Mount, Barrick, and Strauss (1994) and Judge et al. (1999) papers illustrate the benefits of using observer ratings to assess personality.

RELEVANCE OF BIG FIVE TO
ORGANIZATIONAL BEHAVIOR

The Big Five have been related to a variety of fundamental organizational behavior variables, including JOB SATISFACTION, LEADERSHIP, performance, and MOTIVATION. We consider meta-analytic results for each of these in turn.

Job satisfaction   Judge, Heller, and Mount (2002), in a meta-analysis of 334 correlations from 163 independent samples, reported that, as a set, the Big Five traits had a multiple correlation of .41 with job satisfaction. Specifically, neuroticism, conscientiousness, and extraversion displayed the strongest correlations with job satisfaction ($= -.29$, .26, and .25, respectively). Agreeableness and openness to experience were more weakly related to job satisfaction, with estimated true score correlations of .17 and .02, respectively. Moreover, the relationships between neuroticism and extraversion with job satisfaction generalized across studies. Thus, the results of this meta-analysis suggest that the Big Five are important determinants of individual job satisfaction.

Leadership   Judge, Bono, et al. (2002) meta-analyzed 222 correlations from 73 independent samples to derive the relationships between the Big Five and leadership. As a set, the Big Five traits had a multiple correlation of .48 with leadership. Specifically, extraversion displayed the strongest relationship with leadership (= .31), followed by conscientiousness (= .28), neuroticism (= −.24), openness to experience (= .24), and agreeableness (= .08). Across studies and across the different leadership criteria (i.e., leader emergence and leader effectiveness), extraversion emerged as the most consistent predictor. Overall, these results indicate strong support for traditional trait approaches to the study of leadership.

Performance   One of the most popular applications of the five factor model has been to the area of job performance, where numerous meta-analyses have been conducted (e.g., Barrick and Mount, 1991; Hurtz and Donovan, 2000; Robertson and Kinder, 1993; Salgado, 1997). The most cited of these meta-analyses is Barrick and Mount (1991). In reviewing the literature on the relationship between personality and job performance, these authors noted:

> The overall conclusion from these studies is that the validity of personality as a predictor of job performance is quite low . . . However, at the time these studies were conducted, no well-accepted taxonomy existed for classifying personality traits. Consequently, it was not possible to determine whether there were consistent, meaningful relationships between particular personality constructs and performance criteria in different occupations. (Barrick and Mount, 1991: 1–2)

Motivation   Judge and Ilies (2002) demonstrated that the Big Five traits are related to three types of performance motivation: GOAL-SETTING motivation, expectancy motivation, and SELF-EFFICACY motivation. In a meta-analysis of 150 correlations from 65 studies, Judge and Ilies (2002) reported that, as a set, the Big Five had an average multiple correlation of .49 with performance motivation. Specifically, neuroticism (= −.31) and conscientiousness (= .24) were the strongest, most consistent correlates of overall performance motivation. The relationships between the remaining Big Five traits, however, were not as consistent. Extraversion was more strongly related to self-efficacy motivation than expectancy motivation. Agreeableness was positively related to expectancy motivation but negatively related to goal-setting motivation. Openness to experience was positively related to goal-setting motivation and self-efficacy motivation but negatively related to expectancy motivation. Taken together, these results suggest that the Big Five are important correlates of performance motivation.

See also *individual differences*

Bibliography

Barrick, M. R. and Mount, M. K. (1991). The Big Five personality dimensions and job performance: A meta-analysis. *Personnel Psychology*, 44, 1–26.

Costa, P. T., Jr. and McCrae, R. R. (1985). *The NEO Personality Inventory Manual*. Odessa, FL: Psychological Assessment Resources.

Costa, P. T., Jr. and McCrae, R. R. (1992). *Revised NEO Personality Inventory (NEO-PI-R) and NEO Five-Factor Inventory (NEO-FFI) Professional Manual*. Odessa, FL: Psychological Assessment Resources.

Goldberg, L. R. (1992). The development of the Big-Five factor structure. *Psychological Assessment*, 1, 26–42.

Hurtz, G. M. and Donovan, J. J. (2000). Personality and job performance: The Big Five revisited. *Journal of Applied Psychology*, 85, 869–79.

John, O. P., Donahue, E. M., and Kentle, R. L. (1991). *The Big Five Inventory – Versions 4a and 54*. Berkeley, CA: University of California, Institute of Personality and Social Research.

Judge, T. A. and Ilies, R. (2002). Relationship of personality to performance motivation: A meta-analytic review. *Journal of Applied Psychology*, 87, 797–807.

Judge, T. A., Bono, J. E., Ilies, R. and Gerhardt, M. W. (2002). Personality and leadership: A qualitative and quantitative review. *Journal of Applied Psychology*, 87, (4), 765–80.

Judge, T. A., Heller, D., and Mount, M. K. (2002). Five-Factor model of personality and job satisfaction: A meta-analysis. *Journal of Applied Psychology*, 87, 530–41.

Judge, T. A., Higgins, C. A., Thoresen, C. J., and Barrick, M. R. (1999). The Big Five personality traits, general mental ability, and career success across the life span. *Personnel Psychology*, 52, 621–52.

Mount, M. K., Barrick, M. R., and Strauss, J. P. (1994). Validity of observer ratings of the Big Five personality factors. *Journal of Applied Psychology*, **79**, 272–80.

Norman, W. T. (1963). Toward an adequate taxonomy of personality attributes: Replicated factor structure in peer nomination personality ratings. *Journal of Abnormal and Social Psychology*, **66**, 574–83.

Robertson, I. T. and Kinder, A. (1993). Personality and job competencies: The criterion-related validity of some personality variables. *Journal of Occupational and Organizational Psychology*, **66**, 226–44.

Salgado, J. F. (1997). The five factor model of personality and job performance in the European Community. *Journal of Applied Psychology*, **82**, 30–43.

Saucier, G. (1994). Mini-markers: A brief version of Goldberg's unipolar Big Five markers. *Journal of Personality Assessment*, **63**, 506–16.

force field analysis

Dale E. Zand

This is a technique for organizing and analyzing information about the forces maintaining a current condition, such as a group's performance or an individual's relationship to his or her superior, and planning change to improve the situation, attributable to Kurt Lewin (1951). The current condition is viewed as a quasi-stationary equilibrium, a changeable state maintained by a balance of dynamic (i.e., variable) forces, much like an aircraft in level flight. Force is a psychological construct, a perception of a factor and its influence. Forces have direction, driving or resisting movement toward the desired condition, and magnitude or psychological intensity (see figure 1).

Lewin proposed several fundamental propositions which subsequent research confirmed:

1 Adding or increasing driving forces arouses an increase in resisting forces; the current equilibrium does not change but continues under increased tension.

2 Reducing or removing resisting forces is preferable because it allows movement without increasing tension.

3 GROUP NORMS are a critical force in change efforts. Individuals who value their membership in a group will resist change to the degree that they must deviate from the group's norms. Changing a group's norms

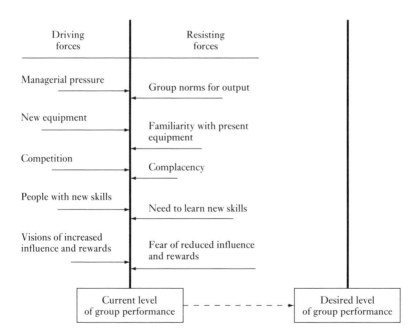

Figure 1 Force field diagram

will reduce this key source of individual resistance.

4   Induced, internal forces such as goal consensus are more powerful, enduring motivators of change than imposed, external forces such as management pressure.

Force field analysis with its propositions, a legacy of Lewin's seminal contributions to change theory and research, is and will continue to be a valuable, readily understandable tool for diagnosing and planning change.

See also *organization development; organizational change*

Bibliography

Burke, W. W. (1982). *Organization Development: Principles and Practices.* New York: Little, Brown.

Lewin, K. (1951). *Field Theory in Social Science.* New York: Harper.

Fordism

see ORGANIZATIONAL DESIGN

formal organization

see ORGANIZATIONAL DESIGN; ORGANIZATIONAL STRUCTURE

formalization

see ORGANIZATIONAL DESIGN; ORGANIZATIONAL STRUCTURE

functional design

see ORGANIZATIONAL DESIGN; ORGANIZATIONAL STRUCTURE

fundamental attribution error

see ATTRIBUTION

G

gain-sharing

see INCENTIVES

game theory

J. Keith Murnighan

Game theory analyzes how rational actors react to potentially conflictual, interdependent interactions (*see* CONFLICT AND CONFLICT MANAGEMENT). Games (i.e., any strategic interactions among interdependent parties) are defined by the players involved, the payoffs, and the rules of the game. These core elements allow the players to choose a variety of strategies, and it is the interaction of possible strategies that becomes a central focus of game theory.

Games are either cooperative, in which the players can make and expect binding COMMITMENTS, or non-cooperative, in which the players cannot make or expect binding commitments. Non-cooperative games typically assume that the payoffs of a game subsume all of the issues that a player might find valuable. In other words, the payoffs should represent the players' utilities for different outcomes.

This way of analyzing games comes from their initial formalization by John von Neumann, an applied mathematician, and Oskar Morgenstern, an economist, in their groundbreaking and amazingly comprehensive *Theory of Games and Economic Behavior* (1947). They contended that "this theory of games of strategy is the proper instrument with which to develop a theory of economic behavior." Their book then presented an exposition of both utility theory and game theory. Since then, game theory has been used to analyze matters as weighty and diverse as international nuclear strategy, local and global environmental concerns, and global trade and monetary issues, and utility has been a cornerstone of decision theory. Game theory's models consider a variety of structural conflicts, ranging from two- to n-party games (*see* COALITION FORMATION), from complete to incomplete information games, and from static to dynamic games (*see* GROUP DYNAMICS). It is probably safe to say that von Neumann and Morgenstern were correct: game theory has revolutionized economics; after almost 60 years since the appearance of their classic book, it has become the central model of microeconomics.

One early and important breakthrough in game theory was John Nash's proposal of the since-called Nash equilibrium (Nash, 1950), in which each of the parties in an interaction selects a strategy that is optimal, given the others' strategies (*see* NEGOTIATION). The Nash equilibria of a game are particularly compelling, as none of the parties have an incentive to change their strategies once they have all chosen an equilibrium strategy, since doing so would reduce a player's payoffs.

Although game theory and its domain of inquiry seem immediately relevant for the study of cognitions and behavior both between and within organizations (*see* MANAGERIAL AND ORGANIZATIONAL COGNITION), organizational behavior has paid little or no attention to game theory, even though game theory is currently undergoing exciting expansion, both theoretically and empirically.

Game theory involves and has been defined as the problem of exchange (von Neumann and Morgenstern's original definition, 1947; *see* EXCHANGE RELATIONS), decisions in conflict situations (Rapoport, 1973), the interaction of rational decision-makers (Myerson, 1991) (*see*

DECISION-MAKING; RATIONALITY), or multi-person decision problems (Gibbons, 1992). "The essence of a 'game' . . . is that it involves decision-makers with different goals or objectives whose fates are intertwined" (Shubik, 1964: 8). Game-theoretic reasoning is "a mathematical shortcut" that theorists use to determine what intelligent, adaptive, rational players will do when they are faced with conflict (Camerer, 1991).

Although its potential applicability may be far-reaching, a strict interpretation of game theory is restricted to an analytical, theoretical approach to conflict situations. A game theorist makes assumptions, considers their logical consequences, and proves theorems which, given the assumptions, are true. Theoretical game theorists "examine what ultrasmart, impeccably rational, super-people should do in competitive, interactive situations" (Raiffa, 1982: 21).

Theoretical game theory is precise and clean, mathematically precise. Like the physical sciences, it investigates human interaction as if it were in a vacuum. And also like the physical sciences, its greatest successes produce truly beautiful, elegant models.

Game theory's theoretical domain is neither descriptive nor normative: it neither describes everyday people's actions nor tells them what to do. Instead, it is analytic: "game theorists analyze the formal implications of various levels of mutual rationality in strategic situations" (Aumann, 1991). By its very nature, theoretical game theory is not refutable: it analyzes limited problems in specifically bounded domains and solves them mathematically (see THEORY).

Game theoretic analysis has, quite naturally, been extended to the realm of empirical predictions. These predictions have been tremendously successful at predicting behavior in market interactions (Smith, 2002). In bargaining and other interpersonal interactions, however, extensions of game theory's analyses to predict behavior have been much less successful. Experiments on the Prisoner's Dilemma game, for instance, which number in the thousands, uniformly indicate that the participants do not defect on every round in finite plays of the game, as the Nash equilibrium indicates that rational people should. Instead, typically about 50 percent of the time, even in one-shot games, people cooperate (Rapoport, 1988).

Another example of the failures of directly extending game theory's analysis to behavior comes from the results testing game theory's strong prediction in ultimatum bargaining. In a standard experimental treatment of an ultimatum game (e.g., Pillutla and Murnighan, 1995), one person receives an amount of money (say $50) and must offer some of it to another person. They can either accept or reject the offer. If the second person accepts, they receive the amount offered and the first person receives the remainder ($50 minus the amount offered). If they reject the offer, both people receive nothing. Game theory uses backward induction (i.e., starting at the end and working backward, to the first choices in an interaction) to predict that, since something is better than nothing, the second person should accept any positive offer and, therefore, the offerer should make a small offer that is accepted. Not surprisingly, this strong theoretical prediction is upheld for few respondents and almost no offerers. (Research indicates that, although some people will accept offers as small as a penny, many offers approach 50–50, and many respondents reject offers that have positive value, sometimes considerable.) Although game theory's prediction is not supported empirically, its logic is unassailable (given its assumptions), and its ability to provide a basis for generating interesting games like the ultimatum game has spawned the exciting new area of behavioral game theory (see the following).

These examples show how empirical extensions of game theory "test" its theoretical principles. The messy realities of everyday human interaction make the empirical domain (and most other social scientific endeavors) less deterministic than the theoretical domain.

Current game theory is expanding its horizons to encompass the general analysis of potentially conflictual interactions. Models are now being developed to accommodate the foibles and psycho-logic of real, rather than strictly rational, human actors (e.g., Raiffa, 1982).

Much of this development has been spurred by the empirical work on game theory. The field of experimental economics has grown exponentially since its early days (e.g., Smith, 1962). This has led to an exciting interplay of experimental observations that inform new game theoretic models, which incorporate assumptions designed to handle some of the peculiarities (i.e., departures from rationality) of everyday human behavior. This developing area of intense experimental activity has recently been called behavioral game theory (Camerer, 2003). Behavioral game theory includes a wide array of experiments on a variety of intriguing games, including the ultimatum game (mentioned above), the dictator game, trust games, asymmetric information games, dominance-solvable games, signaling games, coordination games, and reputation games, to mention a few (Camerer, 2003). These economically motivated experiments shed light on what have previously been topics at the center of the domain of social psychology, including fairness, altruism, and learning. The combination of game theory and experimental methods has provided an important bridge between the fields of economics and psychology (Murnighan and Ross, 1999). The intermingling of these two previously disparate fields provides considerable promise for both theoretical and empirical advances.

Unfortunately, game theory continues to suffer considerable criticism from other social scientists (see Murnighan, 1994). Some social scientists confuse the analytical and behavioral domains of game theory; some are put off by game theory's difficult mathematics; others reject game theory's rational approach. Although game theory may not describe the behavior of the general public, its attention to sophisticated, experienced, knowledgeable, and strategic actors, and its recent attempts to accommodate non-equilibrium behavior, provide us with insights that are unattainable from more mundane analysis. In addition, a number of easily read treatments make game theory understandable without sophisticated mathematics (e.g., Gibbons, 1992; McMillan, 1992).

Most business strategy decisions fit within the broader scope of game theory (Camerer, 1991). Dynamics, communication (see COMMUNICATION), and differential perceptions of the game are all now part of game-theoretic investigations – making it much more appropriate for applicability to research in organizational behavior and strategy. Game theorists' strong theory should provide researchers with potent tools for advancing understandings of conflict and POWER. Its influence is clearly evident in the frameworks it

provides for analyzing the political dynamics of coalition behavior, the dilemma of volunteering (Murnighan, 1994), and broad scale international interactions. These are just some of the examples of areas where little progress has been achieved prior to the recent use of game theoretic models.

Game theory has grown and, from an economic point of view, has become increasingly useful throughout the social sciences. As Myerson (1992: 62) notes: "Game theory provides a fundamental and systematic way of thinking about questions that concern all of the social sciences."

See also *behavioral decision research; bounded rationality; prospect theory; risk taking*

Bibliography

Aumann, R. (1991). Irrationality in game theory. In D. Gale and O. Hart (eds.), *Economic Analysis of Markets and Games*. Cambridge: Cambridge University Press.

Camerer, C. (1991). Does strategy research need game theory? *Strategic Management Journal*, 12, 137–52.

Camerer, C. (2003). *Behavioral Game Theory: Experiments in Strategic Interaction*. New York: Russell Sage Foundation.

Gibbons, R. (1992). *Game Theory for Applied Economists*. Princeton, NJ: Princeton University Press.

McMillan, J. (1992). *Games, Strategies, and Managers*. New York: Oxford University Press.

Murnighan, J. K. (1994). Game theory and organizational behavior. In L. Cummings and B. M. Staw (eds.), *Research on Organizational Behavior*. Greenwich, CT: JAI Press.

Murnighan, J. K. and Ross, T. (1999). On the collaborative potential of psychology and economics. (The introduction to a special issue). *Journal of Economic Behavior and Organization*, 39, 1–10.

Myerson, R. (1991). *Game Theory: Analysis of Conflict*. Cambridge, MA: Harvard University Press.

Myerson, R. (1992). On the value of game theory social science. *Rationality and Society*, 4, 62–73.

Nash, J. (1950). The bargaining problem. *Econometrica*, 28, 155–62.

Pillutla, M. M. and Murnighan, J. K. (1995). Being fair or appearing fair: Strategic behavior in ultimatum bargaining. *Academy of Management Journal*, 38, 1408–26.

Raiffa, H. (1982). *The Art and Science of Negotiation*. Cambridge, MA: Harvard University Press.

Rapoport, A. (1973). *Two-Person Game Theory*. Ann Arbor: University of Michigan Press.

Rapoport, A. (1988). Experiments with n-person social traps I: Prisoner's dilemma, weak prisoner's dilemma, volunteer's dilemma, and largest number. *Journal of Conflict Resolution*, **32**, 457–72.

Shubik, M. (1964). *Game Theory and Related Approaches to Social Behavior*. New York: Wiley.

Smith, V. (1962). An experimental study of competitive market behavior. *Journal of Political Economy*, **70**, 111–37.

Smith, V. (2002). Constructivist and ecological rationality in economics. *American Economic Review*, 93, 465–508.

Von Neumann, J. and Morgenstern, O. (1947). *The Theory of Games and Economic Behavior*. Princeton, NJ: Princeton University Press.

garbage can model

Henrich R. Greve

The garbage can model is a simulation model of organizational DECISION-MAKING under ambiguity (Cohen, March, and Olsen, 1972). It examines how decisions are made when individual preferences are uncertain, cause–effect relations are unclear, and participation in decision-making is fluid. Uncertain preferences and unclear causal relations are found in organizations with unclear TECHNOLOGY and loosely defined goals, such as universities, in subunits of organizations with well-defined overall goals, and when making decisions that do not have an obvious link with the organizational goal. The garbage can is a descriptive model of how decision-making unfolds under some simple assumptions of individual responses to ambiguity. First, solutions are independent of problems rather than answers to problems. Second, participants and choice opportunities are independent of both problems and solutions. Decisions happen when these four flows meet and decision-makers have sufficient energy to deal with the problem.

Findings from the garbage can model include high sensitivity to the authority structure and level of slack resources, a high percentage of decisions that do not solve problems, and frequent association of problems with specific individuals. The model predicts which decision-making structures would likely be effective under different levels of organizational resources and environmental adversity. The main features of the model correspond well with the qualitative evidence from university decision-making processes that inspired the garbage can model.

The garbage can model is a classic in the organizational simulation literature, which now is quite large (Lomi and Larsen, 2001). It is often used to interpret observations of chaotic decision-making processes (Levitt and Nass, 1989), and its predictions have also seen some testing in quantitative studies (Hendrick, 1998). In theoretical work, it is often cited to support the arguments that solutions are not necessarily results of problems, but may be independently or jointly developed, and that decision-maker attention is a scarce resource with great consequences for decision-making. Both statements are consistent with the model and cement its place as an important building block of organizational decision-making under ambiguity. It is used primarily in the fields of organizational theory and political science.

Because the model contradicts rational choice theory (*see* RATIONALITY), it is associated with some controversy, especially in political science (Bendor, Moe, and Shotts, 2001), where rational choice theory is more prominent than in organizational theory. Rational choice theorists will tend to reject its assumptions of the independence of problem and solution flows and decision-making without clearly defined goals. Suggested rational-choice alternatives tend to be incompatible with the original garbage can model because they replace ambiguity of goals with uncertainty about consequences, which alters the interpretation.

The garbage can model has a unique place in organizational theory through its ability to make counter-intuitive predictions of the conditions under which organizations will make fewer or more decisions. With the widespread availability of research methods on the timing of events, one should expect tests of the garbage can model on the timing of decisions in addition to its current use in field research.

See also *behavioral decision research; learning organization*

Bibliography

Bendor, J., Moe, T. M., and Shotts, K. W. (2001). Recycling the garbage can: An assessment of the research program. *American Political Science Review*, **95**, 169–90.

Cohen, M. D., March, J. G., and Olsen, J. P. (1972). A garbage can model of organizational choice. *Administrative Science Quarterly*, **17**, 1–25.

Hendrick, R. (1998). The impact of federal grants and other funds on general fund expenditure decisions: A detailed analysis of one city. *Journal of Public Administration Research and Theory*, **8**, 353–89.

Levitt, B. and Nass, C. (1989). The lid on the garbage can: Institutional constraints on decision-making in the technical core of college-text publishers. *Administrative Science Quarterly*, **34**, 190–207.

Lomi, A. and Larsen, E. R. (eds.) (2001). *Dynamics of Organizations: Computational Modeling and Organizational Theories*. Palo Alto, CA: AAAI Press.

When compared with the more peripheral group members, research has shown that gatekeepers reported significantly higher feelings of participation, satisfaction, responsibility, and commitment to the final group product.

See also *organizational design; power; role*

Bibliography

Lewin, K. (1947). Frontiers in group dynamics: Concepts, method, and reality in social science: social equilibria and social change. *Human Relations*, **1**, 5–41.

White, D. M. (1950). The "gatekeepers": A case study in the selection of news. *Journalism Quarterly*, **27**, 383–90.

gatekeepers

W. Warner Burke

Like many concepts in organizational behavior, that of gatekeepers is metaphorical. When thinking literally of *gate*, one typically imagines a movable object that either stops or allows the flow of physical movement. Gatekeepers, a term originated by Lewin (1947), are persons who either facilitate or impede information flow between people. Gatekeepers are therefore at the nexus of exchange among individuals interpersonally, in groups, or within and across organizations. The term has even influenced thinking in the world of journalism. Editors of newspapers, for example, are seen as gatekeepers, since they determine what gets printed for the public and what does not (White, 1950).

From an organizational behavior perspective, middle managers may occupy the most important roles as gatekeepers in organizations. They pass or do not pass information up, down, and across the hierarchy in organizations. As gatekeepers they can determine whether and what kind of information flows throughout organizations.

The term has been used primarily in group dynamics. Gatekeepers are group members who either help the well-being and maintenance of the group or hinder such processes. By seeking people's ideas and opinions (opening the gate for information flow and participation), gatekeepers effectively facilitate the group's work toward its objectives.

gender

Barbara A. Gutek, Layne Paddock, and Jessica Bagger

The concept of gender, as used in the study of women and men at work, originated in the 1970s in order to differentiate biological differences between men and women from social roles performed by men and women (see Korabik, 1999). Until that time, both differences in ability to bear children and ability to be a manager, for example, were considered sex differences: women were suited to bearing children and men were suited to managing the affairs of business and state. Women and men who did not exhibit sex-typed characteristics or interests were presumed to be psychologically maladjusted. Behavioral scientists in the 1970s applied the label of "gender" to refer to mutable social roles played by the two sexes, leaving the concept of "sex" to refer to biological differences between men and women. This differentiation between sex and gender allowed researchers and theoreticians to question how many of the characteristics and behaviors assumed to be part of men's and women's natures (biological essentialism) were in fact socially constructed. Furthermore, if there is no biological reason why women cannot succeed at any CAREER, then presumably there should be no social impediment (such as not allowing women to enter MBA programs) to their becoming managers and succeeding in that role or in any other role they might choose. As a result, many opportunities previously closed to women were now opened to them.

As the concept of gender became accepted, one-dimensional theories like biological essentialism gave way to more complex models. Sex and gender are now considered theoretically independent constructs. According to an early popular model (Bem, 1974), masculinity and femininity were not polar opposites as they had been conceptualized for decades, but instead they represented two dimensions on which both men and women varied. Furthermore, if masculinity and femininity were separate dimensions, one might score high on both (labeled androgynous), high on one or the other, or low on both (not very common). Androgyny was held out as a model for career success because androgynous people of both sexes should have at their command the whole repertoire of behaviors considered appropriate for men and women. Such a person could be both aggressive and warm, for example.

Many jobs are gendered, in that men more often hold certain kinds of jobs (auto mechanic, neurosurgeon) and women more often hold other jobs (secretary, dietician). In the case of service delivery, both the service provider role and the customer role are gendered (Gutek, Cherry and Groth, 1999). That is, while men and women tend to hold different service delivery jobs (e.g., selling life insurance versus selling children's clothing), men and women also play different customer roles. Men are more likely than women to buy life insurance, boats, or tickets to football games, while women are more likely to buy children's clothing and decorative items for the home, or have their hair colored. Both employees and customers can be gender congruent or gender incongruent (i.e., in a field considered unusual or inappropriate for someone of their gender). Job characteristics may also be gendered. Men may be viewed as especially suited to jobs that are high on task characteristics while women may be viewed as especially suited to jobs that are high on socio-emotional characteristics (see JOB DESIGN).

Researchers interested in gender may study one or more of five kinds of differences between men and women, including: physical differences (such as differences in upper body strength), differences in traits (differences in scores on aggressiveness), or differences in behavior (differences in amount of aggressive behavior). Another is differential treatment (including levels of compensation, rate of career progression). For example, female managers may be treated as secretaries while male secretaries may be assumed to be managers; female medical doctors may be treated as nurses while male nurses may be treated as medical doctors. A fifth area is differential reactions to men and women (differences in evaluation). For example, whereas a certain level of aggressiveness in a man might be evaluated positively, the same level of aggressiveness on the part of a woman might be evaluated negatively. While the first of these differences (physical differences) is clearly a function of sex, and differential treatment and differential reactions to men and women are clearly a function of gender, differences in traits and behavior may be a function of both sex and gender.

Feminist critics point out that the existing body of organizational theory is itself gendered in that it implicitly assumes that managers and workers are male, with stereotypically male attitudes, obligations, and power (see Calás and Smircich, 1996). For example, in the past, family obligations were rarely considered because the manager or employee is assumed to be a man who has few family obligations that would impose on his usual work hours (see NON-WORK/WORK). Perhaps because the study of gender is not a mainstream topic in organizational behavior, some researchers focusing on gender use non-traditional research methods such as deconstruction, a research method borrowed from literature (Martin, 1990). In addition, a number of researchers interested in gender have argued that the field of organizational behavior should also pay more attention to the concepts of ethnicity and race and researchers should also consider gender when they focus on ethnicity or race (see Ferdman, 1999).

An interest in the study of gender in organizational behavior has opened up the field to some new areas. Role identities provide an example of the way in which the study of gender has evolved. It is widely believed that women identify less with their job and more with their family roles than do men, for whom work role is their primary identification, but this is not necessarily true. Likewise, it is often assumed that retirement will be associated with greater role loss for men than women and that it will affect men more than women, but that, too, is not necessarily true.

Work and family issues provide another example of the way the study of gender has opened new areas to the field of organizational behavior. Increasingly, young professionals are choosing to have children later and to focus on career first; however, this does not alleviate work–family conflict for most employed women (see Hochschild, 1997). Organizations hoping to attract and retain women can take several different approaches. Some are implementing policies associated with work–family balance, known as family friendly policies (e.g., flextime, job sharing, etc.), which allow for greater integration of paid work and family demands. Research on family friendly policies focuses on positive work outcomes associated with specific policies and the relationship of other work variables like perceived fairness to policy effectiveness.

See also *career development; critical theory; discrimination; personality; women at work; women managers*

Bibliography

Bem (1974). The measurement of psychological androgyny. *Journal of Consulting and Clinical Psychology*, 42, 155–62.

Calás, M. and Smircich, L. (1996). From "the woman's" point of view: Feminist approaches to organization studies. In S. Clegg, C. Hardy, and W. Nord (eds.), *Handbook of Organizational Studies*. London: Sage, 222–34.

Cooper, C. L. and Lewis, S. (1999). Gender and the changing nature of work. In G. Powell (ed.), *Handbook of Gender and Work*. Newbury Park, CA: Sage, 37–46.

Ferdman, B. M. (1999). The color and culture of gender in organizations. In G. Powell (ed.), *Handbook of Gender and Work*. Newbury Park, CA: Sage, 17–34.

Gutek, B. A. (2001). Women and paid work. *Psychology of Women Quarterly*, 25, 379–93.

Gutek, B. A., Cherry, B., and Groth, M. (1999). Gender and service delivery. In G. Powell (ed.), *Handbook of Gender and Work*. Newbury Park, CA: Sage, 47–68.

Hochschild, A. R. (1997). *The Time Bind*. New York: Metropolitan Books.

Korabik, K. (1999). Sex and gender in the new millennium. In G. Powell (ed.), *Handbook of Gender and Work*. Newbury Park, CA: Sage.

Maier, M. (1999). On the gendered substructure of organization: Dimensions and dilemmas of corporate masculinity. In G. Powell (ed.), *Handbook of Gender and Work*. Newbury Park, CA: Sage, 69–93.

Martin, J. (1990). Deconstructing organizational taboos: The suppression of gender conflict in organizations. *Organizational Science*, 1 (4), 339–59.

Powell, G. (ed.) *Handbook of Gender and Work*. Newbury Park, CA: Sage.

Stroh, L. K., Brett, J. M., and Reilly, A. H. (1992). All the right stuff: A comparison of female and male managers' career progression. *Journal of Applied Psychology*, 77, 251–60.

generalization

Richard Klimoski

The goal of much of organizational science is generalization. Scholars (and reflective practitioners) wish to establish principles or theories of organizational behavior (OB) that are usually correct for a class of cases (e.g., new workers, large organizations) or situations (e.g., during mergers). However, the evidence or data available from research or experience is often limited. What we know may derive from a single case, study, type of measure, investigator, or even from a single nation. Thus, writers in OB (especially textbook writers) are usually making a generalization when they assert (or teach) that a functional relationship exists between two factors, a practice will have a particular consequence, or a particular business policy will have a specified impact (*see* THEORY). The correctness of any generalization will be a function of such factors as the number and breadth of cases for which there is particularized knowledge; consistency of the findings across such cases; degree of bias in the observer; quality of the research (*see* RESEARCH METHODS) or measures (*see* RELIABILITY); and degree of similarity between the instances on which the inferences are built and the individual, organization, or situation to which the generalization is being made.

See also *error; levels of analysis; research design; statistical methods; validity*

Bibliography

Cook, T. D., Campbell, D. T., and Peracchio, L. (1990). Quasi experimentation. In M. D. Dunnette and L. M. Hough (eds.), *Handbook of Industrial and Organizational Psychology*. Palo Alto, CA: Consulting Psychologists Press, 491–576.

Schmitt, N. W. and Klimoski, R. J. (1991). Research methods in human resources management. Cincinnati, OH: South-Western University Press.

goal orientation

Miriam Erez

Goal orientation originated in the educational psychology literature in the early 1980s, and has recently been applied to the work context (VandeWalle, Cron, and Slocum, 2001). Goal orientation represents a personal disposition to pursue either learning or performance goal orientations in achievement situations (Dweck, 1999). A learning goal orientation is associated with the belief that ability can be developed. In contrast, a performance goal orientation is associated with the belief that ability is fixed, and difficult to develop. A learning goal orientation motivates individuals to increase their competence and to master challenging situations. On the other hand, a performance goal orientation motivates individuals to establish the adequacy of their ability in the eyes of others and to avoid situations where they may appear inadequate. More recently, performance goal orientation was further divided into two distinct constructs: proving and avoidance (VandeWalle, Cron, and Slocum, 2001). Proving goal orientation focuses on demonstrating one's competence, and gaining favorable judgments from others. Avoiding goal orientation focuses on ways of avoiding negation of one's competence as well as unfavorable judgments by others. In the context of complex tasks, a learning goal orientation leads to higher performance level than a performance goal orientation, mainly by influencing the mediating variables of goal level, effort, and self-efficacy, and by feedback seeking.

Goal orientation can also be examined as a state. Research demonstrates that setting a learning goal is more effective than setting a performance goal in complex rather than simple tasks, and in situations where primarily the acquisition of ability rather than an increase in motivation is required.

See also *goal setting; motivation; performance appraisal/management*

Bibliography

Dweck, C. S. (1999). *Self-Theories: Their Role in Motivation, Personality, and Development*. Philadelphia, PA: Psychology Press.

VandeWalle, D. M., Cron, W. L., and Slocum, J. W. (2001). The role of goal orientation following performance feedback. *Journal of Applied Psychology*, **86**, 629–40.

goal setting

Miriam Erez

The goal setting theory of MOTIVATION is "the single most dominant theory in the field, with over a thousand articles and reviews published on the topic in over 35 years" (Mitchell and Daniels, 2003: 231). The theory proposes that goals are the immediate regulators of behavior and setting specific and difficult goals leads to higher performance levels than general "do your best" or easy goals. These effects are subject to two necessary conditions: goal COMMITMENT, and FEEDBACK on performance (Locke and Latham, 2002). In line with goal setting theory, social cognitive theory (Bandura, 2001) asserts that specific and high goals create negative discrepancies to be mastered, and this discrepancy mobilizes resources based on anticipatory estimates of what is necessary for goal attainment. The application of goal setting theory to the group level in the last decade confirmed that, similar to the effects at the individual level, group goals have a strong and positive effect on group performance (Latham and Pinder, 2005).

A *goal* is the aim of an action; for example, to attain a specific standard of proficiency on a given task, usually within a specified time limit (increase annual sales by 10 percent or reach an executive position within 10 years). Goals could be *proximal*, leading to immediate action, or *distal* and long term, with interim goals. A vision set by a leader is a distal goal. Goals could either be self-set, participatively set, or externally assigned. Self-set goals are anchored in a person's value system, which is a cognitive representation of basic needs and motives. When assigned by others, goal congruence with a person's motives and values assures goal acceptance.

Goals regulate behavior through four mechanisms (Locke and Latham, 2002; Mitchell and Daniels, 2003). First, goals *direct* effort and other resources towards goal-relevant activities. Second, goals have an *energizing* function, which sets the intensity of effort investment. Third, goals affect *persistence*, with specific hard goals leading to greater persistence in the face of obstacles than general or easy goals. Fourth, goals affect *strategy* development, mainly in highly complex tasks.

The goal setting theory has continuously developed over the last 35 years. The original model (Locke, 1968) posited a sequential five phase process:

Environmental stimuli→ Cognition→ Evaluation→ Intentions/Goals→ Performance

A more recent model of the high performance cycle (Locke and Latham, 2002) incorporates the moderators of goal commitment, feedback, goal importance, SELF-EFFICACY, and task complexity, and recognizes the mediators of strategy development and self-regulatory processes (*see* SELF-REGULATION).

Originally, goal-setting research (Locke, 1968) focused on goals and intentions as the immediate regulators of action and performance. This focus on proximal goals yielded a strong empirical base to the theory, which proposed that specific and difficult goals lead to higher performance levels compared to easy or general "do your best" goals. Once these basic relationships were established, the research progressively explored the three distal phases in the model: evaluation, cognition, and environmental stimuli.

The *evaluation phase* reflects the self-regulatory processes, including goal choice and direction, behavior monitoring, and the evaluation of goal accomplishment. The criteria used for evaluating goal choice and goal accomplishment are anchored in the value system that represents basic motives. Research in this domain identified four important factors in the evaluation process: feedback, goal commitment, self-efficacy, and expectancies. The former two moderate the goal–performance relationships and the latter two mediate the goal–performance relationships. *Feedback* pertains to performance evaluation relative to the goal, and was identified as a necessary condition for goals to affect performance. The combination of feedback and goals leads to the highest performance level. Feedback may have negative effects on performance when it shifts resources to off-task ego-centered processes, in particular for individuals with low levels of self-efficacy.

Goal acceptance refers to initial agreement with the goal, whereas *goal commitment* refers to adherence to the goal, and resistance to changing the goal at a later point in time. Commitment is most important and relevant when the goal is difficult. Goal commitment moderates the effect of goal difficulty on performance. A significant drop in performance is observed as goal commitment declines in response to increasingly difficult goals (Locke and Latham, 2002). Feedback and goal commitment were identified as the two necessary conditions for goals to affect performance. The important role played by goal commitment has led to a growing interest in the antecedents of goal commitment. Participation in goal setting was found to be an effective approach for enhancing goal commitment, and for stimulating information exchange, which positively affected performance (Locke and Latham, 2002).

Self-efficacy is a judgment of one's capability to accomplish a certain level of performance (Bandura, 2001). Goal difficulty positively affects perceptions of self-efficacy, which further affect intentions, personal goals, and performance. Specific and difficult goals lead to high self-efficacy, which further influences goal commitment. Research clearly demonstrated that efficacy beliefs influence the level of motivation and performance (Stajkovic and Luthans, 1998). At the group level, group efficacy is consistently related to group performance (Mitchell and Daniels, 2003).

Expectancies reflect the evaluations people make of their chances of reaching their goals. For a given level of goal difficulty, individuals with high rather than low expectancies are more likely to obtain their goals (Locke and Latham, 2002).

Values determine what people want or what they consciously consider beneficial to their welfare. Values are the motivation core that mediates between needs which stimulate the motivation cycle, and goals, which are the applications of values to specific situations. Need-based theories explain why a person must act, while VALUES explain why specific goals and actions are chosen in specific situations to obtain specific outcomes. Values affect goals and self-efficacy, which further influence performance. There is a growing interest in how personal values are modified, and what is the role played by personality and by the sociocultural context in shaping values.

Interest in *cognition*, which precedes the evaluation phase in the original goal setting model, has increased in parallel to the continuous research on the evaluation phase. Cognition draws attention to the complexity of tasks, and multiple goals. The magnitude of goal effects on performance decreases as task complexity increases. This is because performance of highly complex tasks depends not only on effort or persistence, but also on the cognitive understanding of the task and the strategy or plan necessary for completing it. In complex task situations people move towards their goals by developing strategies about when, where, and how goal attainment will be reached. Research on goal setting effects in the complex task paradigm reveals that goals affect performance to the extent that they lead to the development of effective plans and strategies. Difficult goals affect performance through their effect on strategies (Locke and Latham, 2002).

However, sometimes goals generate pressure for immediate results and they become counterproductive when planning and strategy development are required, and in particular at initial stages of skill acquisition. In this context, setting a "do your best" goal resulted in higher performance than setting a specific high performance goal. Furthermore, setting a learning goal, in terms of discovering appropriate strategies, resulted in higher self-efficacy and goal commit-

ment than setting a performance goal (Latham and Pinder, 2005).

Research on the multiple goals is guided by the assumption that the human organism has a limited pool of resources. As a result, there is a trade-off in the performance of multiple goals. Empirical research has demonstrated that more resources are shifted to the attainment of specific and difficult goals than general or easy goals, and to the attainment of performance goals, which are supported by feedback. Of special interest is the potential trade-off between goals set in terms of quantity, quality, and innovation. Research has demonstrated that generating high expectancy of success, and providing an organizational culture that supports innovation, attention to detail, and outcome orientation enabled the coexistence of innovative, high quality, and efficient performance outcomes.

The fifth phase in the original five phase goal setting model draws attention to effects of *environmental stimuli* on the goal setting process. Research in this area has increased dramatically in the last decade, looking at goals in different contextual levels: individual, group, and organizational goals, as well as examining the influence of national culture on goal behavior (Erez and Earley, 1993; Erez, 2000). National culture shapes distal sources of motivation, including personal beliefs, values, achievement orientation, LOCUS OF CONTROL, and RISK TAKING. People use their cultural values, as they are represented in their selves, for evaluating the meaning of goal accomplishment to their sense of self-worth and well-being. They are motivated to accomplish goals that enhance their self-worth, and to avoid goals that hinder it (Erez and Earley, 1993; Erez, 2000). Therefore, the meaning of certain goals for a person's sense of self-worth and well-being may vary across cultures.

Monetary rewards serve as one of the situational factors that influence the goal–performance relationship. Monetary incentives increase goal commitment, but at the same time they inhibit the attainment of complementary goals that are not compensated for (Mitchell and Daniels, 2003; Latham and Pinder, 2005).

Although *personality factors* were not part of the original goal setting model, research in this area has increased dramatically, demonstrating the effects of self-monitoring dispositions on goal choice, goal commitment, and performance. Various typologies of motivational dispositions have recently been developed, testing these effects on goal setting and performance. Among these typologies are the four core self-evaluation factors, consisting of self-esteem, locus of control, neuroticism, and generalized self-efficacy; motivational dispositions of achievement versus anxiety; learning versus performance goal orientation; and prevention versus promotion regulatory focus (Latham and Pinder, 2005). In essence, all these typologies capture McClelland's ideas of approach and avoidance orientations. The "approach" self-monitoring disposition revealed a robust positive relationship with job performance (Day et al., 2002). Goal orientation is also a state. Setting high learning goals in complex task situations resulted in higher performance levels than setting performance goals. Furthermore, in the presence of specific goals, the effect of dispositional goal orientation disappeared, suggesting that specific and difficult goals create a strong situation (Locke and Latham, 2002).

To summarize, over 36 years goal setting theory has continuously developed to become deeper and more complex than in its first phase, which focused on the immediate goal–performance relationships. Staying close to the explained variable in the first phase of theory development, and then progressing towards understanding mediators, moderators, and antecedents of goals, proved to be an effective approach for theory development, and a potential model for other theoreticians. Furthermore, the theory has grown from the individual level to the levels of groups, organizations, and nations. While the vast majority of the empirical research has focused on goal accomplishment, future research should further enrich our understanding of goal choice, the interplay between proximal and distal goals, and the interaction effects of situational factors and motivational dispositions on goal choice and goal accomplishment.

See also *learning, individual; performance appraisal/performance management; personality*

Bibliography

Bandura, A. (2001). Social cognitive theory: An agentic perspective. *Annual Review of Psychology*, 52, 1–26.

Day, D. V., Schleicher, D. J., Unckless, A. L, and Hiller, N. J. (2002). Self-monitoring personality at work: A meta-analytic investigation of construct validity. *Journal of Applied Psychology*, 87, 390–401.

Dweck, C. S. (1999). *Self-Theories: Their Role in Motivation, Personality, and Development*. Philadelphia, PA: Psychology Press.

Erez, M. (2000). Make management practice fit the national culture. In E. A. Locke (ed.), *Basic Principles of Organizational Behavior: A Handbook*. Oxford: Blackwell, 418–34.

Erez, M. and Earley, P. C. (1993). *Culture, Self-Identity, and Work*. New York: Oxford University Press.

Latham, G. P. and Pinder, C. C. (2005). Work motivation theory and research at the dawn of the 21st century. *Annual Review of Psychology*.

Locke, E. A. (1968). Toward a theory of task motivation and incentives. *Organizational Behavior and Performance*, 3, 157–89.

Locke, E. A. and Latham, G. P. (2002). Building a practically useful theory of goal setting and task motivation: A 35-year odyssey. *American Psychologist*, 57, 705–17.

Mitchell, T. R. and Daniels, D. (2003). Motivation. In W. C. Borman, D. R. Ilgen, and R. J. Klimoski (eds.), *Handbook of Psychology, Vol. 12: Industrial Organizational Psychology*. New York: Wiley and Sons, 225–54.

Stajkovic, A. and Luthans, F. (1998). Self-efficacy and work-related performance: A meta-analysis. *Psychological Bulletin*, 124, 240–61.

governance

Donna J. Wood

Organizational governance concerns "how a corporation is structured, what policies and objectives it seeks to fulfill, how it is managed, and which stakeholder interests it serves" (Wood, 1994). The term "includes specific issues arising from interactions among senior management, shareholders, boards of directors, and other corporate stakeholders" (Cochran and Wartick, 1988).

The basic questions of governance are of power, benefit, and accountability: Who controls the actions of an organization? For what purposes, and to whose benefit, does the organization act? Who is accountable for the consequences of an organization's actions? Governance issues are particularly salient in many large business organizations because the separation of ownership from management control (Berle and Means, 1932) changes the agent–principal relationship, granting much autonomy to managers and little voice to owners. Managers can often avoid accountability for organizational actions, making it difficult for STAKEHOLDERS (including owners/stockholders) or society at large to insure that their legitimate interests are being met.

Reviewing the governance literature, Cochran and Wartick (1988: 22–3, paraphrased) offer this list of board responsibilities:

- Strategic planning: establishing long-range objectives and policies.
- Board renewal: nominating and orienting new board members.
- Supervision of the chief executive officer (CEO): hiring, oversight, compensating, firing.
- Public image maintenance: guarding the firm's legitimacy.
- Overseeing major organizational transformations such as mergers, acquisitions, and divestments.
- Guarding corporate assets: maintaining fiduciary responsibility for appropriate use of assets and ensuring that controls and record keeping practices do not allow for illegal acts.

Individual directors also have responsibilities: (a) a duty of loyalty, expressed by placing the organization's interests above personal interests and avoiding conflicts of interest; and (b) a duty of care, expressed by acting prudently, in good faith, with the organization's best interests in mind.

Current issues in governance have to do with changing definitions of who should control business organizations and for whose benefit they should function. Governance issues include business–government relationships, accommodation of stakeholder interests, executive compensation, financial conflicts of interest, the role of institutional investors, the balance and respective roles of executive vs. outside directors on boards, stakeholder representation, interlocking boards, the board's role in linking mission with structures and incentive systems, and the board's role in monitoring organizational social performance and ethics.

In the wake of widespread corporate financial scandals, stakeholder pressures to reform corporate governance are likely to change many things about how companies are run. For example, the post-Enron legal requirements of the Sarbanes-Oxley Act in the US are spreading to other regulatory regimes, including countries in the European Union. Furthermore, many executives are accustomed to thinking of social responsibility as something to attend to *after* meeting profit goals, but governance reforms could legitimize the relationship between social responsibility and day-to-day operating procedures. A third example is found in the success of institutional investors such as large pension funds in gaining a voice in management and board decisions. Finally, international social and political issues may push closer coordination of governance and social performance in multinational business organizations (Windsor and Preston, 1988).

See also *corporate social performance; values*

Bibliography

Berle, A. A. and Means, G. C. (1932). *The Modern Corporation and Private Property*. New York: Macmillan.

Cochran, P. L. and Wartick, S. L. (1988). *Corporate Governance: A Review of the Literature*. Morristown, NJ: Financial Executives Research Foundation.

Windsor, D. and Preston, L. E. (1988). Corporate governance and social performance in the multinational corporation. In L. E. Preston (ed.), *Research in Corporate Social Performance and Policy*, Vol. 10. Greenwich, CT: JAI Press, 45–58.

Wood, D. J. (1994). *Business and Society*, 2nd edn. New York: Harper Collins.

government and business

John L. Campbell

There is a vast literature about the relationship between government and business in advanced capitalist societies. Central here are three questions: Why does government promulgate the business related policies that it does? How does government affect business? How are government–business relations organized?

Sociologists and political scientists have long debated why governments make business policy as they do. Some assert that governments make policy because members of the business community capture, dominate, or otherwise influence the policy-making process. Others maintain that policy-making reflects a more balanced set of influences, including business, labor, consumers, environmentalists, and voters. Still others argue that policy is a more autonomous response by government officials to market failures, business cycles, and other macroeconomic phenomena. These debates have provoked intense theoretical disagreement as well as an enormous amount of empirical work (e.g., Martin 1991; Vogel 1989).

Regardless of who influences government, government always influences business – even in the most *laissez-faire* situations (Fligstein, 2001). First, governments provide and allocate *resources* to business through subsidies, infrastructure investment, and procurement, which create incentives for firms to engage in many kinds of behavior. Second, governments establish *property rights* and regulate firms in ways that affect not only their behavior, but also their organization. Antitrust law, for instance, influences whether firms form cartels or merge. Third, government *structure* affects business. For example, decentralized states provide different opportunities for firms to relocate their operations than do centralized states (Campbell, Hollingsworth, and Lindberg, 1991; Fligstein, 1990).

The complex relationship between government and business takes different institutional forms in different societies. (On the importance of institutions for business organizations more broadly, *see* INSTITUTIONAL THEORY.) Generally speaking, scholars recognize three varieties of capitalism. First is the *liberal* model (e.g., United States), where government tends to maintain an arm's length relationship to business, grants much freedom to markets, pursues relatively vigorous antitrust policy to insure market competition, and tries not to interfere directly in the activities of firms. Second is the *statist* model (e.g., Japan, South Korea), where government is much more involved in the economy and exercises much greater influence over firms, such as by providing finance and credit

directly to them. Third is the *corporatist* model (e.g., Germany, Northern Europe), where government promotes bargaining among well organized social partners, notably centralized business associations and labor unions, in order to promulgate policies that benefit all groups in society. In short, sometimes government can be an arm's length regulator, a strong economic player, or a facilitator of bargained agreements (Katzenstein, 1978).

These variations matter in terms of the ability of firms to compete successfully and the ability of governments to manage macroeconomic problems such as inflation and unemployment. However, there is much disagreement as to which variety is best. Many economists and conservatives maintain that the liberal model is the best because it insures relatively unbridled market activity, which, following neoclassical economics, is the most efficient and surest way to achieve positive economic performance. Many political scientists and sociologists tend to favor the other two models, reasoning that coordinated economic activity will more effectively mitigate market failures and social ills like inequality and poverty. Recently, scholars have begun to acknowledge that different varieties of capitalism have their own strengths and weaknesses. For instance, liberal economies enable firms to compete by making decisions quickly, keeping costs low, and moving capital rapidly from sector to sector and region to region. The other varieties enable firms to compete by producing high quality products and by adjusting flexibly to shifts in market demand. Why? Because government provides a well educated labor force, insures that business and labor cooperate, and offers generous welfare supports to facilitate the sort of economic restructuring that enhances flexibility and enables business to be competitive, especially internationally (Hall and Soskice, 2001).

Since the mid-1970s, economic activity has become increasingly internationalized. In particular, capital has gained the ability to move from one place to another faster than ever. This has generated much concern that the ability of business to rapidly shift investments internationally has undermined the institutional differences associated with the three varieties of capitalism. Many have warned that governments will need increasingly to compete against each other to retain and attract capital investment. To do so, it is argued, they will have to realign their institutional arrangements with the liberal model – that is, grant business more autonomy to do as it pleases without having to worry about the interests of government, labor, or other actors. If governments fail to do so, then capital flight will result and precipitate a host of economic problems.

This has become a popular mantra among politicians who seek to roll back business regulation, welfare spending, and taxes. Nevertheless, researchers have shown that there is little sign of institutional convergence on the liberal model, or that serious economic problems result for countries that fail to adopt it. Instead, the relationship between government and business and the institutional basis by which business competes continue to evolve along a variety of trajectories. Why? Because institutional change tends to proceed in path-dependent ways. Even when governments try to mimic institutional practices observed elsewhere, they typically translate them into local contexts in ways that do not fully supplant current practices (Campbell, 2004: ch. 5; Garrett, 1998).

See also *contracts; governance; organizational design; values*

Bibliography

Campbell, J. L. (2004). *Institutional Change and Globalization*. Princeton, NJ: Princeton University Press.

Campbell, J. L., Hollingsworth, J. R., and Lindberg, L. N. (eds.) (1991). *Governance of the American Economy*. New York: Cambridge University Press.

Fligstein, N. (1990). *The Transformation of Corporate Control*. Cambridge, MA: Harvard University Press.

Fligstein, N. (2001). *The Architecture of Markets*. Princeton, NJ: Princeton University Press.

Garrett, G. (1998). *Partisan Politics in the Global Economy*. New York: Cambridge University Press.

Hall, P. A. and Soskice, D. (eds.) (2001). *Varieties of Capitalism*. New York: Oxford University Press.

Katzenstein, P. J. (ed.) (1978). *Between Power and Plenty*. Madison: University of Wisconsin Press.

Martin, C. J. (1991). *Shifting the Burden*. Chicago: University of Chicago Press.

Vogel, D. (1989). *Fluctuating Fortunes*. New York: Basic Books.

group cohesiveness

Sarah Ronson and Randall S. Peterson

Group cohesiveness is the extent to which group members are motivated to stay in the group (Cartwright, 1953; Festinger, 1950). It expresses how much group members value their membership in the group. Cohesiveness can arise from attraction between individual group members, or the attraction that each member feels towards the group itself due to some quality of the group, such as its prestige. Based on this definition, cohesiveness has been operationalized in terms of group member motivation towards group goals, interpersonal attraction among group members, member evaluations of the attractiveness of the group, or sense of identification with the group (Cartwright, 1953). The use of these many different measures also implies that cohesiveness may be multidimensional. Hogg (1993), for example, suggests differentiating cohesion into at least two constructs – one based on personal or social attraction of group members, and the other based on the attraction or IDENTIFICATION members feel to the group because membership in that group implies the individual is a person of worth and value.

Minimal levels of cohesiveness can be created by simply assigning members to a group (Hogg, 1993). How much cohesiveness the group achieves will be a function of the extent to which group members must depend on one another as reference points for making judgments to create a social reality, and the extent to which cohesion will enable the group to achieve its goals (Festinger, 1950). Cohesiveness is also affected by the attractiveness of the group to its members, the motivation of individual members, how attractive the outcomes are that members expect to receive as a result of membership, and how favorably group membership compares to membership in other groups. Attractive groups tend to be those with similarity among members, high degrees of cooperation, clear group goals, relatively small group size, decentralized communication networks, democratic or participative leadership, and intrinsically rewarding group tasks (Cartwright, 1953).

Cohesiveness helps group survival by motivating members to stay in the group, increasing participation, enhancing member loyalty, and giving the group more power to influence individual behavior. Cohesive groups can also benefit their individual members by providing support and reducing anxiety (Cartwright, 1953). There is also some evidence that cohesion has a small positive impact on group performance (Mullen and Copper, 1994). However, there are two problems with the cohesion–performance relationship. First, high levels of cohesion may actually impede group performance. For example, pressure for uniformity may build to the point that they prevent group members from adequately challenging one another's information and opinions, resulting in poor decisions (Janis, 1982). Secondly, where cohesion and performance are found to be correlated in groups, it may be that effective group performance enhances the sense of cohesion rather than cohesion causing improved performance (cf. Peterson and Behfar, in press). These issues suggest that mediators and moderators of cohesion and performance may exist. For example, the effect of cohesion on performance may depend on the nature of group norms: when norms support productivity or high performance, cohesive groups exert a greater influence over individual members, encouraging more individual effort than non-cohesive groups.

See also *collaboration; group dynamics*

Bibliography

Cartwright, D. (1953). The nature of group cohesiveness. In D. Cartwright and A. Zander (eds.), *Group Dynamics: Research and Theory*. New York: Harper and Row.

Festinger, L. (1950). Informal social communication. *Psychological Review*, **57**, 271–82.

Hogg, A. (1993). Group cohesiveness: A critical review and some future directions. *European Review of Social Psychology*, 85–111.

Janis, I. L. (1982). *Groupthink: Psychological Studies of Policy Decisions and Fiascos*. Boston, MA: Houghton-Mifflin.

Mullen, B. and Copper, C. (1994). The relation between group cohesiveness and performance: An integration. *Psychological Bulletin*, **115**, 210–27.

Peterson, R. S. and Behfar, K. J. (in press). The dynamic relationship between performance feedback, trust, and conflict in groups: A longitudinal study. *Organizational Behavior and Human Decision Processes*.

group decision-making

Michael A. West

We use WORK GROUPS/TEAMS to make decisions because we believe that the quality of the decision will be better than if the decisions are left to any one individual. TOP MANAGEMENT TEAMS have to decide whether to merge with another company; production and R&D teams decide which new product to invest in; management teams have to decide which of several interviewees to select. Research into group decision-making reveals that where there is a right answer, truth will tend to win out but only if at least two other people advocate it. But in most decision-making situations in organizations there is no well-defined unequivocal right answer. And in these situations a majority verdict decision rule seems to almost always apply (Laughlin, 1996). However, a good deal of research has shown that in coming to their decisions, groups are subject to social processes which undermine their DECISION-MAKING effectiveness:

1   The hidden profile is the powerful but unconscious tendency of team members to focus on information all or most team members already share and ignore information that only one or two team members have (even though it may be brought to the attention of the group during decision-making and may be crucial). Teams can avoid this by ensuring that members have clearly defined roles so that each is seen as a source of potentially unique and important information, by ensuring that members listen carefully to colleagues' contributions in decision-making, and by ensuring that leaders alert the team to information that is uniquely held by only one or two members (Stasser, Vaughan, and Stewart, 2000).

2   PERSONALITY factors such as shyness of individual members can affect quality of group decision-making. Some individuals may be hesitant to offer their opinions and knowledge assertively, thereby failing to contribute fully to the group's store of knowledge.

3   Group members are subject to social CONFORMITY effects causing them to withhold

opinions and information contrary to the majority view.

4   The group may be dominated by particular individuals who take up disproportionate "air time" and argue so vigorously with the opinion of others that their own views prevail. It is noteworthy that "air time" and expertise are correlated in high performing groups and uncorrelated in groups that perform poorly.

5   Status and hierarchy effects can cause some members' contributions to be valued and attended to disproportionately. When a senior executive is present in a meeting his or her views are likely to have an undue influence on the outcome.

6   Janis (1982), in his study of policy decisions and fiascos, identified the phenomenon of GROUPTHINK, whereby tightly knit groups may err in their decision-making as a result of being more concerned with achieving agreement than with the quality of group decision-making.

7   The SOCIAL LOAFING effect is the tendency of individuals in group situations to work less hard than they do when individual contributions can be identified and evaluated. In organizations, individuals may put less effort into achieving quality decisions in meetings, as a result of the perception that their contribution is hidden in overall group performance.

8   The study of BRAINSTORMING groups shows that quantity and quality of ideas produced by individuals working separately, consistently exceed quality and quantity of ideas produced by a group working together. This is partly due to a "production blocking" effect. Individuals are inhibited from both thinking of new ideas and offering them aloud to the group by the competing verbalizations of others.

9   Another difficulty besetting group decision-making is the tendency of groups to "satisfice" or make *minimally acceptable decisions* (*see* SATISFICING). Observations of group decision-making processes repeatedly show that groups tend to identify the first minimally acceptable solution or decision in a particular situation, and then spend time searching for reasons to accept that decision and reject other possible options.

Recently, researchers have begun to identify ways in which some of these deficiencies may be overcome. Leaders can be trained to be participative, seeking the contributions of individual members before offering their own perceptions. Moreover, they should encourage the expression of alternative opinion and criticisms in a cohesive climate. Training group members in information search techniques and advising them not to form a strong adherence to the decision they first thought of are also aids to effective group decision-making.

Rogelberg, Barnes-Farrell, and Lowe (1992) have offered a structured "stepladder technique" for overcoming some of these deficiencies. In this procedure each group member has thinking time before proposing any decisions. Then pairs of group members present their ideas to each other and discuss their respective opinions before making any decisions. The process continues with each subgroup's presentation being followed by time for the group to discuss the problem and ideas proposed. A final decision is put off until the entire group has presented.

This is consistent with the finding that fostering disagreement in a structured way in organizations leads to better decisions (Tjosvold, 1998). Finally, there is some evidence that work groups which take time out to reflect upon and appropriately modify their decision-making processes through "reflexivity" are more effective and innovative than those which do not (West and Hirst, 2003).

Group decision-making is more complex than is commonly understood within organizational settings but too little research has been conducted on decision-making processes among intact groups and teams in organizations. Researchers are now examining cognitive perspectives on team decision-making by focusing on problem framing, information processing, and issue interpretation and by examining sensemaking at the team level. They are exploring the concept of team mental models and team cognitions to advance our understanding of group decision-making (Glynn and Barr, 2003).

There is a huge potential payoff for organizations if researchers can identify the most effective ways of improving group decision-making in organizations.

See also *group dynamics; group norms; minority group influence; nominal group technique*

Bibliography

Brown, R. (2000). *Group Processes*, 2nd edn. Oxford: Blackwell.

Glynn, M. A. and Barr, P. S. (2003). Team decision-making in organizations. In M. A. West, D. Tjosvold, and K. G. Smith (eds.), *International Handbook of Organizational Teamwork and Cooperative Working*. Chichester: John Wiley, 211–29.

Janis, I. L. (1982). *Groupthink: Psychological Studies of Policy Decisions and Fiascos*. Boston, MA: Houghton-Mifflin.

Laughlin, P. R. (1996). Group decision-making and collective induction. In E. H. Witte and J. H. Davis (eds.), *Understanding Group Behavior, Vol. 1: Consensual Action by Small Groups*. Mahwah, NJ: Lawrence Erlbaum Associates, 61–80.

Rogelberg, S. G., Barnes-Farrell, J. L., and Lowe, C. A. (1992). The stepladder technique: An alternative group structure facilitating effective group decision-making. *Journal of Applied Psychology*, **77**, 730–7.

Stasser, G., Vaughan, S. I., and Stewart, D. D. (2000). Pooling unshared information: The benefits of knowing how to access information distributed among group members. *Organizational Behavior and Human Decision Processes*, **82**, 102–16.

Tjosvold, D. (1998). Cooperative and competitive goal approaches to conflict: Accomplishments and challenges. *Applied Psychology: An International Review*, **41**, 285–342.

West, M. A. and Hirst, G. (2003). Cooperation and teamwork for innovation. In M. A. West, D. Tjosvold, and K. G. Smith (eds.), *International Handbook of Organizational Teamwork and Cooperative Working*. Chichester: John Wiley, 297–320.

group dynamics

Sarah Ronson and Randall S. Peterson

Group dynamics is the study of the nature and development of small groups. Small groups are collectives of individuals who are contained by some boundary that enables them to identify themselves as a member of the group, who interact with and influence one another, and who jointly interact with and influence their environment. The term "group dynamics" was originated and popularized by Kurt Lewin, and his work, along with several other key projects in the 1930s, set the stage for development of the field (see Cartwright and Zander, 1953). In 1936 Sherif demonstrated in a laboratory setting that individuals use others as a reference point in making judgments where no objective information exists, and that the group norms that develop for this purpose influence the individual's behavior both in and outside of the group. From 1935–9 Newcomb similarly demonstrated in a naturalistic setting that membership at a liberal university impacted conservative students' political attitudes. Whyte, in 1939, used an ethnographic study to show the importance of social groups in members' lives in the slums of Boston. Finally, Lewin, Lippit, and White, from 1937–40, studied differences between groups of boys under the influence of democratic, autocratic, and *laissez-faire* leadership styles.

The study of group dynamics since this time has been dominated by an input–process–output model, which holds that group outcomes can be understood as a function of the resources group members bring to the group, and the processes that transform these inputs. The primary inputs into a group are its size, structure, and composition. Many processes then operate within groups, but key issues in transforming inputs into group performance, member satisfaction, and other group outputs are social processes such as cohesion and CONFLICT, and the strategies for processing information used by the group. Attention has recently shifted away from the traditional input–process–output model, towards an understanding of groups based on their relationships with external constituents. The external perspective provides insight into group development, identification with the group, and the drivers of group performance.

At the most basic level, the size of the group can have a significant impact on group interactions and performance. As groups become larger, leadership becomes more directive, member participation decreases, conflict increases, and adherence to group norms is less. Increasing coordination and motivation losses as groups become larger can offset the potential benefits that these groups can provide in terms of additional resources (see Moreland, Levine, and Wingert, 1996).

Beyond size, the composition of the group can have a major impact on its development, interactions, and outcomes. While certain abilities or characteristics may be desirable or undesirable in a group member, a more complex perspective on composition considers the fit of members with one another and type of task being undertaken (Moynihan and Peterson, 2001). Fit may be based on a variety of characteristics, such as demographic profile, experience and organizational role, interpersonal needs, or personality. Research on the benefits and drawbacks of diversity in group composition has revealed that diversity in demographic characteristics can have a negative impact on TURNOVER, COMMUNICATION between group members, and performance (Williams and O'Reilly, 1998), while heterogeneity in experience, SKILLS, or personality variables can improve decision-making and creativity (Milliken and Martins, 1996). Group composition may not be stable over time, as members enter and exit the group, although research has tended to neglect the dynamic nature of group membership. One exception is Moreland and Levine (1982), who posit that group members transition through several roles in the group as they continually evaluate the group and alter their level of commitment based on this evaluation.

While composition is based on the members of the group themselves, group structure sets out the pattern of relationships that exist among members. Group structure tends to be established relatively early in group life, and it changes slowly (Levine and Moreland, 2000). Status systems define the relative power of different group members. Expectation theorists suggest that group members make quick cognitive evaluations of each member's likely contribution, and assign higher status to those they expect to make a significant contribution, while dominance theory suggests that cues from each group member elicit dominant or submissive behavior from other members (Ridgeway,

1984). Group structure can also be described in terms of member ROLES, which can be both formally assigned or can develop informally as members find their place in the group. Two types of informal roles can develop: task roles, related to achieving the group's main task, and socio-emotional roles, related to maintaining group harmony (Burke, 1967).

Group composition and structure help us to define the nature of a given group, and provide the context in which a group will interact. However, even groups with an "ideal" composition and structure can fail to achieve optimal outcomes because of process losses that occur in the course of their interaction (Steiner, 1972). For this reason, the study of group interaction is essential to understanding group dynamics. Early theorists viewed group interactions as a result of unconscious forces, such as dependency of members on one another, fight–flight behavior, and pairing of relationships between group members (Bion, 1961). Today, a wide variety of topics covers the nature of group interactions. Social processes between group members have significant impacts on groups. For example, the amount of cohesiveness between group members can impact their experience in the group and group outcomes (e.g., Mullen and Copper, 1994). The amount of conflict in a group also has serious implications for group outcomes. Jehn (1995) elaborated the role of conflict types in groups; she found that relationship conflict can be detrimental to both member experiences in groups, as well as group performance, while task related conflict can benefit groups involved in more complex, non-routine tasks.

Beyond social factors, the strategies groups use for combining member information also impact their outcomes. Typically, all members of the group do not have identical information, and when this information must be combined to make a judgment, group members can influence and be influenced by one another. Several biases have been uncovered in the way that groups make these decisions. For example, group members tend to focus their discussion on information that is held by all group members, rather than trying to extract unique information held by only one member, thus limiting the size of the potential information pool they could use in making a decision (Wittenbaum and Stasser, 1998).

The emergence of external perspectives on group interaction has shed new light on the influences on group development and performance. Early research on group development over time indicated that groups had to move through a series of development stages in sequence. McGrath, Kelly, and Machatka (1984) introduced the idea that groups match the pace and rhythm of work to that demanded by their work environment. This effect is called ENTRAINMENT. Gersick (1988) later built on this work and developed a punctuated equilibrium model of group development to challenge traditional models of set phases of group development; she suggested that groups settle on a way of interacting early in group life, but that this way of interacting is different for each group, and at approximately the midpoint of the group calendar, the group goes through a transition to a new strategy.

Group identity can also be understood in terms of the group's relationship to its environment. While identity with the group is a function of an individual's sense of identification with the group, this sense of identification comes in part as a result of categorization and social comparison with other groups that the individual is not part of (Hogg and Abrams, 1988). Thus, identity cannot be understood without reference to other constituents in the group's environment. A great deal of recent work has focused on how these identity processes affect both group performance and processes (e.g., shared identity boosts cohesion and performance) (see IDENTITY, PERSONAL).

Finally, the external perspective shifts focus away from internal group processes as determinants of success. Ancona (1990) has suggested alternatively that group performance can be understood in terms of the group's success at managing relationships with other parties in the organization.

Three areas will be of particular importance in future research on group dynamics. First, integrating the internal and external perspectives will be essential for gaining a complete and complex understanding of groups. In particular, there is a need to understand the degree to which group focus on internal versus external relationships detracts or enriches each other (e.g., Peterson, Ronson, Rodgers, in progress). Second, the traditional input–process–output model of groups can be altered in various ways to provide new insights into groups. It may be that our traditional conception of causality in group outcomes is incomplete; positive outcomes may actually lead to more positive processes, rather than the reverse (e.g., Peterson and Behfar, in press). For example, Mullen and Copper (1994) have suggested that cohesion is enhanced by good group performance because positive outcomes make belonging to the group more rewarding for members, and they become more attracted to the group. Third, researchers will likely focus increasingly on groups in applied and organizational settings, and continue to move away from zero history, artificially constructed laboratory groups in order to study the external perspectives on groups. The use of bona fide groups, with stable yet permeable boundaries and an interaction with their environmental contexts, can allow us to ask more complex questions about groups that will provide us with a deeper and more accurate understanding of group behavior (Putnam and Stohl, 1990).

See also *group cohesiveness; levels of analysis; minority group influence; power*

Bibliography

Ancona, D. G. (1990). Outward bound: Strategies for team survival in the organization. *Academy of Management Journal*, 33, 334–65.

Bion, W. R. (1961). *Experiences in Groups*. London: Tavistock.

Burke, P. J. (1967). The development of task and socio-emotional role differentiation. *Sociometry*, 30, 379–92.

Cartwright, D. and Zander, A. (1953). Origins of group dynamics. In D. Cartwright and A. Zander (eds.), *Group Dynamics: Research and Theory*. New York: Harper and Row.

Gersick, C. J. G. (1988). Time and transition in work teams: Toward a new model of group development. *Academy of Management Journal*, 31, 9–41.

Hogg, M. A. and Abrams, D. (1988). *Social Identifications: A Social Psychology of Intergroup Relations and Group Processes*. New York: Routledge.

Jehn, K. A. (1995). A multimethod examination of the benefits and detriments of intragroup conflict. *Administrative Science Quarterly*, **40**, 256–82.

Levine, J. M. and Moreland, R. M. (2000). Small groups. In D. Gilbert, S. Fiske, and G. Lindzey (eds.), *The Handbook of Social Psychology*, 4th edn. Boston, MA: McGraw-Hill.

McGrath, J. E., Kelly, J. R., and Machatka, D. E. (1984). The social psychology of time: Entrainment of behavior in social and organizational settings. *Applied Social Psychology Annual*, 5, 21–44.

Milliken, F. J. and Martins, L. L. (1996). Searching for common threads: Understanding the multiple effects of diversity in organizational groups. *Academy of Management Review*, 21, 402–33.

Moreland, R. L. and Levine, J. M. (1982). Socialization in small groups: Temporal changes in individual–group relations. In L. Berkowitz (ed.), *Advances in Experimental Social Psychology*, Vol. 15. 137–92.

Moreland, R. L., Levine, J. M., and Wingert, M. L. (1996). Creating the ideal group: Composition effects at work. In E. White and J. Davis (eds.), *Understanding Group Behavior, Vol. 2: Small Group Processes and Interpersonal Relations*. Hillsdale, NJ: Lawrence Erlbaum Associates.

Moynihan, L. M. and Peterson, R. S. (2001). A contingent configuration approach to understanding the role of personality in organizational groups. *Research in Organizational Behavior*, 23, 327–78.

Mullen, B. and Copper, C. (1994). The relation between group cohesiveness and performance: An integration. *Psychological Bulletin*, 115, 210–27.

Peterson, R. S. and Behfar, K. J. (in press). The dynamic relationship between performance feedback, trust, and conflict in groups: A longitudinal study. *Organizational Behavior and Human Decision Processes*.

Putnam, L. L. and Stohl, C. (1990). Bona fide groups: A reconceptualization of groups in context. *Communication Studies*, 41, 248–65.

Ridgeway, C. L. (1984). Dominance, performance, and status in groups: A theoretical analysis. In E. J. Lawler (ed.), *Advances in Group Processes*, Vol. 1. Greenwich, CT: JAI Press, 59–93.

Steiner, I. D. (1972). *Group Process and Productivity*. New York: Academic Press.

Williams, K. and O'Reilly, C. (1998). Demography and diversity in organizations: A review of 40 years of research. *Research in Organizational Behavior*, 20, 77–140.

Wittenbaum, G. M. and Stasser, G. (1998). Management of information in small groups. In J. L. Nye and A. M. Brower (eds.), *What's Social about Social Cognition? Social Cognition Research in Small Groups*. Newbury Park, CA: Sage.

group norms

Sarah Ronson and Randall S. Peterson

Norms are the unwritten rules that provide guidelines for acceptable behaviors by members of a group. Certain behaviors develop into norms or expectations for all group members over time for a number of reasons, including an influential group member or leader expressing them, group members imitating the actions of others, socially rewarding certain behaviors, group members developing a shared script for events, etc. (Feldman, 1984; Bettenhausen and Murnighan, 1991). Norms can affect not only behavior within a group, but can also influence an individual member's behavior or attitude outside of the group (Sherif, 1966). Norms tend to develop informally and gradually, and to be stable. Situations that are uncertain or unstable are particularly likely to lead to the development of group norms because group members use the group as a reference point for making subjective judgments (Sherif, 1966). Thus, norms tend to serve some function for group members, such as providing information about subjective reality and about how to behave. Norms also benefit the group as a whole. They can (1) define and help enforce behavior that will enable the group to survive (Feldman, 1984); (2) improve group efficiency and effectiveness by making group member behavior predictable (Feldman, 1984); (3) improve member satisfaction by helping members avoid behaviors that the group would not approve of (Feldman, 1984); and/or (4) express the central values of the group (Feldman, 1984; Bettenhausen and Murnighan, 1991).

Norms are generally measured by expressed member attitudes or member behaviors, which raises difficulties in operationalizing this construct. For example, where norms are measured as behaviors, is the behavior simply accepted by the group? Is failure to enact the behavior deviant? When norms are measured as member descriptions, does lack of consensus indicate nonexistence of a norm? Or can there be compliance to a norm without conscious awareness? To clarify these issues, it is generally necessary to define different attributes of norms, such as their strength, importance to the group, or degree of agreement around them.

Research on group norms to date has tended to focus on the effects of norms on individual member behavior or the development and change of norms themselves. The effects of norms on group level outcomes deserves further attention. Some evidence suggests that norms of behavior both within a group, and between groups, can enhance a group's effectiveness (e.g., Bettenhausen and Murnighan, 1991). The effect of norms on group outcomes is not likely to always be positive, however; the nature of the norm should have a substantial impact on outcomes. Argyris (1994), for example, argues that groups tend to develop both positive and negative norms or what he calls "process routines." Routines themselves are often neither positive nor negative, but depend on the situation for interpretation. For example, a norm of "being nice" and respectful to others can have damaging consequences when conflict could help the group to make a better quality decision. Clearly, negative norms can also develop and persist, and even be in conflict with what members believe to be true about effective group behavior, simply because a powerful group member persists in the behavior.

See also *consensus; group cohesiveness; group dynamics; organizational culture*

Bibliography

Argyris, C. (1994). Good communication that blocks learning. *Harvard Business Review*, 72, 77–85.
Bettenhausen, K. L. and Murnighan, K. (1991). The development of an intragroup norm and the effects of interpersonal and structural challenges. *Administrative Science Quarterly*, 36, 20–35.
Feldman, D. (1984). The development and enforcement of group norms. *Academy of Management Review*, 47–53.
Opp, D. (1982). The evolutionary emergence of norms. *British Journal of Social Psychology*, 139–49.
Sherif, M. (1966). *The Psychology of Social Norms*. New York: Harper and Row.

group polarization

Michael A. West

Until the 1960s, researchers assumed that group decisions produced a rough average of the opinions of individual members. At that point social psychological research suggested that, in potentially risky situations, individual group member decisions were less risky than the final decision of the group as a whole. Groups appeared to shift risk in the decision-making process. The risky shift phenomenon attracted much research interest, since it suggested that GROUP DECISION-MAKING might produce dangerous decisions at all organizational levels (e.g., within the nuclear power or defense industries) as a result of unconscious group processes. Subsequent research has indicated that the shift to risk is, in fact, a shift to extremity. Groups shift away from a neutral point beyond the average of the decisions initially favored by individuals in the group; in other words, shifts to caution as well as risk occur. This phenomenon of *group polarization* influences attitudes as well as decisions.

Explanations range from social comparison to persuasion processes. Individuals compare themselves with others and tend to move along the scale in the same direction as the group tendency partly because of a "majority rule" influence – the largest subgroup tends to determine the group decision. Through such social comparison some find that they are farther from the modal position than they anticipated, while others may be more extreme but in the same direction as the majority view. The former will shift their positions more than the latter, resulting in an overall shift towards greater risk or greater conservatism (Myers and Lamm, 1976; Moscovici and Doise, 1974; Isenberg, 1986). These processes may be exacerbated by the tendency of groups to ignore information held uniquely by one member and focus on information held by most or all (Stasser, Vaughan, and Stewart, 2000). Polarization may also occur as a consequence of persuasion and influence attempts by group members during the information processing stage of group decision-making. In organizations the dangers of polarization are most likely when the group has just been formed or when the group is confronted with an unusual (often a crisis) situation (*see* CRISES/DISASTERS).

It is significant to note that almost all studies of group polarization have been conducted in laboratories with ad hoc groups of students focusing on hypothetical decisions. In the most relevant organizational study, Semin and Glendon (1973) replicated the RESEARCH DESIGN from the laboratory in an organization by observing the processes of a job consultation committee charged with grading jobs. On 28 grading decisions over the course of a year the average group job evaluation was identical to the mean of the individual evaluations of the committee members prior to group members coming together to agree a grading. This suggests that the imperatives of organizational life and the experience of intact teams that have a history of interaction may mitigate the effects of group polarization in "real" settings. Further organizationally based research will help us to understand how much of a threat group polarization processes really are in organizations and how much we need to do to train employees to prevent them.

See also *minority group influence; risk taking*

Bibliography

Isenberg, D. I. (1986). Group polarization: A critical review and meta-analysis. *Journal of Personality and Social Psychology*, **50**, 1141–51.

Moscovici, S. and Doise, W. (1974). Decision-making in groups. In C. J. Nemeth (ed.), *Social Psychology: Classic and Contemporary Integration*. Chicago: Rand McNally, 250–88.

Myers, D. G. and Lamm, H. (1976). The group polarization phenomenon. *Psychological Bulletin*, **83**, 602–27.

Semin, G. and Glendon, A. I. (1973). Polarization and the established group. *British Journal of Social and Clinical Psychology*, **12**, 113–21.

Stasser, G., Vaughan, S. I., and Stewart, D. D. (2000). Pooling unshared information: The benefits of knowing how access to information is distributed among group members. *Organizational Behavior and Human Decision Processes*, **82**, 102–16.

group roles

Sarah Ronson and Randall S. Peterson

Group members contribute to the group in different ways. An individual's ROLE in a group is comprised of a set of behaviors that group members expect from the individual. In this way, roles are analogous to a group norm that applies to a given individual or a group of individuals fulfilling the same function. Along with other norms and status systems within the group, roles help to define the structure of the group. This definition makes evident the overlap between the notions of group roles, norms, and structure, and explains why empirically differentiating between the constructs is difficult. Similar to norms and structure, roles have been measured through observation of member behaviors or explicit descriptions from members.

Group roles have been theorized in two general ways. The first is with a functional approach that asks what function(s) a group needs fulfilled and how group members can accomplish them. The most established of the functional approaches is the idea that member contributions to a group can be either task or socio-emotional based (e.g., Bales, 1953). Task roles move the group closer to its goals, while socio-emotional roles maintain interpersonal relations and reduce tension or hostility between members. Task roles tend to develop first. Socio-emotional roles emerge only when the demands of the task go beyond what is perceived as reasonable by some group members and hostility results. The extent to which a group member is likely to take a task versus socio-emotional role may depend on the dispositional preference of the particular group member – with certain personality characteristics being more suited to specific types of roles. For example, group members who are high on agreeableness are more likely to take socio-emotional roles in a group because of their tendency towards cooperative (versus competitive) behavior.

The second approach to group roles research focuses on what individual members contribute to the group. From this perspective, roles may be transferred from similar situations, or be developed in relation to a status system. Probably the best known of this approach is Belbin's (1993) team roles notion, particularly within consulting. A somewhat different approach has taken hold in scholarly circles. The theoretical work of Moreland and Levine (1982), for example, describes how a member's ROLE TRANSITIONS over time as a process of mutual evaluation of commitment between the individual and the group. Individuals move from prospective members, to new members, to full members, to marginal members, to ex-members, with each transition signifying a change in the relationship of the individual to the group.

Recent research suggests that changes in roles can cause at least two interrelated problems. The first is that artificial or assigned roles in groups can be ineffective because they are perceived as disingenuous by group members (e.g., Nemeth and Connell, 2001). The second is that conflict can arise as a result of group roles. For example, a group can feel less committed to the individual than vice versa, and thus a transition from full to marginal member could be forced by the group before it is desired by the individual. People may deal with unwanted roles or transitions by proactively trying to change the requirements of the role to match their needs, but may be unsuccessful and be forced to change themselves in response to the role (Nicholson, 1984).

See also *group development; group dynamics; personality*

Bibliography

Bales, R. F. (1953). The equilibrium problem in small groups. In T. Parsons, R. F. Bales, and E. A. Shils (eds.), *Working Papers in the Theory of Action.* New York: Free Press.

Belbin, R. M. (1993). *Team Roles at Work: A Strategy for Human Resource Management.* Oxford: Butterworth, Heinemann.

Moreland, R. L. and Levine, J. M. (1982). Socialization in small groups: Temporal changes in individual–group relations. *Advances in Experimental Social Psychology*, 15, 137–92.

Nemeth, C. J. and Connell, J. B. (2001). Improving decision-making by means of dissent. *Journal of Applied Social Psychology*, 31, 48–9.

Nicholson, N. (1984). A theory of work role transitions. *Administrative Science Quarterly*, 29, 172–91.

group size

see GROUP DECISION-MAKING; GROUP DYNAMICS

group structure

see GROUP DECISION-MAKING; WORK GROUPS/TEAMS

groupthink

Glen Whyte

DEFINITION

Groupthink has been the leading explanation for crucial group decision failure ever since Irving Janis first proposed it in the early 1970s. According to Janis, groupthink describes "a mode of thinking that people engage in when they are involved in a cohesive in-group, when the members' striving for unanimity overrides their motivation to realistically appraise alternative courses of action" (1982: 9).

This powerful concurrence -seeking tendency underlies groupthink and is manifested by a variety of symptoms in crucial DECISION-MAKING. These symptoms involve positive distortions in how the group views itself, closed-mindedness, and conformity pressures (*see* MINORITY GROUP INFLUENCE). These symptoms prevent the group from engaging in many of the basic elements of effective decision-making, including identifying objectives, generating alternatives, gathering and accurately analyzing information, identifying risks, and formulating contingency plans. The lack of such procedures in crucial decision-making almost inevitably leads to avoidable errors of judgment, excessively risky choices, and poorly crafted policies that are ripe for failure.

STATE OF KNOWLEDGE

Despite the dominance of groupthink in the decision-making literature as an explanation for decision fiascos, several researchers have questioned its validity and proposed alternative explanations. These explanations reflect a lack of research support for the traditional groupthink model wherein moderate or high GROUP COHESIVENESS is a necessary but insufficient condition for groupthink to occur, and psychological stress and procedural and organizational faults are contributing factors (Park, 1990; Tetlock et al., 1992). The influence of Janis's (1982) explanation for groupthink is thus waning.

Another view suggests that the excessive preference for risk characteristic of groupthink-type decision-making derives from a group framing its choice to appear to be in the domain of losses

(Whyte, 1989). This occurs when people perceive the decision to involve a choice between either a sure loss or potentially even larger losses combined with a chance to avoid losses altogether. Such perceptions typically induce preferences for the latter option due to loss aversion (*see* PROSPECT THEORY).

Groupthink-type decision-making may also stem from bloated perceptions of collective efficacy (Whyte, 1998). Such perceptions refer not to actual capacity but to group members' beliefs about their capacity to successfully perform some task. These beliefs often reflect past performance, which if high may reduce motivation to engage in sound analysis in future related decisions. Success-induced complacency in crucial decision-making greatly increases the chance of subsequent failure.

CURRENT SIGNIFICANCE

Groupthink is a memorable name for an important phenomenon that requires a good explanation. Janis was successful in describing groupthink but not in developing a robust explanation for it. The development and testing of other causes of groupthink remain the primary challenges ahead for researchers. Many suggestions offered to reduce groupthink, however, are broadly applicable regardless of its root causes.

Groupthink as a phenomenon will matter as long as making wise choices about important issues is a primary task of management, and incidents of disastrous decision-making remain commonplace. A better understanding of groupthink, and particularly those conditions that foster it, will further enhance the quality of collective judgment and choice in crucial decision-making.

See also *behavioral decision research; group decision-making; group dynamics*

Bibliography

Janis, I. L. (1982). *Groupthink*, 2nd edn. Boston, MA: Houghton-Mifflin.

Park, W. W. (1990). A review of research on groupthink. *Journal of Behavioral Decision-Making*, 3, 229–45.

Tetlock, P. E., Peterson, R. S., McGuire, C., Chang, S., and Feld, P. (1992). Assessing political group dynamics: A test of the groupthink model. *Journal of Personality and Social Psychology*, 63, 403–25.

Whyte, G. (1989). Groupthink reconsidered. *Academy of Management Review*, 14, 40–58.

Whyte, G. (1998). Recasting Janis's groupthink model: The key role of collective efficacy in decision fiascos. *Organizational Behavior and Human Decision Processes*, 73, 185–209.

H

halo effect

Ivan Robertson

This is said to occur when people are assigned the same or similar ratings on different characteristics, (i.e., the ratings between the different characteristics are correlated). There is much research evidence to suggest that raters are prone to make ERRORS by allowing their general impressions of a person to influence ratings of specific qualities. If this happens during the completion of a rating form the separate characteristics rated will be given more similar ratings than they should be and halo error will be present. It is important to distinguish between the halo effect and halo error. One of the difficulties in doing this is that many human qualities are indeed related and accurate ratings of these qualities should correlate. Halo error is present only when the observed correlations between the characteristics involved are bigger than the true correlations. Unfortunately, it is often impossible to tell whether the correlations between variables are a reflection of the true level of relationship between the variables or due to error on the part of the rater (*see* RESEARCH DESIGN). Probably the best way to avoid halo error is to train raters well and insure that they are aware of the possibility of halo error, though this does not always work. Traditionally, halo error has been seen as a widespread problem with ratings. More recent views suggest that this may not be so (Murphy, Jako, and Anhalt, 1993).

See also *bias; impression management; performance appraisal/performance management*

Bibliography

Murphy, K. R., Jako, R. A., and Anhalt, R. L. (1993). Nature and consequences of halo error: A critical analysis. *Journal of Applied Psychology*, **78**, 218–25.

hardiness

Nigel Nicholson

The concept of hardiness enjoyed some popularity in the 1980s and 1990s after it was introduced by Khoshaba and Maddi to denote individuals who were more constitutionally resilient to STRESS and better able to adjust to change. Its elements were conceived as a mix of positive commitments, a sense of control over one's life, and an orientation to change as a challenge for creative response. Despite its attractiveness, the idea suffered from problems of measurement and empirical validation. Alternative ways of viewing the phenomenon can be found in ideas of trait-like positive and negative emotionality within PERSONALITY theory and measurement, and conservation of resources in stress theory.

See also *burnout; emotion in organizations*

Bibliography

Funk, S. C. (1991). Hardiness: A review of theory and research. *Health Psychology*, **11**, 335–45.
Maddi, S. R., Khoshaba, D. M., Persico, M., Lu, J., Harvey, R., and Bleecker, F. (2002). The personality construct of hardiness II: Relationships with comprehensive tests of personality and psychopathology. *Journal of Research in Personality*, **36** (1), 72–85.

Hawthorne effect

Daniel R. Ilgen

This effect, observed in field experiments, occurs when:

1   one or more changes or manipulations are made by researchers in a field setting;
2   the persons in the target sample experiencing the change(s) are aware of the experimental manipulations; and
3   the latter alter their behavior *not because of the specific variables manipulated* but because of the attention they receive.

As a result, the researchers may falsely attribute the observed effects on behavior to the variables manipulated rather than the attention. The effect gets its name from the research studies in which it was identified and labeled.

In the late 1920s and early 1930s, several studies were carried out at Western Electric's Hawthorne Works in Chicago, Illinois (*see* HUMAN RELATIONS MOVEMENT). The research, conducted by E. Mayo, F. J. Roethlisberger, W. J. Dickson, T. N. Whitehead, and others from the Graduate School of Business Administration at Harvard University, in cooperation with a number of persons at the Hawthorne Works, began as an investigation of the effects of illumination intensity on employees, particularly on employee performance. The goal of the research was to find the optimal level of illumination for work involving the assembly and inspection of relays used in telephone equipment. Therefore, the researchers simply varied the amount of illumination over time and measured changes in performance, among other things. The unanticipated finding was that performance did not covary with illumination but continued to improve over the course of the experiment, even when the illumination was reduced to very low levels. The post hoc explanation for the observed pattern of results was that the employees very much appreciated the attention that they received from the researchers, management, and others for being part of the experiment, and their improved performance was one way in which they expressed their appreciation. The explanation stuck, and the phenomenon has been known as the Hawthorne effect ever since.

Ironically, the Hawthorne effect was discovered only because, in the eyes of the researchers, their research had "failed." Had performance decreased as the amount of light decreased and vice versa, the Hawthorne effect would not have been discovered. Since the effects on performance of illumination and those of attention were in opposite directions, the pattern of results fit one explanation, that of the Hawthorne effect, and not the other.

Often in organizational behavior research in the field, the phenomenon of interest is manipulated in a way that leads to predicted changes in behavior that are in the same direction as those that would result from the Hawthorne effect. For example, interventions designed to empower workers, enrich jobs, increase SELF-EFFICACY, focus on quality, or in some other way impact positively on performance may be implemented in such a way that they create a Hawthorne effect. In such cases, if performance changes as is predicted, based on the construct of interest (empowerment, increased self-efficacy, etc.), the tendency is to attribute the effect to the construct under investigation; the alternative explanation of a Hawthorne effect is often ignored. At the very least, when the Hawthorne effect is a possible cause of results that are found, it should be mentioned. Better yet, multiple studies and carefully designed research should be conducted to insure that effects attributed to constructs of interest are, most likely, caused by those constructs and not other common variables confounded with the constructs of interest, particularly those variables considered to cause the Hawthorne effect.

See also *bias; performance appraisal/performance management; research design; research methods*

Bibliography

Roethlisberger, F. J. and Dickson, W. J. (1939). *Management and the Worker*. Cambridge, MA: Harvard University Press.

hierarchy

see ORGANIZATIONAL DESIGN; ORGANIZA-
TIONAL STRUCTURE

high reliability organizations

Karlene H. Roberts

High reliability organizations (HROs) are
organizations in which ERRORS can have catastrophic consequences, but which avoid them.
In such organizations reliability is as much a
part of the bottom line as is productivity.
These organizations are often technologically
complex, making their management more
challenging than is true for "garden variety"
organizations.

In 1984 Charles Perrow published *Normal
Accidents*, in which he described accidents that
could not be prevented (i.e., were normal). He
identified a number of organizations that he
thought were so potentially dangerous that they
should be eliminated. Perrow provided two concepts that are important in more recent literatures: tight versus loose coupling (borrowed
from the social psychologist Karl Weick) and
complex interactions. While smatterings of
other investigations complementary to the
HRO work have been around for some time,
research on HROs began in 1985 by a group of
scholars from the University of California at
Berkeley. These scholars represented several
social sciences (political science, sociology, and
organizational behavior). Over the years a
number of other scholars have engaged in research on organizations that should behave reliably (some that have and some that have not).
This group takes a more positive view than does
Perrow.

One of the first findings in this general area
was that front line operators are not usually the
perpetrators of catastrophes because catastrophes require the resources no single individual has at his or her command (Turner, 1978).
Organizational processes that augment reliability include pushing decision-making to the
lowest hierarchical level commensurate with

the nature of the problem (the person with
the most accurate information rather than the
person at the highest level makes important decisions), the relaxation of hierarchy, structural
flexibility (Roberts, 1990), process auditing (including periodic safety checks), appropriate
reward systems (that is, not rewarding behavior
A while hoping for behavior *B*), avoiding quality
degradation, being constantly aware that risk
exists, and engaging in human resource behaviors that encourage these and other processes
(Roberts and Bea, 2001). An important outcome
of this research was identifying elements that
support a culture of safety and reliability
(Weick and Sutcliffe, 2001). After the space
shuttle *Challenger* accident in 1986, Diane
Vaughan (1996) did an extensive investigation
of NASA and added more concepts to the organizational reliability vocabulary. Chief among
them was her finding that NASA engaged in
the "normalization of deviance" (see DEVI-
ANCE). That is, O rings had previously failed
and NASA convinced itself that this was normal
and nothing catastrophic would happen because
nothing catastrophic had happened. At about the
same time, Scott Sagan (1993) pitted normal
accidents theory against high reliability theory.
Both normal accidents and high reliability
theory proponents see the two positions not
as adversarial but as complementary to one
another.

Today, the research flourishes, although it has
not been well tied to mainstream organizational
theory. Researchers are beginning to understand
that not just single organizations are responsible
for error but that the organization usually resides
within systems of organizations (clients, regulators, customers, etc.) that can contribute to massive error. The work has been applied in a
number of industries, including air traffic control, commercial and military aviation, commercial nuclear power production, healthcare,
financial institutions, and chemical production.
One author states that the reason the area is
important is because "in a generation or two
the world will probably need thousands of high
reliability organizations running ... electrical
grids, computer and telecommunication net-

works, financial networks, genetic engineering, nuclear waste storage, and many other complex, hazardous technologies" (Pool, 1997: 276).

See also *crises/disasters; group decision-making; incentives; learning organization*

Bibliography

Perrow, C. (1999) [1984]. *Normal Accidents: Living With High Risk Technologies*. Princeton, NJ: Princeton University Press.
Pool, R. (1997). *Beyond Engineering: How Society Shapes Technology*. New York: Oxford University Press.
Roberts, K. H. (1990) Some characteristics of one type of high reliability organization. *Organization Science*, 1, 160–76.
Roberts, K. H. and Bea, R. (2001). When systems fail. *Organizational Dynamics*, **29**, 179–91.
Sagan, S. (1993). *The Limits of Safety: Organizations, Accidents, and Nuclear Weapons*. Princeton, NJ: Princeton University Press.
Turner, B. M. (1978). *Man Made Disasters*. London: Wykeham Press.
Vaughan, D. (1996). *The Challenger Launch Decision: Risky Technology, Culture, and Deviance at NASA*. Chicago: University of Chicago Press.
Weick, K. E. and Sutcliffe, K. M. (2001). *Managing the Unexpected: Assuring High Performance in an Age of Complexity*. San Francisco: Jossey-Bass.

human relations movement

John Kelly

This body of theory and practice is popularly associated with the sociologist Elton Mayo (1880–1949), whose basic idea was that workers had strong social needs which they tried to satisfy through membership of informal social groups at the workplace. Managerial attempts to improve JOB SATISFACTION and work MOTIVATION had to take account of these needs and could not treat workers simply as economic individuals wanting to maximize pay and minimize effort (*see* SCIENTIFIC MANAGEMENT).

Human relations thinking emerged from a series of experiments conducted between 1924 and the early 1940s in Chicago which claimed to have found positive associations between work-group cohesion (*see* GROUP COHESIVENESS), participative supervisory styles (*see* MANAGERIAL ROLES), job satisfaction, and job performance. These ideas led to a substantial body of research on WORK GROUPS, on supervisory style, and on worker attitudes (mostly in the 1950s and early 1960s) and the main impact of the movement in organizations was through programs of supervisory training.

Many OB theorists are suspicious of the concept of social need; research on supervision has shown that a participative style does not always produce higher satisfaction and/or performance; and cohesive groups can promote low, as well as high, levels of performance: for these reasons the ideas of the movement have largely fallen out of favor.

See also *participation; Theory X and Y*

Bibliography

Rose, M. (1988). *Industrial Behavior: Theoretical Development since Taylor*, 3rd edn. London: Penguin Books.

hygiene factors

see EXTRINSIC AND INTRINSIC MOTIVATION; JOB SATISFACTION

I

identification

Daniel C. Feldman

Identification is the part of an individual's self-concept which derives from his or her membership in a social group (Tajfel, 1981). To the extent that individuals identify with a group, they experience the successes and failures of the group as their own and incorporate the dominant attitudes and VALUES of the group as their own (Ashforth and Mael, 1989). The term *identification* is also used to refer to the process by which this change in self-concept takes place (Kelman, 1961; Freud, 1949).

Traditionally, identification has been viewed as a voluntary response to group membership rather than as a coercive or instrumental response (*see* CONFORMITY). Individuals who identify with their groups adjust to group expectations not out of fear of PUNISHMENT or for instrumental reasons, but because they find relationships with other group members intrinsically satisfying and want to express attitudes that others in the group will find compatible. While identification has not been closely linked to productivity outcomes, it has been more consistently associated with altruistic behavior, cooperative behavior, and GROUP CO-HESIVENESS (Turner, 1984) (*see* ALTRUISM). For example, in organizational settings, individuals with high identification may be more likely to volunteer to work over-time, to recruit for the group, and to publicize the group in a positive way to outsiders.

Although there has been considerable theoretical speculation on the processes by which identification takes place, there has been relatively little empirical research on this topic. Organizational behavior research has concentrated on examining how identification results from escalating emotional investment in the group (Burke and Reitzes, 1991; Ashforth and Mael, 1989) (*see* COMMITMENT, ESCALATING). In contrast, clinical and developmental psychology has focused on how identification results from the renunciation of the demands of competing groups and personal sacrifices for the group (Freud, 1949; Eysenck, 1960).

See also *attitude theory; group decision-making; group dynamics; group norms; groupthink; identity, personal*

Bibliography

Ashforth, B. E. and Mael, F. (1989). Social identity theory and the organization. *Academy of Management Review*, **14**, 20–39.

Burke, P. J. and Reitzes, D. C. (1991). An identity theory approach to commitment. *Social Psychology Quarterly*, **54**, 239–51.

Eysenck, H. J. (1960). The development of moral values in children: The contribution of learning theory. *British Journal of Educational Psychology*, **30**, 11–22.

Freud, S. (1949). *An Outline of Psychoanalysis*. New York: Norton.

Kelman, H. C. (1961). Processes of opinion change. *Public Opinion Quarterly*, **25**, 57–78.

Tajfel, H. (1981). Human groups and social categories: Studies in social psychology. Cambridge: Cambridge University Press.

Turner, J. C. (1984). Social identification and psychological group formation. In H. Tajfel (ed.), *The Social Dimension: European Developments in Social Psychology*, Vol. 2. Cambridge: Cambridge University Press, 518–38.

identity, organizational

Mary Jo Hatch

While the study of personal identity is long-standing, organizational identity is just coming into its own. Because organizational identity research is both new and focused on a highly complex phenomenon, a certain amount of disagreement over theoretical framing and research methods is understandable and healthy.

What is organizational identity? Albert and Whetten's (1985) widely used definition – "that which is central, distinctive, and enduring about an organization" – suggests both synchronic and diachronic answers. Appreciated synchronically, "central" and "distinctive" invite characterizing the organization using appropriate descriptive terms. For example, in 1960 IBM was a large, bureaucratic, mainframe computer manufacturing company whose representatives were known for wearing blue suits and white shirts. In contrast, "enduring" must be approached diachronically. Only by assessing organizational identities over time can you say what endures or what disappears from their attribute mix. For IBM today, bureaucratic and mainframe manufacturing have disappeared, while large and computer-related endure. White shirts and blue suits no longer define IBM's dress code, but when ex-CEO Gerstner wrote about transforming the company, he appeared on his book's dustjacket in traditional IBM attire.

Methodologically speaking, synchronically defining an organization's central and distinctive attributes most often produces lists analyzed to find the attributes most strongly or widely associated with the organization, or to ask what it is without which the organization would no longer be recognizable (e.g., can Singer be Singer without sewing machines?). Carroll and Hannan (2000) provide an example of synchronic thinking when they equate identity with organizational forms (e.g., microbrewery or brew-pub vs. traditional brewery or restaurant). However, the synchronic approach can encourage confusion of categorical descriptors of identity (identifying labels or identity claims) with identity itself, and, when multiple data points of this sort are collected, researchers easily confuse competing or contradictory labels or claims

with multiple organizational identities (e.g., Pratt and Rafaeli, 1997). In my view, however, competing or contradictory attributes signify the complexity of organizational identities; they speak to the multi-faceted and ever-changing, rather than plural, nature of organizational identities.

Diachronically assessing identity content raises other questions, such as: What do temporal changes in attributes signify about identity's enduring aspect? Gioia, Schultz, and Corley (2000) argue that organizational identity need not endure, interpreting changes in identity attributes as adaptive responses to environmental shifts. They see instability in organizational identities such as Singer's, a company that continued with the same name and many of the same stakeholders after selling its core sewing machine business. These researchers claim that finding adaptive instability in organizational identity undermines Albert and Whetten's definition since, if what is central and distinctive does not endure, it is not central and distinctive. I would argue, however, that "former maker of sewing machines" remains part of Singer's identity, and thus the instability Gioia, Schultz, and Corley observe results from not appreciating identity in its historical context (i.e., not fully activating the diachronic perspective).

The quandary over whether or not organizational identities endure suggests creating a historically rich, diachronic theory of organizational identity able to address the question: How does what is central and distinctive about the organization shift over time in ways that provide continuity while permitting change? Addressing this question offers a solution to the puzzle presented by empirical indicators of multiple identities – a single identity can manifest in multiple ways by being constituted from many, temporally shifting points of view. This perspective leads me to conclude that organizational identity is socially constructed as it emerges, is maintained and transformed via the distributed awareness (no one person or vantage point contains all the cues needed to define a particular identity) and collective consciousness (organizational identity is indicated by collective reference: "we" or "they") of its stakeholders (both internal and external to the organization).

Whether particular organizational identities are continuous or discontinuous, enduring or not, are thus matters for longitudinal empirical study.

Foucault (1972) addressed the diachronic problem of accounting simultaneously for change and stability in organizational identities when, in presenting himself, he stated: "Do not ask who I am and do not ask me to remain the same." By not asking about the content of organizational identity, but instead focusing on processes by which the meanings constituting identity shift over time, we find a very different solution to the problem of defining organizational identity – articulating the dynamics of organizational identity, which is what we were trying to do in Hatch and Schultz (1997, 2000, 2002) when we theorized organizational identity in relation to culture and image.

Hatch and Schultz (2002) defined organizational identity dynamics as a conversation between organizational culture (contextualizing symbolism that serves as an organizational "self") and STAKEHOLDER images (providing fluid interpretations of organizational symbols, including actions, indicating how the organization is considered by others whose contexts are not, strictly speaking, the organization's). Identity continuously emerges from the ongoing conversation via processes of *expressing* organizational beliefs and values, *impressing* others with organizational identity claims, *mirroring* feedback from stakeholders, and *reflecting* upon outsiders' images of the organization in relation to what insiders believe it truly is or should be.

The dynamic approach allows for continuity without consistency (*both* stability *and* change): what remains the same in identity content between time$_1$ and time$_2$ is not necessarily what remains the same between time$_2$, time$_3$ and time$_4$, yet identity$_1$ in relation to identity$_2$ etc., defines a trace that, over time, is recognizable as one (or one's) identity. This idea resembles Czarniawska's (1997) proposition that organizational identities are serial narratives that unfold like soap operas.

Although empirical studies (notably Dutton and Dukerich 1991) helped to establish the field, most organizational identity researchers agree that more empirical work is needed in order to refine and redirect theory and better engage practice. At present, empirical efforts extend identity research into corporate branding and reputation; mergers, acquisitions, joint ventures, and other organizational restructuring activities; and personal identity (via links with organizational identification research). Because of the fundamental nature of identity questions, I expect the concept of organizational identity to prove valuable to additional areas of organizational study as the field matures.

See also *organizational climate; organizational design; organizational effectiveness; symbolism; values*

Bibliography

Albert, S. and Whetten, D. A. (1985). Organizational identity. In L. L. Cummings and M. M. Staw (eds.), *Research in Organizational Behavior*, 7, 263–95.

Carroll, G. R. and Hannan, M. T. (2000). *The Demography of Corporations and Industries*. Princeton, NJ: Princeton University Press.

Czarniawska, B. (1997). *Narrating the Organization: Dramas of Institutional Identity*. Chicago: University of Chicago Press.

Dutton, J. and Dukerich, J. (1991). Keeping an eye on the mirror: Image and identity in organizational adaptation. *Academy of Management Journal*, 34, 517–54.

Foucault, M. (1972). Introduction. *The Archeology of Knowledge*, trans. A. M. Sheridan Smith. London: Tavistock.

Gioia, D. A, Schultz, M., and Corley, K. (2000). Organizational identity, image and adaptive instability. *Academy of Management Review*, 25, 63–82.

Hatch, M. J. and Schultz, M. (1997). Relations between organizational culture, identity and image. *European Journal of Marketing*, 31, 356–65.

Hatch, M. J. and Schultz, M. S. (2000). Scaling the Tower of Babel: Relational differences between identity, image and culture in organizations. In M. Schultz, M. J. Hatch, and M. H. Larsen (eds.), *The Expressive Organization: Linking Identity, Reputation, and the Corporate Brand*. Oxford: Oxford University Press, 13–35.

Hatch, M. J. and Schultz, M. S. (2002). The dynamics of organizational identity. *Human Relations*, 55, 989–1019.

Pratt, M. G. and Rafaeli, A. (1997). Organizational dress as a symbol of multilayered social identities. *Academy of Management Journal*, 40, 862–98.

identity, personal

Blake Ashforth

Identity refers to one's self-definition ("who I am"). An identity anchors and situates a person, strongly influencing many self-relevant processes, ranging from what the person finds motivating, to whom the person compares himself or herself with.

There are at least three "levels" of identity: personal, interpersonal, and collective (Brewer and Gardner, 1996). The personal (or individual) level focuses on oneself as a unique being – on the attributes that describe and help differentiate oneself from others. As such, a personal identity may include traits, VALUES, beliefs, knowledge, skills, abilities, goals, characteristic behaviors, and so on. In contrast, the interpersonal (or relational) level of identity focuses on one's ROLE related relationships, such as supervisor–subordinate and co-worker–co-worker. The collective (or social/group) level focuses on oneself as a prototypical member of a group, such as a department, or a social category, such as gender. Indeed, demographic attributes such as gender and age can be viewed as either collective identities in the sense that prototypes of the attributes are inferred, or as personal identities in the sense that they help distinguish one individual from another (*see* ORGANIZATIONAL DEMOGRAPHY). Collective identities are most salient in intergroup contexts (when one's own group is at least implicitly compared with others), interpersonal identities are most salient in role related contexts, and personal identities are most salient in intragroup contexts (when everyone shares the same collective identity) (Turner et al., 1994).

The concept of personal identity has been used in organizational studies as a counterpoint to the other levels of identity, particularly collective identity, and as a critical variable in research on SOCIALIZATION and personal development (e.g., Ibarra, 1999; Hall, 2002). However, organizational scholars can use the concept in relation to any individual difference variable and any organizational process that capitalizes on such differences. For example, research on PERSONALITY, attitudes, person–organization fit, selection, IMPRESSION MANAGEMENT, and GOAL SETTING could be reframed using an identity lens. The advantage of doing so is that identity speaks to one's core sense of self, often implicating those attributes that one cares most deeply about (whether positively or negatively) and that strongly affect how one enacts one's roles and interacts with others (*see* ENACTMENT). Thus, an identity lens may illuminate what aspects of an organization are most likely to foster person–organization fit and positive attitudes, how individuals are likely to present themselves and behave in group settings, what goals are most likely to be chosen, and related issues.

The concept of personal identity has particular promise in two areas. First, INDIVIDUAL DIFFERENCES are typically researched in atomized form. The notion of personal identity implies that multiple individual differences may be combined into more holistic gestalts. Thus, identity may some day provide a synergistic shorthand for capturing more of the totality of the individual. Second, Markus and Nurius (1986) argue that individuals harbor "possible selves," that is, potential identities that they hope to realize or to avoid. The notion of possible selves adds a dynamic and future oriented flavor to the typically static view of most individual differences, suggesting that such selves may actively motivate, say, the pursuit of developmental opportunities or how one responds to positive and negative feedback.

See also *feedback; learning, individual*

Bibliography

Brewer, M. B. and Gardner, W. (1996). Who is this "we"?: Levels of collective identity and self-representations. *Journal of Personality and Social Psychology*, 71, 83–93.

Hall, D. T. (2002). *Careers In and Out of Organizations.* Thousand Oaks, CA: Sage.

Ibarra, H. (1999). Provisional selves: Experimenting with image and identity in professional adaptation. *Administrative Science Quarterly*, 44, 764–91.

Markus, H. and Nurius, P. (1986). Possible selves. *American Psychologist*, 41, 954–69.

Turner, J. C., Oakes, P. J., Haslam, S. A., and McGarty, C. A. (1994). Self and collective: Cognition and social context. *Personality and Social Psychology Bulletin*, **20**, 454–63.

ideology

Stewart Clegg

An ideology is a coherent set of beliefs, attitudes, and opinions. The meaning is often pejorative, with a contrast drawn between ideology and science. Marxist thinkers developed the concept from the critique of the *ancien régime* made by radical French scholarship (*Les ideologues*) in the eighteenth century. In this account an ideology describes the belief systems of people unaware of their real class interests, who suffer from "false consciousness." Gramsci (1971) refers to this state of affairs as "hegemony," where people think through dominant concepts, a view popular in organization theory influenced by Burawoy (1979). From this perspective, organizations routinely manufacture consent to their standard practices as a part of organizational behavior.

Abercrombie, Hill, and Turner (1980) argue, on the contrary, that dominant ideologies are not used to organize the relatively powerless. Instead, the lower participants of organizations are characterized as people with plural identities and multiple interests. What ideology does is to organize the interests of the dominant strata. An example of this in action is given in the Nobel economist Joseph Stiglitz's (2002) critique of the way that the International Monetary Fund functions. Dominant theories, such as economic neoliberalism, are examples of ideology because they provide seemingly neutral and technical accounts for what organizations should do that overly reflect a very limited range of views and prescriptions. Management and organization theories have been said to play a similar ideological role. For instance, Fergusson (1984) argues that bureaucracy is an ideological construct that privileges male interests because of the way that it separates the public sphere from the private sphere and elevates the public, as a male space, over the private, a female space.

Foucault (1984: 101–2) questions the relation presumed to exist between ideology and science, as realms of "falsity" and "truth." Instead, he regards truth and falsity as effects of the discursive means that are historically institutionalized for producing knowledge. From this perspective the basis for a truth claim will always be a judgment rooted in a particular theory, opening up the possibility that any theory that claims to be able to provide true grounds for its analysis must of necessity be ideological because it seeks to suppress the play of different perspectives. In this argument there cannot be a singular definitive account of a phenomenon and all accounts must be provisional – a position not too far from the more conventional view of science as being a matter of conjectures and refutations. Provisional but falsifiable accounts that are reasonably honest about their value presuppositions are the best we might hope for. All theory should be subject to critique of its assumptions: in this way ideology will be made evident even if the promise of a social science to deliver definitive knowledge is held in doubt.

See also *critical theory; organizational change; values*

Bibliography

Abercrombie, N., Hill, S., and Turner, B. S. (1980). *The Dominant Ideology Thesis*. London: Allen and Unwin.

Burawoy, M. (1979). *Manufacturing Consent*. Chicago: University of Chicago Press.

Fergusson, K. (1984). *The Feminist Case Against Bureaucracy*. Philadelphia, PA: Temple University Press.

Foucault, M. (1984). *The History of Sexuality: An Introduction*. London: Penguin Books.

Gramsci, A. (1971). *The Prison Notebooks*. London: Lawrence and Wishart.

Stiglitz, J. (2002). *Globalization and Its Discontents*. Victoria: Allen Lane.

impression management

Paul Rosenfeld, Robert A. Giacolone, and Catherine Riordan

Organizational theorists, researchers, and practitioners have increasingly recognized the importance of impression management as an explanatory model for a broad range of organizational phenomena. Impression management refers to the many ways that individuals attempt to control the impressions others have of them: their behavior, motivations, morality, and personal attributes like competence, trustworthiness, and future potential.

The impression management framework employs a "life as theater" or dramaturgic metaphor to describe social and organizational behavior. People are actors, play many roles (e.g., parent, employee, supervisor, author), and are keenly aware of audience reactions to their behaviors (see ROLE). Some of the actors' behavior is an attempt to control or modify the image that relevant audiences have of them and to win their moral, social, and financial support. The impression management framework assumes that a basic human motive, both inside and outside of organizations, is to be viewed by others in a favorable manner and avoid being seen negatively. In their interpersonal behaviors individuals act as amateur politicians or "spin doctors" using enhancing impression management tactics (ingratiation, self-promotion) to look good and protective or defensive impression management (e.g., excuses, apologies) to minimize deficiencies and avoid looking bad.

Impression management has increasingly become a recognized part of organizational behavior theory, research, and practice (Rosenfeld, Giacalone, and Riordan, 2002). Two edited volumes (Giacalone and Rosenfeld 1989, 1991) systematically applied an organizational impression management perspective to topics such as selection interviews, letters of recommendation, performance appraisal, leadership, career strategies, exit interviews, organizational justice, and cultural diversity.

Impression management theory has its roots in the pioneering work of sociologist Erving Goffman. In his classic, *The Presentation of Self in Everyday Life* (1959), Goffman systematically interpreted social behavior utilizing the terminology and methods of the theater. People were seen as social actors attempting to establish, in conjunction with those with whom they were interacting, a "working consensus" through their impression management behaviors. This reciprocal impression management served as a social lubricant: it allowed actors to know how to act and what actions to expect from others.

Beginning in the 1960s, experimental social psychologists (most notably Edward E. Jones's seminal studies of ingratiation) increasingly began utilizing impression management to explain a whole host of research areas, including cognitive dissonance, altruism, and aggression. Rather than having independent theoretical status, however, impression management was often an alternative explanation for established social psychological laboratory phenomena (Baumeister, 1982).

The social psychological legacy of impression management theory also gave it a harsh stigma that it still struggles to overcome. Impression management became synonymous with unscrupulous, reprehensible, nefarious, disingenuous, and deceptive actions. People who practiced impression management did not necessarily believe in the impressions they were claiming, but were saying and doing things to gain favor in the eyes of significant audiences as part of a general motive of manipulative social influence (Tedeschi, 1981).

While this highly pessimistic view of impression management undoubtedly plays a role in explaining some behaviors, it is currently seen by scholars and practitioners alike as portraying only a limited aspect of a broader and more positive impression management motivation. Schlenker and Weigold (1992) distinguished between restrictive and expansive views of impression management. The restrictive view sees impression management as a generally negative and deceptive set of behaviors aimed at illicitly gaining social power and approval. The expansive view sees impression management as a fundamental aspect of social and organizational interactions. As Tetlock and Manstead (1985: 61–2) noted: "Although some writers have used the term impression management to refer to the self-conscious deception of others ... there is no compelling psychological reason why impression management must be either duplicitous or under conscious control. Impression management may be the product of highly overlearned habits or scripts, the original functions of which people have long forgotten." It is perhaps best to view impression management behaviors as falling on a continuum ranging from sincere, accurate presentations to conscious deception.

The popularity of impression management in organizational behavior is a relatively recent phenomenon. While many of the concepts of impression management were utilized in areas such as organizational politics (*see* POLITICS), there were few organizational investigations of impression management before the early 1980s. It is only relatively recently that the organizational impression management literature has expanded into the full range of management and organizational behavior topic areas. With this recent increase in research activity, impression management now provides explanatory power for a wide range of topics across both the social and organizational sciences.

A number of challenges remain for future organizational impression management research, three of which are of note. First, can impression management be trained? Although training in impression management performance and detection has been recommended (Rosenfeld, Giacalone, and Riordan, 2002), impression management has yet to have true research-based practitioner applications. A first step may require viewing impression management as a desirable set of skills rather than a deficit.

Second, are impression management motivation and tactics applicable to a culturally diverse and multinational workforce? As organizations grow increasingly diverse and multinational impression management may be crucial to members of racial/ethnic minority groups, women, immigrants, and expatriates who often need to please majority group members in positions of greater social power. Understanding how impression management behaviors are interpreted by others can also serve as the basis for smoother interactions and a means for solving potential communication problems among individuals from diverse backgrounds.

Third, does impression management play a role in functional and dysfunctional interpersonal relationships at work? Limited impression management research has been done with individuals in ongoing professional relationships. It would be of interest to know what types of impression management behaviors are associated with stable and successful relationships in the areas of organizational citizenship, coaching, mentoring, and in the emerging area of workplace spirituality. At the same time, organizations would benefit from understanding conditions that elicit impression management behaviors that are dysfunctional or destructive from the individual or organizational point of view (e.g., substance abuse, sabotage, withholding of effort).

See also *diversity management; halo effect; influence; performance appraisal/performance management*

Bibliography

Baumeister, R. F. (1982). A self-presentational view of social phenomena. *Psychological Bulletin*, **91**, 3–26.

Giacalone, R. A. and Rosenfeld, P. (eds.) (1989). *Impression Management in the Organization*. Newbury Park, CA: Sage.

Giacalone, R. A. and Rosenfeld, P. (eds.) (1991). *Applied Impression Management: How Image Making Affects Managerial Decisions*. Newbury Park, CA: Sage.

Goffman, E. (1959). *The Presentation of Self in Everyday Life*. Garden City, NY: Doubleday.

Rosenfeld, P., Giacalone, R. A., and Riordan, C. A. (1994). Impression management theory and diversity: Lessons for organizational behavior. *American Behavioral Scientist*, **37**, 601–4.

Rosenfeld, P., Giacalone, R. A., and Riordan, C. A. (1995). *Impression Management in Organizations: Theory, Measurement, Practice*. London: Routledge.

Rosenfeld, P., Giacalone, R. A., and Riordan, C. A. (2002). *Impression Management: Building and Enhancing Reputations at Work*. London: Thompson Learning.

Schlenker, B. R. and Weigold, M. F. (1992). Interpersonal processes involving impression regulation and management. *Annual Review of Psychology*, **43**, 133–68.

Tedeschi, J. T. (1981). *Impression Management and Social Psychological Research*. New York: Academic Press.

Tetlock, P. E. and Manstead, A. S. R. (1985). Impression management versus intrapsychic explanations in social psychology: A useful dichotomy? *Psychological Review*, **92**, 59–77.

incentives

George T. Milkovich and Yoshio Yanadori

Incentives are financial or non-financial inducements offered to influence employees' future behavior. Narrowly defined, incentives are valued returns expected by employees in exchange for achieving various performance levels. Organizations use incentives to motivate employees' behaviors, which lead to better individual and organization performance (Bartol and Locke, 2000; Kanfer, 1990; Lawler, 1990). Organizations can be conceived as networks of incentives, offering various anticipated returns for work (e.g., earnings, promotions, recognition, challenging work, learning opportunities) that motivate certain desirable employees' behaviors (Milkovich and Newman, 2002).

INCENTIVE AND RETURNS

Although valued returns can be labeled as both incentives and rewards, a distinction can be made. Rewards reinforce employees' past behaviors and performance. Incentives influence employees' expectations and future behaviors. A promotion received is a reward. Expecting a promotion acts as an incentive. It is a matter of expectations and timing. These expectations may be formed through experience and formal COMMUNICATION.

INCENTIVE PAY

Incentive pay is widely used in organizations (Watson Wyatt, 2002; Brown and Heywood, 2002). Specific criteria for payment (e.g., performance measure, performance target, payment calculation formula) are determined and communicated to employees. Once the performance target is achieved, employees receive the payment based on the preestablished criteria. The size of payment typically varies depending on performance levels achieved. Incentive pay does not add to base salary, and therefore the payment of an incentive in one period must be re-earned in subsequent periods (Milkovich and Newman, 2002).

Incentive pay plans come in many varieties which can be described on several dimensions. One dimension is whether the payment is based on individual or group performance. Under piece-rate systems or sales commissions, employees receive payment based on their individual performance (e.g., output volume, sales volume). Under profit sharing plans or gain sharing plans, the size of the payment pool varies based on unit or firm performance (e.g., profit, return on assets).

A second dimension is the time frame. Short-term incentives are based on performance in a specific period (one quarter or annually). Profit sharing is a typical short-term incentive since its payment generally depends on annual performance. Stock options, by which recipients can realize financial gains only several years after the grant, is an example of a long-term incentive. The form of an incentive payment can also vary. Some pay in cash; others offer stock or stock options, or even all-expense paid vacations or tickets to concerts.

THEORIES AND RESEARCH

Multiple theories and considerable research in psychology and economics deal with the incentive pay–performance relationship (Gibbons, 1998). Agency theory addresses optimal contracts in which principals delegate work to agents in exchange for valued returns. Due to the divergence of interests, agents may not necessarily act for the principals' benefit. A solution is to establish an incentive tied to outcomes desired by the principal. Employees will be motivated to achieve the outcomes to increase their own earnings.

Expectancy theory also explains the influence of incentive pay on employees' motivation. This theory describes MOTIVATION as a multiplicative function of three factors: expectancy, instrumentality, and valence. Instrumentality is the employees' beliefs that their performance is associated with pay increments. If its instrumentality is greater than non-incentive pay forms (e.g., salary, benefits), incentive pay has greater motivational effect. Valence is the value individuals attach to the amount of incentive pay. Larger amounts tend to have greater valences and therefore larger motivational effects. Furthermore, the performance target itself motivates employees to achieve the goal, as posited by goal setting theory (Bartol and Locke, 2000).

OTHER WORKPLACE INCENTIVES

Various other organization systems also influence employees' behaviors. A future, expected stream of earnings influences employees' intention to stay. For instance, under a seniority-based pay system, younger employees may be underpaid and senior employees may be overpaid relative to their actual productivity. Consequently, employees are more likely to stay in their organizations to offset their lower pay during the early stage of their careers. Deferred pay (e.g., pensions) has a similar incentive effect on employees' behaviors. Employees are unwilling to leave their organizations until they are eligible for the payment (Lazear, 1998).

The expectation of promotion may also motivate employees. TOURNAMENT THEORY argues that pay differentials between two job levels can be regarded as the prize of promotion. Given that larger prizes hold higher valences, the larger the potential pay increase associated with promotion, the greater its motivational effects. Thus, the pay structure across job levels (e.g., entry–associate–middle managers–senior managers) can be viewed as financial inducements motivating employees to seek promotions.

The valence of a promotion is not limited to financial returns. Higher status is attached to higher job levels and titles; consequently, employees may put forth greater efforts to attain not only higher pay, but also higher status. In addition to promotion, several non-monetary returns act as incentives to motivate employees' behaviors. A number of organizations adopt non-monetary recognition such as acknowledging employees' achievement in organization newsletters to reinforce employees' superior behaviors. The expectation of challenging new assignments motivates employees to complete their current assignment. The prospect of improved learning opportunities may also influence employee behaviors.

However, incentives may also motivate unintended behaviors. Individuals may manipulate results by violating accounting practices, collude with customers over fictitious sales, or otherwise behave unethically (Kerr, 1995; Milkovich and Newman, 2002).

Research has yet to focus on understanding the overall incentive network. Under what conditions, external and organizational, are various incentives most likely to work? How do organizations structure their network of incentives? How do the different incentives interact? The various types of incentives tend to be considered separately by both researchers and practitioners.

See also *contracts; equity theory; performance appraisal/performance management*

Bibliography

Bartol, K. M. and Locke, E. A. (2000). Incentives and motivation. In S. Rynes and B. Gerhart (eds.), *Compensation in Organizations*. San Francisco: Jossey-Bass.

Brown, M. and Heywood, J. (2002). *Paying for Performance: An International Comparison*. Armonk, NY: M. E. Sharpe.

Gibbons, R. (1998). Incentives in organizations. *Journal of Economic Perspectives*, **12**, 115–32.

Kanfer, R. (1990). Motivation theory and industrial and organization psychology. In M. D. Dunnette and L. M. Hough (eds.), *Handbook of Industrial and Organization Psychology*, Vol. 2. Palo Alto, CA: Consulting Psychologists Press.

Kerr, S. (1995). On the folly of rewarding *A* while hoping for *B*. *Academy of Management Executive*, **9** (2), 7–14.

Lawler, E., III (1990). *Strategic Pay: Aligning Organization Strategies and Pay Systems*. San Francisco: Jossey-Bass.

Lazear, E. P. (1998). *Personnel Economics for Managers*. New York: John Wiley and Sons.

Milkovich, G. T. and Newman, J. M. (2002). *Compensation*, 7th edn. Burr Ridge, IL: McGraw-Hill/Irwin.

Watson Wyatt (2002). *Incentive Compensation Survey*. New York: Watson Wyatt Worldwide.

individual differences

Lisa M. Moynihan

Individual differences is the term used to denote any characteristic on which individuals can be compared and contrasted, generally referring to enduring rather than transient or ephemeral features of individuality. The study of individual differences and their significance is one of the cornerstones of applied psychology as a discipline and the practice of management.

People can be differentiated from one another on the basis of surface level or deep level individual differences. The former are those that are easily recognizable at first sight or on initial interaction with a person. They include demographic characteristics such as age, gender, "race," nationality, ethnicity, education, functional background, and job and organizational tenure. Deep level individual differences, which are not so readily visible, include PERSONALITY traits, VALUES, work attitudes, skill, and ABILITIES. In organizational research, individual differences may figure as independent variables, moderators, or dependent variables. In the case of some of the deep level constructs (e.g., attitudes) they can be all three simultaneously. Individual differences are also the building blocks of research examining diversity, which is essentially the study of the social effects of variation of individual differences. The diversity of group composition is an important construct in the group process and performance literature.

Surface level individual differences have been found to be predictors of getting a job, attitudes towards work, and career success. For example, individual differences in physical attractiveness and demographic characteristics have been shown to relate to interviewer evaluations. Applicants' physical attractiveness has been found to be consistently positively related to interviewer evaluations (Morrow, 1990), while interviewers' perceptions of their own demographic and attitudinal similarity with the applicant predict favorable evaluation.

GENDER also predicts initial salary level after securing a job offer. Stevens, Bavetta, and Gist (1993) found that male MBA students negotiated higher salaries than women MBA students, as a result of the different NEGOTIATION behaviors they adopted. The research also found that these differences in outcomes can be reduced with negotiation training. Gender differences in pay expectations and behaviors have also figured in research, largely because managers and professionals continue to report a significant gender gap in earnings and/or advancement, especially at higher organizational levels.

AGE has also been found to be related to JOB SATISFACTION. The exact nature of the relationship is not clear, with studies variously reporting curvilinear, null, and linear relations. The mixed results may be a result of the age distribution and gender composition differences of study samples and future research is needed to clarify the relationship (Spector, 1997). Meta-analytic evidence also suggests that age and affective COMMITMENT are significantly, albeit weakly, related (Mathieu and Zajac, 1990). Age and years of work experience have also consistently been associated with objective indicators of CAREER success. There is thus substantial support for the impact of these and other human

capital investments on career success. For example, the level, type, and quality of one's educational background are related to career success. Race is another important surface level individual difference that has implications for career success. In a study of race and career success in three American organizations, Greenhaus, Parasuraman, and Wormley (1990) found that black managers received lower ratings from their supervisors on performance and promotability and had lower levels of career satisfaction than white managers. These and other related studies suggest that although people from a variety of racial backgrounds may have gained greater access to managerial jobs, there is still evidence of widespread DISCRIMINATION.

Deep level individual differences have been found to be predictors of attitudes towards work and employment relationship expectations. They are also important moderators of relationships between job characteristics and management practices and satisfaction and performance outcomes. Attitudes towards work are influenced by personality traits. Internal LOCUS OF CONTROL is positively related to job satisfaction, while negative affectivity predicts job dissatisfaction (Spector, 1997). What people look for in a job is influenced by their work values, and work motives affect people's interpretation of their perception of the balance of inducements and contributions in the employment relationship. For example, one study found individuals high in careerism described themselves as planning to leapfrog across organizations in order to advance their career success (Rousseau, 1995). Deep level individual differences are also important moderators of management practices and job characteristics (see JOB DESIGN). For example, individualism and SELF-EFFICACY moderate the motivation potential of individually oriented compensation practices (Cable and Judge, 1994).

Research has also found that enhancing job characteristics (skill variety, task identity, autonomy, FEEDBACK of results) does not increase motivation for everyone – individual differences such as essential skill and knowledge are important moderators of ability to master challenging tasks. In their absence, job redesign tends to increase STRESS, which may negatively impact performance. Growth need strength is a related individual difference moderator – people who are low on the factor do not benefit so much from job enrichment.

Deep level individual differences also moderate the extent to which people experience stress in a given situation. Two people may be exposed to the same stressor, such as having too many deadlines, yet they experience different stress responses. This occurs for several reasons. One is that each of us perceives the same situation differently. People with high self-efficacy, for example, are less likely to experience stress consequences in that situation because the stressor is less threatening. In a similar fashion, people with pessimistic dispositions (negative affectivity) tend to develop more stress symptoms because they interpret stressful situations negatively.

Individual differences are also implicated in person–organization fit – the idea that people prefer to work for organizations that are compatible with their own preferences, personalities, and values (Kristof, 1996) (*see* PERSON–ENVIRONMENT INTERACTION). Schneider's (1987) attraction–selection–attrition (ASA) model associates person–organization fit with employee preferences to join and stay with organizations they feel are congruent with their own personal characteristics (*see* ORGANIZATIONAL CLIMATE). One of the difficulties in conducting research on this theme is determining which individual differences should "fit," and thus which of the wide variety of possible factors one should investigate in any piece of research.

Finally, group composition effects of individual differences have also long been of interest to researchers concerned with GROUP DYNAMICS and team performance. This research has largely focused on surface level individual differences as "inputs" to group process (e.g., age, "race," gender, and functional background) (for a review, see Williams and O'Reilly, 1998), but personality has not played a central role in this theoretical development. More recently, attention is turning to this theme, with research beginning to examine deep level individual differences of personality composition effects in groups (Moynihan and Peterson 2001).

See also *five factor model of personality; identity, personal*

Bibliography

Cable, D. M. and Judge, T. A. (1994). Pay preferences and job search decisions: A person–organization fit perspective. *Personnel Psychology*, **47**, 317–48.

Greenhaus, J. H., Parasuraman, S., and Wormley, W. M. (1990). Effects of race on organizational experiences, job performance evaluations, and career outcomes. *Academy of Management Journal*, **33** (1), 64–86.

Kristof, A. L. (1996). Person–organization fit: An integrative review of its conceptualizations, measurement, and implications. *Personnel Psychology*, **49**, 1–50.

Mathieu, J. E. and Zajac, D. (1990). A review and meta-analysis of the antecedents, correlates, and consequences of organizational commitment. *Psychological Bulletin*, **108**, 171–94.

Morrow, P. (1990). Physical attractiveness and selection decision-making. *Journal of Management*, **16**, 45–60.

Moynihan, L. M. and Peterson, R. S. (2001). A contingent configuration approach to understanding the role of member personality in organizational groups. *Research in Organizational Behavior*, 327–78.

Rousseau, D. M. (1995). Psychological contracts in organizations: Understanding written and unwritten contracts. Thousand Oaks, CA: Sage.

Schneider, B. (1987). The people make the place. *Personnel Psychology*, **40**, 437–54.

Spector, P. E. (1997). *Job Satisfaction: Application, Assessment, Causes, and Consequences.* Thousand Oaks, CA: Sage.

Stevens, C. K., Bavetta, A. G., and Gist, M. E. (1993). Gender differences in the acquisition of salary negotiation skills: The role of goals, self-efficacy, and perceived control. *Journal of Applied Psychology*, **78**, 723–35.

Williams, K. Y. and O'Reilly, C. A., III (1998). Demography and diversity in organizations: A review of 40 years of research. *Research in Organizational Behavior*, **20**, 77–140.

influence

Rosanna E. Guadagno and Robert B. Cialdini

The term influence, also called social influence, refers to the changing of others' attitudes, beliefs, or behavior due to real or imagined external pressure. Influence is usually distinguished from POWER, in the study of the concept in organization behavior. This is best exemplified by the focus of the field on upward influence tactics and associated outcomes in hierarchical organizations. Kipnis and his colleagues (e.g., Kipnis, Schmidt, and Wilkinson,

1980) have demonstrated that individuals use a variety of influence tactics and the effectiveness of these tactics depends on contingencies such as an individual's level in an organization and the number of years that they have worked there. These tactics included rational persuasion, consultation, ingratiation, exchange, coercion, coalition building, and inspirational appeals. After a burst of interest in this topic with large-scale empirical investigations of the consequences of using these influence tactics in organizations, research has tailed off in this area.

Research by social psychologists who have studied influence for decades now has begun to make an impact in organizational behavior and has revived interest in this topic. In an influential book, Cialdini (2001, originally published 1988) proposed that there are six key principles of influence that underlie attempts to influence others: scarcity, reciprocity, consistency/commitment, authority, social validation, and similarity/liking. These principles can be grouped into three major influence-relevant goals: (1) to enhance DECISION-MAKING effectiveness, (2) to build and maintain social relationships, and (3) to manage self-concept. This framework serves as an important organizing tool for research in organizational behavior and has even been extended to the organizational LEVELS OF ANALYSIS to help account for organizational decisions (e.g., Rao, Greve, and Davis, 2001).

The principles of authority, social validation, and scarcity serve the goal of effectiveness. Individuals want to make effective decisions and often determine the most effective course of action based on input such as authority recommendation, the actions of others, and the rarity of an item or information.

Authority figures influence others because they are perceived as experts. This activates the "believe an expert" decision heuristic. Individuals are more likely to be influenced by those who display the trappings of authority such as title, non-verbal behavior, and attire. For instance, uniforms and business suits convey AUTHORITY. A study on the impact of attire as an authority signifier indicated that people were 3.5 times more likely to jaywalk when they saw another jaywalker who was wearing a business suit rather than casual clothing (Lefkowitz, Blake, and Mouton, 1955).

Social validation, also referred to as social proof, is most influential in situations where individuals look to others to guide their actions. Individuals may choose to engage in certain behaviors or make certain choices because they believe that others would do the same. Providing evidence that others are doing the same thing influences an individual because this feedback suggests that the behavior is the most effective decision to make. For example, homeowners are significantly more likely to recycle their trash when they learn that their neighbors are doing so (Schultz, 1999).

Scarcity refers to situations where items or opportunities are presented as something hard to obtain, for reasons such as a limited supply or a time restriction. This principle relies on the "rare = valuable" decision heuristic and suggests to individuals that selecting the scarce item or making decisions based on scarce, exclusive information will lead to the most effective decision. Research on this influence principle has demonstrated that providing clients with scarce information is a powerful sales tool, particularly when they believe they have been provided this information exclusively.

In a study that examined the value of scarcity, a company that sold meat products had advance information that there would be a shortage of Australian beef. To test the impact of the impending scarcity, the researchers created three versions of the sales script: standard, where customer orders were taken as usual with no mention of the upcoming shortage; scarcity, where customers were told of the upcoming shortage; and scarcity plus exclusivity of information, where customers were told of the upcoming shortage and the company representative made it clear that this information was genuinely not well known in the market. The results revealed that customers in the standard condition ordered an average of ten loads of beef. With the scarcity script, over twice the loads of beef were ordered, and with the scarcity plus exclusivity of information script, over six times the loads of beef were ordered (Knishinsky, 1982), thus illustrating the impact of scarcity and exclusivity of information.

Similarity/liking and RECIPROCITY are influence principles that meet the goal of building and maintaining social relationships.

Similarity/liking tactics capitalize on the tendency of individuals to like those who are physically attractive or similar to themselves. For instance, physically attractive individuals are more influential and earn higher salaries on average than those who are less physically attractive (for a review, see Cialdini and Trost, 1998). Genuine compliments also enhance liking, as do perceptions of similarity.

In all human societies there is a norm for reciprocity that indicates that individuals should return favors to those who have done favors to them (Gouldner, 1960). The principle of reciprocity empowers influence tactics that work because the influence practitioner has done a favor for or made a concession to the target of influence. Individuals are more likely to agree with the request because they feel they "owe" the influence practitioner. For instance, servers at restaurants can significantly increase their tips by giving diners a mint when presenting the bill (Strohmetz et al., 2002).

The final goal that underlies the principles of influence is the goal of managing the self-concept. Commitment/consistency is an influence principle that works because it alters one's self-perception. Individuals often look to their own behavior to understand who they are. However, the outcome of their actions based on this information varies based on the level of internal consistency they desire and the way the request is presented (Guadagno et al., 2001). Thus, agreeing to a small request leads some people to see themselves as likely to agree to other similar requests, consequently this minor act becomes a commitment that makes it more likely that these individuals will agree to later, similar requests.

See also *coalition formation; perception; politics; social comparison*

Bibliography

Cialdini, R. B. (2001). *Influence: Science and Practice*, 4th edn. New York: Harper Collins.

Cialdini, R. B. and Trost, M. R. (1998). Social influence: Social norms, conformity, and compliance. In D. T. Gilbert and S. T. Fiske (eds.), *The Handbook of Social Psychology*, Vol. 2, 4th edn. Boston, MA: McGraw-Hill, 151–92.

Gouldner, A. W. (1960). The norm of reciprocity: A preliminary statement. *American Sociological Review*, 25, 161–78.

Guadagno, R. E., Asher, T., Demaine, L., and Cialdini, R. B. (2001). When saying yes leads to saying no: Preference for consistency and the reverse foot-in-the-door effect. *Personality and Social Psychology Bulletin*, 27, 859–67.

Kipnis, D., Schmidt, S., and Wilkinson, I. (1980). Intraorganizational influence tactics: Explorations in getting one's way. *Journal of Applied Psychology*, 65, 440–52.

Knishinsky, A. (1982). The effects of scarcity of material and exclusivity of information on industrial buyer perceived risk in provoking a purchase decision. Unpublished doctoral dissertation, Arizona State University.

Lefkowitz, M., Blake, R. R., and Mouton, J. S. (1955). Status factors in pedestrian violation of traffic signals. *Journal of Abnormal and Social Psychology*, 51, 704–6.

Rao, H., Greve, R. H., and Davis, G. F. (2001). Fool's gold: Social proof in the initiation and abandonment of coverage by Wall Street analysts. *Administrative Science Quarterly*.

Schultz, P. W. (1999). Changing behavior with normative feedback interventions. *Basic and Applied Social Psychology*, 21, 25–36.

Strohmetz, D. B., Rind, B., Fisher, R., and Lynn, M. (2002). Sweetening the till: The use of candy to increase restaurant tipping. *Journal of Applied Social Psychology*, 32, 300–9.

information technology

see TECHNOLOGY

initiative

see PERSONAL INITIATIVE

innovation

Andrew H. Van de Ven

Few subjects have received as much attention from social scientists, managers, and public policy-makers as innovation. It is the engine for novel changes in organizations and society as a whole. An innovation is the creation and implementation of a new idea. The new idea may pertain to a technological innovation (new technical artifacts, devices, or products), a process innovation (new services, programs, or production procedures), or an administrative innovation (new institutional policies, structures, or systems). The idea may be a novel recombination of old ideas, a scheme that challenges the present order, or an unprecedented formula or approach (Zaltman, Duncan, and Holbeck, 1973). As long as the idea is perceived as new and entails a novel change for the actors involved, it is an innovation. When the people working on a new idea are members of an organization, the venture is typically called an organizational innovation, in contrast to efforts undertaken by independent individuals (entrepreneurship) or by organizations working collectively (joint ventures or networks).

Innovations can vary widely in novelty, size, and temporal duration. Some innovations involve small, quick, incremental, lone-worker efforts. Some are unplanned and emerge by chance, accident, or afterthought. Although the majority of innovations in organizations may be of small scope, larger scale innovations have attracted more attention from practitioners and researchers. In particular, we examine innovations in which most managers and venture capitalists typically invest. They consist of planned, concentrated efforts to develop and implement a novel idea that reflects substantial technical, organizational, and market uncertainty, entails a collective effort of considerable duration, and requires greater resources than are held by the people undertaking the effort.

Studies of organizational innovation tend to examine two kinds of questions:

1   What are the causes and consequences of organizational innovation?
2   How are innovations created, developed, and implemented?

The first question entails a study of the factors and conditions that may explain the propensity of organizations to innovate, and the effects of these innovations on organizational outcomes (performance growth, profitability, etc.). The second question involves a processual study of the temporal order and sequence of events that unfold in the development of a given innovation. A brief overview of research findings on these two questions is presented below.

CAUSES AND CONSEQUENCES OF ORGANIZATIONAL INNOVATIVENESS

Many studies have examined the causes and consequences of organizational innovation by counting the number of innovations of various kinds (typically measured as new products, services, or patents) and then either examining the causal factors (independent variables) that explain statistical variations in innovativeness or the consequences of innovativeness on organizational outcomes (such as growth, profitability, etc.).

With regard to the consequences, Tornatsky and Fleischer (1990) point out that a positive bias pervades the study of innovation. Innovation is often viewed as a good thing because the new idea must be useful – profitable, constructive, or solve a problem. New ideas that are not perceived as useful are not normally called innovations; they are often called "mistakes" or "ERRORS." Objectively, of course, the usefulness of an idea can only be determined after the innovation process is completed and implemented.

Empirically, studies show that most attempts at innovation fail or terminate before they are implemented (Van de Ven et al., 1999), and when they are implemented they can have positive or negative short-run and long-run consequences for organizations. Innovations are often observed to have a J-curve effect on organizational performance, where performance deteriorates for a temporary period because of costs and setbacks experienced in learning, "debugging," and implementing innovations, followed by increases in efficiency and growth in performance (Pettigrew et al., 2003). These disruptions in performance can be especially strong when organizations introduce multiple innovations simultaneously, leading to a temporary increase in the hazard of organizational failure (Barnett and Freeman, 2001). Greve and Taylor (2000) found that innovations introduced by a lead organization can also be a catalyst for imitation by other organizations, which in turn can stimulate further changes by the lead organization. They report that the consequences of innovations vary depending on how managers perceive the innovations as opportunities for further research and development.

The causes of innovation have been studied at individual, organizational, and industry levels of analysis. Amabile (1996), Angle (2000), and Damanpour (1996) summarize many studies indicating that individuals are more likely to be creative (come up with novel ideas) and innovative (develop and implement new ideas) in organizations that both enable and motivate innovation. The design of an organization's structure, systems, and practices influences the likelihood that innovative ideas will be surfaced, and that once surfaced they will be developed and nurtured toward realization. Several organizational structural features are empirically related to innovative activities. The more complex and differentiated the organization, and the easier it is to cross boundaries, the greater the potential number of sources from which innovative ideas can spring. However, as Kanter (1983) discusses, organizational segmentation and bureaucratic procedures accompany increases in organizational size and complexity. These often constrain innovation unless special systems are put in place to motivate and enable innovative behavior.

Key motivating factors include providing a balance of intrinsic and extrinsic rewards for innovative behaviors. Incentive pay (i.e., monetary rewards contingent on performance and in addition to base salary) seems to be a relatively weak motivator for innovation; it more often serves as a proxy for recognition. Angle (2000) reports that individualized rewards tend to increase idea generation and radical innovations, whereas group rewards tend to increase innovation implementation and incremental innovations.

In addition to these motivating factors, the following factors have been found to enable and constrain innovative behavior in organizations:

- Resources for innovation.
- Frequent COMMUNICATIONS across departmental lines, among people with dissimilar viewpoints.
- Moderate environment uncertainty and mechanisms for focusing attention on changing conditions.
- Cohesive work groups with open conflict resolution mechanisms that integrate creative personalities into the mainstream (*see* GROUP COHESIVENESS).

- Structures that provide access to innovation role models and mentors.
- Moderately low personnel TURNOVER.
- PSYCHOLOGICAL CONTRACTS that legitimate and solicit spontaneous innovative behavior.

The size, age, and incumbency of an organization, and accompanying liabilities of newness, adolescence, and obsolescence, have contributed to a common perception that large established firms are less innovative than new small company startups – a perception that Chandy and Tellis (2000) called the "incumbent's curse." Early studies by the US Department of Commerce found that small firms (with fewer than 500 employees) produced 2.5 times as many innovations as large firms per employee, and that small firms bring their innovations to market 27 percent more rapidly than large firms (Charpie, 1967). While Chandy and Tellis (2000) found support for this "incumbent's curse" before World War II, after the war they found that large incumbent firms introduced significantly more radical innovations than small firms and non-incumbents. Chandy and Tellis (2000: 12) conclude that the "incumbent's curse may apply, but to an older economic period."

Other studies have found that organizational age, incumbency, and size have mixed effects on innovation. Sorensen and Stuart (2000) found that as semiconductor and biotechnology organizations age, they generate more innovations (or patents), but these gains in competencies and efficiencies come at the price of a decreasing fit between organizational capabilities and environmental demands. In terms of size, Henderson and Cockburn (1996) found that research programs located within larger pharmaceutical firms are significantly more productive than rival programs located within smaller firms. They argue that the advantages large firms realize from economies of scale and scope – such as sustaining diverse portfolios of research projects that capture internal and external knowledge spillovers – outweigh the efficiency losses attributable to market power of large firms. Finally, with regard to incumbency, Christensen (1997) argued that firms established in a product domain fail to adopt new technologies as a result of inertia in the decision-making processes induced by powerful customers. However, studies by Tripsas (1997), Henderson (1999), and King and Tucci (2002) found that the advantages that established firms have over new entrants – investment resources, technical capabilities, and complementary assets – generally outweigh their handicap of introducing inferior or competence-enhancing product designs in comparison to rival or competence-destroying designs of new entrants. Longitudinal studies by Burgelman (2002) and Chandy and Tellis (2000) show that incumbent organizations can remain nimble and innovative by adopting flexible organizational structures and cultures, intensive inter-organizational relationships to build strong technological competencies, and strategies that cannibalize a company's existing products with innovative products (see ORGANIZATIONAL DESIGN; ORGANIZATIONAL CULTURE).

Studies of patents and patent citations have demonstrated that the knowledge and resources that are relevant to the development of many innovations transcend the boundaries of individual firms, industries, and nation-states. Boundary spanning across organizational and technological boundaries by means of inter-organizational communications, personnel mobility (especially of inventors), and strategic alliances are significant related to organizational innovation learning and knowledge transfer (Mowery, Oxley, and Solverman, 1996; Rosenkopf and Almeida, 2003). In addition, an organization's niche and status in an inter-organizational network shape its competitive position and likelihood of innovation success (Podolny, Stuart, and Hannan, 1996).

At the inter-organizational field or industry level, studies have examined patterns of cooperation and competition among organizations developing similar, complementary, or substitute innovations, as well as the roles of public and private sector actors in the development of an industrial infrastructure for innovation (Nelson, 1993; Ruttan, 2001). According to Van de Ven et al. (1999), this industrial infrastructure includes the four subsystems:

Institutional arrangements: the governmental agencies, professional trade associations, and scientific/technical communities that legitimate, regulate, and standardize a technology.

Resource endowments, which include advancements in basic scientific and technological knowledge, financing and insurance arrangements, and training of competent professionals.

Consumer demand: for new-to-the-world technologies, informed, competent, and responsible consumers do not preexist; the market must be created.

Proprietary activities, which transform the available supply of public resources (scientific knowledge and workforce competence) into proprietary products and services to meet customer demand.

As relationships between these infrastructure components suggest, many complementary innovations in technical and institutional arrangements are usually required to develop and commercialize a technology. This has been demonstrated in studies by Ruttan (2001) of agricultural innovations; by Tushman and Anderson (1986) of technological revolutions in cement, minicomputers, and glass; by Powell (1998) of biotechnology; and by Van de Ven and Garud (1993) of biomedical devices. Developments in other complementary technologies and institutions often explain bottlenecks and breakthroughs in the development of a given technology. An infrastructure for innovation represents a collective achievement; it develops through the accretion of numerous events and involves many public and private sector actors over an extended period of time.

THE PROCESS OF ORGANIZATIONAL INNOVATION

Perhaps the most widely known model of the innovation process was proposed by Rogers (2003). It represents four decades of Rogers's own research and a synthesis of over 4,000 published innovation studies. This model portrays the process of innovation as consisting of three basic stages:

1 Invention of novel idea, which comes from a recognition of market or user needs and advances in basic or applied research.
2 Its development, or the sequence of events in which the new idea is transformed from an abstract concept into an operational reality.

3   Implementation, or the adoption and diffusion of the innovation by users.

Specialized fields of study have emerged to examine each innovation stage in greater detail. For the idea invention stage, an extensive literature has developed on individual and group creativity, primarily by psychologists (e.g., Amabile, 1996; Angle, 2000), and on "TECHNOLOGY push" versus "demand pull" by economists (e.g., Ruttan, 2001). Although less extensively studied than the other stages, the development stage is gaining more research attention from management scholars (e.g., Tushman and Romanelli, 1985; Van de Ven et al., 1999; Burgelman, 2002). Finally, Rogers (2003) notes that no area in the social sciences has perhaps received as much study as the implementation stage (*see* INNOVATION DIFFUSION).

While a conducive organizational context sets the stage for innovation, the developmental process itself is highly uncertain, ambiguous, and risky. The sequence of events in developing innovations from invention to implementation does not unfold in a simple linear sequence of stages or phases (Van de Ven et al., 1999). Instead, the innovation journey tends to unfold in the following ways.

In the beginning, seemingly coincidental events occur that set the stage for initiating an innovation. Some of these gestating events are sufficiently large to "shock" certain attentive people to launch an innovative venture.

Soon after work begins to develop the venture, the process proliferates from a simple unitary sequence of activities into a divergent, parallel, and convergent progression. Some of these activities are related through a division of labor among functions, but many are unrelated in any noticeable form of functional interdependence. Many component ideas and paths that were perceived as being related at one time are often reframed or rationalized as being independent and disjunctive at another time when the innovation idea or circumstances change. Problems, mistakes, and setbacks frequently occur as these developmental paths are pursued, and they provide opportunities either for learning or for terminating the developmental efforts.

The innovation journey ends when the innovation is adopted and implemented by an organization, or when resources run out, or when political opposition prevails to terminate the developmental efforts.

These messy and complex processes that are being found in longitudinal studies of innovation development are leading researchers to reconceptualize the process of innovation, because the observed processes cannot be reduced to a simple sequence of stages or phases as most models in the literature suggest. We may never find one best way to innovate because the innovation process is inherently probabilistic and because there are myriad forms and kinds of innovations. In particular, the characteristics of the innovation processes described above are more pronounced or more complex for innovations of greater novelty, size, and duration.

Researchers have found the innovation process to be more disorderly for technically complex innovations than they are for technically simple innovations (Poole et al., 2000). Relationships between innovation processes and outcomes are much weaker for highly novel radical innovations than they are for less novel incremental innovations. Some organizations appear more successful in developing certain types of innovation. Tushman and Anderson (1986) found that competence-destroying technologies tend to be initiated by new entrants, while competence-enhancing innovations are undertaken by existing established organizations in the product market. Some organizations that value and reward individualism may have an advantage in radical innovation, while a more collectivist system may do better at an incremental one (Katz, 2004). However, across these organizations' differences, studies show that temporal transitions from innovation invention to development and implementation often entail shifts from radical to incremental and from divergent to convergent thinking (Poole et al., 2000). As innovations become institutionalized, they become more structured and stabilized in their patterns and less differentiated from other organizational arrangements.

The developmental pattern and eventual success of an innovation are also influenced by its temporal duration (Gersick, 1994). Initial investments at the startup of an innovation represent an initial stock of assets that provides an innovation unit a "honeymoon" period to perform its work. These assets reduce the risk of terminating the innovation during its honeymoon period when setbacks arise and when initial outcomes are judged unfavorable. The likelihood of replenishing these assets is highly influenced by the duration of the developmental process. Interest and commitment wane with time. Thus, after the honeymoon period, innovations terminate at disproportionately higher rates, in proportion to the time needed for their implementation (Schoonhoven and Romanelli, 2001).

See also *creativity; innovation diffusion; motivation; organizational effectiveness*

Bibliography

Amabile, T. M. (1996). *Creativity in Context: Update to the Social Psychology of Creativity*. Boulder, CO: Westview Press.

Angle, H. A. (2000). Psychology and organizational innovation. In A. Van de Ven, H. Angle, and M. S. Poole (eds.), *Research on the Management of Innovation: The Minnesota Studies*. New York: Oxford University Press, 135–70.

Barnett, W. P. and Freeman, J. (2001). Too much of a good thing? Product proliferation and organizational failure. *Organization Science*, **12** (5), 539–58.

Burgelman, R. A. (2002). Strategy as vector and inertia of coevolutionary lock-in. *Administrative Science Quarterly*, **47**, 325–57.

Chandy, R. K. and Tellis, G. J. (2000). The incumbent's curse? Incumbency, size, and radical product innovation. *Journal of Marketing*, **64**, 1–17.

Charpie, R. (1967). *Technological Innovation: Its Environment and Management*. Report 0-242–736. Washington, DC: US Department of Commerce.

Christensen, C. M. (1997). *The Innovator's Dilemma: When New Technologies Cause Great Firms to Fail*. Boston, MA: Harvard Business School Press.

Damanpour, F. (1996). Organizational complexity and innovation: Developing and testing contingency models. *Management Science*, **42** (5), 693–701.

Gersick, C. J. G. (1994). Pacing strategic change: The case of a new venture. *Academy of Management Journal*, **37** (1), 9–35.

Greve, H. R. and Taylor, A. (2000). Innovations as catalysts for organizational change: Shifts in organizational cognition and search. *Administrative Science Quarterly*, **45**, 54–80.

Henderson, A. D. (1999). Firm strategy and age dependence: A contingent view of the liabilities of newness, adolescence, and obsolescence. *Administrative Science Quarterly*, **44**, 281–314.

Henderson, R. and Cockburn, I. (1996). Scale, scope, and spillovers: The determinants of research productivity in drug discovery. *RAND Journal of Economics*, **27** (1), 32–59.

Kanter, R. M. (1983). *The Change Masters*. New York: Simon and Schuster.

Katz, R. (2004). *The Human Side of Managing Technological Innovation: A Collection of Readings*, 2nd edn. New York: Oxford University Press.

King, A. A. and Tucci, C. L. (2002). Incumbent entry into new market niches: The role of experience and managerial choice in the creation of dynamic capabilities. *Management Science*, **48** (2), 171–86.

Mowery, D. C., Oxley, J. E., and Solverman, B. S. (1996). Strategic alliances and interfirm knowledge transfer. *Strategic Management Journal*, **17** (winter special issue), 77–91.

Nelson, R. R. (1993). *National Innovation Systems: A Comparative Analysis*. New York: Oxford University Press.

Pettigrew, A. M., Whittington, R., Melin, L., Sanchez-Runde, C., van den Bosch, F., Ruigrok, W., and Mumagami, T. (2003). *Innovative Forms of Organizing*. London: Sage.

Podolny, J. M., Stuart, T. E., and Hannan, M. T. (1996). Networks, knowledge, and niches: Competition in the worldwide semiconductor industry, 1984–1991. *American Journal of Sociology*, **102** (3), 659–89.

Poole, M. S., Van de Ven, A. H., Dooley, K., and Holmes, M. E. (2000). *Organizational Change and Innovation Processes: Theory and Methods for Research*. New York: Oxford University Press.

Powell, W. W. (1998). Learning from collaboration: Knowledge and networks in the biotechnology and pharmaceutical industries. *California Management Review*, **40** (3), 228–40.

Rogers, E. (2003). *Diffusion of Innovations*, 5th edn. New York: Simon and Schuster.

Rosenkopf, L. and Almeida, P. (2003). Overcoming local search through alliances and mobility. *Management Science*, **49** (6), 751–66.

Ruttan, V. W. (2001). *Technology, Growth, and Development: An Induced Innovation Perspective*. New York: Oxford University Press.

Schoonhoven, C. B. and Romanelli, E. (2001). *The Entrepreneurship Dynamic: Origins of Entrepreneurship and the Evolution of Industries*. Stanford, CA: Stanford University Press.

Sorensen, J. B. and Stuart, T. E. (2000). Aging, obsolescence, and organizational innovation. *Administrative Science Quarterly*, **45**, 81–112.

Tornatsky, L. G. and Fleischer, M. (1990). *The Processes of Technological Innovation*. Lexington, MA: D. C. Heath.

Tripsas, M. (1997). Unraveling the process of creative destruction: Complementary assets and incumbent survival in the typesetter industry. *Strategic Management Journal*, **18** (summer special issue), 119–42.

Tushman, M. L. and Anderson, P. (1986). Technological discontinuities and organizational environments. *Administrative Science Quarterly*, **31**, 439–65.

Tushman, M. and Romanelli, E. (1985). Organizational evolution: A metamorphosis model of convergence and reorientation. In B. Staw and L. Cummings (eds.), *Research in Organizational Behavior*, Vol. 7. Greenwich, CT: JAI Press.

Utterback, J. M. (1994). *Mastering the Dynamics of Innovation: How Companies Can Seize Opportunities in the Face of Technological Change.* Boston, MA: Harvard Business School Press.

Van de Ven, A. H. and Garud, R. (1993). Innovation and industry development: The case of cochlear implants. *Research on Technological Innovation, Management, and Policy*, Vol. 5. Greenwich, CT: JAI Press, 1–46.

Van de Ven, A. H., Polley, D. E., Garud, R., and Venkataraman, S. (1999). *The Innovation Journey.* New York: Oxford University Press.

Zaltman, G., Duncan, R., and Holbeck, J. (1973). *Innovations and Organizations.* New York: Wiley.

innovation adoption

see INNOVATION; INNOVATION DIFFUSION

innovation diffusion

David Strang

Much organizational research examines the process by which new ideas and practices spread. Protections against hostile takeovers like the "poison pill" are shown to be communicated through director interlocks. Japanese quality control circles spread at first through inter-corporate study visits, and later via management consultants and the business press. Public sector initiatives like privatization diffuse as governments observe their consequences and carriers like Chicago School economists obtain positions within national ministries.

In an authoritative review of the field, Rogers (1995: 11) provides a definition: "Diffusion is the process by which (1) an INNOVATION (2) is communicated through certain channels (3) over time (4) among the members of a social system."

The several components of this definition share an elective affinity with each other. The novelty of an "innovation" implies a substantial role for information exchange, since without direct experience one must learn from others. COMMUNICATION and INFLUENCE occur over time, establishing a sequential ordering that can be studied. And meaningful contact is only plausible when action takes place within a social system.

Main questions in the study of innovation diffusion include: Why are some individuals (or organizations) pioneers while others are laggards? What sort of relational linkages provide channels along which diffusion spreads? What characteristics of innovations facilitate or retard their communication? What characteristics of populations promote more or less rapid diffusion? How can professional "change agents" intervene to accelerate the process?

Like other social products, studies of innovation diffusion come in waves. The last fifteen or so years has seen a pretty large wave, perhaps the most substantial one within the subfield of organizational studies. Several factors seem centrally implicated: a sense of the rapid pace of change and need for organizations to innovate; organizational sociology's shift of focus from theories of organizational structure to theories of organizational environments; and the development of methodological tools for the study of temporal processes.

The study of innovation diffusion is empirically rich but theoretically underdeveloped. Each innovation is studied splendidly in isolation, a strategy that generates many mechanisms but few overarching insights (Strang and Soule, 1998). Recent studies seek to redress the balance. Haunschild and Miner (1997) point to the simultaneous operation of multiple forms of imitation, while Davis and Greve (1997) develop comparative insights into why different innovations spread in different ways. These beginnings of a movement toward theoretical integration suggest the opportunity for not only quantitative elaboration but also qualitative advance.

See also *learning organization; learning, organizational; organizational effectiveness; technology*

Bibliography

Davis, G. F. and Greve, H. R. (1997). Corporate elite networks and governance changes in the 1980s. *American Journal of Sociology*, **103**, 1–37.

Haunschild, P. R. and Miner, A. S. (1997). Modes of inter-organizational imitation: The effects of outcome salience and uncertainty. *Administrative Science Quarterly*, **38**, 564–92.

Rogers, E. M. (1995). *Diffusion of Innovations*. New York: Free Press.

Strang, D. and Soule, S. A. (1998). Diffusion in organizations and social movements: From hybrid corn to poison pills. *Annual Review of Sociology*, **24**, 265–90.

institutional theory

Walter W. Powell

Much of the research on organizations since the 1970s focuses on the structure and composition of organizational environments. The idea that organizations are deeply embedded in wider institutional environments suggests that organizational practices are often either direct reflections of, or responses to, rules and structures found in those environments. This line of institutional analysis traces its origins to research by John Meyer on the effects of education as an institution (Meyer, 1977; Meyer and Rowan, 1977); work by Meyer, Scott, and colleagues (Meyer and Scott, 1983) on the dependence of educational organizations on wider cultural and symbolic understandings about the nature of schooling; research by Zucker (1977, 1983) on the taken-for-granted aspects of organizational life; and work by DiMaggio and Powell (1983) on the formation of organizational fields. Institutional theory and research has grown markedly over the past two decades, and empirical analyses cover topics as diverse as affirmative action policies, accounting rules, diversification strategies in large corporations, the expansion of the European Union, due process policies in US companies, and the global spread of human rights legislation.

Although ecological and institutional approaches differ markedly in the weight they assign to organization adaptation and managerial cognition, these approaches share a number of key insights. Both focus on the collective organ-ization of the environment, insisting that the environment of organizations is made up of other organizations and that processes of legit-imation and competition shape organizational behavior. But ecologists attend to demographic processes – organizational foundings, transform-ations, and deaths (*see* ORGANIZATIONAL ECOLOGY). Institutionalists, in contrast, ana-lyze the creation, diffusion, and elaboration of organizational policies and structures.

Institutional theory combines a rejection of the optimizing assumptions of rational actor models popular in economics with an interest in institutions as independent variables. The constant and repetitive quality of much of or-ganizational life results not from the calculated actions of self-interested individuals but from the fact that many practices come to be taken for granted. The model of behavior is one in which "actors associate certain actions with certain situations by rules of appropriate-ness" (March and Olsen, 1984: 741). Individuals in organizations face choices all the time, but in making decisions they seek guidance from the experiences of others in comparable situations and by reference to standards of obligation.

The unit of analysis in institutional research is the organizational field or societal sector. The assumption is that organizations exist in socially bounded communities composed of similar or-ganizations that are responsible for a definable area of institutional life. Fields have been de-fined as "a network, or a configuration, of rela-tions between positions" (Bourdieu, 1992) or as an arena in which competing interests negotiate over the interpretation of critical issues and events (Hoffman, 2001). An organizational field includes key suppliers, consumers, regulatory agencies, and professional and labor associations, as well as other organizations that produce a similar service or product. (Excellent studies of the formation of organizational fields include DiMaggio, 1991; Ferguson, 1998; Scott et al., 2000; Hoffman, 2001; and Thornton, 2004.)

DiMaggio and Powell (1983) argue that the process by which an organizational field comes to be formed consists of four stages:

1   an increase in the amount of interaction among organizations within a field;

2 the emergence of well defined patterns of HIERARCHY and coalition;

3 an upsurge in the information load with which members of a field must contend;

4 the development of a mutual awareness among participants that they are involved in a common enterprise.

PROCESSES OF INSTITUTIONALIZATION

How do organizational practices and structures become institutionalized within a field? Scholars have posited several mechanisms that promote isomorphism, that is, structural similarities among organizations within a field. Some of these processes encourage homogenization within a field directly by leading to structural and behavioral changes in organizations themselves. Others work indirectly by shaping the assumptions and experiences of the individuals who staff organizations. DiMaggio and Powell (1983) suggested three general types of institutional pressures: (1) coercive forces that stem from political influence and problems of legitimacy; (2) mimetic changes that are responses to uncertainty; and (3) normative influences resulting from professionalization. Scott and Meyer (1994) emphasized the importance of regulatory pressures, and more recent work has attended to the proselytizing effects of social movements. These various mechanisms often intermingle in specific empirical settings, but they tend to derive from different conditions and may lead to different outcomes. Indeed, institutional pressures may be cross-cutting and lead to conflict, prompting organizational change.

EMPIRICAL RESULTS

A good deal of early institutional studies focused on public sector and non-profit organizations in such areas as education, healthcare, mental health, and the arts. The latter half of the twentieth century witnessed a large-scale expansion of the role of government and the professions in these fields. The more highly organized policy-making became, the more individual organizations focused on responding to the official categories and procedures specified by the larger environment. In order to be perceived as legitimate, organizations adapt their formal structures and routines to conform to institutional norms. Hence to the extent that pressures from the environment are exerted on all members of a field, these organizations will become more similar. But pressures for field-wide conformity may shape only an organization's formal structure (i.e., its organization chart and rules and reporting procedures), while backstage practices may be "decoupled" from official actions.

The concept of isomorphism has been utilized to describe the processes that encourage a unit in a population to resemble other units facing similar circumstances. Such pressures were theorized to be strongest in fields with a weak technical base (e.g., education, the arts, advertising, etc.), with ambiguous or conflicting goals (e.g., professional service firms), and that are buffered from market pressures (i.e., supported by endowment income or public funding, protected by government regulation, etc.). Over the past decade, researchers turned their attention to for-profit firms, examining the adoption of various employment practices, the utilization of different accounting standards, and the diffusion of management policies. This work has proven valuable in extending the reach of institutional analysis to some of the core firms in the global economy, while at the same time showing that organizations do not passively conform to institutional pressures, and may actively shape the policies that guide organizational fields. Rather, government or professional mandates can be contested, negotiated, or partially implemented. Work by Edelman (1992; Edelman, Uggen, and Erlanger, 1999) on civil rights law illustrates that the diffusion of new legal practices is not unidirectional; instead, a complex interaction emerges in which ambiguous government compliance standards are interpreted, shaped, and implemented by corporations.

Most institutional studies have focused on organizational practices as responses to the actions of various governing bodies: legislatures, courts, regulatory agencies, certification and accreditation boards, and professional associations. The advantage of this research is that it permits specification of how the environment shapes organizations, allowing researchers to understand the effects of different types of control systems. These analyses also enhance our understanding of the relationship between environmental COMPLEXITY and internal organizational structure. For example, when environments contain multiple strong centers of authority and legitimacy, we find more levels of administration inside organizations, and greater differentiation across members of a field. When environments are more homogeneous, researchers find less elaborate internal organizational structures and less diversity across organizations.

With its focus on legitimating and diffusion processes, early institutional work tended to portray organizational fields as settled and perhaps conformist. Indeed, to argue that a practice has become institutionalized entails documenting that it has become relatively permanent. More recent work, however, has attended to processes of institutional change and periods of institutional transformation. Two productive lines of work build on the ideas that (1) participants and organizations are often simultaneously embedded in multiple institutional fields, and can apply the logic of one field in another to exploit tensions and contradictions, and (2) organizations are frequently located in nested and/or fragmented environments, with overlapping but partial authority structures that evolve at different rates. In the former example, Edelman (1992; Edelman, Uggen, and Erlanger, 1999) has shown that ambiguity between law on the books and law in action opened space for interpretation and the remaking of affirmative action legislation into diffuse human resource strategies about diversity. In the second case, Scott et al. (2000) show that the transformation of US healthcare from a professional to a market regime occurred in part because professional authority became highly fragmented, and a third party payment system developed as a higher-order system of medical reimbursement.

SUMMARY

Many of the prevailing approaches to ORGANIZATION THEORY assume implicitly that organizations are purposive and are progressing towards more efficient and adaptive forms. The institutional approach takes neither of these assumptions for granted; consequently, it raises a different set of questions, asking how and from where do conceptions of RATIONALITY emerge. This line of work seeks to treat the emergence of modern organizations and

the laws and practices that govern them as the objects of study. Institutionalization, or the "process by which a given set of units and a pattern of activities come to be normatively and cognitively held in place, and practically taken for granted as lawful" (Meyer, Boli, and Thomas, 1987: 13) becomes the subject of inquiry.

See also *contracts; exchange relations; governance; learning, organizational*

Bibliography

Bourdieu, P. (1992). The logic of fields. In P. Bourdieu and L. Wacquant, *An Invitation to Reflexive Sociology*. Chicago: University of Chicago Press, 94–114.

DiMaggio, P. J. (1991). Constructing an organizational field as a professional project: US Art Museums, 1920–40. In W. Powell and P. J. DiMaggio (eds.), *The New Institutionalism in Organizational Analysis*. Chicago: University of Chicago Press, 267–92.

DiMaggio, P. J. and Powell, W. W. (1983). The iron cage revisited: Institutional isomorphism and collective rationality in organizational fields. *American Sociological Review*, 48, 147–60.

Edelman, L. B. (1992). Legal ambiguity and symbolic structures: Organizational mediation on civil rights law. *American Journal of Sociology*, 97, 1531–76.

Edelman, L. B., Uggen, C., and Erlanger, H. S. (1999). The endogeneity of legal regulation: Grievance procedures as rational myth. *American Journal of Sociology*, 105, 406–54.

Ferguson, P. P. (1998). A cultural field in the making: Gastronomy in nineteenth-century France. *American Journal of Sociology*, 104, 597–641.

Hoffman, A. J. (2001). *From Heresy to Dogma: An Institutional History of Corporate Environmentalism*. Stanford, CA: Stanford University Press.

March, J. G. and Olsen, J. (1984). The new institutionalism: Organizational factors in political life. *American Political Science Review*, 78, 734–49.

Meyer, J. W. (1977). The effects of education as an institution. *American Journal of Sociology*, 83, 55–77.

Meyer, J. W. and Rowan, B. (1977). Institutionalized organizations: Formal structure as myth and ceremony. *American Journal of Sociology*, 83, 340–63.

Meyer, J. W. and Scott, W. R. (eds.) (1983). *Organizational Environments: Ritual and Rationality*. Beverly Hills, CA: Sage.

Meyer, J. W., Boli, J., and Thomas, G. (1987). Ontology and rationalization in the Western cultural account. In G. Thomas, W. Meyer, F. O. Ramirez, and J. Boli (eds.), *Institutional Structure*. Beverly Hills, CA: Sage, 12–37.

Powell, W. W. and DiMaggio P. J. (eds.) (1991). *The New Institutionalism in Organizational Analysis*. Chicago: University of Chicago Press.

Scott, W. R. and Meyer, J. W. (1994). *Institutional Environments and Organizations*. Thousand Oaks, CA: Sage.

Scott, W. R., Reuf, M., Mendel, P. J., and Caronna, C. (2000). *Institutional Change and Health Care Organizations*. Chicago: University of Chicago Press.

Thornton, P. (2004). *Markets from Culture*. Stanford, CA: Stanford University Press.

Zucker, L. G. (1977). The role of institutionalization in cultural persistence. *American Sociological Review*, **42**, 726–43.

Zucker, L. G. (1983). Organizations as institutions. In S. Bachrach (ed.), *Research in the Sociology of Organizations*. Greenwich, CT: JAI Press, 1–47.

institutions

Walter W. Powell

The study of institutions, long an area of interest in the social sciences, has burgeoned of late. The many diverse lines of current research display wide variation in key definitions and concepts. Two lines of research – the new institutional economics (Langlois, 1986; North, 1990) and the new institutionalism in organizational analysis (March and Olsen, 1989; Powell and DiMaggio, 1991) – are of most relevance to scholars of organizations. The economists treat institutions as regularities of behavior understandable in terms of rules and routines. They are "perfectly analogous to the rules of the game in a competitive team sport" (North, 1990: 4). In this view, institutions reduce uncertainty by providing a stable, but not necessarily efficient, structure to guide interaction and exchange.

Institutional economists do not assume that institutions represent optimal solutions to problems of exchange and production, but they do build their theory on the basis of individual choice (*see* EXCHANGE RELATIONS). Institutions, thus, are the products of human design. In contrast, research in sociology and ORGANIZATION THEORY views institutions as the result of human activity, but not necessarily the product of human design and intention. In this view, "institutions are frameworks of programs or rules establishing identities and activity scripts for such identities" (Jepperson, in Powell

and DiMaggio, 1991: 146). Viewed more broadly, institutions are meaning systems, based on symbolic representations and enforced by both formal and informal conventions, standards, and regulations. To say that a practice or model is institutionalized means that it has become a taken-for-granted assumption around which organizational activity is constructed. In contrast to the economist's view, the sociological approach sees organizational action as less based on intentions, and more on identifying normatively appropriate behaviors (March and Olsen, 1989).

See also *bureaucracy; governance; institutional theory*

Bibliography

Langlois, R. N. (1986). The new institutional economics. In R. N. Langlois (ed.), *Economics as a Process*. New York: Cambridge University Press, 1–25.

March, J. G. and Olsen, J. (1989). *Rediscovering Institutions*. New York: Free Press.

North, D. C. (1990). *Institutions, Institutional Change, and Economic Performance*. New York: Cambridge University Press.

Powell, W. W. and DiMaggio, P. J. (eds.) (1991). *The New Institutionalism in Organizational Analysis*. Chicago: University of Chicago Press.

instrumentality

see MOTIVATION

intelligence

see PRACTICAL INTELLIGENCE

interest groups

see POLITICS; SOCIAL COMPARISON

intergroup relations

Roderick M. Kramer and Dana A. Gavrieli

The classic definition of intergroup relations was originally provided by Sherif (1966), who suggested: "Whenever individuals belonging to one group interact, collectively or individually, with another group or its members in terms of their group identification, we have an instance of intergroup behavior" (p. 12). Within ORGANIZATION THEORY, the term *intergroup relations* refers to both individual interactions involving members from different groups and the collective behavior of groups in interaction with other groups, at either the intra- or inter-organizational level (*see* LEVELS OF ANALYSIS). The study of intergroup relations has recently enjoyed a considerable resurgence from social scientists (e.g., Brett and Rognes, 1986; Brewer, 2003; Brown and Gaertner, 2001; Mackie and Smith, 2001; Sedikides, Schopler, and Insko, 1998). This resurgence has been driven in part by contemporary international conflicts that have highlighted the importance of understanding the origins of intergroup tensions and how those tensions can be reduced or eliminated. It reflects also increasing recognition of the importance of intergroup cooperation, especially in large, multinational firms (*see* COLLABORATION).

Several important traditions distinguish how intergroup relations have been conceptualized in organizational theory (for useful reviews, see Alderfer and Smith, 1982; Kramer, 1991). Sociological theory and research has generally focused on the structural determinants of intergroup behavior. Organizational scholars in this tradition have emphasized, for example, how differences in goals, task structures, POWER, and status affect intergroup relations. In addition, they have examined the impact of social processes such as communication patterns and social norms on intergroup behavior. In contrast, political perspectives on intergroup relations have focused on how strategic processes such as bargaining, COALITION FORMATION, and collective action influence intergroup relations. Finally, psychological theories have construed intergroup relations primarily in terms of basic intra-individualistic processes, such as interpersonal attraction, social perception, and interpersonal TRUST. These theories emphasize the importance of cognitive factors such as stereotyping, as well as motivational underpinnings of intergroup behavior, including the presumed desire on the part of group members to

maintain positive social group identities (Brewer and Kramer, 1985). According to these theories, such psychological processes influence intergroup behavior by affecting social judgment and behavior in intergroup contexts (Messick and Mackie, 1989).

The major theories of intergroup relations illustrate these differing emphases. *Realistic conflict theory* posits that intergroup relations are influenced not so much by cognitive and motivational processes as they are by the inherent competition between groups for crucial but scarce resources. In this framework, interdependence is viewed as the basis of intergroup cooperation and CONFLICT. Other theories, in contrast, afford greater importance to the psychological and social processes that influence how individuals in social groups construe their interdependence with other groups. For example, *social categorization theory* focuses on how social and organizational processes that categorize people into distinctive groups foster competitive and conflictual orientations at the intergroup level. Research in this vein has shown that categorization results in a tendency for individuals to view members of their own group (the "ingroup") more positively than individuals from other groups (the "outgroups"). Along similar lines, it has been shown that, when allocating scarce resources such as rewards, individuals tend to confer more favorable treatment on members of their own group over those from other groups. A major presumption of this framework is that an understanding of cognitive processes alone is sufficient to account for intergroup phenomena such as stereotyping and discrimination.

In contrast to this view, *social identity theory* argues that a variety of motivational processes, such as the desire to maintain a positive social identity, also play a formative role in intergroup relations (Tajfel, 1982). According to this perspective, enhancement of the ingroup and derogation of the outgroup serve the important psychological function of bolstering individual self-esteem and the collective esteem of the ingroup. *Relative deprivation theory* examines the role that social comparison processes play in understanding intergroup relations. This theory views intergroup relations as shaped to a large extent by people's comparisons between what their own group possesses relative to other groups within an organization. When individuals feel that their group is receiving favorable treatment relative to other groups, satisfaction is likely to be high. In contrast, when they believe their own group is relatively deprived or disadvantaged, discontent is likely to result. A more recent theory, *system justification theory* (Jost and Burgess, 2000), seeks to explain how and why members of disadvantaged groups provide cognitive and ideological support for the status quo. According to this theory, members of low status groups internalize unfavorable stereotypes about their ingroup and favorable stereotypes about the outgroup in order to justify the current hierarchy. This theory attenuates social psychological processes that emphasize ingroup favoritism and outgroup derogation, and suggests that this process depends on the group status.

These perspectives are important because of the insight they provide with respect to two central concerns in the study of intergroup relations: intergroup conflict and cooperation. Theory and research on intergroup conflict has attempted to identify the origins and dynamics of conflict between various groups. For example, there exists a considerable literature pertaining to intergroup conflict in industrial settings (usually under the rubric of labor-management conflict). Much of this literature draws attention to the role perceptual and social processes – such as ethnocentrism and ingroup bias – play in the development and escalation of intergroup conflict. As Blake and Mouton (1989: 192) noted: "The striking conclusion from [this] research is that when groups are aware of one another's psychological presence, it is natural for them to feel competition . . . [suggesting] a very basic incipient hostility is operating at the point of contact between primary groups." These insights, in turn, suggest a number of perspectives on reducing intergroup competition and conflict. These perspectives generally take as given the pervasiveness of intergroup rivalry and conflict, and then attempt to address the problem of how to promote cooperation between groups.

Several approaches to increasing intergroup cooperation have been proposed, and reasonable evidence is available to suggest the efficacy of each. First, introduction of superordinate (shared) goals to reduce competition has been shown to help attenuate or override competitive tendencies between groups. Second, certain forms of intergroup contact have been shown to enhance cooperation (Stephan, 1985). Of particular importance is contact in which status differences and interaction patterns that reinforce negative stereotypes are minimized or controlled. In addition, the use of "BOUNDARY SPANNERS" (individuals who have roles in both groups) can help correct misperceptions, improve communication and coordination, and reduce distrust between groups. Another important approach has emphasized the positive consequences of "recategorization" as a strategy for achieving intergroup cooperation. The recategorization approach is predicated on the assumption that the deleterious consequences associated with ingroup favoritism and outgroup derogation can be reduced by categorizing individuals in terms of shared, collective identities that draw attention to interpersonal similarities and that increase social attraction between individuals from different groups. Another major approach is on behavioral strategies designed to elicit cooperative interaction and build TRUST between groups, including the use of reciprocity-based influence strategies, such as tit-for-tat (Axelrod, 1984). Finally, recent theory and research have focused on the use of conflict resolution processes such as negotiation (Kramer and Carnevale, 2001), including the use of integrative bargaining involving the groups themselves, as well as various third-party interventions such as mediation and arbitration. This area is currently one of the most active and promising new directions in the study of intergroup relations.

A promising new approach to understanding the origins and dynamics of intergroup relations has been the study of intergroup emotions. Research in this area includes studying, for example, the impact of intergroup affect on the willingness of individuals to engage in intergroup contact and the form such contact takes (Dovidio et al., 2001). Another promising approach explores the effects of perceived status and competition on intergroup emotions, which in turn influence intergroup behaviors (e.g., Fiske, Cuddy, and Glick, 2001).

See also *group cohesiveness; group dynamics; interorganizational relations*

Bibliography

Alderfer, C. P. and Smith, K. K. (1982). Studying intergroup relations embedded in organizations. *Administrative Science Quarterly*, **27**, 33–65.

Axelrod, R. (1984). *The Evolution of Cooperation*. New York: Basic Books.

Blake, R. and Mouton, J. (1989). Lateral conflict. In D. Tjosvold and D. Johnson (eds.), *Productive Conflict Management*. Edinia, MN: Interaction.

Brett, J. M. and Rognes, J. K. (1986). Intergroup relations in organizations. In P. Goodman (ed.), *Work Group Effectiveness*. San Francisco: Jossey-Bass.

Brewer, M. B. (2003). *Intergroup Relations*, 2nd edn. Buckingham: Open University Press.

Brewer, M. B. and Kramer, R. M. (1985). The psychology of intergroup attitudes and behavior. *Annual Review of Psychology*, **36**, 219–43.

Brown, R. and Gaertner, S. (2001). *Blackwell Handbook of Social Psychology: Intergroup Processes*. Malden, MA: Blackwell.

Dovidio, J. F., Esses, V. M., Beach, K. R., and Gaertner, S. L. (2001). The role of affect in determining intergroup behavior: The case of willingness to engage in intergroup contact. In D. M. Mackie and E. R. Smith (eds.), *From Prejudice to Intergroup Emotions*. Philadelphia, PA: Psychology Press, 153–72.

Fiske, S. T., Cuddy, A., and Glick, P. (2001). Emotions up and down: Intergroup emotions result from perceived status and competition. In D. M. Mackie and E. R. Smith (eds.), *From Prejudice to Intergroup Emotions*. Philadelphia, PA: Psychology Press, 247–64.

Jost, J. T. and Burgess, D. (2000). Attitudinal ambivalence and the conflict between group and system justification motives in low status groups. *Personality and Social Psychology Bulletin*, **26**, 293–305.

Kramer, R. M. (1991). Intergroup relations and organizational dilemmas: The role of categorization processes. In B. M. Staw and L. L. Cummings (eds.), *Research in Organizational Behavior*, Vol. 13. Greenwich, CT: JAI Press.

Kramer, R. M. and Carnevale, P. M. (2001). Trust and intergroup negotiation. In R. Brown and S. Gaertner (eds.), *Blackwell Handbook of Social Psychology: Intergroup Processes*. Malden, MA: Blackwell, 431–50.

Mackie, D. M. and Smith, E. R. (2001). *From Prejudice to Intergroup Emotions*. Philadelphia, PA: Psychology Press.

Messick, D. M. and Mackie, D. (1989). Intergroup relations. *Annual Review of Psychology*, **40**, 45–81.

Sedikides, C., Schopler, J., and Insko, C. A. (1998). *Intergroup Cognition and Intergroup Behavior*. Mahwah, NJ: Lawrence Erlbaum Associates.

Sherif, M. (1966). *In Common Predicament: Social Psychology of Intergroup Conflict and Cooperation*. New York: Houghton Mifflin.

Stephan, W. G. (1985). Intergroup relations. In G. Lindsey and E. A. Ronson (eds.), *The Handbook of Social Psychology*, Vol. 2, 3rd edn. New York: Random House.

Tajfel, H. (1982). Social psychology of intergroup relations. *Annual Review of Psychology*, **33**, 1–39.

interlocking boards

James R. Lincoln

Interlocking boards refers to ties formed among organizations when the same individuals serve as directors on multiple boards.

Perhaps the oldest tradition of substantive interlock research addresses the class or elite cohesion hypothesis. Here, board interlocks are seen as *in* organizations but not really *of* them. They are merely a device for reinforcing the cohesion of the economic elite, much in the fashion of exclusive clubs, big-city high society, and elite private schools. CEOs put their friends and acquaintances on their CORPORATE BOARDS – people with whom they associate in other venues and whose values and beliefs they share. Such ties crisscross major corporations, foundations, and government offices, but they are not driven by organization-level dynamics.

Other perspectives ascribe an organizational rationale to interlocking, but not at the level of dyadic exchange. Neo-Marxist bank control/hegemony theory holds that interlocks, most of which link financials to industrials, enable large banks to orchestrate the activities of industrial firms (e.g., Mintz and Schwartz, 1985). A substantively similar but normatively different story is the principal–agent view of banks (particularly in German or Japanese "stakeholder" capitalism) as "delegated" monitors of the corporate economy. A third, less purely organizational theory is that of "business scan": CEOs invite to their boards, not representatives of the companies with whom they do business (which might pose antitrust problems), but knowledgeable and experienced executives able to supply generalized managerial expertise (Useem, 1984).

The final set of theories portrays interlocking as a control or governance mechanism for managing a bilateral or dyadic exchange. Resource dependence theory casts board interlocking as a *co-optive* device: one organization absorbs another on which it is dependent into its decision-making machinery with the intent of disarming a potential threat. TRANSACTION COST ECONOMICS agrees that outsider board seats constitute governance structure, but paints them less as co-optation managed by the receiving party than as strategy on the part of the sender to monitor an investment (debt, equity, knowledge) in the receiver.

Much of the empirical literature on interlocks speaks to these issues, but Palmer (1983) may have best adjudicated between the resource dependence and class cohesion/business scan alternatives. Reasoning that an interlock that manages a resource dependency will be replaced if severed by the incumbent's resignation or death, he found a relatively low incidence of replacement, although "direct" interlocks (a manager from firm *I* is on the board of firm *J*) were reconstituted more than "indirect" (third party) ties.

Still, a number of studies do find interlocks materializing between transactionally intertwined firms. In Asia and continental Europe, the resource dependence rationale is demonstrably strong, owing to relaxed antitrust regulation and the structuring of the economy by business groups and other stable corporate ties (Lincoln, Gerlach, and Takahashi, 1992).

Interlock research has recently shifted to inter-organizational diffusion processes. There is strong evidence that corporate practices such as the "poison pill" takeover defense spread through interlock networks. This pattern supports two perspectives, which differ as to whether the diffusion process is believed relevant to the business of the receiving firm. One is the business scan hypothesis: interlocks serve to aggregate and distribute to individual corporations generalized information on best practice. The other is neo-institutional theory, which sees mimetic processes such as fashion or regulatory and professional (e.g., consultant) pressures operating to channel practices through the network that have little real relevance to the adaptation or performance needs of individual firms.

See also *CEOS; governance; institutional theory; top management teams*

Bibliography

Davis, G. F. (1991) Agents without principles? The spread of the poison pill through the intercorporate network. *Administrative Science Quarterly*, 36, 583–613.

Lincoln, J. R., Gerlach, M. L., and Takahashi, P. (1992). Keiretsu networks in the Japanese economy: A dyad analysis of intercorporate ties. *American Sociological Review*, 57, 561–85.

Mintz, B. and Schwartz, M. (1985). *The Power Structure of American Business*. Chicago: University of Chicago Press.

Palmer, D. (1983). Broken ties: Interlocking directorates and intercorporate coordination. *Administrative Science Quarterly*, 28, 40–55.

Useem, M. (1984). *The Inner Circle*. New York: Oxford University Press.

inter-organizational relations

Paul Ingram

Inter-organizational relations are non-transitory interactions between two or more organizations. They are already foundational to organizational study, and are becoming even more important. The increasing attention to inter-organizational relations is due to changes in both business and research practice. In business, there is renewed interest in smaller and simpler (more focused) organizations. This trend was seeded by the discovery that large organizations are slow to change, and by evidence of the dismal performance of conglomerates. Simultaneously, there is a growing belief that smaller and simpler organizations can reap some benefits of scale and scope through inter-organizational relations. In the United States, support for these ideas comes from the success of interconnected firms at innovation in the biotech industry, and in Silicon Valley. Elsewhere, the Japanese keiretsu, Italian industrial districts, and business groups in developing countries such as India and Mexico, are held up as examples in favor of affiliations between small and/or simple organizations.

Research on inter-organizational relations predates these business trends and shows that the phenomenon is not new. A persistent theme has been that inter-organizational relations are a source of control in the economy and society (Pfeffer and Salancik, 1978). The construction of this research program has accelerated rapidly due to advances in network analysis, many attributable to Harrison White, Ron Burt, and their students and associates. These advances have led to a flurry of recent work, which can be organized by the type of inter-organizational relations studied, and by the effects identified.

Types of inter-organizational relations vary according to the mode of governance employed and the structure of alignment between the related organizations. Governance may rely primarily on social mechanisms, such as TRUST, affect, and family, or on more formal agreements, including CONTRACTS. There are as yet no conclusions as to when one GOVERNANCE form is better than the other, but there is good evidence that social mechanisms can be very effective for governing inter-organizational relations (e.g., Granovetter, 1994; Uzzi, 1996; Ingram and Roberts, 2000). These findings are notable in the face of economic theories that predict exploitive self-interest in the absence of formal control over relationships. Research on formal governance is going in the direction of specifying more precisely what contracts should look like, depending on the types of organizations and the goals of their relationship.

There are three alignment structures for organizational relations, and these are orthogonal to governance, in that there are social and formal instances of each. The first is vertical, describing relations between organizations that occupy buyer/supplier roles relative to each other. Research on vertical relations has shown that they produce cheaper interactions, or allow the organizations to work more closely to address problems that may have been unsolvable at arm's length (Uzzi, 1996). The second alignment, horizontal, describes organizations that occupy equivalent positions in the economy – typically, competing organizations from the same industry. This category has received less research attention than the other two, although there are important examples of horizontal relations, including industry associations and research consortia. These examples reflect two implications of horizontal alignment: that it creates shared political interests and opportunities for learning. Horizontal relations also present the opportunity for collusion, and attempts to conceal collusion probably explain the relative

lack of attention they have received (Ingram and Roberts, 2000). The third alignment form is non-interdependent, describing organizations that have neither competitive nor buyer/supplier relationships. Non-interdependent relations are represented by a large literature on board interlocks which occur when the boards of directors of two organizations share at least one member. These connections are argued to be paths through which innovations such as the multidivisional structure and the poison pill salve against takeover diffuse (e.g., Davis, 1991). They have also been identified as a source of power for dominant classes (e.g., Palmer, Friedland and Singh, 1986).

The most commonly identified effects of inter-organizational relations appear above: vicarious learning, innovation, efficient transactions, and political power. Less familiar others may be as important. Stuart, Hoang, and Hybels (1999), for example, show that endorsements are implied by inter-organizational relations, and that well connected organizations enjoy enhanced reputations. Research on business groups in developing countries, and on the keiretsu, identifies a form of social insurance, whereby organizations that are performing well help struggling relations. Negative effects of inter-organizational relations are also apparent. Most common is overdependence, where one organization relies so heavily on relations with another that it comes to suffer (e.g., Uzzi, 1996). Related, and more compelling, is the loss of autonomy. As in other types of relations, inter-organizational relations often allow one party to exert influence over the other to achieve a range of ends. This possibility has received substantial theoretical attention (e.g., Pfeffer and Salancik, 1978) and, more recently, is an increasing subject of empirical work (e.g., Simons and Ingram, 1997).

There is no doubt that the future will see much more research on inter-organizational relations. Old questions such as "when are informal relations better than formal relations?" and "which types of relations do more to facilitate learning?" are still worth additional research. It is also true that we need to know more about the origins of inter-organizational relations (Gulati and Gargiulo, 1999). However, the most exciting work on this topic will address new questions.

Most obviously, research must catch up to practice by treating inter-organizational relations in the cohesive sets that they often appear in, as the basis of new, inter-organizational forms of economic activity: groups, clusters, districts, keiretsu, families, and networks, rather than merely counts of dyadic ties (e.g., Powell, Koput, and Smith-Doerr, 1996). If current trends in the economy continue, a decade from now dictionaries and academic departments may focus on inter-organizational behavior rather than organizational behavior. A second promising topic for the future is that organizational groupings often cohere around concepts that are tangential to organizational functioning such as family, ideology, or ethnicity (Granovetter, 1994). Incorporating these bases of cohesion into our research will show that inter-organizational relations play a substantial role in the pursuit of the most fundamental social goals (e.g., Simons and Ingram, 1997).

See also *collaboration; organizational design; organizational geography*

Bibliography

Davis, G. F. (1991). Agents without principles? The spread of the poison pill through the intercorporate network. *Administrative Science Quarterly*, 36, 583–613.

Gulati, R. and Gargiulo, M. (1999). Where do inter-organizational networks come from? *American Journal of Sociology*, 104, 1439–93.

Granovetter, M. (1994). Business groups. In N. J. Smelser and R. Swedberg (eds.), *The Handbook of Economic Sociology*. Princeton, NJ: Princeton University Press, 453–75.

Ingram, P. and Roberts, P. (2000). Friendships among competitors in the Sydney hotel industry. *American Journal of Sociology*, 106, 387–423.

Palmer, D., Friedland, R., and Singh, J. V. (1986). The ties that bind: Organizational and class bases of stability in a corporate interlock network. *American Sociological Review*, 51 (6), 781–97.

Pfeffer, J. and R. Salancik, G. R. (1978). *The External Control of Organizations*. New York: Harper and Row.

Powell, W. W., Koput, K. W., and Smith-Doerr, L. (1996). Inter-organizational collaboration and the locus of innovation: Networks of learning in biotechnology. *Administrative Science Quarterly*, 41, 116–45.

Simons, T. and Ingram, P. (1997). Organization and ideology: Kibbutzim and hired labor, 1951–1965. *Administrative Science Quarterly*, 42, 784–813.

Stuart, T. E., Ha Hoang, and Hybels, R. C. (1999). Inter-organizational endorsements and the performance of entrepreneurial ventures. *Administrative Science Quarterly*, 44, 315–49.

Uzzi, B. (1996). The sources and consequences of embeddedness for the economic performance of organizations: The network effect. *American Sociological Review*, 61, 674–98.

interpersonal skills

John D. Bigelow

Whereas the term SKILLS refers generally to an individual's capability for effective action, interpersonal skills refers to the capability to accomplish individual and/or organizational goals through interaction with others. In organizations, many types of goals are accomplished primarily through interaction, and each of these goal types corresponds to a certain type of interpersonal skill. For example, individuals in organizations must accomplish the goal of communicating effectively with others. The capability to accomplish this goal is referred to as COMMUNICATION skill. As another example, individuals are sometimes in a position where they want to insure the success of a group meeting. The capability to accomplish this goal may be referred to as team facilitation skill. Goals may be stated broadly or specifically, and so may skills (e.g., "interpersonal" versus "reflective listening" skills).

Interpersonal skills are distinguished in principle from other types of skills that are also pertinent to organizational life. These include:

1 *intrapersonal* skills, where goals involve self-change, such as self-awareness, time management, or STRESS management;
2 *learning* skills, where goals involve obtaining and using new information;
3 *cognitive* skills, where goals are accomplished primarily through cognitive processes;
4 *job* skills, where goals involve effective performance of specific job tasks.

Interpersonal skills are a type of "action" skill, wherein goal accomplishment requires significant exercise of behavior. While the skill types listed above are conceptually distinct, they are typically used in concert in organizations.

IMPORTANCE OF INTERPERSONAL SKILLS

Interpersonal skills are a uniquely important subset of the skills considered as valuable in organizations. Much of human intelligence is believed to have evolved to cope with the complexities of human interaction. Thus we would expect the exercise of interpersonal skills to involve a large part of intrinsic human capability. The importance of interpersonal skills is also underscored by its inclusion as one aspect of wisdom.

In understanding the relevance of interpersonal skills to organizations it is important first to understand the types of goals that may be accomplished through the exercise of interpersonal skills. These goals can generally be classified as direct and indirect. Direct goals have to do with changes in others as a direct result of interaction (e.g., in others' orientation, COMMITMENT, TRUST, support, knowledge, MOTIVATION, etc.). Indirect goals have to do with the larger impact of direct goal accomplishment. For example, interaction with another may result in the other's support for a policy (direct change), which in turn leads to a majority organizational vote to adopt the policy (indirect change).

Managers accomplish their work largely through the indirect effects of their interactions. Consequently, most of managerial time is spent in interpersonal interactions (e.g., via phone, email, meetings, and face-to-face interchanges) (*see* MANAGERIAL ROLES) (Mintzberg, 1975). Interpersonal skills, therefore, are critical for managerial effectiveness. Moreover, modern organizations have shifted toward more decentralized, interactive, and participatory designs (*see* MATRIX ORGANIZATION; MECHANISTIC/ORGANIC; SOCIOTECHNICAL THEORY). In them, those doing the primary work of the organization are meeting more, doing more work in groups, and taking on greater managerial responsibilities (*see* WORK GROUPS/TEAMS; PARTICIPATION; EMPOWERMENT; NETWORKING; QUALITY CIRCLES; SELF-MANAGING TEAMS). For this reason interpersonal skills are becoming an increasingly important aspect of performance for organizational members at all levels (SCANS, 1991; Motowidlo, Borman, and Schmit, 1997).

SKILLS AND COMPETENCIES

Some authors have used the terms COMPETENCY and "skill" interchangeably. The two are similar, but by no means identical. They are alike in that both are regarded as individual attributes which contribute to situational effectiveness. They differ, however, in two important ways. First, the relation between skills and situational effectiveness is closer, since a skill has to do with effective action in relation to a particular goal. The relation between competencies and situational effectiveness is less direct: many competencies may contribute to effectiveness in accomplishing a particular goal, and a particular competency may contribute to effectiveness in accomplishing a variety of goals.

The second difference is that competencies include a wider variety of individual attributes than do skills. Whereas the concept of skill has only to do with the capability for effective action, competencies may also include motives (e.g., concern for impact), traits (e.g., self-control), and social roles (e.g., oral presentations).

TYPES OF INTERPERSONAL SKILLS AND THEIR RELATIONSHIPS

Much of the study of interpersonal skills has centered around the identification of skills that are important in organizations. At this point, four major types of interpersonal skills can be distinguished, each centering around a basic type of goal, and each including one or more skills:

1 *Communication*. Goal: Establishing effective communication between self and others, and among others. Skills include establishing a supportive climate, listening, NETWORKING, giving FEEDBACK, oral and written communication, use of COMMUNICATIONS TECHNOLOGY, and language.
2 *Influence*. Goal: Effecting changes in others. Skills include persuading, asserting, MOTIVATION, PERFORMANCE APPRAISAL, MENTORING, counseling, delegation, and disciplining (*see* PUNISHMENT).
3 *Negotiation* and CONFLICT MANAGEMENT. Goal: Developing beneficial agreement among parties. Skills include bargaining, diagnosing the other party's pos-

ition, assessing negotiation sessions, mediation, and employing negotiation tactics (*see* CONFLICT AND CONFLICT MANAGEMENT).

4   *Facilitation*. Goal: Helping groups and organizations to operate effectively. Skills include conducting a meeting, TEAM BUILDING, participative problem solving, GROUP DECISION-MAKING, facilitation (*see* SOCIAL FACILITATION), ORGANIZATIONAL CHANGE, and LEADERSHIP.

The importance and expression of these skills can be expected to vary among organizations and over time. Remember that interpersonal skills are means of accomplishing certain types of goals. As organizations and their structures change, different kinds of goals may become more or less important. For example, as organizations become increasingly international and diverse, the ability to enter and establish effective work relationships in a culturally diverse environment is becoming increasingly important (*see* DIVERSITY MANAGEMENT). Thus, "entry" and "diversity" skills may appropriately be added to the list of important interpersonal skills. Moreover, as information TECHNOLOGY develops, new methods of interpersonal interaction have become available. For example, the use of groupware as a communication medium affects the dynamics of group interaction, requiring the development of computer group session management, or "chauffeuring" skills for the group to be effective.

NATURE OF INTERPERSONAL SKILLS

While the concept of skill has been in widespread use for many years, its primary users have been practitioners, such as educators, job trainers, and therapists working with the handicapped. Their interests have generally been in enabling their target groups to enact fairly straightforward behavioral routines. These practitioners have tended, often implicitly, to place skills in a behaviorist context (*see* LEARNING, INDIVIDUAL; BEHAVIORISM). A basic premise of this context is that behaviors are learned and maintained by a system of stimuli, which elicit a desired set of behaviors, or "skill" responses, which are followed in turn by reinforcements.

Initial efforts to put interpersonal phenomena into a skills framework have tended to place them in a behaviorist context as well. Thus, interpersonal skills have been regarded as a set of fairly specific behavioral routines, and interpersonal skillfulness equated with the accurate demonstration of these behaviors upon the appropriate cue. These early efforts have met with limited success, and this has led to a closer examination of the nature of interpersonal skills (Bigelow, 1995). The conclusion: the phenomenon of interpersonal skillfulness departs from behavioral premises in a number of ways:

1   *Response inspecificity*. Whereas a behaviorist approach requires clear descriptions of desired behaviors, skillful interaction is interactive and complex, often involving multiple and possibly conflicting goals and resulting dilemmas. It is usually not possible either to identify one best response or to describe desired responses behaviorally. Thus, the set of possibly appropriate interpersonal behaviors is not closed, but open, requiring CREATIVITY and problem solving.

2   *Lack of cues*. Whereas a behaviorist approach requires cueing of behaviors, it is usually not possible to discern unambiguous cues for behavior in interpersonal situations. Thus, a part of interpersonal skillfulness consists of the ability to "cue" one's own behavior.

3   *Cognition*. Whereas a behaviorist approach does not include cognition, skilled interaction often requires significant cognition. For example, during an interaction a person may be weighing the implications of what the other said, vicariously projecting the impact of various tactics, assessing the success of a line of action, or considering modifying his or her goals for the interaction. Thus, a part of interpersonal skill learning must include development of associated cognitive processes.

4   *Learning resistance*. Whereas a behaviorist approach assumes the skill learner is neutral to the content of what is learned, interpersonal skill learners have already developed orientations and practice theories (i.e., implicit behavioral programs driving their behavior) (*see* DOUBLE-LOOP LEARNING) (Argyris and Schon, 1978), upon which

their interactions are based. The learner may be reluctant to abandon previously successful behaviors, and this can interfere with attempts to develop more effective ones. Thus, the learning of interpersonal skills must include the surfacing, examination, and assessment of what the individual has already learned.

These conclusions change our image of interpersonal skillfulness from that of a relatively simple conditioned response to situational cues, to one that involves more complexity and intelligence. Some researchers have proposed that the innate human intelligence underlying interpersonal skillfulness is of a different kind than that underlying other kinds of intelligent activities, and that individuals vary in the fundamental interpersonal intelligence that they bring to situations (e.g., Gardner 1983; Goleman, 1995). Just as a person's physique affects his or her ability to excel at a sport, these researchers argue that the degree to which a person possesses interpersonal intelligence will influence the extent to which the person's learning efforts will result in actual skillfulness.

In sum, our picture of the interpersonally skilled practitioner has become much richer. Interpersonally skilled people are able to orient themselves intelligently to situations. They take into account not only the situation, but also their prospective broader impact beyond the encounter itself. They have developed a repertoire of interaction tactics and are able to draw on them as needed, or may develop new tactics as the situation warrants. During interaction, they monitor their progress, and may change tactics or goals if necessary. They are able to learn on their own, both from their own encounters and from the encounters of others (*see* LEARNING ORGANIZATION).

SKILL LEARNING

An increased reliance on interpersonal skills in organizations has led to concern as to where organizations will obtain interpersonally skilled participants. Many candidates for organizational positions are not very interpersonally skilled, by reason of youth and/or inexperience. This is particularly the case in individualistic cultures such as the United States (Adler, 1991: 26–8),

which do little to prepare individuals to operate effectively in group or organizational settings.

In response, many organizations have developed skill training programs for employees, and have attempted to enhance on-the-job learning. Moreover, some have suggested that colleges of business, which have traditionally emphasized cognitive skills, should also address interpersonal skills in their curriculum. Currently, a number of approaches to classroom learning are in use. These include:

1   A *social learning* approach, based on Bandura's (1977) model, involving the steps of self-assessment, conceptual learning, skill modeling, application to cases and practice situations, and application to life situations.
2   A *self-managed* learning approach, which empowers individuals to take responsibility for their own learning (*see* SELF-REGULATION; EMPOWERMENT).
3   A *situational learning* approach, which focuses on practice in holistic situations and the development of "skillfulness," as opposed to development of separated skills. This is similar to a problem-based learning approach (Duch, Groh, and Allen, 2001).

These approaches are not entirely distinct, in that each has elements that could be used in other approaches, and each has its own pros and cons (Bigelow, 1995).

Perhaps the thorniest problem faced in skill learning is the assessment of results. Traditional assessment methods involving objective or essay exams are more geared towards assessing cognitive than interpersonal skill accomplishment. Even when unbiased self-assessment can be obtained through self-administered instruments or portfolios, learners often do not have the insight to assess their own skills. The most promising approach appears to be the "action" or "performance" examination, in which learners are required to demonstrate their skill. Yet these require considerable investment in training of examiners and are time consuming to administer. Moreover, they measure skill capability only, and not disposition to actually use skills. Until viable and reasonably accurate measures of skill accomplishment are developed it will be difficult for educators to improve their pedagogy, and for institutions to make claims about the interpersonal skillfulness of their graduates.

See also emotional intelligence; impression management; trust

Bibliography

Adler N. J. (1991). International Dimensions of Organizational Behavior. Boston, MA: PWS-Kent.

Argyris, C. and Schon, D. (1978). Organizational Teaming: A Theory of Action Perspective. Reading, MA: Addison-Wesley.

Bandura, A. (1977). Social Learning Theory. Englewood Cliffs, NJ: Prentice-Hall.

Bigelow, J. D. (1991). Managerial Skills: Explorations in Practical Knowledge. Newbury Park, CA: Sage. [Provides a variety of viewpoints on skills.]

Bigelow, J. D. (1995). Teaching managerial skills: A critique and future directions. Journal of Management Education, 19 (3).

Boyatzis, R. R. (1982). The Competent Manager: A Model for Effective Performance. New York: Wiley.

Bradford, D. L. (ed.) (1983). Special issue on "Teaching managerial competencies." Organizational Behavior Teaching Journal, Vol. 2. [A seminal issue, much of which continues to be relevant.]

Duch, B., Groh, S., and Allen, D. (2001). The Power of Problem-Based Learning: A Practical "How To" for Teaching Undergraduate Courses in Any Discipline. Sterling, VA: Stylus Publishing.

Gardner, H. (1983). Frames of Mind. New York: Basic Books.

Goleman, D. (1995). Emotional Intelligence. New York: Bantam.

Mintzberg, H. (1975). The manager's job: Folklore and fact. Harvard Business Review, 53, 49–71.

Motowidlo, S., Borman, W., and Schmit, M. (1997). A theory of individual differences in task and contextual performance. Human Performance, 10 (2), 71–83.

SCANS: Secretary's Commission on Achieving Necessary Skills (1991). What Work Requires of Schools: A SCANS Report for America 2000. Washington, DC: US Department of Labor.

interviewing

see RESEARCH METHODS

intrinsic satisfaction

see EXTRINSIC AND INTRINSIC MOTIVATION; JOB SATISFACTION

introversion

see FIVE FACTOR MODEL OF PERSONALITY; PERSONALITY

investor capitalism

Michael Useem

Shares of publicly traded companies in most major economies are now more often found in the portfolios of institutions than individuals. This has been the product of a worldwide trend during the last two decades of the twentieth century in which stocks were increasingly managed by professional money managers.

When mutual funds, pension systems, and other institutional investors acquire stock, they are typically doing so on behalf of individuals. Households, not institutions, are the ultimate beneficiaries for most institutional investing. But the difference lies in who ponders which stocks to buy, hold, or sell. In earlier years, individuals decided; now, professional money managers do so.

When millions were buying and selling shares, they rarely met one another, let alone the company executives in whom they were entrusting their family wealth. To the individual stockholder, other market players were as remote as the functionaries of Franz Kafka's castle. By concentrating large assets in a small number of hands, however, institutional investing personalized the impersonal, leading company executives to become directly acquainted with the money managers.

These institutional owners are more demanding and less patient than individual holders; they look for company competitiveness and clamor for change when firms fall short. And the concentration of ever more stockholding in ever fewer hands has given the professional investors unprecedented influence on the firm. Individual shareholders had been relatively powerless to change under-performing company management, but professional investors acquired the clout and mastered the strategies for doing so.

The corporate world has changed from one in which company executives were dominant to one in which money managers are increasingly central. In other words, the managerial capitalism that had come to the fore in the middle decades of the twentieth century was displaced by investor capitalism by century's end.

In response, publicly traded companies in the United States, the United Kingdom, and other countries have restructured their operations to enhance shareholder return, personalized their relations with large holders, and revised executive compensation to align with investors. Company executives also mastered new skills for leading in an environment increasingly defined by a relatively small number of large investors. This entailed above all a capacity to communicate a compelling strategy for sharevalue growth to money managers and, ultimately, delivering that value to them.

The institutional transformation in the equity market has been followed by an internationalization of company shareholding that accelerated in the 1990s and continued into the twenty-first century. It has been facilitated by the privatization of state enterprise, deregulation of domestic stock markets, and cross-listings of stocks on foreign exchanges. It has been driven above all by financial advantages that accrue to investors and companies alike from greater diversification of stock ownership across the international equity market.

Since institutional investors increasingly compare investment opportunities worldwide, companies and their executives are judged less against their domestic neighbors and more against the best firms and managers worldwide. And managements with a demonstrated commitment to working with the international investment community enjoy an edge in the growing competition for global capital. The corporate world is becoming one of international investor capitalism.

See also *CEOs; corporate boards; governance; institutional theory*

Bibliography

Berle, A., Jr., and Means, G. C. (1932). *The Modern Corporation and Private Property*. New York: Macmillan.

Roe, M. J. (1994). *Strong Managers, Weak Owners: The Political Roots of American Corporate Finance*. Princeton, NJ: Princeton University Press.

Useem, M. (1996). *Investor Capitalism: How Money Managers Are Changing the Face of Corporate America*. New York: Basic Books/Harper Collins.

isomorphism

see INSTITUTIONAL THEORY

job characteristics

see JOB DESIGN

job design

Toby D. Wall and Chris Clegg

Jobs are created by people for people. Whether deliberately or by default, choices are made about which tasks to group together to form a job, the extent to which job holders should follow prescribed procedures in completing those tasks, how closely the job incumbent will be supervised, and numerous other aspects of the work. Such choices are the essence of job design, which may thus be defined as the specification of the content and methods of jobs. Although the term implies an individual job level of analysis, in practice it is also used to cover group or team work. Other terms often used as synonyms for job design include "job" and "work restructuring," "work design," and "work organization," though there is a tendency to use "work" in preference to "job" to imply a broader perspective linking job design to the wider organizational context.

In principle, the concept of job design applies to all types of work and job properties. Within OB, however, a more particular emphasis has evolved, which has three aspects. First, attention has been directed mainly at lower level jobs, such as those involving clerical and especially shop-floor work. Second, there has been a concentration on a limited number of generic job characteristics such as the variety of tasks or skills, or the degree of autonomy or responsibility. Finally, interest has mostly focused on the impact of job design on employee well-being (e.g., job satisfaction, strain) and behavior (e.g., performance, absence). These emphases are best understood in the context of the history of job design in manufacturing.

HISTORICAL CONTEXT

Since the turn of the twentieth century, the trend in job design in manufacturing has been one of JOB DESKILLING or job simplification. The move from craft-based industries to larger factories, the emergence of mass production, together with the application of the principles of SCIENTIFIC MANAGEMENT, are among the influences that led to the design of narrow jobs with closely prescribed tasks. The reasoning was that simplifying work in this way would reduce costs by minimizing the risk of ERRORS, allowing less skilled (i.e., cheaper) labor to be used, and reducing training requirements.

Concern about the human costs of job simplification inspired some of the earliest research in OB. In the UK this was the focus of work conducted during the 1920s under the auspices of the government-funded Industrial Fatigue Research Board. That research, involving such jobs as cigarette making and bicycle chain assembly, focused on the psychological effects of highly repetitive work, not surprisingly showing that employees found this dissatisfying and boring. Evidence then began to accumulate in the UK, USA, and elsewhere of more serious consequences in terms of a link between repetitive work and employee STRESS or mental health. Studies in the 1950s and 1960s extended the agenda by considering also how the restriction of autonomy inherent in job simplification affected jobholders, and showed similar and often stronger psychological effects.

JOB REDESIGN

Evidence of the negative effects of job simplification fostered initiatives in *job redesign*. This denotes the attempt to reverse the deleterious effects of job simplification by building into jobs more task variety, autonomy and associated characteristics. Suggestions for job redesign naturally parallel the history of job design research. Thus, one of the earliest proposals, focused on reducing repetitiveness by increasing the number of different tasks experienced by employees, was for job rotation. This entails moving employees at regular intervals *between* different (simplified) jobs. Another was for "horizontal job enlargement," which increases task variety by including a wider range of tasks *within* jobs.

Job redesign proposals in the 1960s and 1970s were for JOB ENRICHMENT (also called "vertical job enlargement"). This reflects the concern about the low levels of discretion in simplified jobs, and focuses on increasing employees' autonomy over the planning and execution of their work (e.g., by giving responsibility for decisions otherwise undertaken by support and supervisory staff). The term job enrichment was originally coined by Herzberg (1966), on the basis of his motivator-hygiene theory, but is now used more generally. Another proposal aimed at enhancing the discretionary component of work, but that differs in taking the WORK GROUP rather than the job as the main unit of analysis, derives from SOCIOTECHNICAL THEORY (see also below) and is for autonomous WORK GROUPS/TEAMS or SELF-MANAGING TEAMS.

MAIN THEORETICAL APPROACHES

Two theoretical approaches have dominated research on job design, and have yet to be superseded. One, concerned with individual job design, is the job characteristics model (Hackman and Oldham, 1976). This specifies five "core job characteristics," namely skill variety, task identity, task significance, autonomy, and feedback from the job itself, as determinants of work MOTIVATION, JOB SATISFACTION, work performance, labor TURNOVER, and absence (*see* ABSENTEEISM). The strength of the effects of the job characteristics on the outcomes is predicted to be affected by INDIVIDUAL DIFFERENCES, being stronger for employees with greater growth need strength and (in later formulations) also for those with higher contextual satisfaction and greater knowledge, skill, and ability.

The other dominant approach derives from sociotechnical theory. The emphasis in this case is on the design of work for teams, with the key proposal being for the implementation of autonomous work groups. Six criteria specified for such groups are that the work should (1) be reasonably demanding and provide variety; (2) afford the opportunity to learn and continue learning; (3) include an area of decision-making that employees can call their own; (4) offer social support and recognition; (5) be of wider social relevance; and (6) lead to a desirable future (Cherns, 1987). Note that the characteristics for autonomous work groups are similar to those specified by the job characteristics model.

RESEARCH APPROACHES

Studies of job design have been of two main types, by far the most common being cross-sectional field studies. These generally confirm the expected relationships between job characteristics and outcomes, but provide a weak base for inferring causality. The second type involves change studies, which are exemplified by two field experiments by Wall, Clegg, and colleagues (Wall and Martin, 1994). In the first, previously simplified individual jobs in a confectionery department were redesigned into autonomous work groups. Team members were given expanded responsibilities, such as allocating tasks among themselves, setting their own work pace, and resolving operational problems. Effects, over 18 months, showed substantial improvements in output, job satisfaction, and mental health. The second study compared the introduction of autonomous work groups with a traditional job design at two sites within the same parent company. Change over 30 months showed that job satisfaction increased, output per person stayed constant, but productivity improved because fewer support staff were needed.

More recent field experiments have focused on job redesign for operators of complex automated and computer-based manufacturing technologies (Parker and Wall, 1998). For systems exhibiting greater uncertainty, these studies suggest increased performance results from two mechanisms. One is a logical benefit arising from operators being able to resolve operational faults immediately rather than having to wait for support staff to do so. The other is a learning mechanism through which operators develop the ability to diagnose and prevent faults. The latter finding is reinforced by a recent field experiment showing that job redesign results in greater job knowledge and self-efficacy (Leach, Wall and Jackson, 2003).

CURRENT ISSUES AND FUTURE DIRECTIONS

Interest in job design peaked in the 1970s and waned in the 1980s. It is now resurfacing in response to changes in the topography of work and new strategies, practices, technologies, and forms of work. There has been a decline in manufacturing and a rise in service work (e.g., call centers), and change in the composition of the workforce (e.g., more older, female, and ethnically diverse employees). Organizations are placing increased emphasis on enhancing their competitiveness through improved quality and responsiveness to customer (or client) demand; and they are supporting this through the use of computer-based technology, just-in-time, TOTAL QUALITY MANAGEMENT, business process reengineering and other initiatives. Equally, recent developments in human resource management emphasizing EMPOWERMENT and employee involvement incorporate core principles of job design within a wider context. The emergence of new classes and types of work, such as virtual teams, knowledge work, and portfolio working, is also relevant. In the light of the above changes, and the limitations of research to date, five main lines of development for the study and practice of job design have been identified (Parker, Wall, and Cordery, 2001).

1   *Antecedents*. Existing theory largely ignores context, either that external (e.g., the uncertainty of the environment, nature of the labor market) or internal (e.g., human resource management strategy, type of technology) to the organization. Yet such contextual factors can influence the choice

and effectiveness of job design initiatives. Moreover, there is a need to understand the link so that job design principles can be incorporated into design processes to insure new systems and technologies do not preclude potentially beneficial alternative job designs (i.e., "prospective design") (see Clegg et al., 1996).

2   *Work characteristics*. There is a need to expand the range of job content variables beyond traditional ones such as autonomy. For employees in call centers, for example, electronic performance monitoring and emotional labor *(see* EMOTION MANAGEMENT*)* are likely to be important considerations; and, for portfolio and knowledge workers, social networks and skills development opportunities may be especially relevant.

3   *Outcomes*. To traditional concerns with well-being and job performance should be added other outcomes such as contextual performance (e.g., helping and sharing knowledge with others) and safety. With respect to the latter, for example, little is known about how job design affects safety attitudes and behavior.

4   *Mechanisms*. Theory to date has largely assumed job design operates through enhancing employee MOTIVATION. Recent research, however, points to other potential underlying mechanisms such as learning and, especially for team-based initiatives, social skills.

5   *Contingencies*. Similarly, theory has been largely universalistic. Yet work is beginning to suggest that particular forms of job redesign will be more effective under some circumstances than others. The degree of task interdependence can influence the effectiveness of self-managed teams; and job redesign appears to have a stronger performance effect where there is greater uncertainty in work processes.

A futher issue now emerging addresses the criticism that job design is often treated as a static phenomenom and as an independent variable. Three propositions that challenge these assumptions are: (1) job holders are active crafters of their own job designs; (2) peers and supervisors may well be involved in such negotiation processes; (3) job performance is a predictor of the opportunities that job holders have for such crafting. These ideas point to a more social, negotiated, and dynamic view of job design in which performance is a predictor of job design as well as an outcome (Wrzesniewski and Dutton, 2001).

See also *organizational design; organizational effectiveness; technology*

Bibliography

Cherns, A. (1987). The principles of sociotechnical systems design revisited. *Human Relations*, **40**, 153–62.

Clegg, C. W., Coleman, P., Hornby, P., Maclaren, R., Robson, J., Carey, N., and Symon, G. (1996). Tools to incorporate some psychological and organizational issues during the implementation of computer-based systems. *Ergonomics*, **39**, 482–511.

Hackman, J. R. and Oldham, G. R. (1976). Motivation through the design of work: Test of a theory. *Organizational Behavior and Human Performance*, **15**, 250–79.

Herzberg, F. (1966). *Work and the Nature of Man.* Cleveland, OH: World Publishing.

Leach, D. L., Wall, T. D., and Jackson, P. R. (2003). The effect of empowerment on job knowledge: An empirical test involving operators of complex technology. *Journal of Occupational and Organizational Psychology*, **76**, 27–52.

Parker, S. K. and Wall, T. D. (1998). *Job and Work Design.* Thousand Oaks, CA: Sage.

Parker, S. K., Wall, T. D., and Cordery, J. L. (2001). Future work design research and practice: Towards an elaborated model of work design. *Journal of Occupational and Organizational Psychology*, **74**, 413–40.

Wall, T. D. and Martin, R. (1994). Job and work design. In C. L. Cooper and I. T. Robertson (eds.), *Key Reviews in Organizational Behavior: Concepts, Theory and Practice.* Chichester: Wiley.

Wrzesniewski, A. and Dutton, J. E. (2001). Crafting a job: Revisioning employees as active crafters of their work. *Academy of Management Review*, **26**, 179–201.

job deskilling

Stephen J. Wood

Deskilling is the process by which SKILL levels of either jobs or individuals are reduced. Particular attention in the social sciences has focused on the way in which, with the rise of modern industry, jobs become increasingly routinized and devoid of any real skill content (i.e., they become deskilled). The paradigm case of deskilling is assembly line jobs, which have very short job cycles (often well under a minute) and minimal training times. While technological developments such as Ford's moving assembly line and increased levels of automation are considered important causes of deskilling, so too are methods of management and, in particular, Taylor's SCIENTIFIC MANAGEMENT.

Taylor's stricture that the conception of tasks should be divorced from their execution, and moreover that management should have sole responsibility for determining job content, implied that jobs would be deskilled and workers would have no autonomy or control over their work. Insofar as Taylor's methods were being applied we would expect the number of deskilled jobs would increase. With the growth of mass production methods, first in the United States in the 1920s and subsequently throughout the world, there has been accordingly a great concern about the deskilled nature of work. Certainly, the antagonistic industrial relations in industries such as automobile manufacture has part of its roots in such conditions, but low-skilled work should not automatically be associated with industrial CONFLICT, as many textile industries throughout the world, for example, despite being characterized by highly routinized work, are also characterized by low levels of overt conflict.

As the levels of automation and use of computers increased, largely from World War II onwards, a belief began to emerge that the number of deskilled jobs would reduce. Research by Blauner in the United States, for example, suggested that at higher levels of automation higher levels of skills would be demanded. Also, jobs in the expanding service sector were widely thought to require higher levels of skill than the average factory job. These ideas prompted criticism – most notably from Braverman (1984), also in the United States – who argued that deskilling was the dominant tendency in modern capitalism and that Taylorist principles would still apply at high levels of automation and would be increasingly applied in the growing service sector, as well as to conventional clerical work. Widespread deskilling arises because the division of labor into narrow routinized tasks is cheaper, and control of workers – a major objective of management within capitalism – is made easier. Accordingly, the initial pursuit of scientific management in the twentieth century was, for Braverman, very much about taking control from craft workers who previously were responsible for both conceiving and executing their tasks.

The deskilling thesis has been questioned most fundamentally on the grounds that control of labor need not become an end in itself for management and the achievement of their prime objective, profitability, may not always be furthered by deskilling work. The more fragmented the structure of tasks and the more limited the range of aptitudes possessed by individual workers, the greater the requirement for expensive managerial skills to coordinate the overall production system. More difficult also may be the problems of the organization in adjusting to fluctuating product market conditions. In the twentieth century the numbers of skilled workers has not, in fact, declined to the extent implied by the deskilling thesis, and the main consequence of mass production was a whole new set of semi-skilled occupations and not the substitution of craftwork by routinized labor. Such jobs are not devoid of skills, many of which may be tacit; and the degree of discretion given to people may vary and not correlate perfectly with their skill level. Nor should the extent of the skills of the artisan be exaggerated. Relative to the nineteenth century, overall skill levels of individuals have increased, as the majority of workers then lacked basic skills such as literacy which are now, perhaps mistakenly, taken for granted.

Certainly, taken over a long historical period, net changes in skill levels will reflect the changing occupational and industrial composition in the economy more than changes within particular jobs. Analysis of industrial and occupational shifts in the twentieth century suggests that overall the direction of change has been toward higher skilled industries and occupations, the opposite of deskilling. Deskilling within jobs is often accompanied by upskilling on other dimensions of the job. Survey work in the UK (Felstead, Gallie, and Green, 2002; Gallie et al., 1998) has confirmed the increasing level

of the average skills required in the economy. If we take the insurance industry as an example, though technical change did take away certain skills, there was a net increase in skill levels. The technical developments largely absorbed the skills of certain low level jobs, and as the industry itself expanded rapidly following World War II, the numbers of higher level jobs expanded disproportionately.

Nevertheless, much work in the twenty-first century, as in the twentieth century, remains low skilled: there have been clear cases where TECHNOLOGY has reduced the skill level and discretion required in particular jobs (e.g., in engineering); and many of the jobs created in the past 20 years with the great growth in the service sector are low skilled (e.g., work in fast-food chains), though not necessarily routinized. Though deskilled work may not be the current or emerging norm, there are sufficient numbers of jobs with low skill and/or low discretion to make for relatively low levels of MOTIVATION and COMMITMENT among a significant number of the working population. Several theories of motivation accord skill and autonomy a prime role (job characteristics, Herzberg's motivator-hygiene theory), and Fox (1974) in particular placed the low skill content of jobs at the center of his explanation of the problems of industrial relations in postwar Western economies. There is little evidence of any widespread commitment of managements to genuinely enlarge the skills of jobs through conscious job redesign (see JOB ENRICHMENT). Nor is it clear that some of the latest developments in management, such as TOTAL QUALITY MANAGEMENT, Japanese-style lean production, business process re-engineering, and teamworking, significantly alter the level of skills or autonomy attached to low level jobs in organizations. They may, however, add new skills to low level jobs (e.g., when assembly workers do testing) as well as affect the skill mix of higher level jobs (e.g., when design engineers engage in procurement and engineers in project management, or nurses take on doctors' functions).

Current concern for deskilling jobs has particularly focused on call centers, which are often presented as modern sweatshops where customer service representatives have calls automatically fed to them, deal with customers through menu-driven instructions and pre-set scripted replies, and have little or no discretion over working arrangements. However, while there are cases of such low skilled jobs (e.g., in telephone directory inquiries), the skills and discretion given to operators can vary immensely across call centers. In some cases the operator is involved with the customer in a complex interactive process, as when designing adverts for newspapers. Technology advances are again changing the skill mix, eliminating some of the simplest dimensions of jobs and upskilling other jobs, particularly those involving sales. The movement of some of the call center work from the USA, UK, and other advanced economies to Asia and particularly India is not a consequence or cause of their being deskilled and has not been confined to the low skilled jobs; rather, it is about differential wage costs for the same skill levels.

See also *job design; technology*

Bibliography

Attewell, P. (1987). The deskilling controversy. *Work and Occupations*, **14**, 323–46.

Braverman, H. (1984). *Labor and Monopoly Capitalism*. New York: Monthly Review Press.

Felstead, A., Gallie, D., and Green, F. (2002). *Work Skills in Britain 1986–2001*. London: Department of Education and Skills.

Fox, A. (1974). *Beyond Contract*. London: Faber and Faber.

Gallie, D., White, M., Cheng, Y., and Tomlinson, M. (1998). *Restructuring the Employment Relationship*. Oxford: Oxford University Press.

Wood, S. (1982). *The Degradation of Work?* London: Hutchinson.

job enlargement

see JOB DESIGN; JOB ENRICHMENT

job enrichment

Greg R. Oldham and Markus Baer

Job enrichment involves expanding a job's content to provide increased opportunities for employees to experience personal responsibility and meaning at work, and to obtain more informa-

tion about the results of their work efforts. Job enrichment often focuses on improving a job's standing on several job characteristics: autonomy, task FEEDBACK, task significance, skill variety, and task identity. Hackman and Oldham (1980) have identified five "implementing principles" that might be used to boost a job on these characteristics and, therefore, to enrich the job itself. These are:

1   *Combining tasks*. This refers to putting together existing, fractionalized tasks to form new and larger work modules. Following this principle, all tasks required to complete a piece of work are performed by one employee, rather than by a series of individuals who do separate parts of the job.

2   *Forming natural work units*. This involves giving the employee continuing responsibility for all work that has been arranged into logical or meaningful groups. For example, the employee might be given responsibility for work within a particular geographical area or for work that originates in one department of an organization.

3   *Establishing client relationships*. This refers to putting the employee in direct contact with the "clients" of his or her work (e.g., customers or employees in other departments) and giving the employee responsibility for managing relationships with those clients.

4   *Vertical loading*. This involves giving the employee increased control over the work by providing responsibility and authority that were once reserved for management. Thus, the employee might be given an opportunity to set schedules, determine work methods, and decide how to check the quality of work produced.

5   *Opening feedback channels*. This involves removing obstacles that isolate the employee from data about his or her work performance. Thus, the employee might be given the opportunity to inspect his or her own work and offered standard summaries of performance records.

Although numerous studies have provided support for the beneficial effects of job enrichment on employee satisfaction and motivation, the evidence with respect to behavioral outcomes (e.g., job performance) is less consistent (Parker, Wall, and Cordery, 2001). Many studies that have examined the impact of job enrichment on behavioral outcomes, however, have tracked changes in these outcomes for time periods of less than 12 months, and it may be that such time periods are too short to observe effects on employee behavior. In support of this view, Griffin (1991) found that job enrichment had no immediate effects on employee performance but significantly improved it after 24 and 48 months. A study by Rentsch and Steel (1998) demonstrating the durability of enriched jobs as predictors of ABSENTEEISM over a six-year period also highlights the importance of considering longer time periods when evaluating the effects of job enrichment.

With job enrichment continuing to play an important role in organizational efforts to enhance employee effectiveness and satisfaction (Parker, Wall, and Cordery, 2001), more research is needed to determine if allowing employees to participate in the enrichment process (e.g., by generating ideas for changing their own jobs) results in more positive responses to job enrichment. In addition, work is needed that examines the effects of job enrichment on nonwork outcomes (e.g., employees' use of alcohol and illicit drugs) (Oldham and Gordon, 1999).

See also *job design; job rotation; self-managing teams; sociotechnical theory*

Bibliography

Griffin, R. W. (1991). Effects of work design on employee perceptions, attitudes, and behaviors: A long-term investigation. *Academy of Management Journal*, **34**, 425–35.

Hackman, J. R. and Oldham, G. R. (1980). *Work Redesign*. Reading, MA: Addison-Wesley.

Oldham, G. R. and Gordon, B. I. (1999). Job complexity and employee substance use: The moderating effects of cognitive ability. *Journal of Health and Social Behavior*, **40**, 290–306.

Parker, S. K., Wall, T. D., and Cordery, J. L. (2001). Future work design research and practice: Towards an elaborated model of work design. *Journal of Occupational and Organizational Psychology*, **74**, 413–40.

Rentsch, J. R. and Steel, R. P. (1998). Testing the durability of job characteristics as predictors of absenteeism over a six year period. *Personnel Psychology*, **51**, 165–90.

job redesign

see JOB DESKILLING; JOB ENRICHMENT

job rotation

Greg R. Oldham and Diana Jimeno-Ingrum

Job rotation refers to an employee moving at regular intervals from one job assignment to another, either on a mandatory or a voluntary basis (Parker and Wall, 1998). Thus, in a three person unit, an employee would work on one job for a specified period before rotating to the second and third jobs.

The objectives of job rotation include reducing employees' boredom, providing relief from repetitive movements, and enhancing the acquisition of new skills (Campion, Cheraskin, and Stevens, 1994). Although few studies have empirically evaluated the effectiveness of job rotation, evidence suggests that it can have positive effects on skill acquisition and on the reduction of fatigue, but has little impact on boredom or job performance. One explanation for the latter results is that job rotation, unlike JOB ENRICHMENT, focuses on changing job assignments rather than changing the nature of the job itself. Therefore, job rotation could involve employees moving between a series of routine jobs without any increases in autonomy or personal ACCOUNTABILITY.

Research is now needed to examine whether rotating between enriched, complex jobs has desirable consequences for the employee and organization, and whether job rotation can be an effective strategy to boost the skill acquisition of employees in managerial positions.

See also *job design; motivation*

Bibliography

Campion, M. A., Cheraskin, L., and Stevens, M. J. (1994). Career-related antecedents and outcomes of job rotation. *Academy of Management Journal*, **37**, 1518–42.

Parker, S. and Wall, T. (1998). *Job and Work Design*. Thousand Oaks, CA: Sage.

job satisfaction

Richard D. Arvey

Job satisfaction is probably one of the most researched constructs in organizational behavior. Literally thousands of articles have been written about its definition and meaning, its antecedents, and its consequences. Job satisfaction may be defined as the emotional state resulting from the appraisal of one's job and as such can be negative, positive, or neutral. A basic element in this definition is that job satisfaction has to do with an affective state or how one "feels" about one's job in contrast to simply describing a job (*see* EMOTION IN ORGANIZA-TIONS).

There are a variety of theories that help explain how job satisfaction comes about. One theoretical structure suggests that job satisfaction is a function of what one expects from a job compared to what is actually present in the job. Another theoretical structure suggests that job satisfaction is a function of the degree to which individuals' needs are fulfilled; still another argues that satisfaction is a function of the degree to which a job fulfills important work values. All these connote some degree of fit or misfit between people and jobs.

Although job satisfaction may be thought of as an "overall appraisal" of one's job, the construct can be broken down into several different job facets, such as achievement, working conditions, advancement opportunities, etc. Some controversy exists regarding whether an overall measure of job satisfaction has the same meaning as measuring satisfaction on different job facets and summing over these facets to obtain a composite measure. In addition, research also suggests that job satisfaction may be described along two relatively independent dimensions: (1) intrinsic satisfaction, which involves achievement, recognition, and other features associated with the work itself, and (2) extrinsic satisfaction, which involves working conditions, supervision, and other components of the environmental context in which the work is performed (*see* EXTRINSIC/INTRINSIC MOTIVATION). An important early framework was developed by Frederick Herzberg, who argued that these two general independent types of events affect satisfaction and dissatisfaction differently. He argued that intrin-sic factors (called motivators) could only enhance job satisfaction, and that extrinsic factors (called hygiene factors) would only operate to reduce or eliminate job dissatisfaction. This theory, known as the "two-factor" motivator-hygiene theory, was used as a starting point for JOB ENRICHMENT and enlargement efforts on the part of organizations. Subsequent research has shown that this model was perhaps too simplistic and that both intrinsic and extrinsic factors operate to influence both satisfaction and dissatisfaction.

There have been a variety of efforts to measure job satisfaction. Perhaps two of the best-known efforts are:

1 The Minnesota Job Satisfaction Questionnaire (MSQ), which assesses job satisfaction along 20 separate job facets where separate composites are computed for intrinsic, extrinsic, and general job satisfaction.
2 The Job Description Index (JDI), where satisfaction is assessed along the following dimensions: work, pay, promotions, co-workers, and supervision.

Many factors have been hypothesized to contribute to job satisfaction. These may be broken roughly into two major categories: individual or person factors and environmental factors. Individual or person factors include demographic variables such as AGE, "race," GENDER, etc., as well as trait factors associated with individuals (e.g., IQ, self-esteem, dominance, etc.). Research evidence has established that job satisfaction is significantly associated with general mental health indices, with several PERSONAL-ITY variables, age, and even genetic factors (Arvey et al., 1989). Such personal variables are sometimes labeled dispositional factors referring to trait-like, stable, and reliable individual differences that correlate with satisfaction. Environmental variables are facets associated with the job and organization such as working conditions, variety in the work, pay, autonomy, interpersonal relations among co-workers, etc. A voluminous body of research has established significant relationships between a variety of these environmental factors and job satisfaction. For example, skill variety in jobs, the degree of task or work significance, and the degree of FEEDBACK are significantly associated with job satisfaction. One of the ongoing debates today is how much independent and joint influence do these two broad factors (trait and environmental) have in determining job satisfaction (Dormann and Zapf, 2001).

There is also a sizable research base examining the consequences of job satisfaction. One of the more closely studied relationships has been between job satisfaction and job performance. While some have argued that high job satisfaction leads to higher levels of job performance, others have suggested that the relationship is reversed and that high performance leads to high satisfaction, but only if performance is rewarded. A sizable number of research studies have been conducted to investigate the empirical relationship, and the findings indicate that the relationship is modest but generally significant. For example, a recent meta-analysis conducted on 312 samples with a combined sample size of over 50,000 subjects showed the estimate of the true correlation between job satisfaction and job performance to be .30 (Judge, Thoresen, et al., 2001). Other research studies show a similarly modest relationship between satisfaction and ABSENTEEISM, but a more substantial relationship between satisfaction and TURNOVER. In addition, satisfaction has been shown to be significantly associated with the COMMITMENT individuals have with the organization, and overall citizenship within the organization (see OR-GANIZATIONAL CITIZENSHIP BEHAVIOR). Finally, there has been research showing that many findings concerning job satisfaction and its correlations with various outcomes and antecedents generalize across international and cross-cultural contexts (Judge, Parker, et al., 2001).

See also *attitude theory; job design*

Bibliography

Arvey, R. D., Bouchard, T. J, Jr., Segal, N. L., and Abraham, L. A. (1989). Job satisfaction: Environmental and genetic components. *Journal of Applied Psychology*, 74, 187–92.
Arvey, R. D., Carter, G. W., and Buerkley, D. K. (1991). Job satisfaction: Dispositional and situational influences. In C. L. Cooper and I. T. Robertson (eds.), *International Review of Industrial and Organizational Psychology*, 6, 359–83.
Dorman, C. and Zapf, D. (2001). Job satisfaction: A meta-analysis of stabilities. *Journal of Organizational Behavior*, 22, 483–504.
Judge, T. A., Parker, S., Colbert, A., Heller, D., and Ilies, R. (2001). Job satisfaction: A cross-cultural review. In N. Anderson, D. Ones, H. K. Sinangil, and C. Viswesvaran (eds.), *International Handbook of Industrial and Organizational Psychology*. London: Sage, 25–52.
Judge, T. A., Thoresen, C. J., Bono, J. E., and Patton, G. K. (2001). The job satisfaction–job performance relationship: A qualitative and quantitative review. *Psychological Bulletin*, 127, 376–407.
Locke, E. A. (1985). The nature and causes of job satisfaction. In M. D. Dunnette (ed.), *Handbook of Industrial and Organizational Psychology*. Chicago: Rand McNally, 1297–1349.

justice, distributive

Jerald Greenberg

Based on Homans' (1961) seminal theory of social exchange, distributive justice refers to the perceived fairness of a distribution of rewards. The study of distributive justice focuses on the decisions allocators make when distributing reward, as well as the reactions of the recipients of the rewards received.

Traditionally in work settings, a reward distribution is said to be distributively just to the extent that it reflects the proportional differences in status or work contributions between the parties involved. People generally strive to maintain distributive justice on the job and respond to distributive injustices as specified by EQUITY THEORY.

Other norms of distributive justice focus on distribution criteria other than contributions (Deutsch, 1985). For example, equal distributions of rewards are considered distributively just in situations in which social harmony is being promoted, such as when sharing resources among spouses. Another distributive norm, based on a Marxian notion of justice, calls for distributing rewards based on need, which is considered distributively just in some settings (e.g., triage decisions in hospital emergency rooms).

See also *contracts; justice, procedural; negotiation*

Bibliography

Deutsch, M. (1985). *Distributive Justice*. New Haven, CT: Yale University Press.

Homans, G. C. (1961). *Social Behavior: Its Elementary Forms*. New York: Harcourt, Brace, and World.

justice, procedural

Jerald Greenberg

Procedural justice refers to the perceived fairness of policies and procedures used as the basis for making decisions. In contrast to distributive justice, which focuses on the perceived fairness of outcome distributions, procedural justice focuses on the perceived fairness of the manner in which those distribution decisions are made.

The concept was first proposed by Thibaut and Walker (1975) in their comparative studies of legal dispute resolution procedures. They found that the legal procedures recognized by disputants as being the fairest were ones that gave litigants control over the way their cases were handled (i.e., process control) even if they left direct control over the outcomes in the hands of third parties, such as judges. Today, the importance of granting voice in decision-making procedures as a way of promoting perceptions of procedural justice in organizations has been well established.

Leventhal, Karuza, and Fry (1980) expanded Thibaut and Walker's (1975) notion of procedural justice beyond dispute resolution settings by identifying six additional criteria of procedural justice: *consistency* (consistent use of procedures across people and over time), *bias suppression* (elimination of self-interest), *accuracy* (reliance on accurate information), *correctability* (opportunities to modify decisions as needed), *representativeness* (decisions reflecting the concerns of all parties), and *ethicality* (decisions based on prevailing moral standards). Subsequent research has established the importance of these rules as determinants of perceived fairness in organizations.

Early procedural justice research primarily established the importance of procedural considerations in perceptions of fairness in organizations, indicating that "procedural justice matters." Taking the role of procedural justice for granted in organizations, more recent investigations have focused on analyzing the cognitive processes underlying people's perceptions of fairness as well as the interrelationship between procedural justice and distributive justice (for a review, see Greenberg and Colquitt, 2004). Recent efforts also have established the importance of procedural justice perceptions in a wide variety of organizational phenomena, such as layoffs, performance appraisals, and the acceptance of smoking bans and drug testing programs. Perceptions of unfair procedures also have been found to play a key role in triggering DEVIANCE in the workplace. These theory driven and practical-based efforts have been spurred by the development of a carefully validated self-report measure of various aspects of procedural justice (Colquitt, 2001).

See also *exchange relations; justice, distributive; trust*

Bibliography

Colquitt, J. A. (2001). On the dimensionality of organizational justice: Construct validation of a measure. *Journal of Applied Psychology*, 86, 386–400.

Greenberg, J. and Colquitt, J. A. (2004). *Handbook of Organizational Justice*. Mahwah, NJ: Lawrence Erlbaum Associates.

Leventhal, G. S., Karuza, J., and Fry, W. R. (1980). Beyond fairness: A theory of allocation preferences. In G. Mikula (ed.), *Justice and Social Interaction*. New York: Springer-Verlag, 167–218.

Thibaut, J. and Walker, L. (1975). *Procedural Justice: A Psychological Analysis*. Hillsdale, NJ: Lawrence Erlbaum Associates.

K

kaizen

see CONTINUOUS IMPROVEMENT

knowledge management

Timothy Morris

For scholars, the question of what exactly is meant by knowledge is central to epistemological and ontological inquiry. This debate has spilled over into work on the area of knowledge management where differences persist over how to define knowledge and what knowledge management entails. In much of the empirical work on knowledge management, researchers have defined knowledge in the terms established by their research subjects. Conceptually, some work has run dangerously close to tautology by suggesting organizational knowledge is that which is known in an organizational setting. Otherwise, the distinctions between data, information, and knowledge have been widely acknowledged. Data are the basic organized stream of signals or sequences of events; information is organized data such that the relation between components of the data are evident; knowledge is judgment of the significance of information via theory or contextualization. Using this schema, some researchers have stressed how knowledge is anchored in or structured by the beliefs and values of its holder. Of importance here is the emphasis on the role of actors in interpreting meaning from information, and the relation to action that follows from knowing: knowledge is used to make sense of the world, to solve problems, and to enact change (*see* ENACTMENT).

Knowledge management implies, at the least, an intent to organize or coordinate knowledge that is held by individuals or groups who are members of an organization. More ambitiously, it can imply a component of interpretation by the organization that is designed to affect future actions by its members and enhanced efficiency and/or effectiveness. Managing knowledge therefore refers to the development and implementation of organizational policies to capture, structure, and distribute forms of knowledge held by individuals and groups, primarily within the organization itself but also from other organizations. In practice, as well, knowledge can be broken down into several elements. The most common of these are *know-how*, which refers to procedural knowledge or ways of doing things, routines, and best practices, and *know-what*, which implies a substantive base to knowledge associated with facts or expertise and even social capital in terms of knowing who knows what in an organizational setting.

In recent years many organizations have become interested in managing their knowledge. There appear to be a number of reasons for this. One is the broad context of the development of knowledge-based industries, in which expertise of various types offers the key to future sources of value. Another is the desire of firms to learn from internal as well as external sources in order to adapt to more unpredictable environments. A third reason has been the development of computer-based technologies that have facilitated the coding and distribution of knowledge in digital form and a fourth is the influence of resource-based ideas of strategic advantage. It can also be argued that knowledge management has become a fad through the influence of carriers of management ideas, such as consulting firms, gurus, and business schools, which have stressed the need for organizations to manage their knowledge bases and proposed a range of strategies for doing this.

Several themes underpin the knowledge management literature. One is organizational learning, particularly on the question of how knowledge is generated in individuals and groups (see LEARNING, ORGANIZATIONAL). Another underpinning is the resource-based theory of the firm and it is probably no coincidence that the growing influence of this view has paralleled the interest among managers in knowledge management. Knowledge is seen as a resource of the firm which is economically valuable because it is unique and difficult to imitate and, crucially, because it can contribute to the creation and delivery of valued products or services. According to the resource-based view, knowledge can be valuable because it is a stock of the firm and access to superior stocks of knowledge may offer competitive advantage. In addition, knowledge may be valuable not just as a stock but as a source of INNOVATION (i.e., an input factor), which depends on unique processes at the firm level to be effectively used. However, one important assumption of much of the resource-based literature is to treat knowledge as an objectively definable commodity that can be traded between individuals and can be viewed as a strategic asset of the firm. Clearly, not all of what is claimed to be knowledge can be treated thus: firms may stake intellectual property claims, but it remains difficult for them to assert ownership of much of what is, in effect, informally coordinated know-how among employees, particularly where this is "sticky" (i.e., difficult to transfer or to capture).

In the more popular managerial literature, there is something of a bifurcation between work that tends to focus on organizational issues and work that concentrates on technical solutions. The former has been concerned with how organizations might recognize and share employee knowledge that is usually developed on the job, either individually or collectively, through appropriate structures, systems of COMMUNICATION and INCENTIVES and supportive cultures (see ORGANIZATIONAL CULTURE). Key terms, discussed further below, are tacit knowledge and communities of practice. Another popular literature has focused primarily on creating and sustaining digital systems that collect, codify, and distribute on demand potentially massive amounts of knowledge in an effi-

cient way. Key questions concern how to collect knowledge efficiently, how to sort it into useful categories according to different criteria and needs, how to redistribute quickly and in ways that allow searchers for knowledge to access solutions easily, how to update the knowledge base, and how to balance comprehensiveness and knowledge overload. None of these is trivial. For example, in collecting knowledge does the organization seek to capture everything it can or does it search and collect more selectively? If the latter, who is best placed to do the selection – those in the operating core, supervisors and managers, or expert gatekeepers? In practice, knowledge systems can easily become swamped with trivia; outdated or simply difficult to search efficiently, wherein they fall into disrepute. One solution is to create an electronic database, such as "yellow pages" of resident experts, documenting who holds what knowledge and providing a means of connecting different parts of a knowledge network. This does not obviate the need for frequent updating of databases, however. Most systems probably combine both codification of substantive knowledge and the building of digital records of social NETWORKS.

Underlying the activities of knowledge management is the assumption that knowledge amounts to more than the sum of that which has been made explicit or codified through rules or norms of operations within organizations. Hence, a common (and over-simplified) dichotomy is between tacit and explicit knowledge. Explicit knowledge is that which is codified or documented in a set of procedures, rules, or guidelines and held by (or an asset of) the organization for use by its members. Tacit knowledge is that which is personal, uncodified, and possibly unarticulated. The value of tacit knowledge is that it represents the sort of working know-how that enables an organization's members to perform effectively the many routines underpinning its ongoing operations. The purported danger is that without codification unplanned disruptions or loss of tacit knowledge through labor turnover may diminish the future effectiveness of the organization. In these terms, knowledge management is essentially, but not solely, concerned with the transformation of tacit into explicit knowledge.

Probably the best known of the schema to explain how transformation occurs is that of

Nonaka and Takeuchi (1995). Their model outlines four different processes of knowledge creation and sharing, depending on the type of knowledge *ex ante* and *ex post*: tacit knowledge can be transferred and remain tacit through interpersonal contact, called socialization, or it can be made explicit, which they call externalization (and is commonly called codification). Explicit knowledge can be combined with other forms of explicit knowledge and converted into new knowledge. Finally, explicit knowledge can be changed into tacit knowledge through internalization. Key assumptions here are that tacit knowledge can indeed be transformed into an explicit form in a meaningful way; that individuals and groups are sufficiently reflexive to be able to render their own knowledge explicit; and that they would be prepared to do this even if it implied a loss of status and power. If tacitness is variable and we do indeed know more than we can say, not all knowledge is capable of this transformation.

Another major assumption concerns where knowledge resides and is created. At one extreme it can be argued that only individuals can be knowers or knowledgeable, because knowledge implies human agency and every individual has the capacity to interpret information differently. From this position, the notion of organizational knowledge, independent of the knowledge held by its members, is reification. Knowledge management therefore becomes no more than the collection of the stock of knowledge held by the organization's members, but this stock cannot be renewed or extended by the organization alone. At the other extreme, it has been argued that organizations can know or be knowledgeable, in the sense that they possess more knowledge than the sum of their individual members. Such a position is consistent with organization learning theorists who see knowledge embedded in routines and standard operating procedures (*see* LEARNING ORGANIZATION). A further and very popular position is that groups of co-workers can develop shared understandings or (more or less tacit) knowledge based on their experience. Often called communities of practice, their knowledge allows them to overcome the deficiencies of formally documented knowledge or bureaucratic rules, as in the case of the Xerox repair technicians studied by Orr (1996).

Much of the popular literature extolling the benefits and the importance of knowledge management for firms in the last 15 years has been built on the value to be gained from exploiting such localized, heuristic know-how.

Finally, it is worth noting the more critical stream of literature on knowledge management coming largely in European organization theory (*see* CRITICAL THEORY). Starting from the position that knowledge is not a commodity or a fixed asset that can be objectively defined and captured, knowledge management is seen as an aspiration of managers to appropriate value which is likely to be overambitious in practice. This stream emphasizes the provisional nature of what passes for knowledge even in areas of science and among so-called experts. The highly intangible and processual nature of working knowledge is emphasized. Knowledge in organizational settings is socially constructed and based around the interactions of workers, who are frequently not formally designated as knowledgeable. While this literature adopts a more critical tone, it does not conclude that knowledge management is a wholly mistaken venture. Rather, it tends to stress that knowledge management can more realistically be seen as a strategy to document and support the development of localized employee know-how, rather than a grander plan of codification. While connecting to some of the popular contributors that have focused on the experiential nature of knowledge of communities of practice, this literature also represents a useful antidote to various simplistic assumptions about organizational knowledge and its management.

This discussion has focused on knowledge management as an activity that is concerned with knowledge stocks and flows internal to the organization. Among the empirical issues that deserve more attention is how knowledge is managed in complex, multi-unit firms that seek to share this resource, particularly across different national and cultural settings. Work on the implications for knowledge management of the range of partnering networks and joint venture arrangements in which organizations participate would also be valuable. Linked to the latter point is the need to understand more about the implications for knowledge management of the transfer of ideas from outside the firm. To what extent, for example, do policies to adopt best practices from elsewhere conflict with or even destroy internal knowledge, or can they be complementary? More broadly, one may ask whether knowledge management will end up as a management fashion with a relatively short shelf life, particularly as organizations come to recognize that it involves much more than an investment in an IT system and a Chief Knowledge Officer, and that the benefits of knowledge management are hard to observe, never mind to calculate in terms of profit and loss.

See also *double-loop learning; feedback; learning, individual; professional service firms*

Bibliography

Barney, J. (1991). Firm resources and sustained competitive advantage. *Journal of Management*, 17, 99–120.

Boisot, M. (1998). *Knowledge Assets*. Oxford: Oxford University Press.

Brown J. S. and Duguid, P. (1991). Organizational learning and communities of practice: Towards a unified view of working, learning, and innovation. *Organization Science*, 2, 40–57.

Davenport, T. and Prusak, L. (1998). *Working Knowledge*. Cambridge, MA: Harvard University Press.

Grant, R. (1996). Towards a knowledge-based theory of the firm. *Strategic Management Journal* (winter special issue), 17, 109–22.

Leonard-Barton, D. (1995). *Wellsprings of Knowledge: Building and Sustaining the Sources of Innovation*. Cambridge, MA: Harvard Business School Press.

Nonaka, I. and Takeuchi, H. (1995). *The Knowledge-Creating Company: How Japanese Companies Create the Dynamics of Innovation*. New York: Oxford University Press.

Orr, J. (1996). *Talking about Machines*. Ithaca, NY: ILR Press/Cornell University Press.

Polanyi, M. (1962). *Personal Knowledge*. Chicago: University of Chicago Press.

Swan, J. and Scarborough, H. (2001). Editorial: Knowledge management: Concepts and controversies. *Journal of Management Studies*, 38, 913–21.

Teece, D. (1998). Capturing value from knowledge assets: The new economy, markets for know-how, and intangible assets. *California Management Review*, 40 (3), 55–79.

Tsoukas, H. and Vladimirou, E. (2001). What is organizational knowledge? *Journal of Management Studies*, 38, 973–93.

knowledge of results

see FEEDBACK

labor process theory

see CRITICAL THEORY

labor turnover

see TURNOVER

leadership

Jay Conger

The examination of leadership as a group and organizational phenomenon has been the focus of both theoretical and empirical analysis for more than half a century (Bass, 1990; Yukl, 1994). Literally thousands of articles, papers, and books on the topic have examined and probed leadership from every conceivable angle. Social scientists of many persuasions such as organizational theorists, political scientists (e.g., Burns, 1978), psychoanalysts (e.g., Zaleznik and Kets de Vries, 1975), psychologists (e.g., Hollander and Offermann, 1990), and sociologists (e.g., Bradley, 1987) have explored the enigmatic nature of leadership. They have proposed various analytical frameworks and focused on different content and process aspects of leadership across a broad range of contexts. As a result, there is a wide range of theories of leadership with supporting empirical studies within each advocacy group. These multidisciplinary approaches have also spoken different languages specific to their own disciplines. Their levels of analyses are equally diverse: behavioral and organizational, individual and interactional, process and structural. That said, there are certain basic assumptions that are widely shared across this diverse range of leadership scholars.

BASIC ASSUMPTIONS UNDERLYING LEADERSHIP THEORY AND RESEARCH

Researchers in social and organizational psychology have come to accept leadership as a group or organizational phenomenon. The phenomenon is observed as a set of ROLE behaviors performed by an individual. Leadership occurs when the situation demands that an individual INFLUENCE and coordinate the activities of a group or members of an organization towards the achievement of a common goal. This individual is called the "leader," and the focus on his or her behaviors characterizes a behavioral perspective on leadership. It is also possible that several individuals could share leadership roles within a group setting.

Before the behavioral approach, leadership was viewed in terms of the "great man" or "trait" theory of leadership, which essentially proposed that the success of a leader could be attributed solely to their personality and physical characteristics without regard to their manifest behavior in a given situation (Cowley, 1928). Numerous studies, however, failed to identify a set of traits common to all leaders. The trait approach was therefore considered too simplistic an explanation. Thus, instead of studying leadership as a cluster of stable PERSONALITY traits in isolation from their context, today we view leadership as a set of role behaviors by individuals in the context of the group or organization to which they belong. As Cartwright and Zander (1968: 304) point out, leadership consists of actions such as "setting group goals, moving the group toward its goals, improving the quality of interactions among the members, building cohesiveness of the group, and making resources available to the group."

From this description of leadership follows the second assumption that leadership is both a relational and an attributional phenomenon (*see* ATTRIBUTION). The existence of a leader depends upon the presence of one or more followers and the kind of status or POWER relationship that develops between them. However, leadership comes into being when followers perceive the leader's behavior in a certain way, accept the leader's attempt to influence them, and then attribute leadership status to that individual. Without the followers' perceptions, acceptance, and attributions, the phenomenon would simply not exist.

Thirdly, it is assumed that leadership can be studied in terms of its "contents" (or elements) and its "processes" (or relationships among the elements). The study of the content of leadership involves the identification of specific sets of leader role behaviors that serve to achieve the group's objectives through influencing the attitudes and behaviors of group members. The study of contents also permits us to identify the perceived attributes of leaders and the properties of followers and situations – such as the task, the social climate, and so on – that facilitate or hinder the manifestation of leadership. Therefore, content refers to the types of leader role behaviors, and the presence of specific attributes of leaders, followers, and the situation. By leadership processes, we refer to the types of social influence processes between the leader and the led, and the psychological dynamics underlying them. Thus, leadership implies the exercise of influence over others by utilizing various bases of social POWER, reinforcers, tactics, and so on in order to elicit the group members' compliance with certain norms and their commitment to achieving the group's objectives.

The distinction between content and process in leadership research leads to another assumption. This assumption is that in order to understand the leadership phenomenon, one must analyze the properties of the basic leadership elements and the major relational processes between them. The basic leadership elements are the leader, the followers, and the situational context. The major relational processes are the leader–follower influence process, the leader–context relational process, and the context–follower relational process.

The final assumption is therefore that the role behaviors of a leader are intended to directly influence followers' attitudes and behavior within a group or organization. Thus leadership effectiveness should be measured in terms of the degree to which a leader promotes (a) instrumental attitudes and behaviors that encourage the achievement of group objectives; (b) followers' satisfaction with the task and context within which they operate; and (c) followers' acceptance of their leader's influence. This last dimension of the leader's influence is often manifested through the followers' emotional bond with the leader, by their attributions of favorable qualities to him or her, by their compliance behaviors, and by their commitment to attitudes and values espoused by the leader.

MODAL ORIENTATIONS IN LEADERSHIP PARADIGMS

The modal orientation of the past leadership research has been to address three specific issues related to the constructs of the "leader" and "leadership effectiveness." A concern for understanding the *leader* has led to identifying leader role behavior in groups. A similar concern for understanding *leadership effectiveness* has led to identifying contingencies for leadership role behaviors by studying the interactions between role behaviors and the characteristics of followers and the situational context. Interest in understanding leadership effectiveness furthermore has led to explorations analyzing the underlying mechanisms of the leader–follower influence process itself.

Leader role behavior   Early research studies which aimed at identifying leader role behaviors analyzed small formal and informal groups in both laboratory and field settings. These investigations (Cartwright and Zander, 1968) converged on the thesis that leader role behaviors were functionally related to two broad group objectives: group maintenance and group task achievement. A group member in an informal group, or an appointed leader in a formal group, is perceived to be acting as a leader when he or she engages in activities that promote group maintenance and/or insures the performance of tasks and the achievement of goals.

Following in this vein, later studies of supervision and leadership in organizations (Yukl,

1994) identified two major leadership roles: a consideration or people orientation (also known as the social role) and an initiating structure or task orientation (also known as the task role). The first role – that is, a consideration or people orientation – reflects the social-emotional side of leadership: "the degree to which the leader's behavior towards group members is characterized by mutual trust, development of good relations, sensitivity to the feelings of group members, and openness to their suggestions." The second role – initiating structure in the group – reflects task oriented leadership: "the degree to which a leader is bent on defining and structuring the various tasks and roles of group members in order to attain group results" (Andriessen and Drenth, 1984: 489).

A third leadership role dimension related to decision-making was identified by the works of Lewin and his associates (Lewin, Lippitt, and White, 1939). These researchers studied autocratic and democratic leadership roles in groups and their impact on decision-taking and decision implementation. In providing direction, or problem solving, or providing interaction opportunities for group members, a leader could implement such decisions by involving group members in providing solutions or by the leader's own decision-taking. In other words, they could choose to engage in either participative or autocratic behavior. Research on these three role dimensions dominated the field from the 1940s until the 1980s.

Leadership contingencies Fiedler (1967) suggested that leadership roles are contingent upon situational conditions for their effectiveness. Fiedler's contingency model suggested that in certain situations with certain types of tasks, follower attitudes, and position power, leaders exhibiting initiating structure behavior would be more effective than leaders exhibiting consideration behavior, while in other situations with different types of tasks, follower attitudes, and position power, consideration oriented leaders would be more effective than initiating structure leaders. In another contingency approach, Kerr and Jermiar (1978) identified two kinds of situational factors referred to as substitutes or neutralizers of leadership influence on subordinates. Their "substitutes for leadership"

specify a set of characteristics of followers, tasks, and organizational contexts that reduce or nullify the effects of relationship and task oriented leadership roles. For example, highly experienced subordinates or an unambiguous task might substitute for the need for leadership.

Building upon Lewin's classic studies of autocratic and democratic leadership, another school of contingency theorists emerged. These researchers explored the effects of autocratic, consultative, and participative leadership behavior on the effectiveness of a leader in achieving group objectives. Using a continuum of styles from autocratic to consultative to participative, these researchers identified the appropriateness of each style depending upon the situational characteristics of both task and follower attributes (Vroom and Yetton, 1973).

Leader–follower influence process The third research issue dealt with how and why leaders become effective in influencing their followers. The goal has been to understand the underlying psychological mechanisms that explain the link between a leader's role behavior and the followers' compliance and commitment to achieving group or organizational objectives. Psychological mechanisms have been explored from three different theoretical perspectives: (1) the bases of social power, (2) the nature of social exchange, and (3) the motivational dynamics (*see* MOTIVATION).

Exploring the reasons for leadership power and influence, Cartwright (1965) suggested that leadership effectiveness stems from the followers' perception that their leader possesses and controls resources that they value. Control over such resources forms the bases of power of all leaders. Most studies of leadership effectiveness using this perspective, however, have used a formulation of five kinds of resources that form the bases of social power: reward, coercive, legal, expert, and referent power bases. The first three bases of social power are often assumed to stem from one's formal authority position within a group or an organization. Hence, they are referred to as position power bases. The last two, expert and referent power bases, are considered as residing in the leader's personal and idiosyncratic ways of influencing followers. Hence they are termed personal power or idiosyncratic power bases. The use of personal power by a leader has an incremental influence on followers over and above the influence that results from the use of the leader's position power. This incremental influence on followers is reflected in the followers' performance beyond an organization's prescribed performance expectations.

The second theoretical perspective used to explain leadership influence makes use of social exchange theory (Blau, 1974) in human interactions. Leaders gain status and influence over group members in return for demonstrating task competence and loyalty to the group. Hollander and Offermann (1990: 181) call this type "a process oriented transactional approach to leadership . . . It emphasizes the implicit social exchange or transaction over time that exists between the leaders and followers, including reciprocal influence and interpersonal perception." Using this approach, Hollander (1986) has advanced the "idiosyncratic credit" model of leadership that explains why the innovative ideas of leaders gain acceptance among followers. According to this model, leaders earn these credits in the eyes of followers when a leader demonstrates good judgment. For example, if a leader's innovative proposal is quite successful, followers' trust in their leader's expertise is confirmed. In turn, followers become more willing to suspend their judgment and go along with the leader's innovative ideas (see INNOVATION). The more successes a leader has, the more credits he or she gains. A leader can then utilize such credits that, in effect, represents followers' trust in order to influence followers' compliance and commitment to innovative goals.

Finally, a leader's influence over followers has also been explained by analyzing the motivational processes governing follower satisfaction and performance. A path–goal theory of leadership was first proposed by Evans and later advanced by House (1971) using the expectancy theory of motivation to account for leadership effectiveness. According to House and his associates, each of the four types of leadership role behavior (directive, achievement oriented, supportive, and participative) influences followers by increasing the personal payoffs to them for group task accomplishments and "making the path to these payoffs easier to travel by clarifying it, reducing roadblocks and pitfalls, and increas-

ing the opportunities for personal satisfaction en route" (House, 1971: 324). Similar motivational explanations for the effectiveness of various leadership activities have also been suggested by Oldham, who observed that leadership activities such as rewarding, setting goals, designing job and FEEDBACK systems heighten followers' motivation. Other researchers have explained leadership effectiveness in terms of the behavior modification principles of contingent reinforcement. This approach to maintaining influence over followers through the use of contingent reinforcement has also been interpreted as a form of transactional leadership (see TRANS-FORMATIONAL/TRANSACTIONAL LEADER-SHIP).

In summary, these modal trends have led researchers to focus on three major leadership role dimensions: (1) a people concern that manifests itself in a relationship orientation and through activities that emphasize the leader's consideration and supportiveness; (2) a task concern which focuses on achievement and through activities that emphasize initiating structure, GOAL SETTING, and facilitating task performance; and (3) a concern for making and implementing decisions, which includes behavior such as facilitating interaction and implementing appropriate decision-making styles that range from autocratic and directive to consultative and participative. These specific role dimensions have been studied in situational contexts involving varied characteristics of three distinct elements: (1) tasks, (2) followers, and (3) groups and organizations. Most contingency theories of leadership consider these three elements as the possible contingencies for understanding leadership effectiveness.

Finally, the nature of the leader–follower influence process is also understood in terms of three theoretical perspectives: control over valued resources, social exchange processes, and motivational dynamics (see EXCHANGE RELATIONS). During the last quarter of a century, leadership contingency models dealing with the three behavior dimensions, the three situational elements, and the three classes of explanations discussed above have dominated the scientific literature both in the East (Misumi, 1988) and in the West (Fiedler, 1967; Vroom and Yetton, 1973).

Recently, these earlier leadership models have been considered to be too narrow and sterile. Disappointment has been expressed about their failure to move beyond the simple social versus task dimensions or autocratic versus participative dimensions that underscored the work of early theorists. Many scholars who pursued the modal trends of past leadership research seemed to have ignored certain core aspects of leader role behavior. These core aspects include (1) the leader's role in the critical assessment of the environment and status quo; (2) the formulation and articulation of a future vision or the formulation of goals for the followers; (3) the building of trust and credibility in the minds of followers which is so crucial to developing commitment to a vision.

The act of leading implies that a future vision or goal for the group or organization must be formulated on the basis of an environmental assessment and that followers have to be led to achieve such a goal. One cannot lead when the status quo is satisfactory, and when there is no future goal to pursue. Also, leading implies fostering changes in followers through the building of trust and credibility. In turn, trust enables and builds enduring commitment in the pursuit of a future goal. Leading does not exist when followers' routine compliance is obtained simply to maintain the group's or the organization's status quo.

The limits of the existing theories and research on leadership are also reflected in the inadequate attention given to the study of followers' behavior, their perceptions and motivations in submitting to their leaders. As Hollander and Offermann (1990: 182) point out: "Although the study of leadership has always presumed the existence of followers, their roles were viewed as essentially passive." There is a significant need for follower-centered approaches to leadership research.

The narrowness of the leadership models discussed so far stems from the three research strategies employed to understand the phenomenon. First, these models are based principally upon observations of small groups. When leadership is studied in small groups, whether in a laboratory or in an organization, certain elements of leadership as observed in large corporations or in religious, social, and political organizations are overlooked. For example, studies based on small groups can easily overlook the formulation of a mission or a strategic vision since group goals are often more tactical and mundane.

Second, studies of supervision in organizations have always used follower attitudes and behaviors as dependent variables, rather than as antecedents or explanations for the leadership phenomenon. Consequently, these studies have neglected to utilize follower-centered approaches. As a result, understanding leadership as an attributional process remained incomplete.

Third, most leadership studies in organizational contexts have, in actual fact, been studies of supervision or day-to-day routine maintenance rather than true leading behaviors observed among leaders. The core element of supervision or managership is the effective maintenance of the status quo, whereas a core element of leadership is to bring about improvements, changes, and transformations in the existing system and in its members.

In view of such differences, the focus of leadership research is shifting from a preoccupation with supervisory or managerial styles (task, people, participative role orientations) to the study of other leader role behaviors such as formulating a vision, articulating the vision, and developing strategies to achieve the vision – activities which are observed in leaders who bring about profound changes in their organizations and in their members (Bass, 1990; Conger and Kanungo, 1998). Likewise, follower-centered approaches with an emphasis on follower perceptions, attributions, and value transformations in the leader–follower relational dynamics need greater attention (Hollander and Offermann, 1990). This type of paradigm shift is already taking place, as can be seen by the recent emergence of interest in charismatic and transformational leadership (Bass and Avolio, 1993; Conger and Kanungo 1987, 1998), follower attributions, and EMPOWERMENT (Conger and Kanungo, 1998; Hollander and Offermann, 1990).

See also *CEOs; charismatic leadership; executive derailment; leadership, contingencies*

Bibliography

Andriessen, E. J. H. and Drenth, P. J. D. (1984). Leadership: Theories and models. In P. J. D. Drenth,

H. Theirry, et al. (eds.), *Handbook of Work and Organizational Psychology*. New York: Wiley.

Bass, B. M. (1990). *Bass & Stodgill's Handbook of Leadership*, 3rd edn. New York: Free Press.

Bass, B. M. and Avolio, B. (1993). Transformational leadership: A response to critiques. In M. M. Chemers and R. Ayman (eds.), *Leadership Theory and Research: Perspectives and Directions*. New York: Academic Press.

Blau, P. M. (1974). *Exchange and Power in Social Life*. New York: Wiley.

Bradley, R. T. (1987). *Charisma and Social Structure: A Study of Love, Wholeness, and Transformation*. New York: Paragon House.

Burns, J. M. (1978). *Leadership*. New York: Harper and Row.

Cartwright, D. (1965). Leadership, influence, and control. In J. G. March (ed.), *Handbook of Organizations*. Chicago: Rand McNally.

Cartwright, D. and Zander, A. (1968). *Group Dynamics: Research and Theory*, 3rd edn. NewYork: Harper and Row.

Coch, L. and Raven, J. R. P. (1948). Overcoming resistance to change. *Human Relations*, 1, 512–32.

Conger, J. A. and Kanungo, R. N. (1987). Toward a behavioral theory of charismatic leadership in organizational settings. *Academy of Management Review*, 12, 637–47.

Conger, J. A. and Kanungo, R. N. (1998). *Charismatic Leadership in Organizations*. Thousand Oaks, CA: Sage.

Cowley, W. H. (1928). Three distinctions in the study of leaders. *Journal of Abnormal and Social Psychology*, 23, 144–57.

Fiedler, F. (1967). *A Theory of Leadership Effectiveness*. New York: McGraw-Hill.

Hollander, E. P. (1986). On the central role of leadership of process. *International Review of Applied Psychology*, 35, 179–89.

Hollander, E. P. and Offermann, L. R. (1990). Power and leadership in organizations. *American Psychologist*, 45.

House, R. J. (1971). A path–goal theory of leadership effectiveness. *Administrative Science Quarterly*, 16, 321–39.

Kerr, S. and Jermiar, J. M. (1978). Substitutes for leadership: Their meaning and measurement. *Organizational Behavior and Human Performance*, 22, 375–403.

Lewin, K., Lippitt, R., and White, R. K. (1939). Patterns of aggressive behavior in experimentally created social climates. *Journal of Social Psychology*, 10, 271–301.

Likert, R. (1961). *New Patterns of Management*. New York: McGraw-Hill.

Misumi, J. (1985). *The Behavioral Science of Leadership: An Interdisciplinary Japanese Research Program*. Ann Arbor: University of Michigan Press.

Vroom, V. H. and Yetton, P. W. (1973). *Leadership and Decision-Making*. Pittsburgh: University of Pittsburgh Press.

Yukl, G. (1994). *Leadership in Organizations*, 3rd edn. Englewood Cliffs, NJ: Prentice-Hall.

Zaleznik, A. and Kets de Vries, M. (1975). *Power and the Corporate Mind*. Boston, MA: Houghton Mifflin.

leadership, contingencies

Jay Conger

The contingencies of leadership denote the aspects of a situation that can determine the role requirements of LEADERSHIP. Expanding upon the earlier constructs of a leader's social and task role behaviors, Fiedler (1967) suggested a contingency model of leadership roles. He operationalized a model in which two key leadership attributes were called high and low Least Preferred Co-worker (LPC). These closely resembled consideration vs. initiating structure or social vs. task role preferences in leadership style. Fiedler's contingency model suggested that in situations with certain profiles of tasks, follower attitudes, and position power, low LPC leaders (or initiating structure behavior) would be more effective than high LPC leaders (or consideration behavior) and in other situations with different types of tasks, follower attitudes, and position power, high LPC leaders would be more effective than low LPC leaders. So, for example, in situations where the task is highly structured, relations with subordinates are good, and the leader has substantial position power, the low LPC leader is most effective. With good relations but an unstructured task and weak position power, the high LPC is more effective. In a similar vein, the path–goal theory of leadership (House, 1971) examines follower satisfaction and MOTIVATION through a set of contingency variables. For example, the work environment, the nature of the task, and subordinate characteristics determine what types of leadership behavior are most effective for enhancing subordinate satisfaction and effort.

Building upon Lewin's classic studies of autocratic and democratic leadership (Lewin, Lippitt, and White, 1939), another school of contingency theorists has examined DECISION-MAKING styles in light of contingencies. These researchers explored the effects of autocratic, consultative, and participative leadership behavior on the effectiveness of a leader in achieving group objectives. Their published findings in both the social psychological and organizational behavior literature (Coch and French, 1948; Tannenbaum and Schmidt, 1958; Vroom and Yetton, 1973) suggested that the extent to which a leader involved followers in their decision-making was a critical factor in leadership role effectiveness. Using a continuum of styles from autocratic to consultative to participative, these researchers identified the appropriateness of each style depending upon the situational characteristics of both task and follower attributes. So, for example, when a decision is important and subordinates possess relevant knowledge and information lacked by the leader, an autocratic decision would be inappropriate (Vroom and Yetton, 1973).

In another contingency approach, Kerr and Jermiar (1978) identified two kinds of situational factors referred to as substitutes or neutralizers of leadership influence on subordinates. Their "substitutes for leadership" specify a set of characteristics of followers, tasks, and organizational contexts that reduce or nullify the effects of relationship and task oriented leadership roles. For example, highly experienced subordinates or an unambiguous task might substitute for the need for leadership.

Most of the contingency theories were formulated in the 1970s and are generally complex. Some have questioned their overall effectiveness for practicing managers given the tremendous variety of rapidly shifting situations managers find themselves in. These models often do not provide enough guidance in the form of simple principles for managers to recognize appropriate leadership requirements and choices in the flow of day-to-day demands facing most managers (Yukl, 2002).

See also *charismatic leadership; contingency theory; job satisfaction; participation*

Bibliography

Coch, L. and French, J. R. P., Jr. (1948). Overcoming resistance to change. *Human Relations*, 1, 512–32.
Fiedler, F. (1967). *A Theory of Leadership Effectiveness*. New York: McGraw-Hill.
House, R. J. (1971). A path–goal theory of leadership effectiveness. *Administrative Science Quarterly*, 16, 321–39.
Kerr, S. and Jermiar, J. M. (1978). Substitutes for leadership: Their meaning and measurement. *Organizational Behavior and Human Performance*, 22, 375–403.
Lewin, K., Lippitt, R., and White, R. K. (1939). Patterns of aggressive behavior in experimentally created social climates. *Journal of Social Psychology*, 10, 271–301.
Tannenbaum, R. and Schmidt, W. H. (1958). How to choose a leadership pattern. *Harvard Business Review*, 36, 95–101.
Vroom, V. H. and Yetton, P. W. (1973). *Leadership and Decision-Making*. Pittsburgh: University of Pittsburgh Press.
Yukl, G. (2002). *Leadership in Organizations*. Upper Saddle River, NJ: Prentice-Hall.

leadership style

see LEADERSHIP; TRANSFORMATIONAL/ TRANSACTIONAL LEADERSHIP

learned helplessness

see ATTRIBUTION; STRESS

learning, individual

James R. Bailey and D. Christopher Kayes

Human learning is the acquisition of knowledge and/or SKILLS that serve as an enduring platform for adaptive development. That is, learning integrates cognitive, emotional, and behavioral components that are both derived from, and determine, a cumulative experience base. Learning allows individuals to acquire technical and social skills that enable them to comprehend and navigate novel problems. Although learning's rich and varied theoretical foundation has been widely adopted in organizational behavior, the implications for practice remain underdeveloped.

Learning differs from intelligence. Although intelligence, which emphasizes cognitive ability, is related to the capacity to learn, and therefore delineates the upper potential of what can be learned, learning itself requires self- and social awareness and goal directed MOTIVATION that is not typically captured in narrower concepts. Growing interest in alternative forms of intelligence, such as social and EMOTIONAL INTELLIGENCE, is testimony to the confluence of factors that effect learning (Sternberg, 2003).

Two distinct approaches to learning – the *cognitive* and *behavioral* – provide differing theoretical and practical traditions that are rooted in Gestalt and behaviorist psychology, respectively.

The Gestalt, or phenomenological, approach rests on cognitive assumptions inasmuch as it is concerned with mental models or frameworks that represent the world and, consequently, serve as a basis of interpretation and action. Here, learning arises from the initial formation and subsequent alteration of mental models based on the acquisition of new information. In this way, Gestalt approaches resemble the "theory building" process addressed in the philosophy of science. As a cognitive process, Gestalt approaches typically involve three elements: (1) assessment (framing and causality); (2) anticipation (speculative prediction); and (3) action (proper behavioral response given one's goals). The Gestalt tradition originated with Koffka (1935) and can be seen in the work of such scholars as Argyris (2002) and Weick (1995). Criticisms of the Gestalt approach focus on the lack of measures and replicability of learning events.

As the name implies, BEHAVIORISM focuses on observable behavior. The stimulus (environmental trigger), response (behavior), and consequence (contingent, contiguous reinforcement) sequence has proven extraordinarily adaptable to a wide range of phenomena. Best represented by reinforcement or reward theory, and manifested in the slogan "behavior is a function of consequences," learning is defined as the demonstration of new or changed behavioral patterns brought about by the introduction of consequences. Usually associated with training and skill development, modern behaviorism is the brainchild of B. F. Skinner (1974) and can be seen in the work of Locke (Locke and Latham, 1990) and most compensation theorists (*see* INCENTIVES). The distinction between Gestalt and behaviorist traditions is, of course, artificially severe for illustrative purposes (for a review, see Hogan and Warrenfeltz, 2002). As

pointed out by the pragmatist school of thought, one learns by doing, which views cognition as guiding behavior and behavior as evidence of changes in cognition.

This approach leads to a more integrated approach to learning as problem solving, and is represented in the experiential and social approaches to individual adaptation. Experiential learning describes the process by which individuals draw on experience to create new knowledge. A variety of experiential approaches exists, but they share a common belief that learning involves creating orderliness out of the complex and changing events encountered throughout life. Experiential approaches often involve iterative cycles of individual experience, reflection, conceptualization and action, as represented in Kolb's well-known work (Kolb, 1984). The cyclical nature places attention on the process of learning as opposed to various outcomes that might result. Experiential approaches tend to be holistic in the sense that they account for multiple learning processes including biological (which include emotional and hormonal variation), behavioral, cognitive, and ideological components. Experiential approaches have been criticized for neglecting the social and cultural aspects of individual learning (Kayes, 2002).

Whereas experiential approaches focus on the individual, social approaches describe the processes through which individuals learn from one another and thus place greater emphasis on context. The roots of social learning theory in organizational behavior can be traced to Bronfenbrenner (1979), who draws heavily on the work of Russian psychologist Lev Vygotsky (1978). Social learning theory emphasizes the role of language in transferring knowledge (either spoken or unspoken) between individuals engaged in problem solving. Renewed interest in social approaches can be seen in the study of groups and teams through the concepts of social cognition and shared mental models. Criticisms of social learning theory focus on its emphasis on social and cognitive components while giving relatively little attention to issues of emotion and PERSONALITY.

Recently, the CRITICAL THEORY tradition has received greater attention. Drawing on the Frankfurt School of philosophy, the critical school has been influential in Europe and Australia and is gaining attention in the United States. Critical theory is skeptical of the pragmatic traditions, which it sees as a commonsense recapitulation of the status quo. Critical approaches to individual learning emphasize questioning assumptions and coming to terms with one's social, historical, and political context. Learning emerges as one begins to understand how these factors influence one's view of the world. As individuals become less apt to engage in generalizations about the world and more likely to understand their contextual nature, they become "emancipated" from their own assumptions (see Mezirow, 1991). Critics have remarked on the difficulty of achieving emancipation, and have suggested that critical approaches have unwittingly created elitism by privileging a liberation that lies outside the reach of average individuals.

To enhance its relevance, learning theory faces three interrelated challenges associated with transforming theory into practical learning curricula. First, the gap between THEORY and practice can be expressed as the need to develop a pedagogy of management learning, which includes educational and illustrative techniques, materials, and frameworks. Second, that pedagogy should be intimately informed by careful assessment of COMPETENCIES that contribute to effective managerial practice and that transcend the "knowing–doing gap" – the separation of analytic skills from concrete intervention. Third, improved methods of outcomes assessment for measuring the efficacy of learning are called for. The rich history and diversity in approaches to individual learning promise to continue to inspire fruitful theoretical and practical developments.

See also *double-loop learning; emotion in organizations; learning, organizational; learning organization*

Bibliography

Argyris, C. (2002). Double-loop learning, teaching, and research. *Academy of Management Learning and Education*, 1 (2), 206–19.
Bronfenbrenner, U. (1979). *The Ecology of Human Development: Experiments by Nature and Design*. Cambridge, MA: Harvard University Press.
Hogan, R. and Warrenfeltz, R. (2002). Educating the modern manager. *Academy of Management Learning and Education*, 2 (1), 74–84.
Kayes, D. C. (2002). Experiential learning and its critics: Preserving the role of experience in management learning and education. *Academy of Management Learning and Education*, 1 (2), 1–13.
Koffka, K. (1935). *Principles of Gestalt Psychology*. London: Lund Humphries.
Kolb, D. A. (1984). *Experiential Learning: Experience as the Source of Learning and Development*. Englewood Cliffs, NJ: Prentice-Hall.
Locke, E. and Latham, G. (1990). *A Theory of Goal Setting and Task Performance*. Englewood Cliffs, NJ: Prentice-Hall.
Mezirow, J. (1991). *Transformative Dimensions of Adult Learning*. San Francisco: Jossey-Bass.
Skinner, B. F. (1974). *About Behaviorism*. New York: Knopf.
Sternberg, R. (2003). WISC: A model of leadership in organizations. *Academy of Management Learning and Education*, 2 (4), 386–401.
Vygotsky, L. S. (1978). *Mind in Society: The Development of Higher Psychological Processes*. Cambridge, MA: Harvard University Press.
Weick, K. (1995). *Sensemaking in Organizations*. Thousand Oaks, CA: Sage.

learning, organizational

Stephen J. Mezias

Work in the behavioral tradition of organizational learning is summarized well by Levitt and March (1988: 319), who describe organizations as experiential learning systems that are "routine-based, history-dependent, and target-oriented." A brief exposition of these three characteristics summarizes the key points of the organizational learning perspective.

The first characteristic is that organizations are routine-based systems that respond to experience. Models of organizations as experiential learning systems typically focus on three categories of routines: search, performance, and change (Mezias and Glynn, 1993):

Search routines. Models of search routines address the process by which organizations attempt to discover adaptive opportunities in an ambiguous world via a costly and routinized process of search.

Performance routines. Models of performance routines suggest that organizations compare actual outcomes against a moving target: an aspired level of performance that changes over time in response to experience. The functional forms guiding the adaption of aspiration levels and empirical evidence for these different forms is presented in some detail by Lant (1992).

Change routines. Models of change routines suggest that ORGANIZATIONAL CHANGE, whether an attempt to refine current capabilities or to implement new and different capabilities, is a stochastic response to experience.

The second characteristic of models of organizations as experiential learning systems is an emphasis on the fact that the learning process is history-dependent; there are no unique equilibria or closed form solutions. Past behavior constrains the path that future behavior by organizations can take in a way that is difficult to specify *a priori*. The prime example of this is the effect of increasing competence with current routines (e.g., the well-known learning curve). It is well established that over time, organizations improve their performance with new TECHNOLOGY but at a decreasing rate. This is one reason why organizations may be reluctant to innovate: they will lose the competencies they have built using the status quo (*see* INNOVATION). As a result, inferior alternatives with which the organization has competence might be preferred to superior alternatives with which the organization lacks competence. Indeed, this notion is at the heart of concepts like the competency trap (Levitt and March, 1988) and the distinction between competence-enhancing and competence-destroying technological change (Tushman and Anderson, 1986).

The third and final characteristic of models of organizations as experiential learning systems is an emphasis on the importance of aspiration levels in mediating the execution of change routines. Organizations are more likely to persist in activities associated with success and desist activities associated with failure. The importance of aspiration level is in determining whether a particular level of performance is defined as success or failure: performance above aspiration level is defined as success, while that below aspiration level is defined as failure. Thus, organizational change will be more likely under conditions of failure than under conditions of success.

See also *community ecology; exchange relations; learning organization; organizational ecology*

Bibliography

Cyert, R. M. and March, J. G. (1963). *A Behavioral Theory of the Firm.* Englewood Cliffs, NJ: Prentice-Hall.

Lant, T. K. (1992). Aspiration level updating: An empirical exploration. *Management Science,* 38, 623–44.

Levitt, B. and March, J. G. (1988). Organizational learning. *Annual Review of Sociology,* 14, 319–40.

Mezias, S. J. and Glynn, M. A. (1993). The three faces of corporate renewal: Institution, revolution, and evolution. *Strategic Management Journal,* 14, 77–101.

Tushman, M. T. and Anderson, P. (1986). Technological discontinuities and organizational environments. *Administrative Science Quarterly,* 31, 439–65.

learning organization

John G. Burgoyne

The concept of the learning organization became popular around 1990 with the publication in the USA of Senge's (1990) *Fifth Discipline* and in the UK of Pedler, Burgoyne, and Boydell's (1991) *Learning Company.* From this time it has become a popular theme for thinking about managing ORGANIZATIONAL CHANGE. It connotes continuous collective learning for the adaptation of organizations to their environments, enhancing their ability to shape their environments and the improvement of their practices and processes.

The central idea is that organizations can learn at the collective level, and this has advantageous consequences for their performance, survival, and goal achievement. Senge's work draws upon systems theory, conceiving organizations as both adapting to and shaping their environments. The central idea in Pedler, Burgoyne, and Boydell (1991) is of organizations being capable of collective discovery.

Organizational learning creates organizational knowledge as a major resource, so learning organization change initiatives have led onto systematic approaches to organizational knowledge management. Organizational knowledge management is approached by a mix of "hard" database systems and "soft" social engineering approaches that seek to facilitate dialogue and informal social processes of knowledge production, sharing, and use. Organizations face new problems of knowledge dependent strategies arising from the nature of knowledge as difficult to protect and own, expensive to generate but easy to copy, distribute, and share. This calls for new approaches to LEADERSHIP (Pedler, Burgoyne, and Boydell, 2003), which emphasize mutual knowledge production and use, aligning the motives of knowledge workers with the organization, and strategic approaches to the newly networked contexts of organizations.

See also *knowledge management; learning, individual; networking*

Bibliography

Pedler, M., Burgoyne, J. G., and Boydell, T. (2003). *A Manager's Guide to Leadership*. Maidenhead: McGraw-Hill.

Pedler, M. J., Burgoyne, J. G., and Boydell, T. (1991). *The Learning Company: A Strategy for Sustainable Development*. Maidenhead: McGraw-Hill.

Senge, P. (1990). *The Fifth Discipline: The Art and Practice of the Learning Organization*. New York: Doubleday.

legitimacy

see INSTITUTIONAL THEORY

leisure

see NON-WORK/WORK

levels of analysis

Gary Johns

This term concerns the level at which data are described or analyzed, where *level* refers to a hierarchy comprising, for example, individuals, dyads, groups, departments, organizations, and industries. It also refers to the theoretical level at which some phenomenon is supposed to exist. In orthodox usage, PERSONALITY is an individual level construct, GROUP COHESIVENESS is a group level construct, and ORGANIZATIONAL CULTURE is an organization level construct. Organizations are inherently multilevel, and conditions at higher levels of analysis provide context for processes at lower levels.

Level of analysis can be distinguished from level of measurement (Rousseau, 1985). The latter refers to the level at which data are collected, as opposed to the level at which they are summarized or analyzed. For example, in studying team productivity, a researcher might add the productivity of individual team members to produce a team level index. Here, the level of measurement is the individual, but the level of analysis is the team. Although the level of measurement need not always correspond to the level of analysis, researchers must clearly justify the logical linkages among their levels of measurement, analysis, and theory.

Not all variables are easily assigned to a theoretical level of analysis. Thus, there is debate about whether LEADERSHIP style is an individual, dyadic, or group level variable. This issue frequently arises when individual responses are used to describe constructs that might exist at some higher level. For instance, is JOB DESIGN best represented as a higher level property of the job or the lower level perceptions of individual job holders? A related problem occurs when attempting to determine the degree of isomorphism between variables at different levels. To what extent is organizational learning similar to individual learning? (*See* LEARNING, INDIVIDUAL.)

There has been longstanding concern about how to insure that level of measurement is logically tied to level of analysis so that the measure fairly represents the variable under consideration. One approach is to match the level of measurement precisely to the level of analysis. For example, an organization's technology might be measured globally by classifying firms according to their production processes. The alternative is to measure technology at some lower level (e.g., individual perceptions of automation) and then aggregate these measures to represent the variable at a higher level. For perceptual variables, there should be reasonable agreement among respondents before their responses are aggregated. By extension, there should generally be differences between units at the higher level.

Relationships that hold at one level of analysis might not hold at another. For example, a correlation between job satisfaction and absenteeism at the individual level does not guarantee that teams with lower morale will have higher absence rates. However, considerable interest has emerged about whether variables at one level of analysis can have an impact at another level. For example, can a group's "absence culture" affect the absence behavior of its individual members (Xie and Johns, 2000)? Such downward cross level effects can be examined in two ways (Klein and Koslowski, 2000). The cross level operator technique uses hierarchical multiple regression in which the dependent variable is at the lower level of analysis. Independent variables include any lower level predictors and higher level predictors in which people in higher natural units (such as teams) are all assigned the same value on that variable. If higher level variables account for variance beyond that accounted for by lower level variables, a cross level effect can be inferred. Alternatively, hierarchical linear modeling calculates regression parameters for the lower level of analysis for each higher level unit and regresses them on the higher level variable. A significant effect indicates cross level influence.

See also *research design; research methods; theory*

Bibliography

Chan, D. (1998). Functional relations among constructs in the same content domain at different levels of analysis: A typology of composition models. *Journal of Applied Psychology*, 83, 234–46.

Klein, K. J. and Koslowski, S. W. J. (eds.) (2000). *Multilevel Theory, Research, and Methods in Organizations: Foundations, Extensions, and New Directions*. San Francisco: Jossey-Bass.

Morgeson, F. P. and Hofmann, D. A. (1999). The structure and function of collective constructs: Implications for multilevel research and theory development. *Academy of Management Review*, 24, 249–65.

Rousseau, D. M. (1985). Issues of level in organizational research: Multilevel and cross level perspectives. *Research in Organizational Behavior*, 7, 1–37.

Xie, J. L. and Johns, G. (2000). Interactive effects of absence culture salience and group cohesiveness: A multilevel and cross level analysis of work absenteeism in the Chinese context. *Journal of Occupational and Organizational Psychology*, 73, 31–52.

liability of newness/smallness etc.

see ORGANIZATIONAL ECOLOGY

life cycle

see CAREER STAGE; ORGANIZATIONAL ECOLOGY

life stages

see CAREER DEVELOPMENT

line/staff

Lex Donaldson

The line refers to the hierarchy of personnel who perform the primary task of the organization; for instance, in an army, the soldiers who do the fighting and the hierarchy of sergeants, captains, and generals. The staff performs the secondary tasks, thereby supporting the line, such as, in an army, the cooks, signalers, and medics. The line has authority over the lower level operational personnel (e.g., the soldiers), but the staff merely gives advice to the line. The terms are little used today, seeming old fashioned, because "staff" may have more influence and "line" managers may be less authoritative.

See also *management, classical theory; organizational design*

Bibliography

Chandler, A. D., Jr. (1962). *Strategy and Structure: Chapters in the History of the American Industrial Enterprise*. Cambridge, MA: MIT Press.

locus of control

Paul E. Spector

The locus of control is a personality construct denoting people's generalized expectancies for control of reinforcements or rewards. People who believe that they can control reinforcements in their lives are termed internals. People who believe that fate, luck, or other people control reinforcements are termed externals. The locus of control concept is most frequently attributed to Rotter (1966). He also developed the most commonly used scale to assess the construct.

Locus of control has been one of the most popularly studied PERSONALITY variables in the organizational behavior domain. In his review of organizational studies, Spector (1982) noted that internality is associated with high levels of effort, MOTIVATION, job performance, and JOB SATISFACTION. Internals tend to exhibit initiative on the job and prefer participative supervisory styles. Externals, on the other hand, are more conforming to AUTHORITY and prefer directive supervisory styles. Research has found that externality (feeling that one has little control) is associated with counterproductive behavior in response to frustration. Externals are more likely than internals to respond to frustrating events at work by engaging in aggression against others, sabotage, starting arguments, and stealing (see Perlow and Latham, 1993).

The higher performance of externals has been explained by the concept of expectancy from vie theory. Internals tend to have greater expectancies than externals that they can be effective in task accomplishment. If they see the job as leading to desired rewards, internals should be more motivated to perform. Research has shown, however, that internals may not always be better performers. Blau (1993) found that internals did better at job tasks requiring initiative, but externals did better in highly structured routine tasks. Thus, internals and externals may be suited for different kinds of jobs, depending upon their need for compliance or initiative.

Since Rotter's initial work, scales have been developed to assess locus of control in specific domains relevant to organizations, including economic locus of control, health locus of control, safety locus of control, and work locus of control (Spector, 1988). These specific scales tend to correlate more highly with variables within their domains than does the general Rotter scale. Spector (1988), for example, found that work locus of control had stronger correlations than general locus of control with work related variables, such as JOB SATISFACTION.

See also *identity, personal; self-regulation*

Bibliography

Blau, G. (1993). Testing the relationship of locus of control to different performance dimensions. *Journal of Occupational and Organizational Psychology*, **66**, 125–38.

Perlow, R. and Latham, L. L. (1993). The relationship between client abuse and locus of control and gender: A longitudinal study in mental retardation facilities. *Journal of Applied Psychology*, **78**, 831–4.

Rotter, J. B. (1966). Generalized expectancies for internal versus external control of reinforcement. *Psychological Monographs*, **80** (1, Whole No. 609).

Spector, P. E. (1982). Behavior in organizations as a function of employees' locus of control. *Psychological Bulletin*, **91**, 482–97.

Spector, P. E. (1988). Development of the work locus of control scale. *Journal of Occupational Psychology*, **61**, 335–40.

loose coupling

Mariann Jelinek

Relationships that are not well specified or frequently monitored, but nevertheless persist, simultaneously characterized by responsiveness and autonomy, are "loosely coupled." Loose coupling is a metaphoric description of association (and can be applied to links between or among individuals, units, hierarchical levels, organization and environment, intention and action, IT systems, plans and action, and cause and effect among others) rather than a precisely measured, unidimensional variable. Carefully structured links, well specified in advance, predictable, frequently and assiduously maintained, can be characterized as "tightly coupled." Relationships that are less structured, where linked activities are partially independent of one another, may be characterized as "loosely coupled." Tight coupling implies less autonomous and more carefully coordinated action; loose coupling, more freedom. Yet the simple opposition of "loose" and "tight" coupling ignores important aspects of the idea.

Loose coupling highlights the apparent paradox of partial autonomy across links that endure, between individuals or units or items that do respond to one another; when the links break down or responsiveness ceases, the units or individuals are said to be decoupled. The concept also directs attention to more nuanced and complex relationships of partial control, willing cooperation, self-directed collaboration, and mutual causality which can be essential to effective organizational performance (see COMMUNI-CATION). Loose coupling enables activities to diverge in detail yet to coordinate despite local disruption, whereas units tightly coupled to one another will all fall into disarray if any one of them does, and decoupled units will not coordinate.

Loosely coupled activities can also be judged by different criteria – manufacturing efficiency in operations, and customer complaints in sales – to respond more effectively to local criteria and situations, fragmented environments, or conflicting demands. Loose coupling may also describe relationships among organizations not formally dependent upon one another that nonetheless coordinate their activities, such as joint ventures, coalitions, alliances, federations, or inter-organizational systems (see COALITION FORMATION; INTER-ORGANIZATIONAL RELATIONS).

Loosely coupled individuals, units, or activities may decouple where local goals assume primacy, or local criteria and tasks are optimized at the expense of broader joint aims. Decoupling between individual incentives and group activities can lead to perverse outcomes when individual actions that undercut group goals are rewarded. These characteristics may discourage system change. In cause–effect linkages, loose coupling indicates ambiguous means–ends connections (which may be due to selective perception, BOUNDED RATIONALITY, haste, uncertainty, or intangibility, among other

sources). Decoupling signals the breakdown of causal links.

Some critiques of loose coupling – widely used to characterize IT systems, for example, as well as in military planning – assert that it is "like pornography," recognizable but lacking a rigorous definition. Another criticism is that the concept is "ambiguous, if fruitful" as a metaphor, and that it invites misapplication because of its allusive nature. The power of the loose coupling concept is in directing attention beyond binary logic to the apparent contradiction of links that exist, but are not wholly determinate. Its shortcoming is that it is too easily applied without precision. Especially in understanding complex relationships, iterative, mutual or multilevel causal links, loose coupling holds special promise. This benefit requires users to resist simplifying the concept, however. For organization theorists or managers, the simultaneity of connection and autonomy is pervasive.

Future research opportunities include conceptualizing dimensions of proximity in identifying "loosely" versus "tightly coupled" systems, organizations, or activities, as well as in considering modes of control and communication in increasingly prevalent alliance and network partnerships. Other research extensions include consideration of strategic issues among and between organizational partners – in marketing or design alliances, for example – where traditional links and control mechanisms are inappropriate.

See also *network theory and analysis; organizational design; stakeholders; systems theory*

Bibliography

Hinings, C. R., et al. (2003). Regionalizing healthcare in Alberta: Legislated change, uncertainty and loose coupling. *British Journal of Management*, **14** (S1), S15.

Orton, J. D. and Weick, K. (1990). Loosely coupled systems: A reconceptualization. *Academy of Management Review*, **15** (2), 203–23.

Weick, K. (1976). Educational organizations as loosely coupled systems. *Administrative Science Quarterly*, **21**, 1–19.

management by objectives (MBO)

P. Christopher Earley

One of the most fundamental aspects of the management process is called management by objectives, or MBO. This technique refers to the establishment of specific targets or goals for work activities in a variety of work contexts. MBO incorporates many important aspects of effective management, including coordination of strategic with tactical and operational goals, individual accountability, clear and straightforward work objectives, and superior–subordinate interaction. The concept of MBO is most often credited to Peter Drucker in his management classic *The Practice of Management* published in 1954, based on his extensive work with General Electric Company as well as industrialist Alfred Sloan. A typical MBO program consists of several stages, including:

1 Define and clarify the desired strategic goals of a company or business unit.
2 Develop tactical goals to be implemented by specific personnel in order to determine the strategic goals.
3 Determine the resources needed to accomplish these goals and make them available to key personnel.
4 Communicate strategic objectives with key personnel and solicit their input.
5 Implement work plans and monitor accordingly.
6 Provide FEEDBACK at regular intervals concerning work performance.

More recently, Edwin Locke has refined the general concept of MBO in his GOAL SETTING theory.

Research on the topic of MBO, and its more current manifestation, goal setting, has been extensive and the results clearly support the proposition that people work more efficiently and effectively if they have challenging work objectives or goals with clearly defined time deadlines. MBO programs have been successfully implemented in a number of industries.

See also *decision-making; motivation; organizational effectiveness; performance appraisal/performance management*

Bibliography

Carroll, S. J. and Tosi, H. L. (1973). *Management by Objectives: Applications and Research*. New York: Macmillan.
Odiorne, G. S. (1978). MBO: A backward glance. *Business Horizons*, October 14–24P.

management, classical theory

Mariann Jelinek

Classical management theory springs from early efforts to formalize principles to guide a growing class of professional managers at the end of the nineteenth century. Classical theory sought rationality and order in work through what they called "the one best way," the most logical division of labor, appropriate structure to relate the activities thus divided (in terms of the variety of activities and the levels of supervision), the correct span of control for directing activities, and the proper allocation of responsibility to a designated AUTHORITY. Despite their European and American roots, classical theorists asserted their insights were universally applicable to all organizations. Specialized, subdivided labor, proper direction and coordination, and effective planning would assure efficiency.

Frederick W. Taylor's *Principles of Scientific Management* (1912) separated planning, coordination, and assessment from task accomplishment, specifying these as management responsibilities, Workers were to be provided with proper tools and specific tasks; managers were to identify, plan, and coordinate these tasks, to insure proper results. Taylor's approach, stressing exhaustive time and motion studies, explicit instructions, and unquestioning obedience by workers, reflected both his engineering background and the numerous semiliterate or illiterate immigrants, no less than the numerous laboring jobs in the American workforce of his time. Taylor's philosophy is based on purely economic MOTIVATION, with fair pay for efficient work the aim (*see* EQUITY THEORY).

"Taylorism" was highly popular with some managers, who saw the approach as a rational and systematic form of management. Others, both advocates and critics, saw SCIENTIFIC MANAGEMENT as a means of gaining tight control over workers. Critics attacked Taylor's theory as unduly manipulative and exploitative of workers, and often portrayed Taylor himself as either exploitative or the dupe of greedy managers. Proponents down to the present day argue that Taylor saw himself as the champion of dignity and fair treatment for workers who were necessarily dependent upon managers for their coordination, instructions, and overall work design, an enlightened position for his time. His underlying assumptions of rationality and the importance of structure pervade much organization theory still, as does his preference for the "scientific," emotion-free and quantitative study of organizations.

Henry Fayol, a French mining engineer, typified another thread of classical management, insight distilled from personal experience. His book *Industrial and General Administration* (French edition 1916, first English edition 1930) codified a lifetime of management experience, which he believed could be taught, rather than merely learned on the job. Among Fayol's insights were important classical concepts such as unity of command (the principle that every person should have only one supervisor, and that all persons should be supervised in a consistent hierarchical structure), equity, and orderly division of work. Fayol identified the key management tasks as planning, coordination, and control.

Charles Barnard, former President of New Jersey Bell Telephone and head of important government relief efforts during the American Depression, read widely in the emerging science of sociology (including Vilfredo Pareto and Max Weber in their original French and German editions). His reflective book, *The Functions of the Executive* (1938), moved well beyond the rigidities of rules and structures to emphasize the systemic, affective, and cooperative nature of work in organizations.

German sociologist Max Weber coined the term BUREAUCRACY and first specified its characteristics. Bureaucracy divided the work to define clearly the authority and responsibility of each member as legitimate, official duties. Positions and responsibilities were arranged in a hierarchy of authority constituting a chain of command, with those higher up superior to those below, and every member having a single direct superior. Members were selected for their technical qualifications (not friendship, for instance), and leaders were appointed to their positions by superiors. Administrative officials worked for fixed salaries, and did not own their units. Strict rules controlled and disciplined all members, setting limits to superiors' authority. Rules were impersonally applied to all. Because bureaucracy captures much of the sense and flavor of classical theory, Weber is cited as a classical theorist, although few outside Germany were directly familiar with his ideas until translations appeared in the 1940s.

Others in the classical management school are Mooney, an executive at General Motors and Urwick. One wing of classical theory emphasized time and motion study and engineering efficiency; representatives included Carl Barth and H. L. Gantt, whose Gantt charts mapped out relationships over time between and among related tasks; and Frank and Lillian Gilbreth, consultants on efficiency.

Classical management, even in its time, was complemented by approaches that gave less weight to structure and more to human interactions. Hugo Munsterberg, author of *Psychology and Industrial Efficiency* (1913), is counted as the father of industrial psychology. Munsterberg examined job demands to specify their requisite mental capabilities, in an effort to use psychological testing to find the best candidate for a given job. This aim is quite similar to Taylor's, although the methods differ from scientific management. Mary Parker Follett, an important theorist of the 1920s, asserted the importance of the group as essential for the full realization of individual development. Follett's thinking on integration, common purpose, and the importance of cooperation seem apropos today.

Classical management was succeeded by traditions like the HUMAN RELATIONS MOVEMENT that turned increasingly to the emotional, non-structural aspects of behavior in organizations, themes that endure in organizational behavior and ORGANIZATION DEVELOPMENT. Though less cited today, classical management's attention to division of work and organizational structure profoundly colored later ORGANIZATION THEORY. Modern organization theory's emphasis on structure, rational arrangement of tasks and control, and its tendency to exclude topics like human emotion, interpretation, POWER, and CONFLICT, link back to classical management theory. Contemporary controversies concern cultural differences, a growing body of work on the importance of cognitive and emotional differences (e.g., Nisbett, 2003), the search for logically consistent bridges between these apparently contradictory emphases, and theorizing about complex, non-linear phenomena.

See also *leadership; managerial roles; organizational design*

Bibliography

Barnard, C. I. (1938) [1956]. *The Functions of the Executive*. Cambridge, MA: Harvard University Press.

Munsterberg, H. (1913). *Psychology and Industrial Efficiency*. Boston, MA: Houghton Mifflin.

Nisbett, R. E. (2003). *The Geography of Thought: How Asians and Westerners Think Differently . . . and Why*. New York: Free Press.

Taylor, F. W. (1912). The Principles of Scientific Management. In H. Pearson (ed.), *Scientific Management*.

Hanover, NH: Tuck School of Dartmouth College, 22–55.

Wren, D. A. (1993). *The Evolution of Management Thought*, 4th edn. New York: John Wiley and Sons.

management, information systems

see COMMUNICATIONS

managerial and organizational cognition

Joseph Porac

The study of organizations as cognitive phenomena was stimulated by Simon's (1955; March and Simon, 1958) argument that managerial interpretations of organizational environments are influenced by managerial cognitive capacities and predilections. This argument was a reaction against neoclassical economists who suggested that the managerial mind scanned environments in panoramic fashion and thus was isomorphic with such environments. When one agrees that the same environment can be interpreted in different ways by different managerial observers, managerial cognitive representations become important variables in a theory of organizations. To the extent that this variation is at least a partial function of the internal environment of organizations, then organizations themselves must be viewed as cognitive processes characterized by the collection, collation, and interpretation of environmental stimuli. The study of managerial and organizational cognition has evolved considerably since Simon's early work, and today represents a healthy area of research that is mapping and exploring the cognitive structures underlying organizational activities and outcomes.

In all such work, attention is given to describing the belief structures that shape the perception, interpretation, and meaning of environmental events and conditions. Many different concepts have been used to label these beliefs, such as cause maps, cognitive maps, schemata, worldviews, strategic frames, recipes, dominant logics, mental models, and knowledge structures. Indeed, it is the explicit attention given to mapping systems of managerial and organizational beliefs that distinguishes the study of cognition in organizations from other related areas of research such as organizational learning, organizational knowledge creation, managerial decision-making, ORGANIZATIONAL CULTURE, and the study of institutions.

Researchers have undertaken these mappings at individual, group, organizational, and interorganizational LEVELS OF ANALYSIS. In an early study at the individual level of analysis, for example, Dearborn and Simon (1955) showed how managerial interpretations of organizational problems were influenced by functional backgrounds and experience. In more recent research, Dutton and Jackson (1987) unpacked the constellation of meanings that give substance to the threat/opportunity distinction in the minds of individual managers. At the group level, a number of studies have sought to detail the belief structures of top management teams. For example, Hodgkinson and Johnson (1994) studied the mental models of the competitive environment held by various managers in grocery retailing chains in the UK. Prahalad and Bettis (1986) introduced the notion of "dominant logic" to explain how the managerial teams of multi-business firms make sense of the relationships among their firms' business units. At the organizational level, Lyles and Schwenk (1992) made good use of the distinction between "core" and "peripheral" cognitive structures in suggesting that core beliefs are shared widely across an organization and involve an organization's mission and purpose. Peripheral beliefs are more varied and involve an organization's subgoals and the suggested means for achieving them. At the inter-organizational level of analysis, several studies have mapped managerial beliefs about the structure of markets and rivalry. Porac et al. (1995), for example, showed how markets for specific categories of garments were consensually held by managers of Scottish knitwear firms. These categories parsed the industry into groups of essentially non-overlapping rivalries. Other studies have shown how managerial fads and fashions diffuse through interorganizational communities. For example, Abrahamson and Fairchild (1999) explored the rise and decline of the quality circle logic during the period from 1974 to 1995. Abrahamson and Fairchild suggested that certain concepts and ideas capture the attention of managers, quickly become a fad, but then decline in popularity just as quickly as new ideas and additional fads replace them.

The study of organizations as cognitive phenomena has a long history in organizational science, and continues to be an active area of current research at all levels of analysis.

See also *values*

Bibliography

Abrahamson, E. and Fairchild, G. (1999). Management fashion: Lifecycles, triggers, and collective learning processes. *Administrative Science Quarterly*, **44**, 708–40.

Dearborn, D. C. and Simon, H. A. (1955). Selective perception: A Note on the departmental identification of executives. *Sociometry*, **21**, 140–4.

Dutton, J. E. and Jackson, S. E. (1987). Categorizing strategic issues: Links to organizational action. *Academy of Management Review*, **12**, 76–90.

Hodgkinson, G. P. and Johnson, G. (1994). Exploring the mental models of competitive strategists: The case for a processual approach. *Journal of Management Studies*, **31**, 525–51.

Lyles, M. A. and Schwenk, C. R. (1992). Top management, strategy, and organizational knowledge structures. *Journal of Management Studies*, **29**, 155–74.

March, J. G. and Simon, H. (1958). *Organizations*. New York: Wiley.

Porac, J. F., Thomas, H., Wilson, F., Paton, D., and Kanfer, A. (1995). Rivalry and the industry model of Scottish knitwear producers. *Administrative Science Quarterly*, **40**, 203–27.

Prahalad, C. K. and Bettis, R. A. (1986). The dominant logic: A new linkage between diversity and performance. *Strategic Management Journal*, **7**, 485–501.

Simon, H. A. (1955). A behavioral model of rational choice. *Quarterly Journal of Economics*, **69**, 99–118.

managerial roles

Colin Hales

Consistent with ROLE theory generally, "managerial role" subsumes three aspects of the work of managers, conventionally defined as those given formal responsibility for a work process and those who carry it out: what managers are expected to do (role definition), how managers interpret and construct their role (role perception and enactment), and what managers actually do in the course of their work (role behavior or performance). The concept, therefore, corrals a range of organizational, interpersonal, and individual aspects of managers' work, such as their function, position, job, tasks, responsibilities, and behavior. A somewhat fragmented body of evidence, models, and theories variously describes, analyzes, frames, and seeks to explain managerial roles, about which there are two major debates: first, over the extent to which these roles display similarity or variation; and second, over the extent to which they display continuity or change over time.

Managers' role definitions are often treated implicitly in discussions of the managerial *function*. Disagreement about whether the managerial role is a neutral, technical coordinative one, necessitated by the scale and complexity of large-scale organization, or a tendentious, political exploitative one, necessitated by the structural conflicts and contradictions of capitalist organization, has disguised essential agreement that the function of managers is to plan, organize, motivate, coordinate, and control. Recently, however, it is argued that, as a result of organizational changes associated with post-industrialism (the replacement of functional by business unit or project structures, vertical hierarchies by lateral networks and process by performance controls), these functions have been displaced to empowered workers or teams. The implied consequence is that exclusively *managerial* roles have dwindled or shifted towards more ambiguous, complex leadership or entrepreneurial roles, concerned more with facilitation, collaboration, negotiation, and development. These recent claims, however, tend to be deduced from business trends and they have been challenged by studies pointing to the limited extent of organizational change, continuities in the managerial role, and persisting managerial preoccupations (Hales, 2002). Empirical studies of how the managerial role is defined are relatively few, although a handful of studies have examined how the role is formally defined organizationally or how it is defined more informally by the expectations of the manager's role set.

In contrast, managerial role *behavior* has been the focus of research for over fifty years (Stewart, 1998). Studies have progressively broadened in scope from straightforward description of how "the" managerial role is performed, through correlational studies of the link between different types of role and diverse contextual variables, to richer, ethnographic accounts of managers at work. The resulting findings, though not always commensurable or cumulative, document both commonalities and variations in what managers do (Hales, 1986, 1999).

Activities common to all or most managers are:

Acting as figurehead, representative, or point of contact for a work unit
Monitoring and disseminating information
Networking
Negotiating with a broad constituency
Planning and scheduling work
Allocating resources to different work activities
Directing and monitoring the work of subordinates
Specific human resource management activities
Problem solving and handling disturbances to work flow
Innovating processes and products
Technical work relating to the managers' professional or functional specialism

This work is characterized by:

Short, interrupted, fragmented activities
Reaction to events, problems, and requirements of others
Preoccupation with the exigent and the ad hoc
Nested activities
High levels of verbal interaction
Tension, pressure, and conflict in juggling competing demands
Choice and negotiation over the nature, boundaries, and conduct of the job

A number of areas remain under-researched; for example, managerial work that takes place away from the workplace or is undertaken by non-managers, and the link between work behaviors and effectiveness. Also, there is a paucity of theory to explain managerial role performance.

Managerial roles have also been shown to vary by individual, job, level, function, forms of organization, industry, economic sector, and national culture, and do so in terms of work content, contact patterns, rhythms of work, where work is carried out, dependency on others, and the amount of interaction involved. Studies documenting variation have shown a progressive widening of focus beyond Anglo-Saxon middle managers in large private sector organizations. A key limitation here is the paucity of theory to account for variations in role performance, although some recent studies have attempted to show how these are shaped by forms of organization, sector, national economic systems, or culture (reviewed in Hales, 1999; Nordegraaf and Stewart, 2000).

Generally, theories of managerial role performance tend to be inductive, idiographic accounts of managers in particular settings. Nomothetic theories are comparatively rare, somewhat tentative, and tend to be drawn from a broadly critical perspective. These include attempts to account for what managers do in terms of balancing maintenance and INNOV-ATION in the context of high task and performance ambiguity, balancing cooperation and control in the context of particular socioeconomic institutions, and as engagement in institutionalized routines that draw on and reproduce institutional, organizational, and management resources and rules (reviewed in Hales, 1999).

Linked to the postmodern preoccupation with discourse, narrative, and negotiated orders, a notable recent development has been a research focus on the processes whereby managers come to learn, interpret, make sense of, negotiate, construct, and enact their roles. Here, the emphasis is on the management of meanings, manipulation of symbols, and deployment of rhetoric to render messy, irrational management processes as orderly and rational and create an illusion of managerial control (see, for example, Watson, 1994). Explanatory accounts of these processes tend, perforce, to be situational-specific, although Fondas and Stewart (1994) offer a more generic model of factors impinging on managerial role ENACTMENT.

Indeed, there remains a tendency to develop models that frame, rather than theories that explain, managerial roles. These models include Mintzberg's (1973) Interpersonal, Informational, and Decisional roles; Stewart's (1982) Demands, Constraints, and Choices, and Mintzberg's (1994) "rounded-out" model. Going beyond descriptions and frames to ex-

planations remains a key challenge for work in the area.

See also *CEOs; management, classical theory*

Bibliography

Fondas, N. and Stewart, R. (1994). Enactment in managerial jobs: A role analysis. *Journal of Management Studies*, **31** (1), 83–104.

Hales, C. P. (1986). What do managers do? A critical review of the evidence. *Journal of Management Studies*, **23** (1), 88–115.

Hales, C. P. (1999). Why do managers do what they do? Reconciling evidence and theory in accounts of managerial work. *British Journal of Management*, **10**, 335–50.

Hales, C. P. (2002). Bureaucracy-lite and continuities in managerial work. *British Journal of Management*, **13** (1), 51–66.

Mintzberg, H. (1973). *The Nature of Managerial Work*. New York: Harper and Row.

Mintzberg, H. (1994). Rounding out the managerial job. *Sloan Management Review*, Fall, 11–26.

Noordegraaf, M. and Stewart, R. (2000). Managerial behavior research in private and public sectors: Distinctiveness, disputes, and directions. *Journal of Management Studies*, **37** (3), 427–43.

Stewart, R. (1982). *Choices for the Manager*. Englewood Cliffs, NJ: Prentice-Hall.

Stewart, R. (ed.) (1998). *Managerial Work*. Aldershot: Ashgate.

Watson, T. J. (1994). *In Search of Management: Culture, Chaos, and Control in Managerial Work*, 2nd edn. London: Routledge.

managerial style

see LEADERSHIP; TRANSACTIONAL/TRANSFORMATIONAL LEADERSHIP

mass production

see TECHNOLOGY

matrix organization

N. Anand

Matrix refers to a form of organization design in which two or more distinctive departments are operationally and administratively integrated into one subunit. In the Royal Dutch Shell organization of 1994, for example, the matrix organization integrated roles and responsibilities along three dimensions in order to provide local services (Kramer, 1994): functions (e.g., finance, marketing, research and development, and operations), regions (e.g., Europe, East Asia, Australasia, and Africa), and business sectors (including upstream oil and gas, downstream oil, chemicals, and natural gas). This design emerged with the rise of increasingly complex organizational forms in the late 1950s. Although first observed in large aerospace firms such as Boeing, Rockwell, and Lockheed, the matrix organizational form soon diffused to a range of different industries such as multinational consumer goods, financial services, healthcare, and high technology (Janger, 1979).

What observers noted as distinctive about the matrix form initially was that it violated the traditional organizational principle of hierarchical unity of command. Since the matrix was created to cope with the joint delivery of services of two departments, employees assigned to a matrix were accountable to at least two bosses, not just one. In a pioneering treatise on the matrix form, Davis and Lawrence (1979) cited the government and the family as examples of institutions with plural forms of authority, and contrasted those with the unitary form of authority found in the military, the church, and the monarchy. In their view, the successful implementation of matrix organization needs not only the appropriate structural design, but also supporting systems, culture, and behavior. Likewise, Ghoshal and Bartlett (1998) argue that the matrix organization could easily descend into anarchy if structural change is not accompanied by clarity of purpose, cultural consistency and behavioral COMMITMENT.

In highly uncertain environments, the matrix design improves the information processing capacity of an organization by creating new, lateral channels of COMMUNICATION that complement existing formal ones (Galbraith, 1973). While the implementation of matrix design has been shown to increase the quantity of communication within organizations, evidence of improved information processing quality is lacking (Joyce, 1986). Other benefits associated with this form of the organization include the increased flexibility in the use of human resources and increased individual MOTIVATION, commitment, and personal development (Ford and Randolph, 1992).

A number of disadvantages of the matrix as a form of organizing can be traced to dual authority. Matrix creates ambiguity over resources. In addition, it has the potential to bring functional and project managers into CONFLICT because of differences in functional and cognitive backgrounds (Davis and Lawrence, 1979). There is some empirical support to suggest that such conflict leads to the abandonment of matrix design (Burns and Wholey, 1993). At an individual level, working in a matrix structure can lead to role ambiguity, lack of obvious direction for career development, and the stress of working for multiple bosses (Ford and Randolph, 1992).

Scholars have provided a variety of explanations for the adoption of the matrix form. Kolodny (1979) offers what is called a rational or technical explanation of the evolution of the matrix form in organizations by claiming that as the information processing demands on an organization become more complex, it moves from a simple functional design to a matrix form in order to respond effectively. While Burns (1989) found some support for the rational explanation, he also noted that professional groups that were less powerful in terms of occupational prestige (such as nurses in a hospital subunit vis-à-vis physicians) championed the adoption of the matrix as a political response in aid of achieving more administrative power. Organizations are also likely to adopt the matrix form for institutional reasons such as when prominent organizations in the same sector or region are likely to have adopted the design, or if there is widespread media coverage of adoption in their locality (Burns and Wholey, 1993).

Several scholars have noted that the matrix form is much written about and theorized, but rarely researched, which is somewhat of a pity since anecdotal evidence suggests that it is thriving. The increasing sophistication of markets and rise in the specialization of knowledge bases seem to have led to conditions suitable for the continued relevance of the design, not only in manufacturing organizations (such as electronics or pharmaceuticals) but also in the service sector (e.g., banking, software), in non-profit organizations such as hospitals and emergency rescue agencies, and in professional service firms (consulting, advertising, and law).

See also *management, classical theory; networking; organizational design; professional service firms*

Bibliography

Burns, L. R. (1989). Matrix management in hospitals: Testing theories of matrix structure and development. *Administrative Science Quarterly*, 34, 349–68.

Burns, L. R. and Wholey, D. R. (1993). Adoption and abandonment of matrix management programs: Effects of organizational characteristics and inter-organizational networks. *Academy of Management Journal*, 36, 106–38.

Davis, S. M. and Lawrence, P. R. (1979). *Matrix*. Reading, MA: Addison-Wesley.

Ford, R. C. and Randolph, W. A. (1992). Cross-functional structures: A review and integration of matrix organization and project management. *Journal of Management*, 18, 267–94.

Galbraith, J. R. (1973). *Designing Complex Organizations*. Reading, MA: Addison-Wesley.

Ghoshal, S. and Bartlett, C. A. (1998). *Managing Across Borders: The Transnational Solution*. London: Random House.

Janger, A. R. (1979). *Matrix Organization of Complex Business*. New York: Conference Board.

Joyce, W. F. (1986). Matrix organization: A social experiment. *Academy of Management Journal*, 29, 536–61.

Kolodny, H. F. (1979). Evolution to a matrix organization. *Academy of Management Review*, 4, 543.

Kramer, R. J. (1994). *Organizing for Global Competitiveness: The Matrix Design*. New York: Conference Board.

mechanistic/organic

Lex Donaldson

The mechanistic organizational structure is a top-down, hierarchical structure in which people have clear roles and receive detailed instructions – formalization and centralization are both high. It is suited to stable conditions in which management understands the tasks and promotes task efficiency (Burns and Stalker, 1961). The organic structure is a network structure in which people use their initiative and define their roles through discussion with peers – formalization and centralization are both low. It is suited to unstable conditions that require

problem solving and promotes higher rates of innovation (Brown and Eisenhardt, 1997). The theory helped develop the modern contingency theory (Donaldson, 2001).

The mechanistic and organic types are extremes, being two ends of a continuum, with actual organizations mainly lying at intermediary points along it. It is unlikely that an organization will be completely mechanistic, because formalization tends to be highest in large sized organizations, which tend to be not centralized, but decentralized; that is, they delegate some decisions to middle and lower levels in the hierarchy. Similarly, it is unlikely that an organization will be completely organic, because formalization tends to be lowest in small sized organizations, which tend to be not decentralized, but centralized (e.g., a small firm run by an owner-manager).

Moreover, there can be variations in the degree of "mechanisticness" and "organicness" within the same organization. Some organizational roles, because of the uncertainty of their tasks (e.g., R&D scientist), are less formalized and more autonomous (i.e., more organic), while some other roles (e.g., assembly worker), because of the certainty of their tasks, are more formalized and more directed by management (i.e., more mechanistic). Successful large, innovatory firms, such as in hi-tech (e.g., electronics), tend to have some mechanistic aspects that provide a framework within which there are also organic features.

See also *family firms; organizational design; organizational effectiveness*

Bibliography

Brown, S. L. and Eisenhardt, K. M. (1997). The art of continuous change: Linking complexity theory and time-paced evolution in relentlessly shifting organizations. *Administrative Science Quarterly*, 42, 1–34.

Burns, T. and Stalker, G. M. (1961). *The Management of Innovation*, 2nd edn. London: Tavistock.

Donaldson, L. (2001). *The Contingency Theory of Organizations*. Thousand Oaks, CA: Sage.

media

see COMMUNICATIONS; COMMUNICATIONS TECHNOLOGY

mediation

see CONFLICT AND CONFLICT MANAGE-
MENT

mentoring

Kathy Kram

Mentoring refers to relationships between juniors and seniors that exist primarily to support the personal development and CAREER advancement of the junior person. Early empirical studies demonstrated that these relationships offer a range of career and psychosocial functions, including sponsorship, challenging assignments, protection, coaching, role modeling, counseling, acceptance, confirmation, and friendship (Kram, 1988). These functions foster individual outcomes such as increased self-confidence, clarity of professional identity, increased competence, and career advancement. Subsequent research documented that seniors derive parallel developmental benefits. In recent years, it has been demonstrated that these relationships can foster organizational outcomes including organizational COMMITMENT, retention, succession, performance, and perceived justice (Wanberg, Welsh, and Hezlett, 2003) (*see* JUSTICE, PROCEDURAL).

Workforce diversity has presented a number of challenges to those who seek mentoring and those who wish to provide such developmental assistance (Noe, Greenberger, and Wang, 2002; Kram, 1988). Relationships that involve individuals of diverse backgrounds – in terms of gender, race, or national identity – are more difficult to establish and maintain over time. More often than not, subtle yet powerful dynamics limit trust and effective COMMUNICATION (Ragins and Cotton, 1999). Self-awareness, empathy, and good listening SKILLS are essential emotional competencies for addressing these obstacles effectively. Organizations can maximize the quality of mentoring for diverse employee populations by offering relevant education and training and making sure that reward systems acknowledge the importance of mentoring and these necessary intrapersonal and interpersonal skills.

In the last decade, the landscapes of careers and organizations have changed dramatically. Stable, hierarchical organizations have given way to more flexible, team-based structures in order to meet the changing and complex demands of an increasingly global and technologically sophisticated marketplace. This dramatic change in context has significant implications for mentoring. The instability of organizations and jobs, as well as the critical need for continuous learning and adaptability, have transformed the nature of mentoring. Individuals are less likely to find long-term, hierarchical relationships that provide traditional mentoring, and more likely to find mentoring in several relationships with peers, juniors, and seniors both inside and outside their immediate organization. Consequently, mentoring has been reconceptualized as a network of *developmental relationships* (Higgins and Kram, 2001).

Concurrent with these trends is the recognition that relationships are a key source of learning at all stages of careers, not just for the newcomer, and not just in the traditional hierarchical mentoring relationships. It has also been demonstrated that individuals benefit from diverse developmental networks (Higgins and Kram, 2001). For example, both women and people of color tend to be more successful in terms of career advancement and personal learning when they have the dual support of people who are like them (female and/or minority) and people who are different (white male majority). Similarly, those in the dominant group (white males) learn how to lead and manage their workforces more effectively from their experiences in diverse developmental relationships (Wanberg, Welsh, and Hezlett, 2003).

A number of strategies for enhancing the availability and quality of mentoring exist, ranging from creating a reward system and culture that encourages informal mentoring, to formally assigning individuals to serve as mentors to juniors for a specified period of time. As the focus moves from one-to-one hierarchical mentoring to developmental networks, organizations should consider ways to foster alternatives, including peer coaching, mentoring circles, and mentoring among members of work teams (Noe, Greenberger, and Wang, 2002; Higgins and Kram, 2001).

See also *career development; learning, individual; networking*

Bibliography

Higgins, M. C. and Kram, K. E. (2001). Reconceptualizing mentoring at work: A developmental network perspective. *Academy of Management Review*, **26**, 264–88.

Kram, K. E. (1988). *Mentoring at Work: Developmental Relationships in Organizational Life.* Lanham, MD: University Press of America.

Noe, R., Greenberger, D., and Wang, S. (2002). Mentoring: What we know and where we might go. *Research in Personnel and Human Resources Management*, **21**, 129–73.

Ragins, B. R. and Cotton, J. L. (1999). Mentor functions and outcomes: A comparison of men and women in formal and informal mentoring relationships. *Journal of Applied Psychology*, **84**, 529–50.

Wanberg, C. R., Welsh, E., and Hezlett, S. (2003). Mentoring research: A review and dynamic process model. *Research in Personnel and Human Resources Management*, **22**, 39–124.

mergers and acquisitions

Phanish Puranam

A merger refers to the amalgamation of two independent corporate entities into a single one (eg. Daimler/Chrysler), whereas an acquisition refers to the absorption of one corporate entity into another (eg. Cisco/Stratacom). Mergers and acquisitions (M&A) are among the most dramatic and visible manifestations of corporate strategy. With a single deal, the strategic course of the organizations involved can be altered permanently. Capital market reactions may create enormous changes in shareholder value and the careers of individual managers at all levels may be profoundly affected.

M&A transactions are made for a variety of reasons: to realize economies of scale and scope; to access technology, brands, products, and distribution channels; to build critical mass in growth industries; to remove excess capacity and consolidate a mature industry; or to change the rules of competition as deregulation and technological change trigger convergence across industries. The common theme (and the attraction of M&A strategies) is quick access to and control of a set of resources. However, the difficulties inherent in managing M&A are reflected in their low success rates. About half of these transactions fail, whether measured in terms of capital market reactions, financial results, or employee retention.

There are at least five important aspects of M&A that are of significance to students of organization. (Economists extensively study other aspects of M&A, such as industry concentration and anti-trust implications). First, M&A involve the valuation of the firm as a bundle of resources. The parties to an M&A transaction must agree on a price that reflects the value of the combination of assets across firms. Second, M&A involve changes to the legal boundaries of the firms involved, and the transfer of property rights on underlying assets. Third, M&A represent a means to diversify a firm's product-market scope (Singh and Montgomery, 1987). Fourth, the implementation of M&A involves the integration of elements of formal organization (such as structures, systems, and processes) and informal organization (such as culture and networks) across formerly independent firms (Puranam and Singh, 2002). Fifth, since many firms engage in a program of M&A, multiple M&A transactions can give rise to experience curve effects (Zollo and Singh, 2000).

The extensive engagement of organization scholars with these aspects of M&A is reflected in their popularity as a research setting. In some ways, M&A transactions are to the organization theorist what fruit-flies are to the biologist, as they present a convenient and useful research setting – they are discrete, easily observable events, occur frequently, and it is relatively easy to collect data about them. Since they also have enormous economic significance, M&A transactions represent an opportunity to do theoretically rigorous work that has high impact on practice.

See also *inter-organizational relations; learning, organizational; organizational change*

Bibliography

Puranam, P., and Singh, H. (2002). Technological interdependence, coordination costs and intra-organizational boundaries (working paper): London Business School.

Singh, H., and Montgomery, C. A. (1987). Corporate acquisition strategies and economic performance. *Strategic Management Journal*, 8 **(4)**: 377–86.

Zollo, M., and Singh, H. (2000). The Impact Of Knowledge Codification, Experience Trajectories And Integration Strategies On The Performance Of Corporate Acquisitions: The Wharton School.

meta-analysis

see RESEARCH METHODS; VALIDITY GENERALIZATION

metaphor

John Van Maanen

A metaphor provides a way of seeing or representing one thing in terms of another. It is a ubiquitous figure of speech or master trope in which a word or phrase that typically denotes one kind of object or idea is used to replace another object or idea, thus suggesting an analogy or likeness between them. A metaphor creates a figurative relationship between the two that is often unnoticed in everyday thought and speech. To say that "organizations are machines" is to claim merely that organizations are like machines for the purpose at hand in a given communicative context (*see* COMMUNICATION). The metaphor allows speakers and listeners to consider an organization *as if* it were a machine. By so doing, metaphor asserts similarity in differences and, less obviously perhaps, differences in similarity. Thus, by claiming similarity, a metaphor sets something apart from other things and establishes differences from them (e.g., as a machine, an organization does not live and die but is built and dismantled); but also, by taking an object in terms of the metaphor, the object is provided with selective but distinct characteristics associated with the term of similarity (e.g., as a machine, an organization is predictable, impersonal, functional, and occasionally in need of repair).

Metaphors should be held loosely, for they may well conceal as much as they reveal. For example, the machine metaphor may mislead those who find it attractive by allowing them to read too little into an organization, just as another metaphor such as a "culture" or a "family" may allow its users to read too much into an organization. Popular metaphors are thus seductive. One of the central insights emerging from the study of metaphor and language use is that as a particular metaphor becomes conventionalized (widely communicated, accepted, and virtually taken for granted), users of the metaphor take the relationship it conveys between two objects or ideas to be the obvious, correct, or literal one. The use of other possible metaphors is thus obliterated and one way of seeing becomes a way of not seeing. Metaphors, then, are not merely linguistic or literary devices that decorate speech, but are the conceptual building blocks by which we forge our understandings of the world. They provide the constructive force for representing experience and thus help shape what we know and how we think.

The analysis of metaphor is slowly penetrating organizational studies. Largely imported from the humanities – in particular, literary criticism and theory – a number of organizational behavior scholars are finding the explication of metaphors quite useful for uncovering "deep" patterns or principles that appear to regulate organizational life. When metaphors are extended and generalized they become paradigms, representing broad but relatively cohesive and coherent ways of seeing the world and interpreting situations of both a routine and novel sort. From this perspective, organizations operate in reasonably consistent ways because they provide their members (and customers, clients, suppliers, stockholders, and so on) with action-generating paradigms. Moreover, these paradigms are discoverable through intensive study. Stories, allegories, legends, uniqueness tales, and creation myths can be read by an analyst as organizing metaphors that incorporate histories, VALUES, purposes, and motives of individuals and groups. The epistemological strategy and perspective are structural and, when used to suggest that a given metaphor (or paradigm) is essentially arbitrary rather than "natural" or "real," it is akin to deconstruction. Ironically, the use of metaphor to explain organization behavior has probably been most powerful when applied to the organization behavior research community itself, where it has been argued that most – if not all – of the research and theory groups in the field are more or less trapped by the metaphors that inform their practice, including those who themselves study metaphors. Such is the state – and point – of metaphor analysis.

See also *ideology; organizational culture; postmodernism; symbolism*

Bibliography

Burke, K. (1962). *A Grammar of Motives and a Rhetoric of Motives.* Cleveland, OH: Meridian.

Lakoff, G. and Johnson, M. (1980). *Metaphors We Live By.* Chicago: University of Chicago Press.

Manning, P. K. (1979). Metaphors of the field. *Administrative Science Quarterly*, **24**, 660–71.

Morgan, G. (1986). *Images of Organizations.* Newbury Park, CA: Sage.

Schon, D. (1979). Generative metaphor. In A. Ortony (ed.), *Metaphor and Thought.* Cambridge: Cambridge University Press, 254–83.

White, H. (1980). *Tropics of Discourse.* Baltimore, MD: Johns Hopkins University Press.

M-form organization

see ORGANIZATIONAL DESIGN; ORGANIZATIONAL STRUCTURE

minorities

see DISCRIMINATION; DIVERSITY MANAGEMENT

minority group influence

Michael A. West

Minority group influence is a process whereby a numerical or POWER minority within a group or organization brings about enduring change in the attitudes and behavior of those in the majority through persistent repetition of their minority position.

Moscovici (1976) argued that repeated exposure to a consistent minority view leads to marked and internalized changes in attitudes and behaviors among the majority. When people conform to a majority view they generally comply pub-

licly without necessarily changing their private beliefs. Minorities, in contrast, appear to produce a shift in private views rather than public compliance. Evidence further suggests that even if they do not cause the majority to adopt their viewpoints, minorities encourage greater independence and CREATIVITY in thinking about the specific issues they raise.

Nemeth and Nemeth Brown (2003) show that we explore the view expressed by a minority more thoroughly than we do the view of a majority with which we disagree and this causes us to consider the issue from multiple viewpoints. Because we feel uncomfortable disagreeing with a majority, we tend to seek information that supports the majority's position. When we hear a persistently expressed minority position we think more creatively around the issue because there is no imperative to find reasons to agree.

Minorities therefore stimulate divergent thought by encouraging consideration of issues from multiple perspectives (Nemeth and Nemeth Brown, 2003). Moscovici gives the examples of the impact on public attitudes of the Green and Feminist Movements in the 1970s and 1980s. Research in newly formed teams also demonstrates the phenomenon in organizational settings (De Dreu and West, 2001).

An implication for organizations is that tolerating the expression of deviant views may be important if creativity and adaptability are not to be stifled. The conflict created by minorities can be seen as a valuable source of creative energy within organizations. However, using devil's advocates as a means of encouraging minority influence is not effective, since authentic dissent rather than role playing appears to produce the independent and creative thinking that are the hallmarks of minority influence (Nemeth, Rogers, and Brown, 2001).

Research in social psychology and observation of organizational practice suggests that:

1   Minorities are most influential when they are persistent.
2   A lone deviant is dramatically less effective than a pair expressing minority opinions and, thereafter, the larger the minority group, in general, the greater its influence.
3   The arguments presented by minorities must be coherent and convincing to be influential.

4   The minority must be seen to be acting out of principle, not for ulterior motives or out of self-interest, if they are not to be dismissed.
5   Consistent but flexible minorities are more influential than those which are seen as consistent but rigid.
6   Minority dissent creates conflict but minorities are seen as competent.

Almost all the research in this promising area has been conducted in social psychology laboratory settings rather than in organizations. There is much promise in exploring minority influence processes for understanding team innovation and organizational change (West, in press).

See also *coalition formation; group cohesiveness; group decision-making; groupthink; intergroup relations; politics*

Bibliography

De Dreu, C. K. W. and West, M. A. (2001). Minority dissent and team innovation: The importance of participation in decision-making. *Journal of Applied Psychology*, **86** (6), 1191–201.

Moscovici, S. (1976). *Social Influence and Social Change*. London: Academic Press.

Nemeth, C. J. and Nemeth Brown, B. (2003). Better than individuals? The potential benefits of dissent and diversity for group creativity. In P. B. Paulus and B. J. Nijstad (eds.), *Group Creativity: Innovation through Collaboration*. Oxford: Oxford University Press, 63–84.

Nemeth, C. J., Rogers, J. D., and Brown, K. S. (2001). Devil's advocate vs. authentic dissent: Stimulating quantity and quality. *European Journal of Social Psychology*, **31**, 707–29.

West, M. A. (in press). Dissent in teams and organizations: Lessons for team innovation and empowerment. In P. A. M. Van Lange (ed.), *Bridging Social Psychology*. Amsterdam: KLI.

mission statements

see IDENTITY, ORGANIZATIONAL

modeling

see COMPUTER SIMULATION; RESEARCH METHODS

monotony

see JOB DESIGN; JOB SATISFACTION; STRESS

mood

see EMOTION IN ORGANIZATIONS

morale

see JOB SATISFACTION; ORGANIZATIONAL CLIMATE

motivation

Ruth Kanfer

Motivation refers to the set of psychological processes governing the direction, intensity, and persistence of actions that are not due solely to overwhelming environmental demands that coerce or force action (Vroom, 1964). The field of work motivation seeks to understand, explain, and predict:

1   The person and contextual determinants and consequences of goal choice (direction of action).
2   How much effort an individual allocates and the strategies used to accomplish various salient goals (intensity of action and action strategies).
3   How long an individual perseveres toward goal accomplishment, particularly in the face of difficulties (persistence of action).

The topic of motivation has a long history in the field of basic and applied psychology (e.g., Weiner, 1980). Work motivation represents a specialty area in the broader field of human motivation that focuses directly on theories, research, and practices that have implications for individual behavior in the context of work, and may be applied to a variety of human resource management activities, including selection, training, and managerial/leadership practices.

In the organizational behavior domain, motivation often refers to a critical management activity; that is, to the techniques used by managers for the purpose of facilitating employee behaviors that accomplish organizational goals. Such techniques may be targeted at the individual level or at the team level, such as when leaders seek to enhance motivation and performance of all team members. Managerial practices designed to enhance employee and/or team performance are rarely straightforward applications of particular work motivation theories, but rather are uniquely tailored activities that incorporate motivational principles in the broader context of the organization's culture, team dynamics, and personnel management practices. The tailoring of motivational strategies to the specific work context makes evaluation of the true validity of specific motivation theories to organizational productivity difficult. However, reviews of the utility of motivation paradigms (including, for example, GOAL SETTING, MANAGEMENT BY OBJECTIVES, JOB DESIGN) (Katzell and Guzzo, 1983) provide evidence that motivational techniques used by managers can have substantial effects on organizationally relevant outcomes.

MOTIVATION TENETS

Three assumptions guide contemporary thinking and research on work motivation. First, motivation is not directly observable. What is observed is a stream of behavior and the products of those behaviors. Motivation is inferred from a systematic analysis of how characteristics of the individual, task, and environment influence behavior and aspects of job performance. Second, motivation is not a fixed attribute of the individual. Unlike motives (which are often defined in terms of stable individual differences in motivational orientation or dispositional tendencies), motivation refers to a dynamic, internal state resulting from the independent and joint influences of personal and situational factors. As such, an individual's motivation for specific activities or tasks may change as a consequence of change in any part of the system. In other words, although modern approaches often accord INDIVIDUAL DIFFERENCES in PERSONALITY a prominent role in motivation, motivation is not viewed as an individual trait, but rather as a dynamic state affected by the continuous interplay of personal, social, and organizational factors.

Third, motivation has its primary effect on behavior (covert and overt); that is, what an individual chooses to do and how intensely and persistently an individual works to accomplish his or her goal. The distinction between motivational effects on behavior versus job performance is of critical importance for understanding motivation effects in the work domain. In the workplace, changes in motivation may or may not affect job performance depending on how job performance is defined and evaluated. Programs designed to enhance job performance by increasing employee motivation may be unsuccessful if job performance is not immediately or substantially affected by an individual's on-task effort.

The processes by which motivation influences behavior and performance are best represented as comprised of two interrelated psychological systems: goal choice and goal striving (or self-regulation) (e.g., Heckhausen, 1991; Kanfer and Hagerman, 1987; Kanfer, 1990). Cognitive theories of motivation describe goal choice as a decision-making/COMMITMENT process in which choice is determined jointly by personal factors and the individual's perceptions of the situation. The product of this process, an individual's intentions or goals, provides a mental representation of a future situation that signifies a desired end-state. Relative to intentions, goals define more specific end-states. Commitment to a goal serves to direct the individual's attention, mobilize the individual's effort toward goal attainment, and support goal persistence. Intentions and goals may relate to the individual's immediate behavior (e.g., my goal is to write two reports today) or to a longer-term outcome (e.g., my goal is to obtain a promotion). Person and situation characteristics influence goal choice as well as the specificity at which goals are articulated.

Theories that describe the decision-making process with respect to goal choice (e.g., Vroom, 1964) have frequently been used to successfully predict a variety of behaviors in which goals are readily attainable (e.g., choice among job offers). However, when goals involve multiple tasks or protracted effort in the face of difficulties, prediction of performance requires additional consideration of the individual's commitment to the goal as well as other motivational processes.

Goal striving refers to the motivational mechanisms set into motion with the adoption of difficult goals for which accomplishment requires active self-regulation of one's cognitions, emotions, and/or actions. Goals, such as learning a complex new skill or earning a college degree, require self-regulatory or volitional processes by which the individual can develop subgoals, monitor his or her performance, and evaluate activities with respect to goal progress. Deficits in the goal striving system may thwart successful transition of a goal into action and obscure or weaken the effect of motivation on performance.

WORK MOTIVATION OVERVIEW

Numerous theories of work motivation have been proposed over the past century. Comprehensive reviews by Campbell and Pritchard (1976), Kanfer (1990, 1992), and Mitchell and Daniels (2003) document major advances in work motivation through the mid-1970s, from the mid-1970s through early 1990s, and from the early 1990s to present, respectively. In concert with theoretical advances, a tremendous variety of programs and techniques have been developed for use in organizational settings. Although the popularity of particular motivation theories or techniques waxes and wanes, there is little evidence to indicate any decline in basic or applied interest in the topic over the past century. Motivation theories, research, and practices remain a topic of central importance in industrial/organizational psychology, organizational behavior, executive development, and managerial and job training programs.

HISTORICAL TRENDS

The history of the application of scientific principles for enhancing work performance via changes in an individual's motivation corresponds closely to theoretical and empirical developments in the study of human behavior and the workplace. Early management theories, such as Taylor's SCIENTIFIC MANAGEMENT, made reference to the longstanding practice of using financial compensation to spur motivation and job performance. The emergence of personality and learning theories in psychology during the early to mid-1900s led to the development of motivational programs aimed at enhancing performance by creating organizational conditions that facilitated the match between employee need satisfaction and increased on-task effort. During the 1940s through the 1960s, explosive growth in theorizing and research on the determinants of choice led to the development of models aimed at enhancing prediction of workplace behaviors, such as turnover. During this same period, results of the Hawthorne studies provided striking evidence for the influence of social norms and other non-financial incentives on work motivation and performance.

The rise of behaviorism during the mid-1900s stressed the importance of operant learning and reinforcement as a means of altering workplace behavior. Organizational interventions using behavior modification techniques were developed to enhance performance on a variety of dimensions, such as safety. At the same time, progress in the field of task characteristics led to greater consideration of the motivating potential of jobs. Integration of this work with intrinsic motivation theorizing led to the development of interventions aimed at enhancing motivation and performance through job redesign. Similar in some respects to earlier work by Herzberg that focused on psychological determinants of job satisfaction, job redesign efforts aimed to strengthen employee motivation by creating work environments that promoted a sense of achievement, perceptions of competence, and autonomy.

During the last third of the twentieth century, work motivation researchers focused almost exclusively on goals and the mechanisms by which goals influence action. Numerous studies on goal setting (see Locke et al., 1981) demonstrated the efficacy of goal setting on task performance and facilitated the popularity of management by objective programs. Based on a view of human behavior that espoused goals as the immediate precursors of action, researchers examined the processes by which goals influence behavior and performance using social cognitive theory (e.g., Bandura, 1986), cybernetic control theory (e.g., Carver and Scheier, 1981), and self-regulation theory (e.g., Kanfer and Hagerman, 1987). Findings obtained in this paradigm demonstrate the influence of both person factors, such as SELF-EFFICACY, and situational factors, such as participative goal setting, on goal setting and self-regulation processes that, in turn, influence performance.

Although goal-based approaches continue to dominate the basic and applied literature, recent work has begun to reexamine the influence of individual differences in personal traits on goal choice and goal striving. Using the FIVE FACTOR MODEL OF PERSONALITY to organize the literature, Barrick and Mount (1991) provide strong meta-analytic evidence for relationships between several personality factors and training and performance outcomes across a broad range of jobs. Other researchers have further sought to identify specific classes of personal traits, such as approach and avoidance motivational orientation, that influence goal choice and goal striving processes (e.g., Kanfer and Heggestad, 1997).

Most organizational researchers and practitioners recognize that work motivation entails a complex set of processes and that there is no one "best" theory or program. As a result, there has been a growing trend to develop broad formulations that subsume or complement major tenets of goal choice, behavioral, and goal striving theories of action. From a practical perspective, the broadening of theories has placed a greater burden on practitioners to conduct a careful analysis of the motivational problem in order to select an appropriate intervention perspective.

Technological, economic, and demographic trends have also spurred new practical questions that require consideration of how adult development and new workplace realities may uniquely influence an individual's goals and work effort. Changing work role demands associated with the implementation of new technologies, for example, have raised new practical questions, such as how best to motivate continuous employee learning and motivation among short-term or contract employees and employees working off-site.

KEY PERSPECTIVES

Modern approaches to motivation may be organized into three related clusters:

- Personality-based views
- Cognitive choice/decision approaches
- Goal/self-regulation formulations.

The following section highlights major assumptions, theories, and findings from each perspective.

Personality-based views of motivation emphasize the influence of relatively enduring characteristics of persons as they affect goal choice and striving. Three types of personality-based work motivation perspectives may be distinguished. The first type pertains to models, such as Maslow's (1954) Need Hierarchy Theory. In these approaches, workplace behavior and satisfaction are posited to be powerfully determined by an individual's current need state within a universal hierarchy of need categories. By understanding which needs were most salient to an individual (e.g., affiliation, self-actualization needs), organizations could enhance work performance and satisfaction by creating environments that facilitated need satisfaction. Although this perspective is well known, scientific research has consistently failed to provide support for basic tenets of the model or to demonstrate that this model is useful in predicting workplace behaviors.

The second type of personality perspective derives from considering the influence of a single or small set of universal or psychologically based motives that may affect behavior and performance. A great deal of work in this perspective has focused on the role of individual differences in strength of achievement motives (i.e., need for achievement). Substantial research in this area indicates that individuals who score high on tests of achievement motivation are more likely to select challenging task goals and to persist longer than persons who score low on this trait (Heckhausen, 1991). Progress over the past decade suggests that achievement motivation may further be usefully distinguished in terms of two goal or motivational orientations: approach or appetitive orientation and avoidance or prevention orientation. Initial findings in this area suggest distinct influences for each form of motivational orientation on self-regulatory processes and workplace behaviors (VandeWalle, 1997).

During the mid-1900s, attention also focused on the role of universal motives, such as the need for competence, self-determination, and organizational fairness/justice. In contrast to achievement motivation theories, motive theories such as Deci's Cognitive Evaluation Theory and Adam's EQUITY THEORY do not stress individual differences in the degree of the motive, but rather the conditions that arouse the motive and its influence on behavior. In equity theory, for example, arousal of the justice motive occurs when the individual perceives an imbalance in the ratio of his or her inputs and outcomes relative to others.

Unlike broad personality theory formulations, motive-based theories more fully specify the organizational conditions that instigate motive-based behaviors, as well as the cognitive processes by which the motive affects behavior. Newer formulations of these approaches in the areas of intrinsic motivation and organizational justice enjoy substantial popularity in the work motivation literature.

The third personality perspective on work motivation emerged in the early 1980s as a direct result of advances in basic research on the structure of personality and measurement of basic personality dimensions. The results of this work led to general agreement regarding the existence of five basic personality dimensions, or trait factors: (1) neuroticism, (2) extraversion, (3) openness to experience, (4) agreeableness, and (5) conscientiousness. Of the five factors, conscientiousness represents the trait dimension most closely associated with motivation. Recent investigations of the association between personality dimensions and job performance indicate that conscientiousness shows consistent relations with several dimensions of job performance (e.g., Barrick and Mount, 1991).These results have spurred interest in delineating how individual differences on motivationally related traits affect work behavior and performance, particularly in service sector jobs, such as sales.

Cognitive choice/decision approaches emphasize two determinants of choice and action: (1) the individual's expectations (i.e., the individual's perception of the relationship between effort and performance level, as well as between performance level and salient outcomes); and (2) the individual's subjective valuation of the expected consequences associated with various alternative actions (i.e., the anticipated affect

associated with attainment of various outcomes). These formulations, known as Expectancy Value (E x V) theories, are intended to predict an individual's choice or decisions, not necessarily subsequent performance. In most models, individuals are viewed as rational decision-makers who make choices in line with the principle of maximizing the likelihood of positive affect. (Note, however, that E x V models predict choice behavior on the basis of the individual's perceptions; misperceptions of the environment or relationship between effort, performance, and outcomes may yield "poor" decisions.) In the motivational realm, choices may be made with regard to direction (goal choice), intensity (goal striving), or persistence of a specific course of action.

The popularity of $E \times V$ approaches reached a peak in the early 1980s. During the 1970s and 1980s, organizational research focused on testing key tenets of these models and investigating the predictive validity of various models. Results from this period indicated several limitations and difficulties associated with basic assumptions of the $E \times V$ models, and lower than expected levels of predictive validity for task and job performance criteria (though predictive validity for job choice has been substantially better; for a review, see Mitchell, 1982). Limitations of $E \times V$ models in predicting ongoing workplace behaviors led to a general decline in the use of classic formulations in field research during the 1980s, and to the development of modern, integrative choice frameworks, such as Naylor, Pritchard, and Ilgen's (1980) theory of organizational behavior. The Naylor et al. theory incorporates several of the classic assumptions of $E \times V$ theorizing, but uses a broader framework of decision-making that includes individual differences in personality as well as other motivational processes, such as SELF-REGULATION.

Goal/Self-regulation formulations of work motivation emphasize the processes and factors that affect goal striving, or the translation of an individual's goal into action. In organizational psychology, the best-known goal setting model was developed by Locke and his colleagues (Locke et al., 1981; Locke and Latham, 1990) and focuses on the relationship between goals and work behavior. Other broad formulations that specify the psychological processes involved in goal striving include cybernetic control formulations based on cybernetic control theory (Diefendorff and Lord, 2003), resource allocation theory (Kanfer and Ackerman, 1989), and social-cognitive theory (Gist and Mitchell, 1992).

Early organizational goal setting research examined the effects of explicit goal assignments that varied in difficulty and specificity. The majority of these studies indicated higher levels of performance among persons assigned difficult and specific goals (e.g., make six sales this week), compared to persons assigned "do your best" goals.

Subsequent research has examined the boundary conditions of this robust effect. Results of this research indicate two critical preconditions for demonstration of the positive goal–performance relationship; namely, that the individual adopt the goal assignment and that the individual obtain performance feedback. Several studies indicate that specific, difficult goal assignments may be more effective when used with relatively simple tasks than complex tasks.

Over the past decade, organizational researchers have used social-cognitive, resource allocation, and cybernetic control theories to further delineate how particular attributes of the goal, the person, and the situation influence goal striving and performance. Studies from these theoretical perspectives indicate further conditions that mediate the effect of goals on task performance. Findings suggest that task demands, percepts of self-efficacy, goal commitment, and orientation toward task accomplishment are also important determinants of the effectiveness of goal setting methods.

SUMMARY

The plethora of work motivation theories and motivational techniques underscores both the complexity of understanding and predicting individual behavior as well as the substantial progress that has been made in this domain. Older work motivation theories, such as Alderfer's adaptation of Maslow's Need Hierarchy Theory, and Vroom's Expectancy Theory, have given way to new approaches that build upon advances in cognitive psychology, information processing, personality, and self-regulation. These newer

perspectives, including for example, Locke and Latham's (1990) goal setting theory, Kanfer and Ackerman's (1989) resource allocation model of learning and performance, Naylor, Pritchard, and Ilgen's (1980) theory of behavior, Diefendorff and Lord's (2003) control theory, and Tett and Burnett's (2003) personality-based interactionist model of job performance, often incorporate elements of older theories, but do so in ways that reduce the sharp distinctions between various approaches. New approaches differ from older conceptualizations in other ways as well. For example, contemporary models of motivation place a central emphasis on the role of goals as the primary concept for linking individuals and organizations. In addition, these approaches typically focus on predicting specific job behaviors, rather than an overall job performance or satisfaction criterion.

Although there has been substantial progress in the theoretical field of work motivation, the dynamics of the modern workplace continue to raise important questions and challenges to the field. Two topics of particular relevance for the coming decade are indicated below.

The social/cultural context of work   There is widespread agreement regarding the influence of the social context as an important determinant of work motivation and performance. This has led to the inclusion of broad "social factors" in several motivation models. But, until recently, little attention was paid to understanding the unique and dynamic motivational processes operative in workgroup or team contexts. The growing use of teams in organizations has renewed interest in this facet of motivation theory and research. In response, several ongoing programs of research, aimed at understanding motivation in team contexts, has begun to delineate how attributes of the team and the task affect the goals, motivation, and behaviors of individual team members (e.g., Chen et al., 2002; Sundstrom, 1999).

In a related vein, results of cross-cultural research indicate that the use and effectiveness of motivational techniques depend in part on the congruence of the motivational approach with the cultural values of the society in which it is used. Erez (1993) points out that motivational approaches consistent with collectivistic, group oriented values (e.g., autonomous work groups) tend to be more effective when used in collectivistic cultures such as Japan, China, and Israel. In contrast, motivational programs consistent with individualistic values (e.g., job enrichment, individual goal setting) are more frequently used and reported more effective in individualistic cultures, such as the United States. Erez (1993) suggests that with workforce globalization, the ultimate success of managerial techniques depends critically on their congruence with the cultural values of the particular organization and its social environment.

Managing motivation   Older views of work motivation imply that employees are relatively passive recipients of managerial and organizational efforts to maximize work motivation by providing appropriate work conditions and incentives. Research during the latter part of the twentieth century provides strong support for a different perspective; namely, that individuals operate as active agents in the motivation process. Substantial evidence indicates that employees interpret and seek to influence managerial practices and the workplace in accord with personal goals, schemas, and beliefs. Research in the areas of employee SOCIALIZATION, organizational justice, organizational change, and leadership indicates that motivation is affected not only by what the manager and/or organization offers the individual, but also by the way in which practices are implemented. Procedural justice research, for example, indicates that the process by which incentives are allocated or layoffs are realized exerts an important effect on employee attitudes and behavior, independent of the outcome (*see* JUSTICE, PROCEDURAL).

Second, and perhaps more importantly, demographic, technological, and economic changes in the workplace, forecast to continue for several decades, have focused attention on the identification of work conditions and managerial practices that promote work motivation and job performance in specific segments of the workforce. For example, in developed countries, the emergence of post-industrial economies and the aging workforce has led to greater emphasis on identifying the determinants of motivation for interpersonal effectiveness in the workplace and the person and situation factors that facilitate work motivation among older employees. Similarly, the development of new technologies that permit employees to work in locations far removed from the manager makes traditional supervisory methods for increasing employee motivation more difficult to implement and raises new motivational issues, such as how to encourage work goal commitment and increased task effort in non-traditional work environments, such as the home.

For these reasons, further advances in work motivation theory and practice are most likely to come from integrative approaches that explicitly consider how the employee governs his or her motivation in response to managerial/organizational practices. In this goal striving perspective, motivation may be represented as a job-related competency and employee resource; that is, a resource that organizations can help to develop/direct and that supervisors and employees co-manage. Recent training programs, based on SELF-REGULATION principles aimed at cultivating employee skills in managing work-related goals and actions, for example, represent a promising new avenue for potentially reducing substantial organizational costs associated with supervision, skill obsolescence, and poor performance.

See also *extrinsic and intrinsic motivation; incentives; job design*

Bibliography

Bandura, A. (1986). *Social Foundations of Thought and Action: A Social Cognitive Theory.* Englewood Cliffs, NJ: Prentice-Hall.

Barrick, M. R. and Mount, M. K. (1991). The big five personality dimensions and job performance: A meta-analysis. *Personnel Psychology,* **44,** 1–26.

Campbell, J. P. and Pritchard, R. D. (1976). Motivation theory in industrial and organizational psychology. In M. D. Dunnette (ed.), *Handbook of Industrial and Organizational Psychology.* Chicago: Rand McNally, 63–130.

Carver, C. S. and Scheier, M. F. (1981). *Attention and Self-Regulation: A Control Theory Approach to Human Behavior.* New York: Springer-Verlag.

Chen, G., Webber, S. S., Bliese, P. D., Mathieu, J. E., Payne, S. C., Born, D. H., and Zaccaro, S. J. (2002). Simultaneous examination of the antecedents and consequences of efficacy beliefs at multiple levels of analysis. *Human Performance,* **15,** 381–410.

Cropanzano, R. (ed.) (1993). *Justice in the Workplace*. Hillsdale, NJ: Lawrence Erlbaum Associates.

Deci, E. L. and Ryan, R. M. (1980). The empirical exploration of intrinsic motivational processes. In L. Berkowitz (ed.), *Advances in Experimental Social Psychology*, Vol. 13. New York: Academic Press, 39–80.

Diefendorff, J. M. and Lord, R. G. (2003). The volitional and strategic effects of planning on task performance and goal commitment. *Human Performance*, **16**, 365–87.

Erez, M. (1993). Toward a model of cross-cultural industrial and organizational psychology. In M. D. Dunnette and H. Triandis (eds.), *Handbook of Industrial and Organizational Psychology*, Vol. 4. Palo Alto, CA: Consulting Psychologists Press.

Gist, M. E. and Mitchell, T. R. (1992). Self-efficacy: A theoretical analysis of its determinants and malleability. *Academy of Management Review*, 17, 183–211.

Heckhausen, H. (1991). *Motivation and Action*. New York: Springer-Verlag.

Kanfer, F. H. and Hagerman, S. M. (1987). A model of self-regulation. In F. Halisch and J. Kuhl (eds.), *Motivation, Intention, and Volition*. New York: Springer-Verlag, 293–307.

Kanfer, R. (1990). Motivation theory and industrial/organizational psychology. In M. D. Dunnette and L. Hough (eds.), *Handbook of Industrial and Organizational Psychology*, Vol. 1. Palo Alto, CA: Consulting Psychologists Press, 75–170.

Kanfer, R. (1992). Work motivation: New directions in theory and research. In C. L. Cooper and I. T. Robertson (eds.), *International Review of Industrial and Organizational Psychology*, Vol. 7. London: Wiley, 1–53.

Kanfer, R. and Ackerman, P. L. (1989). Motivation and cognitive abilities: An integrative/aptitude-treatment interaction approach to skill acquisition. *Journal of Applied Psychology – Monograph*, **74**, 657–90.

Kanfer, R. and Heggestad, E. (1997). Motivational traits and skills: A person-centered approach to work motivation. In L. L. Cummings and B. M. Staw (eds.), *Research in Organizational Behavior*, Vol. 19. Greenwich, CT: JAI Press, 1–57.

Katzell, R. A. and Guzzo, R. A. (1983). Psychological approaches to productivity improvement. *American Psychologist*, **45**, 144–53.

Locke, E. A. and Latham, G. P. (1990). *A Theory of Goal Setting and Task Performance*. New York: Prentice-Hall.

Locke, E. A., Shaw, K. N., Saari, L. M., and Latham, G. P. (1981). Goal setting and task performance: 1969–1980. *Psychological Bulletin*, **90**, 125–52.

Lord, R. G. and Kernan, M. C. (1989). Application of control theory to work settings. In W. A. Herschberger (ed.), *Volitional Action*. New York: Elsevier Science, 493–514.

Maslow, A. (1954). *Motivation and Personality*. New York: Harper and Row.

Mitchell, T. R. (1982). Expectancy-value models in organizational psychology. In N. T. Feather (ed.), *Expectations and Actions: Expectancy-Value Models in Psychology*. Hillsdale, NJ: Lawrence Erlbaum Associates, 293–312.

Mitchell, T. R. and Daniels, D. (2003). Motivation. In W. C. Borman, D. R. Ilgen, and R. J. Klimoski (eds.), *Handbook of Psychology*, Vol. 12. Hoboken, NJ: John Wiley and Sons, 225–54.

Naylor, J. C., Pritchard, R. D., and Ilgen, D. R. (1980). *A Theory of Behavior in Organizations*. New York: Academic Press.

Sundstrom, E. (1999). *Supporting Work Team Effectiveness: Best Management Practices for Fostering High Team Performance*. San Francisco: Jossey-Bass.

Tett, R. P. and Burnett, D. D. (2003). A personality trait-based interactionist model of job performance. *Journal of Applied Psychology*, **88**, 500–17.

VandeWalle, D. M. (1997). Development and validation of a work domain goal-orientation instrument. *Educational and Psychological Measurement*, **57**, 995–1015.

Vroom, V. H. (1964). *Work and Motivation*. New York: Wiley.

Weiner, B. (1980). *Human Motivation*. New York: Holt, Rinehart, and Winston.

motivation and performance

Ruth Kanfer

MOTIVATION represents one of several major determinants of performance in work settings. Four features of the relationship between motivation and performance may be noted. First, the two constructs are not synonymous. Motivation refers to the direction, intensity, and persistence of action. Performance typically refers to the evaluation of job related behaviors with respect to organizational objectives. Individuals may be motivated yet perform poorly if the behaviors they enact do not correspond to the established performance criterion. Second, task demands have a substantial influence on the extent to which motivation level may affect task or job performance. Proportionately larger increases in motivation are required for improved performance in well-learned or high complexity tasks, compared to novel tasks. Third, motivation and performance are reciprocally related.

Knowledge of one's performance can weaken or strengthen subsequent motivation, depending on how performance feedback is interpreted. Fourth, motivation is most likely to affect performance when performance is *not* situationally constrained; that is, when changes in effort are directly related to performance. In summary, the relationship between motivation and performance is dynamic and complex, depending on how performance is defined, the nature of the task, how performance FEEDBACK is interpreted, and the extent to which environmental factors may limit performance accomplishments.

See also *organizational effectiveness; performance appraisal/ performance management*

Bibliography

Kanfer, R. and Ackerman, P. L. (1989). Motivation and cognitive abilities: An integrative/aptitude-treatment interaction approach to skill acquisition. *Journal of Applied Psychology – Monograph*, **74**, 657–90.

Vroom, V. H. (1964). *Work and Motivation*. New York: Wiley.

motivator/hygiene theory

see JOB SATISFACTION; MOTIVATION

multi-level analysis

see LEVELS OF ANALYSIS; RESEARCH METHODS

N

natural selection

see EVOLUTIONARY PERSPECTIVES; EVOLU-
TIONARY PSYCHOLOGY

negotiation

Max Bazerman

When two or more parties need to reach a joint
decision but have different preferences, they
negotiate. They may not be sitting around a
bargaining table; they may not be making explicit offers and counter-offers; they may not even
be making statements suggesting that they are on
different sides. However, as long as their preferences concerning the joint decision are not identical, they have to negotiate to reach a mutually
agreeable outcome.

Over the last decade the topic of negotiation
has captivated the field of organizational
behavior, and more broadly, business schools.
It has grown to be one of the most popular
topics of instruction, and the current state of
research is very different as a result of the interest in this topic. This review will highlight the six dominant areas of research in
negotiation:

1 INDIVIDUAL DIFFERENCES
2 Situational characteristics
3 GAME THEORY
4 Asymmetrically prescriptive/descriptive
5 Cognitive
6 Bringing back social factors

More detailed reviews can be found elsewhere
(Bazerman, Curhan, and Moore, 2000).

INDIVIDUAL DIFFERENCES

During the 1960s and early 1970s, the majority
of psychological research conducted on negotiations emphasized dispositional variables (Rubin
and Brown, 1975) or traits, defined as individual
attributes such as demographic characteristics,
PERSONALITY variables, and motivated behavioral tendencies unique to individual negotiators. Demographic characteristics (e.g., AGE,
GENDER, race, etc.), RISK TAKING tendencies,
LOCUS OF CONTROL, cognitive complexity,
tolerance for ambiguity, self-esteem, authoritarianism, and machiavellianism were all hot research topics in 1960s negotiation literature
(Rubin and Brown, 1975).

Since bargaining is clearly an interpersonal
activity, it seems logical that the participants'
dispositions *should* exert significant influence
on the process and outcomes of negotiations.
Unfortunately, despite numerous studies, dispositional evidence is rarely convincing. When
effects have been found, situational features imposed upon the negotiators often reduce or
negate these effects. As a result, individual attributes typically do not account for significant
variance in negotiator behavior.

A number of authors have reached the conclusion that individual differences offer little
insight into predicting negotiator behavior and
negotiation outcomes: "there are few significant
relationships between personality and negotiation outcomes" (Lewicki and Litterer, 1985).

In addition to the lack of predictability from
individual differences research, this literature
has also been criticized for its lack of relevance
to practice. Bazerman and Carroll (1987)
argue that individual differences are of limited
value because of their fixed nature (i.e., they are

not under the control of the negotiator). Furthermore, individuals, even so-called experts, are known to be poor at making clinical assessments about another person's personality in order to formulate accurately an opposing strategy.

In summary, the current literature on dispositional variables in negotiation offers few concrete findings. Future research in this direction requires clear evidence, rather than intuitive assertions, that dispositions are important to predicting the outcomes of negotiations.

SITUATIONAL CHARACTERISTICS

Situational characteristics are the relatively fixed, contextual components that define the negotiation. Situational research considers the impact of varying these contextual features on negotiated outcomes. Examples of situational variables include the presence or absence of a constituency, the form of COMMUNICATION between negotiators, the relative POWER of the parties, deadlines, the number of people representing each side, and the effects of third parties.

Research on situational variables has contributed much to our understanding of the negotiation process and has directed both practitioners and academics to consider important structural components. For example, situational research has found that the presence of observers in a negotiation can dramatically affect its outcome. This effect holds whether the observers are physically or only psychologically present. Further, whether the observers are an audience (i.e., those who do not have a vested interest in the outcome of the negotiation) or a constituency (i.e., those who will be affected by the negotiation) is of little importance in predicting the behavior of the negotiator (Rubin and Brown, 1975).

One of the main drawbacks of situational research is similar to that of individual differences research. Situational factors represent aspects of the negotiation that are usually external to the participants and beyond the individual's control. For example, in organizational settings, participants' control over third-party intervention is limited by their willingness to make the dispute visible and salient. If and when the participants do, their manager usually decides how he or she will intervene as a third party (Murnighan, 1987)

(*see* CONFLICT AND CONFLICT MANAGEMENT).

The same criticism holds true for other situational factors, such as the relative power of the negotiators or the prevailing deadlines. While negotiators can be advised to identify ways in which to manipulate their perceived power, obvious power disparities, resulting from resource munificence, hierarchical legitimacy, or expertise, are less malleable. Negotiators are often best served by developing strategies for addressing these power differentials instead of trying to change them.

THE ECONOMIC STUDY OF GAME THEORY

The earliest attempts at providing prescriptive advice to negotiators were made by economists. The most well-developed component of this economic school of thought is game theory. In game theory, mathematical models are developed to analyze the outcomes that will emerge in multiparty, DECISION-MAKING contexts if all parties act rationally. To analyze a game, specific conditions are outlined which define how decisions are to be made (e.g., the order in which players get to choose their moves) and utility measures of outcomes for each player are attached to *every* possible combination of player moves. The actual analysis focuses on predicting whether or not an agreement will be reached, and if one is reached, what the specific nature of that agreement will be. The advantage of game theory is that, given absolute RATIONALITY, it provides the most precise prescriptive advice available to the negotiator. The disadvantages of game theory are twofold. First, it relies upon being able to completely describe all options and associated outcomes for every possible combination of moves in a given situation – a tedious task at its best, infinitely complex at its worst. Second, it requires all players to act rationally at all times. In contrast, individuals often behave irrationally in systematically predictable ways that are not easily captured within rational analyses.

ASYMMETRICALLY PRESCRIPTIVE/ DESCRIPTIVE

As an alternative to game theoretic analyses of negotiation which take place in a world of "ultra-smart, impeccably rational, supersmart people,"

Howard Raiffa developed a decision-analytic approach to negotiations – an approach more appropriate to how "erring folks like you and me actually behave," rather than "how we should behave if we were smarter, thought harder, were more consistent, were all knowing" (Raiffa, 1982: 21). Raiffa's decision-analytic approach focuses on giving the best available advice to negotiators involved in real conflict with real people. His goal is to provide guidance for a focal negotiator given the most likely profile of the expected behavior of the other party. Thus, Raiffa's approach is prescriptive from the point of view of the party receiving advice, but descriptive from the point of view of the competing party. Raiffa's approach offers an excellent framework for approaching negotiations. However, it is limited in the insights that it provides concerning the behaviors that can be anticipated from the other party.

Raiffa's work represents a turning point in negotiation research for a number of reasons. First, in the context of developing a prescriptive model, he explicitly acknowledges the importance of developing accurate descriptions of opponents, rather than assuming they are fully rational. Second, by realizing that negotiators need advice, he recognizes that they do not intuitively follow purely rational strategies. Most importantly, he has initiated the groundwork for dialogue between prescriptive and descriptive researchers. His work demands descriptive models which allow the focal negotiator to anticipate the likely behavior of the opponent. In addition, we argue that decision analysts must acknowledge that negotiators have decision biases that limit their ability to follow such prescriptive advice.

Cognitive

The cognitive approach (Neale and Bazerman, 1991; Bazerman, Curhan, Moore, and Valley, 2000) addresses many of the questions that Raiffa's work leaves behind. If the negotiator and his or her opponent do not act rationally, what systematic departures from rationality can be predicted? Building on work in BEHAVIORAL DECISION RESEARCH, a number of deviations from rationality have been identified that can be expected in negotiations. Specifically, Neale and Bazerman's research on two-party negotiations suggests that negotiators tend to:

1   be inappropriately affected by the positive or negative frame in which risks are viewed;
2   anchor their number estimates in negotiations on irrelevant information;
3   over-rely on readily available information;
4   be overconfident about the likelihood of attaining outcomes that favor them;
5   assume that negotiation tasks are necessarily fixed-sum and thereby miss opportunities for mutually beneficial trade-offs between the parties;
6   escalate COMMITMENT to a previously selected course of action when it is no longer the most reasonable alternative (see COMMITMENT, ESCALATING);
7   overlook the valuable information that is available by considering the opponent's cognitive perspective;
8   retroactively devalue *any* concession that is made by the opponent (Ross, 1994).

These tendencies seriously limit the usefulness of traditional prescriptive models' rationality assumption (i.e., the belief that negotiators are accurate and consistent decision-makers). Further, these findings better inform Raiffa's prescriptive model by developing more detailed descriptions of negotiator behavior.

Bringing Back Social Factors

The behavioral decision perspective had a significant influence on the scholarship and practice of negotiation in the 1980s and 1990s. Many authors criticized this perspective for ignoring too many factors that were obviously important in negotiation (Greenhalgh and Chapman, 1995). Recently, research has developed that connects social psychological variables with a behavioral decision research perspective. In this research, the social factors argued to be missing from earlier research on decision-making have become specific topics of study (Bazerman, Curhan, and Moore, 2000). We briefly overview four streams of research in this perspective.

Relationships in negotiations   Relationships as an important ingredient in negotiation have been noted throughout the field's history. The contemporary study of relationships and negotiation can be trichotomized into three basic levels, focusing on the individual, the dyad, and the network. The first level includes studies of how judgment and preferences of individual negotiators are influenced by social context. An example of this work is Loewenstein, Thompson, and Bazerman's (1989), which found that disputants' reported preferences for monetary payoffs were greatly influenced by payoffs to and relationships with their hypothetical counterparts.

A second level explores how social relationships within dyads can influence negotiation processes and outcomes. An example of this work is the result that, given the opportunity to communicate freely, negotiators often appear irrational in their individual decision-making, yet reach dyadic outcomes that *outperform* game theoretic models (Valley, Moag, and Bazerman 1998). Finally, a third level is concerned with the influence of relationships on the broader network of actors. Tenbrunsel et al. (1999) show that people "satisfice" by matching with other people they already know rather than seeking out new partners at a cost to finding better fitting matches.

Egocentrism in negotiation   Negotiators are not objective in assessing a fair agreement. Instead, negotiators overweight the views that favor themselves (Babcock and Loewenstein, 1997). In addition, the more egocentric parties are, the more difficulty they have coming to agreement. This pattern has been replicated both in studies that used financial incentives for performance and across negotiation contexts.

Motivated illusions in negotiation   Most people view themselves, the world, and the future in a considerably more positive light than reality suggests (Taylor, 1989). In the negotiations domain, Kramer, Newton, and Pommerenke (1993) found that 68 percent of the MBA students in a negotiation class predicted that their bargaining outcomes would fall in the upper 25 percent of the class. Negotiators in a prisoner's dilemma act as if their decision will control the simultaneous decision of the other party, even when that is logically impossible (Shafir and Tversky, 1992). This research argues that one reason that parties cooperate in one-shot prisoner dilemma games is the illusion that their own cooperation will create cooperation in the other party.

Emotion in negotiation   We all know emotions matter in negotiation. However, interesting empirical evidence on this topic is quite new. Positive moods tend to increase negotiators' tendencies to select a cooperative strategy and enhance their ability to find integrative gains (Forgas, 1998). Angry negotiators are less accurate in judging the interests of opponent negotiators, and achieve lower joint gains (Allred et al., 1997). Anger makes negotiators more self-centered in their preferences and increases the likelihood that they will reject profitable offers in ultimatum games (Pillutla and Murnighan, 1996). In these experiments, fairly mild manipulations were able to create moderately strong effects. More research is needed on the hot emotions that intuitively convey to us the importance of emotion in negotiation.

Collectively, these six perspectives provide a summary of the recent history and current state of knowledge of the topic of negotiation. Future research is moving in a cognitive direction, which will hopefully serve the need to better resolve disputes in personal, organizational, and societal affairs.

See also *managerial and organizational cognition; trust*

Bibliography

Allred, K. G., Mallozzi, J. S., Matsui, F., and Raia, C. P. (1997). The influence of anger and compassion on negotiation performance. *Organizational Behavior and Human Decision Process*, **70**, 175–87.
Babcock, L. and Loewenstein, G. (1997). Explaining bargaining impasse: The role of self-serving biases. *Journal of Economic Perspectives*, **11**, 109–26.
Bazerman, M. H. and Carroll, J. S. (1987). Negotiator cognition. In B. Staw and L. L. Cummings (eds.), *Research in Organizational Behavior*, Vol. 9. Greenwich, CT: JAI Press, 247–88.
Bazerman, M. H., Curhan, J. R., and Moore, D. A. (2000). The death and rebirth of the social psychology of negotiation. In M. Clark and G. Fletcher (eds.), *Blackwell Handbook of Social Psychology*. Cambridge, MA: Blackwell.
Bazerman, M. H., Curhan, J., Moore, D., and Valley, K. (2000). Negotiations. *Annual Review of Psychology*. Palo Alto, CA: Annual Reviews.
Forgas, J. P. (1998). On feeling good and getting your way: Mood effects on negotiator cognition and bargaining strategies. *Journal of Personality and Social Psychology*, **74**, 565–77.

Greenhalgh, L. and Chapman, D. I. (1995). Joint decision-making: The inseparability of relationships and negotiation. In R. M. Kramer and D. M. Messick (eds.), *Negotiation as a Social Process*. Thousand Oaks, CA: Sage.

Kramer, R. M., Newton, E., and Pommerenke, P. L. (1993). Self-enhancement biases and negotiator judgment: Effects of self-esteem and mood. *Organizational Behavior and Human Decision Process*, **56**, 110–33.

Lewicki, R. J. and Litterer, J. A. (1985). *Negotiation*. Homewood, IL: R. D. Irwin.

Loewenstein, G., Thompson, L., and Bazerman, M. H. (1989). Social utility and decision-making in interpersonal contexts. *Journal of Personality and Social Psychology*, **57**, 426–41.

Murnighan, J. K. (1987). The structure of mediation and "intravention." *Negotiation Journal*, **2** (4), 351–6.

Neale, M. A. and Bazerman, M. H. (1991). *Cognition and Rationality in Negotiation*. New York: Free Press.

Pillutla, M. M. and Murnighan, J. K. (1996). Unfairness, anger, and spite: Emotional rejections of ultimatum offers. *Organizational Behavior and Human Decision Process*, **68**, 208–24.

Raiffa, H. (1982). *The Art and Science of Negotiation*. Cambridge, MA: Belknap Press.

Ross, E. (1994). Psychological barriers to dispute in resolution. In K. Arrow, R. Mnookin, L. Ross, A. Tversky, and R. Wilson (eds.), *Barriers to Conflict Resolution*. New York: Norton.

Rubin, J. Z. and Brown, B. R. (1975). *The Social Psychology of Bargaining and Negotiation*. New York: Academic Press.

Shafir E. and Tversky A. (1992). Thinking through uncertainty: Non-consequential reasoning and choice. *Cognitive Psychology*, **24**, 449–74.

Taylor, S. E. (1989). *Positive Illusions*. New York: Basic Books.

Tenbrunsel, A. E., Wade-Benzoni, K. A., Moag, J., and Bazerman, M. H. (1999). The negotiation matching process: Relationships and partner selection. *Organizational Behavior and Human Decision Process*, **80**, 252–83.

Valley, K. L., Moag, J., and Bazerman, M. H. (1998). A matter of trust: Effects of communication on the efficiency and distribution of outcomes. *Journal of Economic Behavior and Organization*, **34**, 211–38.

network theory and analysis

James R. Lincoln

Network theory and analysis deals with patterns of relations or *ties* among a set of actors or *nodes* such as individuals, groups, organizations, and industries, or even regions and countries.

Once an arcane field mainly addressed to methodology, network analysis has assumed a high profile in organizational studies. Much research examines organizational structures, both formal and informal, in network terms (e.g., White, 1961). Not often acknowledged is the role network analysis played in classical management theory. The dictum that spans of control should not exceed 5–6 subordinates was based on Graicunas's (1934) network calculation that relational complexity explodes with small increases in the number of subordinates. Network models in which all ties route through one central node (versus the case of each node linking directly to all others) supplied an efficiency rationale for administrative hierarchy. As for informal structure, managers as well as scholars see in network analysis a tool for assessing how interaction patterns conform to prescribed ways. In recent years, numerous practitioner oriented cases and exercises in network analysis have become available (Krackhardt and Hanson, 1993).

Not surprisingly, studies of INTER-ORGANIZATIONAL RELATIONS (e.g., human service networks, strategic alliances, or financial/commercial transactions) make wide use of network theory and methods. ORGANIZATIONAL LEARNING and INNOVATION research has recently turned to network analysis in mapping knowledge flows from firm to firm. Some studies are also examining how organizational cultures emerge from the aggregation of employee values and beliefs through network processes.

While the methodological work continues to advance in sophistication, pure methods is today much less the hallmark of network analysis than was true some twenty years ago. Nor are programming skills the barrier to entry they once were. The advent of UCINET and other software packages have greatly eased the tasks of handling and analyzing network data (Borgatti, Everett, and Freeman, 2002).

DATA COLLECTION

Ethnographic Qualitative network methods – participant observation and unstructured interviewing (e.g., use of a key informant – "tribal elder" – to map the network) – are mostly the province of social anthropology, which in the 1950s embraced the network idea as an alternative to images of society and culture as fixed, bounded systems (Mitchell, 1974). Qualitative network research is rare in organizational studies, but some strong examples exist (e.g., Barley, 1990).

Survey The oldest tradition of quantitative network research is *sociometry*, pioneered in the 1930s by Moreno (1934), and famous for its questionnaire methodology ("Name your three best friends") and graphic representations ("sociograms"). The gathering of network data with survey questionnaires presents some thorny problems, however. Standard "closed population" surveys (each person surveyed may choose or be chosen by every other) demand that all respondents' identities be disclosed. Another vexing problem is the number of response choices. Restricted choice constrains the number of ties artificially and may cause important ones to be omitted. Yet unrestricted choice poses problems as well, such as large and implausible individual differences in choice volume. "Open population" ego-network surveys, wherein each respondent reports both on his or her direct ties *and* the ties among those alters as well, skirt these problems and can be conducted on a very large (e.g., national) scale. Yet because the network cannot be rendered as a square matrix whose rows and columns array the same nodes, many standard network analytic techniques are foreclosed. Still, ego-network data can be useful and informative, as in Burt's (1992) influential work on "structural holes" in managerial career networks.

Archival data Much contemporary organizational network research uses archival data to study, for example, cross-shareholdings and board interlocking; financial and commercial exchange; merger and acquisition; strategic alliances; and the like. Such data often have the considerable virtue of being longitudinal, even cross-national. The downside is that the investigator must make do with the data available. Moreover, information on the methods of data collection may be incomplete or non-existent.

LEVELS AND METHODS OF DATA ANALYSIS

Technical network analyses are classifiable according to level of analysis, specifically (1) nodal; (2) dyad or triad; (3) sub-network or whole network.

Nodal Most network studies in organizational behavior are pitched at the most micro-analytic level: the node. Nodes (e.g., persons, groups, organizations) are assigned measurements reflecting their positions in the network. *Centrality* is the most common of these. A node is central if it is close in network space to all alters. Some centrality indices give added weight to nodes tied to alters who themselves are central (Bonacich, 1987). Other measures, like Freeman's (1977) "betweenness" centrality, tap the role of a node in bridging or brokerage relations. Centrality studies enjoy data-analytic simplicity, as conventional STATISTICAL METHODS can be applied (Ibarra, 1992). Yet the independent random sampling assumption required by such methods is hard to justify, since centralities greater than zero imply that at least some nodes are interconnected, hence autocorrelated.

A solution to the non-independence problem in node level statistical analysis is the network autoregression model. In a standard regression of the sort: $y = X\beta + \varepsilon$, ε, the vector of error terms is modeled as $\varepsilon = \rho W\varepsilon$, where W is a matrix of proximities among the nodes. Variations on this model have seen important use in diffusion studies (Burt, 1987).

Dyad and triad A higher level of analysis takes the *dyad* or pair of nodes as unit of observation and models the relation between the pair as a function of explanatory dyad and node level variables. Dyad regression models typically address hypotheses about *homophily* or *complementarity* in how attributes of the nodes combine to shape the likelihood or form of the relation. Again, the independent sampling assumption required by OLS regression is not warranted. Solutions include Lincoln's (1984) adaptation of the network autoregression model to dyad analysis and Krackhardt's (1988) Quadratic Assignment Procedure. QAP can be implemented within UCINET.

An important distinction in dyad analysis is that of cohesion versus structural equivalence. In the cohesion framework, two nodes are related in a network if one can reach the other through some chain of intermediaries. "Path distance" is the number of steps – direct ties – separating the pair, where "1" is a direct link. If one node is not reachable from another via any possible path, the distance is infinity. "Small world" studies address the path distance between two randomly selected persons in a large population (e.g., the United States). These are found to be remarkably small: six or seven links. Other dyad level relational properties that have a cohesion flavor include multiplexity (ties of diverse content link the same nodes), reachability (the probability that two nodes are directly or indirectly linked), and reciprocity (the probability that a tie from I to J is matched by one from J to I). Granovetter's (1973) distinction between "strong" versus "weak" ties can be recast in these terms (i.e., proximate versus distant, multiplex versus single stranded, and reciprocated versus unilateral).

Alternatively, the "relation" in a pair of nodes may be defined in terms of structural equivalence: the degree of similarity in how the two link to others (e.g., the population as a whole). Thus, by this criterion, no direct link need exist between the pair, although structural equivalence does imply *indirect* connection. One operational measure of structural equivalence is the correlation between two nodes' rows and/or columns in a matrix representation of the network. An alternative is Euclidean distance, computed as the square root of the sum of the squared differences between the columns and/or rows.

At the triad level, the chief empirical tradition is the "triad census" research program of Davis (1970) and his colleagues, assessing the prevalence of "mutual, asymmetric, and null" triadic configurations. It has yet to find application in organizational research.

Subnetwork and network At the most macro levels of network analysis are supra-triad subnets and the network as a whole. Properties at these levels may be operationalized as sums or averages or dyad level properties: density (the ratio of realized to potential ties); hierarchy (the ratio of asymmetric to symmetric ties); connectivity (the ratio of connected – reachable – dyads to all dyads); clustering (the degree of clumping or cliquing in the network). A few studies have

measured the structural characteristics of whole organizations in such formal network terms (e.g., Shrader, Lincoln, and Hoffman, 1989).

A major focus of the cohesion tradition of network research has been clique detection. Loosely defined, a clique is a cluster of tightly linked nodes. Various clique detection algorithms based on mathematical criteria have been proposed. An alternative is simply to cluster analyze the matrix of distances (or proximities) to reveal patterns of cliquing.

Blockmodeling methodology, premised on the structural equivalence concept, represents a different approach to network clustering. The matrix of equivalences (e.g., zero-order correlations or Euclidean distances) is cluster analyzed (e.g, with blockmodeling's signature algorithm, CONCOR) to yield a set of "blocks" or sets of equivalent nodes. An "image" matrix then portrays the aggregate ties among the blocks, seen in blockmodeling as role relations among structurally defined positions or statuses. A final step is the development of a "relational algebra" with which hypotheses of the following sort can be proposed and tested: $E^2 = F$ or "my enemy's enemy (E^2) is my friend (F)."

THE STATE OF NETWORK THEORY

As a whole, network analysis is an assemblage of concepts, orientations, measures, and techniques, not a "theory" in the usual sense. Yet it provides a distinctive explanatory lens through which organizational phenomena may be viewed; it identifies a set of problems; it offers a set of concepts for thinking about those problems; and it guides the choice of level and form of causal analysis.

One important stream of network theory originated with the sociology of Georg Simmel (Wolff, 1950). In theorizing on the role of numbers in social life – most notably, dyads and triads – Simmel pioneered a distinctive mode of structuralist inquiry: What can be said about a population merely from the number of actors and the pattern of ties?

Social anthropologist S. F. Nadel's structuralist rendering of role theory is another significant theoretical precedent, informing, in particular, the blockmodeling paradigm. In blockmodeling, the substantive content of relations and the attributes of actors are secondary – at the limit, irrelevant – to a representation of the network in purely structural terms as a system of positions and roles.

The question of a uniquely network theory is complicated by the fact that so many fields of organization study deal, at least implicitly, with ties and networks. Such work has given strong impetus to formal network analysis, which supplies a set of operations and analytical tools for proposing and testing hypotheses on intra- and inter-organizational relations. Exchange/resource dependence theory has stimulated a considerable body of technical network research. Burt's "structural holes" theory blends resource dependence themes with Simmelian postulates on the strategic role of third parties (*tertius gaudens*) in triadically configured networks. Granovetter's *embeddedness* theory of economic action similarly exploits network imagery and is often recast in formal network terms. Recent advances in organizational ecology use network concepts and methods to operationalize its trademark of niche and community. Neo-institutional theory's focus on mimetic processes has spawned numerous inquiries into the diffusion of organizational forms and practices through inter-organizational networks.

A theoretical issue currently attracting wide interest is that of social capital, a concept whose roots include Granovetter's distinction between strong and weak ties. It was his paradoxical insight that "weak" ties provide superior social capital in terms of returns to the actor in information, influence, and other resources. "Strong" ties, by contrast, give rise to closed and tight-knit cliques, thus circulating redundant information. Yet other views of social capital see it expanding linearly with tie strength and volume, such that actors with more and stronger links have better general access to the network's pools of information and skills. Strategic alliance research routinely finds centrality in interfirm networks functioning to bolster a company's success at finding partners and forging new and better alliances.

Network forms   Another recent and influential application of network thinking is the concept of a network organizational form. It refers to an array of organization types, including (1) the "virtual" Silicon Valley corporation that out-sources most functions and inputs; (2) the localized small business networks observed in Northern Italy, Southern Germany, and Japan; (3) loosely integrated business groups such as the Japanese keiretsu or Chinese guanxi. Network organizations are argued to have permeable boundaries and structures built not on fixed hierarchy and narrow functional roles, but around diffuse and flexible ties of obligation and reciprocity.

See also *intergroup relations; networking; research methods*

Bibliography

Barley, S. R. (1990). The alignment of technology and structure through roles and networks. *Administrative Science Quarterly*, **35**, 61–103.

Bonacich, P. (1987). Power and centrality: A family of measures. *American Journal of Sociology*, **92**, 1170–82.

Borgatti, S. P., Everett, M. G., and Freeman, L. (2002). *UCINET for Windows*. Harvard, MA: Analytic Technologies.

Burt, R. S. (1987). Social contagion and innovation: Cohesion vs. structural equivalence. *American Journal of Sociology*, **92**, 1287–1335.

Burt, R. S. (1992). *Structural Holes: The Social Structure of Competition*. Cambridge, MA: Harvard University Press.

Davis, J. A. (1970). Clustering and hierarchy in interpersonal relations. *American Journal of Sociology*, **35**, 843–51.

Freeman, L. C. (1977). A set of measures of centrality based on betweenness. *Sociometry*, **40**, 35–41.

Granovetter, M. (1973). The strength of weak ties. *American Journal of Sociology*, **78**, 1360–80.

Ibarra, H. (1992). Homophily and differential returns: Sex differences in network structure and access in an advertising firm. *Administrative Science Quarterly*, **37**, 422–47.

Krackhardt, D. (1988). Predicting with networks: Nonparametric multiple regression analysis of dyadic data. *Social Networks*, **10**, 359–81.

Krackhardt, D. and Hanson, J. R. (1993). Informal networks: The company behind the chart. *Harvard Business Review*, **71**, 104–11.

Lincoln, J. R. (1984). Analyzing relations in dyads: Problems, models, and an application to inter-organizational research. *Sociological Methods and Research*, **13**, 45–76.

Mitchell, J. C. (1974). Social networks. *Annual Review of Anthropology*, **3**, 279–99.

Moreno, J. L. (1934). *Who Shall Survive?* Washington, DC: Nervous and Mental Disease Publishing.

Podolny, J. M. and Page, K. L. (1998). Network forms of organization. *Annual Review of Sociology*, 24, 57–76.

Shrader, C. B., Lincoln, J. R., and Hoffman, A. N. (1989). The network structures of organizations: Effects of task contingencies and distributional form. *Human Relations*, 42, 43–66.

White, H. C. (1961). Management conflict and sociometric structure. *American Journal of Sociology*, 67, 185–99.

White, H. C., Boorman, S., and Breiger, R. (1976). Social structure from multiple networks: I. Blockmodels of roles and positions. *American Journal of Sociology*, 81, 730–80.

Wolff, K. H. (1950). *The Sociology of Georg Simmel*. Glencoe, IL: Free Press.

networking

W. Warner Burke

At its most basic, networking is the process of (a) contacting and being contacted by people in one's social or technical/professional world and (b) maintaining these linkages and relationships. A network, then, is a set of relations, linkages, or ties among people. Connections among people consist both of content (type of connection) and form (strength of connection). Content may include information exchange or simply friendship ties. The strength of the connection may be determined by the number of contacts made between people over time. Of course, strength can also be measured by the degree of intensity of the relationship (e.g., how long a singular contact is maintained, compared with the number of contacts made).

Considerable research has been conducted on networks. According to Davis and Powell (1992), the information content, maintenance, and mapping of network ties has received most attention whereas, for example, the consequences of an organization's position in various networks has hardly been studied.

Fischer et al. (1977) have contributed to the field by suggesting that networks can best be understood according to a choice constraint approach; that is, a network is the result of individual choices made within certain social constraints. Social structures such as class deter-

mine whether and to what degree these choices can be made.

Tichy, Tushman, and Fombrun (1979) stated that the study of networks can be traced to three broad schools of thought: sociology, anthropology, and ROLE THEORY. From these studies, the key properties of networks have been identified as:

- Transactional content: what is exchanged between members (e.g., information).
- Nature of the links: the strength and qualitative nature of the relationships (e.g., the degree to which members honor obligations or agree about appropriate behavior in their relationships).
- Structural characteristics : how members are linked, the number of clusters within the network, and certain individuals representing special nodes within the network; in other words, not all members are equally important; some, for example, are GATE-KEEPERS.

With the increase in terrorist activities in recent years, and the use of secretive networking to achieve their objectives, a sense of urgency has emerged to understand this form of collective behavior more deeply. For example, it has been clear that there is little hierarchy and that networks typically consist of nodes where pivotal people serve as connectors and gatekeepers. But with increasing use of the Internet, networking has become more diverse and nodes may not be as fundamental to the process as once thought (Rothstein, 2001). What does seem clear is that highly effective networking is very focused, with clarity of purpose, and built on trust; that is, political and emotional connections among members who must rely on one another to accomplish objectives.

Regarding networking inside organizations, the process is typically informal: the contacts and interactions among people do not follow the formal organization chart. Moreover, many organizational observers and scholars today tend to view the formal hierarchy as more of a hindrance than a help to organizational effectiveness (e.g., Rockart and Short, 1991). The need to coordinate activities of organizational members is significantly greater today than in the past.

Getting products to market more rapidly, providing quality service (which now is more dependent on numbers of people rather than on a single individual), and partnering more with contractors, vendors, and other organizational constituents are but a few of the many forces impinging on organizations to be more rapidly responsive.

It would appear, then, that with the need for more and faster responsiveness, and increasing reliance on information TECHNOLOGY, networking will be of growing importance in organizations.

One final point: understanding and using networks can have practical outcomes, as illustrated by Granovetter (1973). Assume you are looking for a job. You are more likely to be successful via the weak ties in your social network than by the strong ones. Close friends are likely to have many of the same contacts and sources as yourself. More distant acquaintances travel in different circles and therefore provide a link to contacts you would not otherwise have. Thus, while certain kinds of networking may be frivolous (e.g., a set of friends who share with you the same interest in, say, Stephen King novels), other networks in your life may provide highly useful information and assistance.

See also *coalition formation; intergroup relations; network theory and analysis*

Bibliography

Davis, G. F. and Powell, W. W. (1992). Organization–environment relations. In M. D. Dunnette and L. M. Hough (eds.), *Handbook of Industrial and Organizational Psychology*, Vol. 3. Palo Alto, CA: Consulting Psychologists Press, 316–75.

Fischer, C. S., Jackson, R. M., Stueve, C. A., Gerson, K., Jones, L. M., and Baldassare, M. (1977). *Networks and Places: Social Relations in the Urban Setting*. New York: Free Press.

Granovetter, M. (1973). The strength of weak ties. *American Journal of Sociology*, 78, 1360–80.

Rockart, J. F. and Short, J. E. (1991). The networked organization and the management of interdependence. In M. S. S. Morton (ed.), *The Corporation of the 1990s: Information Technology and Organizational Transformation*. New York: Oxford University Press, 189–219.

Rothstein, E. (2001). A lethal weapon with no spider. *New York Times*, October 20, A13, A15.

Tichy, N. M., Tushman, M. L., and Fombrun, C. (1979). Social network analysis for organizations. *Academy of Management Review*, 4, 507–19.

neurosis

see ORGANIZATIONAL NEUROSIS

niche

see COMMUNITY ECOLOGY; ORGANIZATIONAL ECOLOGY

nominal group technique

Randall S. Schuler

The nominal group format is a structured GROUP DECISION-MAKING technique used for the generation of a vast quantity of alternatives relevant to group issues, problems, and concerns (Gustafson et al., 1973). The nominal group technique allows for individual thinking and contribution in a group format. Ideas relevant to an issue, problem, or concern are solicited from group participants individually and silently. The group leader then systematically gathers this information from all participants before an open discussion commences. Ideas are discussed one at a time. Based upon the discussions, possible alternatives may be generated in and by the group. The group leader can then instruct the participants to vote on their preferred solutions. Once again, the leader gathers all this information systematically before commencing open discussion and deliberation. Eventually this group decision-making process may conclude with an acceptable solution.

The nominal group technique to group decision-making generally consumes a substantial amount of time. However, individual PARTICIPATION is very high, allowing for understanding, involvement, and eventual COMMITMENT to the group's decision. In particular, for immediate situations that directly affect the participants, the nominal group technique continues to be an effective decision-making method (Zimmerman, 1985; Murnighan, 1981). This technique, however, can also be used for the generation and evaluation of longer-term and more strategic alternatives. Whether for short-term or longer-term goals, the nominal group technique is generally capable of generating a wider array of alternatives and options than other less systematic techniques. It is also capable of doing this more quickly than Delphi groups. Nevertheless, the nominal group technique need not be thought of as a competing model to other techniques, but rather a complementary alternative.

See also *brainstorming; communication; creativity; Delphi; innovation*

Bibliography

Gustafson, D. H., Shukla, R. K., Delbecq, A., and Walster (1973). A comparative study of differences in subjective likelihood estimates made by individuals in interacting groups, Delphi groups and nominal groups. *Organizational Behavior and Human Performance*, 9, 280–91.

Murnighan, J. K. (1981). Group decision-making: What strategy should you use? *Management Review*, 56–60.

Zimmerman, D. K. (1985). Nominal group technique. In L. R. Bittle and J. E. Ramsey (eds.), *Handbook for Professional Managers*. New York: McGraw-Hill, 604–24.

non-work/work

Linda K. Stroh and Linda M. Dunn-Jensen

Non-work/work refers to the relationship between one's work and non-work life. Work generally refers to activities or attitudes undertaken in an employing organization. Non-work has generally referred to activities and attitudes related to one's family, yet also includes what Zedeck (1992) considers a personal sphere, where leisure activities, hobbies, and health related activities occur. Zedeck also notes that the non-work concept can also include other spheres such as religion, community, and social. It has been over a decade since Zedeck's volume examined diverse perspectives on non-work/work relations. Many important societal changes have

occurred since that time. Research agendas have broadened from "family friendly" to "people friendly" and from "work–family initiatives" to "work–life initiatives." Most now consider the non-work/work arena to be much broader and increasingly more complex than once thought. Consequently, the definition of non-work/work has changed over time, as has the relationship between the two concepts. Lobel and her colleagues identified several recent trends that draw attention to the interdependence and complexity of non-work/work policies and practices (Lobel, Googins, and Bankert, 1999). One trend is the changing family structure. For example, family no longer solely means a male-headed household, but has become broadened to mean two or more people having influence over each other's lives, sharing a sense of identity and shared goals. This new definition encompasses both same and different sex partners. Another recent trend is globalization and the need for organizational flexibility. For example, the demands for global coverage have increased the need for "24/7 workloads," thus resulting in an increased need for non-traditional work schedules. Requirements for organizational flexibility have resulted in team-based organizational structures.

Along with these structural changes, organizations have implemented flexible work arrangements such as telecommuting, job sharing, and personal leaves. These organizational changes have resulted, for many (e.g., homemakers, telecommunicators), in work that is done not only in the traditional work environment, but also within the home environment and on the road. Finally, recent technological advances have blurred the lines between non-work and work. Accordingly, because work can now be done in non-traditional places, it can now infringe on non-work time. These changes in work schedules and work locations have changed the definition of work. With these changes in definitions, it becomes obvious that the way researchers view the non-work/work relationship is evolving as well.

History of Findings

The need for research in the non-work/work area became prevalent with the onset of the industrial revolution and the increasing separation of work from family life. Over time, researchers, employers, and employees have increasingly recognized the interrelatedness of the non-work/work spheres. Research related to non-work/work issues began in the 1930s (Voydanoff, 1989). Findings from this period consistently suggested that male *unemployment* and female *employment* had negative effects on both children and the family. While this era of research recognized a "relationship" between one's non-work and work lives, the primary focus was on the negative effects of work on family. The notion that the family might also influence work life had not yet been considered.

Subsequently, the focus of the non-work/work research slowly began to shift to a position of viewing non-work and work lives as interdependent, and in the 1960s to increased attention on the dual-earner couple. Much of this research focused on the additional STRESS and tradeoffs of dual CAREER couples in both their non-work and work lives (Brett, Stroh, and Reilly, 1992). Research during this era began to recognize the "unpaid contribution" of professionals' and managers' wives to their husbands' careers. Some claim it was often the work of the wife that advanced the husband's career, yet severely constrained the wife's career, due to geographic mobility, and the demands on the wife's time (Stroh, 1999).

While earlier research examined primarily men's *un*employment, women's *em*ployment, and dual career couples, recent research has focused on the structural and psychological characteristics of work, and the relationship between work life integration and both JOB SATISFACTION and life satisfaction. For example, Adams, King, and King (1996) found a positive relationship between these variables. Thus, life satisfaction for some may be the result of having a good job. Non-work/work research has also begun to investigate the relationship between job characteristics and stress and well-being. Structural aspects of the job, such as working hours, compressed work week schedules, and geographic mobility, continue to be aggressively studied areas and have been shown to affect family life. For example, overwork is generally shown to be negatively related to the quality of family life (Hochschild, 1997; Brett and Stroh, 2003).

MODELS TO STUDY NON-WORK/WORK ISSUES

Combined with earlier research on non-work/work issues, Kanter's (1977) influential review encouraged researchers to begin to think of the non-work/work environment as an interface and theorists began to develop models to help explain the relationship. Recent work by Kossek and Lambert (2004) has elaborated on these models with increasing emphasis on work–life integration.

The spillover theory suggests that work related activities/satisfaction can affect non-work life and non-work responsibilities/satisfaction may also affect one's work life. For example, a person's marital satisfaction may affect their relationship to the workplace (Edwards and Rothbard, 2000).

Not all researchers accept the spillover theory. Other research argues in favor of a compensation theory. This theory suggests there is an inverse relationship between non-work/work such that individuals compensate for shortcomings in one domain by satisfying needs in the other. For example, a person who is dissatisfied with their family or non-work life may seek greater levels of satisfaction from their work life environment.

A third model explaining the relationship between non-work/work is the segmentation theory, based on the premise that non-work/work lives are distinct and one domain has no influence on the other. For example, family life satisfies needs for affection, intimacy, and relationships, while work life satisfies needs for competition and instrumental relationships.

A fourth model is the resource drain theory. The resource drain theory considers the constraint in which resources (time, attention, and energy) given to one domain reduce the resources available in the other domain. For example, when an individual works longer hours at work, that individual has less time to pursue non-work activities (Edwards and Rothbard, 2000).

In reality, all four models can be accepted insofar as they describe different relationships that may obtain under particular circumstances.

CONCLUSIONS

The emphasis on the way one's family life can affect one's work life as well as one's work life affecting one's family life has given way to new, more applied research efforts on how to better integrate the work–family interface. The practical implications of such research in terms of human resource policy and working arrangements are varied. Economic and social pressures have forced many organizations to implement more progressive maternity, paternity, and childcare related policies in efforts to attract and retain talented managers who want to create more balance in their lives. Flextime and job sharing are two examples of work restructuring that have been found to be useful in helping employees better integrate their lives (*see* JOB DESIGN).

See also *diversity management; family firms; gender; women at work*

Bibliography

Adams, G. A., King, L. A., and King, D. W. (1996). Relationships of job and family involvement, family social support, and work–family conflict with job and life satisfaction. *Journal of Applied Psychology*, 81, 411–20.

Brett, J. M. and Stroh, L. K. (2003). Working 61+ hours per week: Why do we do it? *Journal of Applied Psychology*, 88, 67–78.

Brett, J. M., Stroh, L. K., and Reilly, A. H. (1992). What is it like being a dual-career manager in the 1990s? In S. Zedeck (ed.), *Work and Families, and Organizations*. San Francisco: Jossey-Bass, 138–67.

Edwards, J. R. and Rothbard, N. P. (2000). Mechanisms linking work and family: Clarifying the relationship between work and family constructs. *Academy of Management Review*, 25, 178–99.

Hochschild, A. R. (1997). *The Time Bind: When Work Becomes Home and Home Becomes Work*. New York: Metropolitan Books.

Kanter, R. M. (1977). *Work and Family in the United States*. New York: Russell Sage Foundation.

Kossek, E. E. and Lambert, S. (2004). *Work and Life Integration: Organizational, Cultural, and Psychological Perspectives*. Mahwah, NJ: Lawrence Erlbaum Associates.

Lobel, S. A., Googins, B. K., and Bankert, E. (1999). The future of work and family: Critical trends for policy, practice, and research. *Human Resource Management*, 243–54.

Stroh, L. K. (1999). A review of relocation: The impact on work and family. *Human Resource Management Review*, 9, 279–308.

Voydanoff, P. (1989). Work and family: A review and expanded conceptualization. In E. B. Goldsmith (ed.), *Work and Family*. London: Sage, 1–22.

Zedeck, S. (1992). Exploring the domain of work and family concerns. In S. Zedeck (ed.), *Work and Families, and Organizations*. San Francisco: Jossey-Bass, 1–32.

norms

see GROUP NORMS

obedience

see INFLUENCE

objectives

see MANAGEMENT BY OBJECTIVES

open systems

Thomas G. Cummings

When applying SYSTEMS THEORY to organizations, OB scholars conceptualize them as being open systems exchanging information and resources with their environment. This perspective draws attention to how organizations and their environments mutually influence each other. It seeks to explain how organizations maintain functional autonomy while adapting to external forces. Recent developments in COMPLEXITY THEORY and chaos theory address how organizations cope with rapidly changing environments through complex adaptive behaviors.

As open systems, organizations seek to sustain an input–output cycle of activities aimed at taking in inputs of information and resources from the environment, transforming them into outputs of goods and services, and exporting them back to the environment. This cycle enables organizations to replenish themselves continually so long as the environment provides sufficient inputs and the organization delivers valued outputs.

Considerable research has gone into understanding how organizations manage these information and resource flows. One perspective focuses on how organizations process information in order to discover how to relate to their environments. Another view concentrates on how organizations compete for resources through managing key resource dependencies (*see* RESOURCE DEPENDENCE). Still another perspective focuses on how organizations gain legitimacy from environmental institutions so they can continue to function with external support (*see* INSTITUTIONAL THEORY).

In managing information and resource flows, organizations, like all open systems, seek to establish boundaries around their activities. These organizational boundaries must be permeable enough to permit necessary environmental exchange, yet afford sufficient protection from external demands to allow for rational operation.

Organizational scholars devote considerable attention to understanding the dual nature of organizational boundaries. They study various BOUNDARY SPANNING roles that relate the organization to its environment, such as sales, public relations, and purchasing. They examine how organizational members perceive and make sense out of environmental input (*see* ENACTMENT), and how organizational boundaries vary in sensitivity to external influences. Research is also aimed at identifying different strategies for protecting transformation processes from external disruptions while being responsive to suppliers and customers.

Viewed as open systems, organizations use information about how they are performing to modify future behaviors. This information FEEDBACK enables organizations to be self-regulating. It enables them to adjust their functioning to respond to deviations in expected performance. According to the system's law of requisite variety, however, organizations must have a sufficient diversity of responses to match the variety of disturbances encountered if self-regulation is to be successful.

Extensive research has been devoted to understanding how organizations control and regulate themselves. Using modern information technology, organizations develop a variety of methods for setting goals, obtaining information on goal achievement, and making necessary changes. They also devise different structures and processes for learning from this information about how to improve performance (see CONTINUOUS IMPROVEMENT; LEARNING, ORGANIZATIONAL; LEARNING ORGANIZATION).

As open systems, organizations display the property of equifinality. They can achieve objectives with varying inputs and in different ways. Consequently, there is no one best way to design and manage organizations, but there are a variety of ways to achieve satisfactory performance (see SATISFICING).

Organizational scholars have devoted considerable attention to identifying different choices for designing and managing organizations. They have identified a range of ORGANIZATIONAL DESIGN options that can achieve success in particular situations (see CONTINGENCY THEORY).

Recently, researchers have focused on the non-linear dynamics underlying how organizations as open systems self-organize and change themselves. They have shown how complex interactions among the highly differentiated parts of an organization can lead to relatively organized behaviors for the total organization (see COMPLEXITY THEORY). Conversely, they have found that small changes in the behavior of those interrelated parts can lead to large-scale, unpredictable organization behaviors. These open system dynamics promote organizational innovation and change; they enable organizations to maintain a delicate balance between being too rigid or too chaotic (see ORGANIZATIONAL CHANGE; INNOVATION).

See also *organization theory; organizational ecology; organizational effectiveness*

Bibliography

Aldrich, H. (1979). *Organizations and Environments*. New York: Prentice-Hall.

Katz, D. and Kahn, R. (1978). *The Social Psychology of Organizations*, 2nd edn. New York: John Wiley.

Organization Science (1999). Special issue: Application of complexity theory to organization science. **10**, 3.

Pfeffer, J. and Salancik, G. (1978). *The External Control of Organizations: A Resource Dependence Perspective*. New York: Harper and Row.

organization development

Richard W. Woodman

Organization development (OD) is an applied behavioral science focused on understanding and managing ORGANIZATIONAL CHANGE. As such, OD is both a field of social and managerial action and a field of scientific inquiry (Cummings and Worley, 2001; Woodman, 1989). As a field of scientific inquiry, OD draws particularly heavily from the psychological and sociological sciences. As a field of managerial action, OD draws from many of the OB topics addressed in this volume, including MOTIVATION theory, LEADERSHIP theory, learning theory, theories of GROUP DYNAMICS, and theories of POWER and political behavior, among others. The field is an interdisciplinary one with many theoretical perspectives and research traditions informing the investigation and management of organizational change processes.

REPRESENTATIVE DEFINITIONS AND DEFINING CHARACTERISTICS

Some representative definitions help to frame the boundaries and identify the focus of the field.

> Organization development is a planned process of change in an organization's culture through the utilization of behavioral science technologies, research, and theory. (Burke, 1994: 12)
>
> Organization development [is] a process that applies behavioral science knowledge and practices to help organizations achieve greater effectiveness, including increased financial performance and improved quality of work life. (Cummings and Worley, 2001: 1)
>
> Organization development is the applied behavioral science discipline dedicated to improving organizations and the people in them through the use of the theory and practice of planned change. (French and Bell, 1999: xiii)

Organization development is a set of behavioral science-based theories, values, strategies, and techniques aimed at the planned change of the organizational work setting for the purpose of enhancing individual development and improving organizational performance, through the alteration of organizational members' on-the-job behaviors. (Porras and Robertson, 1992: 722)

Organization development means creating adaptive organizations capable of repeatedly transforming and reinventing themselves as needed to remain effective. (Woodman, 1993: 73)

These definitions emphasize OD's focus on planful, systemic change, its knowledge base in the behavioral sciences, and the goal of improving organizational performance and effectiveness. Indeed, at some level of abstraction, ORGANIZATIONAL EFFECTIVENESS is the ultimate goal of all planned change interventions. At the same time, OD approaches to change emphasize employee growth and fulfilment in the workplace in addition to the overarching goal of effectiveness. Woodman and Dewett (in press) have addressed this duality, pointing out that to understand organizational change in a scientific sense and to manage change in a practical sense necessarily means that the field requires a duality of theorizing and research that extends across the organizational and individual levels of analysis. Just as individual actors effect change in organizations, so too do organizations change the people who work in them. Planned change efforts, though operating primarily in the service of organizational development, nevertheless provide a major impetus for individual development and change. Organizations change people in many ways, both subtle and not so subtle, both intentionally and unintentionally, over time. Thus, the dual focus of the field on both organizational effectiveness and individual work experience and its consequences makes sense.

Another duality that characterizes OD change efforts is the focus on solving immediate problems and on the development of an adaptive, learning organization capable of effectively addressing the same or similar issues in the future. Further, OD approaches to change tend to emphasize the importance of self-directed change. Individuals and teams are seen as taking responsibility for their own job behaviors

and the design of processes and systems utilized in their work. As such, OD typically utilizes very collaborative ACTION RESEARCH processes in gathering information, data analysis, and action planning. There is an emphasis on creating solutions and adaptive strategies that enjoy widespread support from organizational participants.

ORGANIZATION DEVELOPMENT THEORY

A notable characteristic of the field of OD is the rich diversity of theories that have been employed in attempts to explain organizational change. Porras and Robertson (1987, 1992) have identified two types of organization development theory: change process theory and implementation theory. Change process theory focuses on explaining the dynamics through which organizations change. Implementation theory, most closely related to OD practice, focuses on specific interventions and procedures that can be used to change organizations. This dichotomy reflects the dual nature of the field as one encompassing both scientific inquiry and organizational action. In general, implementation theory is more fully developed than change process theory in OD (Porras and Robertson, 1992). In this vein, Pettigrew, Woodman, and Cameron (2001) have suggested that the field needs to dramatically improve the use of time, history, change process explanations, and multiple levels of analysis in theorizing and research on organizational change. Such a call is fundamentally an appeal to improve change process theory. At the same time, the same authors call for more international comparative work, more research conducted in multiple contexts, and more focus on linking change processes and performance outcomes. These latter ideas suggest that they believe implementation theory could be improved as well.

THE FUTURE OF OD

Organization development grew out of early laboratory training methods, survey research and FEEDBACK methodologies, and participative management (see PARTICIPATION) in the US and SOCIOTECHNICAL THEORY developments in several European countries (most notably Great Britain). (For an overview of the history of the field, see Cummings and Worley,

2001: 6–12; French and Bell, 1999: 32–54.) As a result of these origins, OD has been more micro than macro in orientation, more focused on individual and group behaviors than on organizational processes, and, in the eyes of critics, more focused on the tactics of intervention design and conduct than the strategy of changing whole systems. However, OD continues to broaden its focus. In some quarters, the broader label of "organizational change and development" is increasingly popular as a way of recognizing the expanding boundaries of the field. Among the more notable developments are an increased emphasis on ORGANIZATIONAL DESIGN and structure, organizational strategy, ORGANIZATIONAL CULTURE, and "whole systems" change. Even interventions such as TEAM BUILDING, long a basic CHANGE METHOD in OD, have taken on a more systemic flavor with greater linkages to organizational strategy and goals (cf. Woodman and Pasmore, 2002). However, despite noteworthy change management contributions and progress in theory development, the field continues to suffer from tensions between practice and theory. The schism between the science of organizational change and the art of changing organizations is the single greatest impediment to progress in OD.

See also *change, evaluation; innovation; resistance to change*

Bibliography

Burke, W. W. (1994). *Organization Development: A Process of Learning and Changing*, 2nd edn. Reading, MA: Addison-Wesley.
Cummings, T. G. and Worley, C. G. (2001). *Organization Development and Change*, 7th edn. Cincinnati, OH: South-Western College Publishing.
French, W. L. and Bell, C. H. (1999). *Organization Development: Behavioral Science Interventions for Organization Improvement*, 6th edn. Upper Saddle River, NJ: Prentice-Hall.
Pettigrew, A. M., Woodman, R. W., and Cameron, K. S. (2001). Studying organizational change and development: Challenges for future research. *Academy of Management Journal*, 44, 697–713.
Porras, J. I. and Robertson, P. J. (1987). Organization development theory: A typology and evaluation. In R. W. Woodman and W. A. Pasmore (eds.), *Research in Organizational Change and Development*, Vol. 1. Greenwich, CT: JAI Press, 1–57.
Porras, J. I. and Robertson, P. J. (1992). Organizational development: Theory, practice, and research. In M. D. Dunnette and L. M. Hough (eds.), *Handbook of Industrial and Organizational Psychology*, 2nd edn., Vol. 3. Palo Alto, CA: Consulting Psychologists Press, 719–822.
Woodman, R. W. (1989). Organizational change and development: New arenas for inquiry and action. *Journal of Management*, 15, 205–28.
Woodman, R. W. (1993). Observations on the field of organizational change and development from the lunatic fringe. *Organization Development Journal*, 11, 71–4.
Woodman, R. W. and Dewett, T. (in press). Organizationally relevant journeys in individual change. In M. S. Poole and A. H. Van de Ven (eds.), *Handbook of Organizational Change and Innovation*. Oxford: Oxford University Press.
Woodman, R. W. and Pasmore, W. A. (2002). The heart of it all: Group- and team-based interventions in OD. In J. Waclawski and A. H. Church (eds.), *Organization Development: A Data Driven Approach to Organizational Change*. San Francisco: Jossey-Bass, 164–76.

organization theory

John Freeman

Organization theory is a body of scholarship that attempts to explain variations in the structure and operating processes of organizations. Its unit of analysis is the organization itself, or subunits of the organization, not individual people, the units of analysis to which organizational behavior refers (*see* LEVELS OF ANALYSIS). The term "organization theory" is a misnomer because this body of scholarship includes empirical research and prescriptive analyses of managerial problems as well as theory.

The field of organizational behavior emerged as industrial psychologists entered business schools in the United States and sought a term to distinguish their positivistic research from the more normative field of personnel management. When other kinds of social scientists followed, organizational research began to find a broader audience in business schools and other professional schools. People already in the field sought a term to distinguish this new way of looking at organizations from the previous focus on individual behavior. Since this new style of research seemed quite abstract, it came to be known as "organization theory" as a complement to "organizational behavior."

There is, however, a fundamental difference between how these two groups thought about human behavior in organizations. Industrial psychologists generally have not believed human beings think differently when they are in an organizational context. Consequently, their approach has applied theories and methods developed for other purposes to understanding human behavior in organizations. Organizational sociology, in particular, is not an application of some other theory to organizations. Rather, sociologists believe that organizations are units of social organization manifesting phenomena to be explained in ways that differ fundamentally from the explanations offered to account for phenomena manifested by other units of social organization such as families or residential communities.

Organization theory began almost simultaneously in two places in the United States shortly after World War II. In New York City, at Columbia University's Department of Sociology, people began to study organizations as units of analysis, not simply as bureaucracies that were the instruments of political process (see BUREAUCRACY). The inspiration for such a new interest was structural-functional analysis in which social organization develops to satisfy functional requisites or "needs" of society. Formal organizations are important units through which this is done. The other locus of organizational research was the Carnegie Institute in Pittsburgh, where the psychologist Herbert Simon, the political scientist James G. March, and the economist Richard Cyert began to develop a different approach to the study of organizations.

Philip Selznick, trained at Columbia, published *TVA and the Grass Roots* (1949) and *Leadership in Administration* (1957). They appeared at almost precisely the same time as Herbert Simon's *Administrative Behavior* (1948) and March and Simon's *Organizations* (1958).

The Columbia sociology department produced doctoral students who spread out across the United States to develop organizational sociology. While Selznick went to Berkeley, Peter Blau eventually took a job at Chicago, where he trained a series of doctoral students including W. Richard Scott. Their book *Formal Organizations* (1962) was the first textbook devoted exclusively to organization theory. Scott moved to the Stanford sociology department, where he teamed up with another Columbia graduate, John Meyer, to found modern INSTITUTIONAL THEORY. Students from Carnegie-Mellon, as it ultimately came to be called, include Oliver Williamson and Jeffrey Pfeffer (who received an undergraduate degree and MBA from Carnegie).

Organizational theory penetrated business schools in the United States as CONTINGENCY THEORY drew a new audience for learning about organizations. This audience was higher level managers and students who aspired to such high positions. While organizational psychology and its normative cousin, personnel management, were principally about individuals and small groups, with emphasis on the factory work settings, organization theory and its normative cousin, ORGANIZATIONAL DESIGN, were principally about the organization as a whole. This new audience grew as a transition toward more theoretically based material gained impetus in US business schools. As the social sciences invaded business schools and other professional schools as well, social science contributions to organizational studies broadened and became more theoretical. So organizational theory grew rapidly through the 1970s and 1980s.

At about the same time contingency theory emerged as the body of scholarship pushing organization theory itself into the mainstream, SYSTEMS THEORY emerged from engineering and rapidly gained a presence in the field of management science. Systems theory drew attention to the organization as a unit of analysis, and thus was consistent with other strands of organization theory. Furthermore, it treated organizations dynamically, with a focus on operating processes that linked organization with its environment. It also stressed the problems associated with self-regulating systems (sometimes called cybernetic systems), which are the properties of organizations describing their tolerance for and adjustment to environmental and technical change. Systems theory did not penetrate the mainstream of organizational theory very deeply, however. While virtually all organization theorists adopted the metaphors of systems theory, including using the term "system" itself, systems theory never developed a strong empirical base. Many of its more interesting ideas were difficult to render observable in real organizations. In addition, the dynamic nature of the systems conceptualization proved daunting to capture in formal mathematical models. This problem proved a major weakness at the core of systems theory and it ceased to be a major PARADIGM, in management science and operations research as well as in organization theory.

Interest by sociologists in the relationship between organization size and structure developed a literature that made small impact on organization theory as a whole. The main tenet of this work was that larger organizations have more complex structures: more levels in the hierarchy of AUTHORITY, more departments and sections on the horizontal dimension. Probably the most important and lasting contribution of the size and structure literature was to encourage empirical quantitative research on organizations in which large, systematically drawn samples of organizations were used to generate data. This in turn encouraged the use of statistical methods and formalized theories. Organization theory developed methodological sophistication at the same time other branches of scholarship in the social science professional schools developed such methods. This had the effect of keeping the field current with developments elsewhere. It also had the effect of focusing interest on things that were measurable, diverting attention from issues of great interest and importance to many scholars and students of organizations.

In the early 1970s two new branches of organization theory developed, both emanating from the Carnegie school. Pfeffer and Salancik (for a summary, see Pfeffer and Salancik, 1978) began a series of studies drawing attention to the RESOURCE DEPENDENCE of organizations. While contingency theorists wrote about uncertainties imposed on organizations by their environments, resource dependence developed the argument first appearing in Cyert and March (1963) that organizations developed their structures around access to resources. These resources are controlled by other powerful actors whose preferences and practices constrain the organization under study. Control over resources is the primary subject of dispute within organizations and thus conditions POWER structures.

At about the same time, Oliver Williamson was combining the organizational theories of the Carnegie school with the institutional economics of John R. Commons and Ronald Coase to develop a new version of TRANSACTION COST ECONOMICS. While neoclassical economists treated organizations as single, unified actors with clearly evident and consistent preferences, Williamson argued that their internal structures mattered. People in organizations have their own agendas and will pursue them when they can, sometimes to the detriment of the organization as a whole. Organizations are built as attempts to create efficient structures where markets fail to do so.

Each of the strands of theory described thus far, with the exception of systems theory, took it as axiomatic that organizations were to be understood as the purposeful creations of some recognizable individual or group. They were treated as tools to be used to achieve specific purposes. Failure to cooperate, then, is at least implicitly a form of subversion. The inherent conservatism of structural–functional analysis continued in organization theory long after it disappeared in other branches of sociology, political science, and anthropology. The research of the 1960s and 1970s, however, showed that organizational goals are often more apparent than real. Much of what makes an organization organized is the informal system that springs up spontaneously among the people. This organization is often barely recognized and usually misunderstood by higher level managers. By definition, it is not designed by them. So organizations can be seen as having lives of their own. If this is true, how do we understand their structure and operations?

Two branches of organization theory appeared in the late 1970s as an explicit attempt to answer this question. Both grew out of sociological studies of organizations: population ecology of organizations and sociological institutional theory (see ORGANIZATIONAL ECOLOGY).

Population ecology focuses on the tendency of organizations to cluster together in social categories. Observable variations in organizations do not blend smoothly and continuously, so that it makes little sense to refer to a "bank" as compared with a "hospital." The former do not blend seamlessly with the latter, so that in common parlance one is forced to refer to a "more or less bank." The variables on whose dimensions we can distinguish banks from hospitals come distributed in discrete chunks called organizational forms. The organizations manifesting a form are populations of organizations. Among the features these population members share is a common dependence on other organizations for support. In this sense, the members of a population have a shared fate. As resources, cooperation, and opposition from other organizations rise and fall, the population as a whole is advantaged or disadvantaged. The rates of foundings and failure for that population rise and fall. Members of these populations have the odds increasingly with them or against them in consequence. As these populations expand, creating opportunity for organization founders and for existing firms, and contract, signifying tough times for members of those populations, distributions of interesting organizational variables shift. For example, as populations of locally owned and managed banks decline, and nationwide chains of banks expand, the employment opportunities, working conditions, and services offered all change.

Population ecology focuses on the typical case, what population members have in common. As such it provides context against which to gauge behavior of individuals and single organizations, particularly those that are chosen for study because of their unusual features.

While population ecologists tend to stress the resource environments of organizations, institutional theorists stress the cultural and political environments. For them, the societies in which organizations operate impose expectations about structure and operating procedures on the individual organization and its participants. So even if a bank is owned by a single individual, he or she is not perfectly free to organize in any manner that might be possible. A body of social norms, including those formalized in laws and banking regulations, constrains the bank organ-

izer. Further, these patterned expectations include more subtle constraints such as architecture, modes of dress, and styles of interaction. Institutional theorists generally argue that operating efficiency is only one criterion affecting the mode of organization. And efficiency itself is culturally defined. Population ecologists and institutional theorists agree that environmental factors limit the choices available to those who organize and that such decisions are only some of the factors that generate observed organizational patterns.

As population ecology and institutional theory developed in the 1980s, a growing interest in culture and its effects on organization produced related streams of theory and research. Some of this work on culture blended with institutional theory, but some focused more on differences between national cultures and the challenges of organizing across such boundaries (see CULTURE, NATIONAL). Such issues loom larger in the imagination of many European scholars, who can see the political boundaries between societies evaporating, marking the cultural distinctions even more clearly. As European organizations expand across those boundaries, often by constructing joint ventures or by effecting mergers, attempts to understand the consequences have burgeoned. The gropings to understand "Japanese management" and "corporate culture" often missed the point that culture is no more an option to be chosen and designed by chief executives than being Japanese or French is a matter of choice for individuals (see ORGANIZATIONAL CULTURE).

Finally, throughout this period interest in DECISION-MAKING has continued. The Carnegie school began with the assumption of BOUNDED RATIONALITY. This evolved into a critique of organizations as tools designed by rational managers (see RATIONALITY). Organizations face continuing ambiguity as decision-makers face vague COMMUNICATIONS about how imprecise TECHNOLOGY is being used or abused in pursuit of more or less understood goals. All of this leads to a view of organizations as groping through time and space, muddling through rather than conquering strategically chosen obstacles.

See also *critical theory; postmodernism; theory*

Bibliography

Cyert, R. and March, J. (1963). *A Behavioral Theory of the Firm*. Englewood Cliffs, NJ: Prentice-Hall.

March, J. G. and Simon, H. A. (1958). *Organizations*. New York: Wiley.

Mouzelis, N. P. (1968). *Organization and Bureaucracy: An Analysis of Modern Theories*. Chicago: Aldine.

Pfeffer, J. and Salancik, G. (1978). *The External Control of Organizations: A Resource Dependence Perspective*. New York: Harper and Row.

Scott, W. R. (1981). *Organizations: Rational, Natural, and Open Systems*. Englewood Cliffs, NJ: Prentice-Hall.

Selznick, P. (1949). *TVA and the Grass Roots*. Berkeley, CA: University of California Press.

Selznick, P. (1957). *Leadership in Administration*. New York: Harper and Row.

Simon, H. A. (1948). *Administrative Behavior*. New York: Macmillan.

organizational boundaries *see* ORGANIZA-
TIONAL DESIGN; ORGANIZATIONAL STRUC-
TURE; TRANSACTION COSTS ECONOMICS

organizational change

Andrew H. Van de Ven

Organizational change is defined as a difference in form, quality, or state over time in an organizational entity. The entity may be an individual's job, a work group, an organizational subunit, the overall organization, or its relationships with other organizations. Change can be determined by measuring the same entity over two or more points in time on a set of dimensions and then calculating the differences over time in these dimensions. If the difference is greater than zero, we can say that the organizational entity has changed. Much of the voluminous literature on organizational change focuses on the nature of this difference, what produced it, and what are its consequences.

Barnett and Carroll (1995) make a useful distinction between the content and process of change. Content refers to what actually changes in an organizational entity, while process examines how the change occurs. Content studies tend to focus on the antecedents and conse-

quences of organizational change, while process studies examine the sequence of events over time as change unfolds in an organizational entity. Change content and process are interrelated and their effects on organizational outcomes have been difficult to estimate separately. As a result, empirical evidence on the consequences of change is fragmentary and occasionally contradictory (Barnett and Carroll, 1995; Greve, 1999).

THE CONTENT OF ORGANIZATIONAL
CHANGE

Change in organizations can occur at various levels of analysis, including the individual, group, organization, population or networks of organizations, and even larger communities or societies of organizations. Understanding organizational change therefore requires careful focus on what level is being examined, as well as what characteristics or variables are used to measure change at each level. For example, these changes may include the following:

• Changes in composition (e.g., personnel mobility, recruitment, promotion or lay-offs, and shifts in resource allocations among organizational units).

• Changes in structure (e.g., alterations of the organization's GOVERNANCE structure, centralization of DECISION-MAKING, formalization of rules, monitoring and control systems, and inequalities of status or power among units or positions).

• Changes in functions (e.g., organizational or subunit strategies, goals, mandates, products, or services).

• Changes in boundaries (as brought about by mergers, acquisitions, or divestitures of organizational units; establishing joint ventures or strategic alliances; modifying membership admission criteria; or organizational expansions or contractions in regions, markets, products/services, and political domains).

• Changes in relationships among organizational levels and units (e.g., increases or decreases in resource dependencies, work flows, COMMUNICATIONS, CONFLICT, cooperation, competition, control, or culture among organizational entities).

- Changes in performance, including effectiveness (degree of goal attainment), efficiency (cost per unit of output), and morale of participants (e.g., JOB SATISFACTION or quality of work life).
- Changes in the environment (ecological munificence or scarcity, turbulence, uncertainty, complexity, or heterogeneity).

Recognizing that amounts of change in any of these content areas vary widely in an organization over time, much of the literature has distinguished between incremental and radical change. Incremental (first order) change channels an organizational entity in the direction of adapting its basic structure and maintaining its identity in a stable and predictable way as it changes. Radical (second order) change creates novel forms that are discontinuous and unpredictable departures from the past (see review by Meyer, Brooks, and Goes, 1990). Typically, observed changes represent small, incremental, convergent, or continuous differences in localized parts of the organization without major repercussions to other parts of the system. The organization as a whole remains intact, and no overall change of its former state occurs in spite of the incremental changes going on inside. While first order changes may represent radical transformations *of* organizational subunits, they typically represent only incremental or continuous changes *in* the overall organizational system. Indeed, system stability often requires these kinds of incremental changes (*see* ORGANIZATIONAL DESIGN). Occasionally, large differences may occur in all (or at least the core) components of the system, producing a radical transformation or mutation of the overall organization. These second order changes lead us to treat the new organizational system as fundamentally different from the old one.

The borderline between these extremes is somewhat fluid. Incremental changes in organizational units may accumulate and affect the core of the system, producing a radical change of the overall organization. Path dependencies or positive feedback may exist among incremental change events so that the timing of the changes may lead to major transformations. These incremental and radical changes in organizations may also alternate over time. For example, in the punctuated equilibrium model described by Tushman and Romanelli (1985) and Gersick (1991), organizational metamorphosis is explained by long periods of incremental, first order changes that refine an organization's operations, products, and services. These convergent periods are occasionally punctuated by short periods of technological ferment, which may produce radical and discontinuous second order changes in the organization.

THE CORRELATES OF ORGANIZATIONAL CHANGE

Organizational scholars have debated whether organizational changes help or hinder organizational survival. An early population ecology view argued that organizations are imprinted at birth with their identity and structure, and cannot change easily or quickly, and they entail significant risks of failure when they do change. Natural selction at the population level replaces misfit forms of organizations with new forms (Hannan and Freeman, 1984; Freeman, Carroll, and Hannan, 1983) (*see* EVOLUTIONARY PERSPECTIVES). In contrast, adaptation theorists argue that organizational change is driven by the strategic choices, learning, and adaptive responses of managers to shifting environmental demands and opportunities, which lead to reducing organizational mortality rates (Amburgey, Kelly, and Barnett, 1993; Baum and Oliver, 1991; Zajac and Kraatz, 1993).

Empirical studies of organizational change have bridged this debate. For example, in a study of not-for-profit human service organizations in Toronto, Singh, House, and Tucker (1986) found that selection and adaptation are complementary views that explain different kinds of change. Radical or core organizational changes are best explained by an ecological selection view, while incremental or peripheral organizational changes are better described by an adaptation view. Haveman, Russo, and Meyer (2001) bridged the selection and adaptation views in terms of the timing of organizations' responses to discontinuous regulatory changes in California hospital and thrift industries. They found that major industry regulatory change prompted shifts in organizational domains and executive LEADERSHIP. After the shakeup, organizational changes and CEO succession affected subsequent performance. Other researchers (e.g., Lant, Milliken, and Batra, 1992; Virany, Tushman, and Romanelli, 1992; Greve, 1998) have studied the factors that determine organizational reorientations in different environmental contexts. These studies suggest that poor past performance, managerial awareness and interpretations of environments, and turnover of the CEO and TOP MANAGEMENT TEAMS increased the likelihood of organizational reorientations. Greve (1999) found that organizational changes cause performance to decline, as inertia theory predicts, but this is moderated by organizational size and performance before the change. Large and high-performing organizations had greater losses when changing than small and low-performing organizations because of regression toward the market mean. Audia, Locke, and Smith (2000) found that past success led managers to persist in their strategies after a radical environmental change, and such PERSISTENCE induced performance declines. Their laboratory study demonstrated that dysfunctional persistence is due to greater satisfaction with past performance, more confidence in the correctness of current strategies, higher goals, and self-efficacy, and less information seeking from critics. Greve concludes that managers of large and successful organizations may feel confident that they can successfully change their organizations, but it is exactly these organizations that stand to lose by changing (*see* NETWORKS; INTER-ORGANIZATIONAL RELATIONS).

Another factor that appears to moderate the change–performance relationship is inter-organizational ties and network position. Researchers (including Galaskiewicz and Wasserman,1989; Uzzi, 1996; and Kraatz, 1998) found that strong ties to other organizations mitigate uncertainty and promote adaptation by increasing communication and information sharing. Networks can promote social learning of adaptive responses, rather than other less productive forms of imitation between organizations.

Processes of Organizational Change

Scholars have proposed and studied a variety of process theories that may explain how organiza-

tions change. Useful reviews are provided by Weick and Quinn (1999), Poole et al. (2000), and Poole and Van de Ven (2004). We summarize below Van de Ven and Poole's (1995) perspective of four different theories that are often used to explain how and why organizational changes unfold: life cycle, teleology, dialectics, and evolution. These four theories represent fundamentally different explanations of organizational change in any of the substantive content areas listed before. Each theory focuses attention on a different set of generating mechanisms and causal cycles to explain what triggers change and what follows what in a sequence of organizational changes.

Life cycle theory (regulated change)   Many OB scholars have adopted the metaphor of organic growth as a heuristic device to explain changes in an organizational entity from its initiation to its termination (see applications in Huber and Glick, 1993). Witness, for example, often-used references to the life cycles of organizations, products, and ventures, as well as stages in the development of individual careers, groups, and organizations: startup births, adolescent growth, maturity, and decline or death. Life cycle theory assumes that change is immanent; that is, the developing entity has within it an underlying form, logic, program, or code that regulates the process of change and moves the entity from a given point of departure toward a subsequent end that is already prefigured in the present state. What lies latent, rudimentary, or homogeneous in the embryo or primitive state becomes progressively more realized, mature, and differentiated. External environmental events and processes can influence how the immanent form expresses itself, but they are always mediated by the immanent logic, rules, or programs that govern development.

The typical progression of events in a life cycle model is a unitary sequence (it follows a single sequence of stages or phases), which is cumulative (characteristics acquired in earlier stages are retained in later stages) and conjunctive (the stages are related such that they derive from a common underlying process). This is because the trajectory to the final end state is prefigured and requires a specific historical sequence of events. Each of these events contributes a certain piece to the final product, and they must occur in a certain order because each piece sets the stage for the next. Each stage of development can be seen as a necessary precursor of the succeeding stage.

Life cycle theories of organizations often explain development in terms of institutional rules or programs that require developmental activities to progress in a prescribed sequence. For example, a legislative bill enacting state educational reform cannot be passed until it has been drafted and gone through the necessary House and Senate committees. Other life cycle theories rely on logical or natural properties of organizations. For example, Rogers's (2003) theory posits five stages of INNOVATION: need recognition, research on the problem, development of an idea into useful form, commercialization, and adoption and diffusion. The order among these stages is necessitated both by logic and by the natural order of Western business practices.

Teleological theory (intentional change)   Another family of process theories uses teleology to explain development. This approach underlies many organizational theories of planned change, including functionalism, decision-making, adaptive learning, and most models of strategic choice and GOAL SETTING. A teleological theory is based on the assumption that change proceeds toward a goal or end state. It assumes that the organization is populated by purposeful and adaptive individuals. Working alone or with others, they construct an envisioned end state, take action to reach it, and monitor their progress. Thus, this theory views development as a cycle of goal formulation, implementation, evaluation, and modification based on what was learned or intended. This theory can operate in a single individual or among a group of cooperating individuals or organizations who are sufficiently like-minded to act as a single collective entity. Since the individual or cooperating entities have the freedom to set whatever goals they like, teleological theory inherently accommodates creativity; there are no necessary constraints or forms that mandate reproduction of the current entity or state.

Unlike life cycle theory, teleology does not presume a necessary sequence of events or specify which trajectory development will follow.

However, it does imply a standard by which development can be judged: development is that which moves the entity toward its final state. There is no prefigured rule, logically necessary direction, or set sequence of stages in a teleological process. Instead, these theories focus on the prerequisites for attaining the goal or end state: the functions that must be fulfilled, the accomplishments that must be achieved, or the components that must be built or obtained for the end state to be realized. These prerequisites can be used to assess when an entity is developing, when it is growing more complex, more integrated, or when it is fulfilling a necessary set of functions. This assessment can be made because teleological theories posit an envisioned end state or design for an entity, and it is possible to observe movement toward the end state vis-à-vis this standard.

Teleological models of development incorporate the SYSTEMS THEORY assumption of equifinality (i.e., there are several equally effective ways to achieve a given goal). There is no assumption about historical necessity. Changes in organizations are viewed as movements toward attaining a desired purpose, goal, function, or end state. There is no hard and fast order in which the organization must acquire the means and resources to achieve this goal.

While teleology stresses the purposiveness of the individual as the generating force for change, it also recognizes limits on action. The organization's environment and its resources of knowledge, time, money, etc. constrain what it can accomplish. Individuals do not override natural laws or environmental constraints but make use of them in accomplishing their purposes. Once an entity attains this end state, it does not mean it stays in permanent equilibrium. Influences in the external environment or within the entity itself may create instabilities that push it to a new developmental path or trajectory.

Dialectical theory (conflictual change)   A third family, dialectical theories, is rooted in the assumption that the organization exists in a pluralistic world of colliding events, forces, or contradictory values that compete with each other for domination and control. These oppositions may be internal to an organization because it may have several conflicting goals or interest groups competing for priority. Oppositions may also arise external to the organization as it pursues directions that collide with those of others (see Burawoy and Skocpol, 1982).

Dialectical process theories explain stability and change by reference to the relative balance of power between opposing entities. Stability is produced through struggles and accommodations that maintain the status quo between oppositions. Change occurs when these opposing values, forces, or events gain sufficient power to confront and engage the status quo. For example, in the Hegelian process of thesis, antithesis, and synthesis, the relative power of an opposing paradigm or antithesis may mobilize to a sufficient degree to challenge the current thesis or state of affairs and set the stage for producing a synthesis. More precisely, the status quo subscribing to a thesis (A) may be challenged by an opposing entity with an antithesis (Not-A); therefore, the resolution of the conflict produces a synthesis (which is Not Not-A). Over time, this synthesis can become the new thesis as the dialectical process recycles and continues. By its very nature, the synthesis is something new, discontinuous with thesis and antithesis.

An alternative to the Hegelian dialectic is the *tension* dialectic (Bakhtin, 1981), which examines a never-ending series of tensions between dualisms or oppositions. Each side of the dualism requires the other to exist, and there is a constant interplay between the two. Opposing terms mutually imply each other, exist through their opposition, and always remain at work as potential sources of change. Organizations consist of multiple tensions that exist simultaneously, such as pressures for integration–differentiation, exploration–exploitation, and interdependence–independence. Change is shaped by how an organizational unit deals with the dialectic and the challenges and conflicts that it spawns.

Evolutionary theory (competitive change) Although evolution is sometimes equated with change, evolution is used here in a restrictive sense to focus on cumulative and probabilistic changes in structural forms of populations of organizations. As in biological evolution, change proceeds through a continuous cycle of variation, selection, and retention. Variations, the creation of novel forms, are often viewed as emerging by blind or random chance; they just happen. Selection occurs principally through the competition among forms, and the environment selects those forms that optimize or are best suited for the resource base of an environmental niche. Retention involves the forces (including inertia and persistence) that perpetuate and maintain certain organizational forms. Retention serves to counteract the self-reinforcing loop between variations and selection (Aldrich, 1999; Baum and McKelvey, 1999). Thus, evolutionary theory explains changes as recurrent, cumulative, and probabilistic progressions of variation, selection, and retention of organizational entities.

Alternative theories of social evolution can be distinguished in terms of how traits are inherited and whether change proceeds incrementally or radically. A Darwinian view of evolution argues that traits are inherited through intergenerational processes. New organizational forms are determined and imprinted at birth and do not change throughout an organization's life due to organizational inertia (Stinchcombe, 1965). Those who follow a Lamarckian view (e.g., Burgelman, 1991; Baum and Rao, 2004) argue that organizations learn, adapt, and can acquire novel variations at different times throughout their life span.

Social Darwinian theorists emphasize a continuous and gradual process of evolution. In *The Origin of Species* Darwin wrote: "as natural selection acts solely by accumulating slight, successive, favourable variations, it can produce no great or sudden modifications; it can act only by short and slow steps." Other evolutionists posit a saltational theory of evolution, such as Gould and Eldridge's (1977) punctuated equilibrium, which Tushman and Romanelli (1985) and Gersick (1991) introduced to the management literature. Whether an evolutionary change proceeds at gradual versus saltational rates is an empirical matter, for the rate of change does not fundamentally alter the theory of evolution – at least as it has been adopted thus far by organization and management scholars (*see* EVOLUTIONARY PSYCHOLOGY; EVOLUTIONARY PERSPECTIVES).

CONCLUSION

Life cycle, teleology, dialectics, and evolutionary theories provide four useful ways to think about processes of organizational change. The relevance of the four theories depends upon the conditions surrounding the organizational change in question. Specifically, Van de Ven and Poole (1995) propose that the four theories explain processes of organizational change and development under the following conditions.

- Life cycle theory explains change processes within an entity when natural, logical, or institutional rules exist to regulate the process.
- Teleological theory explains change processes within an entity or among a cooperating set of entities when a new desired end state is socially constructed and consensus emerges on the means and resources needed to reach the desired end state.
- Dialectical theory explains change processes between conflicting entities when the aggressor entities are sufficiently powerful and choose to engage the opposition through direct confrontation, bargaining, or partisan mutual adjustment.
- Evolutionary theory explains change processes between a population of entities when they compete for similar scarce resources in an environmental niche.

Thus, to explain organizational change in any content area, one applies the theory that best fits the specific conditions. Organizational change often appears more complex than these process models suggest. This may be due to several reasons.

First, change processes often get bogged down because of errors in implementing any one of the process models. Teleological processes of planned change are subject to individual cognitive biases (Kahneman, Slovic, and Tversky, 1982), errors in critical thinking and decision-making (Nutt, 2002), escalating commitments to failing courses of action (Ross and Staw, 1986), and GROUPTHINK (Janis, 1989). Dialectical processes of change often fail due to dysfunctional methods of conflict resolution and

NEGOTIATION (Bazerman, 1985). Regulated changes in life cycle models are often resisted, resulting in sabotage or mere compliance with mandates rather than internalizing them (Seo, Putnam, and Bartunek, 2004). Finally, evolutionary processes of variation, selection, and retention only work under conditions of competition for scarce resources; they break down when resources are munificent and competition is low (Aldrich, 1999).

Second, errors or omissions in implementing one model of change may trigger the startup of another change model. For example, a failure to reach consensus among leaders of a planned change may bifurcate the leaders into two opposing factions who then engage in dialectical conflict and struggle. So also, age and size may lead to inertia in the life cycles of organizational products, processes, and routines, and make them less responsive to environmental changes. Adaptation failures in these life cycles may trigger an evolutionary process of the environment selecting out the misfit. There are many possible ways that the four process models may trigger, compensate, and complement each other.

A third reason why organizational change is often complex is because positive and negative interactions among several models of change can move an organization towards (1) equilibrium, (2) oscillation, and (3) chaos. Organizational equilibrium results when its routines, goals, or VALUES are sufficiently dominant to suppress opposing minority positions, and thereby produce incremental adaptations flowing toward equilibrium. For example, an existing ORGANIZATIONAL CULTURE, structure, or system can remain intact by undertaking incremental adaptations that appease or diffuse opposing minority positions. Organizational business cycles, fads, or pendulum swings occur when opposing interest groups, business regimes, or political parties alternate in power and push the organization somewhat farther from a stable equilibrium. Such cycles explain recurrent periods of organizational feast and famine, partisan mutual adjustment among political parties, and alternating organizational priorities on efficiency and innovation. Third, seemingly random organizational behaviors are produced when strong oscillations or shifts occur between opposing forces that push the organization out of a single periodic equilibrium orbit and produce multiple equilibria and bifurcations. Currently, there is growing interest in recent advances in chaos theory and nonlinear dynamic models to explain such seemingly random behavior in organizations. Thus, different patterns of interaction between change motors can push an organization to flow toward equilibrium, to oscillate in cycles between opposites, or to bifurcate far from equilibrium and spontaneously create revolutionary changes.

As these complexities and implementation errors imply, it is important to conclude with the caveat that existing theories of organizational change are explanatory but not predictive. Statistically, we should expect most incremental, convergent, and continuous changes to be explained by either life cycle or evolutionary theories and most radical, divergent, and discontinuous changes to be explained by teleological or dialectical theories. But these actuarial relationships may not be causal. For example, the infrequent statistical occurrence of a discontinuous and radical mutation may be caused by a glitch in the operation of a life cycle model of change. So also, the scale-up of a teleological process to create a planned strategic reorientation for a company may fizzle, resulting only in incremental change.

See also *change evaluation; change methods; organizational decline and death; organizational development; organizational effectiveness; role transitions*

Bibliography

Aldrich, H. (1999). *Organizations Evolving.* Englewood Cliffs, NJ: Prentice-Hall.

Amburgey, T., Kelly, D., and Barnett, W. (1993). The dynamics of organizational change and failure. *Administrative Science Quarterly*, 38, 51–73.

Audia, P. G., Locke, E. A., and Smith, K. G. (2000). The paradox of success: An archival and a laboratory study of strategic persistence following radical environmental change. *Academy of Management Journal*, 43 (5), 837–53.

Bakhtin, M. M. (1981). *The Dialogic Imagination: Four Essays by M. M. Bakhtin,* trans. C. Emerson and M. Holquist. Austin: University of Texas Press.

Barnett, W. P. and Carroll, G. R. (1995). Modeling internal organizational change. *Annual Review of Sociology*, 21, 217–36.

Baum, J. A. and McKelvey, B. (1999). *Variations in Organization Science: In Honor of Donald T. Campbell.* Thousand Oaks, CA: Sage.

Baum, J. A. and Oliver, C. (1991). Institutional linkages and organizational mortality. *Administrative Science Quarterly*, 36, 187–218.

Baum, J. A. C. and Rao, H. (2004). Evolutionary dynamics of organizational populations and communities. In M. S. Poole and A. H. Van de Ven (eds.), *Handbook of Organizational Change and Innovation.* New York: Oxford University Press.

Bazerman, M. H. (1985). Norms of distributive justice in interest arbitration. *Industrial and Labor Relations Review*, 38, 558–70.

Burawoy, M. and Skocpol, T. (1982). *Marxist Inquiries: Studies of Labor, Class, and States.* Chicago: University of Chicago Press.

Burgelman, R. A. (1991). Inter-organizational ecology of strategy making and organizational adaptation: Theory and field research. *Organization Science*, 2 (3), 239–62.

Freeman, J., Carroll, G. R., and Hannan, M. T. (1983). The liability of newness: Age dependence in organizational death rates. *American Sociological Review*, 48, 692–710.

Galaskiewicz, J. and Wasserman, S. (1989). Mimetic processes within an inter-organizational field: An empirical test. *Administrative Science Quarterly*, 34, 454–79.

Gersick, C. J. G. (1991). Revolutionary change theories: A multilevel exploration of the punctuated equilibrium paradigm. *Academy of Management Review*, 16 (1), 10–37.

Gould, S. J. and Eldridge, N. (1977). Punctuated equilibria: The tempo and model of evolution reconsidered. *Paleobiology*, 3, 115–51.

Greve, H. R. (1998). Performance, aspirations, and risky organizational change. *Administrative Science Quarterly*, 43, 58–86.

Greve, H. R. (1999). The effect of core change on performance: Inertia and regression toward the mean. *Administrative Science Quarterly*, 44, 590–614.

Hannan, M. T. and Freeman, J. (1984). Structural inertia and organizational change. *American Sociological Review*, 49, 149–64.

Haveman, H. A., Russo, M. V., and Meyer, A. D. (2001). Organizational environments in flux: The impact of regulatory punctuations on organizational domains, CEO succession, and performance. *Organization Science*, 12 (3), 253–73.

Huber, G. P. and Glick, W. H. (1993). *Organizational Change and Redesign: Ideas and Insights for Improving Performance.* New York: Oxford University Press.

Janis, I. L. (1989). *Crucial Decisions*. New York: Free Press.

Kahneman, D., Slovic, P., and Tversky, A. (1982). *Judgment Under Uncertainty: Heuristics and Biases*. Cambridge: Cambridge University Press.

Kraatz, M. S. (1998). Learning by association? Interorganizational networks and adaptation to environmental change. *Academy of Management Journal*, 41 (6), 621–43.

Lant, T. K., Milliken, F. J., and Batra, B. (1992). The role of managerial learning and interpretation in strategic persistence and reorientation: An empirical exploration. *Strategic Management Journal*, 13, 585–608.

Meyer, A. D., Brooks, G. R., and Goes, J. B. (1990). Environmental jolts and industry revolutions: Organizational responses to discontinuous change. *Strategic Management Journal*, 11, 93–110.

Nutt, P. C. (2002). *Why Decisions Fail: Avoiding the Blunders and Traps That Lead to Debacles*. San Francisco: Berrett-Koehler.

Poole, M. S. and Van de Ven, A. H. (2004). *Handbook of Organizational Change and Innovation*. New York: Oxford University Press.

Poole, M. S., Van de Ven, A. H., Dooley, K., and Holmes, M. E. (2000). *Organizational Change and Innovation Processes: Theory and Methods for Research*. New York: Oxford University Press.

Rogers, E. (2003). *Diffusion of Innovations*, 5th edn. New York: Simon and Schuster.

Ross, J. and Staw, B. (1986). Expo 86: An escalation prototype. *Administrative Science Quarterly*, 31, 274–97.

Seo, M., Putnam, L. L., and Bartunek, J. M. (2004). Dualities and tensions of planned organizational change. In M. S. Poole and A. Van de Ven (eds.), *Handbook of Organizational Change and Innovation*. New York: Oxford University Press.

Singh, J. F., House, R. J., and Tucker, D. J. (1986). Organizational change and organizational mortality. *Administrative Science Quarterly* (December), 587–611.

Stinchcombe, A. (1965). Social structure and organizations. In J. March (ed.), *Handbook of Organizations*. Chicago: Rand McNally.

Tushman, M. L. and Romanelli, E. (1985). Organizational evolution: A metamorphosis model of convergence and reorientation. In B. Staw and L. Cummings (eds.), *Research in Organizational Behavior*, Vol. 7. Greenwich, CT: JAI Press.

Uzzi, B. D. (1996). The sources and consequences of embeddedness for the economic performance of organizations: The network effect. *American Sociological Review*, 61, 674–98.

Van de Ven, A. H. and Poole, M. S. (1995). Explaining development and change in organizations. *Academy of Management Review*, 20, 510–40.

Virany, B., Tushman, M. L., and Romanelli, E. (1992). Executive succession and organizational outcomes in turbulent environments: An organizational learning approach. *Organization Science*, 3, 72–91.

Weick, K. E. and Quinn, R. E. (1999). Organizational change and development. *Annual Review of Psychology*, 50, 361–86.

Zajac, E. J. and Kraatz, M. S. (1993). A diametric forces model of strategic change: Assessing the antecedents and consequences of restructuring in the higher education industry. *Strategic Management Journal*, 14, 83–102.

organizational citizenship behavior (OCB)

Robert H. Moorman

OCB describes a type of job performance that is discretionary, not directly recognized by the formal reward system, and helps promote organizational effectiveness (Organ, 1988). Employees who perform OCB are those who may help a co-worker who has been absent from work, adjust their work schedule to fill-in when needed, or show genuine concern and courtesy toward fellow workers.

Most research on OCB performance has focused on its causes and consequences. The causes of OCB performance include a variety of job attitudes (JOB SATISFACTION, perceived fairness, organizational commitment), dispositional variables (agreeableness, conscientiousness, positive affectivity), organizational characteristics (team characteristics, organizational structure), and LEADERSHIP behaviors (transformational leader behaviors, contingent reward behavior) (Podsakoff et al., 2000).

One of the most popular areas of research on the causes of OCB is the study of how job attitudes relate to OCB performance. One explanation of this relationship is based on social exchange theory, which suggests that employees seek to reciprocate benefits received from an organization by contributing various forms of job performance (*see* EXCHANGE RELATIONS). Job attitudes may represent the judgment that the employee has received benefits and these attitudes may then prompt reciprocation in the form of OCB. While there has been much support for relationships between job attitudes and OCB, much more needs to be discovered on the exact process that explains why job attitudes relate to OCB (Moorman and Byrne, 2004) (*see* ATTITUDE THEORY).

Beyond their search for OCB causes, researchers have more recently examined Organ's assumption that OCB performance will benefit an organization. In a meta-analysis of studies examining relationships between OCB and various forms of performance, Podsakoff et al. (2000) provide evidence that the aggregation of employee OCB can translate to more bottom-line performance benefits.

Ironically, issues that have not yet been adequately researched focus mostly on some of the most basic questions about OCB: its construct VALIDITY. Even after decades of research, questions on the definition of OCB remain, as do questions about its dimensionality and measurement. For example, Organ (1997) has recently suggested that OCB might be better thought of as synonymous with contextual performance (Borman and Motowildo, 1993), which is defined as those behaviors that support the psychological and social context in which the task behaviors are performed.

Similarly, the exact dimensionality of OCB continues to evolve and researchers have yet to identify an OCB measure that completely captures the construct. When first conceptualized, OCB consisted of two dimensions labeled ALTRUISM and conscientiousness; however, various models have emerged that contain five or more dimensions. Unfortunately, there is little evidence that these larger models provide either more construct valid conceptions or more valid measures. For this reason, the resolution of definitional and measurement issues remains the greatest challenge to OCB researchers.

See also *commitment; justice, distributive; justice, procedural personality*

Bibliography

Borman, W. C. and Motowildo, S. J. (1993). Expanding the criterion domain to include elements of contextual performance. In N. Schmitt and W. Borman (eds.), *Personnel Selection in Organizations*. New York: Jossey-Bass, 71–98.

Moorman, R. H. and Byrne, Z. S. (2004). What is the role of justice in promoting organizational citizenship behavior? In J. Greenberg and J. A. Colquitt (eds.), *Handbook of Organizational Justice: Fundamental Questions about Fairness in the Workplace*. Mahwah, NJ: Lawrence Erlbaum Associates.

Organ, D. W. (1988). *Organizational Citizenship Behavior: The Good Soldier Syndrome*. Lexington, MA: Lexington Books.

Organ, D. W. (1997). Organizational citizenship behavior: It's construct clean-up time. *Human Performance*, **10**, 85–97.

Podsakoff, P. M., MacKenzie, S. B., Paine, J. B., and Bachrach, D. G. (2000). Organizational citizenship behaviors: A critical review of the theoretical and empirical literature and suggestions for future research. *Journal of Management*, **26**, 513–63.

organizational climate

Benjamin Schneider, Karen Holcombe Ehrhart, and Mark G. Ehrhart

Organizational climate can be defined as employees' shared perceptions or experiences of the policies, practices, and procedures of their workplace and the behaviors that get rewarded, supported, and expected there. Climate exists at the group or organization level of analysis. While the perceptions reside in individuals, they refer to shared contextual phenomena, such as organizational routines, and measured in the aggregate they indicate group or organization phenomena. The usefulness of the concept has been due in part to its ability to capture the human experience in organizations – how organizations look and feel to members – and also to the fact that such shared perceptions are found to be related to important unit outcomes, particularly when climate is operationalized in terms of strategic goals of the organization.

Organizational climate research has its roots in Lewin, Lippitt, and White's (1939) idea that leaders, by their behavior, engender characteristic patterns of behavior and attitudes on the part of followers. They introduced the term "social climate" to refer to the psychological conditions created by group leaders. Writings by numerous commentators in the 1960s elevated the climate construct to common usage.

In the 1960s and 1970s debates emerged over what organizational climate was and how it should be operationalized. With regard to what climate is or to what climate refers, the past two decades have seen a shift from a generic to a strategic conceptualization. Several literature reviews had reported inconsistent research findings regarding the relationship between climate and important organizational outcomes (e.g., Campbell et al., 1970). It was concluded that the variety of foci for climate conceptualizations and the various outcomes with which such data were correlated were the possible causes of the inconsistencies. Schneider (1975) therefore proposed that in order for the concept to be useful, climate should be conceptualized as a climate *for* something. This led to work on a variety of types of strategic climate. For example, safety climate as reported by factory workers was shown to predict on-the-job injuries (Zohar, 2000), and service climate as reported by bank branch employees was shown to predict customer satisfaction (e.g., Schneider, White, and Paul, 1998). Such research has been useful in (a) showing that employee experiences of their workplace relate to important outcomes and (b) identifying the practices and structures most strongly related to outcomes so action might be taken to manage them.

With regard to operationalization issues, climate researchers grappled with issues of level of analysis, including whether climate is an individual or group phenomenon and whether the aggregation of individual climate perceptions to connote larger units is appropriate and reliable. Research has shown that aggregation of carefully designed climate surveys yields both agreement among respondents in a unit and reveals between-unit differences. The challenge has been the design of surveys so as to represent the LEVELS OF ANALYSIS to which the data are to be aggregated (team, branch, organization). The demonstration of commonality in perceptions for such measures shows that climate represents an organizational (unit) not an individual attribute.

Although attention to measurement issues and the demonstration of strategically focused climate–outcome relationships are clear strengths of the climate approach, climate has received less theoretical and empirical attention in recent years, with more attention being directed to ORGANIZATIONAL CULTURE, a related though conceptually distinct construct. Culture researchers typically take more of an anthropological or clinical approach to individuals' experiences of organizations and focus on underlying VALUES, assumptions, and norms of an organization. While these foci are different from the behavioral routines on which climate has focused, our view is that the two are complementary and logically contribute to each other reciprocally (see Schneider, 2000). That is, our perspective is that routines emerge from cultural values and that, in turn, routines influence cultural values. Not everyone shares this view, with some arguing that culture is *not* climate (Martin, 2002), while others see climate as *emerging from* culture (Schein, 2000) with the reverse not mentioned.

Several interesting directions for future research on climate have recently emerged. One example is the work on climate strength. Historically, research on climate was limited to the mean level at which climate existed in a work group or organization (e.g., the extent to which there is a climate for service). Over the last decade, however, research has incorporated the agreement or consensus among individuals' climate perceptions. For example, work on service climate (Schneider, Salvaggio, and Subirats, 2002) and procedural justice climate (Colquitt, Noe, and Jackson, 2002) has shown that climate strength moderates the relationship between climate level and relevant outcomes, such that this relationship is stronger when climate strength is higher.

Interest has also grown with respect to other possible boundary conditions on the expected relationship between climate and outcomes. For example, the relationship between service climate and customer experiences has been shown to be moderated not only by climate strength but also by the frequency of employee–customer contact (Dietz, Pugh, and Wiley, in press). Other moderators of this relationship might include customer expectations, physical proximity to customers, or the importance of service relative to other organizational goals (e.g., efficiency). It is difficult to specify generic boundary conditions that would operate similarly in regards to any strategic climate of interest. However, characteristics of the economy, national culture, and/or human resources practices that are salient for the outcome of interest should be explored as potential moderators of climate–outcome relationships.

In summary, the organizational climate construct has been subjected to extensive conceptual and methodological attention since it was introduced. We have learned that a strategic focus on important organizational outcomes for the measurement of climate is essential if hypothesized relationships are to be found, that a focus on employees' perceptions of organizational routines in such measures is valid, and that an exploration of potential boundary conditions on such relationships is necessary.

See also *attitude theory; identity, organizational; organizational effectiveness*

Bibliography

Campbell, J. P., Dunnette, M. D., Lawler, E. E., III, and Weick, K. E. (1970). *Managerial Behavior, Performance, and Effectiveness.* New York: McGraw-Hill.

Colquitt, J. A., Noe, R. A., and Jackson, C. L. (2002). Justice in teams: Antecedents and consequences of procedural justice climate. *Personnel Psychology,* **55,** 83–109.

Dietz, J., Pugh, S. D., and Wiley, J. W. (in press). Service climate effects on customer attitudes: An examination of boundary conditions. *Academy of Management Journal.*

Lewin, K., Lippitt, R., and White, R. K. (1939). Patterns of aggressive behavior in experimentally created "social climates." *Journal of Social Psychology,* 10, 271–99.

Martin, J. (2002). *Organizational Culture: Mapping the Terrain.* Thousand Oaks, CA: Sage.

Schein, E. H. (2000). Sense and nonsense about culture and climate. In N. M. Ashkanasy, C. P. M. Wilderom, and M. F. Peterson (eds.), *Handbook of Organizational Culture and Climate.* Thousand Oaks, CA: Sage, xxiii–xxx.

Schneider, B. (1975). Organizational climates: An essay. *Personnel Psychology,* **28,** 447–79.

Schneider, B. (2000). The psychological life of organizations. In N. M. Ashkanasy, C. P. M. Wilderom, and M. F. Peterson (eds.), *Handbook of Organizational Culture and Climate.* Thousand Oaks, CA: Sage, xvii–xxii.

Schneider, B., Salvaggio, A. N., and Subirats, M. (2002). Climate strength: A new direction for climate research. *Journal of Applied Psychology,* **87,** 220–9.

Schneider, B., White, S., and Paul, M. C. (1998). Linking service climate and customer perceptions of service quality: Test of a causal model. *Journal of Applied Psychology,* 83, 150–63.

Zohar, D. (2000). A group-level model of safety climate: Testing the effect of group climate on micro-accidents in manufacturing jobs. *Journal of Applied Psychology,* 85, 587–96.

organizational commitment

see COMMITMENT; MOTIVATION

organizational culture

Joanne Martin

Organizational culture is embedded in the everyday working lives of *all* cultural members. Manifestations of cultures in organizations include formal practices (such as pay levels, structure of the hierarchy, job descriptions, and other written policies); informal practices (such as behavioral norms); the organizational stories employees tell to explain "how things are done around here"; RITUALS (such as Christmas parties and retirement dinners); humor (jokes about work and fellow employees); jargon (the special language of organizational initiates); and physical arrangements (including interior decor, dress norms, and architecture). Cultural manifestations also include values, sometimes referred to more abstractly as content themes. It is essential to distinguish values/content themes that are espoused by employees from values/content themes that are seen to be enacted in behavior. All of these cultural manifestations are interpreted, evaluated, and enacted in varying ways because cultural members have differing interests, experiences, responsibilities, and values. Culture consists of the patterns of meanings that link these manifestations together, sometimes in harmony, sometimes in bitter conflicts between groups, and sometimes in webs of ambiguity, paradox, and contradiction. For these reasons, it is much too simple to define culture in unifying, harmonious terms; for example, in terms of values that are espoused by management and supposedly shared by most employees.

The 1980s brought a renaissance of interest in organizational culture. The resulting proliferation of research was accompanied by fundamental and fruitful disagreements about what culture is, whether it should be studied using quantitative or qualitative methods, if its content can be controlled by management, and whether a particular kind of culture can result in stronger organizational performance. This dissension among cultural researchers, regarding such fundamental issues, makes it difficult to define culture and summarize the results of this growing literature in terms of linear progress toward greater, widely accepted knowledge.

THEORETICAL HAIRSPLITTING OR DIFFERENCES OF CONSEQUENCE?

Given this dissension, it is reasonable to ask why applied researchers and practitioners should care about cultural research. Some managers have sought to replicate the supposedly "strong" cultures of profitable companies, while others have tried "engineering values" to generate COM-MITMENT to a philosophy of management, in the hopes of increasing loyalty, productivity, or profitability. Some top executives have sought to create a culture cast in their own image, to perpetuate an organizational culture reflecting their own personal values, thereby attempting to achieve an organizational form of immortality. Usually, practitioners respond to promises of easy solutions and quick fixes with well-deserved skepticism, but organizational culture, at first, seemed immune from such skepticism. Later, disillusionment set in and many dismissed culture as yesterday's fad.

The seesaw between credulity and disillusionment has caused considerable waste of time and money. Practitioners need to know enough to judge – with appropriate skepticism – what researchers and strategic advisors are focusing on and what they are ignoring. Without some understanding of why researchers come to different conclusions about how cultures change and whether transitions can be managed, it is impossible to judge whether the results of a particular study are in some sense valid and whether they have practical applications in a given cultural context. For all these reasons, theoretical differences of opinion are not just hairsplitting debates of interest only to ivory-tower scholars.

OVERVIEW

Three theoretical traditions can be used to describe most organizational culture research to date: the Integration, Differentiation, and Fragmentation perspectives (Martin, 1992). This entry defines the premises of each perspective, summarizes results of representative studies, identifies problems inherent in each viewpoint, and reviews multiple perspective studies that transcend some of the difficulties associated with single perspective studies (Martin, 2002).

Integration perspective Of the three perspectives that have come to dominate organizational culture research, the integration perspective is the most popular and, ironically, the least well supported empirically. Integration studies of culture implicitly or explicitly assume that a culture is characterized by consistency, organization-wide consensus, and clarity. According to Integration studies, consistency occurs because people at the higher levels of an organization articulate a set of espoused values, sometimes in the form of a mission statement; these values are then reinforced by a variety of cultural manifestations that allegedly generate organization-wide value consensus. In Integration studies, there is clarity concerning what the organizational VALUES are and should be, what behaviors are preferable, and what a particular story or ritual means. Organizational members apparently know what they are to do, and they agree why it is worthwhile to do it. In the few instances when ambiguity is acknowledged, or subcultural differences emerge, they are described as "not part of the culture" or as evidence of a failure to achieve a "strong" culture.

For example, Schein (1985) focused attention on individual corporate leaders who attempt to generate company-wide consensus regarding their personal values and corporate goals through a wide range of consistent corporate policies and practices. Using a similarly functionalist approach, Collins and Porras (2002) assume an Integration view of culture and argue that such "strong" (integrated) cultures are a key to firm profitability (see also Kotter, 1992). In contrast to such functionalist research, other Integration studies take a more symbolic approach (Schultz and Hatch, 1996). For example, Barley (in Frost et al., 1991) described how funeral directors use a series of practices and rituals (e.g., putting make-up on a corpse, changing sheets on a death bed, etc.) to reinforce the idea that death can be life-like.

In most but not all Integration studies, culture supposedly originates in the values articulated by top management; these values are then re-inforced by selectively hiring people with similar priorities and by attempting to socialize new employees thoroughly (*see* SOCIALIZATION). The Integration perspective conceptualizes cultural change as an organization-wide cultural transformation, whereby an old unity is replaced – it is hoped – by a new one. In the interim, conflict and ambiguity may occur, but these are interpreted as evidence of the deterioration of culture before a new unity is established. Much of the research that initially generated the renaissance of interest in culture, particularly in the United States, falls within the Integration perspective. This view of culture still has some acceptance, in part because such a harmonious and clear environment is attractive, particularly to executives who would like to think that they could create a vision and enact a culture that would inspire such consensus.

For example, most Integration research takes a "specialist" approach, studying just one (or at most a few) manifestations, usually measures of agreement with a set of espoused values or self-reports of behavioral norms. This limitation creates problems. Self-reports of values and norms are especially liable to reflect halo effects related to overall JOB SATISFACTION, social desirability of particular responses, and IMPRESSION MANAGEMENT considerations. Meanings associated with a small sample of manifestations may not be consistent with meanings associated with the full range of manifestations of a culture. In addition, most Integration studies rely primarily on the views of managerial and professional employees, although it cannot be assumed that the views of this minority of powerful individuals are shared by all employees, particularly given the likelihood of differences of opinion across levels of a hierarchy. Finally, employees' behavioral compliance to top management's preferences or policies cannot be taken as evidence of their personal approval of values, interpretations, or norms. Thus, Integration studies often take evidence of a limited subset of a culture's manifestations or a small and unrepresentative sample of its members, assume consistency and consensus, and generalize from these limited findings to the whole culture, as perceived by all or most of its members. This part–whole error characterizes much Integration

research (Martin, 2002). Because of part–whole errors, Integration studies run the risk of tautology: culture is defined in terms of consistency, consensus, and clarity, and data regarding any manifestations, interpretations, or cultural members that do not conform to this view are excluded as not part of the culture or dismissed as evidence of a "weak" culture.

Because of part–whole errors, and because so many other variables (economic, marketing, and strategic) affect firm performance, oft-repeated claims that "strong" cultures are a key to improved organizational profitability should be regarded as, at best, unproved (Siehl and Martin, 1990). Many critics of Integration research make a stronger claim: that it is highly unlikely that any organizational culture, studied in depth, would exhibit the consistency, organization-wide consensus, and clarity that Integration studies have claimed to find (e.g., Alvesson, 2002; Martin, 1992, 2002; Turner, 1986). Thus, Integration studies offer managers and researchers a seductive promise of harmony and value homogeneity that is empirically unmerited and unlikely to be fulfilled.

Differentiation perspective Differentiation studies describe organizations as composed of overlapping, nested subcultures that coexist in relationships of intergroup harmony, conflict, or indifference. For example, in a Differentiation study, Bartunek and Moch (in Frost et al., 1991) show how five subcultures in a food production firm reacted differently to management's imposition of a quality of working life intervention. Top management was primarily concerned with control. In-house consulting staff members were cooperative. The management of the local plants where the program was implemented was paternalistic, using imagery of employees as "children" to managerial "parents." Line employees exhibited a dependent reaction, following management's preferences. Machinists, historically an active, independent, and comparatively well-paid group, actively resisted the intervention. Thus, in Differentiation studies, to the extent that consensus exists, it exists within subcultural boundaries.

A hierarchical alignment of subcultures is also evident in Van Maanen's (in Frost et al., 1991) study of ride operators at Disneyland. Food vendors ("pancake ladies" and "coke blokes") were allocated to the bottom of status ranking and male operators of yellow submarines and jungle boats shared high status. Tension between ride operators, customers, and supervisors was evident, as ride operators arranged for obnoxious customers to be soaked with water when submarine hatches opened and supervisors were foiled in their constant attempt to catch operators breaking rules. In Young's (Frost et al., 1991) study of "bag ladies" in a British manufacturing plant, tensions between management and labor were evident, and the younger and older workers fissioned into different subcultures. As these examples indicate, subcultures often appear along lines of functional, occupational, and hierarchical differentiation. Also evident in these studies is a subtext: many of these subcultural differences also reflect demographic differences (e.g., class, race, ethnicity, AGE, and GENDER), creating working environments that are racially segregated (Cox, 1993) and/or deeply gendered (e.g., Gherardi, 1995; Aaltio and Mills, 2002).

Inconsistency across cultural manifestations is also evident in Differentiation studies. For example, in the food production firm studied by Bartunek and Moch, top management said one thing to employees and did something different. At Disneyland, ride operators appeared to conform to management's rules, while doing what they pleased. In a particularly detailed examination of the effects of such inconsistencies on individuals, Kunda (1991) studied engineers' reactions as they conformed to a company ritual designed to exhibit commitment to supposedly shared company values. During moments of ease while "off stage," the engineers used humor and sarcastic side remarks to express their disapproval, skepticism, or ambivalence. As these examples indicate, espoused values, behavior mandated by formal policies, and informal norms are often observed to be inconsistent. Whereas some Differentiation studies describe subcultures in functionalist terms, as reflections of occupational socialization, other Differentiation studies take a more critical approach (Alvesson, 2002; Wilmott, 1993), conceptualizing culture as a partially successful attempt by management to exercise hegemonic control over lower ranking employees, eliciting a mix of compliance and resistance.

To summarize, a Differentiation study includes evidence of inconsistency between one cultural manifestation and another. Consensus is evident, but only within the boundaries of a subculture. Within a subculture all is clear, but ambiguities do appear at the interstices where one subculture meets another. When viewed from the Differentiation perspective, the organization is no longer seen as a cultural monolith; instead, it is a collection of subcultures. Some of these subcultures enthusiastically reinforce the views of the top management coalition or operate cooperatively with each other. Others become pockets of ignorance or resistance to top management initiatives.

From the Differentiation perspective, change is localized within one or more subcultures, alterations tend to be incremental, and change is triggered (if not determined) by pressures from an organization's environment. That environment is likely to be segmented, so different subcultures within the same organization experience different kinds and rates of change. Of the three perspectives, the Differentiation viewpoint is most congruent with research that emphasizes environmental determinants of organizational behavior.

As is the case with Integration research, the methodological choices made in Differentiation studies partially determine what results are found. For example, as can be seen in the Disneyland and "bag lady" studies, there is a tendency for Differentiation research to focus on relatively low-ranking employees or first-line supervisors – people who are less likely to share the views of top management. And within any subculture, there is a tendency to focus on the ways subcultural members share the same views, rather than on the ways subcultural members' views differ or what they find ambiguous. As a result, Differentiation studies do not distance themselves far enough from the oversimplifications and distortions of the Integration view; within a subculture, consistency, consensus, and clarity still predominate, and ambiguities are relegated to the interstices among subcultures.

Fragmentation perspective In Fragmentation studies of culture, claims of clarity, consistency, and consensus are shown to be idealized oversimplifications that fail to capture the confusing complexity of contemporary organizational functioning. The Fragmentation perspective offers a quite different alternative. Rather than banning ambiguity from the cultural stage (the Integration view) or relegating ambiguity to the interstices between subcultures (the Differentiation view), Fragmentation studies see ambiguity as the defining feature of cultures in organizations. In these studies, ambiguity is defined to include multiple meanings, paradox, irony, and inescapable contradictions. Such ambiguity pervades all but the most routine and trivial aspects of organizational functioning. Therefore, the meanings that different cultural members attach to particular cultural manifestations are neither clearly consistent nor clearly in conflict. There are many plausible interpretations of any one issue or event, making the idea of a single clear, shared cultural reality highly unlikely. To the extent that consensus exists, it is issue specific and transient: problems or issues get activated, generate positive and negative reactions, and then fade from attention as other issues take center stage, creating temporary, issue specific networks of connection that disappear and reconfigure themselves in a constant flux. From the Fragmentation perspective, culture looks less like a monolith, and less like a collection of subcultural islands, and more like a room full of spider webs, constantly being destroyed and rewoven.

For example, Feldman (in Frost et al., 1991) studied federal policy analysts who analyze policy options, write reports that never get read, and if they are read, probably never will impact policy decisions. Robertson and Swan (2003) studied highly educated consultants working within a knowledge-intensive firm where project work was inherently fluid, complex, and uncertain, embracing ambiguity. Meyerson (in Frost et al., 1991) studied the ambiguities of social work. Goals were unclear; there was no consensus regarding the appropriate means to achieve those goals; success was hard to define and even harder to assess. For social workers, ambiguity was the salient feature of their working lives and any cultural description that excluded ambiguity would be dramatically incomplete.

Whereas the Fragmentation studies described above focused on occupations coping successfully with ambiguous work, Weick (in Frost et al., 1991) has used the Fragmentation perspective in a context where the effects of ambiguities were less benign – a foggy airport in Tenerife where one airplane was attempting to land while another waited to take off. Weick focused on talk among pilots, cockpit crews, and air traffic controlers, as they coped with the complexities of making themselves understood across barriers created by differences in native language, occupational and national prestige, and incompletely shared knowledge. Hundreds of passengers died in the ensuing crash, making this study a powerful illustration of the conclusion that most Fragmentation studies draw: that an understanding of ambiguities should be a central component of any cultural study that claims to encompass the full range of cultural members' working lives.

In Fragmentation studies of culture, POWER is diffused broadly at all levels of the hierarchy and throughout the organization's environment. Culture has no specific point of origin; fleeting affinities are issue specific. Change is a constant flux, rather than an intermittent interruption in an otherwise stable state. Change is largely triggered by the environment or other forces beyond an individual's control, so that Fragmentation studies of change offer few guidelines for those who would normatively control the change process.

The methodological choices made in Fragmentation research enable these kinds of conclusions to be drawn. For example, Fragmentation studies tend to focus on highly ambiguous occupations (i.e., social worker, policy analyst) and contexts (e.g., cross-national communication, literally in the fog). As noted regarding research conducted from the other two perspectives, Fragmentation studies exhibit a form of methodological tautology: these researchers define culture in a particular way and then find what they are looking for.

Advantages of using multiple perspectives in a single study   These problems of methodological tautology, and the theoretical blind spots associated with any single perspective, can be minimized if a single cultural context is studied from each of the three perspectives, permitting a more complete understanding to emerge. While most studies utilize only one of the three perspectives, more recent research indicates that *any* organizational culture contains elements congruent with all three viewpoints (Martin, 2002). If any organization is studied in enough depth, some issues, values, and objectives will be seen to generate organization-wide consensus, consistency, and clarity (an Integration view). At the same time, other aspects of an organization's culture will coalesce into subcultures that hold differing opinions about what is important, what should happen, and why (a Differentiation view). Finally, some problems and issues will be ambiguous, in a state of constant flux, generating multiple, plausible interpretations (a Fragmentation view).

A wide range of organizational contexts have been examined using the three perspective framework, including studies of a temporary educational organization for unemployed women in England, a newly privatized bank in Turkey, the problem of truancy in an urban high school in the United States, changing organizational cultures in the Peace Corps/Africa, a search for a university provost, and professional subcultures in an Australian home care service (e.g., Bloor and Dawson, 1994; Eisenberg, Murphy, and Andrews, 1998).

A SUBJECTIVE APPROACH

Sometimes the three perspective framework is mistakenly taken to mean that some organizations will be correctly described by an Integration viewpoint, while other contexts may better fit the Differentiation or Fragmentation perspectives. This is a misunderstanding. Although these perspectives are empirically derived from the perspectives of cultural members, they are not objective representations of the views of cultural members. Who a researcher is affects what he or she sees and what questions she or he seeks to address. And the identity of a cultural member affects what information they are exposed to, what information they absorb, and what reactions they exhibit. The measurement, collection, and interpretation of qualitative or quantitative cultural data are inevitably affected by subjective factors, whether quantitative or qualitative methods are used (*see* RESEARCH METHODS).

This subjective orientation is counter-intuitive for many. Often, one theoretical perspective, labeled the "home" viewpoint, is easy for cultural members and researchers to see, while the other two perspectives can be more difficult to access. The harder it is to see applicability of a particular perspective, the more likely it is that, in changed circumstances, insights from that perspective may be crucial for organizational survival. For example, if most cultural members would like to see their organization as strongly Integrated, perhaps around the personal values of a well-respected leader, they may repress, or avoid "seeing," evidence of any kind of subgroup conflict. If then that leader were to leave the organization, subcultural conflicts might surface in a totally unanticipated way. As this example illustrates, awareness of the perspectives that are less easily seen may provide a key to anticipating, or at least understanding, organizational change.

This brief review has explained why and how many cultural researchers have disagreed about such fundamental ideas as to what culture is, how it should be studied, and whether it generates (and reflects) harmony, conflict, and/or ambiguity. These disagreements have been fruitful. In part because of the efforts of culture researchers, qualitative methods are now more broadly accepted in organizational studies. Novel applications of quantitative methods have been used to study aspects of culture (e.g., Kilduff and Corley, 2000, on network measures of the three theoretical perspectives). New approaches to writing about cultural theory have been developed (e.g., Czarniawska, 1999), and innovative theoretical approaches are being explored (e.g., Strati, 1999, on aesthetics of organizing). Poststructural cultural theorists (e.g., Jeffcutt, 1995; Wilmott, 1993) (*see* POSTMODERNISM) have shown how cultural studies can reveal the hidden biases and the silenced voices in organizational accounts, broadening the scope of our inquiries to include a wider range of contradictory theories and a greater number of cultural members' viewpoints, without coming to any single conclusion about the superiority or predominance of any of these theoretical views. As hoped by its early proponents in the 1980s, the study of culture has brought fresh ideas into organizational studies, showing how theoretical and methodological dissension can breed new insights.

See also *critical theory; culture, national; identity, organizational; organizational climate; symbolism*

Bibliography

Aaltio, I. and Mills, A. (eds.) (2002). *Gender, Identity and the Culture of Organizations*. New York: Routledge.

Alvesson, M. (2002). *Understanding Organizational Culture*. London: Sage.

Bloor, G. and Dawson, P. (1994). Understanding professional culture in organization context. *Organization Studies*, 15, 275–95.

Collins, J. and Porras, J. (2002). *Built to Last: Successful Habits of Visionary Companies*. New York: Harper Business.

Cox, T. (1993). *Cultural Diversity in Organizations: Theory, Research, and Practice*. San Francisco: Berrit-Koehler.

Czarniawska, B. (1999). *Writing Management: Organization Theory as a Literary Genre*. London: Oxford University Press.

Eisenberg, E., Murphy, A., and Andrews, L. (1998). Openness and decision-making in the search for a university provost. *Communication Monographs*, 65, 1.

Frost, P., Moore, L., Louis, M., Lundberg, C., and Martin, J. (eds.) (1991). *Reframing Organizational Culture*. Newbury Park, CA: Sage.

Gherardi, S. (1995). *Gender, Symbolism, and Organizational Cultures*. London: Sage.

Jeffcutt, P. (1995). *Culture, and Symbolism in Organizational Analysis*. Newbury Park, CA: Sage.

Kilduff, M. and Corley, K. (2000). Organizational culture from a network perspective. In N. Ashkanasy, C. Wilderom, and M. Peterson (eds.), *Handbook of Organizational Culture and Climate*. Thousand Oaks, CA: Sage, 211–21.

Kotter, J. (1992). *Corporate Culture and Performance*. New York: Free Press.

Kunda, G. (1991). *Engineering Culture: Control and Commitment in a High-Tech Corporation*. Philadelphia, PA: Temple University Press.

Martin, J. (1992). *Cultures in Organizations: Three Perspectives*. New York: Oxford University Press.

Martin, J. (2002). *Organizational Culture: Mapping the Terrain*. Newbury Park, CA: Sage.

Robertson, M. and Swan, J. (2003). "Control – what control?" Culture and ambiguity within a knowledge intensive firm. *Journal of Management Studies*, 40, 831–58.

Schein, E. (1985). *Organizational Culture and Leadership*. San Francisco: Jossey-Bass.

Schultz, M. and Hatch, M. J. (1996). Living with multiple paradigms: The case of paradigm interplay in organizational culture studies. *Academy of Management Review*, 21, 529–57.

Siehl, C. and Martin, J. (1990). Organizational culture: The key to financial performance? In B. Schneider (ed.), *Organizational Climate and Culture*. San Francisco: Jossey-Bass, 241–81.

Strati, A. (1999). *Organization and Aesthetics*. London: Sage.

Turner, B. (1986). Sociological aspects of organizational symbolism. *Organizational Studies*, 7, 101–15.

Wilmott, H. (1993). Strength is ignorance; slavery is freedom: Managing culture in modern organizations. *Journal of Management Studies*, 30, 515–52.

organizational decline and death

Robert I. Sutton

Much research on organizational decline and death was published in the 1980s and 1990s, largely in response to economic downturns in North America and Europe. Decline is a two step process in which deteriorating environmental adaptation leads to reduced internal financial resources (Cameron, Sutton, and Whetten, 1988). An organization has environmental support when it has favorable EX-CHANGE RELATIONS with groups and individuals that hold critical resources and when its actions are endorsed by powerful external groups and individuals (*see* RESOURCE DEPENDENCE). Lost environmental support results from the intertwined deterioration of an organization's image and its resource base.

Following writings on sociobiology, deterioration in environmental support can be "k-type" or "r-type." Deterioration of the k-type occurs when an organization is part of an industry, or population, with a shrinking resource base and a decaying image; such deterioration threatens all organizations in the niche. Conversely, r-type deterioration occurs when an organization is in a stable or growing niche, but takes action that causes deterioration of its specific external resource base and image.

Both kinds of deterioration lead to reduced financial resources in the organization. Decline results in pressure to reduce costs through means including workforce reduction, or "DOWNSIZING." Although sometimes used interchangeably, downsizing is distinct from decline (Sutton, 1990). Workforce reduction may reflect increased technical efficiency or be used to please external constituencies rather than in response to shrinking financial resources. Downsizing is also best viewed as a symptom rather than a cure for decline. At best, downsizing reduces the need for internal resources. At worst, it hastens decline. Departures of key personnel can harm an organization's image or its ability to produce quality products or services. Downsizing may also increase costs when displaced employees are replaced with more expensive external contractors.

If decline persists, then organizational death may occur because there are not enough resources to support core activities. Organizational death has, however, proved difficult to define and operationalize. The disappearance of an organization's name from a population is often used as the measure of death (or "mortality") in population ecology research. But it is debatable whether an organization that has "disappeared" because of a name change or merger, but otherwise continues operating, is dead. Furthermore, an organization may halt operations, but not disappear from the listed population, because it persists as a legal entity (Hannan and Freeman, 1989).

Organizational death is unambiguous to the extent that two conditions are met (Sutton, 1987). First, past participants agree that the organization has disappeared. Second, the activities once accomplished by the organization have stopped or been transferred to two or more organizations. This second condition is necessary for an unambiguous death because an organization's activities may continue intact even though it is widely construed to have disappeared as a result of a merger or name change. Unambiguous deaths often unfold through a process where the organization is first construed as a permanent entity that can live indefinitely, then as a temporary entity that is disbanding the people, things, and activities that compose it, and finally as a defunct entity.

See also *crises/disasters; organizational change*

Bibliography

Cameron, K. S., Sutton, R. I., and Whetten, D. A. (1988). Readings in Organizational Decline: Frameworks, Research, and Prescriptions. Boston, MA: Ballinger.

Hannan, M. T. and Freeman, J. (1989). *Organizational Ecology*. Cambridge, MA: Harvard University Press.

Sutton, R. I. (1987). The process of organizational death: Disbanding and reconnecting. *Administrative Science Quarterly*, **32**, 542–69.

Sutton, R. I. (1990). Organizational decline processes: A social psychological perspective. In B. M. Staw and L. L. Cummings (eds.), *Research in Organizational Behavior*, Vol. 12. Greenwich, CT: JAI Press, 205–53.

organizational demography

Anne S. Tsui and Aimee Ellis

The term organizational demography denotes the composition or distribution of a group or organization on attributes such as age, company tenure, gender, "race," educational level, and functional background. It entered the management and organization literature through a conceptual article by Pfeffer (1983) As objective proxies for underlying attributes, demographic variables are preferable to psychological constructs.

There are two major approaches to demographic analysis: the compositional and the relational (Tsui and Gutek, 1999). The compositional approach focuses on the distributions or compositions of demographic attributes within the group. A work unit could range from very homogeneous (everyone is similar to each other) to highly heterogeneous (everyone is different from others) on any demographic attribute. The experience of individuals in the heterogeneous units would be similar to each other but different from individuals in the homogeneous units. The association between company tenure heterogeneity and turnover at the firm level or between race composition and intergroup communication illustrate the composition approach.

The relational demographic approach studies the relationship between an individual's demographic attributes and the demographic attributes of others in the work unit. The other could be a single individual (e.g., the supervisor or peer) or all other members of a work unit. For example, the experience of a woman in a team with five men may be different from the experience of the men in the same unit even though both the woman and the men are situated in the unit with the same compositional demography.

Demographic attributes can be classified into surface level (e.g., AGE, GENDER), easily detectable (e.g., company tenure, occupation), and deep level (e.g., PERSONALITY, sexual orientation). The coefficient of variation (for attributes with a continuous scale such as age or tenure) and the Blau index (for attributes measured by categorical scales such as ethnicity or occupation) are used most often for measuring compositional demography. The Euclidian Distance measure is used most often to measure relational demography (for a discussion of these measures, see Tsui and Gutek, 1999). The similarity attraction paradigm (Byrne, 1972), social categorization (Turner and Associates, 1987), and social identity (Tajfel, 1982) theories explain how demographic differences affect social outcomes such as interpersonal liking, group cohesion, and organizational attachment. The information and resource-based theories explain how demographic heterogeneity affects task outcomes such as innovation or firm performance (*see* RE-SOURCE DEPENDENCE).

A major criticism of early organizational demography was that it infers processes not directly measured (Lawrence, 1997). Recent research has addressed this criticism by focusing on the mediating processes between demographic heterogeneity and outcomes. Mediating processes include social categorization followed by impersonalized attraction, social identification accompanied by interpersonal attraction, communication, and discovery of knowledge, skills, and perspectives. Recent advances also include using moderators at both the individual (e.g., personality, values) and context levels (e.g., business strategy, national culture) to sharpen the prediction of demographic effects.

Organizational demography, which attempts to understand the experiences of all individuals in relation to their group members, offers a significant theoretical framework through which to comprehend the effects of demographic heterogeneity in organizations.

See also *conflict and conflict management; diversity management; organizational culture*

Bibliography

Byrne, D. (1972). *The Attraction Paradigm*. New York: Academic Press.

Lawrence, B. S. (1997). The black box of organizational demography. *Organization Science*, 8 (1), 1–22.

Pfeffer, J. (1983). Organizational demography. In L. L. Cummings and B. M. Staw (eds.), *Research in Organizational Behavior*, Vol. 5. Greenwich, CT: JAI Press, 299–357.

Tajfel, H. (1982). *Social Identity and Intergroup Relations*. Cambridge: Cambridge University Press.

Tsui, A. S. and Gutek, B. A. (1999). *Demographic Differences in Organizations: Current Research and Future Directions*. Oxford: Lexington Books.

Turner, J. C. and Associates (1987). *Rediscovering the Social Group: A Self-Categorization Theory*. Oxford: Blackwell.

organizational design

N. Anand

Organizational design encompasses two distinctive sets of ideas. The first is descriptive and theoretical. It relates to how organizations come to acquire a particular structure (i.e., how organizations are, so to speak, "designed"). The second is more pragmatic and practical. It is concerned with the principles for deriving the ideal organizational structure for a given set of circumstances (i.e., how organizations should be designed).

THEORIES OF ORGANIZATIONAL DESIGN

Theories of variation in organizational design can be traced back to the writings of classical scholars of sociology and political economy. Max Weber observed that distinctive AUTHORITY systems in society led to different modes in which work was assigned, accomplished, and monitored. He described three ideal types of organization: charismatic, feudal, and bureaucratic. Emile Durkheim noted that as a society becomes more developed, tasks and occupations become more specialized and complex organizational forms evolve. Adam Smith, who was a contemporaneous observer of the industrial revolution, provided a memorable description of a pin factory in extolling the advantages of the division of labor. He argued that when compared to an organization where a single individual accomplished all the tasks of pin making, the organization in which the task was divided up among four or five individuals was several hundred times more productive.

Theories of organizational design can be grouped into three approaches: rational, natural, and OPEN SYSTEMS (Scott, 1998). From the rational systems approach, organizations are seen as formal mechanisms for executing tasks that accomplish a desired goal. SCIENTIFIC MANAGEMENT is one strand. Henri Fayol, a practicing manager, was interested in the formalization of roles and responsibilities. Fredrick Taylor, a management consultant, was concerned with efficiency in attaining goals. Max Weber's description of the BUREAUCRACY organization is another strand. Bureaucracy is ultimately rational because of its emphasis on depersonalization of office, efficiency, calculability, predictability, and control (Ritzer, 1993). March and Simon (1958) provided a critique and refinement of this approach by revealing cognitive factors and political interests that shape the manner in which decisions are made in the rational pursuit of goals in organizations.

From the natural systems approach, organizations are seen as social collectives where members are interlinked both formally and informally and pursue multiple and sometimes contradictory goals. The human relations view of management, with its focus on the needs and motivations of members that might be at cross-purposes with organizational goal attainment, exemplifies this approach. Elton Mayo argued that informal structures are vital to an organization's functioning. Chester Barnard envisioned organization as a cooperative enterprise wherein the compliance of followers, rather than being taken for granted, should be secured by creating appropriate systems of belief. Philip Selznick argued that although organization is a rational instrument for task accomplishment, due to social commitments of members it becomes infused with value and takes on an institutional character.

The open systems approach inspired by Ludwig van Bertalanffy views organizations as a set of interlinked elements enclosed within a boundary but embedded in a dynamic exchange with the external environment. The relationship between organizations and environment is reciprocal, comprising action, FEEDBACK, and adaptation. While the rational and natural systems approaches have made their mark in thinking about organizational design, many of the contemporary schools explicitly follow on from the open systems approach, and these are enumerated below.

Contemporary schools of organizational design Research on effective design was spurred by the work of Thompson, who developed a number of postulates on adapting to environmental uncertainty and to types of task interdependence. This led in part to the development of a structural contingency school, which holds that organizations need to be structured differently contingent upon factors such as size, dominant technology, task interdependence, and amount of environmental uncertainty (Donaldson, 2001). CONTINGENCY THEORY holds that there is no one best way of organizing, but also that any way of organizing is not equally effective (Galbraith, 1973). For example, if the environment is highly stable and simple, a mechanistic structure might be more effective than an organic one (Burns and Stalker, 1961). While contingency theory has been the dominant paradigm in explaining the variation in organizational design, it also has been criticized for not developing an adequate concept of agency or strategic choice (Child, 1982) and also for not integrating concerns of legitimacy and authority raised by the classical sociologists and natural systems theorists.

The information processing school of design began by recasting organization and environment as an informational problematic and by assuming that organizations process information to reduce uncertainty (Galbraith, 1973). In this view, organizational hierarchies are seen as a vertical information processing system, while linking or coordinating activity is seen as a horizontal information processing system. Environments and tasks pose information processing requirements and different organizational designs provide different types of information processing capacity. The overall function of organization design is conceptualized in terms of three information related activities: scanning the environment, interpreting its implications, and responding with the appropriate structural adaptation (Daft and Weick, 1984). Daft and Lengel (1986) showed that different types of organizational structure, specifically the type of media used for communication, differ in their ability to provide appropriate interpretations of ambiguous task or environmental conditions. Lean media, such as written policy guidelines, are less capable of providing complex interpretations when compared to rich media, such as face-to-face meetings. The information processing school follows contingency theory in suggesting that organizational effectiveness results where there is a fit between the information processing requirements and capacity (Nadler and Tushman, 1997).

The RESOURCE DEPENDENCE approach follows Thompson in viewing organizations as needing to exchange resources in order to survive (Pfeffer and Salancik, 1978). It is the one school most sensitive to the political context within which organizations operate and hence helps explain the origin and variation in buffering structures that are designed to manage various external dependencies such as administrative units dealing with donors or financial supporters (Tolbert, 1985), interlocking directorates (Mizruchi and Stearns, 1988), and hybrid career systems (Scherer and Lee, 2002).

INSTITUTIONAL THEORY is a somewhat distinctive school of design in that it looks at organizations from the outside in, theorizing about how cultural rules operating in society at large dictate the appropriate form that an organization should take. Meyer and Rowan (1977) argued that publics dealing with an organization hold certain expectations of the legitimate structure that it ought to have. Consequently, an organization's effectiveness, to a certain degree, depends on being able to fulfil those expectations by being responsive to external cultural and symbolic influences. DiMaggio and Powell (1983) likewise theorized that organizations are embedded in fields that mutually shape structural, cultural, and cognitive processes and thereby influence decisions about design. Application of this theory can be found, for example, both in the explanation for the adoption of the

multidivisional form among American corporations (Fligstein, 1985) between 1919 and 1979, as well as the abandonment of the form in the 1980s (Davis, Diekmann, and Tinsley, 1994).

Organizational ecology is another school that has exerted considerable influence in the thinking about organizational design. Research studies from the ecological perspective show that there are tremendous constraints on organizations' ability to change and adapt due to selection pressures at the time of organizational founding and inertia thereafter (Hannan and Freeman, 1977). Ecologists have also provided great insight into how certain designs get imprinted on a population of organizations at the time of founding owing to concerns of legitimacy and competition. The ecological perspective also suggests that organizational forms evolve not merely by adapting but also through demographic processes such as when one organizational form within a population "dies" and is supplanted by a new form (Amburgey and Rao, 1996) (see EVOLUTIONARY PERSPECTIVES; ORGANIZATIONAL ECOLOGY).

Network theory is the one school of organizational design that coalesced and flowered in the late 1990s as theorists turned their attention to the design of inter- and intra-organizational relationships (Anand and Jones, 2003). Following from Granovetter's (1985) ideas on embeddedness of economic action and social structure, Uzzi proposed that organizations need to develop an optimal mix of close and distant interorganizational ties in order to adapt and survive. The architecture of internal networks in organizations and their contribution to an organization's ability to respond and learn has been highlighted in the work of Krackhardt (1990) and Hansen (1999).

Organizational economics is another school that has exerted tremendous influence on the theory and practice of organizational design. Specifically, transaction cost theory's concern about where the efficient boundaries of the firm lie have forced the consideration of "make or buy" decisions with respect to organizational design – that is, whether it is more efficient for a set of activities to be coordinated and produced within a firm or bought through a market transaction. Pisano's research on pharmaceutical firms' decision to internalize or externalize the procurement of research and development provides one example of how the imperative for economic efficiency shapes organizational design.

The sociotechnical school of design was based in the studies of the Tavistock Institute in England carried out in the 1940s and 1950s, most notably of self-managed coal workers (Trist and Bamforth, 1951). This school was unique in assuming that individuals are intrinsically motivated and in its belief in the potential of self-organized teamwork. Many of the principles developed by socio-technologists inform us about the nature of "organic" structures and remain strikingly contemporary (Cherns, 1976): when designing tasks or structures, minimal numbers of rules should be applied; variance from a required standard should be controlled at the source of the work or output; variety and flexibility of the organization should be boosted where possible by multiskilling and rotation of employees; boundaries should be located such that interdependent units are housed close to each other; communication should flow freely within the organization and should be channeled to accomplish tasks and solve problems; and organizational redesign efforts should be participative (*see* SOCIOTECHNICAL THEORY; MECHANISTIC/ORGANIC).

PRINCIPLES OF ORGANIZATIONAL DESIGN

The field of organizational design has also benefited from writers with a somewhat more practical bent who are keen to prescribe the principles of efficient and effective design. The principles of organizational design concern two broad and interrelated sets of decisions: (1) How should the division of labor and coordination of activities be accomplished? (2) How should the organization cope with growth and development?

Division of labor and coordination Depending on the type of task and size of the organization, a number of structural options are available for creating the appropriate division of labor (Daft, 2001). These include: functional structure, with groupings based on specialization of tasks such as manufacturing, marketing, financing, and research and development; divisional structure, where groupings are based on similarity in markets, product lines, or geographic regions; matrix structure, where groupings combine functional and divisional structures; and horizontal structure, where groupings comprise teams structured around specific organizational processes. The tradeoffs involved in choosing an option for the division of labor can be assessed through the following criteria (Nadler and Tushman, 1997): To what extent is resource utilization maximized? How does grouping affect specialization and economies of scale, measurement and control issues, and the organization's capacity to utilize resources with flexibility? How responsive is each option to important competitive demands?

The choice made for the division of labor within an organization needs to be matched by an appropriate mechanism for coordination and control. In the abstract, there are five coordination mechanisms: direct supervision, standardization of work processes, standardization of skills, standardization of outputs, and mutual adjustment (Mintzberg, 1983). In practice, coordination is achieved by designing lateral mechanisms that range from simple to complex (Galbraith, 2002): voluntary processes such as interdepartmental rotation, co-location, and mutually consistent policies; electronic or virtual coordination through information technology-enabled enterprise or customer management tools; formal coordination through hierarchy or cross-unit teams; full time integrator or liaison roles; and horizontal organization (Ostroff, 1999). The appropriateness of each coordination mechanism can be assessed through the following criteria (Nadler and Tushman, 1997): How costly is it in terms of money and other resources? How complementary or dependent is it on the informal organization? How effective is it in terms of providing the required level of information processing capacity?

Choices in respect of division of labor and coordination need to fit the overall context of the organization. A number of other factors moderate the appropriateness of design options. These include the business strategy of the organization, nature of its external environment, culture and values, incentive systems, mechanisms for social control, and the amount of centralization, politics, and conflict (Daft, 2001). In this sense, design choices are not discrete, but part of a holistic configuration of complementary elements.

Organizational growth and development   An organization passes through somewhat predictable life-cycle stages during the course of its evolution (Greiner, 1972). Four typically encountered stages are those of (1) new venture creativity; (2) development and expansion; (3) consolidation and professionalization; and (4) elaboration and decline. Organizations have to be designed appropriately to handle each stage. Greiner (1972) cautions that a design that is relevant to one stage often conceals the seeds of failure for a later stage. The transition of each phase is accompanied by a revolution or crisis of sorts unless the organization is adequately prepared for it. For example, the evolution from the creative stage to that of development is accompanied by a crisis of leadership that requires the replacement of a freewheeling, entrepreneurial authority structure by a more bureaucratic, goal oriented one. Most transitions involve the redefinition and redesign of ROLE of the founder or leader so that direction provided from the top energizes the organization instead of impelling it towards decay (Adzies, 1998).

For each stage, the design emphasis is different (Flamholtz, 1990). In the creativity stage, the organization has to be designed to define a market niche and develop products and resources. In the development stage, organizational design should support the acquisition of resources and implementation of operation systems. In the professionalization stage, design should focus on the recruitment, socialization, and development of management systems. In the elaboration stage, corporate culture and values need attention in order to revitalize the organization and prevent decline. At points of transition the task of organizational redesign has be accomplished with political astuteness to cope with political dynamics, behavioral skill to quell anxiety, and a modicum of participation and communication to facilitate acceptance (Nadler and Tushman, 1997).

Not all transitions in organizational design are orderly and incremental. Some are discontinuous and extremely disruptive. For example, the large-scale replacement of hierarchy-based human information processing systems by information technology led to what is known as the reengineering revolution. Reengineering provided a radically different way of thinking about organizations in terms of information TECHNOLOGY enabled processes (Hammer and Champy, 1993). Its widespread and fad-like adoption led to abrupt changes in the design of organizations due to downsizing. Other instances of disruptive change that force organizational redesign include the introduction of competence destroying technology, sweeping new regulation, and the rapid development of global labor markets.

One prescription provided for coping with such change is to nurture the development of an ambidextrous design; that is, an organization that is capable of pursuing both incremental and discontinuous innovation by hosting multiple and contradictory strategic imperatives, structures, processes, and cultures (Tushman and O'Reilly, 1997). A related suggestion provided by Brown and Eisenhardt (1998) involves the design of two aspects: (1) semi-structures, which are organizational units where some features are prescribed or determined (such as responsibilities, project priorities, milestones) but other aspects probe a different or changing context, and (2) mechanisms for choreographing transitions from current projects to future ones. In this sense, ambidexterity can be understood as a mindset rather than manifest structure, such that each individual in an organization is focused on delivering value at the current time and also simultaneously capable of looking out for changes in the environment and appreciating the adaptive redesign that needs to be carried out (Gibson and Birkinshaw, 2004).

See also *matrix organization; organizational change; organizational effectiveness; structuration*

Bibliography

Adzies, I. (1998). *Corporate Life-Cycles*. Englewood Cliffs, NJ: Prentice-Hall.
Amburgey, T. L. and Rao, H. (1996). Organizational ecology: Past, present, and future directions. *Academy of Management Journal*, 39, 1265–86.
Anand, N. and Jones, B. C. (2003). Organization design: A network perspective. In E. A. Mannix and R. Peterson (eds.), *Understanding the Dynamic Organization*. Mahwah, NJ: Lawrence Erlbaum Associates.

Brown, S. L. and Eisenhardt, K. M. (1998). *Competing on the Edge*. Boston, MA: Harvard Business School Press.

Burns, T. and Stalker, G. M. (1961). *The Management of Innovation*. London: Tavistock.

Cherns, A. (1976). The principles of sociotechnical design. *Human Relations*, **29**, 783–92.

Child, J. (1982). Organizational structure, environment, and performance: The role of strategic choice. *Sociology*, **6**, 1–22.

Daft, R. L. (2001). *Organization Theory and Design*, 7th edn. Cincinnati, OH: South-Western.

Daft, R. L. and Lengel, R. H. (1986). Organizational information requirements, media richness and structural design. *Management Science*, **32**, 554–71.

Daft, R. L. and Weick, K. E. (1984). Toward a model of organizations as interpretive systems. *Academy of Management Review*, **9**, 284–95.

Davis, G. F., Diekmann, K. A., and Tinsley, C. H. (1994). The decline and fall of the conglomerate firm in the 1980s: The deinstitutionalization of an organizational form. *American Sociological Review*, **59**, 547–70.

DiMaggio, P. J. and Powell, W. W. (1983). The iron cage revisited: Institutional isomorphism and collective rationality in organizational fields. *American Sociological Review*, **48**, 147–60.

Donaldson, L. (2001). *The Contingency Theory of Organizations*. Thousand Oaks, CA: Sage.

Flamholtz, E. G. (1990). *Growing Pains*. San Francisco: Jossey-Bass.

Fligstein, N. (1985). The spread of the multidivisional form among large firms, 1919–1979. *American Sociological Review*, **50**, 377–91.

Galbraith, J. R. (1973). *Designing Complex Organizations*. Reading, MA: Addison-Wesley.

Galbraith, J. R. (2002). *Designing Organizations*. San Francisco: Jossey-Bass.

Gibson, C. and Birkinshaw, J. (2004). The antecedents, consequences, and mediating roles of organizational ambidexterity. *Academy of Management Journal* (forthcoming).

Granovetter, M. (1985). Economic action and social structure: The problem of embeddedness. *American Journal of Sociology*, **91**, 481–510.

Greiner, L. E. (1972). Evolution and revolution as organizations grow. *Harvard Business Review*, July–August, 37 16.

Hammer, M. and Champy, J. (1993). *Reengineering the Corporation*. New York: Harper.

Hannan, M. T. and Freeman, J. (1977). The population ecology of organizations. *American Journal of Sociology*, **82**, 929–64.

Hansen, M. T. (1999). The search–transfer problem: The role of weak ties in sharing knowledge across organizational sub-units. *Administrative Science Quarterly*, **44**, 82–111.

Krackhardt, D. (1990). Assessing the political landscape: Structure, cognition, and power in organizations. *Administrative Science Quarterly*, **35**, 342–69.

March, J. G. and Simon, H. A. (1958). *Organizations*. New York: Wiley.

Meyer, J. W. and Rowan, B. (1977). Institutionalized organizations: Formal structure as myth and ceremony. *American Journal of Sociology*, **83**, 340–63.

Mintzberg, H. (1983). *Structure in Fives: Designing Effective Organizations*. Englewood Cliffs, NJ: Prentice-Hall.

Mizruchi, M. and Stearns, L. B. (1988). A longitudinal study of the formation of interlocking directorates. *Administrative Science Quarterly*, **33**, 194–210.

Nadler, D. A. and Tushman, M. L. (1997). *Competing by Design: The Power of Organizational Architecture*. New York: Oxford University Press.

Ostroff, F. (1999). *The Horizontal Organization*. New York: Oxford University Press.

Pfeffer, J. and Salancik, G. R. (1978). *The External Control of Organizations: A Resource Dependence Perspective*. New York: Harper and Row.

Ritzer, G. (1993). *The McDonaldization of Society*. Thousand Oaks, CA: Pine Forge Press.

Scherer, P. D. and Lee, K. (2002). Institutional change in large law firms: A resource dependence and institutional perspective. *Academy of Management Journal*, **45**, 102–19.

Scott, W. R. (1998). *Organizations: Rational, Natural, and Open Systems*, 4th edn. Upper Saddle River, NJ: Prentice-Hall.

Tolbert, P. (1985). Institutional environments and resource dependence: Source of administrative structure in institutions of higher education. *Administrative Science Quarterly*, **30**, 1–13.

Trist, E. L. and Bamforth, K. W. (1951). Some social and psychological consequences of the longwall method of coal-getting. *Human Relations*, **14**, 3–38.

Tushman, M. and O'Reilly, C. (1997). *Winning Through Innovation: A Practical Guide to Leading Organization Change and Renewal*. Boston, MA: Harvard University Press.

organizational ecology

Martin Ruef

Organizational ecology is a research paradigm that explains organizational outcomes in terms of the demographic composition – size and distribution – of organizational populations. The perspective was introduced in 1977 by Michael Hannan and John Freeman, who argued that the prevailing emphasis on adaptation among individual organizations needed to be supplemented by a population-level perspective, which acknowledges that much of the aggregate change observed in organizational structures occurs through entry and exit processes. Extensions to organizational ecology have since investigated a host of other processes empirically, including organizational aging, growth, differentiation, performance, and diversity (Carroll and Hannan 2000).

Contemporary research in organizational ecology typically proceeds at one of two levels of analysis:

1   *The organizational population:* a set of organizations in a defined geographic region assuming a common form (e.g., US acute-care hospitals).
2   *The organizational community:* a spatially or functionally bounded set of related populations (e.g., the American healthcare sector).

POPULATION ECOLOGY

Within the ecological perspective, organizations are grouped together in populations when they assume a common "organizational form," a cluster of features (structural or relational) that serve as a cognitive identity for those organizations and as cultural constraints that limit their transformation (Pólos, Hannan, and Carroll, 2002). In theory, analysts recognize the existence of an organizational form when external audiences enforce that identity through sanctions. In practice, organizational forms tend to be defined on the basis of common labels applied to organizations in industry censuses, trade directories, newspapers, phone books, and other archival sources.

The favored observation plan in population ecology is one that identifies all organizations in a population from its origins. In contrast to designs that emphasize representative samples of organizations, the single population census enables complete historical coverage, the observation of all vital events (such as foundings and failures), and careful measurement of industry and institutional context (Carroll and Hannan, 2000). Models of evolution in organizational populations address the impact of the social environment, population density, and segregation within the population. They also address hetero-

geneity in population composition, considering characteristics such as organizational age, size, internal demography, and efforts at transformation (*see* ORGANIZATIONAL DEMOGRAPHY).

Organizational environments   From its inception, organizational ecology has recognized that the environment of an organization – both resource-based and institutional – impacts its life chances. The range of exogenous environmental conditions affecting a population are typically summarized as its "carrying capacity," referring to the maximum number of organizations of that form that could conceivably be sustained by the environment.

In addition to serving as a selection mechanism, research has identified "environmental imprinting" as another process whereby organizations are impacted by their environments. The idea of imprinting was first discussed by Stinchcombe (1965), who noted that organizational forms tend to reflect the social features that dominate at the time of their emergence. Extending this idea, Baron, Hannan, and Burton (1999) found that the employment models maintained by organizational founders had long-term effects on the human resource structure of their companies. More generally, research on environmental imprinting reflects an interest in organizational path dependency among ecologists.

Density dependence   A major insight of organizational ecology is that a population's vital events tend to depend on the existing number of organizations (i.e., density) within the population. The model of "density dependence" maintains that population density generates effects on founding and disbanding rates through two mechanisms: cognitive legitimacy and competition (Hannan and Carroll, 1992). In its earliest stages an organizational form tends not to be recognized and thus lacks cognitive legitimacy. Growth in density increases legitimacy, possibly up to some ceiling where a form is so prevalent in a society as to be taken for granted. At low densities, population growth only marginally intensifies competition. At a high density, on the other hand, population growth does little to enhance legitimacy but markedly increases competition due to overcrowding in the niche. In combination, the two mechanisms imply that organizational populations tend to exhibit an "S-shaped" pattern of growth.

While empirical support for density dependence is considerable, a number of researchers have criticized the model for its inability to account for decline and resurgence in mature organizational populations. Two extensions to density dependence attempt to bridge this gap – the "density delay" model of Carroll and Hannan (1989) and the "competitive intensity" model of Barnett (1997). The density delay mechanism suggests that organizations founded in high density conditions are more frail and evidence higher rates of disbanding over their entire lifetime. These organizations suffer an adverse form of environmental imprinting, which contributes to the decline of organizational populations from their peak density. In his model of competitive intensity, Barnett proposes that organizations generate different amounts of competition based on their age and size. Mature populations feature larger and older organizations and therefore evidence greater levels of aggregate competition than populations in earlier stages of evolution. The model also recognizes that organizations that are *both* large and old may be relatively innocuous entities in terms of competitive intensity. This interaction can yield a pattern of resurgence in the density of some mature industries.

Segregation The empirical dilemma of resurgence in mature organizational populations has contributed to an alternative modeling approach, emphasizing the segregation of a population's environment into distinct niches. Carroll's (1985) model of "resource partitioning" is one effort to explain this process of segregation. The model relies on the classic ecological distinction between specialists – organizations occupying a narrow resource niche – and generalists – organizations occupying a broad resource niche. When organizational populations mature, they often become concentrated, with a small number of generalists controlling most of the population's productive capacity. Carroll argues that this leads the generalists to become oriented toward the mass market, while abandoning more specialized niches. As a result, the increasing concentration tends to be associated with increases in the viability of specialist organizations and a pattern of resurgence in population density.

Aside from niche width, ecological research has identified other bases for the segregation of a population's environment. These include "size-localized" competition (Hannan and Ranger-Moore, 1990), which considers the tendency of organizations of similar scale to compete more intensely with one another, and "spatial agglomeration" (Sorenson and Audia, 2000), which addresses the tendency of populations to become concentrated in different geographic regions.

Age and size dependence The ecological perspective acknowledges that a host of organizational attributes may impact vital events at the population level, particularly rates of mortality. Following Stinchcombe (1965), researchers have hypothesized that young organizations tend to be especially vulnerable, since their core technologies are unproven, routines must be developed, and members must be socialized. This "liability of newness" can be contrasted with two other typical age dependent patterns. In the "liability of adolescence," organizational founders are thought to begin with an endowment of resources and trust; as this endowment is depleted, the risk to the venture increases in the short term, only to be reversed at later stages of development. In the "liability of senescence," on the other hand, organizations acquire administrative rules and oligarchy with age, consistently becoming more prone to failure (Barron, West, and Hannan, 1994).

Disentangling these age dependent processes presents both an empirical and a logical challenge. As Barron and colleagues note in their research, many studies of age dependence have neglected to control for the "liability of smallness" – the tendency for small organizations to be at disproportionate risk of failure. Hannan (1998) suggests that divergent findings can be sorted out logically once other underlying properties of organizations – such as endowments, capabilities, and inertia – are accounted for.

Internal demography A recent strand of organizational ecology recognizes that the internal demographic composition of organizations – their membership or leadership profile – may also prove fateful for their life chances. In the "genealogical" approach to internal demography, the process of interest involves the transfer of resources and routines from old to new organizations. Phillips (2002) emphasizes the movement of high-ranking employees who stop being members of one organization (a "parent") to become founders of another (its "progeny"). He finds that greater transfers between parents and progeny decrease the life chances of the parent organizations but increase the life chances of their progeny.

Other work in this vein makes causal inferences in the other direction, considering the impact of organizational ecology on the demography of the workforce. Haveman (1995) shows that organizational foundings, dissolutions, mergers, and acquisitions have a pronounced impact on the tenure distribution of managers, as well as their rates of hiring and turnover.

Organizational change   A central claim in organizational ecology is that there are substantial constraints on the ability of an organization to adapt. "Structural inertia" arises due to internal factors, such as the sunk costs associated with an organization's investments, and external factors, such as the difficulty associated with acquiring information about the environment. Moreover, organizations tend to be favored by society for their reliable performance and ability to account for their actions. These properties are most likely to be found in highly inert organizations that exhibit stable routines and structures (Hannan and Freeman, 1984).

Barnett and Carroll (1995) revisit the issue of inertia, distinguishing between two aspects of organizational transformation. One involves the "process" of change, which typically entails disruption and reduced risk of survival while core features of an organization are being modified. The other aspect involves the "content" of change, which addresses how survival chances are affected after a change in core features has been accomplished. Some students of organizational ecology remain open to the possibility that the content of strategic change can provide long-term survival advantages once the hazard of the change process wears off.

COMMUNITY ECOLOGY

Although the interaction of multiple organizational forms has been of interest to organizational ecologists from the beginning, empirical research has, until recently, been limited to a small number of related populations. Community ecologists examine larger sets of populations, seeking to account for the emergence of new organizational forms, the disappearance of existing forms, and the structure of interdependence – both commensalistic and symbiotic – among forms (Aldrich, 1999).

Analysts conducting research on organizational communities typically confront many of the same issues as population ecologists, simply at a higher level of analysis. Boundaries are drawn around the community according to spatial criteria (e.g., all of the organizations in a given town) or functional criteria (e.g., all organizations contributing to a particular sector). Constituent organizational forms are identified and demographic information must be collected for each. In contrast to observation plans focusing on individual populations, multi-population censuses tend to offer more limited temporal coverage and less information on vital events (Carroll and Hannan, 2000).

Emergence of organizational forms   Multi-population models suggest that the process of form emergence is subject to density dependent dynamics similar to those driving vital events in existing populations (Ruef, 2000). The aggregate density of organizations with similar identities increases the probability of form emergence up to a point (cross-form legitimation). However, when there are a large number of organizations adopting a similar form, the emergence of a new form becomes unlikely (cross-form competition). Under this ecological condition, the features of incipient forms are likely to be subsumed within existing organizational arrangements.

An extension of the density dependence model considers whether density per se is sufficient to ensure the cognitive legitimation and, thus, emergence of an organizational form. McKendrick and colleagues (2003) argue that form emergence is also contingent on the existence of organizations with "focused identities." Lack of focus tends to result when the organizations that enter a population are also involved in other populations within an ecological community. Such *de alio* entrants can be contrasted with *de novo* entrants, which are founded with an exclusive orientation toward a particular population's resource niche.

Issues in community ecology   As the newest branch of the ecological perspective, community ecology confronts a number of substantive issues. One is that the distinctions drawn between forms in a community are largely rooted in the cultural perceptions of organizational audiences. Reconciling this perceptual conceptualization with the historical emphasis of population ecology leads to challenges in measurement and theorizing. Theoretical frameworks also remain to be developed to predict when organizational forms are likely to disappear and when forms will have competitive, mutualistic, or symbiotic interdependencies within a community.

See also *community ecology; evolutionary perspectives; organizational change; organizational decline and death; organizational design; resource dependence*

Bibliography

Aldrich, H. E. (1999). *Organizations Evolving*. Thousand Oaks, CA: Sage.

Barnett, W. P. (1997). The dynamics of competitive intensity. *Administrative Science Quarterly*, **42**, 128–60.

Barnett, W. P. and Carroll, G. R. (1995). Modeling internal organizational change. *Annual Review of Sociology*, **21**, 217–36.

Baron, J., Hannan, M. T., and Burton, M. D. (1999). Building the iron cage: Determinants of managerial intensity in the early years of organizations. *American Sociological Review*, **64**, 527–47.

Barron, D., West, E., and Hannan, M. T. (1994). A time to grow and a time to die: Growth and mortality of credit unions in New York, 1914–1990. *American Journal of Sociology*, **100**, 381–421.

Carroll, G. R. (1985). Concentration and specialization: Dynamics of niche width in populations of organizations. *American Journal of Sociology*, **90**, 1262–83.

Carroll, G. R. and Hannan, M. T. (1989). Density delay in the evolution of organizational populations: A model and five empirical tests. *Administrative Science Quarterly*, **34**, 411–30.

Carroll, G. R. and Hannan, M. T. (2000). *The Demography of Corporations and Industries*. Princeton, NJ: Princeton University Press.

Hannan, M. T. (1998). Rethinking age dependence in organizational mortality: Logical formalizations. *American Journal of Sociology*, **104**, 124–64.

Hannan, M. T. and Carroll, G. R. (1992). *Dynamics of Organizational Populations: Density, Legitimation, and Competition*. New York: Oxford University Press.

Hannan, M. T. and Freeman, J. (1977). The population ecology of organizations. *American Journal of Sociology*, **83**, 929–84.

Hannan, M. T. and Freeman, J. (1984). Structural inertia and organizational change. *American Sociological Review*, **49**, 149–64.

Hannan, M. T. and Ranger-Moore, J. (1990). The ecology of organizational size distributions: A microsimulation approach. *Journal of Mathematical Sociology*, **15**, 67–90.

Haveman, H. A. (1995). The demographic metabolism of organizations: Industry dynamics, turnover, and tenure distributions. *Administrative Science Quarterly*, **40**, 586–618.

McKendrick, D. G., Jaffee, J., Carroll, G. R., and Khessina, O. M. (2003). In the bud? Analysis of disk array producers as a (possibly) emergent organizational form. *Administrative Science Quarterly*, **48**, 60–93.

Phillips, D. J. (2002). A genealogical approach to organizational life chances: The parent–progeny transfer and Silicon Valley law firms, 1946–1996. *Administrative Science Quarterly*, **47**, 474–506.

Pólos, L., Hannan, M. T., and Carroll, G. R. (2002). Foundations of a theory of social forms. *Industrial and Corporate Change*, **11**, 85–115.

Ruef, M. (2000). The emergence of organizational forms: A community ecology approach. *American Journal of Sociology*, **106**, 658–714.

Sorenson, O. and Audia, P. G. (2000). The social structure of entrepreneurial activity: Geographic concentration of footwear production in the United States, 1940–1989. *American Journal of Sociology*, **106**, 424–62.

Stinchcombe, A. L. (1965). Social structure and organizations. In J. March (ed.), *Handbook of Organizations*. Chicago: Rand McNally.

organizational effectiveness

Kim Cameron

Organizational effectiveness has been defined in a variety of ways, but no single definition has been accepted universally. This is because organizational effectiveness is inherently tied to the definition of what an organization is. As the conceptualization of an organization changes, so does the definition of effectiveness, the criteria used to measure effectiveness, and frameworks and theories used to explain and predict it. For example, if an organization is defined as a goal seeking entity, effectiveness is likely to be defined in terms of the extent to which goals are accomplished. If an organization is defined as the central purveyor of a social contract among constituencies, effectiveness is likely to be defined in terms of constituency satisfaction with the objectives of the CONTRACT. To understand what is generally agreed upon about organizational effectiveness, it is helpful to discuss several of its important attributes. In particular, effectiveness is:

1   a construct,
2   grounded in the values and preferences of evaluators, and
3   required to be bounded to be measured.

As a *construct*, effectiveness cannot be observed directly. This is because constructs are abstractions, "constructed" to give meaning to an idea. In other words, organizational effectiveness cannot be pinpointed, counted, or objectively manipulated. It is an idea rather than an objective reality. In addition, effectiveness is reflective of the VALUES and preferences of various constituencies. What one group may prefer or label as effective may not be the same as that of another group. Moreover, preferences may knowingly or unknowingly change, sometimes dramatically, over time among evaluators. The attachment of effectiveness to goodness or to excellence makes judgments of effectiveness inherently subjective and value based. This helps explain why no single definition of effectiveness is universal. Different evaluators have different preferences, different values, and different evaluation criteria.

This does not mean, of course, that effectiveness cannot be measured. But in order for acceptable criteria of effectiveness to be identified, the boundaries of the construct must be clearly delineated. This means that seven questions must be answered which specify the construct boundaries:

1   From whose perspective is effectiveness being judged (e.g., employees, customers, stockholders)?

2   On what domain of activity is the judgment focused (e.g., employee loyalty, financial return, market share)?
3   What level of analysis is being used (e.g., individual satisfaction, organizational profitability, industry competitiveness)?
4   What is the purpose for judging effectiveness (e.g., to move up in the rankings, to calculate net worth, to eliminate waste)?
5   What time frame is being employed (e.g., immediate snapshot indicators, long-term trend lines)?
6   What type of data are being used for evaluations (e.g., employee perceptions, financial results, customer satisfaction)?
7   What is the referent against which effectiveness is judged (e.g., comparisons to an ideal standard, past improvement, stated goals)?

Every judgment of effectiveness must answer these seven questions, either explicitly or implicitly, in order to reach a conclusion. When the answer to each question is clearly specified, then acceptable criteria of effectiveness can be identified. Unfortunately, in the organizational studies literature few writers have been careful enough to specify their answers to each of these questions, so comparable measurements of effectiveness have been difficult to find.

Certain common approaches to the definition and measurement of organizational effectiveness have emerged over time, and each "era" has created its own underlying definition of effectiveness. For example, the earliest models of organizational effectiveness emphasized "ideal types": an approach to effectiveness that emphasized the achievement of certain attributes. Max Weber's characterization of bureaucracy as the ideal form of organization is an obvious and well-known example. The most common criterion of effectiveness under this model is efficiency (maximum output with minimum input). The more nearly an organization approaches the ideal bureaucratic characteristics – which are designed to produce maximum efficiency – the more effective it is. In particular, the more routinized, predictable, stable, and standardized, the better.

Subsequent models of ideal organizing challenged this bureaucratic model, however, suggesting that many effective organizations are highly non-bureaucratic. The most effective or-ganizations, they argue, are cooperative and par-ticipative. Effective organizations satisfy the needs of their members by providing adequate inducements to sustain required contributions. They control and motivate employee activities via goals, participation, or teamwork, not rules. They become legitimated by linking their role to social values (Likert, 1967). Over the years, sev-eral ideal type approaches have been widely used. The most common model uses organiza-tional goal accomplishment as the ideal indicator of effectiveness. If stated goals are achieved, the organization is effective.

Advocates of a "natural systems" view of or-ganizations, however, argue that effectiveness ultimately depends on obtaining critical re-sources (*see* RESOURCE DEPENDENCE). The more resources acquired (e.g., revenues, social capital, recognition), the more effective the or-ganization. Others emphasize the organization's COMMUNICATION and interpretation systems, the satisfaction of organization members, the achievement of profitability, the learning ac-quired, or the consistency of activities with prin-ciples of social equity. The common ingredient among all these viewpoints is an advocacy of a single definitive, universal definition and set of criteria for assessing organizational effective-ness. Organizations are effective if they are char-acterized by the ideal criteria.

Challenges to this universalistic approach to effectiveness, coupled with mounting frustration over the truth of the claims of competing models, gave rise to the "CONTINGENCY THEORY" approach to effectiveness (e.g., Law-rence and Lorsch, 1967). This approach argues that effectiveness is not a function of the extent to which an organization reflects the qualities of an ideal profile; rather, it depends on the match between an organization's performance and its environmental conditions. Definitions of effect-iveness are built on the idea of fit between envir-onmental characteristics and organizational characteristics, such as between mechanistic or-ganizational forms and stable, simple environ-ments, or between organizational forms and rapidly changing complex environments. "Con-gruence models" of effectiveness (Nadler and Tushman, 1997) adopt a similar approach in advocating an alignment between various elem-ents inside and outside the organization (e.g., structure, culture, strategy, market demands, leadership style). Organizations are effective to the extent that they achieve congruence.

The critical difference between the ideal type and the contingency approaches to effectiveness is that the former assumes that one model is universally applicable – effectiveness organiza-tions are distinguished by a universal set of attri-butes – whereas the contingency approaches argue that organizations are effective to the extent to which they have alignment with condi-tions of the environment and among various organizational elements.

A third approach to effectiveness arose when the focus shifted away from the dimensions and attributes of the organization itself to the expect-ations of the organization's constituencies. In this approach, effective organizations are those that have accurate information about the expect-ations of strategically critical constituencies and that have adapted internal processes, goals, and values to meet constituency expectations. Pro-ponents of the "strategic constituencies" per-spective view organizations as highly elastic entities in a dynamic force field of constituencies that can manipulate organizational performance (Connolly, Conlon, and Deutsch, 1980). The organization is flexible enough to respond to the demands of powerful interest groups such as stockholders, unions, regulators, customers, and top managers (*see* CEOs). Effectiveness is linked, therefore, to concepts such as customer satisfaction, learning, adaptability, and legitim-acy. The assumption is that organizations are effective if they satisfy their customers, or if they continually learn, or if they adapt to changing constituency demands, or if they acquire legitimacy with their publics (*see* STAKEHOLDERS).

When the expectations of these various con-stituencies diverge from or contradict one an-other, however, organizations are faced with a dilemma. Which constituencies should the organization satisfy, and which criteria should be emphasized? Four alternatives have emerged in the literature (Zammuto, 1984):

1 Strive to provide as much as possible to each constituency without harming any other constituency.

2   Strive to satisfy the most powerful or dominant constituency first.
3   Favor the least advantaged constituencies who are most likely to be harmed.
4   Adapt to the changing set of constituency expectations, and respond as rapidly as possible to all of them.

Conscious choices are required under this approach regarding which constituency or set of demands receives priority.

The strategic constituencies approach to effectiveness, then, differs from the previous two approaches – ideal type and contingency model – by emphasizing dynamic criteria of effectiveness. Rather than relying on archetypal attributes or on an appropriate environmental fit to define effectiveness, this approach relies on key constituencies to determine the most appropriate criteria.

A recent visible manifestation of the strategic constituencies approach has been the quality movement. The term *quality* replaced the concept of effectiveness during much of the 1990s as the construct of choice in describing and assessing desirable performance in the organizational studies literature. This represented a significant change, since prior to the late 1980s, quality was treated as a predictor of effectiveness, not a substitute for it. Quality referred to error rate in goods-producing organizations, REPUTATION in educational organizations, ambiance or talent in arts organizations, recovery rates in healthcare organizations, and customer satisfaction in service organizations. Quality was one of the desired attributes organizations wanted to pursue, and it was used as an adjective associated with other outcomes (e.g., quality products, quality education, quality arts, or quality healthcare). However, "total quality" came to be seen as the ultimate objective for organizations, and it was primarily defined as: "The customer defines quality." All organization processes, behaviors, and achievements were seen as relevant only if they were defined as such from the eyes of the customer (Cameron and Whetten, 1996) (*see* TOTAL QUALITY MANAGEMENT).

The recognition, however, that tensions exist among the various demands placed on organizations, that different customers possess different expectations, and that focusing exclusively on customer satisfaction implies a reactive orientation, gave rise to a fourth approach to effectiveness: a paradox model (Cameron, 1986). This approach emphasizes the paradoxical nature of effective organizational performance. It incorporates elements of each of the three previous models in defining effectiveness as, for example, both adapting to as well as creating the external environment, being both responsive to external constituencies as well as acting independent of them, being both short term and fast as well as long term and deliberate, being both flexible and rigid, being both standardized and creative, and being both efficient and redundant. Organizations are most effective, in this view, when they manifest paradoxical attributes and behavior.

One empirical study concluded, for example, that the presence of simultaneous opposites in organizations produced the highest levels of effectiveness, as well as improvements in effectiveness over time, particularly under conditions of environmental turbulence (Cameron, 1986). It was not just the presence of mutually exclusive opposites that produced effectiveness, but it was the creative leaps, the boundary spanning, and the motivating tension arising from paradoxical attributes that helped account for effectiveness.

Proponents of this approach argue that effectiveness refers not just to matching an ideal profile, nor matching environmental conditions, nor being responsive to constituency expectations. Rather, they emphasize that effectiveness is inherently tied to organizational performance that is paradoxical – that is, simultaneously defensive and aggressive, entrepreneurial and conservative, consistent and inconsistent, reinforcing of and transforming culture, growing and declining, tightly coupled and loosely coupled (Quinn and Cameron, 1988) (*see* LOOSE COUPLING).

One recent adaptation of this paradoxical approach is the "abundance" model arising from the positive organizational scholarship movement (Cameron, Dutton, and Quinn, 2003). This approach incorporates a traditional negative orientation in organizational research (e.g., a focus on factors such as market forces, deficits, problem solving, adversarial NEGOTIATION, uncertainty, resistance, contracting, competitive strategy, and using financial capital as the key indicator of success) with more positive, elevating organizational dynamics. It incorporates factors such as interpersonal flourishing, purpose and meaningfulness, virtuous behaviors, positive emotions, high energy connections, and appreciative inquiry as relevant criteria for judging effectiveness. Effectiveness is equated with unleashing the highest potentiality of human systems. Paradoxically, however, positive phenomena usually cannot be engendered without the presence of their opposites, and positive and negative dynamics are highly correlated. For example, human excellence and flourishing are usually products of difficult and challenging circumstances rather than idyllic and pleasurable circumstances. Positive energy is usually unleashed in demanding circumstances. Hence, the abundance approach to effectiveness accepts the notion that positive and negative elements are often causally intertwined in organizations. Compassion and forgiveness are dependent upon negative or harmful circumstances to become relevant concepts, for example. Self-reinforcing positive emotions and positive interpretations become unrealistic Pollyannaism without balancing negative emotions and interpretations (Cameron and Caza, 2003).

In summary, despite the fact that organizational effectiveness lies at the center of all theories of organizations (i.e., all theories of organization ultimately rely on the fact that a certain way to organize or act is more effective than other alternatives), despite the fact that organizational effectiveness is an ultimate dependent variable in organizational studies (i.e., all relationships among organizational elements assume that achieving effectiveness is an ultimate objective), and despite the fact that individuals and organizations are constantly required to maintain accountability for effectiveness (i.e., individuals and organizations are regularly appraised on their performance, which assumes that one kind of performance is more effective than another), one common definition of effectiveness has remained elusive. However, at least four approaches to effectiveness are currently available, each of which has legitimacy and value.

See also *identity, organizational; organization development; organizational culture; resource dependence; social capital; values*

Bibliography

Cameron, K. S. (1986). Effectiveness as paradox: Conflict and consensus in conceptions of organizational effectiveness. *Management Science*, 32, 539–53.

Cameron, K. S. and Caza, A. (2003). Contributions to the discipline of positive organizational scholarship. *American Behavioral Scientist*, 47, 731–40.

Cameron, K. S. and Whetten, D. A. (1996). Organizational effectiveness and quality: The second generation. *Higher Education Handbook of Theory and Research*, 11, 265–306.

Cameron, K. S., Dutton, J. E., and Quinn, R. E. (2003). *Positive Organizational Scholarship*. San Francisco: Barrett-Koehler.

Connolly, T., Conlon, E., and Deutsch, S. (1980). Organizational effectiveness: A multiple-constituency view. *Academy of Management Review*, 5, 211–17.

Lawrence, P. and Lorsch, J. (1967). *Organizations and Environment*. Cambridge, MA: Harvard University Press.

Likert, R. (1967). *The Human Organization*. New York: McGraw Hill.

Nadler, D. A. and Tushman, M. L. (1997). *Competing By Design*. New York: Oxford University Press.

Quinn, R. E. and Cameron, K. S. (1988). *Paradox and Transformation: Towards a Theory of Change in Organizations*. Cambridge, MA: Ballinger Publishing.

Zammuto, R. (1984). A comparison of multiple constituency models of organizational effectiveness. *Academy of Management Review*, 9, 606–16.

organizational geography

Pino G. Audia

Organizational geography refers to the study of spatial features of organizational activities. Historically, this line of inquiry has not been central in studies of organizations. Starting in the 1960s and 1970s, researchers developed theories that dealt with the relationship between organizations and the environment, but these theories tended to conceive the environment in aspatial terms. Furthermore, research devoted to how organizations structure their activities paid little attention to the spatial dimension; that is, the extent to which organizations disperse their units in space. Reflecting this state of affairs, geography and related concepts, such as space, distance, and propinquity, did not feature in the subject index of influential textbooks by Scott,

Perrow, and Pfeffer. In recent years, however, organizational researchers have started to explore the importance of spatial considerations in a broad range of organizational phenomena (e.g., diffusion of practices, board interlocks, competitive behaviors, organizational learning, INNOVATION, organizational population dynamics). Many of these studies address two questions that can be considered to be the distinctive domain of organizational geography: (1) how do organizational activities come to take on certain spatial configurations and (2) what consequences do spatial configurations of organizational activities have on organizations and other social systems?

Studies addressing the first question point to ecological characteristics of localities and social networks as key factors influencing spatial variation. For example, Kono et al. (1998) studied the spatial configuration of board interlocks, which arise when two organizations share one or more board members. One of their key findings is that organizations were more likely to share board members with organizations located in the same areas if they were located in cities that had a greater number of upper class clubs. They explained this finding by suggesting that upper class clubs are vehicles for the development of trusting relationships that lead to board nominations. Sorenson and Audia (2000) examined the spatial distribution of production in the footwear industry. They found that states that had a heavy concentration of plants in 1940 generally continued to have the heaviest concentration of plants in 1989. Their explanation for this spatial distribution is that new organizations were more likely to be founded in states where similar organizations were present because existing producers serve as training grounds for individuals who start new organizations.

While ecological characteristics such as those identified by Kono et al. and Sorenson and Audia help explain when organizational activities such as board interlocks and production units concentrate in space, social networks spanning across spatial boundaries provide insight into when and how organizational activities disperse. Davis and Greve (1997) found that an organizational practice that allowed firms to protect themselves against hostile takeovers, the poison pill, spread through national networks

that tied organizations that shared board members. Their study is particularly intriguing because they found that another organizational practice, the golden parachute, did not follow the same spatial pattern of diffusion. The golden parachute diffused slowly through regional networks as organizations were more likely to adopt this practice if organizations located in their same area had already done so. They attribute this localized pattern of diffusion to the fact that the golden parachute was a less legitimate practice and that local networks might have been more effective than national networks in helping organizational decision-makers overcome resistance to a practice that was still being questioned. Their argument is similar to that advanced by Hannan et al. (1995) regarding the legitimacy of new organizational forms. These researchers found that the legitimating effect resulting from an increasing number of organizations adopting a new organizational form occurs initially in the areas where the organizational form emerges and then propagates in space, as belief in the viability of the new organizational form spreads through a process of cultural diffusion.

Studies that have addressed the second question about the consequences of spatial distribution suggest that the geographical dispersion of production may have both positive and negative consequences. Audia, Sorenson, and Hage (2001) found that footwear organizations with geographically dispersed production outperformed those that concentrated production. These authors ruled out lower transportation costs as a possible explanation of this advantage because shipping accounts for only a small percentage of total production costs in footwear production. Instead, they suggested that geographic dispersion may have benefited firms by allowing them to diversify location-specific risks. For example, if the labor market tightens in one location, a multi-unit form can shift some portion of production to plants operating in areas where wages remain low, as Romo and Schwartz (1995) have shown. Audia, Sorenson, and Hage (2001) also found that the geographic dispersion of production units hinders organizations' ability to benefit from the accumulation of operating experience, presumably because the difficulty in transferring operational knowledge increases with distance. Chacar and Lieberman

(2003) provide additional evidence of this disadvantage of geographic dispersion in a study of R&D laboratories of US pharmaceutical companies. They found that geographic concentration within the US increased R&D productivity, though having laboratories in foreign countries increased R&D productivity probably because foreign labs allowed them to tap into localized scientific knowledge that was otherwise not available to US labs.

These studies illustrate the growth of interest in organizational geography, but the fact that researchers have been primarily concerned with bringing in geography in the study of specific phenomena rather than with developing theory of organizational geography suggests that the field is still in its infancy. As additional progress is made, researchers interested in organizational geography will continue to benefit from points of contact with related disciplines such as economic geography and regional science. Organizational geography, which appears to be broader in scope than those disciplines because organizational researchers are interested in a wide range of organizational outcomes, may in turn contribute to those disciplines. The breadth of organizational geography research may be an advantage if researchers succeed in integrating insights from different theoretical perspectives and findings regarding different yet related organizational phenomena.

See also *interlocking boards; network theory and analysis; organizational ecology; resource dependence*

Bibliography

Audia, P. G., Sorenson, O., and Hage, J. (2001). Tradeoffs in the organization of production: Multiunit firms, geographic dispersion and organizational learning. *Advances in Strategic Management*, 18, 75–105.

Chacar, A. S. and Lieberman, M. B. (2003). Organizing for technological innovation in the US pharmaceutical industry. *Advances in Strategic Management*, 20, 317–40.

Davis, G. F. and Greve, H. R. (1997). Corporate elite networks and governance changes in the 1980s. *American Journal of Sociology*, 103, 1–37.

Hannan, M. T., Carroll, G. R., Dundon, E. A., and Torres, J. C. (1995). Organizational evolution in multi-

national context: Entries of automobile manufacturers in Belgium, Britain, France, Germany, and Italy. *American Sociological Review*, 60, 509–28.

Kono, C., Palmer, D., Friedland, R., and Zafonte, M. (1998). Lost in space: The geography of corporate interlocking directorates. *American Journal of Sociology*, 103, 863–911.

Romo, F. P. and Schwartz, M. (1995). The structural embeddedness of business decisions: The migration of manufacturing plants in New York state, 1960 to 1985. *American Sociological Review*, 60, 874–907.

Sorenson, O. and Audia, P. G. (2000). The social structure of entrepreneurial activity: Geographic concentration of footwear production in the United States, 1940–1989. *American Journal of Sociology*, 106, 424–62.

organizational neurosis

Manfred Kets de Vries

Notwithstanding the emphasis on rational action in organizational life, organizations are made up of people, and as a wit once said, "everybody is normal, until you know them better." Given the impact of key decision-makers in organizations, and the reality of POWER, organizations are not immune to neurotic behavior patterns. There are a number of PERSONALITY configurations that can contribute to leader and organizational dysfunction. In organizations that have a strong concentration of power, those personality configurations can result in a parallel organizational "pathology." In what can be called "neurotic organizations," one is likely to find a top executive whose rigid, neurotic style is strongly mirrored in ineffective strategies, structures, ORGANIZATIONAL CULTURE, and patterns of DECISION-MAKING.

Taking a psychodynamic perspective (selecting among organizational configurations) one can identify five common types of neurotic organizations: dramatic/cyclothymic, suspicious, detached, depressive, and compulsive (Kets de Vries and Miller, 1984; Kets de Vries, 2001). Table 1 outlines how, in each type of organization, the leader's personal style and inner theater interrelate with the organization's characteristics. Each of the five organizational patterns has strengths as well as weaknesses. In many cases a solid strength (for example, a leader's careful attention to the actions of rivals) becomes a weakness over time (as when healthy wariness becomes unmitigated suspicion), polluting the atmosphere of the organization. When that happens, change is needed if the organization is going to survive. Unfortunately, with corporate styles deeply rooted in history and personality, change processes will take time. Caught in a psychic prison, it is often difficult for leaders of such organiza-

Table 1   The five "neurotic" styles: An overview

Type	Organization	Executive	Culture	Strategy	Guiding theme
Dramatic/ Cyclothymic	Characterized by overcentralization that obstructs the development of effective information systems; too primitive for its many products and broad market; lacking influence at the second-tier executive level.	Attention-seeking; craving excitement, activity, and stimulation; touched by a sense of entitlement; tending toward extremes.	Well-matched as to dependency needs of subordinates and protective tendencies of CEO; characterized by "idealizing" and "mirroring"; headed by leader who is catalyst for subordinates' initiatives and morale.	Hyperactive, impulsive, venturesome, and dangerously uninhibited; favoring executive initiation of bold ventures; pursuing inconsistent diversification and growth; encouraging action for action's sake; based on non-participative decision-making.	"I want to get attention from and impress the people who count in my life."
Suspicious	Characterized by elaborate information processing, abundant analysis of external trends, and centralization of power.	Vigilantly prepared to counter any attacks and personal threats; hypersensitive; cold and lacking emotional expression; suspicious and distrustful; overinvolved in rules and details to secure complete control; craving information; sometimes vindictive.	Fostering "fight or flight" mode, including dependency and fear of attack; emphasizing the power of information; nurturing intimidation, uniformity, and lack of trust.	Reactive and conservative, overly analytical, diversified, and secretive.	"Some menacing force is out to get me. I'd better be on my guard. I can't really trust anybody."
Detached	Characterized by internal focus, insufficient scanning of the external environment, and self-imposed barriers to free flow of information.	Withdrawn and uninvolved; lacking interest in present or future; sometimes indifferent to praise or criticism.	Lacking warmth or emotions; conflict ridden; plagued by insecurity and jockeying for power.	Vacillating, indecisive, and inconsistent; growing out of narrow, parochial perspectives.	"Reality doesn't offer any satisfaction. Interaction with others is destined to fail, so it's safer to remain distant."

Table 1 (*continued*)

Type	Organization	Executive	Culture	Strategy	Guiding theme
Depressive	Characterized by ritualism, bureaucracy, inflexibility, excessive hierarchy, poor internal communications, and resistance to change.	Lacking self-confidence; plagued by self-esteem problems; afraid of success (and therefore tolerant of mediocrity and failure); dependent on "messiahs."	Passive and lacking initiative; lacking motivation; ignorant of markets; characterized by leadership vacuum; avoidant.	Plagued by "decidophobia"; focusing inward; lacking vigilance over changing market conditions; drifting, with no sense of direction; confined to antiquated, mature markets.	"It's hopeless to try to change the course of events. I'm just not good enough."
Compulsive	Characterized by rigid formal codes, elaborate information systems, ritualized evaluation procedures, excessive thoroughness and exactness, and a hierarchy in which individual executive status derives directly from specific positions.	Tending to dominate the organization from top to bottom; insistent that others conform to tightly prescribed rules; dogmatic or obstinate; obsessed with perfectionism,detail, routine, rituals, efficiency, and lockstep organization.	Rigid, inward directed, and insular; peopled with submissive, uncreative, insecure employees.	Tightly calculated and focused; characterized by exhaustive evaluation; slow and non-adaptive; reliant on a narrow, established theme; obsessed with a single aspect of strategy (e.g., cost cutting or quality) to the exclusion of other factors.	"I don't want to be at the mercy of events. I have to master and control all the things affecting me."

tions to identify problems and make new choices.

See also *CEOs; executive derailment; organizational effectiveness; stress*

Bibliography

Kets de Vries, M. F. R. (2001). *The Leadership Mystique.* London: Financial Times/Prentice Hall.
Kets de Vries, M. F. R. and Miller, D. (1984). *The Neurotic Organization.* San Francisco: Jossey-Bass.

organizational identity

see IDENTITY, ORGANIZATIONAL

organizational performance

see ORGANIZATIONAL EFFECTIVENESS

organizational status

James R. Lincoln

Organizational status is the standing or position of an organization in a stratification system based on social honor or esteem. This definition draws on Max Weber's conception of status as a dimension of vertical ordering distinct from those of class (life chances in a market) and power (the capacity to command the actions of others). Weber had in mind people, but his tripartite classification of stratification systems is reasonably applied to organizations as well.

The concept of status in recent organizational study is associated primarily with the writing of Podolny (1993), who views it as a generalized and fungible resource enabling, in his research, leading investment banks to charge their corporate clients higher premia for similar services. However, the idea that organizations may be ranked or stratified by status, prestige, honor, and legitimacy has been floating around organizational theory for some time, if never commanding center stage. Perrow (1961) saw organizations such as hospitals making claims to prestige before various publics as a strategy of managing RESOURCE DEPEND-ENCE. Such claims, he suggested, were especially likely where the organizations' capabilities and outputs were sufficiently complex or ambiguous that they were difficult for outsiders to assess. Building on the resource dependence flavor of Perrow's reasoning, Thompson (1967) expanded the idea that organizations seek prestige as a way of increasing autonomy and diminishing dependence. For him, the notion of prestige was tied to that of "domain": organizations make claims to both and both rest upon a consensus among organizational publics that the claims carry validity. An organization able to stake a successful claim to ownership or dominance of a domain enjoys superior status within the domain (i.e., it commands a degree of legitimacy that organizations making competing claims do not possess).

Outside the sociological tradition, economics has recently paid attention to business REPUTA-TION. Like status, reputation is an intangible asset on which firms actively trade. How does "status" differ? Reputation is an asset derived from the conversion of past performance into present value. Similar to how economists deal with "TRUST" (as an experience-rated bet on a transaction partner's future performance), it is an uncertainty-absorbing extrapolation from the past. An organization that previously dealt fairly and reliably with its customers and partners, providing quality products and services, builds up a stock of reputation, on which it then trades in labor, capital, and product markets. The marketing theorist's notion of brand equity is another intangible asset that, in contrast with reputation, supplements rather than signals product quality and customer service. The concept of organization status or prestige has deeper sociological meaning than either reputation or brand equity. Applied to Podolny's investment banks, some of it had to do with Eastern "old" money, lifestyle, and other cultural considerations. Status thus derives from *institutionaliza-tion*, successful claims to longstanding legitimacy as a purveyor of traditions and values to which the broader community subscribes. Old-line financial services firms such as Citi-Bank or J. P. Morgan enjoy an abundance of status resources, as, obviously, does a Harvard or Princeton in higher education. Status, like brand equity, endows an organization's products and services with value; not the other way around.

Despite variations on the concept of organizational status having periodically resurfaced in organizational study, the volume of systematic research explicitly addressed to it is small. A future challenge for such research is that of sorting out the conceptual similarities and differences among status, reputation, brand equity, and other intangible organizational assets.

See also *identity, organizational; institutional theory; organizational effectiveness*

Bibliography

Perrow, C. (1961). Organizational prestige: Some functions and dysfunctions. *American Journal of Sociology*, 66, 335–41.

Podolny, J. M. (1993). A status-based model of market competition. *American Journal of Sociology*, 98, 829–72.

Simon, C. J. and Sullivan, M. W. (1993). The measurement and determinants of brand equity: A financial approach. *Marketing Science*, 12, 28–52.

Tedelis, S. (1999). What's in a name? Reputation as a tradeable asset. *American Economic Review*, 89, 548–63.

Thompson, J. D. (1967). *Organizations in Action*. New York: McGraw-Hill.

organizational structure

Lex Donaldson

This may be defined as the structure of recurrent relationships between people in an organization. It includes numerous aspects, such as the numbers of departments and hierarchical levels, and the extent of formalization and decentralization. Typically, each aspect can be measured on a quantitative scale.

Much of organizational structure is the formal organization, which is what is officially supposed to happen. However, the informal, i.e., unofficial, organization is also often included in studies of organizational structure.

The Classical School of management made prescriptions about organizational structure, e.g., Taylor's principle that specialization leads to efficiency. However, such universal theories, which state that there is "one best way to organize," have proved unsatisfactory. The more modern approach is that the most effective structure varies according to characteristics of the organization. Thus the effect of structure is contingent upon these characteristics, called contingency factors. The optimal organizational performance is produced by fitting the structure to the contingencies, e.g., size and strategy. This view is referred to as structural CONTINGENCY THEORY.

When organizations conduct the same action repeatedly, such as producing a product or hiring a new employee, organizational routines are created in a process of routinization. It is feasible, and most effective, to pre-program routine decisions, so that organizational members follow rules, in computers or procedure manuals. This ensures efficient operation and avoids each member having to ponder and learn each time a routine decision is made. Formalization is the number of rules that are used in an organization. Repetition, through producing large volumes of products or services, and through having large numbers of members, leads to more rules, so that scale and size are fitted by greater formalization (Blau and Schoenherr, 1971). Task uncertainty, sometimes from the environment of the organization and often resulting from organizational innovation, makes rules counter-productive, so that formalization needs to be lower for organizational sub-units that have higher task uncertainty (e.g., R&D departments). In contrast, formalization needs to be higher for organizational sub-units that have lower task uncertainty (e.g., manufacturing departments) (Burns and Stalker, 1961). The resulting difference between departments in their organizational structures

(sometimes referred to as differentiation) requires integration mechanisms, such as cross-functional task forces (Lawrence and Lorsch, 1967).

As organizations increase in size (i.e., the number of their members), the number of hierarchical levels needs to increase, to avoid exceeding the feasible span of control, that is, the number of direct subordinates of each of the managers. Also, because top managers thereby become remote from the "firing line," they need to delegate decision-making authority down to lower levels of this taller hierarchy. Thus size leads to decentralization, which facilitates faster response to customers and local conditions.

As organizations grow, they specialize to promote efficiency and this leads to an increasing number of departments specialized by function. Thus larger size leads to more departmentation. However, the rate at which new departments are added is non-linear: departments increase at a decreasing rate as size increases. Similar relationships occur between size and many other aspects of organizational structure: span of control of CEO, span of control of supervisors, number of sections per department, division of labor and functional specialization (these aspects are all referred to as structural differentiation). The reason is that size leads to more homogeneous work-groups and to rules, both of which allow larger managerial spans of control and larger organizational subunits (Blau and Schoenherr, 1971).

In summary, small organizations have low formalization, high centralization, and low structural differentiation. Large organizations have high formalization, low centralization and high structural differentiation, a structural pattern which is often referred to as being high on bureaucratization – using that term descriptively rather than pejoratively, and, actually, as entailing efficiency (Child, 1975).

Departmentation changes in type from functional to divisional (or multi-divisional) as the organization changes its strategy by diversifying. Divisionalization may be by product, service customer or area – depending upon which is most diversified. Diversification requires the creation of independent businesses for each separate market, to ensure speed, responsiveness and innovation. Divisions are autonomous profit centres. Hence divisionalization increases decentralization. This decentralization is greater the more the businesses are unrelated. Where the businesses are related in some way, then there is a need for central coordination, often involving central functional staff groups, so that some decisions are taken centrally. At the extreme, where the corporation has several products that are vertically integrated, i.e., highly related, the fitting structure is divisions with limited autonomy and a large, powerful head office (Lorsch and Allen, 1973).

For related diversified companies, they can maximize innovation by divisionalizing, or minimize costs by adopting a functional structure. Thus the product life cycle (PLC) is an additional contingency factor, according to whether the organization is early in the PLC (and so needs to emphasize innovation) or late (and so needs to emphasize cost reduction). If such a company wishes to gain some (but not all) of the benefits of both innovation and cost reduction simultaneously, the product-function matrix is the fit, with each product head orchestrating an innovative team while the functional heads oversee sharing of resources.

If a company has some relatedness of its products (or services or customers) and also of its geographic areas, e.g., countries in a multinational corporation, then a product-area matrix is the fit, allowing some coordination both of products and areas (Davis and Lawrence, 1977). Alternatively, if a company has one product and has some relatedness of its geographic areas, then a functional-area matrix is the fit, allowing some coordination both of functions and areas simultaneously. Thus whether the fitting structure is a functional, divisional or matrix, and which type of those structures, depends upon the degree of relatedness between products, areas etc. A decision-tree model, which gives the fitting structure for the combinations of these contingency factors, offers guidance to managerial practitioners and students making case study recommendations (Donaldson, 1985).

There is a large body of research showing that structures and their contingencies are correlated, e.g., size-formalization, size-structural differentiation, size-decentralization, task certainty-formalization and diversification-divisionalization. There is evidence that some contingency-structure relationships generalize widely: over different types of organizations and national cultures (e.g., Miller, 1987).

Structural contingency theory is a structural-functional type of sociological theory, that is, structures are explained by their positive consequences for effectiveness (Donaldson, 1985) (*see* ORGANIZATIONAL EFFECTIVENESS). Thus a central issue for structural contingency theory is demonstrating that organizations whose structures fit their contingencies perform better than those in misfit. There are fewer of these fit-performance studies, but they are growing in number (Donaldson, 2001). There are methodological issues in ascertaining the effect of fit on performance, which have been discussed (Donaldson, 2001).

The fit of organizational structure to contingency is sometimes stated as a configuration. Configurations are postulated to be few and widely separated in conceptual space, so that organizations are bunched on the contingency and structural variables, and structural change is radical and infrequent (Miller, 1986). However, in structural contingency theory, fit is a line, so that there is a level of the structural variable that fits each level of the contingency variable (this is known as Cartesianism). The empirical evidence supports the Cartesian view of fit, in that organizations are continuously distributed along the structural and contingency variables, fit is a continuous line and organizational change is incremental and frequent (Donaldson, 1996).

Punctuated equilibrium theory holds that organizational change is infrequent and revolutionary (Romanelli and Tushman, 1994). However, disequilibrium theory (Donaldson, 2001) holds that equilibrium produces high performance, often leading to increases in size or diversification etc., which produce recurrent disequilibrium and incremental structural adaptions.

Contingency theory is sometimes criticized for being determinist, because change in contingency causes change in structure, through the imperative to adopt the fitting structure to avoid performance loss. Critics have alleged that contingencies only weakly influence structure, with managers having a wide range of "strategic choice" that reflects their interests and perceptions etc. (Child, 1972). However, many of the criticisms are ill-founded (for a rebuttal see Donaldson, 1996). Structures strongly relate to their contingencies. Moreover, the effect of structural fit on performance is substantial, relative to other factors such as strategy or market concentration, so firms cannot easily ignore the need for structural fit.

Similarly, the functionalism of structural contingency theory has been challenged by political interpretations, such as managerial self-interest. However, a closer examination of the political interpretations reveals them to be invalid (Donaldson, 1996).

Since the development of structural contingency theory, other explanations of organizational structure have been put forward by institutional theory, population-ecology theory and transaction cost economics. These views are subject to active theoretical debate (Donaldson, 1995).

Adaptation of the organizational structure by adopting a structure that better fits the contingencies does not always occur rapidly. Chandler showed in case studies that corporations often failed to change until they had a crisis of low performance and then adapted and thrived. Statistical research on larger samples supports this view (Donaldson, 1987; Ezzamel and Hilton, 1980). This idea has been developed into a formal theory of performance-driven organizational change, which specifies conditions under which adaptation will and will not occur (Donaldson, 1999).

Audia, Locke and Smith (2000) find that organizations persist with formerly successful strategies, after environment changes render them dysfunctional, leading to declining performance. The reasons are that the past successes lead their managers to believe strongly in their current strategies, have SELF-EFFICACY about their ability to continue high performance, have high goals that may induce reliance on old strategies, and avoid use of information from critics of the current strategy. This may help to explain why organizations fail to make needed adaptive changes until their performance becomes poor: because their managers are persisting with previously successful approaches despite them having become dysfunctional. The Audia et al. study is of strategies, so it is a

task for future research to investigate whether this pathological PERSISTENCE psychology applies to organizational structures.

Future research into organizational structure is often equated with studying new organizational structures, with the suggestion that the new structures invalidate the existing structures and contingency theory. However, caution should be exercised, because some investigations searching for new organizational structures have concluded that they are old structures that have merely been modified or redescribed and "hyped" (Eccles and Nohria, 1992). Similarly, the N-form, or network-form (Galbraith, 1998), has been suggested to be a new organizational structure that is replacing existing structures, such as the M-form (multidivisional). However, an organization may have many, strong connections with other organizations and thus be an N-form, while internally remaining a conventionally structured organization, e.g., M-form. Thus the N- and M-forms are not mutually exclusive, so that an increasing number of organizations using the N-form does not necessitate decline or obsolescence of the M-form, or that contingency theory no longer works. Thus "new" organizational structures should be approached carefully, utilizing existing concepts and tools (e.g., decentralization and its measures) and abandoning contingency theory only if it is shown to be unable to explain these structures.

In structural contingency theory, the level of the structural variable that fits a level of the contingency variable produces the highest performance. Traditionally, these fits to the different levels of the contingency variable are considered to produce the same, high performance; this is known as iso-performance (Van de Ven and Drazin, 1985). However, a newer view is that, for some contingency variables (e.g., size), the fits of the structural variable to the different levels of the contingency variable produce different performances. Fit to the high level of the contingency variable produces higher performance, whereas fit to its low level produces lower performance. This is known as hetero-performance (Donaldson, 2001). There is an incentive for an organization to move from one fit to another, e.g., by growing along the size contingency variable. Thus hetero-performance explains why organizations change on these contingency variables. It also recognizes that the contingency variable itself contributes to performance, beyond just that from moderating the effect of structure on performance. Exploring the relative validities of iso- and hetero-performance is a significant agenda for future structural contingency research.

See also *bureaucracy; institutional theory; management, classical theory; organizational design*

Bibliography

Audia, P.G., Locke, E.A. and Smith, K.G. (2000). The paradox of success: An archival and laboratory study of strategic persistence following radical environmental change. *Academy of Management Journal*, **43** (5), 837–53.

Blau, P. M. and Schoenherr, P.A. (1971). *The Structure of Organizations*. New York: Basic Books.

Burns, T. and Stalker, G. M. (1961). *The Management of Innovation*. London: Tavistock.

Child, J. (1972). Organizational structure, environment and performance: The role of strategic choice. *Sociology*, **6** (1), 1–22.

Child, J. (1975). Managerial and organizational factors associated with company performance, Part 2: A contingency analysis. *Journal of Management Studies*, **12** (1), 12–27.

Davis, S. M. and Lawrence, P. R. (1977). *Matrix*. Reading, MA: Addison-Wesley.

Donaldson, L. (1985). *In Defence of Organization Theory: A Reply to the Critics*. Cambridge: Cambridge University Press.

Donaldson, L. (1987). Strategy and structural adjustment to regain fit and performance: In defence of contingency theory. *Journal of Management Studies*, **24** (1), 1–24.

Donaldson, L. (1995). *American Anti-Management Theories of Organization: A Critique of Paradigm Proliferation*. Cambridge, UK: Cambridge University Press.

Donaldson, L. (1996). *For Positivist Organization Theory: Proving the Hard Core*. London, UK: Sage.

Donaldson, L. (1999). *Performance-Driven Organizational Change: The Organizational Portfolio*. Thousand Oaks, CA: Sage.

Donaldson, L. (2001). *The Contingency Theory of Organizations*. Thousand Oaks, CA: Sage.

Eccles, R. G. and Nohria, N. (1992). *Beyond the Hype: Rediscovering the Essence of Management*. Boston, MA: Harvard Business School Press.

Ezzamel, M. A. and Hilton, K. (1980). Divisionalisation in British industry: A preliminary study. *Accounting and Business Research*, **10**, Spring, 197–214.

Galbraith, J. R. (1998). Designing the networked organization: Leveraging size and competencies. In, S. A. Mohrman, J. R. Galbraith, E. E. Lawler III and Associates (eds.), *Tomorrow's Organization: Crafting Winning Capabilities in a Dynamic World*. San Francisco: Jossey-Bass Publishers, 76–102.

Lawrence, P. R. and Lorsch, J. W. (1967). *Organization and Environment: Managing Differentiation and Integration*. Boston: Division of Research, Graduate School of Business Administration, Harvard University.

Lorsch, J. W. and Allen, S. A. (1973). *Managing Diversity and Inter-dependence: An Organizational Study of Multidivisional Firms*. Boston: Division of Research, Graduate School of Administration, Harvard University.

Miller, D. (1986). Configurations of strategy and structure: Towards a synthesis. *Strategic Management Journal* **7**, 233–49.

Miller, G. A. (1987). Meta-analysis and the culture-free hypothesis. *Organization Studies* **8** (4), 309–26.

Romanelli, E. and Tushman, M. L. (1994). Organizational transformation as punctuated equilibrium: An empirical test. *Academy of Management Journal*, **37** (5), 1141–66.

Van de Ven, A. H. and Drazin, R. (1985). The concept of fit in contingency theory. In *Research in Organizational Behaviour*, Vol. 7, 333–65 edited by B. M. Staw and L. L. Cummings. Greenwich, CT: JAI Press.

outsourcing

Phanish Puranam and Kannan Srikanth

Outsourcing is the transfer of responsibility for the execution of any of a company's recurring internal activities or processes to another company. The outsourcing of component production has been historically well established in manufacturing industries such as automobiles and airplanes (Sako, 2003). Outsourcing became popular in the services sector in the late 1980s when firms began relying on specialist companies for ongoing IT support rather than hire employees with IT skills. In essence, the vendor rents its skills, knowledge, technology, and manpower for an agreed-upon price and period to perform functions that the client no longer wants to perform (Adler, 2003).

Outsourcing is not synonymous with "offshoring," which involves the relocation of activities to remote (often low-wage) locations. Firms may continue to use their own employees, albeit in remote locations, or alternatively continue to perform activities in the same physical location but with another firm's employees. Since the 1990s, firms have experienced considerable success in positioning themselves as providers of outsourced services in IT from low-wage offshore locations like India. The early 2000s saw this model being extended to other activities such as the operation of call centers, accounting, auditing, claims processing, and the execution of a range of other back office operations (Dossani and Kenney, 2003).

While offshoring (with or without outsourcing) raises significant concerns about the export of jobs from a country, its proponents argue for the potential advantages of specialization as originally noted by Ricardo in his analysis of comparative advantage. Outsourcing non-core activities allows both the client and vendor firms to focus on what they do best and improve their performance. Hence, often the client firm is able to obtain the same or higher quality levels from the vendor along with significant cost reductions. However, outsourcing also generates risks for both clients and vendors. Firms can find themselves locked into relationships with incompetent or opportunistic partners, and could face difficulties coordinating interdependent activities that are separated by physical and legal boundaries.

Outsourcing has become an interesting empirical setting for testing a variety of organization theories. Since outsourcing results in a redefinition of the economic boundaries of firms and can lead to the emergence of partnerships between clients and vendors, it is of interest to strategy scholars. The transitioning of activities to remote locations and coordinating them offers scope to examine knowledge transfer and inter-organizational coordination issues. HR specialists may find the impact of outsourcing decisions on employees (made redundant, as well as those remaining in the company) noteworthy.

See also *inter-organizational relations; organizational design; transaction cost economics*

Bibliography

Adler, P. (2003). Making the HR outsourcing decision. *MIT Sloan Management Review*, **45** (1), 53–60.

Dossani, R. and Kenney, M. (2003). Went for cost, stayed for quality?: Moving the back office to India. *Berkeley Roundtable on the International Economy*. Berkeley: University of California Press.

Sako, M. (2003). Modularity and outsourcing: The nature of co-evolution of product architecture and organizational architecture in the global automotive industry. In A. Prencipe, A. Davies, and M. Hobday (eds.), *The Business of Systems Integration*. Oxford: Oxford University Press.

P

participant observation

see ETHNOGRAPHY; RESEARCH METHODS

participation

John Cordery

In an OB context, the term *participation* usually denotes EMPLOYEE INVOLVEMENT in DECISION-MAKING within enterprises. Though there has been some debate over the precise meaning of the construct, it is generally accepted to mean the sharing of influence among individuals across different levels of the organizational hierarchy, such that the degree of involvement of organizational members in information processing, problem solving, and decision-making is balanced or equalized (Wagner, 1994). Such a definition, focusing as it does on shared influence, distinguishes participation from authoritative decision-making (the manager makes the decision without consultation), consultation (subordinates' views are sought, but the manager makes the final decision), and delegation (manager transfers complete authority for the decision to subordinates). It may also be differentiated from financial participation (e.g., profit sharing or employee stock ownership), though financial participation and participation in decision-making are frequently clustered together as part of a human resource strategy that seeks competitive advantage by maximizing the competence and commitment (human capital) of employees. A distinction may also be made between participation and EMPOWERMENT practices, the latter being taken to refer to the extent to which decision-making AUTHORITY is transferred to lower levels of the organization.

Within such a broad definition, many different forms of participation are possible (Cotton et al., 1988). First, it may be formal or informal. Formal participation involves set rules and procedures directing the process of decision-making (e.g., process improvement teams; TQM). However, participation may also merely reflect an informal consensus reached between managers and subordinates, and as such can be viewed as a function of a particular LEADERSHIP style. Second, participation may be direct or indirect, depending on the extent to which employees are personally involved in making the decision. Programs of job redesign and structures such as SELF-MANAGING TEAMS typically lead to employees directly participating in the decision-making process. However, this form of participation is to be distinguished from the many which involve some form of collective representation of employee interests, leading to more "distant" involvement of most employees (e.g., an elected worker representative on a company board or a consultative committee). Third, participative mechanisms may also be differentiated in terms of their time span. Some are relatively transient (e.g., a project team or a task force) and some long term (e.g., a self-managing team). Finally, there is the issue of what decisions employees are allowed to participate in. These can include all or some decisions about technical matters and the work itself, employment and other human resource matters, as well as company strategic, economic, and policy matters. Collectively, the structures and mechanisms that give rise to employee participation at the level of the firm and within an industry are often referred to under the label "industrial democracy" (Poole, Lansbury, and Wailes, 2001).

Advocates of participation argue that it affects the behavior of employees via two main mechanisms. In the first instance, participation may influence intrinsic MOTIVATION and psychological well-being, for example by enhancing valued job characteristics such as autonomy and feedback. Cognitive mechanisms are also seen as underlying participation's hypothesized effect on productivity, encouraging better information flow and facilitating knowledge generation. Taken together, these mechanisms suggest a range of positive outcomes for participation, including job satisfaction and organizational commitment, positive mental health, increased motivation and performance, reduced turnover and absenteeism, as well as reduced incidence of industrial conflict. Other proposed benefits include aligning the goals and interests of employees more closely with those of the organization, thereby retaining human capital and maximizing its use. Because of its hypothesized links to affective well-being, it has sometimes been suggested that there is a moral imperative for employee participation, and the need for employee voice mechanisms is frequently identified as a core component of corporate social responsibility. Opponents of this moral view argue that employees differ so significantly in terms of their needs and values that it is impossible to prescribe participation. They point to decisions where employee participation is either unnecessary (employees do not want to become involved and don't care about the outcome) or unproductive (employees do not possess the competence to participate effectively). Other opponents of participation suggest that it has the potential to waste valuable time and resources, encourage free riders, and to interfere unacceptably with managerial control and authority.

Given the number of dimensions on which forms of participation may vary (influence, content of decisions, direct/indirect, formal/informal, short-term/long-term), it is not surprising that studies of the impact of participation on employee attitudes and performance have produced varied results. The impact of participation on productivity and work attitudes has been studied at a number of different levels. At the level of the business unit or firm, meta analyses have concluded that participation has significant, though small and variable, effects on performance and satisfaction (Wagner

1994; Doucouliagos, 1995), which may reflect the influence of contingency factors such as organizational size, technology, and national culture. Other studies have found that the impact of direct "online" forms of participation (e.g., self-managed teams) is potentially stronger with respect to performance and satisfaction than those that are less direct and where decision-making is "offline" (e.g., problem-solving teams, TQM) (Batt and Appelbaum, 1995; Batt, 1999). Multi-industry studies have also suggested that the productivity impact of participation is at worst neutral, while offering significant benefits in terms of promoting positive work attitudes and employee well-being (Freeman and Kleiner, 2000). Clusters of representative and financial participation practices have been associated with 8–9 percent rises in productivity in a number of Japanese industries, though effects took seven years on average to emerge. Despite these findings, industry surveys in a number of countries suggest that, following a sharp rise in the uptake of employee participation schemes in the 1990s, their popularity may have plateaued (Benson and Lawler, 2003). Reasons for this may include growing recognition of the complex system-wide changes that are associated with introducing participation schemes, and because their long-term modest productivity benefits are perceived as relatively unattractive by managers under pressure to achieve short-term results.

See also *influence; job design; job enrichment*

Bibliography

Batt, R. (1999). Work organization, technology, and performance in customer service and sales. *Industrial and Labor Relations Review*, **52**, 539–64.

Batt, R. and Appelbaum, E. (1995). Worker participation in diverse settings: Does the form affect the outcome, and if so, who benefits? *British Journal of Industrial Relations*, **33**, 353–78.

Benson, G. S. and Lawler, E. E. (2003). Employee involvement: Utilization, impacts, and future prospects. In D. Holman, T. D. Wall, C. W. Clegg, and A. Howard (eds.), *The New Workplace: A Guide to the Human Impact of Modern Working Practices*. Chichester: John Wiley.

Cotton, J. L., Vollrath, D. A., Froggatt, K. L., Lengnick-Hall, M. L., and Jennings, K. R. (1988). Employee participation: Diverse forms and different outcomes. *Academy of Management Review*, 13, 8–22.

Doucouliagos, C. (1995). Worker participation and productivity in labor-managed and participatory capitalist firms: A meta-analysis. *Industrial and Labor Relations Review*, 49, 58–77.

Freeman, R. B. and Kleiner, M. M. (2000). Who benefits most from employee involvement: Firms or workers? *The American Economic Review*, 90, 219–23.

Lawler, E., Mohrman, S., and Ledford, G. (1998). *Strategies for High Performance Organizations: Employee Involvement, TQM, and Re-Engineering Programs in Fortune 1000 Corporations*. San Francisco: Jossey-Bass.

Locke, E. A, Schweiger, D. M., and Latham, G. P. (1986). Participation in decision-making: When should it be used? *Organizational Dynamics*, 14, 65–79.

Poole, M. A., Lansbury, R., and Wailes, N. (2001). A comparative analysis of developments in industrial democracy. *Industrial Relations*, 40, 490–525.

Wagner, J. (1994). Participation's effects on performance and satisfaction: A reconsideration of the research evidence. *Academy of Management Review*, 19, 312–30.

path-goal theory

see LEADERSHIP; MOTIVATION

payment systems

see INCENTIVES

perception

Mark Martinko

Perception can be defined as the psychological process by which individuals select, organize, and interpret sensory information. Perception is distinguished from sensation in that sensation is the physiological process by which stimuli are received through the five senses. Perception begins with sensory registration and is the active cognitive process of selecting, organizing, and interpreting the multitude of stimuli that are received.

Perception is of key importance to organizational behavior because people's behavior is a function of their perceived as opposed to their objective world. Although individuals may occupy nearly identical objective realities and receive similar sensory information, their perceptions of reality may differ markedly. These differences in perceptions are important determinants of behavior. Thus, although two individuals may attend the same meeting and receive essentially the same information, they may have very different interpretations and reactions to the information.

Several topics are commonly included in discussions of perception within organizational contexts. Perceptual selectivity addresses the issue of why certain stimuli are perceived and processed whereas others are apparently ignored. Thus it has been found that environmental factors such as size, repetition, familiarity, and contrast increase the probability that individuals will attend to a stimulus. Internal personal factors are also viewed as influencing selection as well as interpretation. These factors include the personality of the perceiver (e.g., thinking versus feeling oriented); learning (i.e., prior experience); motivation (e.g., the effects of needs such as the need for power, mastery, and affiliation); and expectations. Thus, an individual who identifies with an organization's culture, has extensive experience with the culture, and has aspirations for promotion within the organization is likely to view organizational actions more positively than an outsider who has no affiliation with or interest in the organization.

Principles of perceptual organization are concerned with how the information is developed into cohesive patterns and impressions. Principles of perceptual organization include figure–ground relationships, closure, proximity, and similarity.

Recent work has emphasized social perception, which is concerned with the issue of how people form impressions of each other. This area includes the process of social categorization and addresses how information is organized into schemas and stereotypes which provide cognitive "short-cuts" for developing impressions and making decisions about other people. A key aspect of social perception is the ATTRIBUTION process. These causal interpretations about the behavior of others form an important part of people's perceptions of each other. In addition, research on IMPRESSION MANAGEMENT has described how people create and manage specific impressions, thereby enhancing their image to others or reducing their responsibility for poor performance. There is also a fairly extensive literature that describes the development and impact of perceptual errors such as stereotyping and HALO EFFECTS on human resource management processes such as selection and PERFORMANCE APPRAISAL/PERFORMANCE MANAGEMENT.

See also attitude theory; decision-making; self-regulation

Bibliography

Aquino, K., Douglas, S. C., and Martinko, M. J. (2004). Overt expressions of anger in response to perceived victimization by co-workers: Attributional style, hierarchical status, and organizational norms. *Journal of Organizational Health Psychology*, 9 (2).

Carr, J. Z., Schmidt, A. M., Ford, J. K., and DeShon, R. P. (2003). Climate perceptions matter: A meta-analytic path analysis relating molar climate, cognitive and affective states, and individual level work outcomes. *Journal of Applied Psychology*, 8, 605–19.

Gundlach, M. J., Douglas, S. C., and Martinko, M. J. (2003). The decision to blow the whistle: A social information processing framework. *Academy of Management Review*, 128 (1), 107–23.

Onne, J. (2001). Fairness perceptions as a moderator in the curvilinear relationships between job demands, and job performance and job satisfaction. *Academy of Management Journal*, 44, 1039–41.

Thoresen, C. J., Kaplan, S. A., Barsky, A. P., Warren, C. R., and de Chermont, K. (2003). The affective underpinnings of job perceptions and attitudes: A meta-analytic review and integration. *Psychological Bulletin*, 129, 914–45.

performance, individual

see PERFORMANCE APPRAISAL/PERFORMANCE MANAGEMENT

performance appraisal/performance management

Gary P. Latham

The purposes of performance appraisal are at least threefold (Latham and Wexley, 1994).

First, appraisals are the basis for administrative decisions including the promoting, demoting, transferring, compensating, and training of employees. Second, appraisals are conducted for developmental and motivational purposes; they are conducted to instill in people the desire for continuous improvement. The third interrelated purpose for an appraisal is to provide a legal document of the person's performance in regard to the above two objectives, administrative and developmental.

The administrative and developmental purposes of an appraisal have a reciprocal effect on one another. Administrative decisions determine the developmental needs of an employee; the attainment of developmental goals influences administrative decisions that affect an employee's career in an organization. Because of the impact that appraisals have on an employee's career in US law, the appraisal is a legal document that is subject to challenge in a court of law (Arvey and Murphy, 1998).

As a result of performance appraisals, performance can decrease rather than increase. This is because employees often become defensive as a result of the appraisal. Hence, they frequently defend their current behavior rather than focus on ways of improving it.

The reasons for hostility toward the appraisal system are at least threefold. First, people frequently attack the appraisal instrument for its irrelevance to what they do on the job, or for assessing them on metrics for which they have little or no ability to control. The solution is to conduct a systematic job analysis that identifies the behaviors critical to the effective implementation of the organization's strategic plan. These behaviors should constitute the appraisal instrument.

Many strategic plans fail because little or no attention is given as to how to operationalize them in the field. An appraisal instrument that specifies what an employee must start doing, stop doing, or continue doing facilitates coaching an employee as well as self-management. Such an instrument becomes highly relevant for the employee and the appraiser(s) because it specifies the behaviors necessary for the strategic plan to succeed. Moreover, such an instrument is difficult to attack in a court of law.

A second reason for employee hostility toward appraisals is the appraiser. One's supervisor usually lacks the opportunity to obtain a complete picture of the person's performance. Consequently, an appraisal often reflects the biases of the appraiser more than the performance of the person who is being appraised. Moreover, how an employee interacts with the supervisor is not necessarily the way that the employee interacts with peers or subordinates. The solution is 360° FEEDBACK; that is, feedback from multi-sources including peers, subordinates, and even self (Atwater and Waldman, 1998). The responsibility of the supervisor is to collect data from these multi-sources to make administrative and developmental decisions. Multi-source data are not only comprehensive, they also make it more difficult for an employee to argue "I am right, the world is wrong" than it is for an employee to do so when there is only a single appraiser. Multi-source data increase the likelihood that developmental needs will be identified that would otherwise go unnoticed if there is only one source of appraisal. Administrative decisions based on multi-sources are likely to be highly defensible in a court of law.

There are intriguing data on self-appraisals. Research suggests that those whose self-appraisals are aligned with appraisals from others are usually high performers and highly promotable. This appears to be due to the employee's high "self-awareness" (Fletcher, 1997).

A third explanation for the frequent failure of appraisals to bring about a positive change in a person's behavior is that they are done at discrete intervals: quarterly, bi-annually, or annually. Hence, the employee is often surprised by negative feedback that is received, and therefore becomes defensive. The solution is to adopt and adapt from the field of athletics the concept of coaching employees on an ongoing basis. In organizational settings, coaching on an ongoing basis is referred to as performance management. Performance management shifts the administrative emphasis of the appraiser to a developmental one. As is the case in the sports arena, how well and how quickly a person develops in the organization affects administrative decisions "at the end of the season." The formal appraisal at the end of the season is done to document the person's performance throughout the year,

and to set goals to be attained within a specified time period that are aligned with the employing organization's strategic plan.

The principles for conducting an appraisal that bring about a positive change in an employee's performance are the same as those for coaching effectively. The difference is the time frame and the mindset. The time frame for coaching is "ongoing" and the mindset is developmental rather than administrative. For supervisors to excel as both appraisers and coaches requires training in the following areas:

Rater accuracy. Research shows that assessments of others reflects primarily the biases of the assessor rather than the performance of the person who is being assessed (Scullen, Mount, and Goff, 2000). People need to be trained in ways to increase their objectivity.

Feedback. In one third of the interventions, feedback has been shown to decrease performance (DeNisi and Kluger, 2000). To be effective, negative feedback must include specific information on ways to correct performance. Moreover, the emphasis should be on the desired rather than the undesired performance; on the future as to what behaviors should occur rather than on past behaviors, as the past cannot be undone. A cardinal rule in giving constructive feedback is to never confuse honesty with hurtfulness.

Goal setting. Feedback is information only. It has no effect on behavior until it leads to the setting of and commitment to specific high goals. However, the formal appraisal must be on the frequency of the behavior that was demonstrated rather than goal attainment per se, or people will find ingenious ways to set easy goals that appear difficult to administrators.

Organizational justice. In addition to being fair, leaders/coaches must be seen as fair (Greenberg, 1997). Both appraisal and coaching decisions must be based on agreed upon procedures. The logic and sincerity of the appraiser/coach must be apparent to employees. Employees must see that their views are taken into account in the decisions that subsequently affect them in the organization. The data show that to the extent that people perceive that they have "voice," they will support a decision even if they initially disagreed with it.

The coupling of performance management with performance appraisal should lead to a highly trained, highly motivated workforce.

See also *career development; goal setting; learning, individual*

Bibliography

Arvey, R. D. and Murphy, K. R. (1998). Performance evaluation in work settings. *Annual Review of Psychology*, **49**, 141–68.

Atwater, L. E. and Waldman, D. A. (1998). Accountability in 360 degree feedback. *HR Magazine* (May), 96–104.

DeNisi, A. S. and Kluger, A. N. (2000). Feedback effectiveness: Can 360-degree appraisals be improved? *Academy of Management Executive*, **14**, 129–39.

Fletcher, C. (1997). Self-awareness: A neglected attribute in selection and assessment? *International Journal of Selection and Assessment*, **5**, 183–7.

Greenberg, J. (1997). A taxonomy of organizational justice theories. *Academy of Management Review*, **12**, 9–22.

Latham, G. P. and Wexley, K. N. (1994). *Increasing Productivity Through Performance Appraisal*, 2nd edn. Reading, MA: Addison Wesley.

Scullen, S. E., Mount, M. K., and Goff, M. (2000). Understanding the latent structure of job performance ratings. *Journal of Applied Psychology*, **85**, 956–70.

performance related pay

see INCENTIVES

persistence

Pino G. Audia

Persistence is defined by organizational scholars as the continuation of an existing course of action (March and Simon, 1958). Researchers examine different manifestations of persistence within organizations and two common approaches have been to study persistence as continued investment of effort and resources in an ongoing project and persistence as continuation of the organization's current strategy. One of the key empirical findings derived from the theory of learning *(see* LEARNING, ORGANIZATIONAL*)* is that past performance influences the propensity to persist with an existing course of action.

Individuals and organizations are more likely to persist after success, defined as performance that exceeds the aspiration level. This effect arises because individuals become confident in the effectiveness of the current strategy when they find a course of action that produces satisfactory outcomes (Audia, Locke, and Smith, 2000; Lant, Milliken, and Batra, 1992). The idea that reaching a satisfactory level of performance induces persistence implies that failure spurs change by creating the urgency to mend the performance shortfall. Studies, however, suggest that in many circumstances failure does not discourage persistence (Kernis et al., 1982; Ocasio, 1995). Individuals who took actions that led to failure may persist because they are reluctant to admit that their past decisions are incorrect (Staw and Ross, 1987) *(see* COMMITMENT, ESCALATING*)*. Individuals may persist also because they attribute failure to external causes rather than to the poor quality of their decisions (Lant, Milliken, and Batra, 1992) or because very low levels of performance induce STRESS and anxiety that limit their ability to generate new courses of action (Staw, Sandelands, and Dutton, 1981). Finally, irrespective of individuals' responses, failure may be associated with persistence because rigid organizational routines make it difficult to modify existing courses of action (Kelly and Amburgey, 1991). The fact that failure may induce either change or persistence provides an explanation for the kinked performance-change curve found in recent studies (Greve, 2003). The key feature of this curve is that failure increases change less than success suppresses it.

Research has not been limited to the idea that actors decide whether to persist or change depending on the consequences of their past actions. Another key source of learning influencing the decision to persist or change is the actions by others. Organizations may be less likely to persist with the existing course of action as a result of pressures to imitate others who have adopted new approaches, as suggested by INSTITUTIONAL THEORY and studies of diffusion *(see* INNOVATION*)*. Empirical studies, however, suggest that characteristics of the actors who make the change and characteristics of the type of change may influence the likelihood of such mimetic responses (Greve and Taylor, 2000).

The preference for persistence evidenced in empirical studies, especially those focusing on the consequences of performance, is not necessarily a liability for individuals and organizations. Not only are decision makers often evaluated more favorably to the extent that they persist (Staw and Ross, 1987), persistence also benefits organizations by increasing the reliability of operations and by decreasing the risk of adopting incorrect policies (Barnett and Freeman, 2001). Persistence, however, is generally detrimental when performance is poor and adjustments are needed (Staw and Ross, 1987) or when performance is high but changes in the environment call for adjustments to current approaches (Audia, Locke, and Smith, 2000).

Future research on persistence (and change) will benefit from a greater integration of learning theory with the growing body of work on social networks, which allows researchers to theorize on the implications of where individuals are located in social space. Another promising line of inquiry lies in identifying the distinct contribution of psychological processes and structural processes in influencing persistence. By shedding light on how persistence or change unfold within organizations, such studies may help identify ways in which managers can steer organizations in the desired direction.

See also *resistance to change; self-efficacy; self-regulation*

Bibliography

Audia, P. G., Locke, E. A., and Smith, K. G. (2000). The paradox of success: An archival and a laboratory study of strategic persistence following a radical environmental change. *Academy of Management Journal*, 43, 837–53.

Barnett, W. P. and Freeman, J. (2001). Too much of a good thing: Product proliferation and organizational failure. *Organization Science*, 12, 539–58.

Greve, H. R. (2003). *Organizational Learning from Performance Feedback: A Behavioral Perspective on Innovation and Change*. Cambridge: Cambridge University Press.

Greve, H. R. and Taylor, A. (2000). Innovation as catalysts for organizational changes: Shifts in organizational cognition and search. *Administrative Science Quarterly*, 45, 54–80.

Kelly, D. and Amburgey, T. L. (1991). Organizational inertia and momentum: A dynamic model of strategic change. *Academy of Management Journal*, 34, 591–612.

Kernis, M. H., Zuckerman, M., Cohen, A., and Spadafora, S. (1982). Persistence following failure: The interactive role of self-awareness and attributional basis for negative expectancies. *Journal of Personality and Social Psychology*, 43, 1184–91.

Lant, T. K., Milliken, F. J., and Batra, B. (1992). The role of managerial learning and interpretation in strategic persistence and reorientation: An empirical investigation. *Strategic Management Journal*, 13, 585–608.

March, J. G. and Simon, H. A. (1958). *Organizations*. New York: Wiley.

Ocasio, W. (1995). The enactment of economic adversity: A reconciliation of theories of failure induced change and threat rigidity. *Research in Organizational Behavior*, 17, 287–331.

Staw, B. M. and Ross, J. (1987). Understanding escalation situations: Antecedent, prototypes, and solutions. *Research in Organizational Behavior*, 9, 39–78.

Staw, B. M., Sandelands, L. E., and Dutton, J. E. (1981). Threat rigidity effects in organizational behavior: A multilevel analysis. *Administrative Science Quarterly*, 26, 501–24.

person–environment interaction

Amy Kristof-Brown

At its most basic level, person–environment (P-E) interaction argues for study of the relationship between people and their environments. Although these relationships can take many forms, the fundamental idea is that individuals' behaviors and attitudes are determined jointly by personal and environmental conditions. Lewin's (1935) field theory, represented by the equation $B = f (P, E)$ (Behavior is a function of the person and the environment), was one of the earliest and most popularized forms of this approach to organizational behavior. Although the interactional logic is now almost universally embraced, research in the domain of P-E fit represents one of its truest forms.

The concept of P-E fit is that for each individual there are particular environments that are most compatible with his or her personal characteristics. If a person works in those environments, he or she will experience positive consequences, such as improved work attitudes, better performance, and reduced stress. P-E fit has been the foundation for many popular theories, including (1) Holland's (1985) RIASEC model which purports a positive relationship between individual–occupation match and satisfaction, career path stability, and performance; (2) Schneider's attraction–selection–attrition model which proposes that individuals are attracted to, selected by, and likely to remain in organizations where the individual's PERSONALITY matches the modal personality of the organization (*see* SOCIALIZATION); (3) Caplan and Harrison's (1993) P-E theory of stress, in which well-being is thought to result from a match between the demands of the environment and the abilities of the person and/or between the needs of the person and the supplies in the environment; and (4) Chatman's (1989) person–organization fit theory, in which satisfaction and organizational commitment are reportedly maximized when there is congruence between the person and the organization's values. Each of these theories or models has generated prolific streams of research, underscoring the importance of the interactional perspective in organizational behavior.

Recently, research on P-E interaction has been heavily influenced by methodological debate (*see* RESEARCH METHODS). Traditional methods relied heavily on the use of statistical interactions, where the effect of the environment was moderated by the characteristics of the person, or vice versa. Recent approaches to multi-level research, such as hierarchical linear modeling, offer new potential for capturing the simultaneous effects of person and environment on individual and higher level outcomes. In addition, research emphasizing congruence between person and environment (e.g., person–organization fit) traditionally relied on the use of difference scores. In a series of articles in the mid-1990s, Edwards (e.g., Edwards, 1994) critiqued this approach, and instead recommended the use of polynomial regression and surface plot analysis to assess fit relationships. Much current fit research follows this approach, which allows for the examination of conditions of misfit as well as fit. Future research on P-E interaction is likely to be influenced by these methodological advances, as researchers become better able to capture the precise nature of how person and environment interact to influence outcomes.

See also *attitude theory; career development; self-regulation*

Bibliography

Caplan, R. D. and Harrison, R. V. (1993). Person–environment fit theory: Some history, recent developments, and future directions. *Journal of Social Issues*, **49**, 253–75.

Chatman, J. A. (1989). Improving interactional organizational research: A model of person–organization fit. *Academy of Management Review*, **14**, 333–49.

Edwards, J. R. (1994). The study of congruence in organizational behavior research: Critique and a proposed alternative. *Organizational Behavior and Human Decision Processes*, **58**, 51–100.

Holland, J. E. (1985). *Making Vocational Choices: A Theory of Careers*. Englewood Cliffs, NJ: Prentice-Hall.

Lewin, K. (1935). *A Dynamic Theory of Personality*. New York: McGraw-Hill.

person-job fit

see PERSON–ENVIRONMENT INTERACTION

personal initiative

Michael Frese and Doris Fay

Personal Initiative (PI) is behavior characterized by its self-starting nature, its proactive approach, and by being persistent in overcoming difficulties that arise in the pursuit of a goal (Frese and Fay, 2001). Surprisingly, PI was not studied systematically until very recently, although practitioners have often referred to the need to recruit employees with high initiative. Measures have been developed and validated as self-report, peer report, supervisor rating, and an extensive interview procedure. PI is related to INNOVATION because innovation has to be implemented and the implementation phase has to be supported by the PI of the people involved. One consequence of such an active approach is that the environment is changed (e.g., role requirements are altered by the job incumbent as a result of PI) (*see* ENACTMENT; STRUCTURATION). Other concepts that have overlap with PI are proactive behavior (Crant, 2000), voice (Van Dyne and LePine, 1998), taking charge (Morrison and Phelps, 1999), and role-breadth SELF-EFFICACY (Parker, Wall, and Jackson, 1997).

All of these concepts share an emphasis on the active nature of the employee vis-à-vis his or her work. In this way, the PI and related concepts may improve upon passive concepts of performance (e.g., workers perform, if they do what they are told).

Antecedents of PI are the amount of control at work and complexity of the job, the culture/climate of the organization and the CEO's support for PI, PERSONALITY factors such as proactive personality, and related orientations (change orientation, self-efficacy, control expectations, the willingness to take responsibility, and error management (*see* ERRORS)). Modern forms of production, such as just-in-time with its high interdependency and reliance on individuals to self-start, will often produce and require a higher degree of PI (Parker, Wall, and Jackson, 1997). PI has been extended to the climate concept. Climate for initiative enhances firm profitability and interacts with process innovations at work (e.g., just-in-time production); process innovations lead to higher profitability *only* if there is a high PI climate within the firm. There is evidence that PI produces a number of positive effects for individual and firm performance, for CAREER advancement and for the work group, as well as for the whole organization (e.g., profitability and number of innovations) (Frese and Fay, 2001). Interestingly, PI develops in a certain environment, but high PI in turn has a shaping influence on the environment, leading to positive (and vicious) cycles (Frese and Fay, 2001).

PI can be raised by enhancements to an organization's culture, where increased empowerment includes a higher degree of control over work methods, improved management practice, training to raise PI, and PI related incentives and sanctions. Greater awareness of PI and how to raise it could enrich the theory and practice of change management. However, there may also be negative consequences of PI, which have not yet been examined empirically (e.g., coordination problems in team work). Since organizational science has produced a number of rather similar concepts (proactive personality, voice, contextual performance, taking charge, role-breadth self-efficacy, ORGANIZATIONAL CITIZENSHIP BEHAVIOR), more work on the overlap

and distinctions of these concepts is necessary before PI becomes securely established in OB.

See also *motivation; organizational climate; organizational culture*

Bibliography

Crant, J. M. (2000). Proactive behavior in organizations. *Journal of Management*, **26**, 435–62.

Frese, M. and Fay, D. (2001). Personal initiative (PI): A concept for work in the twenty-first century. *Research in Organizational Behavior*, **23**, 133–88.

Morrison, E. W. and Phelps, C. C. (1999). Taking charge at work: Extra role efforts to initiate workplace change. *Academy of Management Journal*, **42**, 403–19.

Parker, S. K., Wall, T. D., and Jackson, P. R. (1997). "That's not my job": Developing flexible employee work orientations. *Academy of Management Journal*, **40**, 899–929.

Van Dyne, L. and LePine, J. A. (1998). Helping and voice extra-role behaviors: Evidence of construct and predictive validity. *Academy of Management Journal*, **41**, 108–19.

personality

Timothy A. Judge and Kevin Miliffe

DEFINITION

Defining something as abstract as personality has proven difficult, and the literature contains multiple definitions of the construct. Although these definitions are distinct in their own ways, they generally can be divided into two approaches: INDIVIDUAL DIFFERENCES and organismic views (Pervin, 1990). The individual differences approach implies personality is reflected in disparities observable in how these individuals react to certain events. The organismic approach views the individual differences approach as incomplete because it fails to consider the dynamic processes occurring *within* individuals. While not denying between-individual differences, the organismic approach requires that all factors be looked at together in order to see the totality of personality. For example:

> Personality exists as an organized whole (system), that is constituted of parts or elements (subsys-

tems), and separated somehow from an environment with which it interacts. (Sanford, 1963: 489)

Mindful of these constrasting approaches, we
would define personality as the dynamic organization of a relatively stable set of traits, thought
processes, and behaviors that give a direction
and a pattern to an individual's life and help
that individual determine his characteristic behavior and thought (Allport, 1961; Pervin,
1990).

HERITABILITY

One of the most important questions arising in
discussions of personality is whether it is genetically determined (nature) or developed over the
life course, particularly in early childhood (nurture). Recent research indicates that a large proportion (roughly 50 percent) of the variance
associated with certain personality characteristics can be explained by genetic variation.
Parents therefore have a great influence on
their children, not necessarily because of the
environment they raise them in, but because of
their genes, though because traits result from
combinations of genes there is a low to zero
correlation between parents and their offspring's
measured personalities, giving rise to the paradox that personality is heritable but does not run
in families.

This conclusion has emerged consistently
from large-scale studies of the heritability of
personality using the twin method. These investigations have analyzed three types of twins:
fraternal twins, identical twins, and twins reared
apart, plus adoptive relationships (to assess pure
environmental effects). Fraternal twins are from
two different fertilized eggs (dizygotic twins),
and thus share only 50 percent genetic material.
This is the same as the genetic relationship between siblings. Identical twins, in contrast, are
practically genetic clones; they are born from the
same fertilized egg (monozygotic twins). Studies
of twins reared apart look primarily at identical
twins that were separated at the beginning of
their life, most often before the end of the second
month.

The results of these studies have strongly
supported the notion that personality traits are
heritable. A study of 850 sets of twins (Loehlin

and Nichols, 1976) found there were high correlations between monozygotes in general ability, special abilities, personality scales, and goals
and interests. Moreover, identical twins' personalities were much more similar than were fraternal twins' personalities. For example, the
correlation between fraternal twins' personality
was .28 compared to a correlation of .50 for
identical twins.

One might criticize this evidence on the
grounds that the observed similarity is due to
the environment in which the twins were raised.
For example, twins reared apart may nonetheless
be raised in similar environments. However,
twin studies have controlled for environmental
factors such as socioeconomic status, education,
geography, and family size. Controlling for these
factors appears to have little effect on the relationship between identical twins' personalities.
Moreover, a shared familial environment explained an average of 13 percent (Tellegen
et al., 1988) of the variance while genetic similarity explained 47 percent of the variance. This
study not only shows that genetics are instrumental in determining an individual's personality makeup, but also that a shared environment
explains little of the variation in personality.
This is not to suggest that personality is wholly
genetic, but it does suggest that genes appear to
be more important to personality than early
childhood experiences.

STABILITY

Our definition of personality was prefaced by the
phrase "relatively stable." Personality traits that
are stable cause similar behavior and reactions
over the course of an individual's life. For
example, an individual who is extremely extroverted is likely to remain extroverted throughout
their life and to behave and make decisions in
ways consistent with that trait. The key to the
stability of personality traits and behaviors is
that there will be a recognizable, consistent pattern throughout an individual's life.

There are two definitions of trait consistency
used by most researchers: mean-level consistency and rank order consistency (Roberts and
DelVecchio, 2000). Mean-level consistency uses
the criterion of whether "groups of people show
reliable mean-level changes over time," while

rank order consistency "refers to the relative placement of individuals within a group." In their meta-analysis, Roberts and DelVecchio (2000) found that in population estimates of trait consistency there was a correlation of .51 for individuals of 18–22 years in age. This correlation was raised to .62 for individuals aged 30–39. The general consensus of their study is that traits are relatively consistent over the course of an individual's life.

Another recent study (Srivastava et al., 2003) set out to determine if specific traits change over time and to see if trait changes might differ by gender. They found that among the traits that comprise the Big Five model (*see* FIVE FACTOR MODEL OF PERSONALITY), conscientiousness and agreeableness both increased after the age of 30. There also were GENDER differences between males and females. Males' neuroticism levels remain relatively constant throughout life, but females' levels of neuroticism steadily decline and continue to do so well beyond the age of 30. The overall findings of this study suggest that personality does change, particularly early in life.

There have been numerous studies looking at the stability of personality traits over time (Costa and McCrae, 1997; Block, 1971). These have found that there is a high correlation in ratings of personality from high school age to adulthood. Block found an average .53 correlation in personality between high school and adulthood for males and .46 for females. Costa and McCrae found median correlations of .34 to .77 in personality trait inventories. Thus, it appears that personality is both stable and changeable at the same time – there is considerable rank order consistency – but mean levels do change.

MEASUREMENT

As there has been considerable debate as to what exactly personality is and is not, there has been a corresponding debate as to how to measure it. At the center of the controversy is the idiographic–nomothetic debate. The idiographic personality approaches are characterized by studying individuals and the ways in which they are unique. In contrast, nomothetic approaches focus on characteristics that are common across all individuals, but for which individuals may vary. The vast majority of research implicitly operates under a nomothetic approach.

Personality assessment can currently be categorized three ways: self-report surveys, observer ratings, and projective measures. There are pronounced differences between these measurement strategies and none has a clear advantage over the others. These assessments can also be classified into implicit and explicit categories. Explicit personality assessments are actual measures that are taken from the individual being studied. Surveys and observer ratings fit into this category. Implicit personality assessments are projective measures. In this case, the respondent is projecting his or her personality onto the question or situation that provoked their response (*see* RESEARCH METHODS).

Survey approaches consist of an individual completing a personality questionnaire measure. Three of the best-known surveys are the NEO, the California Psychological Inventory (CPI), and the 16-PF. One concern with survey approaches is that they are usually based on a single, self-reported questionnaire. There are concerns, especially when using the questionnaire as a basis for employment, that the individual will lie and practice IMPRESSION MANAGEMENT in order to project the best image possible. Though the literature suggests individuals can fake when motivated to do so, it does not appear that faking fatally undermines the validity of personality surveys used in employment decisions. Observer (significant others, co-workers, friends) survey measures have been developed to provide an independent assessment of personality. Though self-rated and observer ratings of personality are correlated (typically around .50), research suggests that observer ratings often explain additional variance in behavior beyond self-reports of personality.

The best examples of projective measures are the Rorschach Inkblot Test and the Thematic Apperception Test (TAT). The Rorschach Inkblot Test consists of several cards of inkblots where the individual says everything that the inkblot looks like. The TAT is a series of pictures (drawings, photos) on cards. The individual being tested writes a story about each individual picture. Clinicians then score the responses. Because projective measures are intended to provide a window into the unconscious, scoring the responses in a reliable and valid manner has proven to be challenging. In a review of the literature, Kihlstrom (2003) concluded that even when projective measures had some validity (which was a rare occurrence in his review), there was no evidence that the findings reflected the person's unconscious mental state.

STRUCTURE

Currently, the best-known and widely used structure of personality is the Big Five. Researchers have found that the Big Five "illustrate that personality consists of five relatively independent dimensions which provide a meaningful taxonomy for studying individual differences" (Barrick and Mount, 1991). These factors are extraversion, neuroticism (also known by its converse, emotional stability), agreeableness, conscientiousness, and openness to experience.

Extraversion typically refers to the extent that an individual is gregarious, sociable, and dominant. Extraverts like talking with others and like to be around other people. Neuroticism is the extent that an individual is depressed, anxious, nervous, and insecure. Agreeableness is the extent to which someone is likeable, friendly, trusting, compliant, and cooperative. Conscientiousness reflects the extent to which individuals are dependable, careful, thorough, responsible, organized, planful, hardworking, achievement oriented, and persevering. The final factor is openness to experience. Open individuals are characterized by non-conformance, creativity, culture, originality, and adaptability.

In the past few years, replacements for the Big Five model have been proposed. Some have argued that five factors are too few to represent human nature. Others prefer a more parsimonious structure, such as three factors. The Big Three factors some prefer consist of extraversion–introversion, emotional stability–neuroticism, and psychoticism (Zuckerman et al., 1993). The third component, psychoticism, is said to be a hybrid of low agreeableness and conscientiousness. In their factor analysis, Zuckerman et al. found evidence that indeed these two scales of the NEO personality inventory, agreeableness and conscientiousness, did negatively load on the psychoticism factor.

Research by Judge and colleagues has proposed another approach, which they term "core self-evaluations." They argue that four traits comprise the core concept of an individual. The four core traits are self-esteem, generalized self-efficacy, locus of control, and emotional stability (the low end of the neuroticism dimension). Research by Judge and colleagues indicates that individuals with positive core self-evaluations are more satisfied with their jobs, are more motivated, and perform better. These researchers have noted that core self-evaluations may be integrated with the five-factor model, in that core self-evaluations may be equivalent to emotional stability, if measures of emotional stability are broadened to assess fundamental aspects of the self-concept.

Other, more specific traits have been proposed by researchers. Depending on the criterion, some of these traits have predictive validity. Thus, one should not construe the support in favor of the five-factor model as closing the door on the investigation of more specific traits. Clearly, in predicting specific criteria, specific traits may be as or more valid.

OUTCOMES IN ORGANIZATIONAL BEHAVIOR

Overall status The popularity of personality research within the field of organizational behavior has increased in the past decade as researchers have begun to conduct studies with personality as the primary variable of interest. In the past, personality research was restricted to playing a secondary role in studies on leadership, work motivation, and attitudes (Weiss and Adler, 1984). The trait method of personality came under attack in the 1960s when Mischel (1968: 301) wrote: "global traits and states are excessively crude, gross units to encompass adequately the extraordinary complexity and subtlety of the discriminations that people constantly make." He also criticized the assumption "that individuals are characterized by stable and broadly generalized dispositions that endure over long periods of time and that generate consistencies in their social behavior across a wide range of situations" (Mischel, 1990).

In response to Mischel's critique, personality research has become more systematic, has better considered the importance of the situation, and has developed better measures (including recognizing the importance of broad, well-validated measures). Moreover, the twin research, as well as recent studies (Srivastava et al., 2003; Roberts and DelVecchio, 2000), have shown that the assumption of relative stability among personality dispositions, contested by Mischel, is valid. Mischel's other concern regarding the global trait method has also been challenged by recent personality research, as evidenced by the numerous studies on the validity of the Big Five and other personality structures, as well as their predictive performance on outcome variables.

Motivation   Personality has been shown to have an effect on an individual's motivation in the workplace. In a recent meta-analysis, Judge and Ilies (2002) found that several of the Big Five factors of personality had a significant relationship with different types of motivation. The factors that had the strongest overall relationships with motivation were neuroticism and conscientiousness. Neuroticism had an average overall relationship of $-.31$ to motivation while conscientiousness had a relationship of .24 to motivation. This shows that highly neurotic individuals are less likely to have high motivation while the converse is true for highly conscientiousness individuals. The other factors of the Big Five were not as strong as neuroticism and conscientiousness, though extraversion did have an overall relationship of .19 with motivation. Thus, it does appear that motivation is, in part, trait based.

Performance   Barrick and Mount's (1991) meta-analysis on the relation of the Big Five personality dimensions and job performance shows that personality and job performance are related under certain conditions. In certain jobs like sales jobs, managerial positions, or any job that requires a lot of social interaction, extraversion was a strong predictor of performance. In other jobs, however, such as skilled/semi-skilled work, it had almost no relation at all. The most significant result of the study was that conscientiousness had a strong relation with each job type studied. The study also included meta-analysis results for personality dimensions and objective and subjective criteria. Conscientiousness once again had the highest relationship

with productivity data as well as to the salary of the individual. Neuroticism was weakly related to the criteria, though more recent meta-analyses have suggested stronger validities.

Job attitudes   The field of organizational behavior has also studied the effects of personality and how it relates to job satisfaction. A recent meta-analysis (Judge, Heller, and Mount, 2002) found that "as a set, the Big Five traits had a multiple correlation of .41 with job satisfaction, indicating support for the validity of the dispositional source of job satisfaction when traits are organized according to the 5-factor model." They found that neuroticism had a strong negative relationship to job satisfaction $(-.29)$. Extraverts appear to be more satisfied with their jobs; the study found a correlation of .25. Conscientiousness also was positively related to job satisfaction, with an overall correlation of .26. In addition to the correlational analysis, Judge, Heller, and Mount performed a regression analysis and found three significant predictors of job satisfaction: neuroticism, extraversion, and conscientiousness (*see* ATTITUDE THEORY).

Leadership   Leadership research has advanced considerably with the addition of personality into the study. The study of leadership in organizational behavior can be divided into two broad categories: leadership emergence and leadership effectiveness. This division is important because different criteria may be necessary to succeed. Leader emergence refers to how leader-like individuals are viewed by a group of individuals that have very little knowledge about their performance. Conversely, leader effectiveness refers to a leader's success in "influencing and guiding the activities of his or her unit toward achievement of its goals" (Judge, Bono et al., 2002). Their meta-analysis found a negative relationship between neuroticism and leader emergence $(-.24)$ and leadership effectiveness $(-.22)$. In the leader emergence criteria, both extraversion and conscientiousness had strong significant relationships with leader emergence (both .33). In a subsequent regression analysis between the Big Five traits and leader emergence, extraversion and conscientiousness also had very high predictive relationships (.30 and .36) with leader emergence success. This shows that in situations where individuals do not have information on performance on potential leaders, these characteristics are significant predictors of a potential leader's success in rising to a leadership position. In this same regression analysis, neuroticism also had a negative relationship with leader emergence. The other criteria, leadership effectiveness, were somewhat similar in that neuroticism had a strong negative relationship ($-.10$) with effectiveness and that extraversion had a strong positive relationship (.18). The difference was that in determining leadership effectiveness, openness to experience was the strongest single predictor.

FUTURE OF PERSONALITY RESEARCH IN OB

Future research on personality in OB could productively pursue several lines of inquiry. First, there is a need for greater integration of research findings with basic research in personality psychology. Much of the research in personality is process oriented, focusing less on the possession of traits and more on the dynamic processes that explain how and why individuals differ. Personality research in OB would benefit from a similar process oriented focus. Second, there has been a growth of research on mood and emotions in OB. This line of research needs to continue, and needs to be integrated with the extant trait research. Third, although most personality research in OB is trait oriented, people are far from fixed entities and indeed respond dramatically to social contexts and processes. More research needs to consider idiographic, dynamic, and within-individual variation in attitudes and behavior.

See also *achievement, need for; affiliation, need for; job satisfaction; motivation; power, need for*

Bibliography

Allport, G. W. (1961). *Pattern and Growth in Personality*. New York: Holt, Rinehart, and Winston.

Barrick, M. R. and Mount, M. K. (1991). The Big Five personality dimensions and job performance: A meta-analysis. *Personnel Psychology*, **44**, 1–26.

Block, J. (1971). *Lives Through Time*. Berkeley, CA: Bancroft.

Costa, P. T., Jr. and McCrae, R. R. (1997). Longitudinal stability of adult personality. In R. Hogan, J. Johnson, and S. Briggs (eds.), *Handbook of Personality Psychology*. San Diego, CA: Academic Press, 269–91.

Judge, T. A. and Ilies, R. (2002). Relationship of personality to performance motivation: A meta-analytic review. *Journal of Applied Psychology*, **87**, 797–807.

Judge, T. A., Bono, J. E., Ilies, R., and Gerhardt, M. W. (2002). Personality and leadership: A qualitative and quantitative review. *Journal of Applied Psychology*, **87**, 765–80.

Judge, T. A., Heller, D., and Mount, M. K. (2002). Five-factor model of personality and job satisfaction: A meta-analysis. *Journal of Applied Psychology*, **87**, 530–41.

Kihlstrom, J. F. (2003). Implicit methods in social psychology. In C. Sansone, C. C. Morf, and A. Panter (eds.), *Handbook of Methods in Social Psychology*. Thousand Oaks, CA: Sage.

Loehlin, J. C. and Nichols, R. C. (1976). *Heredity, Environment, and Personality: A Study of 850 Sets of Twins*. Austin: University of Texas Press.

Mischel, W. (1968). *Personality and Assessment*. New York: Wiley.

Mischel, W. (1990). Personality dispositions revisited and revised: A view after three decades. In L. A. Pervin (ed.), *Handbook of Personality: Theory and Research*. New York: Guilford Press, 111–34.

Pervin, L. A. (1990). A brief history of modern personality theory. In L. A. Pervin (ed.), *Handbook of Personality: Theory and Research*. New York: Guilford Press, 3–18.

Roberts, B. W. and DelVecchio, W. F. (2000). The rank-order consistency of personality traits from childhood to old age: A quantitative review of longitudinal studies. *Psychological Bulletin*, **126**, 3–25.

Sanford, N. (1963). Personality: Its place in psychology. In S. Koch (ed.), *Psychology: A Study of a Science*, Vol. 5. New York: McGraw-Hill, 488–592.

Srivastava, S., John, O. P., Gosling, S. D., and Potter, J. (2003). Development of personality in early and middle adulthood: Set like plaster or persistent change? *Journal of Personality and Social Psychology*, **84**, 1041–53.

Tellegen, A., Lykken, D. T., Bouchard, T. J., Wilcox, K. J., Segal, N. L., and Rich, S. (1988). Personality similarity in twins reared apart and together. *Journal of Personality and Social Psychology*, **54**, 1031–9.

Weiss, H. and Adler, S. (1984). Personality and organizational behavior. *Research in Organizational Behavior*, **6**, 1–50.

Zuckerman, M., Kuhlman, M., Joireman, J., Teta, P., and Kraft, M. (1993). A comparison of three structural models for personality: The Big Three, the Big Five, and the Alternative Five. *Journal of Personality and Social Psychology*, **65**, 757–68.

politics

Roderick M. Kramer and Dana A. Gavrieli

Organizational theorists have long appreciated the central role that political processes play in shaping organizational processes and outcomes (Gandz and Murray, 1980; Simon and March, 1958). Recently, however, there has been renewed interest in this topic (Bacharach and Lawler, 2000; March and Olsen, 1989; Pfeffer, 1992).

DEFINING ORGANIZATIONAL POLITICS

The recognition that organizations can be productively viewed as differentiated social systems comprised of multiple actors with diverse preferences has provided the conceptual foundation for a political view of organizational life (March and Olsen, 1989). From this perspective, organizational decision-making and change are construed not simply as rational or adaptive processes, but rather as end products of political maneuvering, coalitional processes, and bargaining (*see* COALITION FORMATION). Organizations are fundamentally negotiated social orders, and political processes play a central role in that negotiation process.

Consistent with these themes and emphases, Bacharach and Lawler (2000: 4) recently defined organizational politics in terms of "the efforts of social actors (individual and corporate) to strengthen or defend their power positions and to exercise influence over goals, policies, rules, everyday routines, and events that are internal or external to organizations." Bacharach and Lawler's definition is useful in highlighting two important dimensions of political behavior. First, political behavior is presumed to reflect the goal directed and purposive behavior of strategic organizational actors. Second, the definition highlights the pivotal role interdependence plays in political behavior. It is the existence of divergent preferences and conflicting forces within organizations that animate political action (*see* CONFLICT AND CONFLICT MANAGEMENT).

STATE OF KNOWLEDGE

As Bacharach and Lawler (1998) noted in an assessment of the literature, despite the fact that there have been a number of studies of organizational politics, there has been surprisingly little systematic attempt at integrative theory in this domain. As a result, theorizing has been piecemeal and the resulting empirical research scattershot. Despite the obvious importance of the topic, the study of organizational politics remains "a broad rubric of disconnected concepts and research studies, unified primarily by the vague notion that power and influence are important issues for research and theorizing" (Bacharach and Lawler, 1998: 68).

Despite these continuing deficiencies in the research literature, some progress is nonetheless discernible on several fronts. These include recent explorations of the cognitive and behavioral antecedents of political processes, as well as studies examining the effects of political behavior on a variety of important organizational processes and outcomes.

One relatively recent emphasis in the study of organizational politics has been explication of the social cognitive underpinnings of political action (Ferris et al., 2000). Krackhardt (1990), for example, examined how location in an organization influences the accuracy of political PERCEPTION, and Ferris et al. (2000) showed that accuracy, in turn, influences how much power an actor possesses. Kramer (2000), in contrast, examined how location can contribute to systematic forms of inaccurate perception and loss of power. Others have examined the cognitive underpinnings of political judgment (Tetlock, 1992). Along these lines, Gruenfeld (1995) investigated how decision-makers' status and IDEOLOGY influenced the integrative complexity of their political reasoning.

Another promising stream of research has investigated the role political behavior plays in various organizational processes and outcomes. Within this tradition, a particularly important perspective is the bargaining framework articulated most forcefully by Bacharach and Lawler in a series of influential works (1980, 2000). According to this view, political success or failure is largely a function of the skillful use of bargaining strategies and tactics to mobilize support for political objectives and to overcome or thwart resistance to such objectives. A second, and closely related, perspective focuses on the role strategic alliances and coalition formation play in influencing organizational processes and outcomes (March and Olsen, 1989; Riker, 1962).

Finally, another major thrust of recent research has been identification of the macro-structural foundations of organizational politics. For example, March and Olsen (1989) investigated how rules and decisions are institutionalized over time. Brass (1984) explored the impact of organizational location on INFLUENCE. Finally, Ashford (1998) elaborated on some of the strategies and tactics useful for selling controversial issues in organizations.

CURRENT SIGNIFICANCE AND FUTURE DIRECTIONS

Although we suspect few organizational scholars would dispute the importance of political processes, attention to this important topic has continued to lag that afforded to other areas of organizational research. In part, this may reflect a longstanding antipathy towards the study of politics and political processes (Pfeffer, 1992). That picture may, however, be changing in response to recent events. Organizational scandals and fiascos such as Enron, Worldcom, and Arthur Andersen have led to increased concern with political processes and corporate governance. Such abuses of the political process have sparked renewed interest in the ethics of political judgment and decision-making, as well as consideration of the comparative efficacy of various organizational correctives (Cavanagh, Moberg, and Velasquez, 1981; Darley, Messick, and Tyler, 2001).

See also *deviance; influence; power*

Bibliography

Ashford, S. J. (1998). Championing charged issues: The case of gender equity within organizations. In R. M. Kramer and M. A. Neale (eds.), *Power and Influence in Organizations.* Thousand Oaks, CA: Sage, 349–80.

Bacharach, S. B. and Lawler, E. J. (1980). *Power and Politics in Organizations: The Social Psychology of Conflict, Coalitions, and Bargaining.* San Francisco: Jossey-Bass.

Bacharach, S. B. and Lawler, E. J. (1998). Political alignments in organizations: Contextualization, mobilization, and coordination. In R. M. Kramer and M. A. Neale (eds.), *Power and Illusion in Organizations.* Thousand Oaks, CA: Sage.

Bacharach, S. B. and Lawler, E. J. (2000). *Organizational Politics.* Stamford, CT: JAI Press.

Brass, D. J. (1984). Being in the right place: A structural analysis of individual influence in organizations. *Administrative Science Quarterly*, **55**, 518–39.

Cavanagh, G. F., Moberg, D. J., and Velasquez, M. (1981). The ethics of organizational politics. *Academy of Management Review*, **6** (3), 363–74.

Darley, J. M., Messick, D. M., and Tyler, T. R. (2001). *Social Influence on Ethical Behavior in Organizations.* Mahwah, NJ: Lawrence Erlbaum Associates.

Ferris, G. R., Harrell-Cook, G., and Dulebohn, J. H. (2000). Organizational politics: The nature of the relationship between politics, perceptions and political behavior. In S. B. Bacharach and E. J. Lawler (eds.), *Organizational Politics.* Stamford, CT: JAI Press, 89–130.

Gandz, J. and Murray, V. V. (1980). The experience of workplace politics. *Academy of Management Journal*, **23** (2), 237–51.

Gruenfeld, D. H. (1995). Status, ideology and integrative complexity on the US Supreme Court: Rethinking the politics of political decision-making. *Journal of Personality and Social Psychology*, **68**, 5–20.

Krackhardt, D. (1990). Assessing the political landscape: Structure, cognition, and power in organizations. *Administrative Science Quarterly*, **35**, 342–69.

Kramer, R. M. (2000). Political paranoia in organizations: Antecedents and consequences. In S. B. Bacharach and E. J. Lawler (eds.), *Organizational Politics.* Stamford, CT: JAI Press, 88.

March, J. G. and Olsen, J. P. (1989). *Rediscovering Institutions: The Organizational Basis of Politics.* New York: Free Press.

Pfeffer, J. (1992). *Managing with Power.* Boston, MA: Harvard Business School Press.

Riker, W. H. (1962). *The Theory of Political Coalitions.* New Haven, CT: Yale University Press.

Simon, H. A. and March, J. G. (1958). *Organizations.* New York: John Wiley.

Tetlock, P. E. (1992). Good judgment in international politics: Three psychological perspectives. *Political Psychology*, **13**, 517–40.

population ecology

see COMMUNITY ECOLOGY; EVOLUTIONARY PERSPECTIVES; ORGANIZATIONAL ECOLOGY

positivism

see CRITICAL THEORY; THEORY

postmodernism

Karen Legge

Postmodernism is a cultural movement of the late twentieth century that may be defined in opposition to modernism. Modernism is characterized by a rationalistic, positivistic, technological knowledge base which, allied to a belief in metanarratives (large-scale theoretical interpretations of purportedly universal truth and application, e.g., Marxism, capitalism), promised linear progress through rational planning and development, aimed at mass producing standardized goods and private and public services for mass markets/citizens. Modernism is typified by authoritarianism and elitism, through a belief in bureaucratic and hierarchical systems as instruments and guarantors of order, control, and efficiency (*see* BUREAUCRACY; RATIONALITY; SCIENTIFIC MANAGEMENT) and in "art for art's sake," divorced from popular culture, reserved for the appreciation of an artistic establishment. The institutions of modernity are industrialism, capitalism, the nation-state, and surveillance (*see* INSTITUTIONAL THEORY). The individual finds a coherent, if often alienated, identity as a productive worker.

Postmodernism, often seen as a reflection of "disorganized" (i.e., deregulated) global capitalism and time-space compression consequent on information and communication technologies, rejects positivism's tenet of absolute truths in favor of relativism. In Nietzsche's words, "truth is only the solidification of old metaphors." The "real" is not "out there" to be discovered, but is created through discourses emergent from power/knowledge relationships (Foucault). Language is not a neutral vehicle for representing independent "facts," but itself constitutes the "real": "there is nothing outside the text" (Derrida).

Symbol/image/representations can be hyper-real (simulacra) or more real than so-called "reality" (Baudrillard). This ontological position is reflected in a rejection of metanarratives in favor of a plurality of "language games," in which the medium is the message, and both may vary depending on situation and upon which image of our fragmented selves we wish to project (*see* IDEOLOGY; SYMBOLISM). Postmodernists suggest that our shifting identities are defined by our patterns of consumption rather than by our roles as productive workers, but, as postmodernists would assert, it is images we consume rather than purely the use value of products and services. The images are created and transmitted by a new middle class of knowledge workers in the media (e.g., in advertising, PR, and TV). Postmodernists suggest that our tastes, erasing distinctions between high and popular culture, are eclectic, playful, and transient, focusing on style rather than substance and on immediate gratification rather than long-term aspiration. Further, that time-space compression disrupts any sense of linear continuity or spatial boundaries (e.g., use of video, the global village). Hence, history becomes a repository of images to be mined by politicians, the leisure industry and advertisers, which are more readily consumed when presented through shock tactics, such as pastiche or collage forms, or as spectacle (e.g., films, Disneyland). Truth and fiction, fact and artifact are confounded, as the "real" world looks a pale copy of a media-created world (e.g., the UK royal family as soap stars; virtual reality). In this fragmented world postmodernists believe that relationships tend to be temporary and that many boundaries are blurred.

Postmodernism provides several insights into organizational behavior and ORGANIZATION THEORY. It suggests that our focus should not be so much on the "organization of production," as the modernists would assert, but on the "production of organization"; on "organizing," not on "organization" (Cooper and Burrell, 1988). It suggests the end of rationalistic planning, based on extrapolation from the past, and points to emergent strategy formation, concerned with scenario painting of future shock and strategy conceptualization based on metaphor (Cummings and Wilson, 2003). It recognizes an enacted rather than discovered environment (*see* ENACTMENT). It points to why managerial fashions and fads, enticingly packaged by consultants, are consumed as the "in" diet for organizational "lean" fitness. It suggests that the popularity of gurus lies not in the substance of their messages so much as in the images they project of the transformational leader as hero. It proposes that in managing corporate cultures (*see* ORGANIZATIONAL

CULTURE) such leaders engage in stylish media-based performances to sell a vision – often about customer awareness, including the employee as customer – that legitimizes DECISION-MAKING based on hunch rather than rationality. This is necessary because postmodernism's relativism calls into question AUTHORITY based on bureaucratic hierarchies while recognizing that pure rationality is impossible in a world characterized by uncertainty and accelerating rates of change (*see* ORGANIZATIONAL CHANGE).

Postmodernism would consider that new loosely coupled organizational forms such as teams, partnerships, alliances, and joint ventures, as well as moves to functional flexibility and flexible specialization, reflect the blurring of boundaries. It regards such phenomena as delayering, downsizing, career breaks, and numerical flexibility as expressions of the increasing temporariness of relationships. In blurring boundaries and confounding "truth" and fiction, postmodernism is comfortable with the contradictions embedded in organizations. For example, relationships with "outsiders," such as partners, may be more permanent than those with "insiders," such as employees; TOTAL QUALITY MANAGEMENT may represent labor intensification rather than EMPOWERMENT (*see* EMPLOYEE INVOLVEMENT; CONTINUOUS IMPROVEMENT).

Postmodernism has its critics, particularly critical theorists (*see* CRITICAL THEORY). They assert that it overestimates the role of language/discourse in constituting organizational reality; that it degenerates into extreme subjectivism/relativism in which "anything goes"; that it leads to depoliticization, a quiescent "playfulness"; and that it underestimates modernity's "unfinished projects" as a force for good.

See also *identity, organizational; metaphor; theory*

Bibliography

Cooper, R. and Burrell, G. (1988). Modernism, postmodernism and organizational analysis: An introduction. *Organization Studies*, 9, 91–112.
Cummings, S. and Wilson, D. (eds.) (2003). *Images of Strategy*. Oxford: Blackwell.
Eagleton, T. (1996). *The Illusions of Postmodernism*. Oxford: Blackwell.
Hancock, P. and Tyler, M. (2001). *Work, Postmodernism and Organization: A Critical Introduction*. London: Sage.
Harvey, D. (1989). *The Condition of Postmodernity*. Oxford: Blackwell.
Lyotard, J. F. (1984). *The Postmodern Condition*. Manchester: Manchester University Press.

power

Roderick M. Kramer and Dana A. Gavrieli

Few concepts in the organizational sciences are evoked with the same ease or used so readily to explain so much organizational phenomena as *power*. The concept of power has been viewed as central to understanding a variety of major organizational processes, including DECISION-MAKING, CONFLICT, LEADERSHIP, and ORGANIZATIONAL CHANGE, to name just a few. The concept of power has been used to explain, for example, the control of attention and stereotyping (Fiske, 1993), the emergence of various forms of assertive or disinhibitive behavior (Galinsky, Gruenfeld, and Magee, 2003), and organizational paranoia (Kramer, 2000), to name just a few (for a comprehensive review of the literature, see Keltner, Gruenfeld, and Anderson, 2003). The concept of power is routinely invoked, moreover, not only to explain why events do happen in organizations but also why they don't.

DEFINING POWER

As March (1994: 140) noted, many conceptions of power reflect "the intuitive notion of struggle, with outcomes determined by the relative strength of contending forces." This force metaphor finds considerable resonance in attempts to understand what happens and why when trying to explain both intra- and inter-organizational events. Wrong's (1979: 2) definition is representative of this view, characterizing power as the "capacity of some persons to produce intended and foreseen effects on others." Exchange conceptions of power also highlight this notion of relative force. For example, Blau (1964: 115) conceptualized power as a form of influence in EXCHANGE RELATIONS, such that actors possess power when they can "induce others to accede to wishes by rewarding them for doing so."

Despite the appeal of conceptualizing power as a kind of force, critics have been quick to point out problems with this notion (March, 1994). One major problem with operational definitions of power as a force is that they tend to be applied *ex post* and used in an ad hoc fashion to explain already observed events. In this sense, there is a tautological quality to the term's use: we infer that social actors have power by observing what they are able to obtain. We explain what they actually obtain, in turn, by invoking the notion of power.

These concerns notwithstanding, the concept of power nonetheless continues to be widely used to understand many organizational processes and outcomes. Indeed, Russell's (1938) observation that power remains a "fundamental concept" in the social sciences remains as true today as it did when he first uttered it.

State of Knowledge and Research

Research on power in organizations has taken a variety of approaches. These include (1) identifying the psychological, social, and institutional bases of organizational power, and (2) examining the effects or consequences of power.

Bases of power   Research on the antecedents or determinants of organizational power has focused on several broad categories of variables. First, a number of studies have focused on identifying individual attributes and correlates of power, including such things as a target individual's perceived expertise or legitimacy (e.g, French and Raven, 1959; Pfeffer, 1992). Other scholars have focused on the importance of social perceptiveness in assessing the political landscape as a basis of power (Krackhardt, 1990). According to these conceptions, power accrues to those who know how to locate sources of power and who are more adept at assessing emerging opportunities and threats. Finally, numerous studies have highlighted the role bargaining skills and coalitional power play in determining who has power and their effectiveness at using it (*see* COALITION FORMATION).

Institutional and structural analyses of the bases of power highlight the importance of individuals' location in an organizational system as a major source of power (Salancik and Pfeffer, 1977). Location influences the ability of organizational actors to monitor events and broker information, thereby increasing their social capital (Burt, 1992). Access to and control over critical resources, including financial resources, informational resources, and social resources constitute another important source of power. Pfeffer (1992: 83) went so far as to characterize this relationship as the "New Golden Rule" in organizations, observing: "The person with the gold makes the rules."

Institutional theorists (*see* INSTITUTIONAL THEORY) have elaborated on the broader, macro-level determinants of organizational power, including the role legitimation processes play in the attribution and conferral of power. Such perspectives foster an appreciation of the fact that power comes not only from within the organization, but from external sources of validation and reinforcement as well.

Effects of power   Another major focus of recent research has been identifying the consequences of power. This research has taken several directions. First, a number of recent studies have examined how power affects those who hold it. Fiske (1993) and her colleagues explored, for instance, how power affects social perception, including asymmetries in the stereotyping tendencies among the powerful and the powerless. Bargh and his associates (e.g., Bargh and Alvarez, 2001) have examined the effects of nonconscious processes on the tendency to misuse power. Galinsky, Gruenfeld, and Magee (2003) documented that power salience or orientation significantly increases action orientation. Finally, Keltner, Gruenfeld, and Anderson (2003) have documented a variety of intriguing effects related to what they characterize as the disinhibiting effects of power on powerholders. Other studies have examined how power affects important macro-level variables, such as the allocation of departmental resources (Salancik and Pfeffer, 1977).

Current Significance and Future Directions

Historically, much of the early work on power focused attention on those in positions of power or power elites. Currently, there is considerable interest in the effects of powerlessness on judgment and behavior within organizations. Ashforth and Mael (1998) investigated how relatively powerless individuals in organizations sustain valued but threatened identities. Bies and Tripp (1998) examined how feelings of powerlessness influence anti-social coping behavior within organizations. Kramer (1996) documented the deleterious effects of low power on social information processing by organizational members.

One promising direction of current research is examining the relationship between gender and power. For example, Martin and Myerson (1998) recently examined women's reactions to oppressive organizational cultures, investigating strategies for resistance, confrontation, and conformity. Along related lines, Ashford (1998) explored strategies women used to champion and sell "charged" or political issues. Rudman (1998) investigated the role of gender in the efficacy of impression management and INFLU-ENCE within organizations.

Another fruitful line of recent research has explored the relationship between power and emotions. For example, using imaginative laboratory experiments, Tidens, Ellsworth, and Mesquuita have explored the relationships among power, status, and affect. Other related studies have examined the relationship between power and the emotions more generally (Clark, 1990).

Although organizational theorists have clearly appreciated the importance of the concept of power since the field's inception, there will likely be renewed interest in this topic because recent events, such as Enron and Worldcom, as well as the corruption of once trusted financial institutions such as Arthur Andersen, has drawn renewed attention to the importance of power and its potential for use and misuse, including delineating the ethical dimensions of power use (Lee-Chai and Bargh, 2001).

See also *politics; resistance to change; resource dependence*

Bibliography

Ashford, S. (1998). Championing charged issues: The case of gender equity within organizations. In R. M. Kramer and M. A. Neale (eds.), *Power and Influence in Organizations*. Thousand Oaks, CA: Sage, 349–80.

Ashforth, B. E. and Mael, F. A. (1998). The power of resistance: Sustaining valued identities. In R. M. Kramer and M. A. Neale (eds.), *Power and Influence in Organizations*. Thousand Oaks, CA: Sage, 89–120.

Bargh, J. and Alvarez, J. (2001). The road to hell: Good intentions in the face of non-conscious tendencies to misuse power. In A. Lee-Chai and J. Bargh (eds.), *The Use and Misuse of Power: Multiple Perspectives on the Causes of Corruption*. Philadelphia, PA: Psychology Press.

Bies, R. J. and Tripp, T. M. (1998). Two faces of the powerless: Coping with tyranny in organizations. In R. M. Kramer and M. A. Neale (eds.), *Power and Influence in Organizations*. Thousand Oaks, CA: Sage.

Blau, P. M. (1964). *Exchange and Power in Social Life*. New York: Wiley and Sons.

Burt, R. S. (1992). *Structural Holes: The Social Structure of Competition*. Cambridge, MA: Harvard University Press.

Clark, C. (1990). Emotions and micropolitics in everyday life: Some patterns and paradoxes of "place." In T. D. Kemper (ed.), *Research Agendas in the Sociology of Emotions*. Albany: State University of New York Press, 305–33.

Fiske, S. T. (1993). Controlling other people: The impact of power on stereotyping. *American Psychologist*, **48**, 621–8.

French, J. R. P. and Raven, B. H. (1959). The bases of social power. In D. Cartwright (ed.), *Studies in Social Power*. Ann Arbor: University of Michigan Press, 150–67.

Galinsky, A., Gruenfeld, D. H., and Magee, J. (2003). From power to action. *Journal of Personality and Social Psychology*, **85**, 453–66.

Keltner, D., Gruenfeld, D. H., and Anderson, C. (2003). Power, approach, and inhibition. *Psychological Review*, **110** (2), 265–84.

Krackhardt, D. (1990). Assessing the political landscape: Structure, cognition, and power in organizations. *Administrative Science Quarterly*, **35**, 342–69.

Kramer, R. M. (1996). Divergent realities, convergent disappointments in the hierarchic relation: Trust and the intuitive auditor at work. In R. M. Kramer and T. Tyler (eds.), *Trust in Organizations: Frontiers of Theory and Research*. Thousand Oaks, CA: Sage, 216–45.

Kramer, R. M. (2000). Organizational paranoia: Origins and dynamics. In B. M. Staw and R. I. Sutton (eds.), *Research in Organizational Behavior*. New York: Elsevier, 1–42.

Lee-Chai, A. and Bargh, J. (2001). *The Use and Misuse of Power: Multiple Perspectives on the Causes of Corruption*. Philadelphia, PA: Psychology Press.

March, J. G. (1994). *A Primer on Decision Making: How Decisions Happen*. New York: Free Press.

Martin, J. and Myerson, D. (1998). Women and power: Conformity, resistance, and disorganized coaction. In

R. M. Kramer and M. A. Neale (eds.), *Power and Influence in Organizations*. Thousand Oaks, CA: Sage.

Pfeffer, J. (1992). *Managing with Power: Politics and Influence in Organizations*. Boston, MA: Harvard Business School Press.

Rudman, L. A. (1998). Self-promotion as a risk factor for women: The costs and benefits of counter-stereotypical impression management. *Journal of Personality and Social Psychology*, **74**, 629–45.

Russell, B. (1938). *Power: A New Social Analysis*. London: Allen and Unwin.

Salancik, G. R. and Pfeffer, J. (1977). Who gets power – and how they hold on to it: A strategic-contingency model of power. *Organizational Dynamics*, 2–21.

Wrong, D. H. (1979). *Power: Its Forms, Bases, and Uses*. Oxford: Blackwell.

power, distance

see POWER

power, need for

Nigel Nicholson

The need for power is one of a trio of needs, along with achievement and affiliation, extensively studied by David McClelland and followers. People identified as high in nPow have been found to be motivated by a desire to acquire status and to INFLUENCE others. McClelland saw power motivation of central importance to management, and more predictive of LEADERSHIP effectiveness than either of the other needs, especially in middle and high level positions. High nPow is also seen as associated with stress, and high levels of power motivation can bring the risk of derailment, when power is exercised aggressively or in pursuit of exclusive self-interest.

See also *achievement, need for; affiliation, need for; executive derailment; personality; power*

Bibliography

McClelland, D. C. and Boyatzis, R. E. (1982). The leadership motive pattern and long-term success in management. *Journal of Applied Psychology*, **67**, 737–43.

power bases

see POWER

practical intelligence

Robert Wood

Practical intelligence is the ability of individuals to solve real world problems, including being able to size up situations and to determine effectively how to achieve goals (Sternberg et al., 2000). It is a component of Sternberg's triarchic theory of successful intelligence along with creative and analytical intelligences. Practical intelligence differs from traditional notions of intelligence. It is specific to cultures and other contexts, plus it is a developing expertise and trainable. Practical intelligence is measured by tests of tacit knowledge that include responses to situational judgment problems and short answers to case problems that are rated for quality, instead of the structured problems with one correct answer used in standardized intelligence tests. The two types of measures of intelligence are only weakly correlated. Practical intelligence scores have been related to indicators of success in different contexts, including practical problem solving by housewives and street children, leadership achievements and extent of networks of MBA students, and salary levels and job performance of managers. They also decrease less with aging than standardized intelligence measures. Critics argue that the concept is loosely defined, available evidence does not support the claims made by Sternberg and others, and measures of tacit knowledge have not been properly validated. Practical intelligence has popular appeal as an explanation for high school or college dropouts who become successful entrepreneurs and other popular late-bloomer stories.

See also *individual differences; learning, individual; skill*

Bibliography

Sternberg, R. J., Forsythe, G. B., Hedlund, J., Horvath, J. A., Wagner, R. K., Williams, W. M. et al. (2000). *Practical Intelligence in Everyday Life*. Cambridge: Cambridge University Press.

prejudice

Stella M. Nkomo

Prejudice can be defined as a negative attitude toward a social group and members of that group, usually based upon a faulty and inflexible generalization or stereotype (Fiske, 1998). Prejudice is the most affective component, while discrimination is the most behavioral component, of category-based reactions to people who are perceived to be different from one's own group (Fiske, 1998: 357).

Modern social psychology theories for explaining prejudice include social identity theory, social categorization theory, ATTRIBUTION theory, and the contact hypothesis. These theories assume that prejudice underlies racism and DISCRIMINATION and focus on explaining the origins, functioning, and reduction of intergroup conflict (Pettigrew, 1998).

The phenomenological approach of social identity and social categorization theory postulates that individuals depend on social group (e.g., men, women, blacks, whites, etc.) membership for their identity, and they tend to strive for a positively valued social identity (Tajfel, 1981). The evaluation of one's own group is determined with reference to specific other groups through social comparisons in terms of value laden attributes and characteristics. Categorization and cognitive biases result in stereotypes and the mere categorization of persons into ingroup and outgroup membership is sufficient to affect interpersonal perceptions of behavior (Guinote and Fiske, 2003). The solution to prejudice is a reduction in the salience of group boundaries.

Social attribution theory refers to how members of different social groups explain the behavior, outcomes of behavior, and the social conditions that characterize members of their own group (ingroup) and other (the outgroup) social groups (Tajfel, 1981).

The contact hypothesis suggests that an increase in intergroup interaction will result in a reduction in prejudice under certain conditions. While its VALIDITY has been partially established in laboratory studies, there has been less support in field studies (Fiske, 1998).

Theoretical controversy centers on the dominance of cognitive approaches (individual level of analyses) to the neglect of structural and institutional influences (Fiske, 1998). Some scholars argue for an approach that combines cognitive and structural elements of prejudice. Research also suggests that there are contradictions in the way individuals hold prejudiced attitudes and their subsequent behavior. Some scholars have proposed constructs that capture new forms of racism and the persistence of prejudice. These constructs include symbolic racism, modern racism, and aversive racism, and identify a new form of racial prejudice composed of a blend of anti-black affect and the traditional moral values embodied in the Protestant ethic and egalitarian beliefs (Dovidio and Gaertner, 1986; Pettigrew and Meertens, 1995).

Much of the research on racial prejudice in organization settings can be found under the literature on discrimination. Additionally, there is a substantial body of literature that has demonstrated the relationship between social categorization and prejudiced behavior. The simple creation of group boundaries resulting in ingroups and outgroups can create prejudiced attitudes and behaviors. Individuals who are members of the ingroup tend to see outgroup members as more similar to one another and may think of them in stereotyped terms or evaluate them negatively.

See also *conflict and conflict management; group norms*

Bibliography

Dovidio, J. F. and Gaertner, S. L. (1986). *Prejudice, Discrimination, and Racism.* Orlando, FL: Academic Press.

Fiske, S. T. (1998). Stereotyping, prejudice and discrimination. In D. T. Gilbert, S. T. Fiske, and G. Lindzey (eds.), *The Handbook of Social Psychology*, Vol. 1, 4th edn., 357–411.

Guinote, A. and Fiske, S. T. (2003). Being in the outgroup territory increases stereotypic perceptions of outgroups: Situational sources of category activation. *Group Processes and Intergroup Relations*, **6**, 323–34.

Pettigrew, T. (1998). Intergroup contact theory. *Annual Review of Psychology*, **49**, 65–85.

Pettigrew, T. and Meertens, R. W. (1995). Subtle and blatant prejudice in Western Europe. *European Journal of Social Psychology*, **25**, 57–75.

Tajfel, H. (1981). *Human Groups and Social Categories.* Cambridge, MA: Cambridge University Press.

prisoner's dilemma

see GAME THEORY

procedural justice

see JUSTICE, PROCEDURAL

process consultation

Dale E. Zand

There is a subtle but important difference between process and content which is fundamental to process consultation. *Process* refers to how something is done by an individual, a group, or an organization; for example, how goals are set, how decisions are made, or how conflicts are managed – who is involved, when, how, their actions, power, and interpersonal style. What are their beliefs, attitudes, communication skills, and influence, whom do they represent, and so on? *Content*, on the other hand, is subject matter, the "specifics" of a task; for example, a goal such as a market share target, or decision such as which of three marketing plans should we select to reach our target, or conflict such as who should implement each component of the plan with how much of the budget.

Process consultation posits that how something is done – process – determines the content of decisions, their quality, and the effectiveness of implementation. For example, a WORK GROUP with a poor GOAL SETTING, DECISION-MAKING, or conflict management process (*see* CONFLICT AND CONFLICT MANAGEMENT) will be hobbled by unclear, uncoordinated goals, low quality decisions, or difficulty in confronting and solving its serious work conflicts.

Process consultation consists of identifying, analyzing, and improving faulty processes to increase individual, group, or organization effectiveness, usually with the aid of an uninvolved third party or consultant. There are many processes that may be diagnosed as faulty and become targets of learning and change. For example: COMMUNICATION – who communicates with whom, about what, when, arousing what emotions; who is ignored, who is interrupted. In a work team do members or the leader send double messages with significant differences between the manifest, stated content and the latent, real meaning, thus causing confusion, cynicism, or feelings of being manipulated? How well a group functions depends on how well members and the leader perform task roles such as initiating issues or proposals, seeking and giving facts and opinions, and evaluating conclusions, as well as maintenance roles such as keeping sufficient harmony so members continue to work together, encouraging and supporting the expression and consideration of divergent views which are often the source of creative solutions, and gate keeping to enable the PARTICIPATION and contribution of hesitant, diffident members who are easily pushed aside by expressive, powerful members.

LEADERSHIP styles can vary from directive, coercive command through consultative concurrence to total delegation and self-direction. What is the leader's style, how flexible is it, and how well does it fit the characteristics of the followers and the situation? Decision making in a group or organization can vary from ignoring a proposal and allowing it to die by lack of response, through individual, unilateral edict, then on to minority, subgroup rule, majority rule, consensus, and unanimity. How well do the decision modes in use lead to high quality decisions and effective, timely implementation?

Other facets of process consultation include problem solving, goal setting, TRUST development, conflict management, norms, interaction patterns, group cohesion, group growth, ROLE conflict, POWER, INFLUENCE, reward systems, intergroup competition, SOCIALIZATION, and culture.

A primary goal of process consultation is to increase the client's process awareness and skills so that with co-workers he or she can analyze and improve processes and become less dependent on the consultant. The transfer of process analysis skills to a client is best accomplished by using the joint diagnosis consulting model. The client learns to see and solve process problems by participating in diagnosing process difficulties and generating a solution. In the joint diagnosis model, the client and consultant jointly gather data, diagnose the situation, define change goals, and design and implement change. This contrasts with the expert model of consulting, such as the conventional purchased services or doctor–patient relationship, in which the hired expert unilaterally gathers data, diagnoses the situation, and generates a solution and the client is expected to accept and use the hired expert's conclusions.

The knowledge and skills an effective process consultant needs primarily come from the areas of GROUP DYNAMICS, sensitivity training, leadership, ACTION RESEARCH, and ORGANIZATION DEVELOPMENT. Methods to describe and analyze a current process include observation of behavior in meetings, interviews, and other forms of data gathering, FEEDBACK, joint diagnosis, FORCE FIELD ANALYSIS, and SOCIOTECHNICAL THEORY. Methods to facilitate change include modeling, in which the consultant or group leader exhibits the desired new behavior, simulations, exercises, counseling, coaching, TEAM BUILDING, confrontation meetings, training, and open systems analysis.

Process consulting depends on a voluntary relationship between client and consultant. Managers who feel forced into process analysis become defensive and strongly resist learning because they are not prepared to examine their leadership or relationships with co-workers, subordinates, or superiors. The consulting relationship itself is a critical, changing process which client and consultant must continually review as goals and methods change and as the client's process skills increase. Client and consultant must develop a mutually trusting relationship that will facilitate the client's process learning and increased self-sufficiency.

Process analysis originated in group dynamics research and sensitivity training in the 1940s and for several decades included a fairly deep examination of one's personal awareness and interpersonal skills. This personal focus was gradually discontinued as process consultation was applied in organizational settings where it was considered inappropriately probing and not vital to organizational improvement. However, the personal focus is still useful for many individuals seeking to improve their self-awareness and emotional insight to develop their leadership skills and is available in personal counseling, coaching, and sensitivity training programs that

bring strangers together outside of their work organization.

Process analysis is now an integral part of the organization change literature and is widely accepted by managers, although it was considered pioneering and controversial when it emerged in the mid-1900s. The extensive need for process consultation and its ready acceptance poses a serious problem. Many managers and others who have read some of the literature believe that they are qualified to act as consultants. Process consultation, however, involves much more than knowledge. It requires skill in observing and diagnosing complex behavior and action skills to intervene appropriately in dynamic interpersonal, group, and organizational situations. Would-be process consultants should be aware that like would-be aircraft pilots there is a big difference between reading about the aerodynamics of flight and the skills needed to pilot a plane. Without the necessary skills one can inflict considerable harm.

Process analysis is so effective and pervasive that one can expect to find a need for some of its elements in almost every organizational change effort.

See also *consultancy; influence; resistance to change*

Bibliography

Dyer, W. G. (1995). *Team Building: Current Issues and New Alternatives*, 3rd edn. Reading, MA: Addison-Wesley.

French, W. L. and Bell, C. H. (1998). *Organization Development: Behavioral Science Interventions For Organization Improvement*, 6th edn. Upper Saddle River, NJ: Prentice-Hall.

Schein, E. H. (1987). *Organization Culture and Leadership*, 2nd edn. San Francisco: Jossey-Bass.

Schein, E. H. (1987). *Process Consultation: Lessons for Managers and Consultants*. Reading, MA: Addison-Wesley.

Schein, E. H. (1988). *Process Consultation: Its Role in Organization Development*, 2nd edn. Reading, MA: Addison-Wesley.

Schein, E. H. (1998). *Process Consultation Revisited: Building the Helping Relationship*. Upper Saddle River, NJ: Prentice-Hall.

Walton, R. E. (1987). *Managing Conflict: Interpersonal Dialogue and Third-Party Roles*, 2nd edn. Reading, MA: Addison-Wesley.

process technology

see TECHNOLOGY

productivity

see ORGANIZATIONAL EFFECTIVENESS

professional service firms

Timothy Morris and N. Anand

The term professional service firm (PSF) refers to an organization that trades on the knowledge of its human capital (comprising owners and employers) to develop and deliver solutions to client problems (*see* SOCIAL CAPITAL). The term applies to organizations involved in a variety of sectors such as accounting, law, consulting, and architecture. In some of these sectors, such as accounting, employees have to be accredited as professionals; in other sectors, such as management consulting, they do not have to be. The outputs of PSFs are intangible, relatively idiosyncratic, and customized to particular client problems. Such firms typically apply different types of expertise residing in the firm with the close involvement of professional staff in delivering the product, generally in conjunction with the client and over an extended time period.

A PSF operates by balancing two markets: client market, where it seeks to offer services that will be profitable, and the labor market, where it seeks professional staff of appropriate quality. PSFs manage the client market by generating and maintaining demand for services. Maister (1993) identifies three generic strategies for professional service: (1) procedure based, which relies on repeatedly completing the same or similar routines for a variety of clients (e.g., filing corporate income tax); (2) experienced based, which consists of providing services in which professionals have particular, but not very distinctive, experience (e.g., implementing reengineering programs); and (3) expertise based, where professionals provide relatively unique service that is not offered by too many competitors (e.g., designing a "poison pill" to prevent hostile takeover). PSFs generally (but not always) manage the labor market through a partnership form of governance that comprises information about the performance of the firm, consultation over major decisions, and rights to a share of the profits (Greenwood, Hinings, and Brown, 1990). The CAREER ladder that takes a professional up to partner level works on the basis of both intrinsic motivation (such as opportunity to pursue interesting work) and competition for a limited number of partnership seats (*see* TOURNAMENT THEORY). A PSF signals its reputation in the labor market primarily through its promotion decisions (Morris, 2000).

Interest in professional service firms developed in the mid-1950s as part of sociological concern with the role of professions in social systems. Central to this program was the question of how bureaucratic systems of management control, based on hierarchical authority and management discretion over methods of working, could be reconciled with professional models of organization where the individual professional controlled decisions about their own work, including task execution and desired goals (Abbott, 1988). This problem was seen to be becoming more pressing as firms become larger and introduced bureaucratic systems to cope. Empirical work showed that they developed hybrid models of management referred to as a professional BUREAUCRACY (Mintzberg, 1983), where bureaucratic control could coexist with professional control but, particularly, that the latter mode dominated the area of task execution.

Subsequent work by organization scholars has returned to this theme of management control in recent years, in the context of the development of complex, multi-unit and multi-disciplinary professional service firms, especially in the areas of accounting and management consulting. Drawing on STRUCTURATION theory, work by Greenwood et al. (1990) proposed the concept of a professional service firm archetype, which they called the P^2 (professional, partnership), wherein an interpretive scheme or set of professional values informed and was reflected in a structural form and set of management systems. The distinctiveness of the archetype derived from the fact that the owners/partners were also the key producers and managers of the client relationships in the firm. The job of management was rendered difficult by the simultaneous need to serve these partners and the need to coordinate and control the firm's activities. A style of management based heavily on CONSENSUS building and persuasion and with minimal hierarchy was likely to result. Indeed, in practice, management is often accorded low status in these firms and seen as a necessary evil. From the notion of a professional firm archetype much recent work has examined to what extent and in what ways a more modern archetype, sometimes called the Managed Professional Business, has displaced the earlier one. This research has been part of a general theme of examining problems and processes of change among professional service firms through the lens of institution theory and other more micro-processual concepts (Greenwood, Suddaby, and Hinings, 2002).

Another major area of research, often undertaken by economists and based on models of the firm driven by transaction cost and AGENCY THEORY perspectives, has been concerned with incentives and the appropriation of value (Gilson and Mnookin, 1985). This type of research examines what holds firms of professionals together under conditions where it is difficult and costly to monitor the performance of the work of fellow professionals and there is a substantial risk of free-riding or capturing valuable clients of the firm and leaving. Two systems have been seen to be important here. One is the promotion to partner system, which is a deferred reward that provides a powerful incentive for young professionals to work hard under conditions of limited supervision (Morris, 2000). The other is the sharing of profits between partners. Here, the puzzle is that many firms operate with lockstep or sensitivity systems of reward rather than allocate profits on the basis of individual performance. While lockstep offers no individual incentives its benefits may be in building collective COMMITMENT and cooperation; it also minimizes on management costs in defining and allocating rewards equitably and, where it is backed by control over shirking through informal peer pressure, may even be seen to have collective incentive properties (Morris and Pin-

nington, 1998). Although data are hard to come by, there is no clear evidence to suggest highly geared individual incentive systems result in higher firm performance.

Further work on professional service firms is likely to reflect the major changes that these organizations are undergoing. These include decisions about ownership form, internationalization, the regulation of professions, and labor market changes (Brock, Powell, and Hinings, 1999). Ownership questions concern the shift away from partnership and the implications this has for governance as well as for the relationship to the client market. Does incorporation push a professional service firm to pursue strategies that ensure short-term earnings increases, for example? Some work on the internationalization strategies of PSFs has been done, but more is needed to understand the consequences for performance (and other outcomes) of different modes and processes of internationalizing. The external regulation of professional service firms has already had important structural consequences for the large accounting/business advisory firms. Regulation is worthy of study both for its effects on the boundaries of professional service firms and for the implications it has for our understanding of the term professional, for example, when a whole class of occupational workers obtains access to the client market owing to a relaxation of certification norms (Scherer and Lee, 2002).

Research on labor market change and their effects on PSFs remains an important area for further work. This includes changing attitudes among young professionals to careers in PSFs, particularly under conditions of work intensification, the implications for career systems of a high proportion of female professionals, and the greater openness of many labor markets allowing more frequent switching across firms. Finally, work that investigates how innovation in knowledge-based products as well as in organization form occurs, both at the level of the professional service firm and the professional sector, is important, particularly as the expertise on which these firms trade quickly commodifies and has to be replenished.

See also *governance; organizational design*

Bibliography

Abbott, A. (1988). *The System of Professions: An Essay on the Division of Expert Labor*. Chicago: University of Chicago Press.

Brock, D., Powell, M., and Hinings, C. R. (1999). *Restructuring the Professional Organization: Accounting, Health Care And Law*. London: Routledge.

Gilson, R. and Mnookin, R. (1985). Sharing among the human capitalists: An economic enquiry into the corporate law firm and how partners split profits. *Stanford Law Review*, 37, 313–92.

Greenwood, R., Hinings, C. R., and Brown, J. (1990). "P2 form" strategic management: Corporate practices in professional partnerships. *Academy of Management Journal*, 33, 725–55.

Greenwood, R., Suddaby, R., and Hinings, C. R. (2002). Theorizing change: The role of professional associations in transforming institutionalized fields. *Academy of Management Journal*, 45, 58–80.

Maister, D. (1993). *Managing the Professional Service Firm*. New York: Free Press.

Mintzberg, H. (1983). *Structure in Fives: Designing Effective Organizations*. Englewood Cliffs, NJ: Prentice-Hall.

Morris, T. (2000). Promotion policies and knowledge bases in the professional service firm. In M. Peiperl, M. Arthur, R. Goffee, and T. Morris (eds.), *Careers Frontiers: New Conceptions of Working Lives*. Oxford: Oxford University Press, 138–52.

Morris, T. and Pinnington, A. (1998). Patterns of profit-sharing in professional firms. *British Journal of Management*, 9, 23–31.

Scherer, P. D., and Lee, K. (2002). Institutional change in large law firms: A resource dependency and institutional theory perspective. *Academy of Management Journal*, 45, 102–19.

profit sharing

see INCENTIVES

promotion

see CAREER DEVELOPMENT

promotion/prevention focus

E. Tory Higgins

Regulatory focus theory (Higgins, 1997, 2002) assumes that SELF-REGULATION operates differently when serving fundamentally different needs, such as the distinct survival needs of nurturance (e.g., nourishment) versus security (e.g., protection). Nurturant social regulation engenders a *promotion focus*, in which self-regulation is concerned with the presence and absence of positive outcomes (gains/non-gains), with advancement, aspirations, and accomplishments. Security social regulation engenders a *prevention focus*, in which self-regulation is concerned with the absence and presence of negative outcomes (non-losses/losses), with protection, safety, and responsibilities. Both chronic situations, such as those that are institutionalized in organizations, and momentary situations, such as those found in a specific organizational meeting or while working on a particular task, are capable of inducing either promotion focus concerns or prevention focus concerns.

When in a promotion focus, individuals prefer to use *eager* approach means because they ensure the presence of positive outcomes (insure hits; look for means of advancement) and insure against the absence of positive outcomes (insure against ERRORS of omission; do not close off possibilities). When in a prevention focus, individuals prefer to use *vigilant* avoidance means because they insure the absence of negative outcomes (insure correct rejections; be careful) and insure against the presence of negative outcomes (insure against errors of commission; avoid mistakes). Individuals in a promotion versus a prevention focus, respectively, respond to success/failure with cheerful/dejected emotions versus quiescent/agitated emotions, have a "risky" versus "conservative" bias in DECISION-MAKING, generate many versus few alternatives when hypothesis testing, and prefer speed (quantity) versus accuracy (quality).

See also *feedback; managerial and organizational cognition; perception*

Bibliography

Higgins, E. T. (1997). Beyond pleasure and pain. *American Psychologist*, 52, 1280–1300.

Higgins, E. T. (2002). How self-regulation creates distinct values: The case of promotion and prevention decision-making. *Journal of Consumer Psychology*, 12, 177–91.

prospect theory

Don Moore

Prospect theory (Kahneman and Tversky, 1979; Tversky and Kahneman, 1992) has been one of the single most influential behavioral theories of choice, not only in organizational behavior but also in psychology and in economics. It lays out a clear, positive, descriptive theory of how people value different prospects or outcomes. The classic 1979 paper that first articulated prospect theory was published in an economic journal and intended as a critique of expected utility theory. Prospect theory addresses some of the most glaring shortcomings of normative theories such as expected utility theory, which assume that people are rational utility maximizers. Instead, prospect theory offers a more descriptively accurate model of choice.

The best-known feature of prospect theory is the value function it proposes, which specifies the relationship between objective outcome and subjective utility. The S-shaped value function describes decreasing marginal utility to gains and to losses: finding $10 on the street is good, but finding $20 is not twice as pleasurable; likewise, losing $10 is painful, but losing $20 is not twice as painful. The decreasing marginal utility to gains and losses implies that people will be more risk seeking in their attempts to avoid potential losses than they will in their pursuit of potential gains. In order to understand why this is so, consider the choice between $10 for sure and a 50 percent chance at $20. Both options have the same expected value. Nevertheless, because a gain of $20 is not valued twice as much as a gain of $10, doubling the amount does not sufficiently offset halving the probability of winning, and so the sure $10 is preferable: risk aversion. Conversely, because a loss of $20 is not twice as bad as a loss of $10, halving the probability more than offsets the smaller amount of the sure loss, and people prefer the chance: risk seeking.

The value function accords special significance to the reference point from which gains or losses are considered. This reference point is most often the status quo. However, in the "framing" phase of the choice process, people may be vulnerable to the influence of arbitrary or manipulative influences in their selection of a

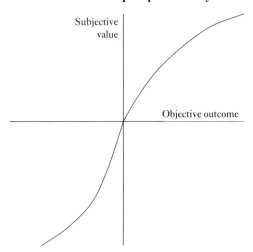

Figure 1 Prospect theory value function

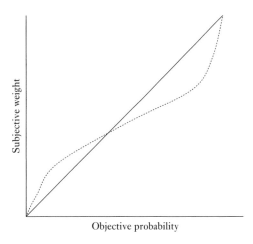

Figure 2 Prospect theory probability weighting function

reference point (Tversky and Kahneman, 1986). For example, the tendency to be risk seeking in the domain of losses and risk averse in the domain of gains has been illustrated perhaps most famously in the "Asian disease problem" that uses a simple framing manipulation (Tversky and Kahneman, 1981). Those given the gain frame were asked: Imagine that the US is preparing for the outbreak of an unusual Asian disease, which is expected to kill 600 people. Two alternative programs to combat the disease have been proposed. Assume that the exact scientific estimate of the consequences of the program are as follows:

If Program A is adopted, 200 people will be saved.

If Program B is adopted, there is a 1/3 probability that 600 people will be saved, and 2/3 probability that no people will be saved.

Given these options, 72 percent of people chose Program A and 28 percent chose Program B. Those given the loss frame were given these two options:

If Program C is adopted 400 people will die.

If Program D is adopted there is a 1/3 probability that nobody will die, and 2/3 probability that 600 people will die.

Given these options, 22 percent of people chose Program C and 78 percent chose Program D.

Prospect theory does not articulate a formal theory of how people select a reference point. Although this ambiguity can make it difficult to predict exactly how a specific individual will value a specific prospect, the ease with which the reference point may be manipulated gives rise to a number of strategic implications. For example, the theory predicts that gains will be enjoyed more to the extent that they are segregated into a set of distinct small gains. On the other hand, losses will be felt less acutely when they are lumped together into one large loss. The Prospect theory notion of asymmetries in gains and losses has been applied in a number of research domains in organizational behavior. For example, research in the area of managerial negotiations has shown that individuals in a gain frame (who see anything better than their outside alternative as a gain) are more concessionary than negotiators in a loss frame, who tend to engage in more risk-seeking NEGOTIATION strategies (Neale and Bazerman, 1985).

A second important attribute of the value function is its greater steepness in the loss domain than in the gain domain. This feature describes the tendency to be loss averse: a loss is more painful than a gain of equivalent magnitude is pleasurable. Loss aversion has a number of important implications. It implies that people will be vulnerable to endowment effects in which they become particularly attached to whatever it is that they happen to possess (Kahneman, Knetsch, and Thaler, 1990), since forgoing the potential gain of trade is less painful than incurring the loss. Loss aversion has also been used to explain some important anomalies in the behavior of stock market investors (Benartzi and Thaler, 1995; Odean, 1998).

The usefulness of prospect theory value function has made it an extremely influential theory in a number of fields, including organizational behavior. Subsequent research has borne out its major predictions (Kahneman and Tversky, 2000). However, it has been argued that the theory contradicts the existence of two important industries. Purchasing insurance to mitigate losses is risk averse behavior in the domain where prospect theory predicts risk seeking. Gamblers, on the other hand, make the risk seeking choice in the domain of gains by paying for a possible win. This contradiction is resolved by prospect theory's subjective probability weighting function. The theory holds that people tend to under-weight high probabilities and over-weight low probabilities. If people over-weight low probabilities such as being robbed or winning the lottery, it can explain their willingness to purchase both insurance and lottery tickets.

See also *behavioral decision research; decision-making; risk taking*

Bibliography

Benartzi, S. and Thaler, R. H. (1995). Myopic loss aversion and the equity premium puzzle. *Quarterly Journal of Economics*, **110** (1), 73–93.

Kahneman, D. and Tversky, A. (1979). Prospect theory: An analysis of decision under risk. *Econometrica*, **47** (2), 263–91.

Kahneman, D. and Tversky, A. (2000). *Choices, Values, and Frames*. New York: Russell Sage Foundation.

Kahneman, D., Knetsch, J. L., and Thaler, R. H. (1990). Experimental tests of the endowment effect and the Coase Theorem. *Journal of Political Economy*, **98** (6), 1325–48.

Neale, M. A. and Bazerman, M. H. (1985). The effects of framing and negotiator overconfidence on bargaining behaviors and outcomes. *Academy of Management Journal*, **28** (1), 34–49.

Odean, T. (1998). Are investors reluctant to realize their losses? *Journal of Finance*, 53 (5), 1775–98.

Tversky, A. and Kahneman, D. (1981). The framing of decisions and the psychology of choice. *Science*, **211** (4481), 453–8.

Tversky, A. and Kahneman, D. (1986). Rational choice and the framing of decisions. *Journal of Business*, **59** (4), S251–78.

Tversky, A. and Kahneman, D. (1992). Advances in prospect theory: Cumulative representation of uncertainty. *Journal of Risk and Uncertainty*, **5** (4), 297–323.

psychological contract

Denise M. Rousseau

Psychological contract refers to the system of beliefs individuals hold regarding their exchange relationship with another; in particular, subjective understandings regarding reciprocal promises or obligations (Rousseau, 1995). Psychological contracts arise in voluntary EX-CHANGE RELATIONSHIPS, typically made between worker and employer, customer and supplier, or client and service provider, among others. (The concept of psychological contract does not apply to non-voluntary activities such as the duties derived from societal roles like parent/child or citizen/state.) These beliefs are understood to be mutual, where an individual's psychological contract reflects his or her understanding of each party's obligations. These obligations derive from promises conveyed via verbal statements and actions each party has made, along with social cues and human resource practices associated with the exchange relationship's setting, typically an organization.

An individual's psychological contract with another is based upon the presumption of mutual agreement, but perceived agreement does not mean that there is necessarily mutuality in fact. For example, managers and workers can have different psychological contracts regarding their relationship (Coyle-Shapiro and Kessler, 2002). However, degree of mutual agreement between parties has considerable impact on the quality of their exchange relationship and its outcomes. Mutual or shared psychological contracts result in higher performance, continuity/retention, satisfaction, and psychological contract fulfillment (Dabos and Rousseau, 2003). Mutuality is greater where parties hold common information, interact regularly, can negotiate with each other when conditions change, and where practices in the larger environment reinforce agreement, such as coherent human resource practices and strong corporate culture (Rousseau, 2001) (*see* ORGANIZATIONAL CULTURE).

The significance of psychological contracts for organizations resides in the greater impact on individual behavior and attitudes that psychological contracts have in contrast to other non-promissory beliefs and expectations. Individuals are more likely to rely upon psychological contracts than on other beliefs in making decisions regarding the exchange relationship (e.g., to join an organization, seek promotion, or decide how much effort to invest on a job). Individuals experience psychological contract fulfilment as a positive, bringing them promised benefits, while lack of fulfilment is associated with loss of those benefits. Individuals react aversely to the failure of others to honor terms of the psychological contract. Such reactions include negative attitudes (e.g., mistrust) and emotions (e.g., anger), along with reduced performance and commitment to the relationship (Rousseau, 1995). Lack of psychological contract fulfilment is commonly associated with organizational change and downsizing (Rousseau, 1995).

Several trends are relevant to the future of psychological contracts. Individually negotiated idiosyncratic terms of employment have expanded relative to standardized terms, due to higher worker mobility, particularly among knowledge workers, and reduced unionism. Employers are challenged to fulfill idiosyncratic psychological contract terms while maintaining a sense of fairness within the firm. Greater use of distributed work, where workers and employers do not interact face to face, may require new ways of creating mutual agreement to promote functional psychological contracts. Global firms with multinational workforces face challenges in creating mutual psychological contracts where local society shapes the psychological contracts of workers (Rousseau and Schalk, 2000).

See also *commitment; contracts; employee involvement; job satisfaction*

Bibliography

Coyle-Shapiro, J. A.-M. and Kessler, I. (2002). Exploring reciprocity through the lens of the psychological contract: Employee and employer perspectives. *European Journal of Work and Organizational Psychology*, **11**, 69–86.

Dabos, G. E. and Rousseau, D. M. (2003). Mutuality and reciprocity in the psychological contracts of employees and employers. *Journal of Applied Psychology.*

Rousseau, D. M. (1995). *Psychological Contracts In Organizations: Understanding Written and Unwritten Agreements.* Thousand Oaks, CA: Sage.

Rousseau, D. M. (2001). Promise, schema, and mutuality: The building blocks of the psychological contract. *Journal of Occupational and Organizational Behavior.*

Rousseau, D.M. and Schalk, R. (2000). *Psychological Contracts in Employment: Cross-National Perspectives.* Thousand Oaks, CA: Sage.

punishment

Richard D. Arvey

The concept of punishment in organizations has to do with the delivery of some aversive event to an employee (or employees) contingent on behavior, or the withdrawal of some valued work outcome as a result of behavior which has violated organizational rules, policies, and practices, as well as sometimes unstated norms. Two elements are central here. First, there are the kinds and types of sanctions and aversive events delivered as punishment. Second, there is the process by which aversive sanctions are delivered. While punishment, and the related concept of discipline, is generally thought of as a formal procedure involving such sanctions as formal warnings, dismissal, and oral warnings by management, it can also be informal, such as supervisors withholding information, delaying actions on requests, and shouting at employees.

Punishment and discipline have received surprisingly little research attention compared to positive reward systems. While there is a good deal of speculation, little solid research evidence exists establishing the empirical correlates of punishment, even when "everybody knows" punishment exists in organizations and has some kind of impact. On the other hand, there is a large body of information based on labor law and arbitration hearings establishing principles of fair treatment in the delivery of penalties associated with discipline in organizations.

Punishment and discipline in organizations may serve several different functions. It may serve as a direct behavior control system by which employees learn through their experiences not to violate specific policies, practices, and procedures, as set out by the organization. Disciplinary systems, formal and informal, also serve to provide indirect cues and signals to employees concerning what is acceptable and what is unacceptable, through social learning processes from observing other employees. The process of punishment involves several related steps. First, there must be a perception by a disciplinary agent of a rule infraction. Research has developed taxonomies of the kinds of behaviors likely to trigger punishment (Arvey and Jones, 1985). The most common are ABSENTEEISM, tardiness, dishonesty, incompetence, violation of safety rules, intoxication, fighting, horseplay, trouble making, insubordination, and disputes with supervisors. Recently, researchers are identifying counter-productive or deviant behaviors as well as "misbehavior" in workplace settings that also might trigger punitive or disciplinary action (Warren, 2003; Vardi and Wiener, 1996). Most disciplinary policy manuals in organizations set out the major classes of behaviors that constitute violations. Second, there must be a decision to take some punitive action. Studies have identified a number of variables that influence the decision to take action. Punitive action is more likely to be taken when infractions involve high cost and/or risk to the organization, when the employee has a history of poor job performance and/or disciplinary history, when there is a poor relationship with the supervisor, and when the infraction is thought to be volitional and under the control of the employee. Third, there is the choice of what kind of punishment is to be administered. Research and theory suggest that punishment which is applied soon after an infraction, is administered consistently, is accompanied by a clear explanation for the punishment, and is not unduly harsh, will be more effective than punishment administered haphazardly, with little explanation, or a long delay after the infraction (Arvey, Davis, and Nelson, 1984).

There is conflicting research evidence concerning the impact and effect of punishment in organizational settings. The literature generally supports the proposition that when punishment is administered contingently, a relationship develops or exists between punishment and satisfaction and/or performance. However, when punishment is viewed as random or non-contingent, there is no relationship. Perhaps when punishment is non-contingent employees turn to other mechanisms to escape, avoid, or gain retribution and it is these conditions that lead to frustration, apathy, sabotage, or employee theft. However, research has tended not directly to examine the impact of punishment on the specific behaviors associated with rule violations, but instead on more broad band job performance criterion measures (e.g., overall job performance). Punishment and disciplinary systems in organizations will also affect perceptions of employees regarding the fairness and justice of such systems. Recent research has discussed the role of procedural justice (how the punishment is carried out) and outcome justice (the relative fairness of the sanctions) on these perceptions (see JUSTICE, PROCEDURAL). In addition, labor arbitration cases and principles also emphasize procedural and outcome issues in relation to the fairness of specific disciplinary acts and systems. Generally speaking, disciplinary systems are perceived as just when there appears to have been good cause, when prior notice has been given, when the sanctions are not unduly harsh, when proper investigative procedures are employed, and when consistent and equal treatment is applied (Koven and Smith, 1992).

See also *deviance; feedback; learning, individual*

Bibliography

Arvey, R. D. and Jones, A. P. (1985). The use of discipline in organizational settings: A framework for future research. In L. L. Cummings and B. M. Staw (eds.), *Research in Organizational Behavior*, Vol. 7. Greenwich, CT: JAI Press, 367–408.

Arvey, R. D., Davis, G. A., and Nelson, S. M. (1984). Use of discipline in an organization: A field study. *Journal of Applied Psychology*, **69**, 448–60.

Koven, A. M. and Smith, S. L. (1992). *Just Cause: The Seven Tests*, 2nd edn. Revd. by D. F. Farwell. Washington, DC: Bureau of National Affairs.

Podsakoff, P. M. (1982). Determinants of a supervisor's use of rewards and punishments: A literature review and suggestions for further research. *Organizational Behavior and Human Performance*, **29**, 58–83.

Vardi, Y. and Wiener, Y. (1996). Misbehavior in organizations: A motivational framework. *Organizational Science*, **7**, 151–65.

Warren, D. E. (2003). Constructive and destructive deviance in organizations. *Academy of Management Review*, **28**, 622–32.

quality

see CONTINUOUS IMPROVEMENT; QUALITY CIRCLES; TOTAL QUALITY MANAGEMENT

quality circles

Gerald E. Ledford, Jr.

A quality circle (QC) is a small group of employees from a common work area who meet regularly to solve problems they encounter in their work. Specific characteristics include the following (Ledford, Lawler, and Mohrman, 1988; Van Fleet and Griffin, 1989).

Membership typically is voluntary, although often only nominally so in Japan. Usually, only some employees in a work area are QC members. The group is responsible for *making suggestions* to management, and does not have the power to decide about implementation. The *goals* of QCs in Japan focus almost exclusively on quality, but also focus on productivity and costs in the US. *Meetings* usually are held on company time in the US, on personal time in Japan. A typical circle meets for an hour per week. QC members receive one to five days of *training* in GROUP DECISION-MAKING techniques. A staff of *facilitators* conducts training, assists with group process, provides communication links to the organization, and administers the program. The organization usually offers no financial *rewards* for group suggestions, except normal suggestion awards, although there may be extensive non-financial recognition. The circle typically receives *information* specifically relevant to its problem.

QCs belong to a class of employee PARTICIPATION groups that provide employees with *suggestion involvement*. Such groups are special collateral organization structures that are dependent on the formal organization for the implementation of changes. Other types of suggestion involvement groups may differ from QCs along one or more of the design dimensions listed above. Suggestion involvement is more limited than *job involvement*, which builds employee decision-making power into the job through JOB DESIGN. It is also more limited than a *high involvement* design, which systematically reinforces employee involvement through various human resource practices (Lawler, 1988).

By the early 1980s, several million Japanese were QC members. Western firms began borrowing QC designs from successful Japanese competitors in the late 1970s. In 1999 more than half of Fortune 1000 firms reported using QCs, and more than 20 percent of employees were members in about one-fourth of the firms (Lawler, Mohrman, and Benson, 2001). However, use of QCs had gradually declined in the prior 12 years, and QCs have become less common than other types of employee participation groups. Other designs were being used by 85 percent of the sample in 1999.

Several key questions remain about QCs (Ledford, Lawler, and Mohrman, 1988; Van Fleet and Griffin, 1989). First, how effective are they? The practitioner literature on QCs is much larger and more positive than the research literature. Research indicates that quality circles sometimes improve organizational performance, but tend not to have strong effects on employee attitudes such as JOB SATISFACTION. Second, how sustainable are QCs? QC programs typically survive only a few years in the US. QC designs appear to generate self-destructive forces even when they succeed. Third, what organizational conditions and types of employees are conducive to QC effectiveness? Not enough research has been conducted to answer these questions definitively, although existing research provides a number of models and suggestions.

See also *employee involvement; errors; work groups*

Bibliography

Lawler, E. E., III. (1988). Choosing an involvement strategy. *Academy of Management Executive*, **2** (3), 197–204.

Lawler, E. E., III, Mohrman, S. A., and Benson, G. (2001). *Organizing for High Performance: Employee Involvement, TQM, Reengineering, and Knowledge Management in the Fortune 1000*. San Francisco: Jossey-Bass.

Ledford, G. E., Jr., Lawler, E. E., III., and Mohrman, S. A. (1988). The quality circle and its variations. In J. P. Campbell and R. J. Campbell (eds.), *Productivity in Organizations: New Perspectives from Industrial and Organizational Psychology*. San Francisco: Jossey-Bass, 255–94.

Van Fleet, D. D. and Griffin, R. W. (1989). Quality circles: A review and suggested future directions. In C. L. Cooper and I. Robertson (eds.), *International Review of Industrial and Organizational Psychology 1989*. New York: John Wiley and Sons, 213–33.

quasi-experimental design

Thomas D. Cook

Quasi-experiments usually test the causal consequences of long-lasting treatments outside of the laboratory. But unlike "true" experiments where treatment assignment is at random, assignment in quasi-experiments is by self-selection or administrator judgment. All experiments seek to identify whether a treatment made a difference in a particular outcome rather than to explain why the difference occurred. Experiments can be made more explanatory by selecting theory relevant treatment and outcome variables or by adding measures of potential moderator or mediator variables. Yet the structure of all experiments, including quasi-experiments, implies a more important goal for causal description than causal explanation.

Campbell and Stanley (1966) explicated some of the validity threats that random assignment rules out but that have to be explicitly probed in quasi-experiments to insure they were not artifically responsible for results. Cook and Campbell (1979) added more validity threats, arguing they should be ruled out by experimental design rather than through measuring them and then statistically manipulating the data to purge their influence from the treatment–outcome relationship. As Cook, Campbell, and Peracchio (1990) illustrate with many examples from organizational behavior, quasi-experimental designs are stronger for descriptive causal inference:

1 the more pretreatment (and posttreatment) measures they have on the dependent variables under examination so as to estimate the most immediate time trends;

2 the better matched are comparison groups so as to minimize the initial difference from treatment groups;

3 the more instances there are of a treatment that has been implemented at different times on different sets of respondents.

Some scholars within econometrics (Heckman and Hotz, 1989) still maintain it is possible to adjust statistically for all the initial differences between non-equivalent treatment groups. But empirical research on the selection adjustment techniques they prefer has shown them to be fallible. Statisticians prefer direct measurement of the selection process whereby different kinds of persons come to be in different treatment groups, since there is no doubt that a *fully known* selection model can lead to unbiased treatment effects. Indeed, the randomized experiment is effective, not because it creates initially comparable groups, but because the differences between these groups are fully known. The regression discontinuity design – where a quantitative score on a scale (say, of individual productivity) is used to determine which members of an organization deserve special treatment because of their exceptionally high level of merit (or need) – is another instance where selection into treatment is therefore completely known. Hence, unbiased treatment effect estimation is also potentially possible in this case (*see* BIAS). However, in all other contexts it is not easy to assume that the selection model is completely known and that unbiased treatment estimates are possible.

Over the last 25 years (Cook, 1991) we have come to see that causal inferences are superior under two conditions. First, when obtained data patterns corroborate causal predictions that are point specific (i.e., the outcome is predicted to change either at a predicted time point – as with the interrupted time series design – or at a predicted point along the continuous variable used for determining treatment assignment – as with regression discontinuity. Second, causal inferences are generally superior when the causal hypothesis under test has multiple empirical implications. This happens when a quasi-experimental design has multiple comparison groups, multiple pretreatment time points, multiple introductions of the treatment at different times, or some dependent variables which theory says should change because of the treatment and other dependent variables which theory says should not change. It will be rare for an alternative interpretation to predict the specific data patterns associated either with interventions at a specific time or point or with interventions that have multiple causal implications. But it will not be impossible.

See also *generalization; research design; research methods; statistical methods*

Bibliography

Campbell, D. T. and Stanley, J. C. (1966). *Experimental and Quasi-Experimental Design for Research*. Chicago: Rand McNally.

Cook, T. D. (1991). Clarifying the warrant for generalized causal inferences in quasi-experimentation In M. W. McLaughlin and D. Phillips (eds.), *Evaluation and Education at Quarter Century*. 1991 Yearbook. Chicago: National Society for the Study of Education.

Cook, T. D. and Campbell, D. T. (1979). *Quasi-Experimentation: Design and Analysis Issues for Field Settings*. Boston, MA: Houghton-Mifflin.

Cook, T. D., Campbell, D. T., and Peracchio, L. (1990). Quasi-experimentation. In M. D. Dunnette and L. M. Hough (eds.), *Handbook of Industrial and Organizational Psychology*, 2nd edn. Palo Alto, CA: Consulting Psychologists Press.

Heckman, J. J. and Hotz, J. (1989). Choosing among alternative non-experimental methods for estimating the impact of social programs: The case of manpower training. *Journal of the American Statistical Association*, 84, 862–74.

R

rationality

Paul L. Koopman

Rationality denotes the selection of preferred behavioral alternatives in terms of systems of values through which the consequences of behavior can be evaluated. Especially in the disciplines of economics and statistics, rational behavior is defined as making a decision that, after a review of all the alternatives, promises to maximize satisfaction or utility. Herbert Simon argued that it is not feasible to attempt a search for each and every alternative. Because of their limited cognitive capacities, decision-makers use only part of the relevant information. Time and money considerations also play a role in determining if there will be a search for more information and how long it will last. The search process generally stops when a "satisficing solution" has been found: alternatives are not studied exhaustively. This is implied by Simon's concept of bounded rationality.

In other words, rational behavior in the decision-making process simply involves the evaluation and selection of some relevant alternatives which offer a perceived advantage to the decision-maker. All that is necessary to make a choice a rational one is that an objective exists and that the decision-maker perceives and selects some alternative which promises to meet the objective (Harrison, 1987: 107).

See also *behavioral decision research; decision-making; garbage can model; postmodernism*

Bibliography

Harrison, E. F. (1987). *The Managerial Decision-Making Process*, 3rd edn. Boston, MA: Houghton-Mifflin.

reciprocal altruism

J. Keith Murnighan

Altruism benefits others but costs actors because, in biological terms, it reduces an individual's ability to procreate. Trivers' (1971) classic article on the evolution of reciprocal altruism – the exchange of altruistic acts over time – shows that altruism can be rational not just among kin (Hamilton, 1964) but also among unrelated individuals and even across species. These effective exchange systems (*see* EXCHANGE RELATIONS) can develop when "the benefit of the altruistic act to the recipient is greater than the cost of the act to the performer." Such systems develop when people have many opportunities to help each other. Cheating (i.e., benefiting from altruistic behavior from another without fully reciprocating) is always tempting but is self-defeating when detection is likely and the benefits from future exchanges of reciprocal altruism are larger than the benefits of short-term cheating. Trivers modeled repeated interactions as iterated prisoners' dilemma games (or as symbiosis), but with a time lag. Humans "in all known cultures" are exemplars: they share food, help the sick, and share implements and knowledge. As our societies have grown and social distance has increased, the temptation of subtle cheating (reciprocating but not in kind) has grown to the point where some think of it as adaptive. This is a common danger of life in organizational systems, which otherwise provide all of the conditions that might encourage reciprocal altruism.

See also *altruism; deviance; game theory; trust*

Bibliography

Hamilton, W. D. (1964). The genetic evolution of social behavior. *Journal of Theoretical Biology*, 7, 1–52.

Trivers, R. L. (1971). The evolution of reciprocal altruism. *Quarterly Review of Biology*, 46, 35–57.

reciprocity

J. Keith Murnighan

Reciprocity is a strong, pervasive, and ancient norm that can be represented by three sayings: one negative ("An eye for an eye; a tooth for a tooth"), one positive ("You scratch my back, I'll scratch yours"), and one general ("Do unto others as you would have others do unto you") (*see* GROUP NORMS). Positive and general reciprocity help create and/or boost social value: if individuals reciprocate and fulfill each other's expectations, their benefits increase (*see* EXCHANGE RELATIONS). Negative reciprocity, as well as positive or general reciprocity not being fulfilled, leads to unmet expectations and the potential for considerable interpersonal conflict (*see* CONFLICT AND CONFLICT MANAGEMENT).

Gouldner (1960) refers to reciprocity as an almost universal norm, which indicates that people should do no harm and "should repay (in kind) what another has provided." Cialdini (1993) notes that all societies subscribe to the norm of reciprocity. Cialdini (1993; Cialdini and Trost, 1998) suggests that felt obligation is a key determinant of reciprocity. Empirical research, for instance, has consistently shown that feelings of obligation and indebtedness and an increased motivation to reciprocate follow the receipt of help, gifts, and favors (*see* RECIPROCAL ALTRUISM). In an experiment on trust and reciprocity, however, Berg, Dickhaut, and McCabe (1995) demonstrated that not everyone reciprocates and how much they reciprocate varies. Gregory (1975) noted that feelings of obligation do not result when recipients (of gifts, concessions, etc.) feel entitled to what was given or when they hold the general belief that those having more should share with those having less.

Interpersonally, acts of reciprocity provide a strong basis for the development of TRUST. In two experiments, Pillutla, Malhotra, and Murnighan (2003) found that reciprocity increased exponentially as a function of the amount a trustor risked, suggesting that trusted parties are sensitive to the size of trusting acts and make stronger attributions of trust when the trusting act increases in significance. Malhotra (2003) refined these conclusions by demonstrating that reciprocity following an act of trust was more likely following large acts of trust because these actions provided greater benefit to the recipients, who were not particularly attuned to the risks taken by the initial trustor. Additional findings showed that trustors who hedged and took small or moderate risks were seen as under-trusting or cheap, attributions that do not generally foster reciprocity (Pillutla, Malhotra, and Murnighan, 2003). In contrast, large, seemingly irrational acts of trust were unambiguous and provided less opportunity for trusted parties to justify non-reciprocity by downplaying the significance of the trustor's act. Relatively small acts of trust, then, set the stage for trusted parties to discount the act, minimizing the chances that the trust will be reciprocated. Larger acts of trust, which leave initial trustors more vulnerable, lead to clearer attributions by trusted parties and a greater likelihood of reciprocity, which can also set the stage for additional increases in trust development.

Organizationally, the strength of the reciprocity norm is easily seen in collective bargaining. The parties to a labor–management agreement are traditionally, if not legally, bound to reciprocate each other's concessions. The difficulty with this almost immutable norm, one that should (theoretically) contribute to the resolution of labor–management conflict, is the likelihood that both parties will overestimate the value of their own concessions and underestimate the value of their counterpart's concessions. This increases the probability that mutually supportive, reciprocal attributions will not be realized, an outcome that is not particularly surprising given the competitive nature of collective bargaining interactions.

Another danger associated with the strength of the reciprocity norm is the fact that reciprocity's positive effects can be used manipulatively (*see* INFLUENCE) by trying to induce individuals who have received a favor to feel obligated to reciprocate. Thus, when the representatives of charitable efforts thrust unwanted items into our possession, we often feel duty-bound to respond by making a contribution. More importantly, in organizations, a subordinate who flatters the boss can establish subtle pressures for the boss to reciprocate. Differentiating between the exchange of relatively equivalent favors (positive reciprocity) and the deceptive action of engaging in low cost entreaties to garner more valuable, reciprocal responses (*see* EXCHANGE RELATIONS) or, conversely, accepting highly beneficial offerings but reciprocating incompletely, means that individuals need to acquire particularly sensitive interpersonal detection skills (*see* INTERPERSONAL SKILLS), as cheating in interpersonal interactions has been understood as tempting and individually beneficial since the times of Plato (Ferris et al., 1994). Because most people's needs for social affirmation encourage flattery, the widely pervasive and particularly powerful norm of reciprocity, which on the one hand provides the potential for enormous interpersonal good, can also tempt people toward ingratiation and interpersonal cheating rather than fair and even-handed reciprocity (*see* IMPRESSION MANAGEMENT).

Extensions of the concept of reciprocity to the societal level, particularly for small societies like tribes, provide the basis for tremendous collective benefit. In particular, Simon (1990) has argued that, at least for relatively small collectivities who can more easily track cheating and establish general reputations for their members, reciprocity can lead to a rational basis for altruism. In essence, people do not appreciate that acting altruistically within such a group may reduce their evolutionary fitness (their ability to reproduce). Instead, they learn how to act appropriately, which, within a small group, may include altruistic action. Also, altruistic acts that increase altruists' reputations can make them more attractive partners for procreation, which then becomes evolutionarily rational. Thus, reciprocity, even in situations that do not presage additional reciprocity (e.g., tipping staff in faraway restaurants), may not be so irrational after all.

See also *exchange relations; game theory*

Bibliography

Berg, J., Dickhaut, J., and McCabe, K. (1995). Trust, reciprocity, and social history. *Games and Economic Behavior*, 10, 122–42.

Cialdini, R. B. (1993). *Influence: Science and Practice.* New York: Harper Collins College Publishers.

Cialdini, R. B. and Trost, M. R. (1998). Social influence: Social norms, conformity and compliance. In D. T. Gilbert, S. Fiske, and G. Lindzey (eds.) *The Handbook of Social Psychology*, 4th edn. New York: McGraw-Hill, 151–92.

Ferris, G. R., Judge, T. A., Rowland, K. M., and Fitzgibbons, D. E. (1994). Subordinate influence and the performance evaluation process: Test of a model. *Organizational Behavior and Human Decision Processes*, 58, 101–35.

Gouldner, A. W. (1960). The norm of reciprocity: A preliminary statement. *American Sociological Review*, 25, 161–78.

Gregory, J. R. (1975). Images of a limited good or expectations of reciprocity? *Current Anthropology*, 16 (1), 73–92.

Malhotra, D. (2003). Trust and the obligation to reciprocate: The differing perspectives of trustors and trusted parties. Working paper, Harvard Business School.

Pillutla, M., Malhotra, D., and Murnighan, J. K. (2003). Attributions of trust and the calculus of reciprocity. *Journal of Experimental Social Psychology*, 39, 448–55.

Simon, H. A. (1990). A mechanism for social selection and successful altruism. *Science*, 250, 1665–8.

reference group

see JUSTICE, DISTRIBUTIVE; SOCIAL COMPARISON

referent power

see POWER

regression toward the mean

Pino G. Audia

Regression toward the mean is a statistical phenomenon which occurs when two quantities are related but imperfectly so (Campbell and Kenny, 1999). The quantities can be repeated observations of the same variable – for example, performance at time t and performance at time $t+1$ – or two distinct variables such as innovation and performance. Regression toward the mean is the tendency for extreme values on the first quantity to be associated with values of the second quantity which are closer to the mean rather than with values that are farther away. Regression toward the mean often arises because extreme quantities are the result of chance events that are unlikely to repeat themselves. In such circumstances those who mistakenly attribute the tendency for extreme quantities to be followed by less extreme quantities to complicated causal theories commit the so-called regression fallacy (Tversky and Kahneman, 1974). Regression toward the mean, however, is not solely due to chance or measurement error. An implication of the fact that regression toward the mean occurs when two quantities have a correlation of less than one is that any factor that weakens the correlation between two variables may be interpreted as facilitating regression toward the mean (Campbell and Kenny, 1999). In line with this logic, organizational researchers have proposed and shown that executives may make it more likely for the performance of firms to regress toward the industry mean by choosing strategic options whose consequences are less certain and that therefore weaken the link between past performance and future performance (Harrison and March, 1984). This is often the result of changing the organization's strategy when there is no clear need to do so (Greve, 1999).

See also *research design; research methods; statistical methods*

Bibliography

Campbell, D. T. and Kenny, D. A. (1999). *A Primer on Regression Artifacts*. New York: Guilford Press.

Greve, H. R. (1999). The effect of core change on performance: Inertia and regression toward the mean. *Administrative Science Quarterly*, **44**, 590–614.

Harrison, J. R. and March, J. G. (1984). Decision-making and post-decision surprises. *Administrative Science Quarterly*, 26–42.

Tversky, A. and Kahneman, D. (1974). Judgment under uncertainty: Heuristics and biases. *Science*, **185**, 1124–31.

regulation

see BOARDS; INSTITUTIONAL THEORY

reinforcement

see BEHAVIORISM

reliability

Richard Klimoski

In the context of organizational research, reliability refers to the degree of self-consistency among the scores earned by an individual on a measure or the degree of consistency that exists among observations made (e.g., of service quality) over repeated attempts to do so. More technically, it is the extent that a set of scores, quantitative descriptions, or observations is free from unsystematic error variation, when some aspect of an individual, organization, or a phenomenon is measured more than once. Reliability is usually estimated from statistical evidence of covariation among a set of items, scores, or observations (*see* STATISTICAL METHODS). Good reliability is a necessary condition for a useful measure or procedure. Evidence of poor or low reliability is a clue that it would be unwise to accept the information, "facts," or data in question at face value (e.g., we should not try to generalize from what we have) (*see* GENERALIZATION). Moreover, low reliability sets limits to the order of magnitude and stability of statistical relationships that we can expect in research. High reliability can be promoted by using appropriate operational definitions, standardized measurement procedures, careful training of observers/recorders, or by choosing to measure phenomena that are not too subtle or elusive.

See also *bias; research design; research methods; validity*

Bibliography

Ghiselli, E. E., Campbell, J. P., and Zedeck, S. (1981). *Measurement Theory for the Behavioral Sciences*. San Francisco: W. H. Freeman.

Schmitt, N. W. and Klimoski, R. J. (1991). *Research Methods in Human Resources Management.* Cincinnati, OH: South-Western.

reputation

Charles Fombrun

Companies rely on both tangible and intangible resources to gain competitive advantage against rivals. Chief among intangible resources is a company's reputation – the salient characteristics that external observers ascribe to a company (Fombrun and Shanley, 1990). When surveyed, senior managers point to a company's reputation as among the most important success drivers and ponder how to induce and maintain favorable assessments of their companies by outside observers. Efforts to understand how corporate reputations develop draw on the perspectives of economics, strategic management, or sociology.

THE ECONOMIC VIEW

Economists adhere to a view of reputation as either a trait or a signal. Game theorists regard reputations as character traits that distinguish among "types" of companies and can explain their strategic behavior (*see* GAME THEORY). Signaling theorists emphasize the informational content of reputations. Both recognize that reputations are perceptions of companies held by external observers.

Weigelt and Camerer (1988: 443) point out: "In game theory the reputation of a player is the perception others have of the player's values ... which determine his/her choice of strategies." Information asymmetry forces external observers to look for proxies to describe the preferences of rivals and their likely courses of action. Consumers rely on a company's reputation because they have less information than managers do about the company's commitment to delivering desirable product features (Stiglitz, 1989). Similarly, since outside investors are less informed than managers about a company's future actions, a favorable reputation increases investor confidence that managers will act in ways that are reputation consistent. For game theorists, reputations are therefore functional: they generate perceptions among employees, customers, investors, competitors, and the general public about what a company is, what it does, and what it stands for.

Signaling theorists concur: reputations derive from the prior resource allocations managers make to first-order activities likely to create a perception of reliability and predictability to outside observers. Since many features of a company and its products are hidden from view, reputations are information signals that increase an observer's confidence in the company's products and services.

Managers can make strategic use of their company's reputation to signal its attractiveness. When the quality of a company's products and services is not directly observable, high quality producers may invest in reputation building in order to signal the greater quality of their products and services (Shapiro, 1983). Their initial investments in building reputation allow them to charge premium prices and earn rents from the repeat purchases that their reputations generate. In contrast, low quality producers avoid investing in reputation building because they do not expect repeat purchases.

Similar dynamics may operate in capital and labor markets. In the capital markets, managers routinely try to signal investors about their company's economic performance. Since investors are more favorably disposed to companies with high and stable earnings, managers often try to smooth quarterly earnings and keep dividend payout ratios high and fixed, despite earnings fluctuations. In the labor market, sometimes companies will also pay a premium price to hire high-reputation auditors and outside counsel. They rent the reputations of their agents in order to signal investors, regulators, and other publics about their company's probity and credibility (Wilson, 1983).

THE STRATEGIC VIEW

When viewed strategically, reputations are mobility barriers (Caves and Porter, 1977) that produce returns to companies because they are difficult to imitate. By circumscribing companies' actions and rivals' reactions, reputations act as a distinct source of industry level structure.

In part, reputations are barriers to competition because they derive from unique internal features of companies that are difficult to duplicate. They describe the history of a company's past interactions with STAKEHOLDERS and so suggest to observers what the company stands for (Dutton and Dukerich, 1991). Reputations are also difficult to replicate because they are externally perceived and therefore difficult to manipulate. Rivals cannot generate the performance results of their better-regarded rivals because, other things being equal, all stakeholders favor the products and services of the more reputable companies. After all, it takes time for a reputation to congeal in observers' minds, and empirical studies show that even when confronted with negative information, observers resist changing their reputational assessments.

Like economists, then, strategists call attention to the competitive benefits of acquiring favorable reputations and support a focus on the longitudinal resource allocations that companies must make to erect reputational barriers to the mobility of rivals. Since primary resource allocations also stand to directly improve organizational performance, however, it proves difficult to isolate their unique impact on performance and reputation. That is why empirical studies have had difficulty untangling a causal ordering: both are produced by the same underlying initiatives (Chakravarthy, 1986).

Although most strategies dwell on the economic and competitive aspects of managerial decision-making, a subset calls attention to the social aspects of these decisions. Social performance theorists tend to take the moral high ground to suggest principles and practices that managers should adhere to in order to induce ethically sound strategic decisions (see CORPORATE SOCIAL PERFORMANCE). However, current approaches now emphasize that companies have diverse stakeholders with valid claims on the strategies that companies pursue, and so advise politically savvy managers to address social concerns in order to secure external legitimacy (Cameron and Whetten, 1983). Implicitly, they suggest that corporate reputations may well gauge the legitimacy of companies' strategic initiatives (Fombrun and Shanley, 1990).

The Sociological View

Sociologists suggest that both economic and strategic models distort the sociocognitive process that actually generates reputational rankings (Granovetter, 1985). To them, rankings are social constructions that come into being through the relationships that a focal company establishes with its stakeholders within an institutional field. Companies have multiple evaluators, each of whom apply different criteria in assessing companies. Reputations come into being as individuals struggle to make sense of a company's past and present actions, so that reputational rankings represent aggregated assessments of institutional prestige and describe the stratification of the social system surrounding companies and industries (Shapiro, 1987).

Faced with incomplete information about a company's actions, observers not only interpret the signals that a company routinely broadcasts, but also rely on the evaluative signals refracted by key intermediaries such as market analysts, professional investors, public interest monitors, and media reporters. These intermediaries are key nodes in an inter-company network that transmits and refracts information among companies and their stakeholders (see NETWORK THEORY ANALYSIS).

An Integrative View

Jointly, these three perspectives suggest that reputations constitute subjective, collective assessments of the credibility and reliability of companies, with the following characteristics:

- Reputations are derivative, second-order characteristics of an industrial social system that crystallize the emergent status of companies in the field.
- Reputations develop from companies' prior resource allocations and histories and constitute mobility barriers that constrain companies' actions and rivals' reactions.
- Reputations crystallize from the bottom-up constructions of diverse evaluators, each applying a combination of economic and social, selfish and altruistic criteria.
- Reputations reconcile the multiple images of companies among all of their stakeholders, and signal their overall attractiveness to employees, consumers, investors, and local communities.
- Reputations embody two key dimensions of companies' effectiveness: an appraisal of

companies' economic performance, and an appraisal of companies' success in fulfilling social responsibilities (Etzioni, 1988).

Thus, a corporate reputation is a collective representation of a company's past actions and results that describes the company's overall attractiveness to its diverse stakeholders.

MEASURING AND MANAGING REPUTATIONS

A wave of corporate scandals since 2001 has increased interest in valuing and managing corporate reputations. Various surveys such as those released annually by *Fortune*, the *Financial Times*, and the *Wall Street Journal* (e.g., Alsop, 1999) now provide benchmarking tools that describe how companies are perceived by managers, CEOs, consumers, employees, or other stakeholders. However, most continue to rely on different definitions of reputation and to sample different publics, so they are not always comparable.

Field research has increased learning about what companies can do to strengthen their reputations. Collins and Porras (1996) show enduring companies are built from core beliefs that are systematically institutionalized internally. Schultz, Hatch, and Larsen (2000) bring together various research projects that describe the strong link that exists between identity, branding, and reputation as companies struggle to "express themselves" to the outside world. Finally, Fombrun and van Riel (2004) describe a set of common elements that highly regarded companies in various countries share.

These recent developments speak directly to the management of reputational risk – the need for companies to balance the upside gains of reputation-building communications and initiatives, against the downside losses that result from scandals and accidents (Rayner, 2003)

See also *family firms; identity, organizational; organizational effectiveness*

Bibliography

Alsop, R. (1999). The best corporate reputations in America. *Wall Street Journal*, September 25. For a compilation of reputation surveys, see www.reputationinstitute.com.

Cameron, K. S. and Whetten, D. A. (eds.) (1983). *Organizational Effectiveness: A Comparison of Multiple Models*. New York: Academic Press.

Caves, R. E. and Porter, M. E. (1977). From entry barriers to mobility barriers. *Quarterly Journal of Economics*, **91**, 421–34.

Chakravarthy, B. (1986). Measuring strategic performance. *Strategic Management Journal*, **7**, 437–58.

Collins, J. and Porras, J. (1996). *Built to Last*. New York: Free Press.

Dutton, J. E. and Dukerich, J. M. (1991). Keeping an eye on the mirror: Image and identity in organizational adaptation. *Academy of Management Journal*, **34**, 517–54.

Etzioni, A. (1988). *The Moral Dimension*. New York: Free Press.

Fombrun, C. J. and van Riel, C. (2004). *Fame and Fortune: How Successful Companies Build Winning Reputations*. Mahwah, NJ: Financial Times/Prentice-Hall.

Fombrun, C. J. and Shanley, M. (1990). What's in a name? Reputation-building and corporate strategy. *Academy of Management Journal*, **33**, 233–58.

Granovetter, M. (1985). Economic action and social structure: The problem of embeddedness. *American Journal of Sociology*, **91**, 481–510.

Rayner, J. 2003. *Managing Reputational Risk*. London: John Wiley and Sons.

Schultz, M., Hatch, M. J., and Larsen, M. H. (2000). *The Expressive Organization: Linking Identity, Reputation, and the Corporate Brand*. Oxford: Oxford University Press.

Shapiro, C. (1983). Premiums for high-quality products as returns to reputations. *Quarterly Journal of Economics*, **98**, 659–81.

Shapiro, S. P. (1987). The social control of impersonal trust. *American Journal of Sociology*, **93**, 623–58.

Stiglitz, J. E. (1989). Imperfect information in the product market. In R. Schmalensee and R. Willig (eds.), *Handbook of Industrial Organization*. Amsterdam: North-Holland, 769–847.

Weigelt, K. and Camerer, C. (1988). Reputation and corporate strategy: A review of recent theory and applications. *Strategic Management Journal*, **9**, 443 51.

Wilson, R. (1983). Auditing: Perspectives from multiperson decision theory. *Accounting Review*, **58**, 305–18.

requisite variety

see OPEN SYSTEMS; SYSTEMS THEORY

research design

Steven G. Rogelberg

Kerlinger (1986: 279) defines research design as "the plan and structure of investigation so conceived as to obtain answers to research questions." Rosenthal and Rosnow (1991: 69) define design as a "blueprint that provides the scientist with a detailed outline or plan for the collection and analysis of data." In both of these definitions, the "plan" includes a researcher's decisions concerning (a) research strategy; (b) research setting; and (c) operational definitions and measurement of the study's constructs of interest. The specific choices within and about these factors influence the internal and external VALIDITY of the conclusions that stem from a study (Stone-Romero, 2002).

RESEARCH STRATEGY

The most common research strategies used in organizational behavior are true experiment, passive observation, and quasi-experiment:

True experiment. In a true experiment the researcher manipulates one or more independent variables to examine their individual and collective effects on a dependent variable. Research participants are randomly assigned to conditions of the study. To improve both the internal and external validity of the study, experimental control of potentially confounding variables is commonly used.

Quasi-experiments. In a quasi-experiment there are typically two or more conditions (e.g., a group that went through downsizing versus a group that did not go through downsizing) that the researcher is interested in studying in relationship to a dependent variable. These conditions are typically naturally occurring rather than overtly manipulated by the experimenter. Participants are not randomly assigned to conditions. The assignment is based on self-selection, happenstance, or convenience. Some experimental control may be undertaken to remove potentially confounding variables.

Nomothetic passive observation. Nomothetic passive observation is a non-experimental strategy in which relations among variables are studied. No variables are manipulated (e.g., treatment conditions) and as a result causal relations among variables are typically difficult to determine. Survey research is the most typical type of nomothetic passive observation research.

Idiographic passive observation. Idiographic passive observation is a non-experimental strategy in which individual variables or cases in and of themselves (rather than relations among variables) are studied/described. Some qualitative oriented research (e.g., "verstehen" and ethnographic studies) can be thought of as following under this research strategy.

Research setting   The most common research settings in which to employ the above strategies are the lab and the field. Laboratory settings are contrived settings created and designed for conducting research. A lab setting maximizes the internal validity (e.g., the setting is controlled, variables can be readily manipulated) of a study. A field setting, by definition, occurs naturally in the environment. It can be an organization, a school, a marketplace, a crowd, etc. The external validity of a field setting is often quite high (greater fidelity). However, this external validity may come at the cost of internal validity (e.g., cannot readily control confounding variables).

Research strategy is crossed with research setting to produce the following designs: lab-based experimental research, lab-based quasi-experimental research, lab-based passive observation research, field-based experimental research, field-based quasi-experimental research, and field-based passive observation research. To be effective, in each of these designs the constructs of interest must be assessed in such ways that validity (the accurateness of inferences made based on the measure; whether the measure accurately and completely represents what it was intended to measure) and reliability (the consistency or stability of a measure) are high. It is also important to recognize that the number of observations and participants in the above research designs can be small or large, collected at one point in time or across time. A few non-traditional research designs exist that do not fit neatly into the above categorization. They are computer simulation research (e.g., models are tested by means of computer generated data) and meta-analyses (e.g., findings across related research studies are accumulated and summarized statistically in order to estimate the true relationship among variables).

Frequency of use Austin, Scherbaum, and Mahlman (2002) coded research studies (on their methodological characteristics) published in the *Journal of Applied Psychology* – one of the premier journals in organizational behavior. Idiographic or nomothetic passive observational designs were used 52 percent of the time. Experimental designs were used 31 percent of the time. With regard to setting, most research was conducted in the field (62 percent). Approximately 25 percent was conducted in the lab. The remaining published research was split relatively equally between simulation research and meta-analytic research.

FUTURE TRENDS IN RESEARCH DESIGN

Consistent with the exhortations of researchers discussing future research design needs (e.g., Rogelberg and Laber, 2002) and journal editors discussing the type of research they want to publish (e.g., Zedeck, 2003), four principal trends in research design are anticipated. The Internet and Intranet will provide great opportunity for exploration into new research methods. Going beyond the online survey, future work will explore and refine methods such as browser-based field experimentation, methods for analyzing Internet archives (e.g., financial reports, job postings, advertisements, vision statements, etc.), methods for automated content analyses of chat room, email, and listproc content, and naturalistic observation methods (e.g., webcams, smartcards). Virtual reality (e.g., business simulations) approaches will also be continually developed and most importantly made readily available to applied researchers. The second anticipated trend concerns triangulation. Triangulation on a social phenomenon of interest through multiple methods provides the most accurate and compelling picture of that phenomenon. Future research designs will likely contain a series of studies, using diverse quantitative and/or qualitative methodologies to examine singular phenomena. Researchers will need to demonstrate the replicability of their findings across methodologies. Third, more research designs with longitudinal and time series data structures are anticipated. These types of data structures are on the rise, both for theoretical reasons (e.g., our models are incomplete without recognizing temporal factors) and methodological reasons (e.g., technological data collection methods allow for easier data collection over time). Finally, consistent with globalization, cross-cultural research teams who conduct concurrent research on the same issue in several international locations should be more prevalent.

See also *bias; quasi-experimental design; research methods; statistical methods*

Bibliography

Austin, J. T., Scherbaum, C. A., and Mahlman, R. A. (2002). History of research methods in industrial and organizational psychology: Measurement, design, analysis. In S. G. Rogelberg (ed.), *Handbook of Research Methods in Industrial and Organizational Psychology*. Oxford: Blackwell.
Kerlinger, F. (1986). *Foundations of Behavioral Research*, 3rd edn. New York: Holt, Rinehart, and Winston.
Rogelberg, S. G. and Laber, M. (2002). Securing our collective future: Challenges facing those designing and doing research in industrial and organizational psychology. In S. G. Rogelberg (ed.), *Handbook of Research Methods in Industrial and Organizational Psychology*. Oxford: Blackwell.
Rosenthal, R. and Rosnow, R. L. (1991). *Essentials of Behavioral Research*. New York: McGraw-Hill.
Stone-Romero, E. F (2002). The relative validity and usefulness of various empirical research designs. In S. G. Rogelberg (ed.), *Handbook of Research Methods in Industrial and Organizational Psychology*. Oxford: Blackwell.
Zedeck, S. (2003). Editorial. *Journal of Applied Psychology*, 88, 3–5.

research methods

Steven G. Rogelberg

Carefully conducted research is the key means to the creation, integration, and appropriate application of new knowledge, without which the advancement of organizational behavior as a scientific discipline would not be possible.

Research can be conceived as comprising four elements: measurement (e.g., conceptualizing the constructs), design (e.g., determining the research setting and strategy), analysis (e.g., analyzing the collected data/information), and report generation. Although many research methodologies exist, historically, they are categorized as being qualitative (e.g., Lee, 1999) or quantitative (e.g., Cook and Campbell, 1976) in nature. This distinction, however, can be overly simplistic in that research typically contains elements of both approaches.

Research is usually designated as qualitative when certain conditions are present. The research mostly takes place in a natural setting. The researchers usually are present in the situation they are researching (i.e., participant observation). In the analysis of information, language indices rather than quantitative indices are preferred as indicators of the constructs of interest. These include observation notes, interview transcripts, diaries, focus group reports, video/audio transcriptions, and organizational documents. Qualitative methods can be highly focused in scope, such as in content analysis where the presence of specified concepts or terms within texts are recorded, in order to make inferences about the messages within the texts, the author(s), the audience, and even the culture and time of which these are a part. A broader qualitative method is ethnography, typically a long-term examination of a social setting based on the participation, or more deeply, the "immersion," of the researcher in the group, providing a detailed exploration of the group, its culture, and activities.

Quantitative research typically involves the use of structured and standardized measures of various types (e.g., questionnaires, ratings of behavior, physiological assessments). The scores produced by the measures can be analyzed with a variety of descriptive and inferential statistical techniques that vary greatly in their sophistication and complexity, from simple tests comparing samples on some measured variable, to methods that assess the fit of an array of data with one or more models specifying a set of causal relationships among variables. Quantitative research can take place in the field or the laboratory, with researchers often seeking to apply experimental or statistical control over potentially confounding variables. The researcher is usually not an actor in the situation they are studying. Common quantitative designs include statistical surveys (e.g., the researcher administers a standardized questionnaire to a randomly selected sample of the population), experiments (e.g., the researcher manipulates one or more variables in a controlled setting to examine their individual and collective effects on another variable), quasi-experiments (e.g., two naturally occurring groups are systematically compared and contrasted on one or more variables), and simulations (e.g., models are tested by means of computer generated data).

In the future, OB research seems likely to use complex methods to accommodate more sophisticated statistical models (e.g., multilevel and longitudinal). The Internet will also shape the future of OB methods as the use of naturalistic observation methods (e.g., webcams, smartcards), virtual reality simulations, and automated content analyses of real time (e.g., chat room) and Internet archives (e.g., financial reports, job postings) increase in use.

See also *computer simulation; quasi-experimental design; regression toward the mean; reliability; research design; validity*

Bibliography

Cook, T. D. and Campbell, D. T. (1976). The design and conduct of quasi-experiments and true experiments in field settings. In M. D. Dunnette (ed.), *Handbook of Industrial and Organizational Psychology*. Chicago: Rand McNally, 223–326.

Lee, T. W. (1999). *Using Qualitative Methods in Organizational Research*. Thousand Oaks, CA: Sage.

resistance to change

Maury Peiperl

Resistance to change denotes active or passive responses on the part of a person or group that militate against a particular change, a program of changes, or change in general. One of the first analyses in the context of ORGANIZATIONAL CHANGE programs was Kurt Lewin's (1951) discussion of FORCE FIELD ANALYSIS, and it has remained a key issue in discussions of business evolution and revolution ever since. *Active* resistance to change may be manifested in voicing disagreement, organizing groups to oppose changes, and direct acts of resistance (such as persistence in using old methods or materials in the face of change requests, sabotaging new equipment, or intentionally spreading false information about change initiatives). *Passive* resistance often involves withholding effort or information, ignoring communications, decreased involvement in the work group, and some manifestations of ABSENTEEISM.

Resistance to change is typically encountered when the affected individual(s) perceive a threat to their position, relationships, power, income, or CAREER prospects. Often, individuals who have not experienced change in a long time, or those who have worked their way up over time to high levels of responsibility and control of resources, are the most resistant. Consequently, it is common to find that in large organizations managers just below board level are more resistant to change than those lower down, who are often stereotyped as unable or unwilling to change.

Resistance to change is usually seen as negative or unconstructive behavior within work organizations. However, it is also often the case that "resistors" understand potential implications of a change program that those driving the program have not considered. In these circumstances it can be thought of as "informed opposition," implying that the appropriate response should be less a matter of decreasing the resistance than of rethinking the change program (Jick and Peiperl, 2003). It has also been suggested that change leaders are themselves resistant to better ways of accomplishing their tasks; that they "resist the very knowledge that would allow them to overcome the resistance to change" (O'Toole, 1995: 158). Resistance to change is therefore often prompted, perhaps needlessly, through a lack of application of best-practice management.

No scientifically valid general theory about resistance to change exists. However, the underlying causes of resistance to change have been explored in depth by (among others) O'Toole (1995: chs. 7–13) and identified as including threats to established power, fear of chaos or discomfort, and loss of control implied by the imposition of the will of others. Perceived inequity can also be a source of resistance, as has been elucidated by Rousseau (1995, esp. ch. 5) in terms of the relationship between an individual and a work organization (*see* EQUITY THEORY). Finally, a biologically based view with organizational implications is proposed by Wheatley (1999), captured in the statement: "Any living thing will change only if it *sees change as the means of preserving itself*." However, organizational evidence suggests that these arguments may be overstated and people who feel secure and optimistic are quite willing and able to embrace change.

See also *change methods; influence; power*

Bibliography

Jick, T. and Peiperl, M. (2003). *Managing Change: Cases and Concepts*, 2nd edn. Burr Ridge, IL: Irwin/McGraw-Hill.

Lewin, K. (1951). *Field Theory in Social Science*. New York: Harper.

O'Toole, J. (1995). *Leading Change: Overcoming the Ideology of Comfort and the Tyranny of Custom*. San Francisco: Jossey-Bass.

Rousseau, D. (1995). *Psychological Contracts in Organizations: Understanding Written and Unwritten Agreements*. Thousand Oaks, CA: Sage.

Wheatley, M. (1999). *Leadership and the New Science: Discovering Order in a Chaotic World*. San Francisco: Berrett-Koehler.

resource dependence

Mikolaj Jan Piskorski and Tiziana Casciaro

Resource dependence theory marked a watershed by positioning power at the core of organizational theory (Pfeffer and Salancik, 1978). The theory establishes two characteristics of actors' structural power: relative power – the difference in the power of each actor over the other; and mutual dependence – actors' total dependence on actors in the dyad. These two characteristics are then related to two outcomes: (1) differences between actors' profits and (2) power balancing operations that aim to change the underlying structure of dependence.

The main hypothesis relating actors' structural power to material inequality between actors suggests that an increase in an actor's power will lead to higher profit for that actor. Burt (1982) provided support for this hypothesis by showing that firms in industries subject to significant constraint from firms in other industries will suffer lower rates of profit. Subsequent tests relating advancement of workers in a professional organization to their constraint yielded similar results (Burt, 1992). Recent developments in this stream of research suggest that mutual dependence may affect the relationship between relative power and profit, such that an increase in actor's power under conditions of high mutual dependence may actually reduce that actor's profit (Piskorski and Casciaro, 2003).

Most research relating actors' structural POWER to balancing operations focused on cooptative devices such as mergers and board interlocks as the main means of changing the underlying structure of dependence. Pfeffer and Salancik (1978) claimed that increases in relative power imbalance and in mutual dependence are likely to lead to such cooptative relationships. Most research has focused on examining the impact of power imbalance and has found mixed evidence for the claim, with stronger results for mergers than for board interlocks. Some of the inconsistency in the results has been attributed to the fact that board interlocks can be thought of as representations of power use, rather than cooptative devices (Pfeffer and Salancik, 1978: 164–5; Palmer, 1983; Mizruchi and Stearns, 1988) (see INTERLOCKING BOARDS). Others have attributed the lack of consistent results to theoretical misspecification linking power imbalance and the likelihood of cooptation, arguing that it is hard to imagine why an increase in a firm's relative power would make it more likely to agree to cooptative action. Recent developments in this stream of research attempt to rectify this issue by explaining why an increase in relative power may actually reduce the likelihood of cooptation, with mutual dependence being the main driver of mergers (Casciaro and Piskorski, 2003).

As evidenced by the recent developments, in the future resource dependence will benefit from full utilization of the two characteristics of structural power. Furthermore, it is hoped that this essentially dyadic perspective will be extended to a triadic (Gargiulo, 1993) and subsequently a network perspective. When this extension occurs, resource dependence should

be integrated with other mechanisms that seek to explain network sources of inequality, such as status. Finally, future extensions will also consider a broader set of dependent variables.

See also *contingency theory; inter-organizational relations; network theory and analysis; networking;*

Bibliography

Burt, R. S. (1982). *Toward a Structural Theory of Action: Network Models of Social Structure, Perception, and Action.* New York: Academic Press.

Burt, R. S. (1992). *Structural Holes: The Social Structure of Competition.* Cambridge, MA: Harvard University Press.

Casciaro, T. and Piskorski, M. J. (2003). Power imbalance and interdependence: Formation of inter-industry mergers. Working Paper, Graduate School of Business, Stanford University.

Gargiulo, M. (1993). Two-step leverage: Managing constraint in organizational politics. *Administrative Science Quarterly*, 38, 1–19.

Mizruchi, M. S. and Stearns, L. (1988). A longitudinal study of the formation of interlocking directorates. *Administrative Science Quarterly*, 33, 194–210.

Palmer, D. (1983). Broken ties: Interlocking directorates and intercorporate coordination. *Administrative Science Quarterly*, 28, 40–55.

Pfeffer, J. and Salancik, G. R. (1978). *The External Control of Organizations: A Resource Dependence Perspective.* New York: Harper and Row.

Piskorski, M. J. and Casciaro, T. (2003). When more power makes you worse off: Turning a profit in the American economy. In D. H. Nagao (ed.), *Proceedings of the Sixty-Third Annual Meeting of the Academy of Management.*

rewards

see INCENTIVES

risk taking

Philip Bromiley

The terms risk, risk taking, uncertainty, and ambiguity have been used in a variety of ways. In the most common usage, a decision-maker must choose between two alternatives (A1 and A2). Under certainty, the decision-maker knows that a given choice results in specific outcomes. Under uncertainty and ambiguity, choosing a given alternative results in one or more of a set of outcomes occurring, but which outcome(s) will occur is not known when the decision is made. If the decision-maker knows all the alternatives and outcomes, and the outcomes' probabilities of occurrence given a specific choice, then the decision involves risk. Alternatively, if the decision-maker does not know all the outcomes and/or their probabilities of occurrence, the decision involves uncertainty or ambiguity. Several literatures have been centrally concerned with issues of risk taking and many of these deal with both risk and ambiguity.

Decision theory develops rational procedures for choices under risk, often based on expected utility theory, although GAME THEORY analyses have also begun to address some such issues. Decision theory techniques address decisions under risk, but have less to say about decisions under uncertainty or ambiguity.

An early literature in psychology looked for personality traits and characteristics of individuals, assuming individuals had stable orientations toward risk (Kogan and Wallach, 1964). This work often related risk taking to sensation seeking. While people clearly have different risk preferences, later research demonstrated that risk preferences do not fully generalize across life activities. Risk takers in one area of life may avoid risk in others.

BEHAVIORAL DECISION RESEARCH (or theory), a branch of psychology, considers risk taking by individuals largely in experimental situations, although often with monetary rewards. Behavioral decision theorists originally explored how actual decision-makers differ from the assumptions of expected utility. The field has progressed rapidly. Numerous studies demonstrate experimentally instances where decision-makers differ from prescriptive models in either assessment of probabilities or choices. The field offers a large inventory of deviations from prescriptive models. The deviations from prescriptive models include biased assessments of probabilities and alternative decision rules (e.g., individuals generally evaluate outcomes relative to a reference point while rational models do not

use reference points). To summarize the general thrust of this field, people in many instances are extremely poor intuitive statisticians and make decisions in ways that are inconsistent with the expected utility maximization model.

Economics and finance theorists use risk as the primary explanation for differential returns in capital markets. A smaller group considers how capital structure influences the risk of bankruptcy. In explaining market returns, risk generally means the risk to stockholders that they cannot eliminate by holding a well-diversified portfolio (systematic risk or beta). Although systematic risk remains widely used in finance, recent research questions the role of beta and has sparked efforts to find alternative measures and models of risk.

Organizational psychologists studying the risky shift phenomenon find that groups make decisions with different apparent risk preferences than their members would prefer individually. In situations where all members of a group may find a given alternative overly risky, the group as a whole may choose that alternative (see GROUP POLARIZATION).

Finally, strategic management researchers consider corporate level risk and performance issues defining risk and performance various ways – capital market risk (returns to shareholders), variability of accounting returns, substantive policy choices, and probability of bankruptcy. Strategic management research on risk has examined numerous topics, including diversification, MERGERS AND ACQUISITIONS, and performance effects. Whereas risk and return appear positively related in capital market models, both positive and negative associations between risk and return have been found when risk is measured by income stream uncertainty. These associations appear to vary over business cycles and across industries.

Across the various areas, some commonalities have emerged. People do not and cannot handle risk in the way prescriptive theories advise. Firms and people both can exhibit risk seeking and risk avoiding behaviors (i.e., we can reject a general assumption of risk avoidance). Firms and people evaluate outcomes relative to reference points and this substantially influences their behaviors. Framing and context strongly influence risk related behaviors.

Overall, these different approaches have made significant progress but have generated confusion by using the term risk to mean quite different constructs. MacCrimmon and Wehrung (1986) demonstrate that differing measures of risk taking gathered from the same individuals at the same time exhibit almost no association. Furthermore, both psychological and organizational research indicates risk related behaviors are quite sensitive to contextual factors. These findings pose serious problems for the development of integrated approaches to risk.

See also *decision-making; game theory; satisficing; trust*

Bibliography

Kogan, N. and Wallach, M. A. (1964). *Risk Taking: A Study in Cognition and Personality*. New York: Holt, Rinehart and Winston.

MacCrimmon, K. R. and Wehrung, D. A. (1986). *Taking Risks: The Management of Uncertainty*. New York: Free Press.

Yates, J. F. (1992). *Risk-Taking Behavior*. New York: Wiley.

risky shift

see GROUP POLARIZATION

rituals

N. Anand

Rituals are a culturally patterned and repetitive rule governed social activity infused with symbolic value for participants and observers (Lukes, 1975). Rituals are one of the primary means by which founders and leaders embed and transmit the values of an organization's culture (Schein 1992). Trice and Beyer (1984) observed that a variety of organizational activity is accomplished through rituals: SOCIALIZATION of newcomers, firing of top executives, collective bargaining, office parties, MOTIVATION seminars, and the announcement of change initiatives. Three theoretical perspectives explain the role of rituals in the creation and maintenance of ORGANIZATIONAL CULTURE.

The functionalist thesis proposed by Durkheim (1965) holds that rituals serve an indispensable role in creating social solidarity and in shaping cultural order. Rituals foster social coherence by providing a focal point for collective action, that is, by providing an opportunity for people to come together to mark a significant occasion. The constant repetition of the symbolic stylized routines that make up rituals are said to constitute tradition. Thus, rituals vitalize and revitalize a group by helping perpetuate customary practice and renewal of a common faith. Rituals impose social control by transmitting messages about appropriate attitudes and behaviors. Rituals help individuals experience social euphoria through the joy of participating in mass social occasions. Deal and Kennedy (1982) highlighted the strategic use of rituals in creating a strong ORGANIZATIONAL CULTURE in corporations such as IBM and Mary Kay Cosmetics. Organizations where rituals underpin strong cultures are said to benefit from richer communication owing to shared symbolic understandings, a heightened need for cooperation as a result of enhanced social interactions, an ability to react more consistently because of shared VALUES, and use of symbolic control systems that improve goal alignment between an organization and its members.

Lukes (1975) argued that a purely functional view of rituals as shared and integrative is both simplistic and incomplete. In the alternative, neo-Marxist view, rituals do not so much affirm unity as express the very real conflicts inherent in society. Rituals help select social groups exert control through the processes of mystification, which refers to the taken-for-granted sanctioning of ritually endowed power that comes from patterning and repetition. Lukes (1975: 301–2) highlights the POWER inherent in the performance of rituals that "helps define as authoritative certain ways of seeing society: it serves to specify what in society is of special significance, it draws attention to certain forms of relationships." Rituals are used by various elements in organizations for largely self-serving political aims, to both channel and repress conflict. Rituals provide not only an opportunity for dominant social groups to strengthen their elite position, but also frequently serve interests of others making claims to authority. Kertzer (1988: 1) asserts that through rituals, "aspiring political leaders struggle to assert their right to rule, incumbent power holders seek to bolster their authority, and revolutionaries try to carve out a new basis of political allegiance." Trice and Beyer (1984) suggest that top managers often use organizational rituals strategically in order to enforce ideological conformity. In his ethnography of a Boston-based hi-tech firm, Kunda (1992) offers a number of examples of organizational rituals, such as top management presentations, training workshops, and formal group meetings, that seem to appear open, informal, and participatory, but in reality serve to exert cultural control on the workforce to conform to the interests of top management.

Finally, the sensemaking perspective on rituals proposes that rituals primarily serve a dynamic, sensemaking function – that of providing symbolic models of the social world that can be internalized as legitimate representations of reality. The enactment of rituals allows for individuals to invoke and internalize collective social categories central to an organization, defining, for example, what is sanctioned and what is taboo, who is an insider and who is not. What gives rituals their efficacy is the ability to provide a shared understanding of social reality as and when rituals are enacted. Bell (1992) views the process of ritualization as part of a repertoire of creative strategies that social actors use to reproduce and reshape their cultural environment. Rites of transition in organizations that serve to socialize, promote, and develop employees operate primarily by helping participants make sense of the significance of various rules that are culturally valued (Ritti and Funkhouser, 1987). Anand and Watson (2004) suggest that cultural rituals such as Oscar and Emmy awards help organizational participants in an industry come together to make sense of who is successful and acclaimed and what trends are popular and worth exploiting. Anand and Watson (2004) show that the Grammy award ceremony played a critical role in the evolution of the popular music industry, since enactment of the ritual provided the occasion to promote the music of award winners and nominees and thus helped deepen the bonds between creative and commercial actors in the field.

See also *enactment; ideology; symbolism*

Bibliography

Anand, N. and Watson, M. R. (2004). Tournament rituals in the evolution of fields: The case of the Grammy awards. *Academy of Management Journal*, **47**, 59–80.

Bell, C. (1992). *Ritual Theory, Ritual Practice*. Oxford: Oxford University Press.

Deal, T. E. and Kennedy, A. (1982). *Corporate Cultures*. Reading, MA: Addison-Wesley.

Durkheim, E. (1965). *The Elementary Forms of the Religious Life*. New York: Free Press.

Kertzer, D. I. (1988). *Ritual, Politics, and Power*. New Haven, CT: Yale University Press.

Kunda, G. (1992). *Engineering Culture: Control and Commitment in a High-Tech Corporation*. Philadelphia, PA: Temple University Press.

Lukes, S. (1975). Political ritual and social integration. *Sociology*, **9**, 289–308.

Ritti, R. and Funkhouser, G. R. (1987). *The Ropes to Skip and the Ropes to Know*. New York: John Wiley and Sons.

Schein, E. H. (1992). *Organizational Culture and Leadership*, 2nd edn. San Francisco: Josey-Bass.

Trice, H. M. and Beyer, J. M. (1984). Studying organizational culture through rites and ceremonials. *Academy of Management Review*, **9**, 653–69.

role

Jeffrey T. Polzer

A role is a delineation of the set of recurrent behaviors appropriate to a particular position in a social system (*see* SYSTEMS THEORY). The social system may range from an informal group to a formal organization. Every social system consists of multiple interdependent positions, each defined by a role. Roles specify many aspects of these relationships, including the AUTHORITY and status relationships within the system. As with social systems, roles can be informal or formal. Informal roles may evolve or be negotiated as a social system such as a group develops. In work organizations, formal roles are often specified by job descriptions.

Roles help us to determine what we should do in order to meet others' expectations, as well as what to expect from others. They are specific to particular positions within particular social systems. Although a person may belong to many different groups and organizations, the role an individual occupies in one social system may be completely different from the role that same individual occupies in other social systems. Furthermore, an individual may occupy more than one role within the same social system.

There are many examples of relatively generic roles that exist in most organizations. The role of boss (i.e., superior, supervisor, manager, etc.) delineates many recurrent behaviors such as evaluating, rewarding, correcting, disciplining, and generally overseeing the work of subordinates in an assertive manner. Likewise, subordinates are expected to behave respectfully and responsively toward their bosses. A person in the role of mentor is expected to be nurturing, patient, and helpful (see MENTORING). A secretary's role includes behaving courteously and in a businesslike manner. While these general roles are fairly universal, many organizational roles delineate much more specific behaviors. However, the exact content of specific role behaviors depends on the particular organization in which the roles are located. For example, a manager in the marketing department of a particular organization may be expected to communicate weekly with a particular production manager, send a summary report to the vice-president of marketing every other week, oversee and evaluate the work of six marketing assistant managers, and entertain certain customers of the company once a month. These specific expectations are unique to the role occupied by the marketing manager in this particular organization.

Because people occupy multiple roles within their social systems, they frequently experience role conflict, when the expectations specified by a person's multiple roles are incompatible. Professionals in organizations often experience role conflict. For example, a corporate lawyer may feel pressures to behave in differing ways from her dual roles as member of the legal profession and employee of the corporation. This latter case is an example of interrole conflict in which there exist incongruent expectations from members of two different role sets. This is distinct from intrarole conflict, which occurs when incongruent expectations are present within a single role set.

Role conflict is one of several role related concepts that facilitate an understanding of the phenomenon of performing a role. Closely related to role conflict is ROLE AMBIGUITY, which is uncertainty about what is expected regarding role performance. Role ambiguity is minimized when role differentiation occurs. Role differentiation refers to the establishment of clear definitions for group members of their specific duties and responsibilities to the group, and how these duties and responsibilities contribute to the realization of the group's goals. Ideally, organizations will go beyond simply making sure that each member has a role and knows what it entails. The roles assigned to group members should also maximize each individual's opportunities to contribute to the objectives of the individual and the social system.

Kahn et al. (1964; Katz and Kahn, 1966) constructed a comprehensive theoretical development of roles. In this conceptualization, each role is surrounded by a role set, which is the collection of people who are concerned with the performance of the occupant of the role. Role episodes consist of role sending, role receiving, and role expectations. When the expectations associated with a particular role are overwhelming to the occupant of the role, role overload occurs. Alternatively, role underload results when there are too few role demands.

Together, these role related concepts form role theory. Role theory is closely related to situated identity theory, which posits that people learn about their role by taking the perspective of others in their role set (Mead, 1934). Because everyone undertakes this process, a mutual understanding develops about what each person's role is. This perspective emphasizes the interpersonal nature of roles; because roles are defined by the expectations of others, conceptually they are an interpersonal phenomenon (Gerth and Mills, 1967). This is true even though roles are often studied with the individual as the unit of analysis.

The concept of role has been very useful to researchers theoretically, but formulating hypotheses about roles requires a specification of which conditions surrounding the role are to be tested. A role is difficult to operationalize without narrowing the inquiry to specific types of role conditions. Thus, research on roles has generally taken the form of looking for correlates of role conditions. Role conditions refer to the role conflict or role ambiguity associated with the role, role overload and role underload, and the other specific concepts discussed above.

Research in several domains of organizational behavior are relevant to roles, for example, research on PERCEPTION, communications, and expectancies. Even though research on these latter topics is not necessarily couched in terms of roles, there are clear connections between these phenomena and role theory.

There are several directions in which research on role conditions could usefully progress. Surprisingly, even after hundreds of studies on various role conditions, there is still debate about the definition of constructs and how best to measure them (King and King, 1990). It is promising that several researchers have been working on conceptually and operationally disentangling these role conditions. As convergence is reached on how to define accurately and measure these constructs, the findings from previous research on correlates of role conditions can be pooled to determine the robustness of these findings (Jackson and Schuler, 1985). As relationships between role conditions and personal and organizational characteristics are determined to be robust, it will be useful to investigate factors that moderate and mediate these relationships to further specify the boundary conditions under which these effects are strongest (for an example of this type of research, see Pierce et al., 1993).

Because of the interpersonal nature of roles and role conditions, integrating the study of networks with the study of roles may increase our understanding of roles within the broader social system. For example, early theorizing on roles suggested that there are objective role conditions and subjective (or perceived) role conditions, but little empirical research investigates the match between objective and subjective role conditions. NETWORK THEORY AND ANALYSIS could shed light on how expectations from other people in the role set match the perceived expectations of the person occupying the role. Similarly, network methods could be used to determine how formal organizational roles (defined by job descriptions, for example) match the informal roles that develop in organizations.

Several current organizational trends may dramatically affect the expectations, and thus the role conditions, of organizational members. For example, how does organizational demography affect role conditions in an increasingly diverse workforce? How does technology, especially regarding communication, affect how role expectations are sent and received? New roles are beginning to emerge in many organizations for people who are technologically proficient. An example of a behavior that is expected from someone in this type of role is to disseminate information about new technologies to less proficient members of the organization. These emerging roles are especially important because surprising degrees of status and power may accompany them. Another important question is how organizational restructuring and the increased use of temporary employees affect the expectations of employees and the patterns of role relationships within organizations. Decreased loyalty to the organization may result in people attaching more importance to their roles outside the organization, especially when role conflict occurs. These issues highlight the importance of furthering our understanding of how roles affect behavior in organizations.

See also *attribution; managerial roles; organizational design; stress*

Bibliography

Ashforth, Blake E. (2001). *Role Transitions in Organizational Life: An Identity-Based Perspective*. Mahwah, NJ: Lawrence Erlbaum Associates.

Gerth, H. and Mills, C. (1967). Institutions and persons. In J. G. Manis and B. N. Meltzer (eds.), *Symbolic Interaction: A Reader in Social Psychology*. Boston, MA: Allyn and Bacon.

Jackson, S. and Schuler, R. (1985). A meta-analysis and conceptual critique of research on role ambiguity and role conflict in work settings. *Organizational Behavior and Human Decision Processes*, **49**, 8–104.

Kahn, R., Wolfe, D., Quinn, R., Snoek, J. and Rosenthal, R. (1964). *Organizational Stress: Studies in Role Conflict and Ambiguity*. New York: Wiley.

Katz, D. and Kahn, R. (1966). *The Social Psychology of Organizations*. New York: Wiley.

King, L. and King, D. (1990). Role conflict and role ambiguity: A critical assessment of construct validity. *Psychological Bulletin*, **107**, 48–64.

Mead, G. (1934). *Mind, Self and Society*. Chicago: University of Chicago Press.

Pierce, J., Gardner, D., Dunham, R., and Cummings, L. (1993). Moderation by organization based self-esteem of role condition-employee response relationships. *Academy of Management Journal*, **36**, 271–88.

role ambiguity

Jeffrey T. Polzer

Role ambiguity denotes uncertainty about the expectations, behaviors, and consequences associated with a particular ROLE. Specifically, a person has a need to know others' expectations of the rights, duties, and responsibilities of the role, the behaviors that will lead to fulfillment of these expectations, and the likely consequences of these role behaviors. Role ambiguity results when these three types of information are non-existent or inadequately communicated. Organizational factors (e.g., rapidly changing organizational structures, job FEEDBACK systems) and individual factors (e.g., information processing biases) may cause role ambiguity. Consequences of role ambiguity may include tension, job dissatisfaction, and TURNOVER. It is useful to distinguish objective role ambiguity from the subjective role ambiguity experienced by the person in the role. A job description is an example of a formal organizational mechanism that may alleviate role ambiguity. Kahn et al. (1964) were the first to extensively develop these elements of role ambiguity within an organizational context. Research indicates that role ambiguity is positively correlated with both anxiety and propensity to leave (the role) and negatively correlated with several factors such as organizational COMMITMENT, EMPLOYEE INVOLVEMENT, and JOB SATISFACTION.

Bibliography

Kahn, R., Wolfe, D., Quinn, R., Snoek, J., and Rosenthal, R. (1964). *Organizational Stress: Studies in Role Conflict and Ambiguity*. New York: Wiley.

role conflict

Catherine Riordan

Role conflict is the experience of contradictory, incompatible, or competing role expectations. It occurs when an individual has two or more salient roles in a situation which include expectations to act in incompatible ways (inter-role conflict), or when expectations within one role are incompatible with each other (intra-role conflict). Conflict between a role and an individual's values or beliefs is also referred to as role conflict. Role conflict is assumed to be an uncomfortable state that individuals are motivated to change.

Current research focuses on characteristic role conflicts like those between family and work, union member and family breadwinner, and foreign and native cultures; the resolution of role conflict; and the evolution of roles within an individual's life. Meta-analyses (*see* VALIDITY; GENERALIZATION) have shown role conflict to be "moderately" ($r = 0.30$) related to dissatisfaction with job content and coworkers (*see* JOB SATISFACTION) and with TURNOVER.

Many studies rely on an eight-item scale, the Role Conflict Scale, developed by Rizzo, House, and Lirtzman (1970). Studies of its construct VALIDITY have concluded it has adequate validity.

See also *conflict and conflict management; job design; role; stress*

Bibliography

Jackson, S. E. and Schuler, R. S. (1985). A meta-analysis and conceptual critique of research on role ambiguity and role conflict in work settings. *Organizational Behavior and Human Decision Processes*, **32**, 16–78.

Rizzo, J. R., House, R. J., and Lirtzman, S. I. (1970). Role conflict and ambiguity in complex organizations. *Administrative Science Quarterly*, **15**, 150–63.

role distancing

Jeffrey T. Polzer

This is behavior (e.g., explanations, apologies, or joking) undertaken by the occupant of a ROLE with the intent of communicating to others that the individual's actions should be attributed to the role rather than to the individual. The person's intention is to create or maintain separateness between herself and the role. The individual is not denying her occupancy of the role; instead, the individual is denying that she would act the same way if it were not for the role. The most likely cause of role distancing is the pressure exerted from another role to act inconsistently from the expectations of the first role (i.e., role conflict). Role distancing behaviors suggest that the individual has some resistance to the role. An example of role distancing is when a teacher explains to students that his disciplinary actions for the student's inappropriate behaviors are not due to him being a mean person, but instead are due to his role as a teacher. The concept of role distancing is embedded in the field of sociology and is most comprehensively developed in Erving Goffman's book *Encounters* (1961).

See also *attribution; self-regulation*

Bibliography

Goffman, E. (1961). *Encounters: Two Studies in the Sociology of Interaction*. Indianapolis, IN: Bobbs-Merrill.

role over/underload

Catherine Riordan

Role overload occurs when an individual experiences excessive role demands. *Quantitative* overload is when role expectations mean there is too much to do. *Qualitative* overload is when the individual does not have the experience or ability to carry out role demands. Having more than one demanding role at the same time, like parent and professional, or a job position with many weighty responsibilities, are frequently researched examples (Marks, 1977). Role underload is the opposite condition in which the individual has very few role demands, or the demands are very easily accomplished. Underload may also be quantitative or qualitative.

Both overload and underload are job stressors. They, in conjunction with other job stressors and the amount of control individuals feel they have over job demands, have been found to be predictive of STRESS related illness. Death from overwork ("karoshi") in Japan or BURNOUT are commonly used examples of the negative consequences of overload. The relationship of overload and underload to variables like ABSENTEEISM, JOB SATISFACTION, and accidents is inconsistent, probably being affected by other moderating variables. Time management techniques are used to deal with problems of quantitative overload.

See also *role; role theory*

Bibliography

Lazarus, R. S. and Folkman, S. (1984). *Stress, Appraisal and Coping*. New York: Springer-Verlag.
Marks, S. R. (1977). Multiple roles and role strain: Some notes on human energy, time and commitment. *American Sociological Review*, **42**, 921–36.

role set

Jeffrey T. Polzer

A role set is the set of people who influence or are concerned with the behavior of the person in a role. A role set typically consists of the people in organizational roles that are directly associated with the focal role, such as those that are adjacent in the work-flow structure or the organizational hierarchy. Members of the ROLE set do not have to be in the same organization as the person in the focal role, however (e.g., customer or salespersons from other organizations can be in the role set).

Role episodes, which include role sending, role receiving, role expectations, and role behavior, occur within the role set. Role expectations are beliefs and attitudes held by members of the role set regarding what behaviors are appropriate for the person in the role. Role sending is the communication of role expectations by members of the role set. Role receiving refers to the perceptions and cognitions by the person in the role of the expectations that are sent by members of the role set. Finally, role behavior refers to the role occupant's recurring actions that are attributable to the role (Katz and Kahn, 1966).

See also *boundary spanning; network theory and analysis; role theory; systems theory*

Bibliography

Katz, D. and Kahn, R. (1966). *The Social Psychology of Organizations*. New York: Wiley.

role taking

Catherine Riordan

ROLE taking, or "taking the role of the other," is a process in which individuals develop an empathetic understanding of other people's roles. George Herbert Mead stated role taking is essential to developing individuals' own role identities. In this sense, roles develop in relation to other people and are influenced by culture (Stone and Stone-Romero, 2004). Theoretically, it is presumed that for interactions to be smooth, interactants must achieve implicit or explicit agreement about their relative roles, although not all research evidence is consistent with this presumption.

Often, situations imply specific roles, which may explain why people familiar with a situation sometimes can predict others' behaviors. Individuals, too, can become identified with the roles they take consistently (e.g., a leader). Some individuals have stronger aptitudes for "role taking."

Perspective taking is a contemporary area of investigation that emerged out of the role taking theories and is being shown to be a moderator of interpersonal interaction and evaluations (Batson et al., 2003).

See also *rituals; role theory*

Bibliography

Batson, C. D., Lishner, D. A., Carpenter, A., Dulin, L., Harjusola-Webb, S., Stocks, E. L., et al. (2003). "As you would have them do unto you": Does imagining yourself in the other's place stimulate moral action? *Personality and Social Psychology Bulletin*, **29**, 1190–1204.

Stone, D. L. and Stone-Romero, E. F. (2004). The influence of culture on role-taking in culturally diverse organizations. In M. S. Stockdale and F. J. Crosby (eds.), *The Psychology and Management of Workplace Diversity*. Malden, MA: Blackwell, 78–99.

role theory

Jeffrey T. Polzer

Role theory specifies the conceptual relationships among several distinct role conditions (*see* ROLE for an extended discussion of these role conditions). Role theory is concerned with the general question of how an individual's behavior is connected to his or her social environment. One of the earlier contemporary conceptions of role theory was enumerated by Kahn et al. (1964). This theory posits that, in most social situations, and especially within organizations, the role that a person takes is "the central fact for understanding the behavior of the individual" (Katz and Kahn, 1966) (*see* ROLE TAKING). The organization is conceptualized as a system of roles, with the ROLE SET of a particular position in an organization consisting of role episodes, which include role sending, role receiving, role expectations, and role behavior.

The greatest contribution of this theory is probably its detailed conceptual description of how people are affected by their social situation, particularly the expectations of the social actors to whom they are connected. Most research related to this theory tests relationships among specific role conditions, organizational and individual characteristics (e.g., hierarchical structure, individual self-esteem), and organizational and personal outcomes (e.g., performance, job satisfaction).

See also *network theory and analysis; managerial roles; systems theory*

Bibliography

Kahn, R., Wolfe, D., Quinn, R., Snoek, J., and Rosenthal, R. (1964). *Organizational Stress: Studies in Role Conflict and Ambiguity*. New York: Wiley.

Katz, D. and Kahn, R. (1966). *The Social Psychology of Organizations*. New York: Wiley.

role transitions

Blake Ashforth

This process refers to the psychological and (if relevant) physical movement between positions in a social system(s), encompassing disengagement from one ROLE (role exit) and subsequent engagement in another (role entry) (Ashforth, 2001; Burr, 1972). The process includes *macro* role transitions between sequentially held roles, such as a student accepting her first full-time job or an assembly worker accepting a promotion to foreman, and *micro* role transitions between simultaneously held roles, such as shifts between one's home and work roles or between one's work roles of subordinate and co-worker. A subtle but important point is that role transitions, whether macro or micro, involve both an exit and an entry and the nature of each affects the other. For example, an involuntary retirement may sour one's acceptance of the retiree role, and a prestigious transfer may help one come to terms with leaving beloved co-workers. Another important point is that role transitions often involve a period of "liminality" (Turner, 1969) where the individual is psychologically if not physically between roles and the grip of each is muted, thereby facilitating personal change and acceptance of that change by others.

Research on macro role transitions is voluminous. First, there is abundant research on specific transitions, particularly job entry, job transfers, and TURNOVER. This research has produced some fairly detailed models of certain transitions, such as school-to-work, international transfers, and involuntary layoffs (e.g., Hom and Griffeth, 1995). However, this work provides little sense of how generalizable these models are to other transitions. Further, this research tends to focus on either role exit or role entry, neglecting their interaction.

Second, there is also abundant research on SOCIALIZATION (e.g., Bauer, Morrison, and Callister, 1998). This research has tended to focus on either the *processes* through which newcomers "learn the ropes" during role entry or the *content* of what they learn. Much of this research has emphasized situational variables (e.g., socialization tactics, information to be learned) and implicitly viewed newcomers as inanimate clay waiting to be molded. More recently, however, research on newcomer information seeking has examined the proactive strategies used by neophytes to learn about and shape their work environments.

Third, there is promising – albeit less – research on generic process models of work role transitions (Ashford and Taylor, 1990; Ashforth, 2001; Brett, 1984; Nicholson, 1984; Stephens, 1994). These models have two major strengths. First, they are applicable to numerous role transitions. For instance, Ashforth (2001) argues that a given transition will tend to be more diffi-

cult for the individual if the contrast between the roles is high, the transition is socially undesirable and irreversible, the transition is involuntary and unpredictable, the individual goes through either exit or entry alone, and the transition period is short. Second, the generic models have a strong interactionist flavor, that is, they include individual and situational variables. For example, the most widely cited of these models – Nicholson's (1984) work role transitions theory – argues that adjustment to a new role involves personal development and/or role development, and that the particular form of adjustment results from combinations of individual traits (desire for control, desire for feedback) and job related variables (discretion, role novelty) (*see* PERSONALITY). However, although these generic models have shed much light on role entry, particularly of organizational newcomers, they have excluded prior role exit (see Ashforth, 2001, for an exception).

In contrast to research on macro role transitions, research on micro transitions has been relatively scant. However, promising leads can be found in studies of commuting and telecommuting, juggling inter-role conflicts, role blurring (e.g., a client becomes a friend), and erecting boundaries between home and work in home office situations (Ashforth, Kreiner, and Fugate, 2000). The major research questions in such studies are how individuals manage recurring transitions between important but typically very different roles, and how inter-role interruptions and conflicts affect one's ability to immerse oneself in and enact a role (*see* ENACTMENT).

Prospects for future research on macro and micro role transitions are very bright. Regarding macro transitions, the increasing turbulence of organizational life suggests that individuals can expect to change jobs and employers more often than in the past. As careers become less stable, research on the psychological dynamics of transitioning becomes more important. For instance, what are the key turning points that precipitate role exit? What role do social referents play as one considers exiting a role or entering a new one? Are there certain rituals, people, and objects that serve as "transition bridges" to facilitate movement between roles? Over time, what personal narratives do individuals create to give prospective and retrospective meaning to their role transitions?

Regarding micro transitions, the same turbulence in organizational life has spawned various flexible work arrangements. As the traditional physical, spatial, and temporal boundaries and routines that divide home and work dissolve, it becomes necessary for individuals to actively attend to the psychological dynamics of role exit and entry. For example, to what extent do individuals prefer to segment rather than integrate their roles and can these preferences be traced to individual difference variables? In the absence of conventional boundaries between home and work, how and to what extent do individuals create idiosyncratic boundaries? In the workplace, how do individuals manage situations where they are required simultaneously to enact multiple roles (e.g., supervisor, co-worker, company representative)? To what extent do individuals develop "transition scripts" to facilitate recurring transitions?

See also *career development; identity, organizational; identity, personal; learning, individual*

Bibliography

Ashford, S. J. and Taylor, M. S. (1990). Adaptation to work transitions: An integrative approach. *Research in Personnel and Human Resources Management*, 8, 1–39.

Ashforth, B. E. (2001). *Role Transitions in Organizational Life: An Identity-Based Perspective*. Mahwah, NJ: Lawrence Erlbaum Associates.

Ashforth, B. E., Kreiner, G. E., and Fugate, M. (2000). All in a day's work: Boundaries and micro role transitions. *Academy of Management Review*, 25, 472–91.

Bauer, T. N., Morrison, E. W., and Callister, R. R. (1998). Organizational socialization: A review and directions for future research. *Research in Personnel and Human Resources Management*, 16, 149–214.

Brett, J. M. (1984). Job transitions and person and role development. *Research in Personnel and Human Resources Management*, 2, 155–85.

Burr, W. R. (1972). Role transitions: A reformulation of theory. *Journal of Marriage and the Family*, 34, 407–16.

Hom, P. W. and Griffeth, R. W. (1995). *Employee Turnover*. Cincinnati, OH: South-Western.

Nicholson, N. (1984). A theory of work-role transitions. *Administrative Science Quarterly*, 29, 172–91.

Stephens, G. K. (1994). Crossing internal career boundaries: The state of research on subjective career transitions. *Journal of Management*, 20, 479–501.

Turner, V. W. (1969). *The Ritual Process: Structure and Anti-Structure*. Chicago: Aldine.

routinization

see ORGANIZATIONAL DESIGN; ORGANIZATIONAL STRUCTURE

rules

see BUREAUCRACY; MANAGEMENT, CLASSICAL THEORY

S

sabotage

see DEVIANCE

satisfaction

see ATTITUDE THEORY; JOB SATISFACTION

satisficing

Susan Miller

Satisficing refers to a choice situation in which decision-makers look for a course of action that is "good enough"; that is, one that satisfies and suffices, rather than selecting the optimum from a full range of alternatives.

Classical theories of DECISION-MAKING see the decision-maker as an economic actor who, when faced with a decision, rationally diagnoses the problem, draws up a complete range of alternative solutions, evaluates each against explicit criteria, and is therefore able to make a choice that maximizes outcomes.

Behavioral decision theory acknowledges that decision-makers often operate in complex environments where there is much uncertainty. Issues compete for attention so that many potential decisions do not get on the agenda. If they do, definition is problematic, many alternative solutions exist, and criteria are often unclear and conflicting.

So the organizational decision-maker has to simplify, and the limitations of human cognitive capacities and constraints of time mean that not every aspect of the situation can be examined in full. The analogy often given is that one is not looking for the sharpest needle in the haystack, only one sharp enough to sew with. Decision-makers therefore operate within a BOUNDED RATIONALITY and satisficing solutions are the result.

See also *behavioral decision research; managerial and organizational cognition*

Bibliography

March, J. G. and Simon, H. A. (1993). *Organizations.* Oxford: Blackwell.
Simon, H. A. (1997). *Administrative Behavior*, 4th edn. New York: Free Press.

scientific management

John Kelly

Scientific management refers to the theory and practice of management originated by Frederick Winslow Taylor (1856–1915), an American engineer best known for his development of time and motion study. Taylor became concerned about the collective controls over output exercised by skilled workers and reinforced by strong social norms (see GROUP NORMS). He attributed management's inability to tackle these problems to its lack of scientific knowledge of the production process and therefore proposed to measure the time required for each element of a job in order to establish the "one best way" of performing that job, and the level of output that was possible. Management would then be able to reassert its control over production and prescribe work methods and output goals. Taylor also believed that jobs should be divided up into small units; workers should be motivated with financial incentives linked to performance (see MOTIVATION); they should be allocated a daily work quota (see GOAL SETTING); they should be subject to close supervision; and factory departments should be reorganized to permit the most efficient flow of work and materials. Henry Ford combined these ideas with a moving assembly line to establish even tighter control of work levels (Kelly, 1982; Littler, 1982; Rose, 1988).

Underlying Taylor's ideas was a set of assumptions referred to as Theory X (*see* THEORY X AND Y): workers are alienated from their work, wish to avoid high levels of effort, are motivated solely or largely by pay, and distrust management. The worker–management relationship is therefore based on low TRUST, although Taylor believed cooperation was possible given high wages, high productivity, and positive attitudes by both parties.

Taylor and his associates measured a wide range of jobs in a range of industries, especially engineering, construction, and transportation, and often raised labor productivity, although the more spectacular claims of 100 percent productivity increases were almost certainly exaggerated. At the same time, Taylor's practices and his authoritarian way of implementing them produced intense hostility from unionized workers, and the use of time and motion study became the focus of bitter conflict until well into the 1960s. Trade unions objected to the deskilling of work (*see* JOB DESKILLING), to increased managerial control, and to the "speed up" or intensification of effort levels.

The popularity of Taylor's ideas has fluctuated over time. Although widely used throughout manufacturing industry in the 1950s, a reaction set in during the following decades. A growing number of firms moved towards job enlargement or multi-tasking and academic theorists of work motivation increasingly emphasized intrinsic work motivation, downplaying the role of pay. Taylor's ideas continue to be criticized in textbooks, but during the past two decades there has nonetheless been renewed interest in many of his principles. Detailed measurement and control of work is commonplace in low-skill growth areas of the economy such as call centers and fast food outlets, as well as in the highly competitive Japanese manufacturing plants (Royle, 2000). Performance related pay is now widely used for many white collar workers, including professionals.

See also *bureaucracy; management, classical theory; organizational effectiveness*

Bibliography

Kelly, J. (1982). *Scientific Management, Job Redesign, and Work Performance*. London: Academic Press.

Littler, C. (1982). *The Development of the Labour Process in Capitalist Societies*. London: Heinemann.

Rose, M. (1988). *Industrial Behavior: Theoretical Development since Taylor*, 3rd edn. London: Penguin Books.

Royle, T. (2000). *Working for McDonald's in Europe: The Unequal Struggle*. London: Routledge.

self-actualization

Paul E. Spector

Self-actualization is the fifth and highest level need of Maslow's (1943) need hierarchy (*see* MOTIVATION). It is the fulfilment of a person's life goals and potential. Maslow defined it as "the desire to become ... everything that one is capable of becoming" (Maslow, 1943: 382). According to theory, self-actualization is a need that motivates people's behavior. A person whose self-actualization need is met is said to be self-actualized, but few are thought to achieve this state. Many famous people in the arts and sciences have been presumed to have achieved self-actualization.

Self-actualization is somewhat akin to the growth need strength component of Hackman and Oldham's (1976) job characteristics theory. Both these concepts share the idea that people have a need for continual development throughout their life. Growth need strength, however, is a PERSONALITY characteristic that varies among people.

See also *creativity; human relations movement; job satisfaction; self-regulation*

Bibliography

Hackman, J. R. and Oldham, G. R. (1976). Motivation through the design of work: Test of a theory. *Organizational Behavior and Human Performance*, 16, 250–79.

Maslow, A. H. (1943). A theory of human motivation. *Psychological Review*, 50, 370–96.

self-efficacy

Paul Spector and Lisa Penney

Self-efficacy is the extent to which a person feels capable and effective in a particular domain in life or in accomplishing a particular task. Self-efficacy theory (Bandura, 1982) states that self-efficacy is a major determinant of individual motivation and performance. People who have high self-efficacy believe that they are able to successfully perform a task and should put forth more effort and persist longer at a task. Individuals who have low self-efficacy, however, do not believe in their ability to perform a task well and as a result, have lower MOTIVATION and put forth less effort.

Self-efficacy is domain/task specific. In other words, a person can have different levels of self-efficacy for various domains/tasks. For example, an engineer may have high self-efficacy for dealing with the technical demands of work, but low self-efficacy for dealing with people. This would explain why some engineers are perceived as having poor social skills, although they make valuable technical contributions. The theory would predict that engineers would put forth greater effort on the technical aspects of their work than the interpersonal aspects.

The concept of self-efficacy is somewhat like the expectancy theory concept of expectancy. The difference is that expectancy concerns people's beliefs about their ability to accomplish a task at a given point in time in a specific situation. Self-efficacy concerns a person's belief about how good they are at a task in general across time and situations.

The process by which self-efficacy affects motivation and performance is similar to a self-fulfilling prophecy. Eden and his associates refer to this as the Galatea effect, wherein individuals' beliefs about their own capabilities lead them to perform better. Self-efficacy may also work through goal setting. In a study of students in a typing course, McIntire and Levine (1991) found that students who had high self-efficacy before the class began set higher goals than students who had low self-efficacy prior to taking the course.

Research on self-efficacy theory has supported its predictions for task performance in a number of situations (Locke and Latham, 1990). For example, Tierney and Farmer (2002) developed a measure to assess creative self-efficacy at work. They found in two separate samples that those who scored high on their measure were rated by supervisors as being high on creative task performance.

The theory has useful implications for organizational effectiveness as it suggests that employee performance can be improved by enhancing self-efficacy. This can be accomplished in a number of ways. Bandura (1982) suggested that self-efficacy is affected by past experiences. Therefore, self-efficacy can be developed by exposing individuals to simple tasks with a high probability for success and gradually increasing the difficulty of the tasks. The early successes should lead to an increase in self-efficacy, which in turn would lead to greater persistence, effort, and success on the more difficult tasks. Moreover, results of a study by Karl, O'Leary-Kelly, and Martocchio (1993) found that providing positive FEEDBACK to individuals low in self-efficacy for a speed reading task raised self-efficacy.

Additional research suggests that self-efficacy can be manipulated through training. Gibson (2001) found that providing nurses with GOAL-SETTING training increased self-efficacy following training, as well as effectiveness on the job. Morin and Latham (2000) reported gains in self-efficacy for employees who participated in communication skills training that involved lectures, observational learning, role playing, and mental rehearsal of the new skills.

Recent work has also shown a link between self-efficacy and stress. Jex et al. (2001) argued that individuals with low levels of self-efficacy would feel less capable of handling work demands, and thus would be more likely to perceive stressors in the work environment, and thus they should experience more strain. Their study of US Army personnel showed that self-efficacy related to perceptions of stressors (work overload) as well as psychological strain (emotional distress) as expected.

See also *job satisfaction; self-regulation*

Bibliography

Bandura, A. (1982). Self-efficacy mechanisms in human agency. *American Psychologist*, 37, 122–47.

Eden, D. and Aviram, A. (1993). Self-efficacy training to speed reemployment: Helping people to help themselves. *Journal of Applied Psychology*, **78**, 352–60.

Eden, D. and Zuk, Y. (1995). Seasickness as a self-fulfilling prophecy: Raising self-efficacy to boost performance at sea. *Journal of Applied Psychology*, **80**, 628–35.

Gibson, C. B. (2001). Me and us: Differential relationships among goal-setting training, efficacy and effectiveness at the individual and team level. *Journal of Organizational Behavior*, **22**, 789–808.

Jex, S. M., Bliese, P. D., Buzzell, S., and Primeau, J. (2001). The impact of self-efficacy on stressor-strain relations: Coping style as an explanatory mechanism. *Journal of Applied Psychology*, **86**, 401–9.

Karl, K. A., O'Leary-Kelly, A. M., and Martocchio, J. J. (1993). The impact of feedback and self-efficacy on performance in training. *Journal of Organizational Behavior*, **14**, 379–94.

Locke, E. A. and Latham, G. P. (1990). *A Theory of Goal Setting and Task Performance*. Englewood Cliffs, NJ: Prentice-Hall.

McIntire, S. A. and Levine, E. L. (1991). Combining personality variables and goals to predict performance. *Journal of Vocational Behavior*, **38**, 288–301.

Morin, L. and Latham, G. P. (2000). The effect of mental practice and goal setting as a transfer of training intervention on supervisors' self-efficacy and communication skills: An exploratory study. *Applied Psychology: An International Review*, **49**, 566–78.

Tierney, P. and Farmer, S. M. (2002). Creative self-efficacy: Its potential antecedents and relationship to creative performance. *Academy of Management Journal*, **45**, 1137–48.

self-esteem

Paul E. Spector

Self-esteem is the attitude that a person has about himself or herself, as a good or bad person, and the extent to which people like themselves. Self-esteem has been considered a PERSONAL-ITY trait, a stable individual difference in the extent to which people hold positive or negative views of themselves. People who are high in self-esteem have been found to be psychologically better adjusted, to perform better in school, to handle criticism more appropriately, and to cope better with failure (Baron and Byrne, 1991).

Tharenou (1979) summarized the research on self-esteem in the work domain. She found that high esteem was positively associated with job satisfaction and intention to stay on the job (*see* TURNOVER). Low esteem was associated with poor employee health, but it is not clear whether esteem affects health. Tharenou suggests that both low self-esteem and poor health may be responses to STRESS on the job. Research has failed to find relations of esteem with job performance in field settings. The more task specific variable of self-efficacy seems to have more promise in explaining and predicting task performance.

See also *persistence; personality; self-regulation*

Bibliography

Baron, R. A. and Byrne, D. (1991). *Social Psychology*. Needham Heights, MA: Allyn and Bacon.

Tharenou, P. (1979). Employee self-esteem: A review of the literature. *Journal of Vocational Behavior*, **15**, 316–46.

self-management

see EMPLOYEE INVOLVEMENT; SELF-MANAGING TEAMS

self-managing teams

John Cordery

A self-managing team is a formally constituted work group whose members perform a set of interdependent tasks, share collective responsibility for a readily identifiable set of outcomes, and who are afforded moderate to high levels of discretion when it comes to regulating the way their work is executed (*see* WORK GROUPS/TEAMS). Sometimes called semi-autonomous work groups, they are commonly associated with sociotechnical systems interventions and commitment oriented human resource management strategies.

In practice, the degree of self-management responsibility exercised by these teams may span three areas of DECISION-MAKING. First, there are decisions associated with regulating the immediate production or work process. Teams may be responsible for determining the pace and order of task performance, for securing a requisite supply of materials and resources, or for liaising with suppliers and customers. Second, there are decisions concerning the internal governance of the team, such as scheduling leave, and hiring and training new members. Third, there are decisions that affect the team's role within the organization, such as determining what gets produced or the type of service that is provided to customers.

Self-managing teams are seen as having a beneficial impact on employee behavior, specifically through the enhancement of MOTIVATION, SKILL utilization, and learning. To the extent that team members are likely to perceive heightened autonomy, identity, and impact associated with their work, they also experience feelings of psychological empowerment (Kirkman and Rosen, 2000), leading to greater effort and PERSISTENCE on tasks. The intrinsic rewards associated with work characteristics experienced by members of self-managing teams may also be reflected in positive work attitudes, particularly JOB SATISFACTION, and affect related behaviors such as absence, extra-role performance, and voluntary TURNOVER. Direct performance benefits may also derive from the fact that the breadth, flexibility, and autonomy associated with work roles within self-managing teams encourages members to make full use of their existing skills and knowledge, while also learning from those around them. There are also significant organizational advantages. Self-managing teams typically reduce the need for administrative, managerial, and technical support staff, reducing indirect labor costs.

While self-managing teams offer these potential benefits, their promise is not always fulfilled. One reason for this is that certain technical and social contexts suit their introduction more than others, for example where task interdependence and operational uncertainty associated with work processes are high, and where cultural values support collectivism. Within the team itself, dysfunctional processes may be fueled by the heightened autonomy afforded the team, leading to concertive control, where undue pressure is exerted on members to conform to internal norms or where the team isolates itself from the rest of the organization and its manage-

ment (Barker, 1993; Levy, 2001). Other reasons for self-managing team failure lie outside the boundaries of the team. External leaders influence the extent to which teams are allowed to exercise sufficient autonomy, as well as helping the team clarify performance goals and strategies and obtain necessary material resources (Hackman, 2002). Rewards systems can also hinder the effective operation of self-managing teams, to the extent that they focus on rewarding individual as opposed to team outcomes.

See also *group dynamics; participation; team building*

Bibliography

Barker, J. R. (1993). Tightening the iron cage: Concertive control in self-managing teams. *Administrative Science Quarterly*, 37, 634–5.

Cohen, S. G. and Bailey, D. E. (1997). What makes teams work: Group effectiveness research from the shopfloor to the executive suite. *Journal of Management*, 23, 239–90.

Hackman, J. R. (2002). *Leading Teams: Setting the Stage for Great Performances.* Boston, MA: Harvard Business School Press.

Kirkman, B. L. and Rosen, B. (2000). Powering up teams. *Organizational Dynamics*, 28, 48–66.

Levy, P. F. (2001). The Nut Island effect: When good teams go wrong. *Harvard Business Review*, March, 51–9.

self-monitoring

see PERSONALITY; SELF-REGULATION

self-regulation

Ginka Toegel and Nigel Nicholson

Self-regulation refers to a set of processes that enable individuals to guide their goal directed activities over time and across changing contexts (Karoly, 1993). As yet this does not constitute a unitary body of knowledge and theory, but a collection of ideas running in parallel from the same core insight. Its insight (whose origins can perhaps even be attributed to Freud in his treatment of the ego) is that the self is the psychological agency that exists in order to coordinate human thought, feeling, and action. Some authors use the terms "self-regulation" and "self-control" interchangeably (Baumeister and Vohs, 2003).

At the core of self-regulation processes is the maintenance of goal directedness and functional integrity. For this reason, it is generally perceptions that shift to adapt to goals, rather than the reverse (Powers, 1973). Processes of self-regulation – modulation of thought, affect, action, and attention – are initiated when a routine is impeded or when goal directedness is made salient, for example by a new challenge or a failure (Karoly, 1993). Much self-regulation seems to be focused on mood control – maintaining positive affect for motivated people, and underpinning negative affect for depressed or helpless people, for whom psychological consistency is a psychological anchor.

Extensive research has focused on the closed loop control models of self-regulation like Test-Operate-Test-Exit and on "if-then" control systems. Enlarging the frame of analysis, Carver and Scheier (1981) introduced a more general control theory, which incorporates the role of self-awareness. The basic premise of their theory is that attention constantly fluctuates between the self and the outside world. Stimuli like audiences or physiological arousal, for example, may focus attention on the self. As a result, a tendency to compare the present state with a behavioral standard is activated. Self-regulation is a dynamic process based on the operation of FEEDBACK. The feedback reflects the information conveyed by the act's consequences. It leads to decisions whether the individual should continue the action, change it, or disengage from it. In that sense, self-regulation is promoted by discrepancy-reducing feedback loops, which imply that the perception of a present condition is compared against a reference value. A perception of discrepancy is followed by a behavior, which aims at the reduction of the discrepancy. The speed of improvement determines the emotional response. Moving towards one's goals makes the individual feel good, while moving too slowly towards the goals, or even away from them, makes people feel bad.

Self-regulation is a complex process. The Regulatory Focus theory (Higgins, 1998), for example, suggests that self-regulation operates differently when serving different needs. While survival needs activate a "promotion focus" of self-regulation (presence or absence of positive outcomes, i.e., gains/non-gains; advancement and accomplishment), security needs lead to a "prevention focus" (absence and presence of negative outcomes, i.e., non-losses/losses; protection, safety, and responsibility). Consequently, there are different means of goal attainment. These theorists say that when in a promotion focus an "eagerness" approach predominates (concern to maintain positive outcomes), while in a prevention focus, the strategy is a "vigilance" approach (energies devoted to avoidance of negative outcomes).

A substantial body of research has examined why people fail at self-regulation. Recent studies have suggested a resource depletion model, which compares self-regulation with a muscle. According to this approach, self-regulation consumes cognitive resources and therefore is vulnerable to temporary depletion as a result of strenuous use (Muraven and Baumeister, 2000).

See also *identity, personal; perception; personality; promotion/prevention focus*

Bibliography

Baumeister, R. and Vohs, K. (2003). Self-regulation and executive function of the self. In M. Leary and J. Tangney (eds.), *Handbook of Self and Identity*. New York: Guilford Press.

Carver, C. and Scheier, M. (1981). *Attention and Self-Regulation: A Control-Theory Approach to Human Behavior*. New York: Springer Verlag.

Higgins, E. (1998). Promotion and prevention: Regulatory focus as a motivational principle. In M. Zanna (ed.), *Advances in Experimental Social Psychology*, Vol. 30. New York: Academic Press, 1–46.

Karoly, P. (1993). Mechanisms of self-regulation: A systems view. *Annual Review of Psychology*, **44**, 23.

Muraven, M. and Baumeister, R. F. (2000). Self-regulation and depletion of limited resources: Does self-control resemble a muscle? *Psychological Bulletin*, **126** (2), 247–59.

Powers, W. (1973). *Behavior: The Control of Perception*. Chicago: Aldine.

sex differences

see GENDER; WOMEN AT WORK

sex roles

see GENDER; WOMEN MANAGERS

sexual harassment

Barbara A. Gutek

Sexual harassment is broadly defined as unwelcome verbal or physical sexual overtures that may be made a condition of employment or otherwise affect one's job or CAREER and/or create a hostile or intimidating work environment. Sexual harassment is treatment based on GENDER, constitutes a form of STRESS for victims, is an impediment to equal opportunity, and thus is a human resource management issue. Most of the research focuses on three questions: (1) How common is it? (2) How do people define it? (3) What do theories such as social identity theory or sex-role spillover contribute to our understanding it? In countries where research has been done, an estimated 25–50 percent of women have been sexually harassed sometime in their work life. Women who work in non-traditional jobs are more likely than other women to be sexually harassed, in part because of the amount of contact they have with men in their work. While men can be and are harassed by both sexes, many fewer men than women are harassed. Although it is somewhat "subjective" in nature, research shows that most people agree that behavior like fondling and sexual overtures accompanied by job threats are sexual harassment. There is, however, disagreement about the less severe behavior. Many researchers have examined the factors such as gender that affect the definition of sexual harassment. Although the gender effect appears to be small, it is widely discussed as evidence that sexual harassment is subjective.

See also *deviance; diversity management; women at work*

Bibliography

Gutek, B. A. and Done, R. (2001). Sexual harassment. In R. Unger (ed.), *Handbook of the Psychology of Women and Gender*. New York: Wiley and Sons.
O'Donohue, W. (1997). *Sexual Harassment: Theory, Research and Treatment*. Needham Heights, MA: Allyn and Bacon.

skill

Joyce Hogan

Skill is proficiency on a specific task. The definition includes an evaluation of the level of proficiency (e.g., highly skilled) and the task to be accomplished (e.g., drive a car). Skills are acquired through learning and experience. Perceptual and motor skills require voluntary coordinated movement to execute a task. Cognitive and social skills require interpreting and controlling COMMUNICATIONS and then responding. In the workplace, basic skills include reading comprehension, active listening, writing, and speaking, as well as mathematics and science. Cross-functional skills for work related tasks include problem solving skills, social skills, technical skills, systems skills, and resource management skills (US Department of Labor, 2001). Current interest in identifying occupational skills stems from the need to prepare workers for jobs of the twenty-first century (Mumford, Peterson, and Childs, 1999).

Skill builds from an ability (talent) foundation of basic COMPETENCY and extends performance proficiency to specific activities. Basic ABILITY is a prerequisite for skill; skills depend on practice FEEDBACK and learning, and they are the product of training. Ability influences the rate of skill acquisition and the level of performance a person can achieve. Measurement of skill is specific to the task under consideration and content valid tests provide accurate assessments. Examples of such evaluations are assessment center exercises, mechanical maintenance tests, and threat detection x-ray image tests. Skill tests, supported by content VALIDITY evidence, are used widely for CAREER counseling, job referral, apprentice training, and personnel selection.

See also *ability; individual differences*

Bibliography

Mumford, M. D., Peterson, N. G., and Childs, R. A. (1999). Basic and cross-functional skills. In N. G. Peterson, M. D. Mumford, W. C. Borman, P. R. Jeanneret, and E. A. Fleishman (eds.), *An Occupational Information System for the 21st Century: The Development of the O*NET*. Washington, DC: American Psychological Association.

US Department of Labor, Employment, and Training Administration (2001). *O*NET Online*. (Online Access: online.onetcenter.org). Washington, DC: Author.

slack resources

Henrich Greve

Slack resources are resources in excess of what is required to reward the dominant coalition that governs the organization (Cyert and March, 1963). Organizations can accumulate slack resources when they earn greater profits than they are expected to distribute. Slack resources relieve scarcity, increase allocation of resources to projects sought by subunits, and reduce monitoring of profitability, allowing greater experimentation. Consequently, slack resources are thought to increase INNOVATIONS and RISK TAKING in organizations. These effects may be contingent on other variables such as the organizational performance. Slack resources are usually operationalized through accounting measures of resources absorbed as extra cost or available as financial reserves (Bourgeois, 1981). Empirical analysis of slack resources has generally shown the predicted effects, but sometimes the findings have been weak. Slack resources are seen as a promising construct with potential to explain organizational changes, and especially changes that have proven difficult to predict from other theories, such as organizational experimentation and innovation. Because slack interacts with other variables affecting organizational decision-making, studies controlling for confounding effects should show stronger results. Future work seems likely to focus on establishing how slack interacts with other variables and developing and testing new measures of slack resources.

See also *organizational change; resource dependence; systems theory*

Bibliography

Bourgeois, L. J. (1981). On the measurement of organizational slack. *Academy of Management Review*, 6, 29–39.

Cyert, R.M. and March, J. G. (1963). *The Behavioral Theory of the Firm*. Englewood Cliffs, NJ: Prentice-Hall.

social capital

Brenda Ghitulescu and Carrie Leana

Social capital refers to the resources available through networks of social relationships possessed by an individual or a social unit. Social capital is a broad concept that describes the value of connections and has been conceptualized in different ways, including network position (Burt, 1992), network structure (Coleman, 1988), shared cognitions (Nahapiet and Ghoshal, 1998), and collective norms and sanctions.

There are two major approaches to the concept. The first, labeled bridging social capital, defines social capital as an attribute of an individual actor or unit and is focused on his or her relative position in a larger network (*see* NETWORK THEORY AND ANALYSIS). The advantages of this type of social capital are realized by actors who span disconnected others within a network, and include faster access to information, stronger influence among peers, and higher compensation and promotions. The second, labeled bonding or organizational social capital (Leana and Van Buren, 1999), defines social capital as an attribute of a collective realized through social relationships among its members. Its advantages are realized through a dense network of relationships that fosters shared norms of reciprocity and trust, and include more efficient collective action, enhanced intellectual capital, better use of information, and collective prosperity.

Social capital's potential benefits are not without potential risks. The potential liabilities of social capital include insulation of the group from diverse sources of ideas, high maintenance costs of relationships, or conformity to GROUP NORMS that undermines INNOVATION (Leana and Van Buren, 1999; Adler and Kwon, 2002). Given these potential negative consequences, investments in bonding social capital within an organization need to be balanced by investments in bridging social capital of individuals, units, and the organization.

Recent models of organizational social capital have proposed multiple dimensions of the concept. The most inclusive model (Nahapiet and Ghoshal, 1998) proposed three dimensions: structural, describing the dimensions of the networks; relational, including shared norms, trust, and obligations; and cognitive, including knowledge, language, and narratives. Social capital differs from other constructs such as GROUP COHESIVENESS, which focuses on affective bonds within a group, or social networks, which consider the structure but not the affective content of relationships. Social capital is generally seen as a value added construct, with the potential to predict performance beyond the effects of other resources, such as human capital.

We know much more about social capital's character and effects than about what explains its formation and maintenance. While self-interest drives individuals in building their bridging social capital because of its direct benefits to individuals, we know less about how successful collective action occurs, because of the less direct benefits for the individual actor. In organizations, management practices that create employee stability are important in the formation and maintenance of organizational social capital, while outsourcing and downsizing lead to its destruction (Leana and Van Buren, 1999).

In light of recent empirical evidence, the prospects of social capital as a value added concept are promising. While there is still a need for more research in this area, recent studies have increasingly pointed to the fact that social capital can be a powerful predictor of performance for individuals, groups, and organizations.

See also *networking; organizational citizenship; professional service firms*

Bibliography

Adler, P. S. and Kwon, S. W. (2002). Social capital: Prospects for a new concept. *Academy of Management Review*, 27, 17–40.
Burt, R. S. (1992). *Structural Holes: The Social Structure of Competition*. Cambridge, MA: Harvard University Press.
Coleman, J. S. (1988). Social capital in the creation of human capital. *American Journal of Sociology*, 94 (supplement): S95–120.
Leana, C. R. and Van Buren, H. J., III (1999). Organizational social capital and employment practices. *Academy of Management Review*, 24, 34–59.
Nahapiet, J. and Ghoshal, S. (1998). Social capital, intellectual capital, and the organizational advantage. *Academy of Management Review*, 23, 242–66.

social comparison

Stuart Albert

The theory of social comparison, developed by Leon Festinger in 1954, is a set of hypotheses, corollaries, and deviations concerned with why, with whom, and to what effect people compare themselves with other people. Festinger (1954b) assumed a motive to know that one's opinions are correct and to know what one is and is not capable of doing. This leads to "derivations" about the conditions under which social comparison processes arise and about its nature. For example, a process of social comparison arises when a person cannot directly evaluate his or her opinions or abilities by objective non-social evidence. When that occurs, individuals use other persons as points of comparison, preferably others who are similar to themselves. One ceases comparison with another person when that person becomes very divergent from one's self.

There have been many recent developments; for example, a focus on the process of downward comparison, that is, comparison with a person who is less well off, rather than the upward comparison (comparison with a person who is better off). Festinger (1954a) believed that under certain conditions one would compare oneself with persons of slightly better ability. Indeed, there has been a recent explosion of interest which is impossible to succinctly summarize. As Buunk and Mussweiler (2001: 172) note, the theory has moved "from a specific, well defined theory, to a broad field of research." The interested reader can find an excellent overview of this expansion in Suls and Wheeler (2000). Although many aspects of the theory have been questioned (for example, there may be other motives for social comparison), social comparison theory remains a classic formulation of social comparison processes with broad impact on issues of health, coping, stress, and personal identity.

Temporal comparison theory (Albert, 1977), derived from social comparison theory, was a set of propositions about when, with whom, and for what reasons one would compare one's self at one point in time with one's self at another point in time. The theory argues, for example, that such comparisons are particularly likely during periods of rapid change as a way to maintain a coherent sense of personal identity. For example, exiting an organization (which is usually viewed as a large and significant change) may evoke memories of the time when the individual first joined the organization. Much less empirical research has been devoted to temporal comparison theory than social comparison theory (for references to relevant work, see Suls and Wills, 1991).

Processes of social and temporal comparison, that is, comparisons with other persons in the light of one's own past and projected future, are highly relevant to judgments of perceived equity and fairness (*see* EQUITY THEORY; JUSTICE, DISTRIBUTIVE). For example, the pain of inequity may be tempered by the fact that all parties are experiencing rapid improvement.

See also *group dynamics; role taking; self-esteem; status incongruence*

Bibliography

Albert, S. (1977). Temporal comparison theory. *Psychological Review*, 84 (6), 485–503.

Buunk, B. P. and Mussweiler, T. (2001). New directions in social comparison research. *European Journal of Social Psychology*, 31, 467–75.

Festinger, L. (1954a). A theory of social comparison processes. *Human Relations*, 7, 117–40.

Festinger, L. (1954b). Motivation leading to social behavior. In M. R. Jones (ed.), *Nebraska Symposium on Motivation*. Lincoln: University of Nebraska Press.

Suls, J. M. and Wills, T. A. (eds.) (1991). *Social Comparison: Contemporary Theory and Research*. Hillsdale, NJ: Lawrence Erlbaum Associates.

Suls, J. M. and Wheeler, L. (eds.) (2000). *Handbook of Social Comparison: Theory and Research*. New York: Kluwer Academic/Plenum.

social desirability

see RESEARCH METHODS

social facilitation

Michael West

The mere presence of others can significantly enhance our performance. Social psychologists have termed this social facilitation. Working with others doing the same simple task on a production line produces better performance than working alone. The presence of others also inhibits performance, as in the case of public speaking, through a process called social inhibition. It is clear from many studies that on simple tasks performance is facilitated by the presence of others but on more difficult tasks it is impaired.

Three principal explanations have been offered for these effects. Zajonc (1965) demonstrated that the presence of others increases arousal in many species (including ants, chickens, cockroaches, fish, fruit flies, monkeys, and humans) and this arousal may facilitate greater effort and therefore effectiveness in task performance. The second explanation proposes that the presence of others is cognitively distracting on complex tasks and leads to performance decrement. A third suggests that evaluation apprehension may interfere with complex task performance.

This research implies that open plan offices will hinder performance when tasks are complex but that on simple tasks, such as call center or assembly line work, the presence of others will facilitate performance. As in most areas of research in social psychology, our understanding of social facilitation would deepen if researchers ventured out to conduct more research in work organizations.

See also *cognitive dissonance; group dynamics; social comparison*

Bibliography

Zajonc, R. B. (1965). Social facilitation. *Science*, 149, 269–74.

social identity theory

see IDENTITY, PERSONAL; PERSONALITY

social learning theory

see LEARNING, INDIVIDUAL; IDENTITY, PERSONAL

social loafing

Jayanth Narayanan and Madan M. Pillutla

The term social loafing refers to the tendency of individuals to expend less effort when working in collectives than when working by themselves. This is also called the Ringelmann effect, after a nineteenth-century French agricultural engineer who noticed that the average force exerted by each individual group member declined as more people were added to a group pulling on a rope. The phenomenon was originally thought to be the result of coordination losses that result from individuals working together. The persistence of the effect even after controlling for these coordination losses led Latane, Williams, and Harkins (1979) to coin the term "social loafing" and propose that declining productivity resulted from reduced efforts by individuals.

Research in this area has tended to focus on contextual factors that affect social loafing. Results suggest that individuals loaf more when their contributions cannot be identified, when they perceive the group task to be easy, and when they belong to less cohesive groups. Increasing individual accountability and group cohesion and designing the right INCENTIVE structures are among the proposed remedies to the problem of loafing.

In contrast to past research focusing on situational factors, recent research suggests that the tendency to loaf might be an individual difference and could be correlated with aspects of PERSONALITY (Smith et al., 2001).

See also *deviance; group cohesiveness; group dynamics*

Bibliography

Latane, B., Williams, K., and Harkins, S. (1979). Many hands make light the work. *Journal of Personality and Social Psychology*, 37, 822–32.
Smith, B. N., Kerr, N. A., Markus, M. J., and Stasson, M. F. (2001). Individual differences in social loafing: Need for cognition as motivator in collective performance. *Group Dynamics: Theory, Research and Practice*, 5 (2), 150–8.

social responsibility

see CORPORATE SOCIAL PERFORMANCE

socialization

John P. Wanous

Organizational socialization involves ROLE TAKING related to important transitions: (1) organizational entry as a new employee; (2) internal movements across functional/divisional lines; (3) moving up in the hierarchy; and (4) moving "inwards" towards increased status and/or POWER (Schein, 1971). Socialization is related to but different from other transitions such as labor force entry, occupational/career entry, entry into a new work group, and the reentry of expatriate employees. Orientation of newcomers is typically considered part of socialization, but differs because (1) it is an event of limited duration vs. a process; (2) it is limited to the organizational entry transition; (3) the level of STRESS is much higher at organizational entry than at other transitions; and (4) there are fewer members of one's ROLE SET.

Organizational socialization refers to changes in newcomers, rather than to changes in the organization, which is a separate process that has been called "personalization." Socialization involves attitude change, CONFORMITY, and organizational COMMITMENT. PSYCHOLOGICAL CONTRACTS and MENTORING are related topics, but are separate because they do not necessarily concern organizational entry.

Socialization is primarily achieved via social learning. Thus, the entire ROLE SET of a newcomer may be involved in the process: co-workers, those in positions of authority, and others with whom one comes in contact, such as those on temporary task forces or those with whom one socializes. Because of the number and variety of people involved in socialization, all sources of INFLUENCE are likely to be involved: legitimate AUTHORITY, reward power, coercion, expertise, referent, and charismatic.

SUMMARY OF RESEARCH

First, socialization tactics include the following six "tactical" dimensions: (1) collective vs. individual; (2) formal vs. informal; (3) sequential vs. random; (4) fixed vs. variable; (5) serial vs. disjunctive; (6) divestiture vs. investiture. If newcomers are socialized according to the first half of each dimension (e.g., formal, sequential, and so on), they tend to adopt an "institutional" orientation, thus conforming to the existing ORGANIZATIONAL CULTURE. Those socialized according to the opposite end of each continuum are said to develop an "individual" orientation as the result. In general, those socialized via the institutional orientation tend to experience less ROLE AMBIGUITY and ROLE CONFLICT, higher JOB SATISFACTION, and greater organizational commitment. Those socialized via the individual orientation tend to attempt more innovation at work and sometimes engage in more self-management.

Second, Reichers (1987) first suggested that proactive behavior by newcomers had been ignored. Up to this point, it had been implicitly assumed that newcomers were passive with respect to socialization tactics. Morrison (1993) was the first to provide empirical support about information seeking behaviors. Research has yet to specify a set of typical newcomer behaviors that is not specific to a particular type of person or organization. Further, the relative importance of newcomer information seeking as compared to socialization tactics, individual differences, and situational differences has yet to be determined, although there have been attempts to do so.

Third, the role of individual differences has received recent attention. Factors such as work experience, PERSONALITY (e.g., SELF-EFFICACY), work VALUES, and even demographic factors have all been studied at least

once. Both high self-efficacy and previous work experience facilitate socialization.

Fourth, the "content" of socialization is another recent development. Chao et al. (1994) is the most ambitious study and is cited most often. They identified six dimensions: (1) performance proficiency; (2) good interpersonal and working relationships; (3) organizational politics and the power structure; (4) language issues such as jargon; (5) organizational goals and values; and (6) learning organizational history, traditions, and customs.

Fifth, the outcomes of met (vs. unmet) expectations on newcomer attitudes and behavior (31 studies representing 17,241 people) were reviewed and meta-analyzed by Wanous et al. (1992). They reported the following mean correlations between met expectations and these attitudes and behaviors: r = .36 for job satisfaction, r = .34 for organizational commitment, r = .29 for intent to remain, r = .12 for job performance, and r = .24 for job survival (i.e., retention).

Sixth, identifying the stages of organizational socialization was initially a popular topic. Wanous, Reichers, and Malik (1984) reviewed and compared all of the stage models, and Wanous (1992) proposed a comprehensive and integrative four stage model: (1) confronting and accepting organizational reality; (2) achieving role clarity; (3) locating oneself in the organizational context; and (4) detecting signposts of successful socialization. Writing about socialization stages has all but ceased in the past 20 years.

Seventh, the role of groups at work has been identified by Wanous, Reichers, and Malik (1984). They noted that individuals are arrayed on two dimensions: (1) the stage of group development and (2) the stage of organizational socialization. An example of someone in a group facing the initial stages of both group development and socialization is a recruit in basic training.

RESEARCH TRENDS

The most recent and comprehensive review of socialization research (Bauer, Morrison, and Callister, 1998) compared two time periods: prior to 1986 covered by an earlier review vs. 1986 to 1998, which they reviewed. Prior to 1986, it had been estimated that no more than

15 well designed empirical studies had been conducted. Further, only a limited sample of occupations had been studied: students, nurses, and police. Finally, prior to 1986 most studies concerned data from only one point in time.

In the 12 years after 1986, many studies (n = 67) were done. Importantly, 47 of the 67 involved the collection of longitudinal data, averaging almost 3 data points per study for up to one year in duration. Students graduating from college, from MBA programs, and from nursing schools account for about 50 percent of the more recently conducted 67 studies. This is unfortunate because there are serious confounding factors, such as entry into the full-time labor force and into an occupation. To avoid this, socialization research should involve experienced persons who switch organizations but not occupations. Of the 67 studies summarized by Bauer, Morrison, and Callister (1998) only two concerned employees who transferred jobs, and the sum total of both samples is less than 50 persons.

See also *career development; learning, individual; organizational culture*

Bibliography

Bauer, T. N., Morrison E. W., and Callister, R. R. (1998). Organizational socialization: A review and directions for future research. *Research in Personnel and Human Resources Management*, 16, 149–214.

Chao, G. T., O'Leary-Kelly, A. M., Wolk, S., Klein, H. J., and Gardner, P. (1994). Organizational socialization: Its content and consequences. *Journal of Applied Psychology*, 79, 730–43.

Morrison, E. W. (1993). Newcomer information seeking: Exploring types, modes, sources, and outcomes. *Academy of Management Journal*, 36, 557–89.

Reichers, A. (1987). An interactionist perspective on newcomer socialization rates. *Academy of Management Review*, 12, 278–87.

Schein, E. H. (1971). The individual, the organization, and the career: A conceptual scheme. *Journal of Applied Behavioral Science*, 7, 401–26.

Van Maanen, J. and Schein, E. H. (1979). Toward a theory of organizational socialization. In B. M. Staw (ed.), *Research in Organizational Behavior*, Vol. 1. Greenwich, CT: JAI Press, 209–64.

Wanous, J. P. (1992). *Organizational Entry: Recruitment, Selection, Orientation, and Socialization*, 2nd edn. Reading, MA: Addison-Wesley.

Wanous, J. P., Poland, T. D., Premack, S. L., and Davis, K. S. (1992). The effects of met expectations on newcomer attitudes and behaviors: A review and meta-analysis. *Journal of Applied Psychology*, 77, 288–97.

Wanous, J. P., Reichers, A. E., and Malik, S. D. (1984). Organizational socialization and group development: Toward an integrative perspective. *Academy of Management Review*, 9, 670–83.

sociotechnical theory

Chris Clegg

Sociotechnical theory is concerned with the analysis and design of work organizations and proposes the need for the joint optimization and concurrent design of their social and technical subsystems. The theory challenges the dominant, longstanding Tayloristic (*see* SCIENTIFIC MANAGEMENT) view of JOB DESIGN.

The ideas originated at the Tavistock Institute in London during the 1950s and 1960s. Trist and Bamforth's (1951) study of coal mining methods is seminal. They compared the impact of a new mechanized method of mining with the group-based method it replaced. The old system incorporated features such as small group working, supervision internal to the group, a sense of responsible autonomy, a complete work cycle, multiskilling, and self-selection. The new system, based on mass production principles, involved a radical change in work organization that effectively destroyed the previous social structure and led to a catalogue of individual, organizational, and performance problems.

Sociotechnical theory is best known for its general proposition (as above), for its underlying design principles (Cherns, 1976, 1987), the innovation of autonomous work groups, and its criteria on job design (*see* WORK GROUPS/TEAMS).

Cherns (1987) articulated a set of sociotechnical design principles, proposing that:

- design processes should be compatible with desired design outcomes (i.e., they should be participative);
- methods of working should be minimally specified;

- variances in work processes should be handled at source;
- organizational boundaries should not be drawn to impede the sharing of information, learning, and knowledge;
- information should support those who need to take action;
- those who need resources should have access to and authority over them;
- ROLES should be multifunctional and multiskilled;
- other systems supporting the focal group should be congruent in their design;
- transitional arrangements between the existing and new system should be planned and designed in their own right;
- redesign should be continuous, with regular review and evaluation.

One of the key innovations to emerge from the sociotechnical approach has been the autonomous work group. The essential feature of such groups is that they are self-managing (see SELF-MANAGING TEAMS), although their autonomy is constrained by the need to meet agreed targets and standards of performance, and by prevailing safety and disciplinary requirements. The role of supervision and management becomes that of managing the boundaries and supporting the group in achieving its goals.

So far as the individual working within a sociotechnical system is concerned, Emery (1964) identified six desirable characteristics for job design:

- A job should be reasonably demanding (in terms other than sheer endurance).
- There should be opportunities to learn and continue learning.
- There should be an area of decision-making the individual can call his or her own.
- There should be a degree of social support and recognition.
- It should be possible to relate what one does to wider life.
- The work should have some desirable future.

These criteria are very similar to those emerging from the work on job characteristics.

The current status of sociotechnical thinking is mixed. It is widely taught; its central proposition is increasingly recognized and accepted; the principles are often cited, and indeed some have wide currency (e.g., that variances should be handled at source); and the job design criteria remain relevant. Nevertheless a number of trenchant criticisms exist (Clegg, 2000).

The major criticisms are that, in practice, most initiatives have identified similar ("one best way") solutions to problems of work organization, stressing the need for employee PARTICIPATION and autonomous work groups. Furthermore, almost all the intervention work has taken the technology as given, redesigning the social systems around an existing technology. The design principles themselves are largely social in content; there is little to guide the design of the technical subsystem. Furthermore, relatively little attention has been paid to the issue of function allocation (i.e., deciding which tasks are allocated to humans, and which to technology). These concerns have largely been left to those working within ergonomics. There is also little support in the form of methods or tools, for those people who wish to engage in sociotechnical design. While there are some exceptions to this (Mumford and Axtell, 2003), these criticisms hold for the new technologies and ways of working, such as ENTERPRISE RESOURCE PLANNING and e-business. There is also a criticism that the theory is too managerial and entails too unitaristic a view of work organization and ORGANIZATIONAL CHANGE (i.e., one based on an assumption of shared objectives and interests). Finally, the theory has proved disappointing in its long-term practical impact. The application of these ideas over several decades has proved to be limited, especially when compared with ideas such as TOTAL QUALITY MANAGEMENT and just-in-time, which have had a more immediate and substantial impact on thinking and practice. To remain salient and become influential, work needs to be done addressing these issues.

One could argue that sociotechnical thinking will become both more difficult and more important as organizations continue to try to make their processes more effective, increase their levels of technological sophistication, and take out slack (tighten coupling) in their operations (Clegg and Walsh, 2004). New sociotechnical interdependencies will emerge and new knowledge will be required. However, it is not evident that work is underway that will help achieve this. Furthermore, some believe that there are many powerful social forces that militate against the widespread adoption of such ideas (Clegg, 1993). Examples include:

- the emphasis within the supply side of the IT industry on new products and new functionality, rather than performance and end user needs;
- the gap that exists in language, understanding, and assumptions between the various interest groups involved in designing, implementing, using, and managing new technologies and the work systems they support;
- the lack of understanding of sociotechncial interdependencies on the part of many senior managers and technical specialists;
- the heavy emphasis in systems development methods on technical concerns;
- the relative lack of attention in research and development programs to human and organizational issues;
- the lack of control and power on the part of end users;
- the apparent ability of end users to cope with whatever system they are given;
- the lack of attention to, and influence over, technology-based innovations on the part of human resource/personnel managers and specialists.

On a more positive note, those engaged in sociotechnical thinking and practice are often actively committed to, and engaged in, the design of work organizations. Too often the contribution of social scientists is assumed to lie in a concern for the human and organizational impacts of new technologies and ways of working (i.e., after the event).

See also *person-environment interaction; systems theory; technology*

Bibliography

Cherns, A. (1976). The principles of sociotechnical design. *Human Relations*, 29, 783–92.
Cherns, A. (1987). Principles of sociotechnical design revisited. *Human Relations*, 40, 153–62.

Clegg, C. W. (1993). Social systems that marginalize the psychological and organizational aspects of information technology. *Behavior and Information Technology*, 12, 261–6.
Clegg, C. W. (2000). Sociotechnical principles for system design. *Applied Ergonomics*, 31, 463–77.
Clegg, C. W. and Walsh, S. (2004). Change management: Time for a change! *European Journal of Work and Organizational Psychology*.
Emery, F. (1964). *Report on the Hunsfoss Project*. London: Tavistock Documents Series.
Mumford, E. and Axtell, C.M. (2003). Tools and methods to support the design and implementation of new work systems. In D. Holman, T. D. Wall, C. W. Clegg, P. Sparrow, and A. Howard (eds.), *The New Workplace: A Guide to the Human Impact of Modern Working Practices*. Chichester: Wiley.
Trist, E. L. and Bamforth, K. W. (1951). Some social and psychological consequences of the longwall method of coal-getting. *Human Relations*, 14, 3–38.

span of control

see ORGANIZATIONAL STRUCTURE; MANAGEMENT, CLASSICAL THEORY

stakeholders

Donna J. Wood

A stakeholder is "any group or individual who can affect or is affected by the achievement of [an organization's] objectives" (Freeman, 1984: 24) (i.e., those who have or could have a *stake* or interest in the organization's activities). The stakeholder concept originates in ROLE theory, which posits a complex interdependent network of relationships for every person, marked by differing interests and expectations for each role relationship. Similarly, stakeholders constitute a complex relational environment for organizations.

An organization's core stakeholders – those with ongoing, intensely interdependent relationships – depend to some extent on the nature of the organization and its activities. Most organizations have the following types of core stakeholders: (1) *constituents* on whose behalf the organization exists and operates (e.g., business owners or voluntary association members); (2) *employees* who conduct the organization's affairs; (3) *customers* who receive the goods or services the organization produces; (4) *suppliers* who provide the input materials for the organization's activities; (5) *government* that guarantees an organization's rights and privileges, enforces its responsibilities, and regulates its behaviors through political processes.

Organizations have many other stakeholders, including local communities, competitors, media, financial analysts and markets, financial institutions, voluntary organizations, environmental and consumer protection groups, religious organizations, military groups, political parties or factions, etc. Depending on the cultural context, any of these stakeholders can be very important to an organization. Furthermore, an organization's stakeholder set changes over time, as stakeholders enter and exit the environment, and as stakeholder interests and interdependencies change.

International business organizations experience a much more complex stakeholder environment than do single-country organizations. An international company will have a different stakeholder set in every country in which it operates. Furthermore, some stakeholders will themselves be international, not tied to a particular country.

Understanding stakeholder relationships gives managers a more realistic view of the organization's environment. An organization's social performance is evaluated with respect to stakeholder expectations; organizational governance occurs in the context of stakeholder interests. Stakeholder analysis and management involve identifying stakeholders and their relationships to the organization, including the nature of each stakeholder's interest in the organization and other characteristics (e.g., the direction, strength, and immediacy of effect; types of power held; single- or multiple-issue orientation; shared values or problems). Then, relationships *among* stakeholders are mapped. Finally, organizational strategies for managing stakeholder relationships are developed and implemented (Wood, 1994).

Current research in stakeholder management concerns questions such as the role of POWER, legitimacy, and urgency in shaping managers' perceptions of stakeholder salience (Mitchell, Agle, and Wood, 1997); processes by which stakeholder expectations are established, communicated, understood, and acted upon; the value bases of differing stakeholder expectations; cross-cultural differences in organizational stakeholder environments; the moral standing of stakeholders; and the relevance of the stakeholder concept for theories of AGENCY, transaction costs, moral behavior, RESOURCE DEPENDENCE, institutional isomorphism, and behavioral or economic explanations of organizational behavior. Eventually, stakeholder research may result in a new, more comprehensive theory of the firm.

See also *corporate social performance; governance; values*

Bibliography

Freeman, R. E. (1984). *Strategic Management: A Stakeholder Approach*. Boston, MA: Ballinger.

Mitchell, R. K., Agle, B. R., and Wood, D. J. (1997). Toward a theory of stakeholder identification and salience: The principle of who and what really counts. *Academy of Management Review*.

Wood, D. J. (1994). *Business and Society*, 2nd edn. New York: Harper Collins.

statistical methods

Kenneth W. Koput

The defining feature of techniques known as statistical methods is that they are designed to sort out what appears as chance in individual units (be they persons, groups, firms, industries, or otherwise) into collective regularities and frequencies. There are two branches into which statistical methods are classified, having developed somewhat separately: descriptive and inferential.

The term "statistics" dates from the early eighteenth century, being "that which statists do." Mostly, statists engaged in describing their states. Accordingly, methods within this original domain now fall under the heading of descriptive statistics, whose range extends beyond states to all manner of populations, whether concrete (e.g., blue collar employees) or abstract (e.g., all possible realizations of a stochastic founding process). Such methods seek to organize large amounts of raw data on individual units into more readily assimilated, population-level summary measures. Descriptive statistical methods are used in organizational research to help researchers get a grasp of what goes on in a population – establishing the existence of phenomena for study. These methods have been used to answer such questions as what are typical levels of TURNOVER, how widely dispersed are values of job satisfaction, how values of organizational size are distributed, and what are the characteristics of Japanese management.

Inferential statistics, the second branch, did not begin to develop until the turn of the nineteenth century. Inferential statistical methods use probability theory to draw conclusions about a population from a sample, or subset, of the individuals comprising the population. We first formulate a hypothesis about the descriptive properties of or relationships between variables characterizing the individuals in the population, then we observe data from a sample. We are uncertain about the hypothesis, but we do know that the data have occurred. Hence, if obtaining the sample data actually observed is a high probability event under some hypothesis, we are inclined to accept that hypothesis; else, we are inclined to favor some alternative.

Many statistical methods are well established in organizational research. The choice of method is determined by the nature of the variables (continuous, discrete) and the hypothesized relationships (cross-sectional, time series, etc.). Analysis of variance, regression, and contingency tables are the most widely used for "static" studies, where the relationship under study is between variables measured concurrently (at the same time). Uses of such methods range from studying the effects of INDIVIDUAL DIFFERENCES on MOTIVATION and performance to testing predictions of CONTINGENCY THEORY about the fit between ORGANIZATIONAL DESIGN variables such as formalization, and such key dimensions of the environment as uncertainty. Where social dynamics are of interest, event history analysis has become a popular way to study discrete dependent variables, as in career transition or organizational birth and death. Time series regression is typically used for longitudinal studies where the dependent variables are continuous, as in organizational economics. Limitations of the data or operationalizations (e.g., level of measurement available) can also influence the choice of technique. Multivariate methods, such as factor or cluster analyses, have been used to infer the existence of unobservable constructs, especially in studies of personality or strategic groups. Choice of a statistical method that is not suited to the characteristics of a study can lead to BIAS.

Despite the mathematical foundation on which inferential statistics is built, which gives the appearance of objectivity, there are four approaches to formalizing the process of inference which have and continue to be the subject of some debate: Fisherian significance testing, Neyman–Pearson hypothesis testing, Bayesian analysis, and a hybrid of the Fisherian and Neyman–Pearson approaches. The hybrid, in which a researcher sets a level of significance against which the probability of the data occurring under a single hypothesis is compared and on the basis of which a clear decision to accept or reject the hypothesis as truth is made, has been dominant in organizational research. The reason is straightforward: it simplifies the process of evaluating research, making editorial decisions, and defining researchers' careers.

However, this "objectification of subjectivity" also has some negative consequences. Some hypotheses suffer premature deaths, even though there may be no well-explicated alternative, while others are born without paying due respect to a stream of prior research to the contrary (*see* ERROR). Neyman and Pearson railed against the first sin, while Bayesians promise salvation from the latter. As for Fisher, he maintained that a hypothesis could never be shown plausible – only implausible – and that the demonstration of a natural phenomenon requires "that we know how to conduct an experiment that will rarely fail to give us a statistically significant result." Attention needs to be paid not only to the choice of statistical methods for particular studies, but also to the way we use the results of these methods in accumulating knowledge across studies.

See also *computer simulation; organizational decline and death; quasi-experimental design; reliability; research design; research methods; validity*

Bibliography

Fisher, R. A. (1990). *Statistical Methods: Experimental Design and Scientific Inference*. Oxford: Oxford University Press.

Gigerenzer, G. et al. (1989). *The Empire of Chance: How Probability Changed Science and Everyday Life*. New York: Cambridge University Press.

Oakes, M. W. (1986). *Statistical Inference: A Commentary for the Social and Behavioral Sciences*. New York: Wiley.

status

see EVOLUTIONARY PSYCHOLOGY; ORGANIZATIONAL STATUS

status incongruence

David L. Deephouse

Status incongruence occurs in two ways. First, a person may be ranked high on some evaluative status dimensions but low on others. A quintessential example is the person with a doctoral degree driving a taxicab; this person has high educational attainment but low occupational prestige. A second type of status incongruence occurs when a person's status characteristics appear inappropriate for the person's position or ROLE. For instance, a marketing person may be put in charge of a production.

Status incongruence can affect the particular person and the person's co-workers. In the first case, status incongruence may engender cognitive dissonance. This, in turn, may influence JOB SATISFACTION and performance. In the second case, the person's co-workers may question the fairness of the person's status. EQUITY THEORY suggests that co-workers may alter their behavior and attitudes in this situation.

See also *cognitive dissonance; role theory; self-esteem*

Bibliography

Mitchell, T. R. (1982). *People in Organizations*, 2nd edn. New York: McGraw-Hill.

strain

see STRESS

stratification

see ORGANIZATIONAL DESIGN

stress

Michael Frese and Sabine Sonnentag

Stress in organizations is common: between 26 and 40 percent of workers in the USA and in Europe experience their work as very stressful. Healthcare costs are 46 percent higher for workers who experienced high levels of stress (Sonnentag and Frese, 2003). Other costs are low organizational COMMITMENT, ABSENTEEISM, disability pensions, and mortality rates. Illnesses that are affected by stress at work include immune system problems, psychosomatic complaints, coronary heart disease, depression, and possibly cancer.

There is disagreement on what stress really is. On the most general level, one can differentiate between three stress concepts: (1) the stimulus concept; (2) the response concept; and (3) the transactional concept. The stimulus concept focuses on situational conditions or events (e.g., stressful life events). The reaction concept concentrates on physiological reactions (i.e., stress exists if an individual shows a specific physiological reaction pattern) (Selye, 1983). Both of these positions have their shortcomings, as they do not take into account that different situations can result in the same physiological response and different physiological reactions may appear in the same situation. The transactional concept brought forward by Lazarus and Folkman (1984) assumes that stress results from a transaction between the individual and the environment, including the individual's perceptions, expectations, interpretations, and coping responses.

Major theoretical models on job stress include the Person–Environment Fit Theory (Edwards, 1991), the Job Demand–Job Control Model (Karasek and Theorell, 1990), the Vitamin Model (Warr, 1987), and the Effort–Reward Imbalance Model (Siegrist, 1996). According to Person–Environment Fit Theory stress occurs because of two types of misfit between the individual and the environment: (1) misfit between the demands of the environment (objective and subjective) and the competencies of the persons (subjective and objective); (2) misfit between the needs of the person and supplies from the environment. The Job Demand–Job Control Model argues that jobs high on stressors and low on decision latitude produce high strain and ill health. This model assumes that decision latitude "buffers" the effects of stressors on ill health because decision latitude reduces the negative effects of the stressors. This model can explain why managers who are high on stressors but also high on job decision latitude do not show negative health effects as strongly as blue collar workers on an assembly line. There is substantial evidence for a model that includes both lack of control or decision latitude and stressors as predictors of ill health; however, the buffer effect is controversial (De Lange et al., 2003). Irrespective of the buffer effect, lack of decision latitude directly affects health negatively.

The Vitamin Model assumes non-linear relationships between work characteristics such as job autonomy, social support, or skill utilization and ill health. For example, the more employees can utilize their skills at work, the better their well-being. However, extremely high degrees of skill utilization are assumed to be detrimental for employee well-being. The Effort–Reward Imbalance Model assumes that an incongruence between the amount of effort invested at work and the (financial and non-financial) rewards received leads to emotional distress and ill health.

Empirically, careful longitudinal studies have shown that stress at work causes ill health. There is substantial evidence that a high workload is detrimental for psychological health. Longitudinal studies identified effects of stressors at work on (psycho-) somatic complaints and cardiovascular indicators. Interestingly, there is some evidence that ill health and poor well-being might cause an increase in stress at work. However, this effect is weaker than the opposite effect of stressors on strains. The size of the effect of stressors on health and well-being is higher than the effect of Ibuprofen on pain reduction and about twice as high as the effect of combat exposure in Vietnam on developing posttraumatic stress disorder.

Resources at work and individual resources attenuate the effects of stressors on health. Besides control at work, social support by supervisors and colleagues is a core resource at work (Frese, 1999). Personal resources comprise problem oriented coping styles, internal locus of control, self-efficacy, HARDINESS, and a sense of coherence (Semmer, 2003a). However, these resources are not effective under all circumstances. For example, problem oriented coping is only beneficial if employees experience job control. Without job control, problem oriented coping cannot be effective (De Rijk et al., 1998).

There are also relationships between stress at work and performance. Laboratory research has shown that stressors affect performance negatively, particularly because they impair basic cognitive processes. Evidence from field research, however, is less conclusive (Jex, 1998). It seems that employees are able to compensate for the stressor effects by exerting more effort, by using different task strategies, and prioritizing the most relevant tasks. The same is also true of fatigue effects: often, people are able to compensate for it, so that the negative effects of fatigue do not always emerge – at least over the short term (Meijman and Mulder, 1998).

There are good treatment and prevention models for stress at work. Interventions can focus on the reduction of stressors, increase of resources, strain reduction, and lifestyle changes. If aiming to reduce stressors, interventions have to change task characteristics, change working conditions (referring to ergonomic features, time related issues, and workload), and improve role clarity (Semmer, 2003b). Increase of resources implies that the employees receive more control over their work situation (empowerment and participation) and receive better social support (particularly from supervisors – this implies that improving leadership skills may also enhance well-being) or increasing COMPETENCIES to deal with the work situation. Strain reduction programs are very common within and outside organizations. Among the most successful interventions are cognitive behavioral interventions (dealing with the thoughts and belief systems of individuals), relaxation training, and multimodal approaches (Murphy, 1996; Van der Klink et al., 2001). Within the group of cognitive behavioral interventions, stress inoculation training has proved to be particularly effective (Saunders et al., 1996). Lifestyle changes imply reduction of consumption of drugs, alcohol, and cigarettes, as well as increasing physical exercise, such as walking up stairs instead of using the elevator.

Scientifically, a lot is known about stress at work. During the past decades longitudinal research has made progress by showing that stress at work indeed negatively affects employee health and well-being. However, there are still areas which are interesting and underexplored, particularly how stress effects unfold over time, how stress at work is related to performance, under which conditions resources work as stress buffers, and how employees can recover from work stress.

See also *burnout; emotion in organizations*

Bibliography

De Lange, A. H., Taris, T. W., Kompier, M. A. J., Houtman, I. L. D., and Bongers, P. M. (2003). "The very best of the millenium": Longitudinal research and the demand–control–(support) model. *Journal of Occupational Health Psychology*, 8, 282–305.

De Rijk, A. E., Le Blanc, P. M., Schaufeli, W. B., and de Jonge, J. (1998). Active coping and need for control as moderators of the job demand–control model: Effects on burnout. *Journal of Occupational and Organizational Psychology*, 71, 1–18.

Edwards, J. R. (1991). Person–job fit: A conceptual integration, literature review, and methodological critique. In C. L. Cooper and I. T. Robertson (eds.), *International Review of Industrial and Organizational Psychology*. Chichester: Wiley, 283–357.

Frese, M. (1999). Social support as a moderator of the relationship between work stressors and psychological dysfunctioning: A longitudinal study with objective measures. *Journal of Occupational Health Psychology*, 4, 179–92.

Jex, S. M. (1998). *Stress and Job Performance: Theory, Research, and Implications For Managerial Practice*. Thousand Oaks, CA: Sage.

Karasek, R. A. and Theorell, T. (1990). *Healthy Work: Stress, Productivity, and the Reconstruction of Working Life*. New York: Basic Books.

Lazarus, R. S. and Folkman, S. (1984). *Stress, Appraisal and Coping*. New York: Springer.

Meijman, T. F. and Mulder, G. (1998). Psychological aspects of workload. In P. J. D. Drenth, H. Thierry, and C. J. De Wolff (eds.), *Handbook of Work and Organizational Psychology*, Vol. 1. London: Psychology Press.

Murphy, L. R. (1996). Stress management in work settings: A critical review of health effects. *American Journal of Health Promotion*, 11, 112–35.

Saunders, T., Driskell, J. E., Johnston, J. H., and Salas, E. (1996). The effect of stress inoculation training on anxiety and performance. *Journal of Occupational Health Psychology*, 1, 170–86.

Selye, H. (1983). The stress concept today, past, present, and future. In C. L. Cooper (ed.), *Stress Research: Issues for the Eighties*. Chichester: Wiley, 1–20.

Semmer, N. K. (2003a). Individual differences, work stress and health. In M. J. Schabracq, J. A. M. Winnubst, and C. L. Cooper (eds.), *Handbook of Work and Health Psychology*, Vol. 2. Chichester: Wiley, 83–120.

Semmer, N. K. (2003b). Job stress interventions and organization of work. In J. C. Quick and L. E. Tetrick (eds.), *Handbook of Occupational Health Psychology*. Washington, DC: American Psychological Association, 325–53.

Siegrist, J. (1996). Adverse health effects of high effort/low reward conditions. *Journal of Occupational Health Psychology*, 1, 27–41.

Sonnentag, S. and Frese, M. (2003). Stress in organizations. In W. C. Borman, D. R. Ilgen, and R. J. Klimoski (eds.), *Handbook of Psychology: Industrial and Organizational Psychology*, Vol. 12. Hoboken, NJ: Wiley, 453–91.

Van der Klink, J. J. L., Blonk, R. W. B., Schene, A. H., and Van Dijk, F. J. H. (2001). The benefits of interventions for work-related stress. *American Journal of Public Health*, 91, 270–6.

Warr, P. B. (1987). *Work, Unemployment, and Mental Health*. Oxford: Oxford University Press.

structuration

Stephen R. Barley

The term "structuration" was coined by Giddens (1984) to refer to the dynamic articulation between structure and action (which Giddens called "agency"). Traditionally, sociologists and organizational theorists have treated structure as an exogenous constraint on action. In turn, they have viewed action as independent of structure and, in many instances, as a phenomenon that exists at a "lower" level of analysis. In organization studies, the implicit gulf between structure and action is reflected in the distinction between micro- and macro-organizational behavior. Giddens argued that action and structure are inextricably linked, that action both "constitutes and is constituted by" structure. From this perspective, human action always instantiates structures. Actions may replicate, but they may also alter, existing structural patterns. The relationship between action and structure is therefore a process that can best be understood when studied over time. The importance of structuration for organization studies is that it provides a theoretical and empirical base for bridging the longstanding gulf between studies of organizational structure and studies of everyday action within organizations (*see* ORGANIZATIONAL DESIGN). Giddens's notion of structuration bears similarities to Strauss's (1978) concept of a "Negotiated order" – the rules, roles, rights, and obligations that individuals and other types of actors establish as they interact with each other over time.

See also *agency theory; enactment; theory*

Bibliography

Giddens, A. (1984). *The Constitution of Society*. Berkeley: University of California Press.
Strauss, A. (1978). *Negotiations*. San Francisco: Jossey-Bass.

succession

see EXECUTIVE SUCCESSION

supervision

see LEADERSHIP

surveys

Paul Rosenfeld, Jack E. Edwards, and Marie D. Thomas

A survey is a method used to obtain self-reported information about the attitudes, behaviors, or other characteristics of a population or sample (*see* STATISTICAL METHODS). Survey information can be gathered with a wide variety of administration methods. Over the last several years, web-based surveys administered over the Internet have gained significantly in popularity, but paper-and-pencil, optical scan, telephone, and face-to-face surveys are also popular for particular applications.

Although surveys of voting preferences or social attitudes may receive most of the attention in the press and popular media, surveys have long been used in organizational settings, including private and public businesses, the military, universities, and medical centers. In organizational or corporate settings surveys allow employees to feel that they are a part of DECISION-MAKING processes. In addition, organizational surveys can provide information that is unavailable from other sources or using other methods. The ability to solicit information anonymously or confidentially can enhance the accuracy of survey answers beyond that which might be available using other methods such as face-to-face interviews. Organizational surveys are also very adaptable; they can be utilized for diverse purposes such as assessing employee needs and attitudes about the workplace, measuring employee morale, motivation, job satisfaction, and intentions to remain with or leave an organization; and determining consumers' opinions and preferences about the goods and services they receive. Surveys can also establish baselines, benchmarks, or norms at the time of an organizational intervention. These standards can be used in future evaluations to determine the effectiveness of new programs and policies.

Recently, textbooks devoted specifically to conducting organizational surveys have begun to appear and supplement descriptions of how to conduct social, political, and marketing surveys. Given the unique methodological issues associated with organizational survey development and implementation, organizational researchers are encouraged to consult textbooks specifically devoted to organizational survey work.

Although conducting a well written, well administered organizational survey can be costly, challenging, and labor intensive, the survey process is also very rewarding. Managers have the satisfaction of seeing a need for information turn into survey items. The items return as data, the data are analyzed and interpreted, and ultimately provide an empirical basis for answering the original questions. For respondents, organizational surveys provide a vehicle that allows employees to communicate their concerns and questions to management (*see* SURVEYS, FEEDBACK).

While the benefits of surveys are many, they also entail dangers and difficulties that will need to be addressed in the future. These include raising unfulfilled expectations, inadequate follow-up communications, suggesting unattainable outcomes, and too few employees completing the survey to make the responses generalizable to the population of interest. Surveys are not a panacea for all organizational ills; expectations of what a survey can do may need to be tempered with the realities of what it cannot accomplish. These potential pitfalls often can be avoided through careful design and administration and an awareness of the organization's culture and interpersonal politics.

See also *attitude theory; research design; research methods*

Bibliography

Church, A. H. and Waclawski, J. (1998). *Designing and Using Organizational Surveys*. Brookfield, VT: Gower.

Edwards, J. E. and Fisher, B. M. (2004). Organizational survey programs. In J. E. Edwards, J. C. Scott, and N. S. Raju (eds.), *The Human Resources Program-Evaluation Handbook*. Newbury Park, CA: Sage, 365–86.

Edwards, J. E., Thomas, M. D., Rosenfeld, P., and Booth-Kewley, S. (1997). *How to Conduct Organizational Surveys: A Step-By-Step Guide*. Newbury Park, CA: Sage.

Kraut, A. I. (ed.) (1996). *Organizational Surveys*. San Francisco: Jossey-Bass.

Rosenfeld, P., Edwards, J. E., and Thomas, M. D. (eds.) (1993). *Improving Organizational Surveys: New Directions, Methods, and Applications*. Newbury Park, CA: Sage.

surveys, feedback

Paul Rosenfeld, Marie D. Thomas, and Jack E. Edwards

Organizations use SURVEYS to gather information on the attitudes, behaviors, and characteristics of employees. Before administering the survey, decisions must be made about which stakeholders (e.g., top management and respondents) will receive information about the survey findings. Such survey feedback will work best when it is tailored to the audience having a need or desire to know. Typical methods for feeding back information include briefings to top management, presentations organization-wide or to small groups, short written synopses distributed in organizational mail or posted on websites, and reports containing in-depth information.

Survey feedback has long been an integral component of ORGANIZATIONAL DEVELOPMENT (OD) method and practice, and employees highly value survey feedback. Thus, one positive outcome resulting from survey feedback may be improved two-way communication between management and workers. Through feedback, surveys can become a way to generate employee commitment, enthusiasm, and involvement in organizational change initiatives that often follow the survey effort. Achieving these goals of survey feedback is a challenge many organizations will continue to face in the future.

See also *action research; learning organization; research methods*

Bibliography

Edwards, J. E., Thomas, M. D., Rosenfeld, P., and Booth-Kewley, S. (1997). *How to Conduct Organizational Surveys: A Step-By-Step Guide*. Newbury Park, CA: Sage.

Rosenfeld, P., Edwards, J. E., and Thomas, M. D. (eds.) (1993). *Improving Organizational Surveys: New Directions, Methods, and Applications*. Newbury Park, CA: Sage.

symbolism

John Van Maanen

Symbolism refers to the manipulation of meaning through the use of symbols. It involves the linking of a sign to a content or referent by some ordering principle. This is a process of coding/decoding, which is a mental and therefore cultural activity. Symbols work to organize experience. In semiotic terms, they are signs that stand for something else. A symbol such as a corporate logo or a political slogan may stand for a particular company or ideological stance. They may also invoke notions of IDENTIFICATION, fealty, and honor, or alienation, disgust, and fear. They often carry denotative and connotative meanings. Denotative meanings refer to the direct, instrumental uses of a symbol – the flag as standing for a given country. Connotative meanings refer to the expressive, more general, and broader uses of a symbol – the flag as standing for law and order. To study symbolism is to learn how the meanings on which people base actions are created, communicated, contested, and sometimes changed.

There are at least four interrelated domains to be explored if the workings of a given symbol are to be understood. First, symbols are cultural objects whose form, appearance, logic, and type can be categorized (although category systems differ and some differ spectacularly). Second, symbols are produced and used by specific people and groups for certain purposes and thus the intentions of symbol creators and users must be understood. Third, symbols are always displayed within particular social contexts and these contexts severely shape (and limit) the possible meanings a symbol may assume. Fourth, symbols typically mean different things to different groups of people, so the receptive competencies and expectations of those who come into contact with given symbols must be examined. Since each domain plays off the others, the interpretation of symbols – even simple ones – can be quite complex.

Take, for example, the Big Mac as a symbol of interest. Consider the audience first. To some McDonald's patrons, the Big Mac is the quintessential American meal, a popular and desirable hamburger served up in a timely and tasty fashion. To others, the Big Mac is food without nourishment, a travesty of a meal served up in a most sterile and unappetizing way. But social context is of considerable importance also. A Big Mac in Tel Aviv is simply not the same cultural object as a Big Mac in Boston. Nor is the history of the Big Mac itself irrelevant to symbolism, for this more or less edible symbol has been around for some time and comes packed with consumer myths, production rules, social standing, snappy advertising, and associated symbols all cross-referenced to an uncountable number of life's little pleasures – "you deserve a break today." Some of this is by design, some accidental, and some circumstantial and fleeting. Symbolism is about how context helps shape meaning; how symbols are created, packaged and, in a variety of ways, understood; how connotative meanings grow from denotative ones and vice versa; and, most critically, how various audiences receive and decode symbols and then act on the basis of the meaning the symbols hold for them.

Symbolism is of great importance when cultural perspectives are used to describe and explain organizational behavior. The interpretation of symbols is at the heart of any cultural analysis, whether the culture being represented is a small and relatively autonomous work group within an organization or a huge multinational firm operating in diverse social, linguistic, and political contexts around the world. Symbolism is also central to studies of virtually all forms of organizational COMMUNICATION, since communication itself rests on a socially constructed coding framework that is shared by at least some if not all organizational members. From this perspective, symbolism reaches into all aspects of organizational behavior because it is the process by which all organizational activities, ceremonies, objects, products, stories, services, roles, goals, strategies, and so on are made sensible and hence logical and perhaps desirable to given audiences both inside and outside recognized organizational boundaries. Leadership can therefore be seen as symbolic action, as can other organizational influence attempts such as selection, SOCIALIZATION, and reward practices. Broadly conceived, symbolism is an elementary or fundamental process that makes organizational behavior both possible and meaningful.

See also *metaphor; organizational culture; rituals*

Bibliography

Blumer, H. (1969). *Symbolic Interactionism.* Englewood Cliffs, NJ: Prentice-Hall.

Feldman, M. S. and March, J. G. (1981). Information in organizations as symbol and signal. *Administrative Science Quarterly*, **34**, 171–86.

Geertz, C. (1973). *The Interpretation of Culture.* New York: Basic Books.

Griswold, W. (1992). *Cultures and Societies in a Changing World.* Thousand Oaks, CA: Pine Forge Press.

Manning, P. K. (1992). *Organizational Communication.* New York: de Gruyter.

Pfeffer, J. (1981). Management as symbolic action. In L. L. Cummings and B. M. Staw (eds.), *Research in Organizational Behavior*, Vol. 3. Greenwich, CT: JAI Press, 1–52.

Swidler, A. (1986). Culture in action: Symbols and stratagems. *American Sociological Review*, **51**, 273–86.

synectics

see CREATIVITY

systems dynamics

see COMPUTER SIMULATION; LEARNING ORGANIZATION

systems theory

Thomas G. Cummings

Systems theory refers to broad meta-theory for describing the structure and behavior of complex wholes called systems. Drawn from diverse work in the physical, biological, and social sciences, systems theory includes laws and principles that apply to all levels of systems, from single cells to societies. Systems theory has endured as a basic framework for studying organizational behavior for over 40 years. It treats organizations as systems, and seeks to explain their parts and interactions among them, how they structure themselves, and how they function to achieve particular results. Recent developments, such as COMPLEXITY THEORY and chaos theory, focus on the more dynamic aspects of organizations, particularly how they self-organize and adapt to rapidly changing environments. They consider organizations as complex adaptive systems whose parts interact non-linearly, thus producing emergent behaviors that are surprising and novel. This can promote organization change and innovation (*see* INNOVATION; ORGANIZATIONAL CHANGE).

OB scholars use systems theory to describe the general properties of organizational systems, such as groups and organizations. These system characteristics have a profound effect on how we view modern organizations.

One key feature has to do with the notion of system itself and how it forms an organized whole. A system is composed of parts and relationships among them. The system provides the framework or organizing principle for structuring the parts and relationships into an organized whole capable of behaving in a way that is greater than merely the sum of the behaviors of its parts.

In organizational systems, this draws attention to identifying the constituent members or subunits of the system and examining relationships among them. Equally important, it forces us to go beyond members and relations to assess the organizing principle through which they are arranged into a coherent whole. GROUP DYNAMICS scholars, for example, have spent considerable time addressing issues of group membership and member interaction. They have discovered different ways of organizing members and relations for performing tasks that members could not achieve working alone, such as SELF-MANAGING TEAMS and QUALITY CIRCLES. Similarly, organization theorists have expended effort identifying the different components of organizations and examining relations among them. They have found different ways to organize the components and relationships for competitive advantage, such as the M-form organization, the BUREAUCRACY, and the MATRIX ORGANIZATION.

A second important feature of systems has to do with whether they are relatively closed or open to their environment. Closed systems do not interact with the environment, and consequently their behavior depends largely on the internal dynamics of their parts. OPEN SYSTEMS, on the other hand, exchange with the environment, and thus their behavior is influenced by external forces.

Early conceptions of organizational systems tended to employ a closed system perspective. Attention was directed mainly at the internal dynamics of groups and organizations, for example, and at how their behaviors could be controlled internally. This led to knowledge of a variety of internal control mechanisms, such as hierarchy, rules/procedures, and functional design. In the late 1960s, OB scholars began to broaden their focus to external forces affecting organizational systems. This open systems view was fueled by growing applications of it to the social sciences, and by realization that the behavior of organizational systems could not be adequately explained without examining environmental relationships and their effects on the system. It has led to considerable research and theory about organizational environments, their dynamics and effects, and how organizational systems interact with them. Moreover, open systems theory has provided a number of powerful concepts for understanding how organizations maintain themselves while adapting to external forces.

A third characteristic of systems has to do with system viability. In order to survive and prosper, open systems need to perform at least four critical functions:

1 Transformation of inputs of energy and information to produce useful outputs.
2 Transaction with the environment to gain needed inputs and to dispose of outputs.
3 Regulation of system behavior to achieve stable performance.
4 Adaptation to changing conditions.

Because these different functions often place conflicting demands and tension on the system, system viability depends on maintaining a dynamic balance among them.

In organizational systems, considerable research is devoted to identifying and explaining how these four functions operate and contribute to ORGANIZATIONAL EFFECTIVENESS and survival. This has led to knowledge about how organizations and groups produce products and services through acquiring, operating, and developing different technologies (see TECHNOL-

OGY); how they protect their technologies from external disruptions while acquiring raw materials and marketing finished products; how they regulate themselves for stable performance while initiating and implementing innovation and change. This research defines a key role of management in organizational systems as sustaining a dynamic balance among these functions; one that allows the organization or group sufficient stability to operate rationally (see RATIONAL-ITY) yet requisite flexibility to adapt to changing conditions.

A fourth key feature of systems that has influenced our conceptions of organizational systems has to do with their multilevel nature. Systems exist at different levels. The levels display a hierarchical ordering, with each higher level of system being composed of systems at lower levels. For example, societies are composed of organizations; organizations are composed of groups; groups are composed of individuals; and so on. Because systems are embedded in other systems, it is necessary to look both upward and downward when describing a system and explaining its behavior. Higher level systems provide constraints and opportunities for how a system organizes its parts, and the nature of those parts affects the system's organizing possibilities.

This multilevel perspective has led OB scholars to identify different levels of organizational systems, and to focus on understanding them and how they interact with each other. Considerable attention is directed at specifying appropriate LEVELS OF ANALYSIS, both for conceptualizing about organizational systems and for aggregating and disaggregating data that apply to different levels. As researchers have developed more extensive theories and more powerful analytical methods, they have made finer distinctions among levels of organizational systems, particularly above the organization level. Today, scholars focus on at least six levels of organizational systems.

1 Individual member (see INDIVIDUAL DIFFERENCES)
2 Group (see WORK GROUPS/TEAMS)
3 Organization
4 Population of organizations and/or alliance among organizations (see INTER-ORGANIZATIONAL RELATIONS)

5 Community of populations and/or community of alliances (*see* COMMUNITY ECOLOGY)
6 Nation (*see* CULTURE, NATIONAL; CROSS-CULTURAL RESEARCH)

See also *management, classical theory; organization development; theory*

Bibliography

Buckley, W. (1968). *Modern Systems Research for the Behavioral Scientist*. Chicago: Aldine.

Cummings, T. (1980). *Systems Theory for Organization Development*. Chichester: Wiley.

Simon, H. (1996). *The Architecture of Complexity*, 3rd edn. Cambridge, MA: MIT Press.

T

tacit knowledge

see PRACTICAL INTELLIGENCE

Taylorism

see SCIENTIFIC MANAGEMENT

team building

W. Gibb Dyer, Jr.

In the general field of ORGANIZATION DEVELOPMENT (OD), the title given to the process of intervening in organizations to improve productivity and morale has been called team building. It was probably the first innovation in the OD movement, advancing the basic premise that before any group of people can begin to improve their performance, group members must be able to work together effectively and collaboratively. Team building, then, is a planned, systematic process designed to improve the collaborative efforts of people who must work together to achieve goals.

Team building methods grew out of an earlier invention called the Training Group (or T-group). This learning process, developed in the late 1940s and 1950s, featured an unstructured group, usually a collection of strangers, for the purpose of allowing interaction to occur without predetermined direction. Out of this interaction participants were trained to observe how the dynamics and structure of a group emerges, and to gain insights into their own and other members' interaction styles. Emphasis was also placed on giving personal feedback to all group members, and as the T-group movement developed, this latter emphasis began to predominate, subordinating group dynamics analysis.

Participants in early T-groups were captivated by the impact the group had on them in terms of increased TRUST, openness, and cohesiveness. In an attempt to transfer these same conditions back to their organizational settings, T-group trainers were asked to conduct the T-group training for organizational work teams. These early practitioners found that the T-Group methodology, which was appropriate for understanding how a group forms and giving feedback to relative strangers, was less suited to groups of employees with specific assignments, common work goals, and a longstanding knowledge of each other. The T-group methodology had to be altered to take into account the conditions found in work groups with common goals, specific assignments, deadlines, allocation of important rewards such as salary and advancements, and often high task interdependence within an organization context where there was a given structure and culture.

The goals of almost all team building efforts are to help group members develop a sense of trust among themselves, open up channels of COMMUNICATION so all relevant issues can be discussed, make sure everyone understands the goals and assignments, make decisions with the commitment of all members, prevent the leader from dominating the group, openly examine and resolve conflicts, carry out assignments and regularly review and critique work activities to improve processes.

While it was recognized early on that groups differed along a series of important dimensions (size, composition, length of life, nature of the task, degree of interconnectedness of individual tasks or assignments, sophistication of team members in group dynamics, time frames and deadlines, management patterns, and organization culture), there has been a tendency to consider all groups (or teams) as being similar and team building methods were commonly applied to all types of groups. Practitioners began to consider that different actions needed to be taken if one was working with a new team, a team rife with conflict, an apathetic team, a team dominated by a boss, or one split into cliques. An expanded set of actions and skills was developed to meet these various conditions and a repertoire of team building models emerged (*see* CONFLICT AND CONFLICT MANAGEMENT).

In recent years, the most dramatic difference in team building methods has been between decision teams and work teams. A decision team such as a management executive committee or a university academic department, or a collection of doctors or lawyers in a clinic or firm, must function as a team primarily to make decisions. These team members do not have to coordinate their daily tasks to accomplish a goal. They do have to make decisions which people can accept and implement with commitment. In contrast, a work team (a hospital operating unit, a police SWAT team, a NASA space crew, and some production units) must coordinate its efforts constantly every day. This has led to a new set of methodologies around building the autonomous or semi-autonomous work team (*see* WORK GROUPS/TEAMS). It is apparent that work teams must also make a range of decisions, so effective decision-making is a central activity.

Another recent phenomenon has been the advent of "virtual teams," which are work teams composed of individuals who work in different locations and therefore must communicate and coordinate team activities primarily through information technologies. This creates unique challenges for creating common goals, values, and effective working relationships in such teams (Thompson, 2004).

Dyer (1995) found that many company executives said they believed team building to be important but few (only 22 percent) actually engaged in any ongoing team building. When asked why team building programs were not being used, the executives listed the following:

Managers did not know how to do team building.
They did not understand the rewards.
They thought it would take too much time.
Team building efforts were not rewarded in the company.
People felt they did not need team building.
People felt it was not supported by their superiors.

Simple team building activities focus on asking team members to address the following questions:

What keeps our work group from being an effective team?
What changes would help us become a better team?
What are we currently doing that helps us work together as a team?

All group members share their responses to the above questions, a list of issues is developed specifying changes needed, and change actions are agreed upon and taken.

Another common design (Role Clarification Model) asks each person in the work group to describe their work or job assignment, obtains clarification from others about the job, and then encourages agreements from every other person about what is needed from them in order for the person in question to get their job done. This is especially useful when work roles are not clear.

A fundamental principle of team building is that it is a process, not an event. Too many companies have a one-time team building event, with no long-lasting results. Research by Boss (1989) has noted that personal management interviews (regular interviews between the team leader and team members concerning team performance) in conjunction with team building activities, reinforce and sustain positive changes in teams over time.

See also *group decision-making*

Bibliography

Boss, R. W. (1989). *Organization Development in Health Care*. Reading, MA: Addison-Wesley.

Dyer, W. (1995). *Team Building: Current Issues and New Alternatives*. Reading, MA: Addison-Wesley.

Fisher, K. (1993). *Leading Self-Directed Work Teams*. New York: McGraw-Hill.

Thompson, L. L. (2004). *Making the Team: A Guide for Managers*, 2nd edn. Upper Saddle River, NJ: Pearson.

Zenger, J. H., Musselwhite, E., and Hurson, K. (1994). *Leading Teams*. Homewood, IL: Business One Irwin.

team roles

see GROUP ROLES

technology

Philip Anderson

Although technology is a central construct in organizational research, it is defined and employed in different ways by different scholars, sometimes causing considerable confusion. Technology is a human activity undertaken by those whose efforts produce material objects (unlike activities such as religion or sports). Derived from the Greek word *techne*, meaning art or skill, technology is a collection of techniques, ways of fabricating things with a useful purpose in mind.

Typically, technology involves the making and using of artifacts. Yet tools or objects are not technology themselves – they embody technology, which is the know-how that underlies making and using them. The body of knowledge and skills required to produce useful artifacts is the technology, and it may reside in people, things, or processes. In essence, technology mediates between people and the objective world.

Technology is a central construct in organizational research because an organization's technology is the means through which work gets accomplished. Technology provides an organization's means of transforming raw materials (human, symbolic, or material) into desirable goods and services. As a result, the technology that an organization adopts, and the technology adopted by other organizations with which it interacts, can hardly be divorced from its strategy, structure, culture, or characteristic pattern of social relations.

Until quite recently, economists defined technology simply, in terms of production possibility frontiers. A curve could be drawn showing the tradeoff inherent in the production of any two goods: for any set of inputs, such an "isoquant" showed all the different combinations of the two goods that could be effected. Technological progress consisted of moving this curve outward, so that with the same inputs, more of either or both outputs could be produced.

Organizational research has adopted a more complex view of technology. Because technology is a human activity and a body of knowledge, it is not treated as a force purely external to the firm; technology both shapes and is shaped by human VALUES. Orlikowski (1992) summarizes the prevailing view that technology is an external force impacting the organization, but these effects are moderated by human actors and the organizational contexts within which they act. Technology is to some extent autonomous of the firm, but its meaning is socially constructed.

Several fine distinctions appear in the organizational literature, although they are not applied consistently. Technology is treated as distinct from science in that technology is oriented toward producing useful artifacts, while science is oriented toward producing new theory and empirical tests of theory. However, the line between the two is not sharp.

Commonly, at least three different types of technology are distinguished. Product technology is the know-how embedded in an artifact, the blueprint of an object. Process technology is the know-how embedded in the sequence of tasks that creates artifacts. Clearly, the distinction depends on the firm's position in a value chain; to a machine tool maker, the skill embodied in a tool is product technology, but to the firm employing the tool to make things, the same skill is process technology. The third form is administrative technology, which is the set of skills underlying the process of coordinating economic production and exchange of goods.

TECHNOLOGY AND ORGANIZATIONAL ENVIRONMENTS

To some extent, the set of technologies available to an organization is external and autonomous, and thus is a critical part of the organizational environment. For example, an organization wishing to produce and sell a wrench has a variety of cutting, forming, and assembly technologies available to it, and their technical characteristics are to a great extent independent of the organization's interpretation of them. In the OPEN SYSTEMS models which prevail in organization theory, the organization must adapt to its environment; hence, it must adapt to the pattern of technology adoption it observes and to changes in technology over time.

Technological change appears to behave like an evolutionary system in punctuated equilibrium (see EVOLUTIONARY APPROACHES). This is to say that technological development is typically characterized by long eras of incremental change, occasionally interrupted by breakthrough technologies. Such discontinuous advances typically inaugurate an era of ferment and flux, in which the new technology displaces the old while various versions of the new technology compete for marketplace acceptance. Eventually, a standard, or "dominant design," typically emerges in response to organizational avoidance of uncertainty. The emergence of a standard creates conditions under which incremental change, focused on improving one general design, can resume. Technological standards have assumed increasing importance in recent times, as the increased interconnection of products into systems, particularly systems interconnected by digital information technology, creates pressure for products to be compatible with one another and able to communicate.

Almost all technologies are brought to economic use by organizations. As a result, technical communities form, and institutional factors often govern the trajectory of a technology's development. Technologies seldom achieve widespread use due to technical superiority alone. The evolution of a technology is not driven by sheer engineering performance; the development of an institutionalized social framework around a technology plays a critical role. It is more accurate to say that technologies and organizations co-evolve than it is to say that technology is solely an autonomous environmental force (see INSTITUTIONAL THEORY).

Additionally, technologies both help to shape and are shaped by cultural forces. The same technologies may have different social conse-quences in different countries, depending on institutional relationships and national sets of values. Although some scholars contend that technology imposes its own value system on humans, the weight of the evidence suggests that all technologies undergo different interpretations in different settings, and thus are socially constructed within a cultural context (Bijker, Hughes, and Pinch, 1987).

TECHNOLOGY AND ORGANIZATIONAL STRATEGY

Since technology is central to the organizational environment, scholars examining the strategies firms use to adapt to their environments frequently examine the impact of technology, particularly technological change, upon strategic choices and outcomes. The effects of INNOVATION adoption is the most widely studied topic in this area. Because much know-how is tacit, firms often find it difficult to adjust to technological change, especially when it is rapid and unpredictable. Thus technology can be a powerful force in reshaping and overturning industry structure. The foundation of most research in this vein is the economist Josef Schumpeter's vision of "creative destruction" – the replacement of a set of dominant firms by another group of rivals employing a radically new technology – as the fundamental engine of capitalist progress.

The rise of digital technologies has also focused attention on the role of standards and network externalities in determining why some technologies and innovators displace others (e.g., Schilling, 2002). Where customers value compatibility among complementary technologies or between old and new technologies, technological variants that acquire a slight lead in an adoption race can crowd out alternatives; Rohlfs (2003) provides many empirical examples. Strategic efforts to influence which standards prevail can influence the performance and life chances of an enterprise (e.g., Rosenkopf, Metiu, and George, 2001).

As technical systems grow more complex and interconnected – due largely to innovations in communications technology and information technology that embed intelligence in different products which must communicate – technological systems and networks assume increasing importance. As a consequence, more techno-logical development is taking place through inter-organizational ventures than appears to have been the case in the past (*see* INTER-ORGANIZATIONAL RELATIONS). Competitive success via technology may depend more and more on the firm's ability to build alliances and partnership networks, not simply on the firm's individual technological prowess, and conse-quently, the study of technology based alliances is one of the most vibrant areas in modern strat-egy research.

Since the 1990s, scholars have studied inten-sively how firms acquire knowledge, partly in order to understand how distinctive capabilities emerge that create enduring differences among rival enterprises. Technology is not the only form of intellectual capital that firms develop, but the study of how firms build technical know-ledge is central to the fast-growing literature on knowledge management. Scholars also have become more interested in understanding how technological knowledge, embodied in patents, is transferred among specialities and domains. For example, Hargadon and Sutton (1997) de-scribe the role of technology brokers in bringing together knowledge from different fields to foster innovation, while Ahuja (2000) examines how the structure of collaboration networks in-fluences the amount of new technical knowledge a firm produces.

TECHNOLOGY AND ORGANIZATIONAL STRUCTURE

The way in which a firm gets work done is a fundamental determinant of organizational structure. Firms devising technically complex and advanced products typically require a com-bination of a flexible structure with close coord-ination to manage the complexity. Firms also tend to develop a higher ratio of supervisors to other employees as the range and technical diffi-culty of their tasks increases (*see* ORGANIZA-TIONAL DESIGN).

The nature of a firm's process technology may also influence its organizational structure. The more a firm relies on mass production to achieve high productivity, the more MECHANISTIC it tends to be. The more it relies on flexible, low-volume batch production, the more organic it tends to be. Computer integrated manufacture may make possible customized batch production that is as economical as mass production. A good deal of scholarly research is aimed at discerning the effect of advanced manufacturing technology on the organizational structures of the future, so far without conclusive results.

The influence of technology on organizational structure generally appears to be far from deter-ministic. Different organizations may respond differently to the implementation of very similar technologies because of their distinctive histories and patterns of social relations. This is not to say that technology has no orderly, regular influence on organizational structure. Rather, it is to say that organizations have considerable latitude in constructing the meaning of new technologies they adopt, and the structural responses they generate depend in large part on the way in which different interpretations structure behav-ior (Orlikowski, 1992).

TECHNOLOGY AND THE NATURE OF WORK

Technology has played a very large part in or-ganizational research on the sociology of work and industrial relations. The key idea underlying much of this research is that technology is not simply a neutral instrument by which knowledge is put to useful purposes. Rather, a firm's choice of technology may well influence the relation-ship between workers and their work, and be-tween workers and the organizations to which they belong.

One aspect of Karl Marx's materialism is the assertion that the organization of the means of production determines the other features of a society. In the Marxist tradition, Blauner (1964) describes a specific relationship between dominant production technology, organizational structure, worker attitudes, and worker con-sciousness. In Blauner's view, the relationship between the worker and his or her job tasks is one of alienation under modern production tech-nology because technology is an instrument of domination, wielded by managers who possess POWER. Other studies suggest that relations between workers and their companies is also significantly affected by the type of production technology employed.

One way in which managers achieve control over people and things is by substituting technical RATIONALITY for human interpretation (Berting, 1993). Thus the contemporary dominance of technology is connected to the rise of universal instrumental rationality as a value. Managing for technical efficiency appears to be rational, and society generally demands from organizations the appearance of rationality. In some industries and societies, pressure to display dispassionate, instrumental rationality had led to the formation of a "technocratic" class of managers, whose control and authority stem from their mastery of a distinctive body of technical know-how. However, technology choices may well hinge on the manager's desire to maintain dominance and avoid dependence on worker idiosyncrasies, not on purely technical considerations (Noble, 1984).

See also *job design; loose coupling; management, classical theory*

Bibliography

Adler, P. S. (1989). Technology strategy: A guide to the literatures. In R. S. Rosenbloom and R. A. Burgelman (eds.), *Research on Technological Innovation, Management and Policy*. Greenwich, CT: JAI Press, 25–151.

Ahuja, G. (2000). Collaboration networks, structural holes, and innovation: A longitudinal study. *Administrative Science Quarterly*, 45, 425–55.

Berting, J. (1993). Organization studies and the ideology of technological determinism. In S. Lindenberg and H. Schreuder (eds.), *Interdisciplinary Perspectives on Organization Studies*. Oxford: Pergamon Press, 183–94.

Bijker, W. E., Hughes, T. P., and Pinch, T. J. (1987). *The Social Construction of Technological Systems: New Directions in the Sociology and History of Technology*. Cambridge, MA: MIT Press.

Blauner, R. (1964). *Alienation and Freedom: The Factory Worker and His Industry*. Chicago: University of Chicago Press.

Hargadon, A. and Sutton, R. I. (1997). Technology brokering and innovation in a product development firm. *Administrative Science Quarterly*, 42, 716–49.

McGinn, R. E. (1978). What is technology? In P. T. Durbin (ed.), *Research in Philosophy and Technology*. Greenwich, CT: JAI Press, 179–97.

Noble, D. (1984). *Forces of Production: A Social History of Industrial Automation*. New York: Knopf.

Orlikowski, W. J. (1992). The duality of technology: Rethinking the concept of technology in organizations. *Organization Science*, 3, 398–427.

Rohlfs, J. J. (2003). *Bandwagon Effects in High Technology Industries*. Cambridge, MA: MIT Press.

Rosenkopf, L. R., Metiu, A., and George, V. P. (2001). From the bottom up? Technical committee activity and alliance formation. *Administrative Science Quarterly*, 46, 748–72.

Schilling, M. A. (2002). Technology success and failure in winner-take-all markets: The impact of learning orientation, timing, and network externalities.

Trist, E. L. and Bamforth, K. W. (1951). Some social and psychological consequences of the longwall method of coal-getting. *Human Relations*, 4, 3–38.

Usher, A. P. (1954). *A History of Mechanical Inventions*. Oxford: Oxford University Press.

technology transfer

Kim Sutherland

TECHNOLOGY transfer involves the movement of an idea, practice, or object from a "source" individual or organization to a "recipient" individual or organization which perceives it as new. Technology transfer is concerned with the diffusion of tools, products, and information together with the associated knowledge regarding their use and application. Successful technology transfer is characterized by recipients being able to use and adapt the technology to their particular requirements and circumstances.

Early work in the 1960s and 1970s tended to portray technology transfer as a linear process whereby products, ideas or techniques moved from their genesis in basic research, to applied research, to development, to commercialization, to diffusion and adoption. Subsequent work has highlighted the complexity of technology transfer processes and recognizes the important roles played by FEEDBACK and iteration, by acceptance of multiple perspectives, and by sensitivity to social, cultural, and assumptive contexts (Munir, 2002).

The literature focuses on three main types of technology transfer:

1 *Intra-organizational technology transfer,* which is concerned with the translation of ideas and prototypes from research related to production related functions within a single organization.

2 *Inter-sectoral technology transfer*, which embodies the movement of technology from research focused "source" organizations such as universities to practice focused "recipient" organizations such as commercial companies.

3 *International technology transfer*, which occurs across geographical boundaries, often from industrialized countries to developing countries.

Much of the literature on technology transfer resonates with that concerned with the diffusion of INNOVATION. Rogers's (1995) influential work on the diffusion of innovation asserts that the adoption of new ideas, techniques, and products is shaped by the interplay between the innovation, the recipient, and the environment. It encompasses a social contagion model of diffusion and asserts that information or innovation transfer occurs via direct social contact and is facilitated by social cohesiveness.

In contrast, research into social networks suggests that densely connected NETWORKS are less efficient than sparse networks (Burt, 1992). "Weak" rather than "strong" ties are seen to be an important factor in the processes of information and technology transfer. Weak ties link individuals to diverse sets of contacts, providing a range of heterogeneous cues and social relations, whereas tightly knit, homogeneous groups receive fewer cues and are characterized by stronger norms and greater conformity and are less open to new ideas and approaches.

Burt's (1992) work on social networks also found that individuals and/or organizations in "structurally similar positions" (i.e., those that have the same patterns of social relations), even in the absence of social contact, are more likely to adopt an innovation if their corresponding entities do so. This finding echoes aspects of INSTITUTIONAL THEORY, particularly the role of fads and fashions and institutional trends towards isomorphism (Powell and DiMaggio, 1991) as factors in technology transfer.

While there are clearly overlaps between these related concepts, technology transfer is differentiated by its focus on more directed and deliberate transfer processes. In most cases, prospective recipients for technology transfer are clearly identified and cognizant participants. The process itself is often characterized by a more inclusive and interactive approach with the use of joint problem solving between those involved with development, adaptation, and use.

Different mechanisms that have been used to facilitate technology transfer mechanisms include:

Spin-offs: new organizations that are formed in order to capitalize on a technology developed within a parent company; often staffed by individuals who were employees of the parent organization.

Licensing: the granting of permission to produce, use, or sell a certain technology.

Publications: the publication of articles in academic journals is widely used by the university sector as a dissemination tool.

Meetings: personal interaction, networks, and associations.

Policy and governmental initiatives: including technology based economic development programs, science parks, technology incubators, and (in the US) cooperative R&D agreements (CRADAs) (Bozeman, 2000).

Temporary organizational alliances such as joint ventures, partnerships, and projects.

The most widely used of these mechanisms, publications, is the least effective (Rogers, Takegami, and Yin, 2001). This finding is unsurprising given our current understanding of the need for communication processes that are iterative and ongoing in effective technology transfer.

In moving from one organizational setting to another, technology transfer processes invariably have to overcome different organizational barriers to change. In the case of intraorganizational transfer from R&D to commercial functions these barriers are often the product of structural and hierarchical boundaries and associated systems for resource allocation and reward. For example, if research and production departments act as self-contained units with tight budgets and resource allocation processes that do not encourage cooperation and joint problem solving, then little effective technology transfer will take place (Dawson, 1995). For intersectoral and international transfer, organizational characteristics such as structure, resourcing, existing technology, and environmental context all represent potential hurdles. An overarching factor which affects all types of technology transfer is organizational culture, particularly the existence of different subcultures; different social context and different sets of mental maps and taken-for-granted assumptions in donor and recipient environments (Bozeman, 2000).

Empirical evidence suggests that successful technology transfer requires the transfer of tacit knowledge along with codified and technical information. Tacit knowledge is transferred through relationships between source and recipient and these relationships are often founded on some sort of common ground such as a shared knowledge base, a similar set of experiences, or shared values, beliefs, and assumptions (Cummings and Teng, 2003). Robust organizational relationships also allow for complex information transfer processes with multiple feedback channels and shared problem solving to occur across the relatively formalized relationship between donor and recipient.

See also *learning, organizational; organizational change; resistance to change*

Bibliography

Bozeman, B. (2000). Technology transfer and public policy: A review of research and theory. *Research Policy*, **29**, 627–55.

Burt, R. (1992). *Structural Holes: The Social Structure of Competition*. Cambridge, MA: Harvard University Press.

Cummings, J. and Teng, B. (2003). Transferring R&D knowledge: The key factors affecting knowledge transfer success. *Journal of Engineering and Technology Management*, **20**, 39–68.

Dawson, S. (1995). Technology transfer. *Encyclopedic Dictionary of Organizational Behavior*. Oxford: Blackwell.

Munir, K. (2002). Being different: How normative and cognitive aspects of institutional environments influence technology transfer. *Human Relations*, **55** (12), 1403–28.

Powell, W. and DiMaggio, P. (eds.) (1991). *The New Institutionalism in Organizational Analysis*. Chicago: University of Chicago Press.

Rogers, E. (1995). *Diffusion of Innovations*, 4th edn. New York: Free Press.

Rogers, E., Takegami, S., and Yin, J. (2001). Lessons learned about technology transfer. *Technovation*, **21**, 253–61.

Williams, R. and Gibson, D. (1990). *Technology Transfer: A Communications Perspective*. London: Sage.

temporal perspective

Sally Blount-Lyon

Temporal perspective refers to a specific point of view or attitude that an actor holds about time (Kirton, Okhuysen, and Waller, 2004). Different actors (i.e., people, groups, organizations, national/ethnic cultures) can hold different temporal perspectives across activities and over time. These may vary regarding how, for example, attention is given to (a) the direction of time (past, present, or future); (b) the interval of elapsed time that is salient (e.g., a minute, hour, week, month, or seven years); (c) the meaning and value attached to a time interval (e.g., lunch time, vacation time, class time, a product life cycle; or billable versus non-billable time); (d) the reference points used to measure and evaluate the passage of time (e.g., an editor's deadline, social norms, or a personal performance goal); and (e) the conscious (or non-conscious) experience of elapsed time (Bluedorn, 2002). Actors' temporal perspectives affect how they evaluate outcomes (e.g., Sara's report was not ready in time for the meeting), experience activities (e.g., Joe was so busy that he did not even notice the time), and formulate expectations and goals regarding how activities are spaced out over time (Blount and Janicik, 2001). Thus, temporal perspectives are integral to human cognition, emotion, and action at multiple levels of analysis. They affect how the past is evaluated, the present is experienced, and the future is planned.

Time itself is often perceived as a valued resource, and across all cultures the control of time (i.e., establishing calendars and schedules) typically resides with the wealthy and political elite. At the group level, the control of time is also a vehicle commonly used to assert one's comparative power – the idea being that in a meeting, for example, the longer that people wait for you, the higher your status (Bluedorn, 2002).

Management research finds that organizations differ regarding temporal norms (e.g., the degree to which punctuality is valued or family time is held sacred) and the degree to which organizations synchronize with their environments (e.g., with the ongoing rates of change in product advancements and production technologies). Groups differ in the degree to which they "entrain" with their environments (i.e., align their own activities to match the pace of surrounding activities versus create their own rhythms) (*see* ENTRAINMENT); demonstrate "mid-point transitions" in structuring work to meet deadlines; and pace their activities depending on their tasks (e.g., compare the workpace of accounting versus creative departments) (Ancona and Chong, 1996). National and organizational cultures (*see* CULTURE, NATIONAL; ORGANIZATIONAL CULTURE), as well as the individuals within them, may also differ regarding whether they are time urgent, past vs. future oriented, and monochromic vs. polychromic (i.e., preferring to work on one activity at a time versus several activities simultaneously).

In sum, the study of temporal perspectives offers a rich lens for interpreting behavior at all levels (Zaheer, Albert, and Zaheer, 1999). However, the topic lacks shared theories and methodologies, and has yet to gain broad institutional acceptance. As these roadblocks are overcome, time-based research will expand, and new avenues will be opened for topics that have traditionally been studied statically.

See also *career; levels of analysis*

Bibliography

Ancona, D. and Chong, C. L. (1996). Entrainment: Pace, cycle, and rhythm in organizational behavior. In B. M. Staw and L. L. Cummings (eds.), *Research in Organizational Behavior*, 18, 251–84.

Blount, S. and Janicik, G. A. (2001) When plans change: Examining how people evaluate timing changes in work organizations. *Academy of Management Review*, 26, 566–85.

Bluedorn, A. C. (2002). *The Human Organization of Time: Temporal Realities and Experience*. Stanford, CA: Stanford University Press.

Kirton, B., Okhuysen, G. A., and Waller, M. J. (2004). A glossary of temporal terms relating to groups and organizations. In S. Blount, M. A. Neale, and E. A. Mannix (eds.), *Research on Managing Groups and Teams – Time in Groups*, 6, 237–66.

Zaheer, S., Albert, S., and Zaheer, A. (1999). Time scales and organizational theory. *Academy of Management Review*, 24 (4), 725–41.

theory

Karl E. Weick

Theory, which is about suppositions that are general, idealized, and abstract, can easily be misunderstood in a field like organizational behavior where pragmatists, practitioners, and positivists worry about practice, profits, and precision. To forestall such misunderstanding, this entry discusses theory in general, what it is, how people approximate it, and the consequences of these approximations.

DEFINITION OF THEORY

If theory is equated with knowledge claims preserved in statements involving concepts, then its nature and importance are captured as well by Kant as anyone: "Perception without conception is blind; conception without perception is empty." For comparison, here are two descriptions that are more prosaic but less elliptical.

1   Theory is "an ordered set of assertions about a generic behavior or structure assumed to hold throughout a significantly broad range of specific instances" (Sutherland, 1975: 9).
2   Theory is "a collection of assertions, both verbal and symbolic, that identifies what variables are important for what reasons, specifies how they are interrelated and why, and identifies the conditions under which they should be related or not related" (Campbell, 1990: 65).

What is common among these descriptions is the idea that theories refer to "specific instances," which provides the perceptions that keep conceptions from becoming empty, and the idea that these references are abstract, general simplifications, which provides labels for perceptions and keeps them from becoming blind. But not all theories are equally successful at removing emptiness and blindness. The reason is that they vary in the degree to which their assertions facilitate sensemaking, move beyond common sense, and approximate the properties of a fully developed theory. Variation in these three dimensions affects the extent to which the theory is able to explain, predict, and delight. We review these dimensions briefly to create a more nuanced understanding of theory.

THEORY AND SENSEMAKING

If sensemaking is defined as "the reciprocal interaction of information seeking, meaning ascription, and action" (Thomas, Clark, and Gioia, 1993; 240), then the affinity between it and theorizing is apparent. Dubin (1976: 26) says as much: "A theory tries to make sense out of the observable world by ordering the relationships among elements that constitute the theorist's focus of attention in the real world." To think more clearly about theory is to take this correspondence seriously.

Blumer (1969) took it seriously in his extended gloss of Kant's aphorism about PER-CEPTION and conception. Blumer argued that conception comes into play when an activity, driven by perception, becomes blocked or frustrated. "A concept always arises as an individual experience, to bridge a gap or insufficiency in perception." This bridging, in the form of a new orientation that reshapes perception and guides action, unfolds similarly in the mind of the theorist and the lay person. Concepts give blocked experience an "understandable character" by referring to something whose existence is presumed, isolated through abstraction, labeled, and shared, even though its character is not fully understood. Perhaps most important, the conception is instrumental. It releases and allows completion of activity, whether that activity be Pasteur solving the problem of anthrax or practitioners solving problems of DOWNSIZING or identity.

To make sense by means of conception is to invent, to bring things into existence. Theorists do this by means of sentences that make knowledge claims. That is less innocent than it

sounds. The tipoff is the word "claims." Van Maanen (1993: 6, 8) captures the issues: "Theorizing is a social practice that represents the construction of reality via the only method at our disposal – language … Theorists produce discourse whose purpose is to persuade readers that they've got it right, have something to say." Theories do not mirror reality. Instead, they create a sense of what is real and unreal, which means they are rhetorical rather than foundational (Mailloux, 1990: 133).

Theorists have no choice but to use sentences if they want to communicate knowledge for purposes of evaluation. Furthermore, only sentences can be evaluated as true or false. There is no such thing as a "true" or "false" experience. Therefore, what is said becomes what we know, which means that how we formulate what we say, determines how systematic and shared the things will be that we claim to know. Thus, ways of writing theory influence what can be done with it.

THEORY AND DISCOVERY

Perception remains relatively blind unless theories tell us something we do not already know. To do this, theorists often deliberately move away from collective social wisdom so that they can gain access to knowledge with a low *a priori* probability of ever being known. Common knowledge is suspended temporarily when people invoke possible worlds such as those created in SIMULATIONS, laboratories, formal models, and thought experiments involving imagination (Weick, 1990). Possible worlds are tools of rhetoric that create a unique sense of what is real and unreal. Nevertheless, their content can be given an empirical interpretation at any time, which means their departures from common knowledge are transient and instrumental. Theorists and practitioners sometimes forget this.

THEORY AND ITS APPROXIMATIONS

Theory in organizational behavior is a dimension rather than an all-or-none activity and it ranges from "guess" to "explanatory system." Merton (1967) suggests possible points along this dimension, all of which represent distinct interim struggles, but none of which represents a final product. To "compare" theories for their usefulness is often a misleading exercise since what is actually being compared are approximations that have developed different parts of a theory.

Theory work is sometimes approximated by *general orientations* to materials. Broad frameworks specify types of variables that people should take into account, but determinate relationships between specific variables are not set forth. References in the organizational behavior literature to "lenses," "images," "perspectives," and "frameworks" typically signal work of this kind. Scott's (1987: 29) three organizational perspectives – rational, natural, and OPEN SYSTEMS – are advanced general orientations since they also embody elaborated concepts and empirical generalizations.

As we saw earlier, much theory work is language work or, as Merton calls it, *analysis of concepts*. As the label suggests, conceptual analysis consists of specification and clarification of key concepts. But a list of concepts and definitions is not a theory. "It is only when such concepts are interrelated in the form of a scheme that a theory begins to emerge" (Merton 1967: 143). Perrow's (1984) development of the idea of a "normal accident" exemplifies conceptual analysis. And his elaboration of this idea in terms of coupling and complexity represents steps toward interrelating variables associated with the concept.

Post-factum interpretation often passes as theory work in organizational behavior because so much of the database is case histories. These interpretations have a spurious adequacy because they are often ad hoc hypotheses, selected because they fit observations, with no systematic exploration of alternative interpretations that are also consistent with the data and no tests of the ad hoc fit with new observations. Weick's (1990) analysis of the Tenerife air disaster as stress induced regression illustrates this tactic, and in doing so is just that, an illustration rather than a test of claims about stress.

Finally, *empirical generalization*, the raw material for theory, may be misidentified as theory itself. However, since the generalization is "an isolated proposition summarizing observed uniformities of relationships between two or more variables" (Merton, 1967: 149), it lacks the crucial property of an interrelated set of propositions. The idea that power flows toward those who reduce significant uncertain-

ties (Salancik and Pfeffer, 1977) represents an empirical generalization in search of related propositions.

By way of conclusion, readers should understand that approximations are the bulk of theory in organizational behavior. Approximations can still supply "substantive ideas about what things mean, how things work, or what the serious problems are" (Campbell, 1990: 67). Those approximations that do so, persuasively, in uncommon ways, that are susceptible to further elaboration, hold the future of the field.

See also *critical theory; innovation; systems theory*

Bibliography

Blumer, H. (1969). *Symbolic Interactionism.* Englewood Cliffs, NJ: Prentice-Hall.

Campbell, J. P. (1990). The role of theory in industrial and organizational psychology In M. D. Dunnette and L. M. Hough (eds.), *Handbook of Industrial and Organizational Psychology*, vol. 1, 2nd edn. Palo Alto, CA: Consulting Psychologists Press, 40–73.

Dubin, R. (1976). Theory building in applied areas. In M. D. Dunnette (ed.), *Handbook of Industrial and Organizational Psychology*. Chicago: Rand McNally, 17–39.

Mailloux, S. (1990). Interpretation. In F. Lentricchia and T. McLaughlin (eds.), *Critical Terms for Literary Study*. Chicago: University of Chicago Press, 121–34.

Merton, R. K. (1967). *On Theoretical Sociology*. New York: Free Press.

Perrow, C. (1984). *Normal Accidents*. New York: Basic Books.

Salancik, G. R. and Pfeffer, J. (1977). Who gets power – and how they hold on to it: A strategic-contingency model of power. *Organizational Dynamics*, 5, 3–21.

Scott, W. R. (1987). *Organizations*, 2nd edn. Englewood Cliffs, NJ: Prentice-Hall.

Sutherland, J. W. (1975). *Systems: Analysis, Administration, and Architecture*. New York: Van Nostrand.

Thomas, J. B., Clark, S. M., and Gioia, D. A. (1993). Strategic sensemaking and organizational performance: Linkages among scanning, interpretation, action, and outcomes. *Academy of Management Journal*, 36, 239–70.

Van Maanen, J. (1993) Theory as style: The uses, abuses and pleasures of organizational theory. Talk presented at Academy of Management, August 10.

Weick, K. E. (1989). Theory construction as disciplined imagination. *Academy of Management Review*, 14, 516–31.

Weick, K. E. (1990). The vulnerable system: Analysis of the Tenerife air disaster. *Journal of Management*, 16, 571–93.

theory X and Y

Bernard M. Bass

According to McGregor (1960), traditional management believed implicitly in Theory X, which postulates that employees are inherently lazy, indifferent to the needs of the organization, and uninterested in doing a good job. Employees should not be expected to do any more than absolutely necessary. As a consequence, management has to direct, motivate, and control the workforces as if they were immature children. Control systems are essential and assignments must be specific. Close monitoring and correction of performance by supervisors is essential. Thinking should be left to superiors. Discipline and fear of PUNISHMENT should be used to maintain standards of performance. Employees should be motivated primarily by "carrots" for good performance and "sticks" for poor performance.

Opposite to belief in Theory X is Theory Y, which postulates that employees essentially want to do a good job. They have ego needs as well as needs for material benefits. They respond positively to being treated like adults and given responsibilities commensurate with their capabilities. Their involvement, loyalty, and COMMITMENT to the organization are important motivators of their performance. Wherever possible, they should be able to participate in decisions affecting their performance (*see* PARTICIPATION).

The two theories are predicated on distinctive assumptions about human behavior. Theory X assumes workers must be persuaded, rewarded, punished, controlled, and directed if the coordination of effort is to be achieved. In fact, no work at all will get done unless there is active intervention by management. This is because employees are naturally lazy and will work as little as possible. They lack ambition, dislike accepting responsibility, and prefer to be led. They are only concerned with their own needs and not with the goals of their organization. They resist change (*see* RESISTANCE TO CHANGE). They are not good decision-makers. As much as possible, all decisions within the organization should be routinized so that under all circumstances the individual will require a minimum of thought without alternatives. Indeed, they must be told in detail what to do or they will not be able to do their job.

They must be prodded with external incentives and close surveillance. While management is responsible for organizing the elements of productive enterprise – money, materials, equipment, people – in the interest of economic ends, employees develop passivity and resistance to organizational needs as a result of their experience in organizations.

Theory Y says that workers have the potential for development, the capacity for assuming responsibility, and the readiness to work for organizational goals. Management makes it possible for workers to recognize and develop these traits. Therefore, management is responsible for arranging organizational processes and conditions so that employees can achieve their own goals by directing their efforts toward organizational objectives. Management creates opportunities, releases potential, removes obstacles, encourages growth, and provides guidance. Belief in Theory Y promotes decentralization, delegation, job enlargement, EMPOWERMENT, participation, and SELF-MANAGING TEAMS.

See also *employee involvement; scientific management; self-actualization; theory z; values*

Bibliography

McGregor, D. M. (1960). *The Human Side of Enterprise.* New York: McGraw-Hill.

theory Z

Bernard M. Bass

Ouchi (1981) introduced the idea of Theory Z to represent the beliefs underlying Japanese management in contrast to THEORY X AND THEORY Y. The management of Theory Z firms is characterized by long-term employment and intensive SOCIALIZATION of their workforce. Objectives and VALUES emphasize cooperation and teamwork. There is slow promotion from within the firm and jobs are rotated. Employees are expected to be generalists rather than specialists. Performance appraisal systems are complex. Emphasis is on WORK GROUPS/TEAMS rather than individuals, open COMMUNICATION, consultative DECI-

SION-MAKING, and a relations oriented concern for employees. In comparison to Theory X organizations, Theory Z organizations are more decentralized and have fewer levels of management. Subordinates exercise more upward influence in dealing with their bosses in the Type Z than in the Type X organizations.

See also *group cohesiveness; group dynamics; organizational culture*

Bibliography

Ouchi, W. G. (1981). *Theory Z: How American Business Can Meet the Japanese Challenge*. Reading, MA: Addison-Wesley.

top management teams

Donald C. Hambrick

The term "top management team" (TMT) has been adopted by organization and strategy theorists to refer to the relatively small group of most influential executives at the apex of an organization – usually the general manager (*see* CEOs) and his or her direct reports. The term does not necessarily imply a formalized management-by-committee arrangement, but rather simply the constellation of, say, the top three to ten executives. A scholarly interest in top management teams emerged in the early 1980s and has been prominent ever since. Stemming from a realization that top management typically is a shared activity, researchers have moved beyond an examination of individual leaders to a wider focus on the senior leadership group.

The underlying assumption is that the collective dispositions and interactions of top managers affect the choices they make (Hambrick and Mason, 1984). The available evidence as to whether the characteristics of the individual top executive or of the entire top team are better predictors of organizational outcomes clearly supports the conclusion that the top team has greater effect. For example, the degree to which all TMT members value innovation (rather than stability) has been found to be more strongly related to the pursuit of innovation strategies

than the values of chief executives alone. Similarly, significant strategic change is more likely to occur following major changes in the composition of the TMT than when only the CEO changes.

TMT HETEROGENEITY

Researchers have also devoted considerable attention to the effects of TMT heterogeneity (or diversity) on organizational outcomes. By examining the diversity of group members on such dimensions as age, tenure in the company, tenure in the industry, and functional background, researchers have explored the conditions under which member variety is helpful or harmful to performance (Bunderson and Sutcliffe, 2002). The general conclusion from this research is that TMT diversity enhances strategic creativity and boldness, but it impairs the organization's speed in making and implementing decisions. Although research results have been far from definitive, there is general belief among scholars that TMT diversity enhances organizational performance when environmental conditions are dynamic, but that it impairs performance when conditions are stable.

BEYOND TMT DEMOGRAPHY

A widely noted limitation of TMT research is that much of it relies on demographic variables and that such explorations do not reveal the operative mechanism(s) that cause TMT profiles to be manifested in organizational outcomes. This failure to get "inside the black box" of demography has led, in turn, to calls for research on the actual dynamics and processes that occur within TMTs. For example, researchers have become interested in how TMT composition affects conflict, cohesion, ease of communications, interpersonal rivalry, and so on (Peterson, Owens, and Martorana, 1999).

The vast majority of research on TMTs has focused primarily on the composition of teams as predictors of organizational outcomes. Unfortunately, other team characteristics have not received as much attention, no doubt because they are more difficult for researchers to observe and measure. A complete portrayal of a TMT, however, would include not only its composition, but also team structure (e.g., size and roles), incentives (e.g., individual vs. group-based financial incentives and succession prospects) (*see* EXECUTIVE SUCCESSION), and team processes (e.g., communication flows and sociopolitical dynamics) (*see* GROUP DYNAMICS), as well as the characteristics and behaviors of the group leader (Hambrick, 1994).

A major dilemma particularly arises in TMT research due to the fact that senior groups vary widely in the degree to which they have the properties of a "team." Very often, such groups consist of loose constellations of executive talent: individuals who rarely come together (and then usually for superficial exchange of information), who rarely collaborate, and who focus almost entirely on their own piece of the enterprise (Katzenbach and Smith, 1991). To the extent that TMTs are highly fragmented, then a research focus on collective team properties will yield weak predictions of organizational outcomes. Researchers have recently become interested in directly examining "behavioral integration" – or the degree of mutual and collective interaction – in top management groups, including attention to the factors that enhance or diminish behavioral integration, as well as the effects of behavioral integration on strategic outcomes and performance (Hambrick, 1994).

DETERMINANTS OF TMT CHARACTERISTICS

Complementing the larger body of work on the effects of TMTs, some research has examined the determinants of TMT characteristics. In this vein, researchers have found that both external factors (such as industry age, growth rate, and munificence) and organizational characteristics (including strategic profile, size, and financial resources) help to explain the characteristics of TMTs. Indeed, one of the major limitations of many studies on TMTs is that the direction of causality has been imputed but not verified. It is most plausible to believe that firms select and promote executives who fit certain critical contingencies; in turn, those executives make choices in line with their particular predispositions and competencies. Over time, a reinforcing spiral probably occurs; therefore, establishing definitive causality will always be a bit difficult.

Available research, however, does allow us to conclude that the biases, blinders, experiences, and interactions of top executives greatly affect what happens to companies. Thus, CEOs or general managers who wish to improve the performance and fitness of their organizations are well advised to focus their attention on the characteristics and qualities of their top teams.

See also *corporate boards; governance; leadership; organizational demography; organizational effectiveness*

Bibliography

Bunderson, J. S. and Sutcliffe, K. M. (2002). Comparing alternative conceptualizations of functional diversity in management teams: Process and performance effects. *Academy of Management Journal*, **45**, 875–93.

Hambrick, D. C. (1994). Top management groups: A conceptual integration and reconsideration of the "team" label. In B. M. Staw and L. L. Cummings (eds.), *Research In Organizational Behavior*. Greenwich, CT: JAI Press.

Hambrick, D. C. and Mason, P. A. (1984). Upper echelons: The organization as a reflection of its top managers. *Academy of Management Review*, **9**, 195–206.

Jackson, S. E. (1991). Consequences of group processing for the interpersonal dynamics of strategic issue processing. In P. Shrivastava, A. Hugg, and J. Dutton (eds.), *Advances In Strategic Management*. Greenwich, CT: JAI Press, 345–82.

Katzenbach, J. R. and Smith, D. K. (1991). *The Wisdom Of Teams*. Boston, MA: Harvard Business School Press.

Peterson, R. S., Owens, P. D., and Martorana, P. V. (1999). Cause or effect? An investigation of the relationship between top management group dynamics and organizational performance. In R. Wageman (eds.), *Research on Managing Groups and Teams*. Stamford, CT: JAI Press, 49–69.

Smith, K. G., Smith, K. A., Olian, J. D., Sims, H. P., O'Bannon, D. P., and Scully, J. A. (1994). Top management team demography and process: The role of social integration and communication. *Administrative Science Quarterly*, **39**, 412–38.

total quality management

Gerald E. Ledford, Jr.

Total quality management (TQM) is a management philosophy and business strategy intended to embed quality improvement practices deeply into the fabric of the organization. It is also a social movement that has become partly institutionalized in many countries. No single authority speaks for the entire movement. Rather, TQM is a diverse collection of related ideas primarily contributed by American quality consultants such as Juran (1988) and Deming (1986), and the Japanese (Ishikawa, 1985; Young, 1992).

Major themes in TQM include the following. First, the entire organization becomes focused on quality, defined as *satisfying customer requirements*. Improving quality is thought to improve productivity, decreases costs, and increases speed to market as well. Quality experts typically estimate that the "cost of quality," including inspection, defects, scrap, rework, and warranty cost, is typically 10–25 percent of product cost.

TQM efforts also attempt to create a culture of CONTINUOUS IMPROVEMENT in which improving quality is the responsibility of every employee. This requires LEADERSHIP by top management. Quality problems are viewed as system problems, not worker motivation problems. A TQM culture requires values, perspectives, and tools that rely on senior management for development. Thus, TQM has a "top-down" flavor. *Planning* to integrate a quality focus in all operations receives a heavy emphasis.

Functional and cross-functional *teamwork* is stressed. QUALITY CIRCLES and JOB DESIGN may enhance teamwork. Using and collaborating with a limited number of quality oriented vendors is encouraged. A major contribution of the quality movement is the development of specific tools for quality analysis and GROUP DECISION-MAKING. These include benchmarking, statistical process control, measurement of the "cost of quality," process analysis, Pareto charts, cause and effect diagrams, control charts, and other tools. A critical part of Japanese management, especially in manufacturing firms using mass production technologies, is just-in-time.

Finally, certain human resource practices are characteristic of TQM efforts. Job designs make employees responsible for inspecting their own work and correcting their errors. However, work simplification and standardization mean that employees do not necessarily gain self-management responsibility in TQM systems. Employees typically receive considerable quality data. Rewards for quality improvement typically are limited to recognition.

Formal TQM programs have declined in the US. For example, only 55 percent of Fortune 1000 firms reported have a TQM program in 1999, versus 66 percent in 1996 and 76 percent in 1993 (Lawler, Mohrman, and Benson, 2001). On average, these programs cover one-third of employees. Nevertheless, many quality practices have become nearly universal. More than 90 percent of firms reported making at least some use of such practices as cost of quality monitoring, work simplification, self-inspection, and collaboration with suppliers on quality.

The quality research literature is vast but unimpressive. Most evidence of TQM effectiveness is anecdotal. Many positive stories tell of drastic reductions in quality problems, millions of dollars of costs eliminated, markets and profits regained, and so on. Other anecdotes point to a high failure rate. Overall, TQM reports are probably overly optimistic (Zbaracki, 1998). TQM does not fit conveniently into existing research domains, and mainstream academics have neglected TQM (Dean and Bowen, 1994). Some research points to difficulties in implementation of such a complex and challenging innovation (Hackman and Wageman, 1995). A large-scale study in the healthcare industry indicates that early adopters of TQM are motivated by the hope of performance gains, while later adopters are motivated more by institutional forces and network effects (Westphal, Gulati, and Shortell, 1997). Since almost any new adopter of TQM is now a late adopter, this finding has interesting implications for the future of the TQM movement.

See also *job design; organizational effectiveness; technology*

Bibliography

Dean, J. W. and Bowen, D. E. (1994). Management theory and total quality: Improving research and practice through theory development. *Academy of Management Review*, **19** (3).

Deming, W. E. (1986). *Out of the Crisis.* Cambridge, MA: MIT Press.

Hackman, R. and Wageman, R. (1995). Total quality management: Empirical, conceptual, and practical issues. *Administrative Science Quarterly*, **40** (2), 309–42.

Ishikawa, K. (1985). *What is Total Quality Control? The Japanese Way*. Englewood Cliffs, NJ: Prentice-Hall.

Juran, J. M. (1988). *Juran on Planning for Quality*. New York: Free Press.

Lawler, E. E., III, Mohrman, S. A., and Benson, G. (2001). *Organizing for High Performance: Employee Involvement, TQM, Reengineering, and Knowledge Management in the Fortune 1000*. San Francisco: Jossey-Bass.

Westphal, J. D., Gulati, R., and Shortell, S. M. (1997). Customization or conformity? An institutional and network perspective on the content and consequences of TQM adoption. *Administrative Science Quarterly*, **42** (2), 366–94.

Young, S. M. (1992). A framework for successful adoption and performance of Japanese manufacturing practices in the United States. *Academy of Management Review*, **17** (4), 677–700.

Zbaracki, M. J. (1998). The rhetoric and reality of total quality management. *Administrative Science Quarterly*, **43** (3), 602–30.

tournament theory

Keith Weigelt

The vast majority of incentive schemes (*see* INCENTIVES) in organizations are based on tournament theory. Tournaments are based on relative, not absolute performance. Hence, an agent's payment is based on her performance, relative to the performance of all others in the tournament. An example of a tournament is the tenure process at most universities. In this process, the work of a professor is judged relative to the work of an identified peer group.

Rosen (1986) models the internal wage structure of business organizations as a sequential elimination tournament. Agents are assigned to their organizational position through participation in the tournament. The structure of most organizations resembles that of a pyramid; as one goes higher in the organization, there are fewer positions available. At the top level (the CEO), generally only one position exists. Let's say we are looking at the agents at the *nth* organizational level. Who do you promote? Rosen claims that most organizations look at the relative performance of agents at that level. Those agents who perform better get promoted to the next organ-

izational level (n-1), where there are fewer positions available. The lower performing agents do not get promoted.

Tournament models are game theoretic in nature (*see* GAME THEORY). Given the relative nature of tournaments, they are modeled as non-cooperative games. While tournament theory can predict the behavior of agents, it says little regarding attributes of the principals. For example, it does not explicitly specify the issues facing the principal, nor does it explain how to optimize the principal's preferences.

There is a growing body of empirical research supporting predictions of tournament models. Several studies support the prediction that differences in compensation and spreads in adjacent levels increase as agents move up the organizational pyramid (Lambert, Larcker, and Weigelt, 1993). Other studies show that hiring from outside the organization is more common at lower organizational levels (Baker, Gibbs, and Holmstrom, 1994). Finally, studies show that within organizations, promotion is essential for salary growth (Bognanno, 2001).

Several experimental papers have examined behavior in asymmetric tournaments. Tournaments can be asymmetric in two ways. In unfair tournaments, one group of agents may be favored over another. Because of this DISCRIMINATION, the agents who are not favored must perform significantly better than those in the favored group. Society has attempted to remedy this discrimination through the use of equal opportunity laws. Tournament theory predicts that when discrimination exists, the effort levels of all participants (both advantaged and disadvantaged) decrease. In a series of experimental papers (see Schotter and Weigelt, 1992), it is shown that in the presence of equal opportunity laws, the effort levels of both advantaged and disadvantaged agents increase. In effect, these laws are both equitable and efficient.

Given the universal use of tournament-like incentive schemes within organizations, additional studies of tournament behavior will continue. Tournaments hold a unique position in that they are situated at the nexus of economics, game theory, and organizational behavior. This interdisciplinary approach has been useful since tournaments not only explain the wage structure within organizations, they also explain how agents are assigned to positions.

See also *career development; equity theory; justice, distributive; justice, procedural*

Bibliography

Baker, G. M., Gibbs, M. and Holmstrom, B. (1994). The internal economics of the firm: Evidence from personnel data. *Quarterly Journal of Economics*, **109**, 881–919.

Bognanno, M. (2001). Corporate tournaments. *Journal of Labor Economics*, **19**, 290–315.

Lambert, R., Larcker, D., and Weigelt, K. (1993). The structure of organizational incentives. *Administrative Science Quarterly*, **38**, 438–61.

Rosen, S. (1986). Prizes and incentives in elimination tournaments. *American Economic Review*, **76**, 701–15.

Schotter, A. and Weigelt, K. (1992). Asymmetric tournaments, equal opportunity laws, and affirmative action: Some experimental results. *Quarterly Journal of Economics*, May, 512–39.

traits

see FIVE FACTOR MODEL OF PERSONALITY; PERSONALITY

transaction cost economics

Edward Zajac

Transaction cost economics has become one of the most influential (and somewhat controversial) theoretical perspectives in organizational and strategy research (Coase, 1937; Williamson, 1975, 1985). Transaction cost economics (TCE) and AGENCY THEORY represent the two major economics-based theories of organizational governance and contracting, and like agency theory, TCE has a broad reach, seeking to explain phenomena across levels of organizational analysis, such as employer–employee relations, the choice of functional vs. divisional organization forms, and the boundaries of the firm. It is in the arena of firm boundaries, however, that TCE has had its greatest influence, as in discussions of topics such as vertical integration (*see* ORGANIZATIONAL BOUNDARIES).

Williamson's (1975) pathbreaking book on markets and hierarchies discusses the organization of economic activity as a decision between markets or hierarchy. He explains vertical integration as the efficient solution to a transaction cost minimization problem, where the costs of market exchange compare unfavorably with the costs of controlling production hierarchically through ownership. Transaction costs are those costs of negotiating, monitoring, and enforcing contractual exchange relationships (*see* EXCHANGE RELATIONS). Thus, TCE is a perspective that examines the efficiency of alternative mechanisms for minimizing the risk of being exploited by one's exchange partner (often referred to as a "hold-up problem") (Milgrom and Roberts, 1998). Transaction costs may be significant, given Williamson's (1975: 9–10) root assumptions regarding two human factors (BOUNDED RATIONALITY and opportunism) and two environmental factors (uncertainty and small numbers).

It is the intensity of the small numbers (of exchange partners) problem that substantively defines the intensity of a transaction cost problem (the other three factors are actually assumptional conditions that do not vary in Williamson's framework). This can be seen in Williamson's (1975: 104) discussion of vertical integration, where he observes that it is "favored in situations where small numbers bargaining would otherwise obtain." It may appear that this emphasis on small numbers has been replaced in Williamson (1985: 56) by an emphasis on asset specificity, which refers to the investments an exchange partner makes that are highly specialized and can be redeployed only by sacrificing productive value (Williamson calls this the "big locomotive to which transaction cost economics owes much of its predictive content"). Asset specificity, however, is central only to the extent that it creates what Williamson (1985: 12) refers to as the "Fundamental Transformation – whereby a large-numbers condition . . . is transformed into a small-numbers condition during contract execution." In other words, the structural dimension of small numbers (i.e., limited exchange partner alternatives) is therefore still of critical importance to Williamson's (1985) transaction cost analysis.

Much of the recent controversy surrounding TCE relates to the inordinate weight placed on transaction cost economizing as underlying organizations' decisions regarding firm boundaries (as typified by Williamson's (1985: 17) claim that the "economic institutions of capitalism have the main purpose and effect of economizing on transaction costs"). Zajac and Olsen (1993), for example, are critical of TCE explanations of formal INTER-ORGANIZATIONAL RELATIONS, such as joint ventures, and argue instead that the recent proliferation of such inter-organizational relations is typically more a function of anticipated value gains, rather than anticipated losses due to hold-up problems. Milgrom and Roberts (1998: 81) also suggest that observed vertical inter-organizational relations are often "directly at odds with transaction cost theory." In addition, Zajac and Olsen (1993) suggest that Williamson's (1985) notion of a "fundamental transformation" is in fact a *process* whose properties are underspecified in the structural perspective of transaction cost analysis. For example, rather than emphasizing the negative implications of one-time structural changes in inter-organizational relations (i.e., the hold-up problem that arises when going from large numbers to a small numbers condition), they stress how vertical inter-organizational relations can also transform *positively* over time, as partners jointly develop better repertoires for inter-firm cooperation, leading to greater expected net benefits for both parties. Given the explosive recent growth in outsourcing, increased reliance on fewer suppliers, and increasingly creative types of strategic alliances, the TCE presumption that hold-up problems drive ownership and governance choices will likely continue to be debated for some time.

See also *game theory; organizational effectiveness; trust*

Bibliography

Coase, R. H. (1937). The nature of the firm. *Economica*, **4**, 386–405.

Milgrom, B. and Roberts, J. (1998). The boundaries of the firm revisited. *Journal of Economic Perspectives*, 12, 73–94.

Williamson, O. E. (1975). *Markets and Hierarchies: Analysis and Antitrust Implications*. New York: Free Press.

Williamson, O. E. (1985). *The Economic Institutions of Capitalism: Firms, Markets, Relational Contracting*. New York: Free Press.

Zajac, E. J. and Olsen C. (1993). From transaction costs to transaction value analysis: Implications for the study of inter-organizational strategies. *Journal of Management Studies*, **30** (13), 1–45.

transformational/transactional leadership

Bernard M. Bass

Before 1980, social and organizational behavior research on LEADERSHIP focused on observable, short-term, leader–follower relations: relations on the micro level. Leadership on the macro level (heads of organizations) and meta levels (leaders of society) was generally ignored (*see* CEOs). Autocratic vs. democratic leadership, task vs. relationship orientation, direction vs. participation, and initiation vs. consideration remained the paradigms of consequence for research and education. In all these paradigms, leadership was conceived as an exchange process. A *transaction* occurs in which followers' needs are met if their performance is as contracted with their leader. Transactional leadership depends on the leader's POWER to reinforce subordinates for their successful completion of the CONTRACT. But a higher order of change in followers is also possible. The *transformational* leader motivates followers to work for transcendental goals for the good of the group, the organization, the community of society as a whole, for achievement and self-actualization, and for higher level needs of the collectivity rather than immediate personal self-interests.

Traditional transactional paradigms and exchange theories of leadership failed to account for the effects on leader–follower relations of vision, SYMBOLISM, and imaging. The transactional leader adapts to the ORGANIZATIONAL CULTURE; the transformational leader changes it. As conceived by Burns (1978), transformational leaders motivate followers to do more than they originally expected to do as they strive for higher order outcomes.

In an early study, 70 South African senior executives were asked if any had experienced a transformational leader in their career: everyone was able to describe such a leader. Their leaders motivated them to extend themselves, to develop, and become more innovative. The executives were motivated to emulate their transformational leader. They were led to higher levels of COMMITMENT to the organization as a consequence of belief in the leader and in themselves. They exerted extra effort for their leader (Bass, 1985).

The executives' statements and those from the literature on charisma (*see* CHARISMATIC LEADERSHIP) and managerial leadership, after refinement and validation studies, formed the basis of the Multifactor Leadership Questionnaire (MLQ). This measures four interrelated factors (the 4 I's):

Idealized influence. Leaders become a source of admiration, often functioning as role models for their followers. They enhance follower pride, loyalty, and confidence and align followers through identification with the leaders around a common purpose or vision.
Inspirational MOTIVATION. Leaders articulate in simple ways an appealing vision and provide meaning and a sense of purpose in what needs to be done.
Intellectual stimulation. Leaders stimulate their followers to view the world from new perspectives; that is, to question old assumptions, values, and beliefs, and move toward new perspectives.
Individualized consideration. Leaders diagnose and elevate the needs of each of their followers. They promote the development of their followers, emphasize equity, and treat each follower as an individual.

Transactional leadership, which involves a reinforcing exchange of reward or PUNISHMENT by the leader for follower compliance, yields the factors of:

Contingent reward (CR): leader clarifies what needs to be done and exchanges psychological and material rewards for services rendered.
Active management-by-exception (MBE-A): leader arranges to monitor follower performance and takes corrective action when deviations from standards occur.

Passive management-by-exception (MBE-P): leader only intervenes when standards are not met.
Laissez-faire leadership (LF): leader avoids intervening or accepting responsibility for follower actions.

Recent large-scale factor analyses indicate the best fitting model combines idealized influence and inspirational motivation into a single factor. Passive management-by-exception and laissez-faire do likewise. Contingent reward breaks into two components: a transformational psychological reward and a transactional material reward (Avolio, Bass, and Jung, 1999; Antonakis, Avolio, and Sivasubramanian, 2003). The factors can be ordered into a full range of leadership types from passive to transformational leadership (Avolio and Bass, 1990). The factors can also be ordered on a second dimension: effectiveness.

A leader has a pattern of frequencies of behavior that is optimally effective when the 4 I's for the leader are highest in frequency and laissez-faire leadership is lowest in frequency. An inactive and ineffective leader's highest frequencies are for laissez-faire leadership and passively managing-by-exception, and the lowest frequencies are for the 4 I's (Avolio and Bass, 1990).

There is a hierarchy of relations among the full range of leadership styles and outcomes in effectiveness, effort, and satisfaction. Transformational leaders are more effective than those leaders who practice contingent reward. Contingent reward is somewhat more effective than active management-by-exception, which in turn is more effective than passive management-by-exception. Laissez-faire leadership is least effective. Research also supports the conclusion that there is a one-way augmentation effect. Transformational leadership adds to transactional leadership in predicting outcomes, but not vice versa. Transformational augments transactional leadership but it does not replace it.

Studies completed in at least a dozen countries suggest that whatever the location, when people think about leadership their prototypes and ideals are transformational (Avolio and Bass, 1990).

See also *leadership contingencies; motivation; organizational change*

Bibliography

Antonakis, J., Avolio, B. A., and Sivasubramanian, N. (2003). Context and leadership: An examination of the nine-factor Full-Range Leadership theory using the Multifactor Leadership Questionnaire. *Leadership Quarterly*, **14**, 261–96.

Avolio, B. J. and Bass, B. M. (1990). *The Full Range of Leadership*. Manual. Binghamton, NY: Center for Leadership Studies.

Avolio, B. J., Bass, B. M., and Jung, D. I. (1999). Reexamining the components of transformational and transactional leadership using the Multifactor Leadership Questionnaire. *Journal of Organizational and Occupational Psychology*, **72**, 441–62.

Bass, B. M. (1985). *Leadership and Performance Beyond Expectations*. New York: Free Press.

Bass, B. M. (1998). *Transformational Leadership: Industrial, Military and Educational Impact*. Mahwah, NJ: Lawrence Erlbaum Associates.

Burns, J. M. (1978). *Leadership*. New York: Harper and Row.

transitions

see ROLE TRANSITIONS; ORGANIZATIONAL CHANGE

trust

Madan M. Pillutla

Trust can be defined as a psychological state comprising the intention to accept vulnerability based upon positive expectations of the intentions or behavior of another (Rousseau et al., 1998). However, this is a concept where the content of a definition is a substantive issue in its own right, and integral to the theoretical and empirical challenge of studying it. Over the years, scholars from several disciplinary perspectives have studied it, including anthropology, economics, psychology, sociology, and political science. As can be expected with such a diversity of scholarship, there are major differences of opinion over the fundamental nature of the challenge the concept presents.

Lewicki and Bunker (1996) suggest that the study of trust may be categorized based on how it is viewed – as an individual characteristic, as a characteristic of interpersonal transactions, and as an institutional phenomenon, each being the province of different social science disciplines. PERSONALITY psychologists have traditionally viewed trust as an individual characteristic (e.g., Rotter, 1971). Within organizational behavior, the focus has been on the contextual factors that enhance or inhibit the development and maintenance of trust in relationships. Economists and sociologists are interested in how institutions and incentives are created to reduce the anxiety and uncertainty (and thus increase trust) associated with transactions among relative strangers (e.g., Uzzi, 1997).

DEFINING TRUST

Rotter (1971) defines trust as "a generalized expectancy held by an individual or group that the word, promise, verbal, or written statement of another individual or group can be relied on" – a definition that is quite close to the *Oxford English Dictionary* definition of trust as "confidence in or reliance on some quality or attribute of a person or thing, or the truth of a statement."

In contrast to Rotter's "generalized expectancy," which denotes a relatively stable personality characteristic, Mayer, Davis, and Schoorman (1995) define trust as "the willingness of a party to be vulnerable to the actions of another party based on the expectation that the other party will perform a particular action important to the trustor, irrespective of the ability to monitor or control the party." This definition suggests that trust is specific to a transaction and the person with whom one is transacting. It also indicates that expectations that others would cooperate or behave benevolently exclusively on account of external INCENTIVES or sanctions, does not count as trust, even though the outcome may be expected and desirable. Within this view, incentives or sanctions (or other legalistic remedies such as bonds or CONTRACTS) are substitutes for trust and are typically used to compensate for lack of trust.

Economists, with the notable exception of Williamson (1993), have no such restrictions on their definitions of trust. Their view is that trust follows from the ability to structure contracts or rewards and punishments so that individuals behave in a pre-specified manner. Economists concern themselves with the costs and benefits of specific behaviors. It is important to note that it is not a requirement of economic models that all people are inherently untrustworthy, but that people maximize the payoffs and minimize the costs of interaction. Kreps (1990) and Dasgupta (1988) are perhaps the best-known examples of the economic modeling of trust and are fairly representative of the approach used. In their models, trust serves less as an inherent concept and more as a label describing an equilibrium behavioral outcome not to behave opportunistically towards one's opponent or partner.

An important and emerging perspective is provided by EVOLUTIONARY PSYCHOLO-GISTS who view trust as an innate, presumably evolved proximate mechanism that is part of our biology and enables cooperation. Within this field, the study of trust is tied closely to the examination of altruism and reciprocal behavior. Early models emphasized the centrality of kinship ties (kin selection) and the repeated nature of exchanges (RECIPROCAL ALTRUISM) in determining reciprocal behaviors. These models led to insights about the evolution of cognitive capacities such as a memory to keep track of good and bad partners and an ability to detect cheating. In conditions where resources are not shared simultaneously, evolution favors the development of a capacity to anticipate future gains, a capacity that is facilitated by a willingness to trust one another.

Recent explorations about how trust can originate when two unrelated individuals have no experience in dealing with each other gives center stage to "strong reciprocity." There is considerable evidence to show that individuals are predisposed to cooperate with others and punish non-cooperators, even when this behavior cannot be justified in terms of extended kinship or reciprocal altruism. Gintis and his colleagues (e.g., Gintis, 2000) have derived simple models showing how strong reciprocity can evolve and persist in evolutionary equilibrium. Their model is based on the plausible idea that in the relevant evolutionary environment human groups faced extinction threats (e.g., wars or environmental catastrophes) with a posi-

tive probability. In such situations, the shadow of the future is weak, making reciprocal altruism an insufficient explanation for cooperation. Kin selection is also not a complete explanation as most human groups are also open to non-kin members. Thus "strong reciprocity" indicates an evolved tendency to be trustworthy and to punish untrustworthiness.

Most conceptualizations of trust agree on the idea that trust cannot exist in an environment of certainty; or if it did, it would do so trivially (see RISK TAKING). Most would also agree on the idea that it reflects an aspect of predictability (i.e., it is expectancy). And finally, they would agree that trust is good.

THE DEVELOPMENT OF TRUST

Despite differences in their orientation to the study of trust, one fundamental question that is common to all approaches is: How is trust engendered? The literature suggests that trust is likely to result when (1) the interests of transacting parties are aligned (Dasgupta, 1988; Kreps, 1990); (2) when a sense of shared identity or solidarity is created (Kramer, 1993; Powell, 1996; Ouchi, 1980), and (3) when care is taken in choosing transaction partners (Powell, 1996).

These ideas correspond to Lewicki and Bunker's (1996) categories of calculus-based, identification-based, and knowledge-based trust, and to Barney and Hansen's (1994) weak, semi-strong, and strong forms of trust. Calculus-based trust refers to expectations based on the rewards or punishments that guide others' behavior, knowledge-based trust refers to the predictability of others' behavior, and identification-based trust refers to an internalization of the other's desires and intentions.

Many theorists (including Lewicki and Bunker 1996; Barney and Hansen, 1994) suggest that the different types of trust correspond to different levels of a trust hierarchy, such that the achievement of trust at one level enables the development of trust at the next level. Specifically, business partners begin with activities that build calculus-based trust (e.g., incentives and complete contracts) and if validated (i.e., the other side is consistent), move on to activities that enable knowledge-based trust development (e.g., seek knowledge about other party's values and preferences) and finally begin to identify with the other party.

This development sequence follows from traditional, incremental models of trust development (e.g., Rempel, Holmes, and Zanna, 1985) that suggest that trust initiators should be careful, because trust involves risk. Thus, it is wise for trustors to take relatively small risks initially, increasing their risks as a relationship develops (see, for example, the tit-for-tat tactic in GAME THEORY). There is very little empirical evidence to support this developmental model of trust, though there is some research that shows that individuals do actually distinguish between different types of trust.

Recent research suggests that the phased approach towards building trust may not work. Trusted parties may view the precautions that individuals take to build calculus-based trust initially (e.g., CONTRACTS) skeptically, wondering if they reflect a lack of trust (Murnighan, Malhotra, and Weber, 2004). They may also view small initial acts of trust negatively, or may not even recognize them as "trusting acts" (Pillutla, Malhotra, and Murnighan, 2003), suggesting that incremental procedures towards building trust could actually signal distrust.

CONSEQUENCES OF TRUST

Despite the lack of agreement about what constitutes trust, the organizational behavior literature is clear about the consequences: trust leads to beneficial outcomes. For parties who have to work together, trust reduces the cost of doing business. Cooperation, in the absence of trust, often requires a system of formal rules and regulations, which have to be negotiated, agreed to, litigated, and enforced, entailing significant transaction costs. Research suggests that when two individuals trust each other, they are more likely to cooperate (Mayer, Davis, and Schoorman, 1995), share information in NEGOTIATIONS (Thompson, 1991), and engage in mutually beneficial relationships. At the organizational level, trust helps resolve agency problems (e.g., Das and Teng, 1998) and mitigates negative reactions to bad outcomes. At the interorganizational level, trust enables parties to take risks (Uzzi, 1997), reduce uncertainty, and facilitate market processes (Arrow, 1974). At the societal level, a high degree of trust will permit a variety of social relationships to emerge, thereby encouraging the development of innovative organizational forms (Fukuyama, 1995).

Current scholarly interest in the concept of trust is very high. The topic is inspiring research in existing domains such as ORGANIZATIONAL DESIGN and organizational economics. In the former field, for example, research interest has been stimulated in information technologies that allow businesses to innovate in the organization of their activities (e.g., by OUTSOURCING some of their non-core activities or by resorting to auctions for supplies). Trust is an important explanatory variable under these conditions. The role of trust in new complex types of intra- and inter-organizational relationships is likely to increase, as well as the emerging and hitherto under-explored topic of how trust can be repaired following a violation.

See also *altruism; evolutionary psychology; stakeholders; values*

Bibliography

Arrow, K. (1974). *The Limits of Organizations*. New York: Basic Books.

Barney, J. B. and Hansen, M. H. (1994). Trustworthiness as a source of competitive advantage. *Strategic Management Journal*, 15 (special issue), 175–90.

Das, T. K. and Teng, B. (1998). Between trust and control: Developing confidence in partner cooperation in alliances. *Academy of Management Review*, 23, 491–512.

Dasgupta, P. (1988). Trust as a commodity. In D. Gambetta (ed.), *Trust: Making and Breaking Cooperative Relations*. Oxford: Blackwell, 49–72.

Fukuyama, F. (1995). *Trust: The Social Virtues and the Creation Of Prosperity*. New York: Free Press.

Gintis, H. (2000). Strong reciprocity and human sociality. *Journal of Theoretical Biology*, 213, 103–19.

Kramer, R. M. (1993). Cooperation and organizational identification. In J. K. Murnighan (ed.), *Social Psychology In Organizations: Advances in Theory and Research*. Englewood Cliffs, NJ: Prentice-Hall, 244–68.

Kreps, D. (1990). Corporate culture and economic theory. In J. Alt and K. Shepsle (eds.), *Perspectives on Positive Political Economy*. Cambridge: Cambridge University Press, 90–143.

Lewicki, R. J. and Bunker, B. (1996). Developing and maintaining trust in work relationships. In R. Kramer and T. Tyler (eds.), *Trust in Organizations*. Newbury Park, CA: Sage, 114–39.

Mayer, R. C., Davis, J. H., and Schoorman, F. D. (1995). An integrative model of organizational trust. *Academy of Management Review*, **20**, 709–34.

Murnighan, J. K., Malhotra, D., and Weber, J. M. (2004). Paradoxes of trust: Empirical and theoretical departures from a (dominant) traditional model. In R. Kramer and K. Cook (eds.), *Trust and Distrust Across Organizational Contexts: Dilemmas and Approaches*. Russell Sage Foundation Series on Trust: Vol 7.

Ouchi, W. G. (1980). Markets, bureaucracies, and clans. *Administrative Science Quarterly*, **25**, 129–41.

Pillutla, M., Malhotra, D., and Murnighan, J. K. (2003). Attributions of trust and the calculus of reciprocity. *Journal of Experimental Social Psychology*, **39**, 448–55.

Powell, W. W. (1996). Trust based forms of governance. In R. Kramer and T. Tyler (eds.), *Trust in Organizations*. Newbury Park, CA: Sage, 51–67.

Rempel, J. K., Holmes, J. G., and Zanna, M. P. (1985). Trust in close relationships. *Journal of Personality and Social Psychology*, **49**, 95–112.

Rotter, J. (1971). Generalized expectancies for interpersonal trust. *American Psychologist*, **26**, 443–52.

Rousseau, D., Sitkin, S., Burt, R., and Camerere, C. (1998). Not so different after all: A cross-cultural discipline view of trust. *Academy of Management Review*, 33, 393–404.

Thompson, L. (1991). Information exchange in negotiation. *Journal of Experimental Social Psychology*, 27, 161–79.

Uzzi, B. (1997). Social structure and competition in interfirm networks: The paradox of embeddedness. *Administrative Science Quarterly*, **42**, 35–67.

Williamson, O. E. (1993). Calculativeness, trust and economic organization. *Journal of Law and Economics*, **36** (1 Pt 2), 453–86.

turnover

Stuart A. Youngblood and Charles R. Williams

Turnover can be defined as voluntary cessation of membership in an organization, and is one of several forms of organizational withdrawal such as ABSENTEEISM and tardiness.

EASE AND DESIRABILITY OF MOVEMENT

Turnover decisions are a function of two factors: ease of movement (how easy it is to find another job) and desirability of movement (whether employees experience enough dissatisfaction to want a different job) (March and Simon, 1958).

Economists focus primarily on labor market determinants of the ease of movement. Firm turnover (quit) rates are best predicted by general economic activity. When the economy is healthy or unemployment is low and jobs plentiful, turnover rates will increase. When economic activity and job growth are slow, turnover rates will generally decline. Economists have also found that most but not all who leave do so for better paying jobs.

Desirability of movement is typically measured by asking workers to report their level of JOB SATISFACTION, which has a small, negative relationship with turnover. Raising levels of job satisfaction can substantially decrease turnover. For example, one year after implementing regular salary reviews, consistent pay policies across departments, and job transfers for clerical workers wanting advancement, Hulin (1968) found sizable increases in satisfaction with pay and promotions and a decrease in turnover from 30 percent to 18 percent.

Research also shows that ease of movement and desirability of movement can jointly affect turnover decisions. When jobs are scarce, many dissatisfied employees who want to leave cannot leave, thus yielding smaller correlations between job satisfaction and turnover. When jobs are plentiful, however, many dissatisfied employees will leave, and the relationship between satisfaction and turnover increases.

Psychological process of leaving   The psychological process of leaving has been conceived as a simple, five factor causal model that begins with job satisfaction and proceeds through a series of decision stages (Steel, 2002). Dissatisfied employees start to have thoughts about quitting, then decide to search for other jobs, and then formalize specific intentions to quit their jobs (Mobley, 1982). However, strong intentions to quit do not always result in turnover. When alternative jobs are scarce, dissatisfied employees, as well as employees with clear intentions to quit, find other, acceptable jobs harder to locate. Realistic job previews and job enrichment can also modestly reduce employee turnover by improving job satisfaction.

Investment Model of Turnover   Another approach to understanding turnover is the investment model, suggesting that turnover increases when employee COMMITMENT decreases (Rusbelt and Farrell, 1983). Commitment decreases when job rewards worsen (e.g., pay, satisfying work, supervision), when job costs increase (e.g., high work load, inadequate resources), when investment decreases (e.g., tenure, organization-specific SKILLS, non-transferable retirement plans, friends at work), and when attractive, alternative jobs are available.

UNFOLDING MODEL OF VOLUNTARY TURNOVER

Not all turnover, however, results from dissatisfaction or other job opportunities. Lee et al. (1999) suggest that quit intentions often occur in response to an event or shock (e.g., expected/unexpected; positive/negative; internal/external), such as organizational mergers, friends leaving, unsolicited job offers, expecting a child, spouse relocation, or administrative changes. Such events or shocks can prompt workers to leave even though they weren't dissatisfied or planning to leave.

Interaction between workers and working environment Another approach to understanding turnover is to examine the interaction between workers and their environments. In general, workers who fit better into their work environments will be less likely to quit.

For example, demographic models (*see* ORGANIZATIONAL DEMOGRAPHY) predict that executives, who differ significantly from their peers in terms of AGE, education, or experience, etc., are more likely to quit. Some interaction/fit models propose reducing turnover at the point of hire. That is, firms can reduce turnover by hiring workers who are similar to existing workers and who have values consistent with the ORGANIZATIONAL CULTURE.

Alternatively, once hired, person/job or organizational fit suggests that employers can reduce turnover by increasing job embeddedness (Mitchell et al., 2001), which has three components: (1) social capital, that is worker attachments to people, teams, and groups; (2) perceptions of fit with the job, organization, and community; and (3) perceptions of what must be sacrificed if the worker leaves the organization. By contrast to most turnover models which focus on *why* workers leave, job embeddedness focuses on the psychological process of why workers *stay*. Mitchell, Holtom, and Lee

(2001) suggest that organizations can strengthen job embeddedness and reduce turnover intentions and turnover by strengthening links to teams within the organization, focusing on person job/organizational fit at the time of hire, and using financial (golden handcuffs) and non-financial incentives (e.g., sabbaticals or other unique perquisites) to magnify the perceived sacrifice an employee must make if they leave.

CONSEQUENCES OF TURNOVER

All of the previous approaches assume that employee turnover is inherently bad, expensive, and should be reduced whenever possible. Yet some kinds and levels of turnover (e.g., when poor performers leave) are beneficial for companies. Dalton, Krackhardt, and Porter (1981) believe that the traditional stay/quit definition overstates the negative consequences of employee turnover and ignores its positive consequences. They defined two kinds of turnover: (1) dysfunctional turnover, where someone valued by the organization leaves, and (2) functional turnover, where a person not valued leaves. The marginal cost implication for employers is to target turnover reduction strategies to prevent only the loss of good performers.

O'Reilly and Pfeffer (2000) argue that the key to success in any organization is retaining key employees through the application of critical people practices, such as highly selective screening (on APTITUDE and PERSONALITY), extensive training and orientation, sharing financial and non-financial information with employees, and by using CAREER management strategies and performance-based reward systems to enhance retention. According to O'Reilly and Pfeffer (2000), organizations succeed because of their people, not necessarily because they possess superior technology or a unique competitive strategy.

See also *incentives; job design; motivation; organizational effectiveness; role transitions*

Bibliography

Dalton, D. R., Krackhardt, D. M., and Porter, L. W. (1981). Functional turnover: An empirical assessment. *Journal of Applied Psychology*, **66**, 716–21.

Griffeth, R. W. and Hom, P. W. (eds.) (2004). *Innovative Theory and Empirical Research on Employee Turnover.* Information Age Publishing.

Hulin, C. L. (1968). Effects of changes in job satisfaction levels on employee turnover. *Journal of Applied Psychology*, **52**, 122–6.

Lee, T. W., Mitchell, T. R., Holtom, B. C., McDaniel, L. S., and Hill, J. W. (1999). The unfolding model of voluntary turnover: A replication and extension. *Academy of Management Journal*, **42** (4), 450–62.

March, J. G. and Simon, H. A. (1958). *Organizations.* New York: Wiley.

Mitchell, T. R., Holtom, B. C., and Lee, T. W. (2001). How to keep your best employees: Developing an effective retention policy. *Academy of Management Executive*, **15** (4), 96–108.

Mitchell, T. R., Holtom, B. C., Lee, T. W., Sablynski, C. J., and Erez, M. (2001). Why people stay: Using job embeddedness to predict voluntary turnover. *Academy of Management Journal*, **44** (6), 1102–21.

Mobley, W. H. (1982). *Employee Turnover: Causes, Consequences, and Control.* Reading, MA: Addison-Wesley.

O'Reilly, C. A. and Pfeffer, J. (2000). *Hidden Value: How Great Companies Achieve Extraordinary Results With Ordinary People.* Boston, MA: Harvard Business School Press.

Rusbelt, C. E. and Farrell, D. (1983). A longitudinal test of the investment model: The impact of job satisfaction, job commitment, and turnover of variations in rewards, costs, alternatives, and investments. *Journal of Applied Psychology*, **68**, 429–38.

Steel, R. P. (2002). Turnover theory at the empirical interface: Problems of fit and function. *Academy of Management Review*, **27** (3), 346–60.

two-factor theory

see JOB SATISFACTION; MOTIVATION

type-A

see PERSONALITY; STRESS

uncertainty

see DECISION-MAKING; RISK-TAKING

V

valence

see MOTIVATION

validity

Richard Klimoski

In the context of organizational research, validity is defined as the appropriateness of the inferences drawn from an observation, test score(s), a study, or a set of studies.

Issues of validity relate to measures, to research designs, or to data. The validity of a *measure* has been further interpreted in terms of its content, relationship to external variables (criteria), or to the constructs it is designed to get at. (A construct is a concept that has been created or adopted for a scientific purpose.) Thus "content" validity is the degree to which responses required by the items of a test or measure are representative of the behaviors or knowledge to be exhibited in the domain of interest. A job knowledge test would be content valid if it fairly assessed the knowledge needed for a job. A measure would have "criterion related" validity if scores received by individuals (groups or organizations) covary with scores on some external standard (criterion). A cognitive ability test might have criterion related validity if its scores correlated with a measure of job performance. A measure would have "construct" validity to the extent that an underlying explanatory concept (e.g., honesty) can account for the scores obtained (i.e., truly honest individuals receive high scores and dishonest individuals receive low scores). Construct validity can be established through careful operational definitions and through the statistical analysis of accumulated empirical evidence regarding the pattern of scores yielded by the measure vis-à-vis scores from other, well-known, or trusted measures.

The validity of *research designs* refers to the extent that the plan for a study and the methods employed allow for accurate inferences or conclusions from the data (*see* QUASI-EXPERIMENTAL DESIGN; RESEARCH METHODS). Usually, this means that the plan deals with (rules out) plausible, rival explanations for the results. If research is designed satisfactorily, one can speak of "internal" validity, the capacity to infer causal relationships, and "external" validity, the capacity to generalize (*see* GENERALIZATION) to other studies or cases. Common threats to the validity of a research design include small or inappropriate samples of subjects (e.g., number of employees or business units), unstandardized research conditions, inappropriate methods, or the failure to recognize the impact of unmeasured factors. Assessing the validity of a research design is usually done through a critical analysis by a competent researcher who is also a subject matter expert.

The validity of *data* is related to both the validity of measures and designs. Thus, we cannot make correct inferences (descriptions or predictions) from data that are derived from poor measures or weak designs. In particular, if scores are derived from unreliable measures with questionable construct validity, obtained from a set of people who are unrepresentative of those who we are really interested in, and/or were gathered in atypical situations, there is little basis on which to claim that we have valid data. Assessing of the validity of data is both a statistical and logical/analytical process.

See also *reliability; research design; research methods; statistical methods; validity generalization*

Bibliography

Cook, T. D., Campbell, D. T., and Peracchio, L. (1990). Quasi experimentation. In M. D. Dunnette and L. M. Hough (eds.), *Handbook of Industrial and Organizational Psychology.* Palo Alto, CA: Consulting Psychologists Press, 491–576.

Ghiselli, E. E., Campbell, J. P., and Zedeck, S. (1981). *Measurement Theory for the Behavioral Sciences.* San Francisco: W. H. Freeman.

Landy, F. J. and Schmitt, N. (1993). The concept of validity In N. Schmitt and W. C. Borman (eds.), *Personnel Selection in Organizations.* San Francisco: Jossey-Bass, 275–309.

Runkel, P. J. and McGrath, J. E. (1972). *Research on Human Behavior: A Systematic Guide for Method.* New York: Holt, Rinehart, and Winston.

Schmitt, N. W. and Klimoski, R. J. (1991). Research methods in human resources management. Cincinnati, OH: South-Western.

validity generalization

Richard Klimoski

Validity generalization is an approach to summarizing what is known about a key characteristic (usually predictive validity) of a test or test type (*see* STATISTICAL METHODS). It is one of a class of meta-analytic techniques which treats the validation study as the unit of analysis. It is based on the assumption that the results from any one study might be misleading, given the potential impact of one or more factors in a piece of research which are known to artificially raise or lower computed correlations.

After a frequency distribution of the results (e.g., VALIDITY coefficients) found in published and unpublished studies is developed, various statistical procedures are applied. Thus, the steps in a validity generalization study are as follows:

1 Identify a set of studies from the research domain of interest. Investigators usually attempt to be as complete as possible in this step.
2 Code key information from each study in a way that would allow one to compute an estimate of effect size.
3 Record any additional information that could plausibly be a factor in affecting the results (e.g., whether it was a study in one type of industry or another, one type of employee, etc).
4 Correct the frequency distribution and/or individual effect size estimates for sources of artifactual variance. Such sources have traditionally included such things as lack of predictor (test) RELIABILITY and size of the sample respondents in the study.
5 If necessary or desired, regress the corrected effect sizes upon those study characteristics coded in order to help to explain the effect sizes (e.g., one might find higher validity for the test in one type of industry).

The end product of the procedure becomes a quantitative index ("a corrected or estimated 'true' correlation") rather than a traditional narrative summary of findings (e.g., "significant correlations were found for the test in most of the studies"). Using this approach permits one to reach a conclusion regarding, for example, whether a particular (employment) test established as useful in one setting (company) would be appropriate to use in another (called transportability). Validity GENERALIZATION analyses are also helpful in resolving ambiguities that exist if one were only to attend to the results of individual studies. An instance of this relates to the usefulness of what are called integrity tests. The authors of a meta-analysis (Ones, Viswesvaran, and Schmidt, 1993) based on 665 (often contradictory) individual validity studies were suprised to find that, collectively, integrity tests do predict a broad range of organizationally disruptive behaviors (including rule breaking incidents and employee theft). Hence they would appear to be useful in employee selection.

One caveat: despite the apparent statistical control of the subjectivity typically found in a narrative summary, numerous judgment calls are involved in conducting a validity generalization study (e.g., just which studies should be included or excluded in the analysis?).

See also *research design; research methods*

Bibliography

Hunter, J. E. and Schmidt, F. L. (1990). *Methods of Meta-Analysis.* Newbury Park, CA: Sage.

Ones, D. S., Viswesvaran, C., and Schmidt, F. L. (1993). Comprehensive meta-analysis of integrity test validities: Findings and implications for personnel selection and theories of job performance. *Journal of Applied Psychology*, **78**, 679–703.

Schmidt, F. L. and Hunter, J. E. (1977). Development of a general solution to the problem of validity generalization. *Journal of Applied Psychology*, **62**, 529–40.

Wanous, J. P., Sullivan, S. E., and Malinak, J. (1989). The role of judgment calls in meta-analysis. *Journal of Applied Psychology*, **74**, 259–64.

values

Elizabeth C. Ravlin

Values are a set of core beliefs held by individuals concerning how they should or ought to behave over broad ranges of situations. Values are generalized beliefs about modes of conduct (Rokeach, 1973) that form a primary component of the self-schema, the "ought" self (as compared to the "actual" or "desired" self). Because beliefs about the self tend to be the most deeply held and influential of cognitions, values are stable and central, and are pervasive in their influence on other cognitions, PERCEPTION, and behavior.

This conceptualization differs from the interpretation of values as preferences for objects that affect responses to those objects (Locke, 1976) (*see* ATTITUDE THEORY). Values, as generalized, "ought-oriented" beliefs, provide the standard that individuals use to determine whether an object has value or should be preferred. Values act as a primary cognitive organizing structure for much of the rest of our belief system, including cognitions commonly perceived to be "facts," and are not simple evaluative responses.

Values also act as motivational elements (*see* MOTIVATION) in that they indicate which behaviors are more desirable to perform than others from an ideal perspective, all other things (such as instrumentality) being equal. Acting on values may fulfill innate needs; however, there is no necessary correspondence between the two.

ACQUIRING VALUES

Values are acquired from societal institutions (family, economic, and political systems) and their cultural context. They are initially learned in isolation, in an absolute fashion. As an individual matures, he or she integrates them into a value system, also based in part on personality (Rokeach, 1973). Because of their societal origin and consequent social desirability, people typically endorse value oriented statements; therefore, individual differences in values lie not so much in the specific values that individuals hold, but in their order of importance within the value system (Ravlin and Meglino, 1987). A small number of value dimensions seems to generalize across national cultures (Schwartz, 1992); thus values are pivotal in understanding cultural differences in such areas as communication, conflict resolution, the psychological contract, and status organizing processes.

VALUE CHANGE

Because values are learned early in life, and occupy a central position in cognitive structure, they are difficult to change during adulthood. Such change requires a change in the self-schema and related beliefs, attitudes, and perceptions acquired over a lifetime. Pitting two conflicting values against one another may produce change, and having violated a value once, individuals may find it progressively easier to violate that value until it has lost its importance. Repeated functional failure of value related behavior may also produce change. These latter propositions seem more likely to explain long-term, cross-situational values change in adults. For example, work ethic values in the US tend to erode as related behaviors, or lack thereof, fail to effect a significant change in lifestyle.

Organizational SOCIALIZATION is one avenue by which values are conveyed to adults. Myths, stories, repetition, and formal socialization processes are often sources of work values. Organizational leaders may set the values of the organization and propagate them among employees. To be acquired, however, a value must serve a function for the individual, or be presented as the only possible interpretation of the situation. Values also may eventually lose their priority if organizational reward systems facilitate their frequent violation (*see* INCENTIVES). Employees bring values to the organization with them, so may at times influence those of the organization rather than the reverse.

EFFECTS ON BEHAVIOR

Values act as a perceptual screen to influence
what we see in our environment, and as a channel to influence behavioral decisions (England,
1967). Goals may mediate the relationship between values and behavior, and moderators,
such as personal discretion and the labeling of a
behavior as value relevant, act to determine
when values will predict behavior. Specific
values play important roles in influencing certain
behaviors. A dominant honesty value produces
more ethical decisions. Collectivism, as a cultural value, influences behavior toward aggregate well-being, as opposed to individual goals
(Triandis, 1995). These relationships between
specific values and behavior typically are
expected to be small at any one point in time,
but stronger over time, as with other individual
differences (Epstein, 1980). Cultural values also
often moderate commonly observed relationships. Additionally, in some instances, individuals use value statements (espoused, as opposed
to in-use, values) to provide legitimacy for behavior that has already occurred.

SHARING VALUE SYSTEMS

Shared value systems (value congruence) have
been shown to positively influence internal
processes (Schein, 1985) such that common cognitive processing leads to less CONFLICT,
less uncertainty, shared goals, and more
predictability, interpersonal TRUST, and satisfaction. This view is consistent with the Attraction–Selection–Attrition (ASA) framework of
Schneider (1987), which holds that organizations tend to attract and retain people with similar views, and thus become more homogeneous
over time. While sharing in-use values tends to
produce the above affective effects, the ability to
articulate espoused values congruent with
organizational management may relate more
consistently to individual performance evaluations and retention.

Alternative views of value sharing drawn from
the ORGANIZATIONAL CULTURE literature include differentiation perspectives, which focus
on the differences in beliefs that exist between
groups within organizations, and fragmentation
perspectives, which note the temporary nature

of shared beliefs generated by multiple belief
systems in complex and ambiguous environments (Martin, 2001). Each of these views can
be used as a lens for examining organizational
value systems that influences what and how research is conducted. Value congruence has been
explored at multiple levels (individual–organization, supervisor–subordinate, between co-
workers, within teams) in studies that primarily
reflect either integration or differentiation
perspectives.

Although evidence consistently shows that
value congruence generates more positive attitudes, the relationship between value sharing
and performance remains unclear. The integration perspective tends to imply that positive
affect generated by value congruence will lead
to higher performance. Other areas of research,
in particular the cross-cultural, GROUP DECI-
SION-MAKING and ASA literatures, suggest
that too much homogeneity of belief systems
may hinder performance in non-routine,
changing situations, and that constructive conflict can be generated by a diversity of task relevant perspectives, enhancing performance on
creative or non-routine tasks. Such conflict
must be managed carefully to positively influence effectiveness.

See also *culture, national; deviance*

Bibliography

England, G. W. (1967). Organizational goals and expected
behavior of American managers. *Academy of Management Journal*, **10**, 107–17.
Epstein, S. (1980). The stability of behavior: II. Implications for psychological research. *American Psychologist*,
35, 790–806.
Locke, E. A. (1976). The nature and consequences of job
satisfaction. In M. D. Dunnette (ed.), *Handbook of
Industrial Psychology*. Chicago: Rand-McNally,
1297–349.
Martin, J. (2001). *Organizational Culture: Mapping the
Terrain*. Thousand Oaks, CA: Sage.
Ravlin, E. C. and Meglino, B. M. (1987). Effect of values
on perception and decision-making: A study of
alternative work values measures. *Journal of Applied
Psychology*, **72**, 666–73.
Rokeach, M. (1973). *The Nature of Human Values*. New
York: Free Press.

Schein, E. H. (1985). *Organizational Culture and Leadership*. San Francisco: Jossey-Bass.

Schneider, B. (1987). The people make the place. *Personnel Psychology*, **40**, 437–53.

Schwartz, S. H. (1992). Universals in the content and structure of values: Theoretical advances and empirical tests in 20 countries. In M. P. Zanna (ed.), *Advances in Experimental Social Psychology*, Vol. 25. San Diego: Academic Press, 1–65.

Triandis, H. C. (1995). *Individualism and Collectivism*. Boulder, CO: Westview Press.

VIE theory

see MOTIVATION

virtual organization

see COMMUNICATIONS; ORGANIZATIONAL DESIGN

women at work

Barbara A. Gutek, Layne Paddock, and
Jessica Bagger

Most women have always been "at work," but traditionally, fewer women than men have engaged in paid work. In 1890, for example, women made up only 17 percent of the US labor force. But that has changed. In 2000, over all, 63.9 percent of Americans aged 16 and older were in the labor force, including 57.5 percent of all women 16 years or older. In the Scandinavian countries, typically 75 percent or more of adult women are in the labor force. In general, during the 1970s and 1980s, women increased their share of the labor force in most countries of the world (United Nations, 1991), although the rate of increase has slowed in the past decade or so. Furthermore, in all areas of the world today, women in the prime childrearing years (25–44) are more likely to be employed than either younger or older women. This represents a change in most of the industrialized countries where, in the past, women in this age band were less likely than either younger or older women to be employed. For many women, this fact has created a double shift, where they work 8 or more hours in paid employment and then work another 4 or so hours at home.

The topic of "women at work" as a coherent subfield is less than 25 years old and it is interdisciplinary, involving researchers from management, psychology, sociology, economics, etc. This body of research tends to focus disproportionately on women in non-traditional jobs (i.e., management and the male-dominated professions) and women at higher organizational ranks (managers and executives). Likewise, the research focuses disproportionately on women who are white and middle or upper class.

These features characterize research on work in general, not just women at work.

In all of the research GENDER figures prominently, and women and their experiences are either overtly or covertly compared with men. Sex differences are a common theme in the research (e.g., Eagly and Johnson, 1990; Eagly, Karau, and Makhijani, 1995); they encompass both differences between men and women and differences between the treatment of men and the treatment of women (such as opportunities for promotion, compensation, and performance appraisal). Women tend to work in "women's jobs," jobs defined in a particular time and place as appropriate for women. Although there are some consistencies across countries, cultures, and organizations (e.g., jobs involving children tend to be labeled women's jobs), examples of one job being a "man's job" in one country, culture, or organization, and a "woman's job" in another, are common. This is true, for example, of medicine, sales, and clerical work.

Women's work is characterized by horizontal segregation (men and women work in different occupations). In the US, sex segregation has declined, and it has done so, not because more men are working in jobs traditionally held by women (they are not), but because women have moved into traditionally male fields such as law, medicine, and management (see Konrad, Winter, and Gutek, 1992). Women's work is also characterized by vertical segregation, which means that men and women are located at different places in the work hierarchy. Women tend to be located in lower level positions in their occupations and in their organizations, whereas men are found in jobs throughout the hierarchy. Women are said to face a glass ceiling in that they are rarely found above certain hierarchical levels. Like horizontal segregation, vertical segregation is also decreasing except at the top.

Research on women at work usually fits into one of three categories: sex differences, problem focused studies, and reports on changes initiated to alleviate problems.

The first of these types of research focuses on differences and similarities between the sexes. Among the topics covered are differences in masculinity and femininity and their implications; differences or similarities in management style or leadership style; sex differences in career choices and career interests; and differences and similarities in achieving style. Early research focused on traits or characteristics believed to be associated with women more than men, such as fear of success. A few areas are notable for the lack of expected sex differences. For example, while an active debate about whether men and women exhibit different leadership styles flourishes, the research suggests that men and women in leadership positions exhibit few differences. In the case of LEADERSHIP styles, Eagly and her colleagues found that men and women differed little, although both lab and field studies revealed that women tend to lead in a more democratic and participative style than men. Another area that is perceived to differ by gender is preference for job characteristics. Men are expected to prefer, for example, high pay and prestigious jobs while women are expected to prefer jobs requiring "people skills." However, a comprehensive review of the research on preferences of various job attributes revealed relatively few sex differences. Konrad et al. (2000) examined 242 samples of more than 600,000 women and men and girls and boys (as young as elementary school) in which they classified and analyzed 40 job attributes for sex differences in preference. In general, sex differences were found in 33 of the 40 job attributes, but in 26 of them the difference was quite small.

A large body of research on women at work focuses on problems faced by women. These topics include biases in selection, placement, PERFORMANCE APPRAISAL/PERFORMANCE MANAGEMENT, and promotion (e.g., Heilman, Block and Lucas, 1992); sexual harassment (Gutek, 1985); obstacles to achievement, advancement, and attainment of positions of leadership (Eagly and Johnson, 1990; Eagly, Karau,

and Makhijani, 1995); lack of mentoring (Ragins and Cotton, 1991); sex discrimination; the pay gap; stereotyping; lack of job mobility; and conflict between work and family responsibilities (see NON-WORK/WORK). Research starting in the late 1970s on the problems faced by tokens (women who are numerically rare), including the problems faced by women when there are few women in top management positions in the organization, continues to be relevant (see Tolbert, Graham, and Andrews, in Powell, 1999). Especially intriguing is Ely's (1994) research using a sample of law firms, suggesting that women have a particularly difficult time when there are few women in senior management.

A third type of research focuses on the success or failure of attempts to alleviate problems faced by working women (e.g., Ely, Foldy, and Scully, 2003), including the impacts of laws and other programs aimed at providing equal opportunity, addressing affirmative action, establishing the comparable worth of jobs, and eliminating sexual harassment. Konrad and Linnehan (1999) identified more than 100 different mechanisms that might assist organizations in reaching affirmative action goals. These activities can be divided into two types: identity blind (such as formal MENTORING programs, flexible work schedules, and employee assistance programs) or identity conscious activities that consider one's sex or race. These include targeting women (or other underrepresented groups) in hiring and promotion considerations, targeting women for management training, establishing a woman's interest group in the workplace, and the like. In general, the identity blind practices and policies are more common and preferred by most people. It is the identity conscious practices, however, that are effective in that only they result in high levels of employment status for minority and majority women and minority men. Thus, working environments that target activities for women result in better outcomes for women. Preferential treatment can, however, have negative consequences on women and minorities if others believe they were hired or promoted only because of their sex or race.

Laws are not the only approach to alleviating problems faced by working women. In general, the type of solution sought depends on the way the problem is defined. Nieva and Gutek (1981) listed four models of problem definition and some problem solving strategies that follow from them. They are (1) the individual deficit model, wherein the problem is defined as problem people; (2) the structural model, wherein organizational structures and policies hamper women; (3) the sex role model, wherein social roles and role expectations and role stereotypes hamper women; and (4) the intergroup model, wherein men and women are viewed as opposing groups fighting over a limited amount of desirable jobs, power, and influence. They conclude that the most commonly proposed solutions fit the individual deficit model. Women are given opportunities to overcome their "deficits" through training and self-help materials targeted at them. Examples include dressing for success, assertiveness training, and how to write a business plan or obtain venture capital. Increasingly, men too are targets of training aimed at sensitizing them to issues like sexual harassment and sex discrimination.

Overall, the topic of women at work has attracted substantial research attention over the past 20 years or so. Recent reviews of the literature can be found in Ely, Foldy, and Scully (2003), Cleveland, Stockdale, and Murphy (2000), and Powell (1999). Comparing the topics covered in these volumes with those reviewed in the first widely cited text on the topic (Nieva and Gutek, 1981) show that some topics of research, like the sex role appropriateness of different occupations, have all but disappeared, while others like sexual harassment, leadership, mentoring, and preferential selection have blossomed – both because there are now a sufficient number of women (for example, holding leadership positions) to make research feasible and a sufficient number of researchers interested in the topic. While the field is not bereft of theory, much of the research continues to be descriptive, an approach well suited to a topic that is fraught with misperceptions and misinformation.

See also *diversity; evolutionary psychology; individual differences; personality; woman managers*

Bibliography

Cleveland, J., Stockdale, M., and Murphy, K. (2000). *Women and Men in Organizations: Sex and Gender Issues at Work*. Mahwah, NJ: Lawrence Erlbaum Associates.

Eagly, A. H. and Johnson, B. T. (1990). Gender and leadership style: A meta-analysis. *Psychological Bulletin*, **108**, 233–56.

Eagly, A. H., Karau, S. J., and Makhijani, M. G. (1995). Gender and the effectiveness of leaders: A meta-analysis. *Psychological Bulletin*, **108**, 233–56.

Ely, R. J. (1994). The effects of organizational demographics and social identity on relationships among professional women. *Administrative Science Quarterly*, **39** (2), 203–38.

Ely, R. J., Foldy, E. G., and Scully, M. A. (2003). *Reader in Gender, Work, and Organization*. Oxford: Blackwell.

Gutek, B. A. (1985). *Sex and the Workplace*. San Francisco: Jossey-Bass.

Gutek, B. A. (1993). Changing the status of women in management. *Applied Psychology*, **43** (4), 301–11.

Heilman, M. E., Block, and Lucas, J. A. (1992). Presumed incompetent? Stigmatization and affirmative action efforts. *Journal of Applied Psychology*, **77**, 536–44.

Knapp, D. E., Faley, R. H., Ekeberg, S. E., and DuBois, C. L. Z. (1997). Determinants of target responses to sexual harassment: A conceptual framework. *Academy of Management Review*, **22**, 687–729.

Konrad, A. M. and Linnehan, F. (1999). Formalized HRM structures: Coordinating equal employment opportunity or concealing organizational practices? *Academy of Management Journal*, **38**, 787–820.

Konrad, A. M., Ritchie, J. E., Jr., Lieb, P., and Corrigall, E. (2000). Sex differences and similarities in job attribute preferences: A meta-analysis. *Psychological Bulletin*, **126** (4), 593–641.

Konrad, A. M., Winter, S., and Gutek, B. A. (1992). Diversity in work group sex composition: Implications for majority and minority members. *Research in the Sociology of Organizations*, **10**, 115–50.

Nieva, V. F. and Gutek, B. A. (1981). *Women and Work: A Psychological Perspective*. New York: Praeger.

Powell, G. (ed.) (1999). *Handbook of Gender and Work*. Newbury Park, CA: Sage.

Ragins, B. R. and Cotton, J. L. (1991). Easier said than done: Gender differences in perceived barriers to gaining a mentor. *Academy of Management Journal*, **34**, 939–51.

United Nations (1991). *The World's Women: Trends and Statistics, 1970–1990, Social Statistics and Indicators*, Series K, no. 8. New York: United Nations.

US Bureau of Census website: www.census.gov/Press-Release/www/2002/dp_comptables.html

women managers

Barbara A. Gutek

Today, women hold a larger share of managerial positions than ever. Women have made the greatest inroads into management in countries where an academic degree (MBA, bachelor's degree in commerce) is a prerequisite for managerial jobs. This includes most European countries and the countries dominated by people of European backgrounds, such as the United States, Canada, and Australia. In countries that do not rely on formal educational programs to prepare people for management, the percentage of women is lower.

Women are significantly more likely than men to have started entrepreneurial enterprises, although these are also disproportionately among the smaller businesses. Similarly, although the numbers of women managers have increased, women are virtually unrepresented in the highest ranking DECISION-MAKING positions in business and government in almost every country in the world. According to the Federal Glass Ceiling Commission (1995), women occupy less than 5 percent of high ranking positions in the United States. There is a lively ongoing debate over whether the gender gap between the lower and higher ranks of management is a temporary or more-or-less permanent phenomenon. Some scholars believe insufficient time has passed for women to move into the top ranks, whereas others disagree (see Northcraft and Gutek, in Fagenson, 1993); both sides are able to marshal some evidence for their position.

Because management continues to be a "nontraditional" job choice for women (*see* WOMEN AT WORK), the traits associated with managers are more likely to be considered masculine than feminine. A series of studies by Schein and colleagues (Brenner, Tomkiewicz, and Schein, 1989) showed that in the mid-1970s both sexes associated the traits of successful managers with stereotypically male traits, but they were independent of stereotypes of female traits. Schein's research suggests this finding is generalizable to many different countries, although by the late 1980s in the United States, women (but not men) were somewhat more likely to associate the traits of successful managers with characteristics associated with both sexes (*see* PERSONALITY). By the beginning of the twenty-first century, women managers were increasingly seen as competent but were judged to be less warm than women in traditional roles. In addition, a meta-analysis by Eagly, Karau and Makhijani (1995) showed that men and women were equally effective leaders although both sexes were more effective in managerial roles associated with their gender.

Another lively debate in the field addresses the issue of managerial style: do women have a unique management style that differs from that typically used by men? Although those who argue that they do rely on "common sense" observations, the bulk of the research evidence suggests that men and women who are in management do not differ in management style (*see* VALIDITY GENERALIZATION). There is more intra- than between-sex variation in management style. In addition, many of the traits traditionally associated with women, such as working well in a team and being supportive of subordinates, are increasingly being recognized as important components of successful managers.

See also *CEOs; discrimination; diversity management; individual differences; organizational culture*

Bibliography

Adler, N. (1999). Global leaders: Women of influence. In G. Powell (ed.), *Handbook of Gender and Work.* Newbury Park, CA: Sage, 239–61.

Brenner, O. C., Tomkiewicz, J., and Schein, V. E. (1989). The relationship between sex role stereotype and requisite management characteristics revisited. *Academy of Management Journal,* **32**, 662–9.

Butterfield, D. A. and Grinnell, J. P. (1999). "Reviewing" gender, leadership, and managerial behavior. In G. Powell (ed.) *Handbook of Gender and Work.* Newbury Park, CA: Sage, 223–38.

Eagly, A. H., Karau, S. J., and Makhijani, M. G. (1995). Gender and the effectiveness of leaders: A meta-analysis *Psychological Bulletin,* **108**, 233–56.

Fagenson, E. A. (ed.) (1993). *Women in Management: Trends, Issues, and Challenges in Managerial Diversity.* Vol. 4 in the Women and Work series. Newbury Park, CA: Sage.

Powell, G. (1993). *Women in Management,* 2nd edn. Newbury Park, CA: Sage.

work and nonwork

see NON-WORK/WORK

work groups/teams

Michael West

Human beings work and live in groups because groups enable survival and reproduction (Baumeister and Leary, 1995). In the evolutionary past, by living and working in groups human beings could share food, easily find mates, and care for infants. They could hunt more effectively and defend themselves against their enemies (*see* EVOLUTIONARY PSYCHOLOGY). The small group is the basic strategy for human survival. Modern work groups refer to both formal and informal collectives of individuals within organizations. Formal groups are those designated as work groups or teams by the organization and whose members usually have shared task objectives. Informal groups are those not defined by the organization as functional units, but which nevertheless have an impact upon organizational behavior. Examples include friendship and pressure groups.

Teams are a particular form of work group. They are groups of people who share responsibility for producing products or delivering services. They share overall work objectives and ideally have the necessary authority, autonomy, and resources to achieve these objectives. Team members are dependent on each other to achieve the objectives and therefore have to work closely, interdependently, and supportively to achieve the team's goals. Members have distinct and clear roles. Effective teams have as few members as necessary to perform the task and are ideally no larger than six to eight members. And the team is recognized by others in the organization as a team (West, 2003).

There are multiple types of teams in organizations:

Advice and involvement teams (e.g., management decision-making committees, quality control (QC) circles, staff involvement groups).

Production and service teams (e.g., assembly teams; maintenance, construction, mining, and commercial airline teams; departmental teams; sales and healthcare teams).

Project and development teams (e.g., research teams, new product development teams, software development teams).

Action and negotiation teams (e.g., military combat units, surgical teams, and trade union negotiating teams).

Key dimensions on which they differ include:

Degree of permanence: project teams have a defined lifetime that can vary from weeks to years; cockpit "teams" are together for only hours.

Emphasis on skill/competence development: breast cancer care teams must develop their skills over time to a high level, whereas decision-making committees usually have little emphasis on skill development.

Genuine autonomy and INFLUENCE*:* manufacturing assembly teams may have little autonomy and influence, whereas top management teams are powerful.

Level of task from routine through to strategic: short haul flights involve cockpit crews in routine tasks, whereas a government cabinet may be determining penal strategy for a ten year period.

The following dimensions describe the tasks that are best performed by teams rather than individuals:

Completeness (i.e., whole tasks): not simply putting the studs on the car wheels but assembling the whole transmission system plus wheels.

Varied demands: team tasks require a range of SKILLS that are held or best developed by a number of different individuals.

Requirements for team member interdependence and interaction: team members interact frequently and mutually depend upon one another in order to complete the task.

Task significance: the importance of the task in contributing to organizational goals or to the wider society.

Opportunities for learning: providing team members with chances to develop and stretch their skills and knowledge

Developmental possibilities for the task: the task can be developed to offer more challenges to the team members, requiring them to take on more responsibility and learn new skills over time.

Autonomy: the amount of freedom teams have over how to do their work.

Why work in teams? In many areas of endeavor, research has shown how team working can lead to greater efficiency or effectiveness. Better patient care is provided when health professionals work together in multidisciplinary teams and the more team working there is in hospitals, the lower the level of patient mortality (West et al., 2002). There is evidence that when students work in cooperative groups rather than individually, they word harder, help less able group members, and learn more (Slavin, 1983). Teams enable organizations to learn (and retain learning) more effectively. When one team member leaves, the learning of the team is not lost. Team members also learn from each other during the course of team working. Cross-functional teams promote improved quality management. By combining team members' diverse perspectives, decision-making is improved. DIVERSITY, properly processed, leads to high quality decision-making and innovation (West, 2002). An analysis of the combined results of 131 studies of organizational change found that interventions with the largest effects upon financial performance were team development interventions or the creation of autonomous work groups (Macy and Izumi, 1993). Applebaum and Batt (1994) reviewed 12 large-scale surveys and 185 case studies of managerial practices. They concluded that team-based working led to improvements in organizational performance on measures both of efficiency and quality.

Much effort has been devoted to understanding the factors which promote group effectiveness and the thinking of most researchers has been dominated by an input–process–output model, mainly because of its simplicity and utility. Inputs include the task of the team, group composition (size, functional and demographic diversity, tenure), and organizational context (such as culture, support for team working, structure). Some processes mediate the relationships between inputs and outputs, such as PARTICIPATION mediating the effects of diversity upon innovation, while some inputs such as organizational context directly influence outputs. Processes include participation (influence over decision-making, interactions and information sharing), leadership, conflict, decision-making, interteam processes, and reflexivity (Hackman, 2002; West, 2003). Team outputs include productivity, INNOVATION, team member well-being, and team learning.

The study of work groups and teams has developed rich understanding of social processes and performance in organizations (West, Tjosvold, and Smith, 2003) and the future for this area is immensely promising. The challenge now is to understand the functioning of team-based organizations (or multi-team systems) and how they can be structured and developed to maximize the benefits of this basic form of human functioning in modern, large, complex organizational settings (Mathieu, Marks, and Zaccaro, 2001)

See also *corporate boards; group dynamics; team building; top management teams*

Bibliography

Applebaum, E. and Batt, R. (1994). *The New American Workplace.* Ithaca, NY: ILR Press.

Baumeister, R. F. and Leary, M. R. (1995). The need to belong: Desire for interpersonal attachments as a fundamental human motivation. *Psychological Bulletin,* 117, 497–529.

Hackman, J. R. (2002). *Leading Teams: Setting the Stage for Great Performances.* Cambridge, MA: Harvard Business School Press.

Macy, B. A. and Izumi, H. (1993). *Organizational Change, Design and Work Innovation: A Meta-Analysis of 131 North American Field Studies – 1961–1991.* Research in Organizational Change and Development, Vol 7. Greenwich, CT: JAI Press, 235–313.

Mathieu, J. E., Marks, M. A., and Zaccaro, S. J. (2001). Multiteam systems. In N. Anderson, D. S. Ones, H. K. Sinangil, and C. Viswesvaran (eds.), *Handbook of Industrial, Work and Organizational Psychology,* Vol. 2. London: Sage, 289–313.

Slavin, R. E. (1983). When does cooperative learning increase student achievement? *Psychological Bulletin,* 94, 429–45.

West, M. A. (2002). Sparkling fountains or stagnant ponds: An integrative model of creativity and innovation implementation in work groups. *Applied Psychology: An International Review*, **51**, 355–87.

West, M. A. (2003). *Effective Teamwork: Practical Lessons from Organizational Research*. Oxford: Blackwell.

West, M. A., Borrill, C., Dawson, J., Scully, J., Carter, M., Anelay, S., Patterson, M., and Waring, J. (2002). The link between the management of employees and patient mortality in acute hospitals. *International Journal of Human Resource Management*, **13** (8), 1299–310.

West, M. A., Tjosvold, D., and Smith, K. G. (eds.) (2003). *International Handbook of Organizational Teamwork and Cooperative Working*. Chichester: John Wiley and Sons.

work role transitions

see CAREER TRANSITIONS

Index

Note: Headwords are in bold type

ability 1
  and aptitude 12
  attribution theory 14
  and competency 54
  individual differences 167
  intellectual 1, 12
  practical intelligence 324
  and skill 367
  social comparison 369
absence culture 3, 218
absenteeism 1–3, 88, 349, 409
  and job design 194
  and job enrichment 199
  and job satisfaction 201, 218
  punishment 334
  and role over/underload 357
  stress-related 378
accountability 3–6
  and corporate social
    performance 73
  and diversity management 94
  and governance 142
  and job rotation 199
accounting methods 26
achievement, need for 6–7
  entrepreneurs 107
  motivation 6, 7, 13
action research 7–8
  and organization
    development 257
action, theories of 95
administrative technology 389
adverse selection 10
aesthetic labor 99–100
Affective Events Theory 100
affect–performance
    relationships 100–1
affiliation, need for 6, 8
affirmative action 419
age 8–9
  career plateauing 31–2

career stages 32
  and commitment 168
  and complexity theory 57
  diversity management 92
  and job design 9, 195
  and job satisfaction 168, 200
  population ecology 287
age discrimination 9
agency theory 10–11, 403
  and accountability 4
  and contracts 70
  and corporate boards 71
  and crises 78
  and decision-making 84
  and executive succession
    119
  and family firms 123
  and professional service
    firms 329
  vertical integration 403
agent–principal
    relationship 142
  and incentives 166
aggregation bias 22
agreeableness 126, 127, 128, 315
Albert, S. 369–70
alienation 103, 391
alliances *see* strategic alliances
alternative dispute resolution 60
altruism 11–12
  agency theory 11
  and identification 159
  in negotiation 116
  and organizational citizenship
    behavior (OCB) 270
  see also reciprocal altruism
Amabile, T. M. 74–7, 121–2
ambiguity
  communications 50
  and risk taking 350–1
  role ambiguity 354, 356

analogy, creativity and 76
Anand, N. 226–8, 280–5,
    328–30, 352–3
anchoring 18
Ancona, D. 105–6
Anderson, P. 389–92
angel investors 108
antitrust law 143, 185
approximations 397
aptitude 12
arbitration 60, 183
Argyris, C. 95–6, 151
Armed Services Vocational
    Aptitude Battery
    (ASVAB) 12
artificial life 58
Arvey, R. D. 200–1, 334–5
Ashforth, B. 162, 358–60
assembly line production 196
attitude
  attitude-shifting 4
  and participation 305
  stereotypical 9
attitude theory 12–13, 316
  cognitive dissonance 4, 43
  and organizational citizenship
    behavior (OCB) 270
attraction–selection–attrition
    (ASA) framework 169, 416
attribution 13–15
  evolutionary psychology
    framework 116
  and leadership 13, 40–1, 208
  and prejudice 325
  and social perception 306
Audia, P. G. 293–5, 309–10,
    341–2
authoritarian personality 15
authority 16
  bureaucratic 25, 222, 321
  charismatic leadership 40

authority (*cont'd*)
  classical management
    theory 221
  delegation 304
  hierarchical 25
  and influence 170
  and locus of control 168
  and organizational design 280
autonomy
  and career anchors 31
  and commitment 45–6
  and creativity 75
  and job design 194
  and job rotation 199
  loose coupling 219–20
  and prestige 298
  self-managing teams 365
  work groups/teams 422, 423

Baer, M. 198–9
Bagger, J. 135–7, 418–20
Bailey, J. R. 213–15
bargaining
  game theory 132
  intergroup relations 182, 183
  political behavior 318
  and power 322
Barley, S. R. 113–14, 380–1
Barnard, C. I. 222, 281
Bass, B. M. 398–9, 404–6
Bazerman, M. H. 17–19, 46–7,
    242–6
behavior modification 20
**behavioral decision
    research 17–19**, 82
  decision-making 361
  evolutionary psychology
    framework 116
  and negotiation 244
  and risk taking 351
behavioral game theory 133
behaviorism 19–22
  and individual learning 214
  interpersonal skills 189
  and motivation 235
bias 22, 337
  and behavioral decision
    research 18–19
  debiasing efforts 19
  decision-making 17, 18–19,
    148–9, 330
  and diversity management 92
  evolutionary psychology
    framework 116
  hindsight bias 18, 111–12
  ingroup bias 183

and organizational
    change 267
  rational 5
  and statistical methods 377
  suppression 202
Big Five model *see* five factor
    model of personality
Bigelow, J. D. 187–91
Blau, P. 219, 259
Blauner, R. 391
blogging 50
Blount-Lyon, S. 394–5
boundaries 23
  and careers 30, 31, 34
  change 39, 262
  and communications
    technology 51
  geographical 53
  organizational 255
  political 261
boundary spanning 23–4
  and communication 48
  and community ecology 53
  and corporate social
    performance 73
  and innovation 174
  intergroup relations 183
  open systems 255
boundaryless careers 30, 31, 34
**bounded rationality 17, 18,
    24**, 339
  and contracts 70
  decision-making 17, 25, 82,
    83, 86, 261, 361
Boyatzis, R. E. 54–6, 101–2
Bradley, J. C. 100–1
brainstorming 24–5
  and group decision-
    making 146
  problem solving 76
Brief, A. P. 100–1
Bromiley, P. 350–2
buck-passing 4
bullying 61, 100
bureaucracy 25–9
  and authority 16
  characteristics 222
  conflict 59
  dysfunctions 27
  ideology 163
  and modernism 320
  and professional service
    firms 328
  public sector 26, 27–8
  rationality 281
  and routinization 68

Weberian 48, 50, 222, 290
Burgoyne, J. G. 216–17
Burke, W. W. 23–4, 135, 250–1
burnout 29
  attribution theory 14
  and conflict 59
  role over/underload 357
business process
    reengineering 197

California Psychology Inventory
    (CPI) 314
call centers 195, 197–8, 362
Cameron, K. 63–4, 96–8,
    289–93
Campbell, J. L. 142–4
capital accounting 26
capital flight 144
capitalism 143, 320
  capital market risk 351
  investor capitalism 191–2
  managerial capitalism 192
career 30
  boundaryless careers 30, 31,
    34
  and commitment 45–6
  dual career families 34, 252
  management career
    strategies 410
  orientations 7
  portfolio careers 30, 31
  success, personality and 127,
    168
career anchor 30–1, 34
career counseling 12
career development 30, 31
  and age 9
career plateau 31–2
career stage 31, 32
  entrainment 106
career theory 30, 31, 32–5
  five factor model of
    personality 127
Cartesianism 300
Casciaro, T. 349–50
catastrophe theory 55
categorization 182, 183
cellular automata 56–7
centralization 299
CEOs 35–7
  boundary spanning 23
  and corporate boards 71–2,
    184
  family firms 123
  "Great Man" view 36, 207
  power 72, 119–20

selection and succession 37, 71, 119–20, 263–4
self-interest 10
span of control 299
change
  change–performance relationship 263, 264
  and charismatic leadership 41
  content/process 262–3
  and continuous improvement 69
  dialectical theory 265–6, 267
  effective 39
  evolutionary theory 266
  implementation theory 40, 299
  incremental 69, 263
  life cycle theory 264–5, 267
  management 38
  methodology 39
  organizational change 262–9
  and organizational culture 275, 276
  and organizational ecology 288
  performance-driven 301
  process theory 257
  radical 69, 263
  resistance to 15, 24, 61, 348–9, 398
  self-directed 257
  technological 38, 216
  teleological theory 265, 267
change, evaluation 37–8
change, methods 38–40
chaos theory 255, 267–8, 384
charismatic leadership 40–1
chief executive officer see CEOs
chief operating officer see COO
Cialdini, R. B. 169–71
circadian rhythms 105
citizenship see organizational citizenship behavior
civil rights legislation 90, 179
clans 84
classical design theory see management, classical theory
Clegg, C. W. 193–6, 373–5
Clegg, S. 79–80, 163
client relationships 198
climate see organizational climate
clique detection 248
closed systems 68, 384–5
coaching 308

coalition formation 41–2, 84, 117
  coalitional power 322
  game theory 131, 133
  intergroup relations 182
  loose coupling 220
  organizational politics 318–19
cognition
  and attitude theory 13
  Cognitive Evaluation Theory 237
  cognitive skills 187
  entrepreneurs 108
  errors 111
  evolutionary psychology framework 116
  and goal setting 140
  heuristics 114
  interpersonal skills 187, 189
  and learning 213–14
  managerial and organizational cognition 223–4
  and negotiation 244
cognitive behavioral interventions 380
cognitive dissonance 4, 43
  and commitment 45
  and equity theory 109
cognitive social psychology 5
  error-and-bias tradition 6
collaboration 43–4, 182
collectivism/individualism 168, 190, 239, 416
commensalism 53
commitment 44–6
  and age 168
  attitude-shifting 4
  and conformity 63
  and consensus 64
  contracts 69–70
  and employee involvement 103
  game theory 131
  goal commitment 138, 139
  and influence 171
  and job deskilling 197
  and job satisfaction 201
  leadership 105
  and mentoring 229
  and motivation 234
  nominal group technique 251
  and organizational culture 273
  and role ambiguity 356
  and stress 378
  theory X and Y 398

  and turnover 409–10
commitment, escalating 5, 46–7, 267, 309
  and identification 159
  and negotiation 244
communication 47–50
  congruence 63–4
  and diversity management 93
  and employee involvement 102
  face-to-face 49, 52, 282
  and game theory 133
  and group dynamics 148
  information and meaning-centered conceptions 47
  and innovation 173, 177
  interactivity 51
  and knowledge management 204
  lateral/vertical 49, 51
  the matrix organization 227
  and negotiation 243
  and organizational design 282
  overload 49, 51
  and process consultation 326
  processes 38
  and role theory 355
  skills 187, 188, 367
  symbolism 383
  team building 387
  trust 387
communications technology 50–2
communities of practice 205
community ecology 52–4, 288–9
comparison, social see social comparison
compensation see payment systems
competency 1, 54–6
  and career anchors 31
  and emotional intelligence 101
  and individual learning 215
  single/clusters 54, 101–2
  and skills 188, 367
  and technology 216
competitive advantage, sources of 79
complexity theory 56–7, 255, 384
  and crises 78
  environmental complexity 179–80
  open systems 256

computational and mathematical
    organization theory
    (CMOT) 58
computational mechanics 58
computer integrated
    manufacture 391
computer simulation 57–8,
    348
  and bias 22
  and decision-making 86
computers
  and communication 50, 51–2
  computational modeling 56
  conferencing 51
  enterprise resource
    planning 104–5
  flaming 51
  groupware 189
  and knowledge
    management 203, 204
conceptions 396
conditioning
  contingent reinforcement 210
  operant 20
  respondent 20
conflict and conflict
    management 38, 59–62
  and absenteeism 2
  and affiliation motivation 8
  asymmetrical conflicts 61
  attribution theory 13, 14
  and communication 50
  and consensus 64
  and diversity management 92
  game theory 131, 133
  group dynamics 147, 148
  and group roles 153
  intergroup relations 183
  interpersonal skills 188–9
  and job deskilling 196
  labor–management
    conflict 183
  leader–member conflicts 15
  levels of analysis 59
  the matrix organization 227
  mediation 5
  and negotiation 243
  prisoner's dilemma 132, 245
  process consultation 326
  reciprocity norm 340
  and socialization 372
  see also role conflict
conflicts of interest 67
conformity 62–3
  affiliation motivation 8
  authoritarian personality 15

group decision-making
    145–6, 153
  and rituals 353
Conger, J. 40–1, 207–13
congruence 63–4
  effectiveness models 291
  goal congruence 139
  value congruence 416
conjunction fallacy 18
conscientiousness 2, 126, 127,
    237, 269, 316
consensual assessment
    technique 74
consensus 64
  goal consensus 130
  professional service firms 329
consolidated accounting 26
construct validity 413
consultancy 64–7
consultancy process 64–5
contact hypothesis 325
content
  content validity 413
  and process 326
contingency theory 67–8, 259
  functionalism 301
  and job design 195
  leadership contingencies 208,
    209, 210, 212–13
  and organizational design 281
  and organizational
    effectiveness 291
  structural 281, 299, 300, 301
continuous improvement
    68–9
  error management 112
  and total quality
    management 401
contracts 69–70
  and agency theory 10
  and governance 186
  psychological contract 70,
    333–4
  and trust 70, 406, 408
  violations 116
control
  bureaucratic 25
  locus of 219, 315
Cook, T. D. 337–8
Cooper, A. C. 106–9
cooperation 60, 174, 182, 183,
    223, 408
  game theory 131
  see also collaboration;
    teamwork; work groups/
    teams

cooptation 6, 350
coordination mechanisms 283
COO (chief operating
    officer) 36
Cordery, J. 304–6, 364–5
corporate boards 71–2
  accountability 6
  and control of managerial
    behavior 10, 71
  decision-making 84
  executive succession 119–20
  interlocking boards 71,
    184–5, 282, 294, 350
  and organizational
    geography 294
  and organizational
    performance 84
  role and responsibilities 10,
    142
corporate entrepreneurship 106,
    107
corporate social
    performance 72–3
  and reputation 344
corporate social
    responsiveness 73
Creative Problem Solving 76
creativity 74–7
  assessment 12, 74
  and career anchors 31
  decision-making 24–5
  enhancement 76, 93
  Intrinsic Motivation
    Principle 75, 122
  minority group influence 232
  and organizational design 284
crises/disasters 77–9
  catastrophe theory 55
  and errors 110, 111, 157
  external crises 27
  group polarization 151
crisis-prone organizations 78
critical theory 79–80
  and consultancy 65
  and individual learning
    214–15
  and knowledge
    management 205
  and postmodernism 321
cross-cultural conflict 61
cross-cultural management 80
cross-cultural research 80,
    347
  motivation theory 238–9
cultural assimilation 90
cultural awareness 54, 94, 102

culture   39
  absence culture   3
  cross-cultural research   80,
    238–9, 347
  definitions   81
  ethnography   113
  interrelated systems   81
  organizational   47, 274–8
  and technology   390
  values   416
culture, national   81, 261
  and motivation   140
Cummings, T. G.   255–6,
  384–6
cybernetics
  cybernetic control
    formulations   235–6, 238
  cybernetic systems   259

De Dreu, C. K. W.   59–62
death, organizational *see*
    organizational decline
    and death
decentralization   78, 143, 188,
  299, 399
decision-making   82–7
  accountability   3, 4, 5
  and agency theory   10
  and altruism   11
  authoritative   304
  barriers to   24
  bias   17, 19, 148–9, 330
  bounded rationality   17, 24,
    82, 83, 261, 361
  brainstorming   24–5, 146
  bureaucratic   25
  CEOs   36
  cognitive perspectives   146
  commitment   46
  and communications
    technology   51
  and conflict management   60
  conformity   63
  contexts   82–4
  corporate boards   72
  creativity   24–5
  Delphi group format   87
  emotion management   100
  employee involvement   304
  entrainment   105
  family firms   123
  game theory   132, 243
  garbage can model   58, 134
  group decision-making
    145–7, 151
  groupthink   153–4

heuristics   17–18, 24, 63, 107,
  170
  identity confirmation   82
  and influence   170
  joint/unilateral   60
  leadership style   209, 210,
    212–13
  and logrolling   84
  maximization   82
  neurotic style   295
  procedural justice   202
  processes   38
  quality circles   336
  rational   17, 83, 339
  risk taking   350–1
  satisficing   24, 82, 83, 361
  self-managing teams   364–5
  strategic choice
    perspective   36
  surveys   381
  uncertainty   24, 67, 361
  visionary   321
  and women   421
Deephouse, D. L.   16, 378
delegation   304
  decision-making   10
Delphi   87
Deming, W. Edwards   68–9
demography *see* organizational
    demography
DeNisi, A.   124–5
density dependence model
  286–7, 288
departmentalization   300
dependence
  mutual   349–50
  overdependence   186
  resource dependence   260,
    278, 349–50
design *see* organizational design
deskilling *see* job deskilling
deviance   87–9, 202
  absenteeism   2, 3
  attribution theory   14
  punishment   334
dialectical theory   265–6, 267
differentiation
  organizational culture   274–5
  organizational design   23
  role differentiation   354
  structural   300
digital technologies   390
DiMaggio, P. J.   178, 179, 282
discipline   334, 398
  see also punishment
discrimination   89–91

age   9
  and diversity management   93
  prejudice   325
  racial   90, 91, 168
  sexism   90, 419
  and tournament theory   402
disequilibrium theory   300
diversification   299–300
  in organizations   92
diversity
  analysis and initiatives   92–5
  consequences   92–3
  content and structure   92
  ethnic and cultural   92
  individual differences   168
  and personal identity   162
  and team working   423
  top management teams   399
diversity management   91–5
  interpersonal skills   189
  and mentoring   229
division of labor   25, 68, 283
  and job deskilling   196–7
divisionalization   26, 299–300
dogmatism   15
Donaldson, L.   218, 228,
  298–302
double-loop learning   95–6
downsizing   96–8
  bureaucratic
    organizations   26, 27
  lack of psychological contract
    fulfillment   333
  and new job creation   106
  and organizational decline
    279
Drucker, P.   221
drug testing programs   202
dual career couples   252
dual concern theory   60
Dunn-Jensen, L. M.   252–4
Durkheim, E.   280, 352
Dyer, W. G., Jr.   387–9
dynamic network   51
dysfunctional behavior   14,
  165
  see also deviance

Earley, C. P.   80, 221
e-business   374
ecology *see* community ecology;
    organizational ecology;
    population ecology
econometrics   337
economics
  experimental   132, 133

economics (*cont'd*)
  institutional   181
  organizational   282, 408
economies of scale and
      scope   230
e-consulting   66
Edwards, J. E.   163–5, 381–2
effectiveness
  abundance model   292–3
  boards   10
  bureaucracies   26, 27
  and career plateauing   32
  change   39
  and competencies   188
  congruence models   291
  feedback   124–5
  group   150, 153–4
  and knowledge
    management   203
  leadership   208, 209, 210, 316,
    324
  organizational
    effectiveness   282, 289–93,
    363
  and organizational
    structure   300
  quality circles   336
  and reputation   344
  strategic constituencies
    approach   291–2
  work groups/teams   423
efficiency
  bureaucracies   26, 27–8, 290
  and downsizing   97
  operational/technical   261,
    391
egocentrism   245
Ehrhart, K. H.   270–2
Ehrhart, M. G.   270–2
elitism   37, 71, 79, 184, 320
Ellis, A.   279–80
email   49, 50, 51
emotion
  attitude theory   13
  attribution theory   14
  and deviant behavior   89
  emotional stability   315
  extraversion   126
  intergroup emotions   183
  in negotiation   245
emotion management
    99–100
emotion in
    organizations   100–1
  job satisfaction   200
  and leadership   209

emotional intelligence   54,
    100, **101–2**, 214
emotional labor   99, 101, 195
empathy   54, 102
employee involvement   102–3
  and empowerment   103
  and job design   195
  participation   304
  quality circles   336
empowerment   103, 304, 321,
    398
  and job design   195
  self-managing teams   365
enactment   103–4
  and careers   30
  and decision-making   84
  and knowledge
    management   203
  managerial role
    enactment   226
  open systems   255
  and personal identity   162
  and postmodernism   320
  and role transitions   359
enculturation   48
enterprise resource
    planning   104–5, 374
entrainment   105–6, 395
  group dynamics   149
entrepreneurship   106–9
  achievement motivation   7
  and charismatic leadership   41
  family firms   123
environment
  assessment   73
  change   263
  and creativity   75–6
  and goal-setting process   140
  imprinting   286, 287
  and job satisfaction   200
  and organizational
    decline   278
  and organizations   68, 260,
    286, 291, 385
  and perception   306
  person–environment
    interaction   30, 100,
    310–11, 378–9
  systems theory   384–5
  work environment, creativity
    and   75–6
equal employment legislation   90
equifinality   256, 265
equilibrium, punctuated   149,
    263, 266, 300,
    390

equity theory   109–10
  and distributive justice   201
  and motivation   237
  and resistance to change   349
  and social comparison   370
  and status incongruence   378
Erez, M.   138–41, 238–9
error   110–11
error management   111–12, 312
errors   111–13
  behavioral decision
    research   20
  and crises   77, 157
  double-loop learning   95
  halo error   155, 307
  and innovations   172, 175
  and job design   193
  of omission   111, 330
  and organizational change
    267
  rational   5
ethics
  board responsibilities   142
  corporate social
    performance   73
  honesty value   416
ethnocentrism   183
ethnography   113–14
  and network theory   246
  qualitative research   348
evolutionary computation   58
evolutionary
    perspectives   114–15
  and organizational
    change   263, 266
evolutionary
    psychology   114, 115–17
  and altruism   11
  and group strategy   422
  and trust   407
exchange relations   117–18,
    278
  game theory   132
  institutional perspective   181
  and leadership   210
  and organizational citizenship
    behavior (OCB)
    269
  and power   321–2
  psychological contract   333
  reciprocity   339, 340, 341
  and transaction cost
    economics   403
executive compensation   10, 37
executive derailment   118–19
executive discretion   36–7

executive succession   119–21
expectancies
  goals   140
  and group dynamics   148
  and job satisfaction   200
  locus of control   219
expectancy motivation   128
expectancy theory   166, 363
expectancy value theory   237
expected utility theory   331
experimental economics   132, 134
extraversion   126, 127, 128, 315, 316
extrinsic and intrinsic motivation   110, 121–2, 237, 362
  job satisfaction   200

face-to-face communication   49, 52, 282
facilitation   187, 189
  quality circles   336
  social facilitation   370
family firms   123–4
  and altruism   11
family-friendly work policies   137, 253
fatigue   379
Fay, D.   311–12
Fayol, H.   222, 281
feedback   124–5
  communication   47
  and decision-making   85
  and empowerment   103
  goal setting   138, 139
  job enrichment   198
  and job satisfaction   201
  and media richness   51
  and motivation   241
  negative   124, 125, 308
  open systems   255
  performance appraisal   76, 308
  and self-efficacy   363
  and self-regulation   366
  and skills   367
  surveys   382
  task focused   7
  and workplace performance   20
Feldman, D. C.   62–3, 159
Fenton-O'Creevy, M.   102–3
Festinger, L.   369
Fineman, S.   99–100
Fisher, R. A.   377

five factor model of personality   15, 116, 126–9, 236, 314, 315, 316
flextime   3, 254
Follett, M. P.   223
Fombrun, C.   343–5
force field analysis   129–30, 348
Ford, Henry   196, 362
formalization   299
Foucault, M.   161, 163, 320
fragmentation studies   275–6
free riders   305, 329
Freeman, J.   52–4, 67–8, 258–62, 285–6
Frese, M.   111–13, 311–12, 378–80
Freud, Sigmund   365–6
Fryer, D.   7–8
functionalism   265, 273, 283, 300, 352
fund accounting   26
fundamental attribution error   111

Galatea effect   363
game theory   131–4
  and coalition formation   42
  decision-making   84
  negotiation   243, 245
  prisoner's dilemma   132, 245
  and reputation   343
  risk taking   351
  and tournament theory   402
  and trust   408
garbage can model   58, 134–5
gatekeepers   135, 204, 250
Gavrieli, D. A.   181–4, 318–19, 321–4
gender   135–7
  attribution theory   14
  discrimination   90
  diversity management   92
  evolutionary psychology   115
  and impression management   323
  and job design   136, 195
  and job satisfaction   200
  and leadership styles   419
  and non-work/work   136, 253
  occupations   135–6, 168, 418
  and personality traits   314
  and power   323
  sexual harassment   367
  women at work   418–20
  work roles   135–6

General Aptitude Test Battery (GATB)   12
generalization   137–8, 342
  empirical   397
  validity generalization   414
Gestalt tradition   214
Ghitulescu, B.   368–9
Giddens, A.   380–1
glass ceiling   91, 418
globalization   55
  and organizational flexibility   118, 239, 252
  and research design   347
goal acceptance   139
goal congruence   139
goal displacement   27
goal orientation   138, 141
goal setting   138–41, 361
  achievement motivation   7
  error   110
  five factor model of personality   128
  goal incongruence   10
  management by objectives   221
  and motivation   128, 234–5, 236, 238
  and performance appraisal   308
  and personal identity   162
  process consultation   326
  and self-efficacy   363
  teleological theory   265
goals   138–9
  and behavior regulation   139
  commitment   44, 234
  and creativity   75
  deviation from   110, 111
  direct/indirect   188
  distal/proximal   139
  formulation   41
  goal commitment   138, 139
  goal consensus   130
  interdependence   60
  and intergroup relations   182
  and interpersonal skills   188
  and motivation   233
  multiple goals   83, 140
  quality circles   336
  self-set   139
  superordinate goals   183
Goffman, E.   164, 357
golden handcuffs   410
golden parachutes   71, 85, 294
governance   141–2
  and agency theory   10

governance (*cont'd*)
  and corporate social
    performance 73
  employee involvement 102
  family firms 123
  inter-organizational
    relations 186
  partnership form 328
  self-managing teams 365
  social mechanisms 186
  and stakeholders 376
**government and
  business 142–4**
  performance appraisal 26
  privatization 26, 28
Greenberg, J. 87–9, 109–10,
  201–2
Greve, H. 82–7, 134–5, 368
Griffin, R. W. 12–13, 43
Griffiths, A. 8–9
group cohesiveness 144–5,
  149, 158, 217, 369
  and consensus 64
  groupthink 153
  and identification 159
  and innovation 173
  and leadership 207
  process consultation 326
**group decision-making
  145–7**
  brainstorming 24–5, 146
  and conformity 63, 153
  consensus 64
  Delphi technique 87
  groupthink 153–4
  individual interaction 85
  nominal group format 251
  and the quality
    movement 401
  risky shift phenomenon 151
  stepladder technique 146
  and values 416
group development 149
group dynamics 147–50
  and coalition formation 41–2
  and consensus 64
  and diversity management 92
  exchange relations 117
  game theory 131
  gatekeepers 135
  and individual
    differences 169
  systems theory 384
  task conflict 59
  top management teams 400
group effectiveness 150, 153–4

group interactions 148
  see also group dynamics
group norms 150–1, 361
  and cohesion–performance
    relationship 145
  force field analysis 129
group polarization 151–2
group roles 152–3
groupthink 93, **153–4**
  and conformity 63
  decision-making 84, 146, 153
growth, bureaucratic 27
growth need strength 168–9,
  362
Guadagno, R. E. 169–71
guanxi 249
Guest, D. 44–6
gurus 320
Gutek, B. A. 135–7, 367,
  418–22

Habermas, J. 79
Hales, C. 224–6
halo effect 155, 274, 307
Hambrick, D. C. 35–7, 399–400
Hannan, M. 285–6, 294
harassment, sexual 367
hardiness 155, 379
Hatch, M.-J. 160–1
Hawley, A. 52–3
Hawthorne effect 156, 235
health
  and absenteeism 2
  and conflict 61, 62
  and self-esteem 364
  and stress 378
Heider, F. 13
helplessness, learned 14
Henik, E. 3–6
Hennessey, B. A. 121–2
Herzberg, F. 194, 200
hetero-performance 301
heuristics 17–18, 24, 63, 107,
  114, 170
hierarchy
  and authority 16, 25
  and brainstorming 24
  bureaucratic 222
  egalitarian 116
  and group decision-
    making 24, 146
  line/staff 218
  and the matrix
    organization 227
  mechanistic organizational
    structures 228

Need Hierarchy Theory 236,
  362
  and networking 250
  and organization size 260, 299
  and organizational
    culture 274–5
  and participation 304
  trust hierarchy 407–8
Higgins, E. T. 330
**high reliability
  organizations 157–8**
Hochschild, A. 99
Hogan, J. 1, 12, 367–8
**human relations
  movement 158,** 223,
  282
human resource management
  commitment approach 44
  competency-based
    practices 55
  and downsizing 97
  and total quality
    management 401
hypothesis testing 110, 377

identification 78, **159**
  and group cohesiveness 144,
    159
  symbolism 383
identity
  collective 162, 183
  dynamics 161
  group 149, 182
  interpersonal 162
  organizational 160–1
  personal 162–3
  and role theory 354
  social 4
  synchronic/diachronic
    approaches 160
identity confirmation 82
**identity, organizational
  160–1**
identity, personal 162–3
  and conformity 63
ideology 163
  absolutist ideologies 15
  and bureaucracy 25, 163
  clans 84
  and coalition formation 42
  and communication 48
  and discrimination 90
  and politics 318
Ilgen, D. R. 156
implementation theory 40, 257
impossibility theorem 83

impression
    management   163–5
    attribution theory   13, 15
    and gender   323
    and organizational
        culture   274
    and perception   306–7
    and personal identity   162
    personality testing   314–15
    and reciprocity norm   341
incentives   165–7
    and accountability   4
    and agency relationships   10
    bureaucratic organizations   25
    and knowledge
        management   204
    and social loafing   371
    tournament theory   402
    see also payment systems;
        rewards
individual differences   167–9
    and ability   1
    attribution theory   14
    and job design   194
    and job satisfaction   200
    motivation and
        performance   234, 236,
        377
    and negotiation   242–3
    and personal identity   162
    and personality   312
    and socialization   372
industrial psychology   223, 256
industrial-organizational
    psychology   126
industrialism   320
inertia theory   264
influence   169–71
    and coalition formation   42
    competency   54
    conflict theory   61
    and consensus   64
    and decision-making   19
    and gender   323
    and group polarization   151
    and innovation   177
    interpersonal skills   188
    leadership influence   207, 210,
        405
    minority group influence
        232–3
    and politics   319
    and power   324
    and reciprocity   340–1
    and socialization   372
    work groups/teams   422

information
    asymmetry   10, 120, 343
    communication   47
    networking   250
    open systems   255
    processing   255, 281–2, 284
information technology
    and business
        reengineering   284
    communications   49
    enterprise resource
        planning   104–5
    networking   251
    and value chain
        management   65
Ingram, P.   185–7
innovation   171–7
    and bureaucracy   27
    and communication   48, 49
    conflict theory   61
    and creativity   74
    entrepreneurship   106, 107
    and inter-organizational
        relations   186
    and knowledge
        management   204
    leadership   210
    life cycle theory   265
    loose coupling   110
    managerial roles   226
    and network theory   246
    and personal initiative   311
    product innovation   23
    and slack resources   368
    and systems theory   384
    and technology   390, 393
    and top management
        teams   399
innovation diffusion   177–8
innovation processes   174–6
Innovative Forms of Organizing
    (INNFORM)   39
institutional discrimination   90
institutional economics   181
institutional investors   72,
        191–2, 343
institutional legitimacy   48, 73
institutional theory   178–81,
        259, 261
    and corporate boards   72
    executive succession   119
    government and business
        143
    open systems   255
    and organizational design   282
    and power   322

and professional service
        firms   329
    and status   298
institutionalization
        processes   179
institutions   181
integration
    and bureaucracy   25
    organizational culture   273–4
    organizational design   23
integrity   4
intelligence
    and ability   1
    decision-making   17
    emotional intelligence   54,
        100, 101–2, 214
    fluid/crystallized   1
    and interpersonal skills   188,
        190
    and learning   214
    practical intelligence   324
    structure of intellect model   1
inter-organizational
        relations   185–7
    boundary spanning   23
    and change   262
    collaboration   44
    communication   48
    loose coupling   220
    and network theory   246
    and organizational
        change   264
    and technological
        development   391
    and technology transfer   392
    and transaction cost
        economics   404
intergroup relations   181–4
interlocking boards   184–5,
        294, 350
international management
    interpersonal skills   189
    and investor capitalism   191–2
    professional service firms
        329
    stakeholders   376
Internet
    conferencing   50
    and research design   347, 348
    web-based surveys   381
interpersonal skills   187–91,
        341
intrinsic motivation see extrinsic
    and intrinsic motivation
investor capitalism   191–2
iso-performance   301

isomorphism   179, 217, 393
issues management   73

Jackson, S. E.   91–5
Jahoda, M.   7
Janis, I. L.   153, 154
Japanese management   69, 197,
    261, 336, 398, 401
Jelinek, M.   219–20, 221–3
Jimeno-Ingrum, D.   199
job attitudes see attitude theory
job characteristics   193, 194, 195,
    362, 374
job description
    boundaries   23
    and role ambiguity   356
Job Description Index
    (JDI)   200
job design   38, 193–6, 217, 336
    age factor   9, 195
    employee involvement   103,
        304
    error   110
    and gender   136, 195
    and individual
        differences   168
    redesign   97, 103, 193–4, 195,
        197, 235
    sociotechnical theory   373–4
    and stress   168, 193
    and teamwork   401
job deskilling   193, 196–8,
    362
job embeddedness   410
job enrichment   194, 198–9
    and absence reduction   3
    employee involvement   102
    motivator-hygiene
        theory   200
    and turnover reduction   409
job performance see performance
job rotation   194, 199
job satisfaction   200–1
    and absenteeism   2, 218
    affect–performance
        relationships   101
    age factor   9, 168
    attitude theory   13
    and employee
        involvement   103
    equity theory   109
    "fit" approach   100
    and job design   194
    and life satisfaction   253
    and locus of control   168, 219
    and motivation   235

and organizational
    culture   274
person–environment
    interaction   100
and personality   127, 316
and quality circles   336
and role ambiguity   356
and role conflict   356
and role over/underload   357
and self-esteem   364
self-managing teams   365
and social needs   158
and socialization   372
and status incongruence   378
and turnover   409
job security   46
job sharing   252, 254
job simplification   193, 194
    see also job deskilling
job stress see stress
Johns, G.   1–3, 217–18
Judge, T. A.   126–9, 312–17
Juran, J. M.   68–9
just-in-time systems   312, 374,
    401
justice, and attribution
    theory   14
justice, distributive   201–2
    and equity theory   109
    and social comparison   370
justice, organizational   308
justice, procedural   116, 202,
    271
    and motivation   239
    and punishment   335

kaizen   69, 112
    see also continuous
        improvement
Kanfer, R.   233–41
Kant, Immanuel   395
Kanter, R. M.   23
Kayes, C.   213–15
keiretsu   185, 187, 249
Kelley's Cube   14
Kelly, J.   158, 361–2
Kets de Vries, M.   295–7
Klimoski, R.   137–8, 342,
    413–15
Kluckhohn, C.   81
knowledge
    commoditization   67
    and consultancy   65
    creation and sharing   205
    management   391
    organizational   205, 216–17

tacit/explicit   204, 205, 394
technical   391, 393
knowledge management
    203–6, 216–17
Koopman, P. L.   339
Koput, K. W.   22, 110–11,
    376–8
Kram, K. E.   229–30
Kramer, R. M.   181–4, 318–19,
    321–4
Kristof-Brown, A.   310–11

labor, division of   25, 68, 283
lateness   1, 2, 409
Latham, G. P.   307–9
Lawrence, B. S.   30–1, 32–5
leadership   39, 207–12, 217
    attribution theory   13, 14, 208
    CEOs   35–7
    charismatic   16, 40–1
    and coalition formation   42
    commitment   405
    communication   48
    and competency   54
    conflict theory   61
    effectiveness   208, 209, 210,
        317, 324
    emotion management   100
    family firms   123
    five factor model of
        personality   128
    gendered   419, 421
    "Great Man" theory   207
    influence   207, 405
    knowledge management
        216–17
    laissez-faire   147, 405
    leader–follower
        dynamics   208, 209–10, 211
    motivation of workforce   405
    neurotic   295–7
    and organizational citizenship
        behavior (OCB)   269
    and organizational climate
        270
    and organizational
        culture   273, 277
    and organizational design   284
    participative   146, 209,
        212–13, 304
    personality   316–17
    power   208, 324, 404
    and process consultation   326
    role behaviors   40, 207, 209,
        210, 211, 212
    symbolic action   383

theory and research   207–8
and total quality
    management   401
transformational/transactional
    leadership   404–6
and trust   41
leadership
    contingencies   208, 209,
    212–13
Leana, C.   368–9
learned helplessness   14
learning
    cognitive/behavioral
        approaches   214
    critical theory   214–15
    double-loop learning   95–6,
        189–90
    and error management   112
    experiential   214, 215–16
    goal orientation   138, 140,
        141
    learning resistance   189–90
    organizational   86, 112, 118,
        119, 204, 205, 216, 246
    self-managed   190
    situational   190
    skills   187, 190
    social learning   190, 214
learning curve   84, 216
learning, individual   213–15
learning, organizational
    215–16
learning organization
    216–17
    and network theory   246
Ledford, G. E., Jr.   68–9, 336–7,
    400–2
Legge, K.   320–1
legitimacy
    and bureaucratic
        organizations   28
    and corporate boards   71
    and employee involvement
        102
    hierarchical   243
    institutional   48, 73
    open systems   255
    and organizational
        behavior   178, 179, 281
    and power   16, 322
    and reputation   344
    and status   298
    value statements   416
levels of analysis   217–18
    and bias   22
    and career theory   33

conflict/conflict
    management   59
    managerial and organizational
        cognition   224
    organization theory   260
    systems theory   385–6
Lewin, K.   7, 40, 129, 147, 348
life cycle theory   264–5, 267, 284
Lincoln, J. R.   184–5, 246–50,
    297–8
line/staff   218
Locke, E. A.   214, 221
locus of control   219, 315
    and creativity   75
    entrepreneurs   107
    and goal setting   140, 141
    and job satisfaction   168
logrolling   60, 84
Lomi, A.   57–8
loose coupling   157, **219–20**
    and innovation   110
    and postmodernism   320
Luthans, B.   19–22
Luthans, F.   19–22

Machiavellianism   242
McLelland, D.   6, 7, 8, 54–5
management by objectives
    (MBO)   221, 235
management-by-exception   405
management, classical
    theory   221–3
    and network analysis   246
    and organizational
        structure   299
managerial behavior
    interpersonal interactions   188
    monitoring   10, 71
    motivational principles   234
    styles   9, 158, 421
    women managers   421
managerial discretion   73
managerial function   225
managerial and
    organizational
    cognition   223–4
managerial roles   224–6
Marcusc, H.   79
Martin, J.   274–8
Martinko, M. J.   13–15, 306–7
Marx, Karl   391
Marxism
    critical theory   79
    and discrimination   90
    distributive justice   201
    hegemony theory   184

ideology   163
    and production
        technology   391
Maslow, A. H.   362
matrix organization   226–8,
    384
    communication   49
    conflict   59
Mayo, E.   158, 281
Mead, G. H.   358
mechanistic/organic
    structures   68, 78, **228**,
    281, 283, 391
media choice theories   51
mediation   60, 183
mentoring   229–30, 354
    and career development   31
    and career plateauing   32
    and career theory   32, 34
mergers and
    acquisitions   230–1
    and downsizing   96, 97
metaphor   48, 76, **231–2**
    gatekeepers   135
    organic growth   264
Meyer, J.   178, 259
Meyer, M. W.   25–9
Mezias, S. J.   215–16
Miliffe, K.   312–17
Milkovich, G. T.   165–7
Miller, S.   24, 361
Milliken, F. J.   78
Minnesota Job Satisfaction
    Questionnaire (MSQ)
    200
minority group
    influence   232–3
minority groups
    and conformity   63
    and discrimination   90, 91
    and impression
        management   165
    preferential treatment   419
mission statements   48
model selection   22, 110
model selection bias   22
modeling   56, 110
modernism   320
modular organizations   51
moods   101
    mood control   366
Moore, D.   331–3
Moorman, R. H.   269–70
moral hazard   10
Morgenstern, O.   131
Morris, T.   203–6, 328–30

motivation   233–40
  and ability   1
  achievement motivation   6, 7,
    13
  affiliation motivation   8
  behaviorist approach   21
  and career plateauing   32
  classical management
    theory   222
  and communication   48
  and creativity   75
  extrinsic/intrinsic   75, 121–2,
    237, 362
  five factor model of
    personality   128
  goal setting   138, 237–8
  incentives   166
  and job design   194, 195
  and job deskilling   197
  leadership   210, 405
  and learning   214
  and locus of control   219
  the matrix organization   227
  motivator-hygiene
    theory   194, 200
  and national culture   140
  need theory   6
  and participation   305
  payment systems   361
  personality-based views   234,
    236–7, 316
  rewards   121
  and self-efficacy   168, 363
  and social needs   158
  values   415
motivation management   239
**motivation and
    performance**   234,
    240–1
Moynihan, L. M.   167–9
Munsterberg, H.   223
Murmann, J. P.   114–15
Murnighan, J. K.   41–2, 64,
    117–18, 131–4, 339–41

Nadel, S. F.   248
Narayanan, J.   371
Nash equilibrium   131
needs
  Need Hierarchy Theory   236,
    238, 362
  need theory   6, 8, 158
  rewards based on   201
  social needs   158, 260
negotiation   242–6
  altruism   116

behavioral decision
    perspective   19, 244
  and communication   49
  and decision-making   19, 84
  Dual Concern Theory   60
  egocentrism   245
  emotions   245
  game theory   131, 243
  gender differences   168
  intergroup relations   183
  skills   188–9
  Theory of Cooperation and
    Competition   61
  and trust   408
neoclassical economics   5, 73,
    223, 260
neo-institutional theory   185
**network theory and
    analysis**   113, **246–50**
  and organizational design   282
  and reputation   344
  and resource dependence   350
  and role theory   355
  and social capital   368
networking   **250–1**
  and career theory   33
  and coalition formation   42
  and collaboration   44
  communication   47
  entrepreneurs   108
  and job design   195
  and knowledge
    management   204
  organic organizational
    structures   228
  and organizational
    change   264
  and organizational
    geography   294
  and relational contracts   70
  social networks   32, 53
  subnets   248
  technology transfer   393
Neumann, J. von   131
neuroticism
  neurotic styles   296–7
  organizational neurosis   295–7
  personality   126, 127, 141,
    314, 315, 316, 317
Nicholson, N.   6–7, 8, 11–12, 15,
    29, 30, 31–2, 103–4, 115–17,
    123–4, 155, 324, 359, 365–6
Nkomo, S. M.   89–91, 325
**nominal group
    technique**   **251–2**
non-work/work   **252–4**

and commitment   46
  and gender   136, 252
norms
  and change   39
  group   150–1, 361
  negative   151
  reciprocity   171, 340
  temporal   395

Ocasio, W.   71–2, 119–21
offshoring   302
Oldham, G. R.   198–9
omitted variable biases   22
O*NET taxonomy of
    occupational information   1
open systems   **255–6**, 397
  and change   69
  enactment processes   104
  and organizational design   281
  systems theory   384–5
  and technology   68, 390
openness to experience   126,
    127, 128, 315
operant conditioning   20
**organization
    development**   223, **256–8**
  conformity   63
  and consultancy   65
  effective change   39
  survey feedback   382
  team building   387–8
organization theory   **258–62**
  and classical management
    theory   223
  computer modeling   58
  decision-making   82
  gendered   136
  institutional approach   180,
    181
  intergroup relations   182
  open systems perspectives   68
  and postmodernism   320
  structural–functional
    analysis   260
organizational behavior
  behaviorism   19–22
  and communication
    technologies   51
  computer modeling   58
  and the five factor model of
    personality   127–8
  and gender   136–7
  generalization   137
  impression management   165
  and motivation   234
  and personality   315–17

symbolism   383
systems theory   384–6
organizational boundaries   255
    see also organizational design;
        transaction cost economics
organizational change   216,
    262–9
computer simulation   86
conflict theory   61
and crises   79
diversity management   93
effective   39
entrainment   105
entrepreneurship   107
evaluation   38
lack of psychological contract
    fulfillment   333
and the learning
    organization   216
and organization
    development   256
and organizational
    ecology   285–6
processes   264–6
punctuated equilibrium
    theory   266, 300
and sociotechnical theory   374
and systems theory   384
**organizational citizenship
    behavior (OCB)   269–70**
and accountability   5
and commitment   45
and deviance   89
and job satisfaction   101, 201
**organizational climate
    270–2**
and personal initiative   312
person–organization fit   162,
    169, 310–11
Organizational Commitment
    Questionnaire (OCQ)   45
organizational culture   217,
    272–8
and attitude theory   12–13
and climate   271
and innovation   174
and knowledge
    management   204
and network theory   246
neurotic   295
and organization
    development   256
and organizational
    change   267
and organizational design   284
and perception   306

and personal initiative   312
and postmodernism   320–1
rituals   352
and socialization   372
and transformational/
    transactional
    leadership   404
and values   410, 416
**organizational decline and
    death   96, 278–9**
**organizational
    demography   279–80**
and community ecology   53
and diversity management
    92
executive succession   119
and personal identity   162
and role theory   355
and turnover   410
organizational design   26, 38,
    259, **280–5**
boundaries   23
bureaucracy   26
and career plateauing   31
and communications
    technology   51
complexity theory   56
congruence   63
and crises   79
divisionalization   26, 299–300
incremental change   263
and innovation   174
modular organizations   51
natural systems
    approach   281, 291
neo-Darwinian
    perspective   116
open systems   256
and organizational
    development   258
principles   283–4
public sector   26
structuration   381
subunits   26, 384
and trust   408
organizational ecology   178,
    285–9
complexity theory   57
and entrepreneurs   108
and network theory   249
and organizational design
    282
    see also community ecology;
        population ecology
organizational economics   282,
    408

**organizational
    effectiveness**   260, **289–93**
and self-efficacy   363
7-S framework   63–4
and systems theory   385
organizational equilibrium
    267–8
**organizational
    geography   293–5**
organizational growth   284
organizational identity   160–1
organizational innovation   172–7
**organizational neurosis
    295–7**
and double-loop learning   95
organizational psychology   259
organizational size   68, 260, 299
organizational sociology   259
organizational status   297–8
**organizational structure
    298–302**
process technology   391
Osborn, R. N.   77–9
Ouchi, W. G.   398
outsourcing   51, 66, **302–3**, 408

Paddock, L.   135–7, 418–20
participation   304–6, 398
employee involvement   102–3
nominal group technique   251
and process consultation   326
quality circles   336
and sociotechnical theory   374
work groups/teams   423
pattern recognition   54, 58
payment systems
deferred pay   167
executive pay   10, 37
gender differences   168
incentive pay   166, 173
performance-related   10, 166,
    361, 362
and tournament theory
    402
Peiperl, M.   32, 348–9
Penney, L.   363–4
perception   306–7
bias   46
and commitment,
    escalating   46
and conception   396
and decision-making   17
and deviant behavior   88
political   318
and role theory   355
social   306, 322

performance
  affect–performance
    relationships 100–1
  age factor 9
  change–performance
    relationship 263, 264
  cognitive dissonance 43
  cohesion–performance
    relationship 145, 149
  feedback effect 20
  five factor model of
    personality 128
  goal orientation 138
  goal–performance
    relationship 139, 140
  group performance 145, 148,
    149
  Hawthorne effect 156
  hetero-performance 301
  and innovation 172
  iso-performance 301
  and job enrichment 199
  and job rotation 199
  and job satisfaction 201
  and locus of control 219
  motivation 234, 240–1
  pay–performance
    relationship 10, 166, 362
  and persistence 309–10
  and personality 316
  punishment effect 20
  self-appraisals 308
  and self-efficacy levels 363,
    364
  self-managing teams 365
  social facilitation 370
  standards 5, 6
  and stress 379
  and structural fit 300
performance appraisal/
  performance
  management 307–9
  attribution theory 13
  and discrimination 90
  feedback 76, 308
  public sector 26
Perrow, C. 77, 111, 157, 298
persistence 309–10
  dysfunctional 264, 301, 309
  self-managing teams 365
personal initiative 311–12
personality 217, 312–17
  and ability 1
  Big Five model 15, 116,
    126–9, 236, 314, 315, 316
  and career success 127

and competency 54
  conformity 63
  core self-evaluations 315
  creativity 75
  deviant behavior 88
  entrepreneurship 107
  and goal setting 140–1
  and group decision-
    making 145
  heritability 313
  individual differences
    approach 162, 167, 312
  and job satisfaction 200
  locus of control 219
  measurement 314–15
  and motivation 234, 236–7
  and organizational
    behavior 315–17
  and organizational
    dysfunction 295
  and personal identity 162
  and personal initiative 312
  and risk taking 351
  self-reporting 127
  and social loafing 371
  stability 313–14
  structure 315
person–environment
  interaction 30, 310–11,
    379
  and job satisfaction 100
  and stress 379
person–organization fit 162,
  169, 311
Peterson, R. S. 118–19, 144–5,
  147–51, 152–3
Pfeffer, J. 259, 260, 322, 349
phenomenology 325
Pillutla, M. M. 69–70, 371,
  406–9
Piskorski, M. J. 349–50
poison pills 71, 177, 185, 186,
  294
politics 318–19
  coalition formation 42
  and consensus 64
  organizational 165, 318–19
  power politics 120
Polzer, J. T. 353–6, 357, 358
Poole, M. S. 47–52
population ecology 28, 52,
  260–1
  age and size dependence
    287
  density dependence 286–7
  internal demography 287–8

and organizational
    change 263, 288
  and organizational
    ecology 286–8
  organizational
    environments 286
  segregation 287
  time aggregation bias 22
Porac, J. 223–4
portfolio careers 30, 31, 195
portfolio management
  strategies 119
positive psychology
  movement 14, 15
postmodernism 320–1
  cultural studies 113
  organizational culture 277
  organizational design 49
Powell, W. W. 178–81, 282
power 321–4
  and authority 16
  bureaucratic 25, 27
  CEOs 72, 119–20
  coalition formation 42
  and communication 48, 49
  conflict theory 61
  and consensus 64
  consequences 322
  and corporate boards 71
  definitions 321–2
  determinants 322
  exchange relations 321–2
  and game theory 133
  and hypothesis testing 110
  imbalance 349, 349–50
  and influence 169
  and intergroup relations 182
  leadership 208, 209, 404
  legitimacy 16
  and negotiation 243
  and organizational
    culture 276
  political 186
  power politics 120
  power/knowledge
    relationships 320
  power–conflict theories of
    discrimination 90
  relationships 117
  and resource dependence 68,
    260, 349–50
  and rituals 352–3
  social 209
power, need for 6, 7, 324
powerlessness 323
practical intelligence 324

prejudice   325
    and discrimination   90, 325
prestige   298
    see also reputation; status
principal–agent relationship   6,
    10
    commitment   44
    information asymmetry   10
    see also agency theory
prisoner's dilemma   132, 245
privatization   26, 28, 177, 192
problem solving
    brainstorming   76
    Creative Problem Solving   76
    group   60–1
    and learning   214
    process consultation   326
process analysis   327
process consultation   38,
    326–7
product innovation   23
product life cycle   300
product specialization   91
product technology   389, 391
productivity
    and participation   305
    team productivity,
        measurement of   217
**professional service
    firms**   84, **328–30**
profitability
    and competency   55
    and enterprise resource
        planning   104–5
promissory contracts   70
**promotion/prevention
    focus   330**
    and self-regulation   366
property rights   143
prospect theory   84, **331–3**
    and crises   78
    and groupthink   154
psychological contract   70,
    333–4
    and career theory   32
    and innovation   173
psychological testing   223
public scrutiny, and
    accountability   5
public sector bureaucracies   26,
    28
punctuated equilibrium   149,
    263, 266, 300, 390
punishment   334–5
    and absence control   3
    potential harm   20

and power   16
    theory X and Y   398
    and workplace
        performance   20
Puranam, P.   230–1, 302–3

quality   292
    see also quality circles; total
        quality management
quality circles   102, 103, 177,
    336–7, 401
**quasi-experimental
    design   337–8**, 346, 348

race
    and career success   168, 229
    and job satisfaction   200
racism   91, 325
Raiffa, H.   244
rational choice theory   134
rational investment theory   85
rationality   339
    bounded rationality   17, 18,
        24, 70, 82, 83, 261, 339, 361
    and bureaucracy   25, 281
    and commitment   46
    decision-making   17, 82–3,
        261
    double-loop learning   95
    game theory   132, 243
    and the garbage can
        model   134
    and systems theory   385
    technical   391–2
Ravlin, E. C.   415–17
reciprocal altruism   339–40,
    340, 341
    and trust   407
reciprocity   340–1
    and influence   170, 171
    strong reciprocity   407
reengineering revolution   284
regression fallacy   342
**regression toward the
    mean**   18, 264, **341–2**
regulation
    professional service firms
        329
    self-regulation   330, 365–6
    social regulation   330
Regulatory Focus Theory   366
relational contracts   70
relative deprivation theory
    182–3
reliability   18, **342–3**
    and change evaluation   38

high reliability
    organizations   157–8
reputation   4, **343–5**
    and consultancy   65
    and organizational status   298
    reduction in   77
    and status   298
reputation management   345
research
    action research   7–8
    cross-cultural   80
    qualitative/quantitative   113,
        348
research design   346–7
    and change evaluation   38
    halo effect   155
    quasi-experimental
        design   337–8, 346, 348
    validity   413
research and development
    and organizational
        geography   295
    and technology transfer   393
research methods   347–8
    multi-level research   311
    quantitative/qualitative   277,
        348
research strategies   346
resistance to change   15, 24,
    61, **348–9**, 398
resource-based theory of the
    firm   203, 204
resource dependence   260,
    278, **349–50**
    and CEO appointment   37
    and corporate boards   71
    entrepreneurs   108
    and executive succession   119
    and interlocking boards
        184–5
    network research   249
    open systems   255
    and organizational design   28,
        282
    and organizational
        effectiveness   291
    and organizational status   298
    and power structures   68, 260,
        322
    slack resources   368
resource drain theory   253
resource partitioning   287
respondent conditioning   20
responsibilities
    attribution theory   13
    boards   142

responsibilities (*cont'd*)
CEOs 35–6
and corporate social
performance 72–3
individual 73
managerial 73
outsourcing 302
public 73
rewards
contingent rewards 405
and continuous
improvement 69
and creativity 75
and distributive justice 201
entrepreneurs 107
equity theory 109
goal–performance
relationship 140
incentives 166, 173
for innovation 173
and intergroup relations 182
intrinsic 7
and motivation 121, 235
non-monetary 167, 235
and power 16
self-managing teams 365
see also payment systems
Ring, P. 43–4
Riordan, C. A. 357
risk taking 350–2
agency theory 10
CEOs 36
and charismatic leadership 41
compensation risk 10
and creativity 75
and crises 78
and decision-making 83,
84–5
entrepreneurs 107, 108
evolutionary psychology
framework 116
and goal setting 140
and groupthink 153
reputational risk 345
risk-return paradox 85, 351
and slack resources 368
and trust 407
risky shift phenomenon 351
rituals 48, 352–3
and organizational
culture 274
Roberts, K. H. 157–8
Robertson, I. 155
Rogelberg, S. G. 346–8
Rogers, E. 174
role 353–5

boundary spanning 23
CEO 36
competencies 54
and gender 136–7
generic roles 354, 359
group roles 152–3
and group structure 148
identities 136–7
impression management 164
integration 23
interpersonal 354
managerial roles 224–6
multiple roles 360
and sociotechnical theory 374
status incongruence 378
role ambiguity 354, 356
and socialization 372
role conflict 23, 354, 356
role differentiation 354
role distancing 356–7
role episodes 354, 357
role over/underload 357
role set 354, 357, 358
and socialization 371–2
role taking 358
and socialization 371
role theory 354, 358
and networking 250
stakeholders 375
role transitions 358–60
career theory 32
and group structure 152
Ronson, S. 118–19, 144–5,
147–51, 152–3
Rorschach Inkblot Test 314–15
Rosenfeld, P. 163–5, 381–2
Rotter, J. B. 219
Rousseau, D. M. 333–4
routinization
bureaucratic 25, 68
and decision-making 83–4
search, performance and
change routines 215–16
Ruef, M. 285–9
rule-based decision-making 83,
85

sabotage 14, 219, 335
sacrifice 5, 41
Salancik, G. 260, 350
sample selection bias 22
satisficing 361
decision-making 24, 82, 83,
86, 146
open systems 256
scapegoating 119

Schneider, B. 270–2
Schuler, R. S. 24–5, 87, 251–2
Schumpeter, J. 390
science, and ideology 163
scientific management 26,
193, 281, **361–2**
and classical management
theory 222
and consultancy 65
and job deskilling 193, 197
and motivation 235
and social needs 158
theory X and Y 352, 398
Scott, B. A. 126–9
Scott, W. R. 259
self-actualization 362
self-appraisals 308
self-awareness 54, 101, 366
self-criticism, preemptive 4
self-efficacy 301, 315, 363–4
attribution theory 14
and empowerment 103
and errors 111
five factor model of
personality 128
goal setting 139, 140, 141
Hawthorne effect 156
and motivation 128, 168, 236
and personal initiative
311–12
problem solving 61
and stress 169
self-esteem 315, 364
attribution theory 14
and conformity 63
and goal setting 141
self-identity 32, 63
self-interest 10, 11, 19, 60, 186
self-managing teams 102,
194, **364–5**
and job design 194
motivation 239
participation 304
and sociotechnical theory 374
team building 388
self-presentation *see* impression
management
self-regulation 330, 365–6
and behaviorism 21
cybernetic systems 259
and enactment 104
evolutionary psychology
framework 116
goal setting 139, 235–6,
237–8
and motivation 235, 239

Selznick, P.   259, 281
semi-autonomous work groups *see*
    self-managing teams
sensemaking   396
    and career theory   34
    and enactment   103, 104
    and rituals   353
7-S framework   63–4
sexism   90, 91, 419
sexual harassment   367
Shannon, C.   47
Shepherd, C.   104–5
Sherif, M.   181–2
shiftwork   105
signaling theory   343
significance testing   377
Simmel, G.   248
Simon, H.   17, 48, 58, 223, 259,
    339, 341
simulation *see* computer
    simulation
situational research   243
size, organization   68, 260, 299
skill   367–8
    and aptitude   12
    assessment   190
    and competencies   188, 367
    congruence   63–4
    cross-functional skills   367
    deficiencies   118
    evaluation   367
    executive derailment   118
    and group dynamics   148
    individual differences   167
    interpersonal skills   187–91
    job deskilling   193, 196–8
    job rotation   199
    and job satisfaction   200
    learning   187, 190, 213
    mentoring skills   229
    skill-building programs   94
    social skills   102
    team skills   197, 422
Skinner, B. F.   20, 214
slack resources   368
small business networks   249
Smith, Adam   280–1
social anthropology   246, 248,
    250
social attribution theory   15, 325
    see also attribution
social capital   368–9
    and network theory   249
social categorization theory   182,
    281, 325
social cognitive theory   138

    and behaviorism   21
    and goal setting   235–6, 238
social comparison   369–70
    and deviant behavior   88
    and equity theory   109
    and exchange relations   117
    and group polarization   151
    and intergroup relations   182
social constructionism   104
social contract   70
social Darwinism   266
social engineering   7, 217
social exchange theory   210, 269
social facilitation   370
social identity   53, 325
Social Identity Theory   182
social influence *see* influence
social inhibition   370
social issues management   73
social loafing   371
    and decision-making   146
social needs   158, 260
social networks *see* networking
social psychology
    creativity experiments   75
    decision-making research   151
    impression management   164
    and intergroup relations   182
    and minority influence   232–3
    and negotiation   244–5
    and prejudice   325
social recognition   20
social responsibility   142
social utility   117
social validation   170
socialization   371–3
    and career development   31
    and career theory   32, 34
    and organizational
        culture   274
    and personal identity   162
    rituals   352
    and role transitions   359
    values   415–16
sociometry   247
**sociotechnical theory   38,
    373–5**
    action research   8
    and job design   194, 373–4
    and organizational design   283
Sonnentag, S.   378–80
Sorenson, O.   56–7
specialization   287, 302–3, 320
Spector, P. E.   219, 362–4
Srikanth, K.   302–3
stakeholders   375–6

alliances   23
and corporate reputation
    344
and critical theory   79
and enactment   104
and governance   142
management   73
Stanford Prison Study   62–3
Starbuck, W. H.   78
statistical methods   376–8
    error   110–11
    reliability estimation   342
    surveys   381
    validity generalization   413,
        414
status
    evolutionary psychology
        framework   116
    and group decision-
        making   146
    and group dynamics   148
    and incentives   167
    and intergroup relations   183
    organizational status   297–8
    stratification systems   297–8
status incongruence   378
stereotyping
    attribution theory   13
    authoritarian personality   15
    and diversity management   92
    gender   75
    negative   183
    and perception   307
    and prejudice   325
    women managers   421
Strang, D.   177
strategic alliances   23
    and network theory   249
    politics   318
strategic choice   36, 104
stress   378–80
    attribution theory   14
    burnout   29
    cognitive dissonance   43
    and commitment   46
    and failure   309
    and hardiness   155, 379
    immunity syndrome   8
    and job design   168, 193
    management by   69
    and need for power   324
    and neuroticism   126
    and non-work/work   253
    and person–environment
        fit   310
    role over/underload   357

stress (*cont'd*)
  and self-efficacy levels   169,
    363
  and self-esteem   364
  sexual harassment   367
  and socialization   371
  stress concepts   378
  treatment and
    prevention   379–80
Stroh, L. K.   252–4
structural inertia theory   288
structural–functional
  analysis   260, 260
structuration   380–1
  and professional service
    firms   328
structure *see* organizational
  design; organizational
  structure
subcultures   274, 277
surveys   381–2
  network research   247
  personality measures   314
  response bias   22
  statistical   348
surveys, feedback   382
Sutherland, K.   392–4
Sutton, R. I.   278–9
symbiosis   53
symbolism   383–4
  and board decisions   72
  CEO roles   36
  and communication   48
  and institutions   181
  rituals   352
synectics   76
system justification theory   183
systematic risk   351
systems theory   259, 384–6
  closed systems   68, 384–5
  and crises   77
  equifinality   265
  and the learning
    organization   216
  levels of analysis   385–6
  open systems   68, 255–6,
    384–5, 390, 397
  and roles   353
systems thinking   54

T-group methodology   387
tasks
  combining   198
  complex task paradigm   140
  entrainment   105
  performance   1

specialization   283
task-oriented leadership   209
task-relationship conflict
  model   59
task roles   152
task uncertainty   299
Taylor, F. W.   196, 222, 281,
  361–2
team building   38, 387–9
  and organization
    development   258
team theory   83
teamwork
  and competency   54
  cross-functional teams   24
  decision-making   83
  facilitation skills   187, 189
  group conflict   59
  motivational processes   238
  and skills   197, 422
technological standards   390
technology   389–92
  and change   38, 216
  communications
    technology   50–2
  and competencies   216
  contingency theory   68
  and entrepreneurship   106
  and job deskilling   197
  non-work time, infringement
    on   252
  and role theory   355
  and systems theory   385, 389
  and uncertainty   134, 390
technology transfer   392–4
telecommuting   51, 252
teleological theory   265, 267
temporal perspective   394–5
tension dialectic   266
Tetlock, P.   3–6, 164
Thematic Apperception Test
  (TAT)   6, 314–15
theory   395–7
theory X and Y   11, 362, 398
theory Z   398–9
Thibaut, J.   202
Thomas, M. D.   163–5, 381–2
Thompson, J. D.   42, 298
tight coupling   77, 111, 157,
  219–20
time
  and career theory   33
  temporal perspective   395
time aggregation bias   22
time and motion study   222
time series regression   377

Toegel, G.   64–7, 365–6
**top management teams   39,
  399–400**
  decision-making   145
  executive succession   119
  and organizational
    culture   274
**total quality
  management   85, 292,
  321, 374, 400–2**
  and continuous
    improvement   68
  and skills   197
**tournament theory   167, 328,
  402–3**
trade unions   362
training
  communications training   363
  goal-setting training   363
  T-group methodology   387
trait affect   101, 200, 207, 313
trait consistency   313–14
**transaction cost
  economics   10, 260, 403–4**
  and bureaucratic
    efficiency   27–8
  and contracts   70
  and interlocking boards   185
  and organizational design   282
  and professional service
    firms   329
  and trust   408
**transformational/
  transactional
  leadership   404–6**
  attribution theory   14
  and commitment   45
  and influence   210
transparency   73
triangulation   347
Trivers, R. L.   339
trust   298, 362, 406–9
  and contracts   70, 406, 408
  definitions   406–7
  and governance   186
  intergroup relations   182, 183
  and leadership   41, 211
  process consultation   326
  and reciprocity   340, 407
  team building   387
Tsui, A. S.   279–80
turnover   93, 409–11
  and absenteeism   1, 2
  and commitment   45
  executive turnover   37, 119
  and group dynamics   148

and innovation   173
and job design   194
and job satisfaction   201
and role ambiguity   356
and role conflict   356
voluntary   365, 409, 410

UCINET   246, 247
uncertainty
   and communication   47, 50
   decision-making   24, 67, 361
   garbage can model   134
   and innovation   173
   and job design   195
   reduction   47, 50, 408
   and risk taking   350–1
   task uncertainty   299, 365
   and trust   408
unions see trade unions
United States
   CEOs   119
   change programs   39
   entrepreneurship   106
   family firms   123
   public sector   26
   scientific management   196
unity of command principle   222
Useem, M.   191–2
utility theory   131

validity   111, **413–14**
   and change evaluation   38, 39
   and research design   346
   social validation   170
   validity threats   337
**validity generalization
   414–15**
value chain management   65
value statements   416
values   415–17
   and authority   16
   and career anchors   30
   cognitive dissonance   43
   and commitment   45

and competency   54
congruence   64
family firms   123
goal setting   140
and identification   159
and individual
   differences   167
organization climate   271
and organizational
   culture   273, 410
and organizational
   effectiveness   290
and technology   389
transmission   352
Van de Ven, A. H.   171–7, 262–9
Van Maanen, J.   231–2, 383–4,
   396
venture capital   108
vertical integration   403
vertical loading   198
vertical segregation   418–19
vicious cycles   27, 78
video conferencing   50
vie theory   219
virtual organization   51, 249
virtual reality   347
virtual teams   195, 388
vision   41, 139, 211

Walker, L.   202
Wall, T. D.   193–6
Wanous, J. P.   371–3
Weber, M.   16, 25, 26, 40, 222,
   280
Weick, K. E.   104, 276, 395–7
Weigelt, K.   402–3
West, M. A.   145–7, 151–2,
   232–3, 370, 422–4
whistleblowing   6
Whyte, G.   153–4
Williams, C. R.   409–11
Williamson, O. E.   260, 403
women at work   418–20
   career success   229

and discrimination   90, 91
diversity management   92
glass ceiling   91, 418
sexual harassment   367
women managers   116, 135–6,
   419, **421–2**
diversity management   92
Wood, D. J.   72–3, 141–2, 375–6
Wood, R.   324
Wood, S. J.   196–8
Woodman, R. W.   37–40, 256–8
work
   and career theory   32–3
   creativity and the work
      environment   75–6
   entrainment   105
   motivation   235
   social/cultural context   238–9
   spillover theory   253
   work–life conflict   45, 101,
      137, 253
   work–life initiatives   252
work groups/teams   38, 158,
   398–9, **422–4**
   creativity   75
   decision-making   145
   diversity management   92
   process consultation   326, 327
   social loafing   371
   subunits   26, 384
   team building   388
   see also self-managing teams;
      teamwork
work units   198, 279–80

Yale Obedience Study   62–3
Yanadori, Y.   165–7
Youngblood, S. A.   409–11
Youssef, C.   19–22

Zajac, E.   10–11, 403–4
Zand, D.   129–30, 326–7